W9-BRW-551

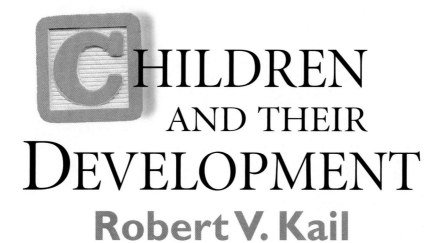

CHILDREN AND THEIR DEVELOPMENT

Robert V. Kail
Purdue University

Prentice Hall, Upper Saddle River, New Jersey 07458

Library of Congress Cataloging-in-Publication Data

Kail, Robert V.
 Children and their development / Robert V. Kail.
  p.   cm.
 Includes bibliographical references and index.
 ISBN 0-13-518903-9
 1. Child development.   2. Child psychology.   3. Memory in children.
 4. Cognition in children.   I. Title.
HQ772.K216   1998   97-26307
305.231—dc21   CIP

Editorial Director: Charlyce Jones Owen
Editor in Chief: Nancy Roberts
Executive Editor: Bill Webber
Acquisitions Editor: Jennifer Gilliland
Assistant Editor: Anita Castro
Director of Production and Manufacturing: Barbara Kittle
Managing Editor: Bonnie Biller
Director of Development: Susanna Lesan
Development Editor: Harriett Prentiss
Editorial/Production Supervision: Mary Rottino
Manufacturing Manager: Nick Sklitsis
Prepress and Manufacturing Buyer: Tricia Kenny
Creative Design Director: Leslie Osher
Interior and Cover Design: Function thru Form, Inc.
Electronic Illustrations: Joseph Rattan Design
Director, Image Resource Center: Lori Morris-Nantz
Photo Research Supervisor: Melinda Reo
Image Permission Supervisor: Kay Dellosa
Photo Researcher: Eloise Donnelly
Editorial Assistant: Tamsen Adams

Acknowledgments for copyrighted material may
be found beginning on p. 443, which constitutes
an extension of this copyright page.

This book was set in 10.5/13 Minion and Gills Sans Bold by TSI Graphics
and was printed and bound by RR Donnelley & Sons Company–Roanoke.
The cover was printed by The Lehigh Press, Inc.

 © 1998 by Prentice-Hall, Inc.
Simon & Schuster/A Viacom Company
Upper Saddle River, New Jersey 07458

Printed in the United States of America
10 9 8 7 6 5 4 3 2

ISBN 0-13-518903-9

Prentice-Hall International (UK) Limited, *London*
Prentice-Hall of Australia Pty. Limited, *Sydney*
Prentice-Hall Canada Inc., *Toronto*
Prentice-Hall Hispanoamericana, S.A., *Mexico*
Prentice-Hall of India Private Limited, *New Delhi*
Prentice-Hall of Japan, Inc., *Tokyo*
Simon & Schuster Asia Pte. Ltd., *Singapore*
Editora Prentice-Hall do Brasil, Ltda., *Rio de Janeiro*

To Laura, Matt, and Ben

Brief Contents

Contents

Cultural Influences

Focus on Research

Making Children's Lives Better

Real Children

Preface

My aim in writing *Children and Their Development* was to create a book that would help students to appreciate both the splendor of child development and the strides that researchers have made in understanding development. At the same time, I wanted to provide students with insights that would make their own interactions with children—as teachers, parents, or simply as citizens—more informed and more fulfilling. The result is a book that presents a broad but selective introduction to child development as a science that is at once basic and applied.

To achieve these ends, I have followed a number of guidelines. Collectively, they form the general orientation of the book.

1. Research, theory, and application are inseparable. The best way to answer a question or solve a problem that involves real-live children is to have a theory that specifies effective solutions, and the best theories are the ones that have been documented with extensive research. Throughout this book, I illustrate the close links between theory, research, and practice.

2. The beauty of child development can truly be appreciated only by examining its many different forms. Some aspects of development reflect the biological heritage that is shared by all children. However, projected on this common biological backdrop are unique trajectories of development that depend upon the cultural context in which the child develops. This variety in child development is emphasized throughout the book.

3. There is a fundamental continuity among all developmental processes. The text is organized topically, so that different aspects of child development can be examined in detail. However, these different aspects are completely interwoven in the lives of real, growing children. Throughout the text, these connections between biological, intellectual, and social components of child development are highlighted.

ORGANIZATION OF THE BOOK

The book begins, in Chapter 1, with a brief description of how to use the book to learn about child development and an introduction to the theories and methods that have guided research in child development. Chapters 2 through 5 are devoted to the genetic and biological bases of human development, and the growth of perceptual and motor skills. Chapters 6 through 9 cover intellectual development—how children learn, think, reason, and solve problems. Chapters 10 through 15 concern social and emotional development—how children acquire customs of their society and learn to play the social roles that are expected of them.

PEDAGOGICAL FEATURES

I have written this book with the student in mind. My aim has been to present the intricacies of child development in a clear and engaging style that never forgets how growing children often delight us with their laughter and sometimes bewilder us with their problems.

The book has several elements designed to help students learn about child development. These are described in detail in Module 1.1, so I'll simply highlight some of them here. Each chapter consists of three or four modules that begin with a set of learning objectives and a vignette that introduces the topic to be covered in the module. Within each module, all figures, tables, and photos are fully integrated, eliminating the need for students to turn pages searching for a graphic. Similarly, boxlike feature material that is set off in other textbooks is fully integrated with the main text and identified by a distinctive icon. Each module ends with several questions designed to help students check their understanding of the major ideas in the module.

The end of each chapter includes several additional study aids. "In Perspective" recaps each module, then links the ideas in the chapter to a major developmental theme. "Thinking about Development" presents questions that encourage students to integrate what they've read. "See for Yourself" suggests activities that allow students to observe topics in child development firsthand. "Resources" includes books, telephone numbers, and sites on the World Wide Web where students can learn more about child development. "Key Terms" is a list of all of the important terms that appeared in the chapter. The "Summary" is organized by module and the primary headings within the module and reviews the entire chapter.

ANCILLARIES

Children and Their Development is accompanied by a superb set of ancillary teaching materials. They include the following:

Instructor Supplements

Instructor's Resource Manual, by Dale Grubb of Baldwin Wallace College. This unusually inclusive manual will be an important resource for new and experienced professors alike. Included in each chapter are: a chapter organizer page; resourceful learning objectives; detailed lecture outlines; up-to-date additional lecture suggestions; creative classroom demonstrations and student activities; a listing of appropriate Prentice Hall transparencies; a complete listing of suggested video resources; and useful handouts that can be removed from the manual and copied for distribution to students.

Test Item File, by Terri T. Combs of Indiana University-Purdue University Indianapolis. This comprehensive manual contains an average of 90 multiple choice questions and 4 short answer/essay questions for each chapter. Also available on Custom Test.

Prentice Hall Custom Tests for Windows, Macintosh, and DOS. A computerized version of the *Test Item File,* Prentice Hall's exclusive testing software supports a full range of editing and graphics options, network test administration capabilities, and greater ease-of-use than ever before. It offers a two-track design for constructing tests: Easytest for novice users and Fulltest for more advanced users. The Custom Testing also offers features such as On-Line Testing and Electronic Gradebook.

Teaching Transparencies for Human Development. A full set of color transparencies add visual impact to the study of child development. Designed in large format for use in lecture hall settings, many of these high quality images are not found in the text.

"800-Number" Telephone Test Preparation Service. A toll-free preparation service is also available. Instructors may call an 800-number and select up to 200 questions from the *Test Item File* available with the text. Prentice Hall will format the test and provide an alternate version (if requested) and answer key(s), then mail it back within 48 hours, ready for duplication.

Videotape Support Materials

ABC News/Prentice Hall Video Libraries
Lifespan Development, 1996
Child Development in Action, 1995
Human Development, 1993

Three video libraries consisting of feature segments from award-winning programs such as *Nightline, 20/20, PrimeTime Live,* and *The Health Show* are available to qualified adopters of *Children and Their Development.*

Student Supplements

Study Guide, by Dea DeWolff of Purdue University, who happens to be my wife. This attractive, highly visual Study Guide reinforces the key pedagogical features of the textbook. The author incorporates both illustrations and design elements from the text. Each of the 15 chapters follows the same modular organization as the text. Common elements for each module include: learning objectives; matching exercises to review key theories, definitions, terms and concepts; practice true/false questions; cumulative "fill-in-the-blank" chapter summaries; an average of 25 practice multiple choice questions, and 3 essay questions.

The New York Times **Supplement for Human Development.** When you adopt *Children and Their Development,* Prentice Hall and *The New York Times* will provide you with a complimentary student newspaper in quantities for your class. This collection of articles is designed to supplement classroom lectures and improve student access to current real-world issues and research.

Website

Additional study aids for students and links to important resources are available at the *Children and Their Development* website: *http://www./prenhall.com/kail*

NEWS
ABCNEWS

The New York Times

ACKNOWLEDGMENTS

Textbook authors do not produce books on their own. I want to thank the many people who have generously given their time and effort to help sharpen my thinking about child development and shape the development of this text. I am especially grateful to the following people who reviewed various aspects of the manuscript: Susan McClure, Westmoreland County Community College; Rebecca Bigler, University of Texas-Austin; Kathleen Fox, Salisbury State University; Rick Medlin, Stetson University; Joan Cook, County College of Morris; Elizabeth Lemerise, Western Kentucky University; Jim Dannemiller, University of Wisconsin-Madison; Mark B. Alcorn, University of Northern Colorado; Vernon C. Hall, Syracuse University; and May X. Wang, Metropolitan State College of Denver. Without their thoughtful comments, this book would be less complete, less accurate, and less interesting.

I also owe a debt of thanks to many people who helped take this project from a first draft to a bound book. My development editor, Harriett Prentiss, taught me much about writing, and did so with wit and grace. Leslie Osher and Function thru Form designed a book that is both beautiful and functional. Mary Rottino skillfully orchestrated the many activities that were involved in actually producing the book. Eloise Donnelly found the marvelous photographs that appear throughout the book. To all of these people, many, many thanks.

Robert V. Kail

About the Author

Robert V. Kail is Professor of Psychological Sciences at Purdue University. His undergraduate degree is from Ohio Wesleyan University and he received his Ph. D. from the University of Michigan. Kail has served as Associate Editor of the journal *Child Development* and is currently Associate Editor of the *Journal of Experimental Child Psychology*. He received the McCandless Young Scientist Award from the American Psychological Association and was named a fellow in the American Psychological Society. He was also named the Distinguished Sesquicentennial Alumnus in Psychology by Ohio Wesleyan University. His research interests are in the area of cognitive development and focus on the causes and consequences of developmental change in the speed of information processing. Kail has also written *The Development of Memory in Children*, and, with John C. Cavanaugh, *Human Development*. Away from the office, he enjoys flying his Cessna 172, playing soccer with his daughter, and arguing with his teenage sons about the relative musical contributions of John Lennon and Kurt Cobain.

CHILDREN AND THEIR DEVELOPMENT

The Science of Child Development

BEGINNING AS A MICROSCOPIC CELL, EVERY PERSON TAKES A FASCI-NATING JOURNEY DESIGNED TO LEAD TO ADULTHOOD. LIKE ANY JOURNEY WORTH TAKING, THE JOURNEY TO ADULTHOOD IS FILLED WITH REMARKABLE EVENTS THAT MAKE THE TRIP both interesting and challenging. In this book, we'll trace this journey as we learn about the science of child development, a multidisciplinary study of all aspects of growth from conception to adulthood. As an adult, you've lived the years that are the heart of this book. I hope that you enjoy reviewing your developmental journey from the perspective of child development research. I expect that this perspective will lead you to new insights into the developmental forces that made you the person that you are today.

Chapter 1 sets the stage for our study of child development. I begin, in Module 1.1, by giving you some tips on how to use this book. In Module 1.2, I describe the theories and themes that are central to child development research. In Module 1.3, I explain the techniques that researchers use to study children and their development.

SING THIS BOOK

In most textbooks, the material on the next few pages appears in a preface entitled "To the Student." But I'm afraid that most students never read this material, so I'm including it here at the beginning of Chapter 1. Please don't skip it now; read on to learn how to use this book. It will save you time in the long run.

I want to begin by explaining the book's modular format, which should help you learn the science of child development.

THE MODULAR FORMAT

Each of the 15 chapters in the book includes three or four modules that are listed on the first page of every chapter. As you can see in the inset page below, each module begins with a set of learning objectives phrased as questions. Next is a brief vignette that introduces the topic to be covered in the module by describing an issue or problem faced by real people. In the margin is a mini-outline listing the major subheadings of the module—a kind of roadmap for reading. The learning objectives, vignette, and mini-outline tell you what to expect in the module.

MECHANISMS OF HEREDITY

MODULE
2.1
Mechanisms of Heredity
— *The Biology of Heredity*
— *Single Gene Inheritance*
— *Polygenic Inheritance*

Learning Objectives
- **What are chromosomes and genes?**
- **What are dominant and recessive traits? How are they inherited?**
- **What is polygenic inheritance? How is it studied in children and adults?**

Leslie and Glenn have decided to try to have a baby. They are thrilled at the thought of starting their own family but also very worried because Leslie's grandfather had sickle cell anemia and died when he was just 20 years old. Leslie is terrified that their baby could inherit the disease that killed her grandfather. Leslie and Glenn wished someone could reassure them that their baby would be okay.

The inset on page 3 shows another important element of each module: All illustrations and tables are integrated with the text. You won't need to turn pages searching for a picture or table that is described in the text; instead, pictures, tables, and words are linked to tell a unified story.

Two other elements are designed to help you focus on the main points of the text. First, whenever a key term is introduced in the text, it appears in ***boldfaced italics like these*** and the definition appears in **boldface type**. This format should make key terms easier for you to find and learn. Second, about half the pages in the book include a sentence in large italicized type that extends into the margin. This sentence summarizes a key point that has been made in the surrounding text. Looking at these sentences as you read will help identify the key points in each module; reviewing them later will help you prepare for exams.

An italicized sentence like this highlights a key point from the surrounding text.

Each module in Chapters 2–15 includes a special feature that expands or highlights a topic. There are four different kinds of features; you can recognize each one by its distinctive icon:

Focus on Research provides details on the design and methods used in a particular research study.

 Cultural Influences shows how culture influences children and illustrates that developmental journeys are diverse.

 Real Children provides a case study that illustrates an issue in child development in the life of a real child.

 Making Children's Lives Better shows how research and theory can be applied to improve children's development.

Each module concludes with "Check Your Learning"—shown in the inset—to help you check your understanding of the major ideas in the module. If you can answer the questions in "Check Your Learning," you are on your way to mastering the material in the module. However, do not rely exclusively on "Check Your Learning" as you study for exams. The questions are designed to give you a quick, spot-check of your reading, not a comprehensive assessment of your knowledge of the entire module.

health care professional is present for home labor and delivery. Sometimes this is a doctor, but more often, it is a trained nurse-midwife like the one in the photo.

For Americans accustomed to hospital delivery, home delivery can seem like a risky proposition. Is it safe? Yes, but with a very important catch. Birth problems are no more common in babies delivered at home than in babies delivered in a hospital, if the woman is healthy, her pregnancy has been problem-free, the labor and delivery are expected to be problem-free, and a trained health care professional is there to assist (Rooks et al., 1989). If there is *any* reason to believe problems requiring medical assistance might occur, labor and delivery should take place in the hospital, not at home.

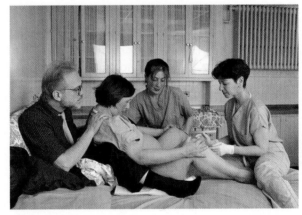

Another alternative to home or hospital birth is the freestanding birth center. Birthing centers are typically small, independent clinics. A woman, her coach, and other family members and friends are assigned a birthing room that is often decorated to look homelike rather than institutional. A doctor or nurse-midwife assists in labor and delivery, which takes place entirely in the birthing room, where it can be observed by all. Like home deliveries, birthing centers are best . . .

Check Your Learning

1. Important general risk factors include a woman's nutrition, _____, and her age.

2. _____ are some of the most dangerous teratogens because a pregnant woman is often unaware of their presence.

3. During the period of the zygote, exposure to a teratogen typically _____.

4. Two techniques used to determine if a fetus has a hereditary disorder are amniocentesis and _____.

Answers: (1) the degree of prolonged stress that she experiences, (2) Environmental hazards, (3) results in spontaneous abortion of the fertilized egg, (4) chorionic villus sampling (CVS)

At the end of each chapter—after the last module—are several additional study aids. "In Perspective" begins by highlighting each of the modules, then links the ideas in the chapter to a major developmental theme. Next is "Thinking about Development," which presents thought questions to help you integrate what you've read. "See for Yourself" suggests some simple activities for exploring issues in child development on your own. "Resources" includes books and sites on the World Wide Web where you can learn more about children and their development. "Key Terms" is a list of all of the important terms that appear in the chapter, along with the page where each term is defined. Finally, drawing the chapter to a close is a "Summary" of the entire chapter, organized by module and the primary headings within the module.

I strongly encourage you to take advantage of these learning and study aids as you read the book. Use the learning objectives, vignettes, mini-outlines and summary boxes to orient yourself to the upcoming material. Use the boldface sentences to guide your highlighting of important terms. Read the text features to expand your understanding of the text material and get you thinking about related issues. Answer the questions in "Check Your Learning" and "Thinking about Development" to determine how well you've learned what you've read.

TERMINOLOGY

Every field has its own terminology and child development is no exception. I will be using several terms to refer to different periods of infancy, childhood, and adolescence. Although these terms are familiar, when I use them, each will refer to a specific range of ages:

Newborn	Birth to 1 month
Infant	1 month to 1 year
Toddler	1 to 2 years
Preschooler	2 to 6 years
School-age child	6 to 12 years
Adolescent	12 to 18 years
Adult	18 years and older

Sometimes for the sake of variety I will use other terms that are less tied to specific ages, such as babies, youngsters, and elementary-school children. When I do, you will be able to tell from the context what groups are being described.

I will also use very specific terminology in describing research findings from different cultural and ethnic groups. The appropriate terms to describe different cultural, racial, and ethnic groups change over time. For example, the terms "colored people," "Negroes," "Black Americans," and "African Americans" have all been used to describe Americans who trace their ancestry to the races that originated in Africa. In this book, I will use the term African American because it emphasizes the unique cultural heritage of this group of people. Following this same line of reasoning, I will use the terms European American (instead of Caucasian or white), Native American (instead of Indian or American Indian), Asian American, and Hispanic American.

These labels are not perfect. Sometimes, they blur distinctions within ethnic groups. For example, the term European American ignores differences between individuals of northern or southern European ancestry; the term Asian American blurs variations among people whose heritage is Japanese, Chinese, or Korean. Whenever researchers identified the subgroups in their research sample, I will use the more specific terms in describing results. When you see the more general terms, remember that conclusions may not apply to all subgroups within the group.

ORGANIZATION

Child development encompasses many aspects of children's lives, including physical growth, intellectual development, personality, and social development. These different topics provide the structure for this book. Chapters 2–5 are devoted to the genetic and biological bases of human development, and the growth of perceptual and motor skills. Chapters 6–9 cover intellectual development—how children learn, think, reason, and solve problems. Chapters 10–15 concern social and emotional development—how children acquire customs of their society and learn to play the social roles expected of them.

Chapters 2–15 include a variety of topics, but they all draw upon the same developmental theories and the same scientific methods. The next module describes the theories that are essential to developmental research. The last module in this chapter covers research methods.

 **HEORIES AND THEMES**

MODULE
1.2
Theories and Themes

Theories of Child Development

Themes in Child Development Research

Learning Objectives

- **What are the major theories of child development? How do they account for change across infancy, childhood, and adolescence?**
- **What are some general conclusions about development that all child development scientists support?**

> *Marcus has just graduated from high school, first in his class. For his proud mother, Betty, this is a time to reflect on Marcus's past and ponder his future. Marcus has always been a happy, easygoing child—a joy to rear. And he's constantly been interested in learning. Betty wonders why he is so perpetually good-natured and so curious. If she knew the secret, she laughed, she could write a best-selling book and be a guest on Oprah!*

Betty is not the first person to ask these questions about children. In fact, such questions have occupied some of the greatest philosophers in history. Nearly four hundred years ago, the English philosopher John Locke (1632–1704) claimed that the human infant is a *tabula rasa*, or "blank slate." Experience then molds the infant, child, adolescent, and adult into a unique individual. Locke's view was challenged by the French philosopher, Jean Jacques Rousseau (1712–1778), who believed that newborns were endowed with an innate sense of justice and morality that would unfold naturally unless experience interfered.

By the middle of the 19th century, progress in science had merged with growing concerns about children's welfare to bring about a new approach to understanding childhood (Sears, 1975). Speculation about the child's "nature" was replaced by efforts to record and to study actual behavior and development. This was the dawn of the modern science of child development. To introduce you to this field, let's look at the major theories that have guided research in child development.

THEORIES OF CHILD DEVELOPMENT

For many people, the word "theory" means "boring." Boring professors make up boring theories that have nothing to do with the real world. But that's not true. If you want to understand children's development, theories are essential because they provide the *why*s for development. What is a theory? **In child development, a *theory* is an organized set of ideas that is designed to explain development.** For example, suppose friends of yours have a baby who cries often. You could imagine several explanations for her crying. Maybe the baby cries because she's hungry; maybe she cries to get her parents to hold her; maybe she cries because she's simply a cranky, unhappy baby. Each of these explanations is a very simple theory: It tries to explain why the baby cries so much. Of course, real developmental theories are much more complicated, but the purpose is the same—to explain behavior and development.

Research in child development is guided by the biological, psychodynamic, learning, cognitive-developmental, and ecological perspectives.

Theories lead to predictions that we can test in research; in the process, the theory is supported or not. Think about the different explanations for the crying baby. Each one leads to unique predictions. If, for example, the baby is crying because she's hungry, we predict that feeding her more often should stop the crying. When results of research match the predictions, this supports the theory. When results differ from the predictions, this shows that the theory is incorrect and needs to be revised.

Perhaps now you see why theories are essential for child development research: They are the source of predictions for research, which often lead to changes in the theories. These revised theories then provide the basis for new predictions, which lead to new research, and the cycle continues.

Many theories guide research and thinking about children's development. Some of these theories share ideas and assumptions about children and their development but differ in their details. These theories are often grouped together to form a theoretical perspective. In the next few pages, I briefly sketch five major theoretical perspectives in child development research: the biological, psychodynamic, learning, cognitive-developmental, and ecological perspectives. As you read about each perspective, think about how it differs from the others in its view of development.

The Biological Perspective. According to the biological perspective, intellectual and personality development, as well as physical and motor development, proceed according to a biological plan. One of the first biological theories, maturational theory, was proposed by Arnold Gesell (1880–1961), shown in the photo. **According to *maturational theory,* child development reflects a specific and prearranged scheme or plan within the body.** In Gesell's view, development is simply a natural unfolding of a biological plan; experience matters little. Like Jean Jacques Rousseau 200 years before him, Gesell encouraged parents to let their children develop naturally. Without interference from adults, Gesell claimed, behaviors like speech, play, and reasoning would emerge spontaneously according to a predetermined developmental timetable.

Other biological theories give greater weight to experience. ***Ethological theory* views development from an evolutionary perspective.** In this theory, many behaviors are adaptive—they have survival value. For example, clinging, grasping, and crying are adaptive for infants because they elicit caregiving from adults. Ethological theorists assume that people inherit many of these adaptive behaviors.

So far, ethological theory seems like maturational theory, with a dash of evolution for taste. How does experience fit in? Ethologists believe that all animals are biologically programmed so that some kinds of learning occur only at certain ages. **A *critical period* is the time in development when a specific type of learning can take place; before or after the critical period, the same learning is difficult or even impossible.**

One of the best known examples of a critical period comes from the work of Konrad Lorenz (1903–1989), a Nobel-prize-winning Austrian zoologist. Lorenz noticed that newly hatched chicks follow their mother about. He theorized that chicks are biologically programmed to follow the first moving object that they see after hatching. **Usually this was the mother, so following her was the first step in *imprinting*, creating an emotional bond with the mother.** Lorenz tested his theory by showing that if he removed the mother immediately after the chicks hatched and replaced it with another moving object, the chicks would follow that object and treat it as "mother." As the photo shows, this included Lorenz himself!

Lorenz also discovered that the chick had to see the moving object within about a day of hatching. Otherwise, the chick would not imprint on the moving object. In other words, there is a critical period for imprinting that lasts about a day; when chicks experience the moving object outside of the critical period, imprinting does not take place. Even though the underlying mechanism is biological, experience is essential for triggering programmed, adaptive behaviors.

Ethological theory and maturational theory both highlight the biological bases of child development. Biological theorists remind us that children's genes, which are the product of a long evolutionary history, influence virtually every aspect of children's development. Consequently, a biological theorist would tell Betty, the mother of the high-school graduate in the module-opening vignette, that her son's good nature and his outstanding academic record are both largely products of heredity.

The Psychodynamic Perspective. This is the oldest scientific perspective on child development, tracing its roots to Sigmund Freud's (1856–1939) work in the late 19th and early 20th centuries. Freud, shown in the photo, was a physician who specialized in diseases of the nervous system. Many of his patients were adults who suffered from ailments that seemed to have no obvious biological cause. As Freud listened to his patients describe their problems and their lives, he became convinced that early experiences establish patterns that endure throughout a person's life. **Using his patients' case histories, Freud created the first *psychodynamic theory* in which development is largely determined by how well people resolve conflicts they face at different ages.**

Two aspects of Freud's theorizing have influenced child development research. The first was his theory of personality. Freud proposed that personality includes three primary components that emerge at distinct ages. **The *id* is a reservoir of primitive instincts and drives.** Present at birth, the id presses for immediate gratification of bodily needs and wants. A hungry baby crying illustrates the id in action. **The *ego* is the practical, rational component of personality.** The ego begins to emerge during the first year of life, as infants learn that they cannot always have what they want. The ego tries to resolve conflicts that occur when the instinctive desires of the id encounter the obstacles of the real world. The ego often tries to channel the id's impulsive demands into socially more acceptable channels. **The third component of personality, the *superego*, emerges during the preschool years as children begin to internalize adult standards of right and wrong.** The superego is the "moral agent" in the child's personality.

A second influential aspect of Freud's work was his account of psychosexual development. He believed that humans want to experience physical pleasure from birth. As children grow, the focus of the pleasure shifts to different parts of the body. The result is a sequence of developmental stages in which each stage is characterized by sensitivity in a particular part of the body or erogenous zone. For example, from birth to the first birthday, infants are in the oral stage. As the name suggests, they seek pleasure orally, usually by sucking.

Freud believed that development proceeds best when children's needs at each stage are met but not exceeded. If children's needs are not met adequately, they are frustrated and reluctant to move to other, more mature forms of stimulation. For example, a baby whose needs for oral stimulation were not met may try to satisfy these needs as an adolescent or adult by smoking. If children find one source of stimulation *too* satisfying, they see little need to progress to more advanced stages. In Freud's view, parents have the difficult task of satisfying children's needs without indulging them.

Freud's student, Erik Erikson (1902–1994), shown in the photo, believed that psychological and social aspects of development were more important than the biological and physical aspects that Freud emphasized. **Erikson proposed a *psychosocial theory* in which development consists of a sequence of stages, each defined by a unique crisis or challenge.** The complete theory included eight stages

The Eight Stages of Psychosocial Development in Erikson's Theory

Psychosocial Stage	Age	Challenge
Basic trust versus mistrust	Birth to 1 year	To develop a sense that the world is safe, a "good place"
Autonomy versus shame and doubt	1 to 3 years	To realize that one is an independent person who can make decisions
Initiative versus guilt	3 to 6 years	To develop the ability to try new things and to handle failure
Industry versus inferiority	6 years to adolescence	To learn basic skills and to work with others
Identity versus identity confusion	Adolescence	To develop a lasting, integrated sense of self
Intimacy versus isolation	Young adulthood	To commit to another in a loving relationship
Generativity versus stagnation	Middle adulthood	To contribute to younger people through child rearing, child care, or other productive work
Integrity versus despair	Old age	To view one's life as satisfactory and worth living

that are shown in the table on page 8. You can see that the name of each stage reflects the challenge that people face at a particular age. For example, the challenge for young adults is to become involved in a loving relationship. Erikson claimed that adults who establish this relationship experience intimacy; those who don't, experience isolation.

Erikson also argued that the earlier stages of psychosocial development provide the foundation for the later stages. For example, adolescents who do not meet the challenge of developing an identity will not establish truly intimate relationships; instead, they will become overly dependent on their partners as a source of identity.

Psychodynamic theories emphasize that development is a product of the child's responses to life's challenges.

Whether we call them challenges, crises, or conflicts, the psychodynamic perspective emphasizes that the trek to adulthood is difficult because the path is strewn with obstacles. Outcomes of development reflect the manner and ease with which children surmount life's barriers. When children overcome early obstacles easily, they are better able to handle the later ones. A psychodynamic theorist would tell Betty that her son's cheerful disposition and his academic record suggest that he has handled life's early obstacles well, which is a good sign for his future development.

The Learning Perspective. Learning theorists champion John Locke's view that the infant's mind is a blank slate on which experience writes. John Watson (1878–1958) was the first theorist to apply this approach to child development. Watson argued that learning determines what children will be. He assumed that with the correct techniques anything could be learned by almost anyone. In other words, in Watson's view, experience was just about all that mattered in determining the course of development.

Watson did little research to support his claims; B. F. Skinner (1904–1990), shown in the photo, filled this gap. **Skinner studied *operant conditioning,* in which the consequences of a behavior determine whether a behavior is repeated in the future.** Skinner showed that two kinds of consequences were especially influential. **A *reinforcement* is a consequence that increases the future likelihood of the behavior that it follows.** Positive reinforcement consists of giving a reward like chocolate, gold stars, or paychecks to increase the likelihood of a previous behavior. The parents of the child whose room is shown in the photograph could use positive reinforcement to encourage her to clean her room. Every time she cleaned her room, they could reinforce her with praise, food, or money. Negative reinforcement consists of rewarding people by taking away unpleasant things. The same parents could use negative reinforcement by saying that whenever she cleaned her room she wouldn't have to wash the dishes or fold laundry.

A *punishment* is a consequence that decreases the future likelihood of the behavior that it follows. Punishment suppresses a behavior by either adding something aversive or by withholding a pleasant event. When the child failed to clean her room, the parents could punish her by spanking (adding something aversive) or by not allowing her to watch television (withholding a pleasant event).

Skinner's research was done primarily with animals, but child development researchers soon showed

that the principles of operant conditioning could be extended readily to children's behavior (Baer and Wolf, 1968). Applied properly, reinforcement and punishment are indeed powerful influences on children. However, researchers discovered that children sometimes learn in ways that are not readily explained by operant conditioning. The most important of these is that children sometimes learn without reinforcement or punishment. **Children learn much simply by watching those around them, which is known as** *imitation or observational learning.* Imitation is occurring when one toddler throws a toy after seeing a peer do so or when a school-age child offers to help an older adult carry groceries because she's seen her parents do the same.

Perhaps imitation makes you think of "monkey-see, monkey-do" in which children simply mimic what they see. Early investigators had this view, too, but research quickly showed that this was wrong. Children do not always imitate what they see around them. Children are more likely to imitate if the person they see is popular, smart, or talented. They're also more likely to imitate when the behavior they see is rewarded than when it is punished. Findings like these imply that imitation is more complex than sheer mimicry. Children do not mechanically copy what they see and hear; instead, they look to others for information about appropriate behavior. When popular, smart peers are reinforced for behaving in a particular way, it makes sense to imitate them.

Albert Bandura (1925–) based his *social cognitive theory* **on this more complex view of reward, punishment, and imitation.** Bandura, shown in the top photo, calls his theory "cognitive" because he believes that children are actively trying to understand what goes on in their world; the theory is "social" because, along with reinforcement and punishment, what other people do is an important source of information about the world.

Bandura also argues that experience gives children a sense of *self-efficacy,* **which refers to children's beliefs about their own abilities and talents.** Self-efficacy beliefs help determine when children will imitate others. A child who sees herself as athletically untalented, for example, will not try to imitate Michael Jordan dunking a basketball, despite the fact that he is obviously talented and popular. Thus, whether children imitate others depends on who the other person is, whether that person's behavior is rewarded, and the children's beliefs about their own talents.

Bandura's social cognitive theory is a far cry from Skinner's operant conditioning. The operant conditioning child who responds mechanically to reinforcement and punishment has been replaced by the social cognitive child who actively interprets events. Nevertheless, Skinner, Bandura, and all learning theorists share the view that experience propels children along their developmental journeys. They would tell Betty that she can thank experience for making Marcus both happy and successful academically.

The Cognitive-Developmental Perspective. The cognitive-developmental perspective focuses on how children think and how their thinking changes over time. Jean Piaget (1896–1980), shown in the bottom photo, was the most influential developmental psychologist of the 20th century and proposed the best-known of these theories. Piaget believed that children naturally try to make sense of their world. Throughout infancy, childhood, and adolescence, youngsters want to understand the workings of both the physical and the social world. For example, infants want to know about objects: "What happens when I push this toy off the table?" And they want to know about people: "Who is this person who feeds and cares for me?"

Piaget argued that in their efforts to comprehend their world, children act like scientists in creating theories about the physical and social worlds. They try to weave all that they know about objects and people into a complete theory. Children's theories are tested daily by experience because their theories lead them to expect certain things to happen. As with real scientific theories, when the predicted events do occur, a child's belief in her theory grows stronger. When the predicted events do not occur, the child must revise her theory. For example, an infant's theory of objects might include the idea that "Toys pushed off the table fall to the floor." If the infant pushes some other object—a plate or an article of clothing—she will find that it, too, falls to the floor and can make the theory more general: "Objects pushed off the table fall to the floor."

Piaget also believed that at a few critical points in development, children realize their theories have basic flaws. When this happens, they revise their theories radically. These changes are so fundamental that the revised theory is, in many respects, a brand-new theory. Piaget claimed that radical revisions occurred three times in development: once at about age 2 years, a second time at about age 7, and a third time just before adolescence. These radical changes mean children go through four distinct stages in cognitive development. Each stage represents a fundamental change in how children understand and organize their environment, and each stage is characterized by more sophisticated types of reasoning. For example, the sensorimotor stage begins at birth and lasts until about 2 years of age. As the name implies, sensorimotor thinking is closely linked to the infant's sensory and motor skills. This stage and the three later stages are shown in the table.

> **Piaget believed that children spontaneously create theories to explain the workings of their physical and social worlds.**

Piaget's Four Stages of Cognitive Development

Stage	Approximate Age	Characteristics
Sensorimotor	Birth to 2 years	Infant's knowledge of the world is based on senses and motor skills. By the end of the period, infant uses mental representations.
Preoperational thought	2 to 6 years	Child learns how to use symbols such as words and numbers to represent aspects of the world, but relates to the world only through his or her perspective.
Concrete operational thought	7 to 11 years	Child understands and applies logical operations to experiences, provided they are focused on the here and now.
Formal operational thought	Adolescence and beyond	Adolescent or adult thinks abstractly, speculates on hypothetical situations, and reasons deductively about what may be possible.

Not all cognitive-developmental theorists view development as a sequence of stages. Information-processing theorists, for example, draw heavily on how computers work to explain thinking and how it develops through childhood and adolescence. **Just as computers consist of both hardware (disk drives, random-access memory, and central processing unit) and software (the programs we use),** *information-processing theory* **proposes that human cognition consists of mental hardware and mental software.** Mental hardware refers to cognitive structures, including different memories where information is stored. Mental software includes organized sets of cognitive processes that allow children to complete specific tasks, such as reading a sentence, playing a video game, or hitting a baseball.

In the information-processing approach, cognitive development reflects change in mental hardware and mental software.

How do information-processing psychologists explain developmental change in thinking? To answer this question, think about improvements in personal computers. Today's personal computers can accomplish much more than a computer that was built just a few years ago. Why? Because today's computer has better hardware (for example, more memory and a faster central processing unit) and because it has more sophisticated software that takes advantage of the better hardware. Like modern computers, older children and adolescents have better hardware and better software than younger children, who are more like last year's out-of-date model. For example, older children typically can solve math word problems better than younger children because they have greater memory capacity to store the facts in the problem and because their methods for performing arithmetic operations are more efficient.

For both Piaget and information-processing theorists, children's thinking becomes more sophisticated as children develop. Piaget explains this change in terms of more sophisticated theories that children create; information-processing psychologists attribute it to more sophisticated mental hardware and mental software. Neither would have much to say to Betty about Marcus's good nature. As to his academic success, Piaget would explain that all children naturally want to understand their worlds; Marcus is simply unusually skilled in this regard. An information-processing psychologist would point to superior hardware and superior software as the keys to his academic success.

The Ecological Perspective. Most developmentalists agree that the environment is an important force in development. However, only ecological theories have focused on the complexities of environments and their links to development. **For** *ecological theory,* **which gets its name from the branch of biology dealing with the relation of living things to their environment and to one another, child development is inseparable from the environmental contexts in which a child develops.** In other words, all aspects of development are interconnected, much like the threads of a spider's web are all intertwined. Interconnectedness means that no aspect of development can be isolated from others and understood independently.

The best-known proponent of the ecological approach is Urie Bronfenbrenner (1917–), shown in the photo. Bronfenbrenner proposes that the developing child is embedded in a series of complex and interactive systems. As the diagram at the top of page 13 shows, Bronfenbrenner (1979, 1989, 1995) divides the environment into four levels: the microsystem, the mesosystem, the exosystem, and the macrosystem. **At any point in life, the** *microsystem* **consists of the people and objects in an individual's immediate environment.** These are the people closest to a child, such as parents or siblings. Some children may have more than one microsystem; for example, a young child might have the microsystems of the family and of the day-care setting. As you can imagine, microsystems strongly influence development.

Microsystems themselves are connected to create the *mesosystem.* The mesosystem represents the fact that what happens in one microsystem is likely to influence others. Perhaps you've found that if you have a stressful day at work or school, you're often grouchy at home. This indicates that your mesosystem is alive and well; your microsystems of home and work are interconnected emotionally for you.

The *exosystem* **refers to social settings that a person may not experience firsthand but that still influence development.** For example, a mother may pay more attention to her child when her work is going well and less attention when she's under a great deal of work-related stress. Although the influence of the exosystem is at least secondhand, its effects on the developing child can be quite strong.

The broadest environmental context is the *macrosystem,* **the subcultures and cultures in which the microsystem, mesosystem, and exosystem are embedded.** A mother, her workplace, her child, and the child's school are part of a larger cultural setting, such as Asian Americans living in Southern California or Italian Americans living in large cities on the East Coast. Members of these cultural groups share a common identity, a common heritage, and common values. The macrosystem evolves over time; what is true about a particular culture today may or may not have been true in the past and may or may not be true in the future. Thus, each successive generation of children develops in a unique macrosystem.

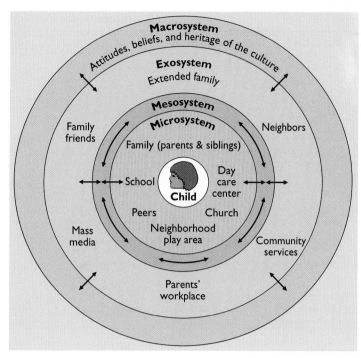

Bronfenbrenner and other ecological theorists would agree with learning theorists in telling Betty that the environment has been pivotal in her son's amiable disposition and his academic achievements. However, the ecological theorist would insist that environment means much more than the reinforcements, punishments, and observations that are central to learning theory. The ecological theorist would emphasize the different levels of environmental influence on Marcus. Betty's ability to balance home and work so skillfully (which meant that she was usually in a good mood herself) contributed positively to Marcus's development, as did Betty's membership in a cultural group that emphasized the value of doing well in school.

The Big Picture Concerning the Five Perspectives. Comparing five major perspectives in 8 pages is like trying to see all of the major sights of a large city in a day: It can be done, but it's demanding and, after a while, everything blurs together. Relax. The table at the top of page 14 gives a capsule account of all five perspectives and their important theories.

Perhaps you're wondering which of the perspectives is right? Actually, no single perspective provides a truly complete explanation of all aspects of children's development. But by drawing upon all of them, we'll be better able to understand the different forces that contribute to children's development. Development *is* complicated, after all, and in many chapters we'll rely upon multiple perspectives to understand why children develop as they do.

Characteristics of Developmental Perspectives

Perspective	Key Assumptions	Specific Theories
Biological	Development is determined primarily by biological forces.	**Maturational theory:** emphasizes development as a natural unfolding of a biological plan.
		Ethological theory: emphasizes the adaptive nature of behavior and the importance of experience during critical periods of development.
Psychodynamic	Development is determined primarily by how a child resolves conflicts at different ages.	**Freud's theory:** emphasizes the conflict between primitive biological forces and societal standards for right and wrong.
		Erikson's theory: emphasizes the challenges posed by the formation of trust, autonomy, initiative, industry, and identity.
Learning	Development is determined primarily by a child's environment.	**Skinner's operant conditioning:** emphasizes the role of reinforcement and punishment.
		Bandura's social cognitive theory: emphasizes children's efforts to understand their world, using reinforcement, punishment, and others' behavior.
Cognitive-Developmental	Development reflects children's efforts to understand the world.	**Piaget's theory:** emphasizes the different stages of thinking that result from children's changing theories of the world.
		Information-processing theory: emphasizes the changes in thinking that reflect changes in mental hardware and mental software.
Ecological	Development is influenced by immediate and more distant environments, which typically influence each other.	**Bronfenbrenner's theory:** emphasizes the influences of the microsystem, mesosystem, exosystem, and macrosystem.

THEMES IN CHILD DEVELOPMENT RESEARCH

We've seen that the five perspectives differ in many key assumptions about development. Nevertheless, if we asked 100 child development experts representing these different perspectives to describe general conclusions concerning development, several would appear on nearly everyone's list. I like to think of these conclusions or themes as a foundation that you can use to organize the numerous specific facts about child development that fill the rest of this book. These conclusions or themes should help you to unify your own understanding of child development. In fact, to help you do this, every chapter (except this one) ends with "In Perspective," where one of the themes is illustrated in detail with research from the chapter.

Here are the four unifying themes.

Early development is related to later development but not perfectly. This theme has to do with the "predictability" of development. Do you believe that happy, cheerful 5-year-olds remain outgoing and friendly throughout their lives? If you do, this shows that you believe development is a continuous process: Once a child begins down a particular developmental pathway, he or she stays on that path throughout life. According to this view, friendly and smart 5-year-olds become friendly and smart 15- and 25-year-olds. The other view—that development is not continuous—is shown in the cartoon at the top of page 15. Sweet and cooperative Trixie has become a demanding, assertive child. According to this view, friendly and smart 5-year-olds may be obnoxious and foolish as 15-year-olds and quiet but wise as 25-year-olds. **Thus, *the continuity versus discontinuity issue* is really about the "connectedness" of development: Are early aspects of development consistently related to later aspects?**

Hi and Lois © 1993. Reprinted with special permission of King Features Syndicate.

In reality, neither of these views is accurate. Development is not perfectly predictable. A friendly, smart 5-year-old does not guarantee a friendly, smart 15- or 25-year-old, but the chances of a friendly, smart adult are greater than if the child were obnoxious and foolish. There are many ways to become a friendly and smart 15-year-old; being a friendly and smart 5-year-old is *not* a required step but it *is* probably the most direct route!

Development is always jointly influenced by heredity and environment. Let me introduce this theme with a story about my sons. Ben, my first son, was a delightful baby and toddler. He awoke each morning with a smile on his face, eager to start yet another fun-filled day. When Ben was upset, which occurred infrequently, we could console him quickly by holding and rocking him. I presumed that his cheerful disposition must reflect fabulous parenting. Consequently, I was stunned when my second son, Matt, spent much of the first year of his life being fussy and cranky. He was easily irritated and hard to soothe. Why wasn't the all-star parenting that had been so effective with Ben working with Matt? The answer, of course, is that Ben's parenting wasn't the sole cause of his happiness. I thought environmental influences accounted for his amiable disposition, but in fact, biological influences also played an important role.

This anecdote illustrates the *nature-nurture issue*: What roles do biology (nature) and environment (nurture) play in child development? Are children like Ben outgoing because of their heredity or because of the experiences they have? Scientists once hoped to answer questions like this by identifying either heredity or environment as *the* cause. Their goal was to be able to say, for example, that intelligence was due to heredity or that personality was due to experience. Today, we know that virtually no aspects of child development are due exclusively to either heredity or environment. Instead, development is always shaped by both; nature and nurture interact. In fact, a major aim of child development research is to understand how heredity and environment codetermine children's development. Biology will be more influential in some areas and environment in others.

Children help determine their own development. Whenever I teach child development, I always ask students their plans for when they have children. How will they rear them? What do they want them to grow up to be? It's interesting to hear students' responses. Most have big plans for their future children. It's just as interesting to watch students who already have children roll their eyes in a "You don't have a clue" way at what the others say. The parent-students in class admit that they, too, once had grand designs about child rearing. What they quickly learned, however, was that their children shaped the way in which they parented.

All aspects of development are determined by the combined forces of heredity and environment.

These two points of view illustrate the *active-passive child issue:* Are children simply at the mercy of the environment (passive child) or do children actively influence their own development through their own unique individual characteristics (active child)? The passive view corresponds to Locke's description of the child as a blank slate on which experience writes, whereas the active view corresponds to Rousseau's view of development as a natural unfolding that takes place within the child. Today, we know that experiences are indeed crucial but not always in the way Locke (and the early learning theorists) envisioned. Often, it's a child's interpretation of experiences that shapes his or her development. Also, a child's unique characteristics may cause him or her to have some experiences but not others. From birth, children are trying to make sense of their world, and in the process, they help shape their own destinies.

Development in different domains is connected. As I explained on page 5, the chapters in this book are organized around different topics of development. Why? Child development research is designed to examine different aspects of development—like physical growth, cognition, language, personality, and social relationships. Describing the findings of this research is much more straightforward when the book is organized around the topics that child developmentalists actually explore. This topical organization does not mean that you should think of each aspect of development as an independent entity, one that is completely separate from the others. To the contrary, our 100 child development experts would definitely agree that development in different domains is always intertwined. Cognitive and social development are not independent; advances in one area affect advances in the other. The same could be said for the many other topics throughout the book.

Now that I've introduced the themes, let me present them together one time before we move on.

- Early development is related to later development but not perfectly.

- Development is always jointly influenced by heredity and environment.

- Children help determine their own development.

- Development in different domains is connected.

You will see these themes frequently because, beginning in Chapter 2, each chapter ends with "In Perspective," where I use research from the chapter to explore a particular theme in detail.

The themes and the five theoretical perspectives will serve you well as we explore the field of child development. However, you need one more essential tool: You need to learn about the methods developmentalists use to conduct research. This is the topic of Module 1.3.

Check Your Learning

1. Ethological theorists claim that _____ is a time when a specific type of learning can take place.

2. The _____ perspective emphasizes the influence of conflicts on children's development.

3. _____ proposes that children use reinforcement, punishment, and others' behavior to learn about the world.

4. According to _____, development is linked to changes in mental hardware and mental software.

5. The influence of multiple levels of the environment is central in _____ theory.

6. The _____ issue concerns whether early development is related to later development.

discontinuity.

Answers: (1) a critical period, (2) psychodynamic, (3) Albert Bandura's social cognitive theory, (4) the information-processing approach, (5) Bronfenbrenner's ecological, (6) continuity-

D OING DEVELOPMENTAL RESEARCH

Learning Objectives

- **How do scientists measure topics of interest in children's development?**
- **What general research designs are used in child development research? What designs are unique to child development research?**
- **What ethical procedures must researchers follow?**

> *Leah and Joan are both mothers of 10-year-old boys. Their sons have many friends, but the basis for the friendships are not obvious to the mothers. Leah believes that "opposites attract"—children form friendships with peers who have complementary interests and abilities. Joan doubts this; her son seems to seek out other boys who are near clones of himself in terms of interests and abilities.*

Suppose that Leah and Joan know you're taking a course in child development, so they ask you to settle their argument. You know, from Module 1.2, that Leah and Joan each have simple theories about children's friendships. Leah's theory is that complementary children are more often friends, whereas Joan's theory is that similar children are more often friends. And you know that these theories should be tested with research. But how? In fact, child development researchers must make several important decisions as they prepare to study a topic. They need to decide how to measure the topic of interest; they must design their study; they must choose a method for studying their topic; and they must decide if their method respects the rights of the individuals who would participate in the research.

Child development researchers do not always stick to this sequence of steps. For example, often researchers consider the rights of research participants as they make each of the other decisions, perhaps rejecting a procedure because it violates the rights of research participants. Nevertheless, for simplicity, I will use this sequence as I describe the steps in doing developmental research.

MEASUREMENT IN CHILD DEVELOPMENT RESEARCH

Research usually begins by deciding how to measure the topic or behavior of interest. For example, the first step toward answering Leah and Joan's question about friendships would be to decide how to measure friendships. Child development researchers typically use one of three approaches: observing systematically, using tasks to sample behavior, and asking children for self reports.

Systematic Observation. As the name implies, *systematic observation* involves watching children and carefully recording what they do or say. Two forms of systematic observation are common. **In *naturalistic observation,* children are observed as they behave spontaneously in some real-life situation.** Of course, researchers can't keep track of everything that a child does, so beforehand they must decide which variables—factors subject to change—to record. Researchers studying friendship might, for example, decide to record where children sit in the lunchroom and who talks to whom. Further, they might decide to observe children at the start of the first year in a middle school because many children make new friends at this time.

In *structured observation,* **the researcher creates a setting that is particularly likely to elicit the behavior of interest.** Structured observations are particularly useful for studying behaviors that are difficult to observe naturally. Some phenomena occur rarely, such as emergencies. An investigator relying upon natural observations to study children's responses to emergencies wouldn't make much progress with naturalistic observation because, by definition, emergencies don't occur at predetermined times and locations. However, using structured observation, an investigator might stage an emergency—perhaps by having a nearby adult cry for help—and observe the child's response.

> *Structured observations are useful for studying behaviors that occur rarely or that typically occur in private settings.*

Other behaviors are difficult for researchers to observe because they occur in private settings not public ones. For example, much interaction between friends takes place at home, where it would be difficult for investigators to observe unobtrusively. However, friends could be asked to come to the researcher's laboratory, which might be furnished to resemble a family room in a typical house. Friends would then be asked to perform some activity typical of friends, such as playing a game together or deciding what movie to see. The researchers would then observe their activity from another room, through a one-way mirror.

Though structured observations allow researchers to observe behavior(s) that would otherwise be difficult to study, investigators must be careful that the settings they create do not disturb the behavior of interest. For instance, observing friends as they play a game in a mock family room has many artificial aspects to it: The friends are not in their own homes, they were told (in general terms) what to do, and they know they're being observed. Any or all of these factors may cause friends to behave differently than they would in the real world. **This issue of whether observations really measure what researchers think they measure is referred to as** *validity.* Are observations of friends in a mock family room telling us about friends' interactions as they occur naturally? If they are, then they are a valid measure of children's behavior. Investigators must take great care to document the validity of their measures.

Sampling Behavior with Tasks. When investigators can't observe a behavior directly, another popular alternative is to create tasks that are thought to sample

the behavior of interest. Digit span is a task that's often used to measure children's memory: Children listen as a sequence of numbers is presented aloud. After the last digit is presented, children try to repeat the digits in order. Another example is shown in the diagram. The child has been asked to look at the photographs and point to the person who is happy. A child's answers on this sort of task are useful in determining children's ability to recognize emotions.

Sampling behavior with tasks is popular with child development researchers because it is so convenient. A major problem with this approach, however, is validity: Does the task really sample the behavior of interest? For example, asking children to judge emotions from photographs may not be valid because it underestimates what they do in real life. Can you think of reasons why this might be the case? I mention several reasons on page 26, just before "Check Your Learning."

Self Reports. The last approach to measurement, self reports, is actually a special case of using tasks to measure children's behavior. *Self reports* **are simply children's answers to questions about the topic of interest.** When questions are posed in written form, the report is a questionnaire; when questions are posed orally, the report is an interview. In either format, questions are created that probe different aspects of the topic of interest. For example, if you believed that children more often become friends when they have interests in common, then research participants might be told the following:

> Tom and Dave just met each other at school. Tom likes to read, plays the clarinet in the school orchestra, and is not interested in sports; Dave likes to watch videos on MTV, tinkers with his car, and is a star on the football team. Do you think Tom and Dave will become friends?

Children would decide, perhaps using a rating scale, if the boys are likely to become friends.

Self reports are useful because they can lead directly to information on the topic of interest. They are also relatively convenient (particularly when they can be administered to groups of subjects). However, self reports are not always valid measures of children's behavior because children's answers are inaccurate. Why? When asked about past events, children may not remember them accurately. For example, an adolescent asked about childhood friends may not remember those friendships well. Sometimes children answer incorrectly due to response bias. That is, some responses may be more socially acceptable than others, and children are more likely to select those than socially unacceptable answers. For example, many children would be reluctant to admit that they have no friends at all. As long as investigators keep these weaknesses in mind, self report is a valuable tool for child development research.

The three approaches to measurement are summarized in the table:

Ways of Measuring Behaviors of Interest in Child Development Research

Method	Strength	Weakness
Systematic observation		
Naturalistic observation	Captures children's behavior in its natural setting	Difficult to use with behaviors that are rare or that typically occur in private settings
Structured observation	Can be used to study behaviors that are rare or that typically occur in private settings	May be invalid if the structured setting distorts the behavior
Sampling behavior with tasks	Convenient—can be used to study most behaviors	May be invalid if the task does not sample behavior as it occurs naturally
Self reports (questionnaires and interviews)	Convenient—can be used to study most behaviors	May be invalid because children answer incorrectly due to forgetting or response bias

Throughout this book, you'll see many studies using these different methods. You'll also see that studies of the same topic or behavior often use different methods. That is, each approach can be used in many different studies. This can be particularly valuable: Because the approaches to measurement have different strengths and weaknesses, finding the same results regardless of the approach leads to particularly strong conclusions.

Representative Sampling. Valid measures depend not only upon the method of measurement, but also upon the children who are tested. **Researchers are usually interested in broad groups of children called *populations*.** Examples of populations would be all American 7-year-olds or all African American adolescents. **Virtually all studies include only a *sample* of children, which is a subset of the population.** Researchers must take care that their sample really is representative of the population of interest. An unrepresentative sample can lead to invalid research. For example, what would you think of a study of children's friendship if you learned that the sample consisted entirely of 8-year-olds who had no friends? You would, quite correctly, decide that this sample is not representative of the population of 8-year-olds and question its results.

Researchers study samples of children to reach conclusions about larger populations of interest.

As you read on, you'll discover that much of the research I describe was conducted with samples of middle-class European American youngsters. Are these samples representative of all children in the United States? Of all children in the world? Sometimes, but not always. Be careful *not* to assume that findings from this group necessarily apply to people in other groups.

GENERAL DESIGNS FOR RESEARCH

Having selected a way to measure the topic or behavior of interest, researchers must then put this measure into a research design. Child development researchers usually use one of two designs: correlational and experimental studies.

Correlational Studies. In a *correlational study,* investigators look at relations between variables as they exist naturally in the world. In the simplest possible correlational study, a researcher measures two variables, then sees how they are related. Imagine a researcher who wants to test the idea that smarter children have more friends. To test this claim, the researcher would measure two variables for each child in the sample. One would be the number of friends that the child has; the other would be the child's intelligence.

The results of a correlational study are usually expressed as a *correlation coefficient,* abbreviated *r,* which stands for the strength and direction of a relation between two variables. Correlations can range from −1.0 to 1.0:

- When $r = 0$, two variables are completely unrelated: Children's intelligence is unrelated to the number of friends they have.

- When r is greater than 0, scores are related positively: Children who are smart tend to have more friends than children who are not as smart. That is, *more* intelligence is associated with having *more* friends.

- When r is less than 0, scores are related, but inversely: Children who are smart tend to have fewer friends than children who are not as smart. That is, *more* intelligence is associated with having *fewer* friends.

A researcher conducting a correlational study determines whether variables are related, but this design doesn't address the question of cause and effect between the variables. In other words, suppose a researcher finds that the correlation between intelligence and number of friends is .7. This means that children who are smarter have more friends than those who are not as smart. How would you interpret this correlation? The diagram shows that three interpretations are possible. Maybe being smart causes children to have more friends. Another interpretation is that having more friends causes children to be smarter. A third interpretation is that neither variable causes the other; instead, intelligence and number of friends are caused by a third variable that was not measured in the study. Perhaps parents who are warm and supportive tend to have children who are smarter and also have many friends. Any of these interpretations could be true. Cause and effect cannot be distinguished in a correlational study. When investigators want to track down causes, they must use a different design, an experimental study.

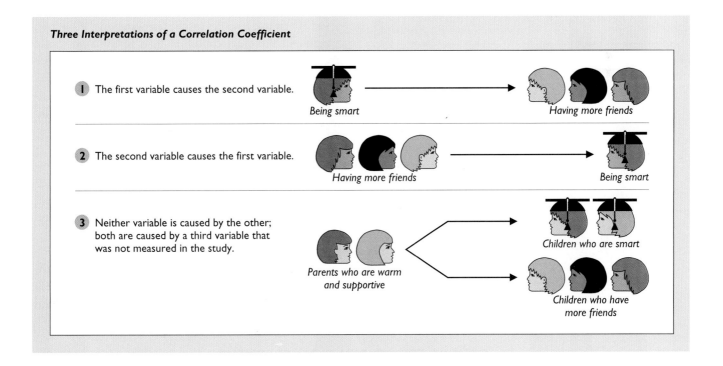

Three Interpretations of a Correlation Coefficient

1. The first variable causes the second variable.
   Being smart → *Having more friends*

2. The second variable causes the first variable.
   Having more friends → *Being smart*

3. Neither variable is caused by the other; both are caused by a third variable that was not measured in the study.
   Parents who are warm and supportive → *Children who are smart* / *Children who have more friends*

Experimental Studies. An *experiment* **is a systematic way of manipulating the key factor(s) that an investigator thinks causes a particular behavior. The factor that is manipulated is called the *independent variable;* the behavior that is measured is called the *dependent variable.*** In an experiment, the investigator begins with one or more treatments, circumstances, or events (independent variables) that are thought to affect a particular behavior. Children are then assigned randomly to different treatment groups. Next, the dependent variable is measured in all groups. Because each child has an equal chance of being assigned to any treatment group (the definition of random assignment), the groups should be the same except in the treatment they receive. Any differences between the groups can then be attributed to the differential treatment the children received in the experiment, rather than to other factors.

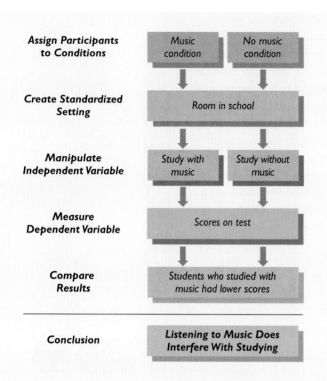

Assign Participants to Conditions	Music condition	No music condition
Create Standardized Setting	Room in school	
Manipulate Independent Variable	Study with music	Study without music
Measure Dependent Variable	Scores on test	
Compare Results	Students who studied with music had lower scores	
Conclusion	**Listening to Music Does Interfere With Studying**	

Suppose, for example, that an investigator believes adolescents can learn more by reading in a quiet room than in a room with loud music playing. The diagram shows how we might test this hypothesis. Adolescents would come to the testing site (perhaps an available room in the school) where they would read a brief story prepared specially for the study. Based on random assignment, individual adolescents would read the story either while the room was quiet or while loud music was played. The loud music would be the same music, played at the same volume, for all adolescents in the loud-music condition. All adolescents would read the identical story under circumstances held as constant as possible except for the presence or absence of the music. They would all get the same amount of time to read the story, and they would all be given the same test afterward. If scores on the test were, on the average, better in the quiet condition than in the loud-music condition, the investigator could say with confidence that the music had an unfavorable effect on learning the story. Conclusions about cause and effect are possible because there was a direct manipulation of an independent variable under controlled conditions.

Child development researchers usually conduct their experiments in laboratory-like settings to control all the variables that might influence the outcome of the research. A shortcoming of laboratory work is that the behavior of interest is not studied in its natural setting. Consequently, there is always the potential problem that the results may be invalid because they are artificial—specific to the laboratory setting and not representative of the behavior in the "real world."

Both research designs used by developmentalists—correlational and experimental—have strengths and weaknesses. There is no one best method. Consequently, no single investigation can definitely answer a question, and researchers rarely rely on one study or even one method to reach conclusions. Instead, they prefer to find converging evidence from as many different kinds of studies as possible.

DESIGNS FOR STUDYING DEVELOPMENT

Sometimes child development research is directed at a single age group, such as the adolescent students in the impact of music study. Or researchers might study mother-infant relationships in 1-year-olds or friendships in fifth graders. With single age groups, after an investigator decides how to measure the behavior of interest and whether the study will be correlational or experimental, he or she could skip directly to the last step—determine if the study is ethical. However, much research in child development concerns changes that occur *as children develop* over a period of time. In these cases, investigators must make one further decision: Will they do a longitudinal study or a cross-sectional study?

Longitudinal Studies. In a *longitudinal study,* **the same individuals are observed or tested repeatedly at different points in their lives.** As the name implies, the longitudinal approach takes a lengthwise view of development and is the most direct way to watch growth occur. The longitudinal approach is well suited to studying almost any aspect of the course of development. More important, it is the only way to answer certain questions about the continuity or discontinuity of behavior: Will characteristics such as aggression, dependency, or mistrust observed in infancy or early childhood persist into adulthood? Will a traumatic event such as being abandoned by one's parents influence later social and intellectual development? How long will the beneficial effects of special academic training in the preschool years last? Such questions can be explored only by testing children early in development and then retesting them later in their development.

Only longitudinal studies can answer questions about the continuity of behavior over development.

The approach, however, has disadvantages that frequently offset its strengths. An obvious one is cost: The expense of merely keeping up with a large sample of individuals can be staggering. A related problem is the constancy of the sample over the course of research. Experience has shown how difficult it is to maintain contact with children over several years (as long as 30 years in some longitudinal studies!) in a highly mobile society. And even among those who do not move away, some lose interest and choose not to continue. These "dropouts" are often significantly different from their more research-minded peers, and this fact may also distort the outcome. For example, a group of children may seem to show intellectual growth between 4 and 7 years of age. What has actually happened, however, is that those who found earlier testing most difficult are the very ones who have quit the study, thereby raising the group average on the next round.

Even if the sample remains constant, though, the fact that children are given the same test many times may make them "test-wise." Improvement over time that is attributed to development may actually stem from practice with a particular test. Changing the test from year to year solves the practice problem but raises the question of how to compare responses to different tests. Because of these and other problems with the longitudinal method, child development researchers often use cross-sectional studies instead.

Cross-sectional Studies. In a *cross-sectional study,* developmental changes are identified by testing children of different ages. In other words, the researcher charts the differences in some attribute between, say, 2-, 4-, 6-, and 8-year-olds. The cross-sectional approach avoids almost all the problems associated with repeated testing, including costly record keeping and sample loss. But cross-sectional research has its own weaknesses. Because children are tested at only one point in their development, we learn nothing about the continuity of development. Consequently, we cannot tell if an aggressive 4-year-old remains aggressive at age 10 because a child would be tested at age 4 or age 10, but not at both ages.

Cross-sectional studies are also affected by *cohort effects,* meaning that differences between age groups (cohorts) may result as much from environmental events as from developmental processes. In a simple cross-sectional study, we compare children from two age groups. If we find differences, we attribute them to the difference in age, but this needn't be the case. Why? The cross-sectional study assumes that when the older children were younger, they were like children in the younger age group. This isn't always true. Suppose, for example, that a researcher measures creativity in 8- and 14-year-olds. If the 8-year-olds are found to be more imaginative than the 14-year-olds, should we conclude that imagination declines between these ages? Not necessarily. Perhaps a new curriculum to nourish creativity was introduced in kindergarten and first grade, before the 8-year-olds entered these grades but after the older children had completed them. Because the younger children experienced the curriculum but the older children did not, the difference between them is difficult to interpret.

The two general research designs and the two designs that are unique to studying development are summarized in the table. When combined, four prototypic designs result: cross-sectional correlational studies, cross-sectional experimental studies, longitudinal correlational studies, and longitudinal experimental studies.

Summary of Designs Used in Child Development Research

Type of Design	Definition	Strengths	Weaknesses
General Designs			
Correlational	Observe variables as they exist in the world and determine their relations	Behavior is measured as it occurs naturally	Cannot determine cause and effect
Experimental	Manipulate independent variable and determine effect on dependent variable	Control of variables allows conclusions about cause and effect	Work is often laboratory-based, which can be artificial
Developmental Designs			
Longitudinal	One group of children is tested repeatedly as they develop	Only way to chart an individual's development and look at the continuity of behavior over time	Expensive, participants drop out, and repeated testing can distort performance
Cross-sectional	Children of different ages are tested at the same time	Convenient—solves all problems associated with longitudinal studies	Cannot study continuity of behavior; cohort effects complicate interpretation of differences between groups

You'll read about studies using these various designs, although the two cross-sectional designs will show up more frequently than the two longitudinal designs. Why? For most developmentalists, the ease of cross-sectional studies compared to longitudinal studies more than compensates for the limitations of cross-sectional studies.

ETHICAL RESPONSIBILITIES

Having selected a way of measuring the behavior of interest and chosen appropriate general and developmental designs, one very important step remains. Researchers must determine whether their research is ethical, that it does not violate the rights of the children who participate. Professional organizations and government agencies have codes of conduct that specify the rights of research participants and procedures to protect those participants. The following essential guidelines are included in all those codes:

Minimize risks to research participants: Use methods that have the least potential for harm or stress for research participants. During the research, monitor the procedures to be sure to avoid any unforeseen stress or harm.

Describe the research to potential participants so they can determine if they wish to participate: Prospective research participants should be told all details of the research so they can make an informed decision about participating. Children are minors and are not legally capable of giving consent; consequently, as shown in the photograph, researchers must describe the study to parents and ask them for permission for their children to participate.

Avoid deception; if participants must be deceived, provide a thorough explanation of the true nature of the research as soon as possible: Providing complete information about a study in advance can sometimes bias or distort participants' responses. Consequently, investigators sometimes provide only partial information or even mislead participants about the true purpose of the study. As soon as it is feasible—typically just after the experiment—any false information must be corrected and the reasons for the deception must be provided.

Keep results anonymous or confidential: Research results should be anonymous, which means that participants' data cannot be linked to their name. When anonymity is not possible, research results should be confidential, which means that the identities of the individuals are known only to the investigator conducting the study.

Researchers must convince review boards consisting of scientists from many disciplines that they have carefully addressed each of these ethical points. Only then can they begin their study. If the review board objects to some aspects of the proposed study, the researcher must revise those aspects and present them anew for the review board's approval.

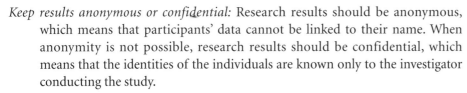

Ethical research minimizes risk and deception, allows individuals to decide if they want to participate, and keeps results confidential.

When the study is complete and the data analyzed, researchers write a report of their work. This report describes, in great detail, what the researchers did and why, their results, and the meaning(s) behind their results. The researchers submit the report to one of several scientific journals that specialize in child development research. Some of these are *Child Development, Developmental Psychology, Journal of Experimental Child Psychology, Infant Behavior and Development, Cognitive Development, Social Development, Journal of Applied Developmental Psychology,* and *Journal of Early Adolescence.* If the editor of the journal accepts the report, it appears in the journal where other child development researchers can learn of the results.

These reports of research are the basis for virtually all the information I present in this book. As you read, you'll see names in parentheses, followed by a date, like this:

(Levine, 1983).

This indicates the person who did the research and the year in which it was published. By looking in the References, which begin on page 425 and are organized alphabetically by the first author's last name, you can find the title of the article and the journal where it was published.

Maybe all of these different steps in research seem tedious and involved to you. For a child development researcher, however, much of the fun of doing research is planning a study that no one has done before and that will provide useful information to other specialists. This is one of the most creative and challenging parts of child development research.

The "Focus on Research" features that appear in each chapter of this book are designed to convey both the creativity and the challenge of doing child development research. Each feature focuses on a specific study. Some are studies that have just recently appeared in the journals; others are classics that defined a new area of investigation or provided definitive results in some area. In each "Focus" feature, we'll trace the decisions that researchers made as they planned their study. In the process, you'll see the ingenuity of researchers as they pursue questions of child development, and you'll see that any individual study has limitations. Only when converging evidence from many studies—each using a unique combination of measurement methods and designs—all points to the same conclusion can we feel confident about research results.

Responses to question on p. 19 about using photographs to measure children's understanding of emotions: Children's understanding of emotions depicted in photographs may be less accurate than in real life because (1) in real life, facial features are usually moving—not still as in the photographs—and movement may be one of the clues that children naturally use to judge emotions; (2) in real life, facial expressions are often accompanied by sounds, and children use both sight and sound to understand emotion; and (3) in real life, children most often judge facial expressions of people that they know (parents, siblings, peers, teachers), and knowing the "usual" appearance of a face may help children determine emotions accurately.

Check Your Learning

1. In _____, children are observed as they behave spontaneously in a real-life setting.

2. A _____ is a group of individuals considered representative of some larger population.

3. The _____ variable is measured in an experiment in order to evaluate the impact of the variable that was manipulated.

4. Problems of longitudinal studies include the amount of time and money to complete the work, loss of research participants over time, and _____.

5. Researchers must submit their plans for research to a review board that determines if the research _____.

Answers: (1) naturalistic observation, (2) sample, (3) dependent, (4) influence of repeated testing on children's performance, (5) preserves the rights of research participants

THINKING ABOUT DEVELOPMENT

1. Of the five perspectives on development presented in Module 1.2 (and summarized in the table on page 14), which are most alike on the continuity-discontinuity issue? Which are most alike on the nature-nurture issue? What about active-passive views of the child?

2. Suppose that you wanted to determine the impact of divorce on children's academic achievement. What would be the merits of correlational versus experimental research on this topic? How would a longitudinal study differ from a cross-sectional study?

SEE FOR YOURSELF

A good first step toward learning about child development research is to read the reports of research that scientists publish in journals. Visit your library and locate some of the child development journals that I mentioned on page 25. Look at the contents of an issue to get an idea of the many different topics that child development researchers study. When you find an article on a topic that interests you, skim the contents and try to determine what design the investigator(s) used. See for yourself!

RESOURCES

For more information about . . .

 the different theories described in Module 1.2, I recommend Patricia H. Miller's Theories of Developmental Psychology (W. H. Freeman, 1993) for its comprehensive account of each of the theoretical perspectives

 *how you can use the research and theory in this book to help improve children's lives,* try calling the Children's Defense Fund, an organization speaking on behalf of children and adolescents, 1-800-275-2222

research articles on topics in child development, visit the Web site of *Child Development Abstracts and Bibliography,* http://www.journals.uchicago.edu/CDAB/

KEY TERMS

active-passive child issue *16*
cohort effects *23*
continuity-discontinuity issue *14*
correlation coefficient *20*
correlational study *20*
critical period *7*
cross-sectional study *23*
dependent variable *21*
ecological theory *12*
ego *7*
ethological theory *6*
exosystem *13*
experiment *21*
id *7*

imitation (observational learning) *10*
imprinting *7*
independent variable *21*
information-processing theory *12*
longitudinal study *22*
macrosystem *13*
maturational theory *6*
mesosystem *13*
microsystem *12*
naturalistic observation *17*
nature-nurture issue *15*
operant conditioning *9*
population *20*

psychodynamic theory *7*
psychosocial theory *8*
punishment *9*
reinforcement *9*
sample *20*
self-efficacy *10*
self reports *19*
social cognitive theory *10*
structured observation *18*
superego *8*
systematic observation *17*
theory *6*
validity *18*

SUMMARY

MODULE 1.1:
USING THIS BOOK

THE MODULAR FORMAT
Each chapter includes three or four modules that begin with learning objectives, a vignette, and a mini-outline. In the text, key terms and their definitions appear in boldface type. Each module includes a special feature that examines a specific topic in depth. The module ends with questions that allow you to check your learning. Each chapter ends with several elements that should encourage you to think about the information in the chapter as well as a summary like the one you're reading now.

TERMINOLOGY
I use specific terms to refer to people of different ages: newborn, infant, toddler, preschooler, school-age child, adolescent, and adult. Also, when describing different ethnic groups, I use terms that identify the unique cultural heritage of each: African American, Asian American, European American, Hispanic American, and Native American.

ORGANIZATION
Chapters 2–5 address biological, perceptual, and motor development. Chapters 6–9 cover intellectual development. Chapters 10–15 concern social and emotional development.

MODULE 1.2:
THEORIES AND THEMES

THEORIES OF CHILD DEVELOPMENT

Theories are important because they provide the explanations for development. Traditionally, five broad theoretical perspectives have guided researchers. According to the biological perspective, development is determined primarily by biological forces. According to the psychodynamic perspective, development is shaped by conflicts that arise at different ages. The learning perspective emphasizes the role of reward and punishment as well as observing and interpreting others' behavior. The cognitive-developmental perspective emphasizes how thinking changes as children grow. According to ecological theories, development is influenced by immediate and more distant environments. No single perspective is entirely correct; instead, each explains some aspects of development well. We will draw upon each throughout the book.

THEMES IN CHILD DEVELOPMENT RESEARCH

Four themes help unify the findings from child development research that are presented throughout this book: 1. Early development is related to later development, but not perfectly. 2. Development is always jointly influenced by heredity and environment. 3. Children help determine their own development. 4. Development in different domains is connected.

MODULE 1.3:
DOING DEVELOPMENTAL RESEARCH

MEASUREMENT IN CHILD DEVELOPMENT RESEARCH

Research typically begins by determining how to measure the topic of interest. Systematic observation involves recording children's behavior as it takes place, either in a natural environment (naturalistic observation) or in a structured setting (structured observation). Researchers sometimes create tasks to obtain samples of children's behavior. In self reports, children answer questions posed by the experimenter. Researchers must also obtain a sample that is representative of some larger population.

GENERAL DESIGNS FOR RESEARCH

In correlational studies, investigators examine relations between variables as they occur naturally. This relation is measured by a correlation coefficient, *r*, which can vary from −1 (strong negative relation) to 0 (no relation) to +1 (strong positive relation). Correlational studies cannot determine cause and effect, so researchers do experimental studies in which they manipulate an independent variable to determine the impact on a dependent variable. Experimental studies allow conclusions about cause and effect but the strict control of all possible variables often makes the situation artificial. The best approach is to use both experimental and correlational studies to provide converging evidence.

DESIGNS FOR STUDYING DEVELOPMENT

To study development, some researchers use a longitudinal design in which the same children are observed repeatedly as they grow. This approach provides evidence of actual patterns of individual growth but has several shortcomings: It is time-consuming and expensive, some children drop out of the project, and repeated testing can affect performance. An alternative, the cross-sectional design, involves testing children in different age groups. This design avoids the problems of the longitudinal design but provides no information about individual growth. Also, what appear to be differences due to age may be cohort effects. Because neither design is problem-free, the best approach is to use both to provide converging evidence.

ETHICAL RESPONSIBILITIES

Planning research also involves selecting methods that preserve the rights of research participants. Experimenters must minimize the risks to potential research participants, describe the research so that potential participants can decide if they want to participate, avoid deception, and keep results anonymous or confidential.

Genetic Bases of Child Development

I **WISH I HAD A DOLLAR FOR EVERY TIME MY PARENTS OR IN-LAWS SAID** ABOUT ONE OF MY CHILDREN, "HE (OR SHE) COMES BY THAT NATURALLY." THE USUAL PROMPT FOR THEIR COMMENT IS THAT THE CHILD HAS JUST DONE SOMETHING EXACTLY AS I OR MY wife did at the same age. By their remarks, grandparents are reminding us that some behavioral characteristics are inherited from parents just as physical characteristics like height and hair color are inherited.

In this chapter, we'll see how heredity influences children and their development. We'll start, in Module 2.1, by examining the basic mechanisms of heredity. In Module 2.2, we'll focus on disorders that some children inherit. Finally, in Module 2.3, we'll see how the environment is crucial in determining the way that heredity influences development.

M ECHANISMS OF HEREDITY

Learning Objectives

- **What are chromosomes and genes?**
- **What are dominant and recessive traits? How are they inherited?**
- **What is polygenic inheritance? How is it studied in children and adults?**

Leslie and Glenn have decided to try to have a baby. They are thrilled at the thought of starting their own family but also very worried because Leslie's grandfather had sickle cell anemia and died when he was just 20 years old. Leslie is terrified that their baby could inherit the disease that killed her grandfather. Leslie and Glenn wish someone could reassure them that their baby would be okay.

How could we reassure Leslie and Glenn? For starters, we need to know more about sickle cell anemia. Red blood cells like the ones in the top photo carry oxygen and carbon dioxide to and from the body. When a person has sickle cell anemia, the red blood cells look like those in the bottom photo—long and curved like a sickle: These stiff, misshapen cells cannot pass through small capillaries, so oxygen cannot reach all parts of the body. The trapped sickle cells also block the way of white blood cells that are the body's natural defense against bacteria. As a result, many people with sickle cell anemia—including Leslie's grandfather and many other African Americans, who are more prone to this painful disease than other groups—often die from infections before the age of 20.

Sickle cell anemia is inherited and because Leslie's grandfather had the disorder, it apparently runs in her family. Would Leslie's baby inherit the disease? To answer this question, we need to examine the mechanisms of heredity.

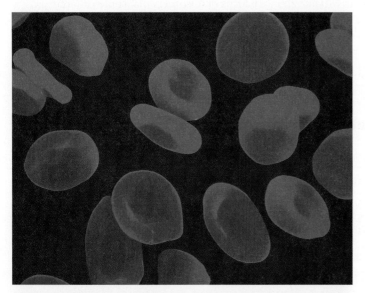

THE BIOLOGY OF HEREDITY

The teaspoon of semen released into the vagina during an ejaculation contains from 200 million to 500 million sperm. Only a few hundred of these actually complete the 6- or 7-inch journey to the fallopian tubes. If an egg is present, many sperm simultaneously begin to burrow their way through the cluster of nurturing cells that surround the egg. When a sperm like the one in the photo on the top of page 33 penetrates the cellular wall of the egg, chemical changes occur immediately that block out all other sperm. **Each egg and sperm cell contains 23 *chromosomes,* tiny structures in the nucleus that contain genetic material.** When a sperm penetrates an egg, their chromosomes combine to produce 23 pairs of chromosomes. The development of a new human being is underway.

For most of recorded history, sexual intercourse was the only way for sperm and egg to unite and begin the development that results in a human being. No longer. In 1978, Louise Brown captured the world's attention as the first test-tube baby—conceived in a laboratory dish instead of in her mother's body. Today, this reproductive technology is no longer experimental; it is a multi-billion-dollar business in the United States (Beck, 1994). Many new techniques are available to couples who cannot conceive a child through sexual intercourse. **The best known, *in vitro fertilization,* involves mixing sperm and egg together in a laboratory dish and then placing several fertilized eggs in the mother's uterus.** The middle photo shows this laboratory version of conception, with the sperm in the dropper being placed in the dish containing the eggs. If the eggs are fertilized, in about 24 hours they are placed in the mother's uterus, with the hope that they will become implanted in the wall of her uterus.

The sperm and egg usually come from the prospective parents, but sometimes they are provided by donors. Occasionally the fertilized egg is placed in the uterus of a surrogate mother who carries the baby throughout pregnancy. In other words, a baby *could* have as many as five "parents": the man and woman who provide the sperm and egg; the surrogate mother who carries the baby; and the mother and father who rear the child.

New reproductive techniques offer hope for couples who have long wanted a child, but there are difficulties. Only about 20 percent of attempts at in vitro fertilization succeed. And, when a woman becomes pregnant, she is more likely to have twins or triplets because multiple eggs are transferred to increase the odds that at least one fertilized egg will implant in the mother's uterus. These problems emphasize that, although technology has increased the alternatives for infertile couples, pregnancy on demand is still in the realm of science fiction.

Whatever the source of the egg and sperm, and wherever they meet, their merger is a momentous event: The resulting 23 pairs of chromosomes define a child's heredity—what he or she "will do naturally." For Leslie and Glenn, this moment also determines whether or not their child inherits sickle cell anemia.

To understand how heredity influences child development, let's begin by taking a closer look at chromosomes. The bottom photo shows all 46 chromosomes, organized in pairs ranging from the largest to the smallest. **The first 22 pairs of chromosomes are called *autosomes;* the chromosomes in each pair are about the same size.** In the 23rd pair, however, the chromosome labeled X is much larger than the chromosome labeled Y. **The 23rd pair determines the sex of the child and,**

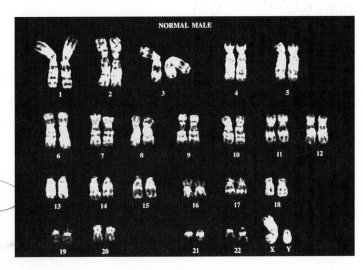

NORMAL MALE

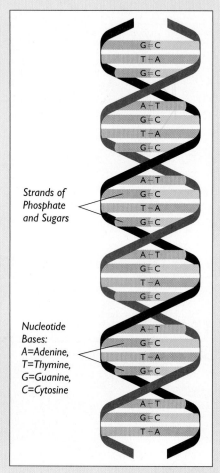

Strands of Phosphate and Sugars

Nucleotide Bases:
A=Adenine,
T=Thymine,
G=Guanine,
C=Cytosine

hence, these two are known as the *sex chromosomes.* An egg always contains an X 23rd chromosome. In contrast, a sperm contains either an X or a Y. When an X-carrying sperm fertilizes the egg, the 23rd pair is XX and the result is a girl. When a Y-carrying sperm fertilizes the egg, the 23rd pair is XY and the result is a boy.

Each chromosome actually consists of one molecule of *deoxyribonucleic acid*—DNA for short. The diagram shows a section of a DNA molecule, which resembles a spiral staircase. The rungs of the staircase carry the genetic code, which consists of pairs of different nucleotide bases: Adenine is paired with thymine, and guanine is paired with cytosine. The order of the nucleotide pairs is the code that causes the cell to create specific amino acids, proteins, and enzymes—important biological building blocks. **Each group of nucleotide bases that provides a specific set of biochemical instructions is a *gene.*** For example, three consecutive thymine nucleotides is the instruction to create the amino acid, phenylalanine.

Altogether, a child's 46 chromosomes include roughly 100,000 genes. Through biochemical instructions that are coded in DNA, genes regulate the development of all human characteristics and abilities. **The complete set of genes makes up a person's heredity and is known as the person's *genotype.*** Genetic instructions, in conjunction with environmental influences, produce a *phenotype,* an individual's physical, behavioral, and psychological features.

In the rest of this module, we'll see the ways in which the instructions contained in genes produce different phenotypes.

SINGLE GENE INHERITANCE

How do genetic instructions produce the misshapen red blood cells of sickle cell anemia? **Genes come in different forms that are known as *alleles.*** In the case of red blood cells, for example, two alleles can be present on chromosome 11. One allele has instructions for normal red blood cells; another allele has instructions for sickle-shaped red blood cells. **The alleles in the pair of chromosomes are sometimes the same, which makes them *homozygous.* The alleles sometimes differ, which makes them *heterozygous.*** In Leslie's case, her baby could be homozygous, in which case it would have two alleles for normal cells *or* two alleles for sickle-shaped cells. Leslie's baby might also be heterozygous, which means that it would have one allele for normal cells and one for sickle-shaped cells.

How does a genotype produce a phenotype? The answer is simple if a person is homozygous. When both alleles are the same—and therefore have chemical instructions for the same phenotype—that phenotype results. If Leslie's baby had alleles for normal red blood cells on both of the chromosomes in its 11th pair, the baby would be almost guaranteed to have normal cells. If, instead, the baby had two alleles for sickle-shaped cells, her baby would almost certainly suffer from the disease.

When a person is heterozygous, the process is more complex. **Often one allele is *dominant,* which means that its chemical instructions are followed whereas those of the other, the *recessive* allele, are ignored.** In the case of sickle cell anemia, the allele for normal cells is dominant and the allele for sickle-shaped cells is recessive. This is good news for Leslie: As long as either she or Glenn contribute the allele for normal red blood cells, her baby would not develop sickle cell anemia.

Genotype refers to a child's hereditary makeup. Phenotype refers to the physical, behavioral, and psychological characteristics that result when a genotype is exposed to a particular environment.

The diagram summarizes what we've learned about sickle cell anemia. The letter *A* denotes the allele for normal blood cells and *a* denotes the allele for sickle-shaped cells. Depending upon the alleles in Leslie's egg and Glenn's sperm, three outcomes are possible. Only if the baby inherits two recessive alleles for sickle-shaped cells is it likely to develop sickle cell anemia. But this is unlikely: Glenn is positive that no one in his family tree has had sickle cell anemia, so he almost certainly has the allele for normal blood cells on both of the chromosomes in his 11th pair.

But even though Glenn's sperm carry the gene for normal red blood cells, this doesn't guarantee that their baby will be healthy. Why? **Sometimes one allele does not dominate another completely, a situation known as** *codominance.* In codominance, the phenotype that results often falls between the phenotype associated with either allele. This is the case for the genes that control red blood cells. **Individuals with one dominant and one recessive allele have** *sickle cell trait:* **In most situations they have no problems but when they are seriously short of oxygen, they suffer a temporary, relatively mild form of anemia.** Thus, sickle cell trait is likely to appear when the person exercises vigorously or is at high altitudes (Sullivan, 1987). Leslie and Glenn's baby would have sickle cell trait if it inherited a recessive gene from Leslie and a dominant gene from Glenn.

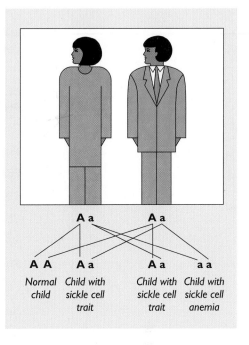

A a   A a

A A   A a   A a   a a
Normal child   *Child with sickle cell trait*   *Child with sickle cell trait*   *Child with sickle cell anemia*

One aspect of sickle cell anemia that we haven't considered so far is why this disorder primarily affects African American children. The "Cultural Influences" feature addresses this point and, in the process, tells more about how heredity operates.

Cultural Influences: WHY DO AFRICAN AMERICANS INHERIT SICKLE CELL ANEMIA?

Sickle cell anemia affects about 1 in 400 African American children. In contrast, virtually no European American children have the disorder. Why? Surprisingly, because the sickle cell allele has a benefit: Individuals with this allele are more resistant to malaria, an infectious disease that is one of the leading causes of childhood death worldwide. Malaria is transmitted by mosquitos, so it is most common in warm climates, including many parts of Africa. Compared to Africans who have alleles for normal blood cells, Africans with the sickle cell allele are less likely to die from malaria, which means that the sickle cell allele is passed along to the next generation.

This explanation of sickle cell anemia has two implications. First, sickle cell anemia should be common in any group of people living where malaria is common. In fact, sickle cell anemia affects Hispanic Americans who trace their roots to malaria-prone regions of the Caribbean, Central America, and South America. Second, malaria is rare in the United States, which means that the sickle cell allele has no survival value to African Americans. Accordingly, the sickle cell allele should become less common in successive generations of African Americans, and research indicates that this is happening.

There is a simple but important general lesson here. The impact of heredity depends on the environment. An allele may have survival value in one environment but not in others. ◼

The simple genetic mechanism responsible for sickle cell anemia, involving a single gene pair, with one dominant allele and one recessive allele, is also responsible for numerous other common traits, as shown in the table:

Some Common Phenotypes Associated with Single Pairs of Genes

Dominant Phenotype	Recessive Phenotype
Curly hair	Straight hair
Normal hair	Pattern baldness (men)
Dark hair	Blond hair
Thick lips	Thin lips
Cheek dimples	No dimples
Normal hearing	Some types of deafness
Normal vision	Nearsightedness
Farsightedness	Normal vision
Normal vision	Red-green color blindness
Type A blood	Type O blood
Type B blood	Type O blood
Rh-positive blood	Rh-negative blood

Source: McKusick, 1995.

In each of these instances, individuals with the recessive phenotype have two recessive alleles, one from each parent. Individuals with the dominant phenotype have at least one dominant allele.

You'll notice that the table includes many biological and medical phenotypes but lacks behavioral and psychological phenotypes. Behavioral and psychological characteristics can be inherited, but the genetic mechanism is more elaborate, as we'll see in the next section.

POLYGENIC INHERITANCE

Traits controlled by single genes usually represent "either-or" phenotypes. That is, the genotypes are usually associated with two (or sometimes three) well-defined phenotypes. For example, a person either has normal color vision or has red-green color blindness; a person has blood that clots normally, has sickle cell trait, or has sickle cell anemia.

But most important behavioral and psychological characteristics are not either-or cases. Instead, an entire range of different outcomes is possible. Take extroversion as an example. Imagine trying to classify 10 people that you know well as either extroverts or introverts. This would be easy for a few extremely outgoing individuals and a few intensely shy persons. Most of your friends and acquaintances, however, are probably neither extroverts nor introverts but somewhere in between. Classifying your friends would probably produce a distribution of individuals across a continuum, from extreme extroversion at one end to extreme introversion at the other.

Many behavioral and psychological characteristics reflect polygenic inheritance in which the phenotype reflects the combined action of many separate genes.

Many behavioral and psychological characteristics are distributed in this fashion, including intelligence and many aspects of personality.

When phenotypes reflect the combined activity of many separate genes, the pattern is known as *polygenic inheritance*.

Because so many genes are involved in polygenic inheritance, we usually cannot trace the effects of each gene. But we can use a hypothetical example to show how many genes work together to produce a behavioral phenotype that spans a continuum. Let's suppose that eight pairs of genes contribute to extroversion and that the allele for extroversion is dominant. Thus, a person could inherit as many as 16 alleles for extroversion or as few as 0. Of course, these extremes would be rare, for the same reason that if you toss a coin 16 times, you rarely get 16 heads or 16 tails. Because each allele is equally likely to be present, most people will inherit about 8 dominant alleles for extroversion and 8 recessive alleles for introversion. The result is the distribution of extroversion shown in the diagram.

Remember, this example is completely hypothetical. Extroversion is *not* based on the combined influence of eight pairs of genes. I merely want to show how several genes working together *could* produce a continuum of phenotypes. Something like our example is probably involved in the inheritance of numerous human behavioral traits, except that many more pairs of genes are involved and the environment also influences the phenotype (Plomin, Owen, & McGuffin, 1994).

If many behavioral phenotypes involve countless genes, how can we hope to unravel the influence of heredity? Twins provide some important clues. **Identical twins are called *monozygotic twins* because they come from a single fertilized egg that splits in two.** Because identical twins come from the same fertilized egg, they have the same genes that control body structure, height, and facial features, which explains why identical twins like those in the photo look alike. **In contrast, fraternal or *dizygotic twins* come from two separate eggs fertilized by two separate sperm.** Genetically, fraternal twins are just like any other siblings—on average, about half their genes are the same. In twin studies, scientists compare identical and fraternal twins to measure the influence of heredity. If identical twins are more alike than fraternal twins, this implicates heredity.

An example will help illustrate the logic underlying comparisons of identical and fraternal twins. Suppose we want to determine whether extroversion is inherited. We would first measure extroversion in a large number of identical and fraternal twins. We might use a questionnaire with scores ranging from 0 to 100 (100 indicating maximal extroversion). Some of the results are shown in the table at the top of page 38.

Look first at the results for the fraternal twins. Most have similar scores: The Aikman twins both have high scores but the Herrod twins have low scores. Looking at the identical twins, their scores are even more alike—typically differing by no more than five points. This greater similarity among identical twins than fraternal twins would be evidence that extroversion is inherited, just as the fact that identical twins look more alike than fraternal twins is evidence that facial appearance is inherited.

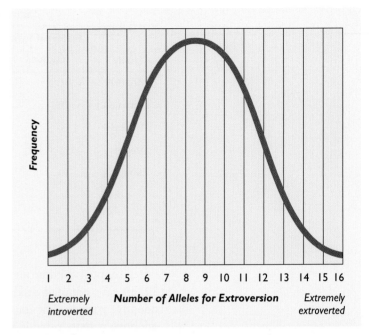

Scores on a Measure of Extroversion

	Fraternal Twins			Identical Twins	
Family	**One Twin**	**Other Twin**	**Family**	**One Twin**	**Other Twin**
Aikman	80	95	Bettis	100	95
Fernandez	70	50	Harbaugh	32	30
Herrod	10	35	Park	18	15
Stewart	25	5	Ramirez	55	60
Tomczak	40	65	Robinson	70	62
:	:	:	:	:	:

Adopted children are another important source of information about heredity. In this case, adopted children are compared with their biological parents and their adoptive parents. The idea is that biological parents provide the child's genes but adoptive parents provide the child's environment. Consequently, if a behavior has genetic roots, then adopted children should behave more like their biological parents than their adoptive parents.

If we wanted to use an adoption study to determine whether extroversion is inherited, we would measure extroversion in a large sample of adopted children, their biological mothers, and their adoptive mothers. (Why just mothers? Obtaining data from biological fathers of adopted children is often difficult.) The results of this hypothetical study are shown in the table.

Scores on a Measure of Extroversion

Child's name	**Child's Score**	**Biological Mother's Score**	**Adoptive Mother's Score**
Anita	60	70	35
Jerome	45	50	25
Kerri	40	30	80
Michael	90	80	50
Troy	25	5	55
:	:	:	:

First, compare children's scores with their biological mothers' scores. Overall, they are related: Extroverted children like Michael tend to have extroverted biological mothers. Introverted children like Troy tend to have introverted biological mothers. In contrast, children's scores don't show any clear relation to their adoptive mothers' scores. For example, although Michael has the highest score and Troy has the lowest, their adoptive mothers have very similar scores. Children's greater similarity to biological than to adoptive parents would be evidence that extroversion is inherited.

Twin studies and adoption studies are not foolproof, however. Maybe you thought of a potential flaw in twin studies: Parents and other people may treat identical twins more similarly than they treat fraternal twins. This would make identical twins more similar than fraternal twins in their experiences as well as in their genes. Adoption studies have their own Achilles heel. Adoption agencies have sometimes tried to place youngsters in homes like those of their biological parents. For example, if an agency believes that the biological parents are bright, the agency may try harder to have the child adopted by parents that the agency believes are bright. This can bias adoption studies because biological and adoptive parents end up being similar.

The problems associated with twin and adoption studies are not insurmountable. Because twin and adoption studies have different faults, if the two kinds of studies produce similar results concerning the influence of heredity, we can be confident of those results.

Studies of twins and adopted children reveal that genetic influence is strongest in three psychological areas: intelligence, psychological disorders, and personality. In the case of intelligence, identical twins' scores on IQ tests are consistently more alike than fraternal twins' scores (Plomin et al., 1994). Research also shows an important heredity component to two major psychological disorders. **In** *depression,* **individuals have pervasive feelings of sadness, are irritable, and have low self-esteem. In** *schizophrenia,* **individuals hallucinate, have confused language and thought, and often behave bizarrely.** Twin studies show remarkable similarity for identical twins for these disorders. In depression, for example, if one identical twin is depressed, the other twin has roughly a 70 percent chance of being depressed. For fraternal twins, the odds are much lower—only 25 percent (Gottesman, 1993; Rowe, 1994).

Research that demonstrates the influence of heredity on personality is the topic of the "Focus on Research" feature.

Heredity is implicated when identical twins are more alike than fraternal twins and when adopted children resemble their biological parents more than their adoptive parents.

Focus on Research: HEREDITARY AND ENVIRONMENTAL ROOTS OF INFANTS' SOCIAL BEHAVIOR

Who were the investigators and what was the aim of the study? Toddlers differ in the ways they interact with others, especially people they don't know well. Some toddlers interact easily and with little hesitation. Other toddlers are reluctant to interact and seem wary of people. This dimension of personality is known as sociability. Robert Plomin and David Rowe (1979) wanted to determine whether a toddler's sociability is determined, in part, by heredity.

How did the investigators measure the topic of interest? Plomin and Rowe decided to study sociability in identical and fraternal twins using structured observation. In the twins' home, an adult not known to the twins spent 5 minutes talking with the mother while the twins were nearby. Then the adult approached the twins and offered them a toy. During this time, two observers recorded the twins' behavior. Each observer was assigned one twin, so that the twins' behavior was assessed independently. The observers recorded many behaviors, but for simplicity, I'll focus on three:

1. the number of times the child spoke positively to the stranger (for example, describing himself or herself),

2. the amount of time spent looking at the stranger, and

3. how quickly the child approached the stranger when he offered the toy.

Who were the children in the study? The researchers obtained measures for 21 pairs of identical twins and 25 pairs of same-sex fraternal twins. Their average age was 22 months.

What was the design of the study? This study was correlational: Plomin and Rowe measured many variables, such as time looking at the stranger, and looked at twins' similarity on these measures. The study focused on a single age group, so it was neither longitudinal nor cross-sectional.

Were there ethical concerns with the study? No. The situations that Plomin and Rowe created were routine in the toddlers' real life, so the children were not at risk. Plomin and Rowe obtained permission from the mothers for the twins to participate.

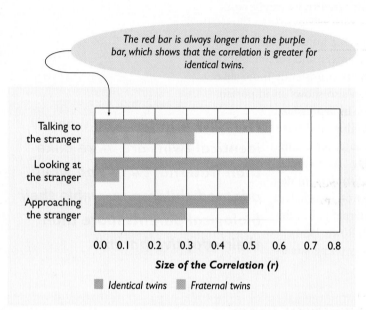

The red bar is always longer than the purple bar, which shows that the correlation is greater for identical twins.

Talking to the stranger

Looking at the stranger

Approaching the stranger

0.0 0.1 0.2 0.3 0.4 0.5 0.6 0.7 0.8

Size of the Correlation (r)

■ Identical twins   ■ Fraternal twins

What were the results? The primary results were expressed as correlations, which are shown in the graph. Each bar shows the size of the correlation for either identical or fraternal twins on one measure. For example, the first bar shows that the correlation for talking to the stranger was nearly .6 for identical twins. This means that if one identical twin talked often to the stranger, the other usually did, too; if one identical twin was quiet, the other usually was also. The important pattern in the graph is that, for each measure, the correlation is greater for identical twins than for fraternal twins. That is, as I described on page 37, the greater similarity among identical twins than fraternal twins is evidence that a behavior is inherited.

What did the investigators conclude? Sociability, at least as reflected in the measures that Plomin and Rowe devised, is influenced by heredity. ■

We will look at personality in greater detail later. For now, keep in mind two conclusions from twin studies like Plomin and Rowe's and from adoption studies. On the one hand, the impact of heredity on behavioral development is substantial and widespread. Research shows that heredity has a sizable influence on such different aspects of development as intelligence and personality. In understanding children and their development, we will always need to think about how heredity may contribute. On the other hand, heredity is never the sole determinant of behavioral development. For example, 50 percent of the differences among children's scores on intelligence tests is due to heredity. But the remaining 50 percent is due to environment. Throughout this book, we'll see that the course of development is controlled by both heredity and environment.

Check Your Learning

1. The first 22 pairs of chromosomes are called _____.

2. In _____, the phenotype often falls between the dominant and the recessive phenotype.

3. _____ reflects the combined activity of a number of distinct genes.

Answers: (1) autosomes, (2) codominance, (3) Polygenic inheritance

GENETIC DISORDERS

Learning Objectives

- **What disorders are inherited?**
- **What disorders are caused by too many or too few chromosomes?**

> *Carolyn and Doug, both 46, hadn't planned to have a baby, but Carolyn soon discovered that her lingering case of the flu was actually morning sickness. She and Doug both knew that with Carolyn's age they risked having a baby with Down syndrome, but they decided not to worry about this. When Carolyn gave birth to a baby boy, it was apparent that he did have Down syndrome. Carolyn and Doug were startled by the news, but it didn't change their joy at being parents. They did want to know more about the special challenges their son would face.*

Like Carolyn and Doug's baby, some children are affected by heredity in a special way: They have genetic disorders that disrupt the usual pattern of development. Genetics can derail development in two ways. First, some disorders are inherited. Sickle cell anemia is one example of an inherited disorder. Second, sometimes eggs or sperm have more or fewer than the usual 23 chromosomes. In this module, we'll see how inherited disorders and abnormal numbers of chromosomes can alter a child's development. **We'll also learn more about *Down syndrome,* an inherited disorder caused by an extra 21st chromosome that results in mental retardation.**

INHERITED DISORDERS

In Module 2.1, we saw that sickle cell anemia is a disorder that affects people who inherit two recessive alleles. **Recessive alleles also cause *phenylketonuria,* a disorder in which babies are born lacking an important liver enzyme.** This enzyme converts phenylalanine—a protein found in dairy products, bread, and fish—into amino acids that are required for normal body functioning. Without this enzyme, phenylalanine accumulates and produces poisons that harm the nervous system, resulting in mental retardation. The alleles for phenylketonuria—PKU for short—are found on chromosome 12 (Mange & Mange, 1990).

Most inherited disorders are like sickle cell anemia and PKU in that they are carried by recessive alleles. Relatively few serious disorders are caused by dominant alleles. Why? If the allele for the disorder is dominant, every person with at least one of these alleles would have the disorder. Individuals affected with these disorders typically do not live long enough to reproduce, so dominant alleles that produce fatal disorders soon vanish from the species. **An exception is *Huntington's disease,* a fatal disease characterized by progressive degeneration of the nervous system.** Huntington's disease is caused by a dominant allele found on chromosome 4. Individuals who inherit this disorder develop normally through childhood, adolescence, and young adulthood. However, during middle age, nerve cells begin to deteriorate, causing muscle spasms, depression, and significant changes in personality (Shiwach, 1994). By the time symptoms of Huntington's disease appear, adults affected with the disease may already have produced children, many of whom will later display the disease themselves.

Inherited disorders that affect development are usually carried by recessive alleles, not dominant alleles.

Fortunately, most inherited disorders are rare. PKU, for example, occurs once in every 10,000 births and Huntington's disease occurs even less frequently.

Nevertheless, adults who believe that these disorders run in their family want to know if their children are likely to inherit the disorder. The "Making Children's Lives Better" feature shows how these couples can get help in deciding whether to have children.

Making Children's Lives Better: **GENETIC COUNSELING**

 Family planning is not easy for couples who fear that children they have may inherit serious or even fatal diseases. The best advice, though, is to seek the help of a genetic counselor before the woman becomes pregnant. With the couple's help, a genetic counselor constructs a detailed family history that can be used to decide whether it's likely that either the man or the woman has the allele for the disorder that concerns them. A family tree for Leslie and Glenn, the couple from Module 2.1, would confirm that Leslie is likely to carry the recessive allele for sickle cell anemia. The genetic counselor would then take the next step, obtaining a sample of Leslie's cells (probably from a blood test). The cells would be analyzed to determine if the 11th chromosome carries the recessive allele for sickle cell anemia. If Leslie learns she has the dominant allele for healthy blood cells, then she and Glenn can be assured their children will not have sickle cell anemia. If Leslie learns that she has the recessive allele, then she and Glenn will know they have a 25 percent risk of having a baby with sickle cell anemia and a 50 percent risk of having a baby with sickle cell trait. Tests can also be administered after a woman is pregnant to determine whether the child she is carrying has an inherited disorder. We'll learn about these tests in Chapter 3. ■

More common than inherited diseases are disorders in which development is disturbed by the wrong number of chromosomes, as we'll see in the next section.

ABNORMAL CHROMOSOMES

Sometimes individuals do not receive the normal complement of 46 chromosomes. If they are born with extra, missing, or damaged chromosomes, development is always disturbed. The best example is Down syndrome, the disorder that affects Carolyn and Doug's son. Like the girl in the photo, persons with Down syndrome have almond-shaped eyes and a fold over the eyelid. Their head, neck, and nose are usually smaller than normal. During the first several months, babies with Down syndrome seem to be developing normally. Thereafter, though, their mental and behavioral development begins to lag behind the average child's. For example, a child with Down syndrome might not sit up without help until about 1 year, not walk until 2, or not talk until 3, months or even years behind children without Down syndrome. By childhood, mental retardation is apparent.

Carolyn and Doug are right in believing that rearing a child with Down syndrome presents special challenges for parents. During the preschool years, children with Down syndrome need special programs to prepare them for school. **In elementary and secondary school, children with Down syndrome (and other children with disabilities) are typically placed in regular classes, a practice known as *mainstreaming*.** Educational achievements of children with Down syndrome are likely to be limited. Nevertheless, as we'll see in Chapter 8, many persons with Down syndrome lead fulfilling lives.

What causes Down syndrome? Individuals with Down syndrome typically have an extra 21st chromosome that is usually provided by the egg (Antonarakis & the Down Syndrome Collaborative Group, 1991). Why the mother provides two 21st chromosomes is unknown. However, the odds that a woman will bear a child with Down syndrome increase markedly as she gets older. For a woman in her late 20s, the risk of giving birth to a baby with Down syndrome is about 1 in 1,000; for a woman in her early 40s, the risk is about 1 in 50. Why? A woman's eggs have been in her ovaries since her own prenatal development. Eggs may deteriorate over time as part of aging or because an older woman has a longer history of exposure to hazards in the environment, such as X-rays, that may damage her eggs.

An extra autosome (as in Down syndrome), a missing autosome, or a damaged autosome always has far-reaching consequences for development because the autosomes contain huge amounts of genetic material. In fact, nearly half of all fertilized eggs abort spontaneously within 2 weeks, primarily because of abnormal autosomes. Thus, most eggs that could not develop normally are removed naturally (Moore & Persaud, 1993).

Abnormal sex chromosomes can also disrupt development. The chart lists four of the more frequent disorders associated with atypical numbers of X and Y chromosomes. Keep in mind that *frequent* is a relative term; although these disorders are more frequent than PKU or Huntington's disease, the chart shows that most are rare. Notice that there are no disorders consisting solely of Y chromosomes. The presence of an X chromosome appears to be necessary for life.

Common Disorders Associated with the Sex Chromosomes

Disorder	Chromosomes	Frequency	Characteristics
Klinefelter's syndrome	XXY	1 in 500 male births	Tall, small testicles, sterile, below-normal intelligence, passive
XYY complement	XYY	1 in 1,000 male births	Tall, some cases apparently have below-normal intelligence
Turner's syndrome	X	1 in 2,500–5,000 female births	Short, limited development of secondary sex characteristics, problems perceiving spatial relations
XXX syndrome	XXX	1 in 500–1,200 female births	Normal stature but delayed motor and language development

Based on Bancroft et al., 1982; Downey et al., 1991; Linden et al., 1988; Plomin et al., 1990.

These genetic disorders demonstrate the remarkable power of heredity. Nevertheless, to fully understand how heredity influences development, we need to consider the environment, which we'll do in Module 2.3.

Check Your Learning

1. _____ is an inherited disorder in which toxins accumulate that harm the nervous system, resulting in mental retardation.

2. Genetic disorders involving dominant alleles are rare because _____.

3. Down syndrome usually is caused by _____.

4. Disorders involving abnormal numbers of sex chromosomes suggest that the presence of _____ chromosome is necessary for life.

Answers: (1) PKU, (2) individuals with these disorders often do not live long enough to have children, (3) an extra 21st chromosome, (4) an X

HEREDITY IS NOT DESTINY

Learning Objectives

- **Does a genotype always lead to the same phenotype?**
- **How does the relation between heredity and environment change as children develop?**

> *Sadie and Molly are fraternal twins. As babies, Sadie was calm and easily comforted, but Molly was fussy and hard to soothe. Their parents wondered if they'd always differ or if they'd become more alike as they grew older.*

Many people mistakenly view heredity as a set of phenotypes that unfold automatically from the genotypes that are set at conception. Nothing could be further from the truth. Although genotypes are fixed when the sperm fertilizes the egg, phenotypes are not fixed. Rather, phenotypes depend on both the genotypes and the environment in which the child develops.

In this module, we'll first look at the range of phenotypes that can result from a single genotype. Then we'll see how genotypes can affect the experiences that children have. In the process, we'll learn if Sadie and Molly became more alike as they grew.

REACTION RANGE

If you read the fine print on a can of diet soda (and some other food products), you'll see the following warning:

> *"Phenylketonurics: contains phenylalanine."*

From Module 2.2, you know phenylketonuria (PKU) is an inherited disorder that results when phenylalanine accumulates and damages the nervous system. But why the warning on diet soda? Today, most American hospitals check for PKU at birth, with a blood or urine test. Newborns who have the disease are immediately placed on a diet that limits intake of phenylalanine, and mental retardation is avoided. Thus, an individual who has the genotype for PKU but is not exposed to phenylalanine has normal intelligence. PKU illustrates that development depends upon heredity *and* environmental factors—in this case, diet.

In general, heredity and environment jointly determine the direction of development. Therefore, a genotype can lead to a range of phenotypes. **Reaction range refers to this fact that a genotype is manifested in reaction to the environment in which development takes place.** The graph on page 45 illustrates how the same genotype can lead to a range of phenotypes, depending upon the environment. When the environment is impoverished, the phenotype is limited; as the environment becomes richer, the phenotype changes, too.

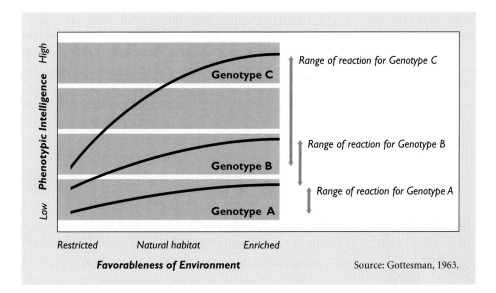

Source: Gottesman, 1963.

Let's see how reaction range can be applied to intelligence. Imagine that a child's genotype for intelligence is perfectly average. Now suppose that the child grows up in an impoverished environment: The parents ignore the child and the environment lacks other sources of intellectual stimulation, such as books. The child will probably develop below-average intelligence because of the limited environment. Now suppose the same child (with the same genotype, obviously) grows up in an average environment: The parents pay attention to the child and the environment includes some books and other sources of stimulation. The child will now develop an average level of intelligence. Finally, suppose the child grows in an enriched environment: The parents actively stimulate the child intellectually, and they are careful that the child experiences other sources of stimulation, such as challenging books, special after-school classes, and academic summer camps. This child will probably develop above-average intelligence.

The conclusion to be drawn from the example is obvious: One genotype leads to three quite different phenotypes, all depending upon the level of intellectual stimulation in the environment. Of course, what makes a "good" or "rich" environment is not the same for all facets of behavioral or psychological development. Throughout this book, you will see how specific kinds of environments influence very particular aspects of development (Wachs, 1983).

One genotype can produce many phenotypes, depending on the environment in which the child develops.

CHANGING RELATIONS BETWEEN NATURE AND NURTURE

How nature (genetics) and nurture (environment) work together partly depends on the child's age. Sandra Scarr (1992, 1993; Scarr & McCartney, 1983) describes three types of relations between heredity and environment. **In the first, a *passive gene-environment relation,* parents pass on genotypes to their children and provide much of the early environment for their young children.** For example, bright parents are likely to transmit genes that make for bright children. Bright parents are also likely to provide books, museum visits, and discussions that are intellectually stimulating. In this case, heredity and environment are positively related: Both foster brighter children. In both respects, children are passive recipients of heredity and environment. This passive type of relation is most common with infants and young children.

In the second type of relation, an *evocative gene-environment relation,* different genotypes evoke different responses from the environment. For example, children who are bright (due in part to their genes) may pay greater attention to their teachers and ask more questions and, in turn, receive greater positive attention in school than children who are not as bright. Or, children who are friendly and outgoing (again, due in part to their genes) may elicit more interactions with others (and, in particular, more satisfying interactions) than children who are not as friendly and outgoing. In the evocative relation, which is common in young children, a child's genotype causes people to respond differently to the child.

In the third type of relation, an *active gene-environment relation,* individuals actively seek environments related to their genetic makeup. Children who are bright (due in part to heredity) may actively seek peers, adults, and activities that strengthen their intellectual development. Similarly, children like the one in the photo, who are outgoing (due in part to heredity), seek the company of other people, particularly extroverts like themselves. **This process of deliberately seeking environments that fit one's heredity is called *niche-picking.*** Niche-picking is first seen in childhood and becomes more common as children get older and can control their environments. The "Real Children" feature shows niche-picking in action.

Real Children: SADIE AND MOLLY PICK THEIR NICHES

Did Sadie and Molly, the twins in the module-opening vignette, become more alike as they grew? No. Even as a young baby, Sadie was always a "people person." She relished contact with other people and preferred play that involved others. Molly was more withdrawn and was quite happy to play alone. When they entered school, Sadie enjoyed making friends while Molly looked forward to the new activities and barely noticed the new faces. These differences reveal heredity in action because sociability is known to have important genetic components (Braungart et al., 1992).

As adolescents, Sadie and Molly continued to seek environments that fit their differing needs for social stimulation. Sadie was in school plays and sang in the school choir. Molly developed a serious interest in crafts, which she pursued by herself. Sadie was always doing something with friends. Molly enjoyed the company of some long-time friends, but she was just as happy to be working alone on some new craft project. Sadie and Molly chose distinctive and very different niches, choices that were influenced by the genes that regulate sociability. ■

The description of Sadie and Molly illustrates that genes and environment rarely influence development alone. Instead, nature and nurture interact. Experiences determine which phenotypes emerge, and genotypes influence the nature of children's experiences.

Much of what we have said about genes, environment, and development is summarized in the diagram. Parents are the source of children's genes and, at least for young children, the primary source of children's experiences. Children's genes also influence the experiences that they have and the impact of those experiences on them. Together, heredity and environment determine behavioral and psychological development.

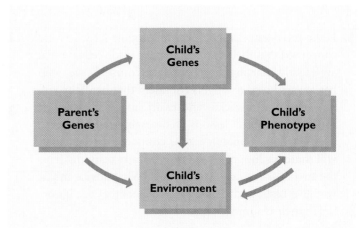

Most of this book is devoted to explaining the links between nature, nurture, and development. We can first see the interaction of nature and nurture during prenatal development, which is the topic of Chapter 3.

Check Your Learning

1. _____ refers to the fact that the same genotype can be associated with many different phenotypes.

2. In _____, children's genotypes cause others to respond differently to them.

3. Older children and adolescents often deliberately seek environments that match their heredity, a process known as _____.

Answers: (1) Reaction range, (2) an evocative gene-environment relation, (3) niche-picking

GENETIC BASES OF CHILD DEVELOPMENT IN PERSPECTIVE

The 46 chromosomes of a fertilized egg are like a road map, guiding development along its path to adulthood. In Module 2.1, we reviewed the mechanisms that regulate genetic functioning. Behavioral development usually follows a pattern of polygenic inheritance, in which behavioral traits reflect the combined effects of many pairs of genes and the environment. In Module 2.2, we saw how heredity can disrupt development. Some children inherit diseases such as sickle cell anemia or PKU. Other children have the wrong number of chromosomes, which can produce disorders like Down syndrome. In Module 2.3, we examined the complexities of the relation between heredity and environment. A single genotype can lead to many phenotypes and genes can influence a child's experiences.

This entire chapter is devoted to a single theme: *Development is always jointly influenced by heredity and environment.* We saw, again and again, how heredity and environment are essential ingredients in all developmental recipes, though not always in equal parts. In sickle cell anemia, an allele has survival value in malaria-prone environments but not in environments where malaria has been eradicated. In PKU, persons who inherit the disorder become retarded when their dietary environment includes foods with phenylalanine but not when their diet lacks phenylalanine. And children with genes for normal intelligence develop below-average, average, or above-average intelligence, depending upon the environment in which they grow. Nature and nurture . . . development always depends on both.

THINKING ABOUT DEVELOPMENT

1. Leslie and Glenn, the couple from Module 2.1 who were concerned that their baby could have sickle cell anemia, are eagerly charting their baby's life course. Leslie, who has always loved to sing, is confident that her baby will be a fantastic musician and easily imagines a regular routine of music lessons, rehearsals, and concerts. Glenn, who is a pilot, is just as confident that his child will share his love of flying; he is already planning trips the two of them can take together. What advice might you give Leslie and Glenn about factors they are ignoring in their planning?

2. As scientists learn more about heredity, we can tell people more about their own, unique genotype. What are some of the benefits of this knowledge? Are there any harmful consequences?

3. On page 39, I describe potential problems of twin and adoption studies. (In twin studies, identical twins may be treated more alike than fraternal twins; in adoption studies, biological parents may be similar to adoptive parents.) How could an investigator conducting either twin or adoption studies determine if these problems affected his or her work?

SEE FOR YOURSELF

The Human Genome Project, launched in the late 1980s by U.S. scientists, aims to identify the exact location of all 100,000 human genes. It is a vast undertaking that first requires determining the sequence of roughly 3 billion pairs of nucleotides like those shown in the diagram on page 34. The Project has produced maps of each chromosome showing the location of known genes. You can see these maps at a Web site maintained by the Human Genome Project. The address is: http://www.ncbi.nlm.nih.gov/science96. At this site, you can select a "favorite" chromosome and see which genes have been located on it. See for yourself!

RESOURCES

For more information about . . .

human heredity, try Robert Shapiro's *The Human Blueprint: The Race to Unlock the Secrets of Our Genetic Script* (St. Martin's Press, 1991), which describes progress in genetics research by focusing on the Human Genome Project

 sickle cell anemia, contact the National Association for Sickle Cell Disease, 1-800-421-8453

 children with Down syndrome, visit the Down syndrome Web site, http://www.nas.com/downsyn

KEY TERMS

active gene-environment relation *46*
alleles *34*
autosomes *33*
chromosomes *32*
codominance *35*
deoxyribonucleic acid (DNA) *34*
depression *39*
dizygotic (fraternal) twins *37*
dominant *34*
Down syndrome *41*

evocative gene-environment relation *46*
gene *34*
genotype *34*
heterozygous *34*
homozygous *34*
Huntington's disease *41*
in vitro fertilization *33*
mainstreaming *42*
monozygotic (identical) twins *37*
niche-picking *46*

passive gene-environment relation *45*
phenotype *34*
phenylketonuria *41*
polygenic inheritance *37*
reaction range *44*
recessive *34*
schizophrenia *39*
sex chromosomes *34*
sickle cell trait *35*

UMMARY

MODULE 2.1:
MECHANISMS OF HEREDITY

THE BIOLOGY OF HEREDITY

At conception, the 23 chromosomes in the sperm merge with the 23 chromosomes in the egg. The 46 chromosomes that result include 22 pairs of autosomes plus two sex chromosomes. Each chromosome is one molecule of DNA, which consists of nucleotides organized in a structure that resembles a spiral staircase. A section of DNA that provides specific biochemical instructions is called a gene. All of a person's genes make up a genotype; phenotype refers to the physical, behavioral, and psychological characteristics that develop when the genotype is exposed to a specific environment.

SINGLE GENE INHERITANCE

Different forms of the same gene are called alleles. A person who inherits the same allele on a pair of chromosomes is homozygous; in this case, the biochemical instructions on the allele are followed. A person who inherits different alleles is heterozygous; in this case, the instructions of the dominant allele are followed whereas those of the recessive allele are ignored. In codominance, the person is heterozygous but the phenotype is midway between the dominant and recessive phenotypes.

POLYGENIC INHERITANCE

Behavioral and psychological phenotypes that reflect an underlying continuum (such as intelligence) often involve polygenic inheritance. In polygenic inheritance, the phenotype reflects the combined activity of many distinct genes. Polygenic inheritance is often examined by studying twins and adopted children. These studies indicate substantial influence of heredity in three areas: intelligence, psychological disorders, and personality.

MODULE 2.2:
GENETIC DISORDERS

INHERITED DISORDERS

Most inherited disorders are carried by recessive alleles. Examples include sickle cell anemia and phenylketonuria (PKU), in which toxins accumulate because of a missing liver enzyme, causing mental retardation. Inherited disorders are rarely carried by dominant alleles because individuals with such a disorder usually don't live long enough to have children. An exception is Huntington's disease, which doesn't become symptomatic until middle age.

ABNORMAL CHROMOSOMES

Most fertilized eggs that do not have 46 chromosomes are aborted spontaneously soon after conception. One exception is Down syndrome, caused by an extra 21st chromosome. Down syndrome individuals have a distinctive appearance and are mentally retarded. Disorders of the sex chromosomes, which are more common because these chromosomes contain less genetic material than autosomes, include Klinefelter's syndrome, XYY complement, Turner's syndrome, and XXX syndrome.

MODULE 2.3:
HEREDITY IS NOT DESTINY

REACTION RANGE

PKU does not lead to mental retardation when individuals with the disorder maintain a diet low in phenylalanine. This demonstrates the concept of reaction range—the same genotype can lead to different phenotypes. The outcome of heredity depends upon the environment in which development occurs.

CHANGING RELATIONS BETWEEN NATURE AND NURTURE

In infants and young children, the gene-environment relation is passive: parents pass on genotypes to their children and provide much of the early environment for their young children. An evocative gene-environment relation increasingly occurs during development as the child's genotype evokes responses from the environment. In older children and adolescents, an active gene-environment relation is common: Individuals actively seek environments related to their genetic makeup.

THREE

Prenatal Development, Birth, and the Newborn

IF YOU ASK PARENTS TO NAME SOME OF THE MOST MEMORABLE EXPERIENCES OF THEIR LIVES, MANY MENTION THE EVENTS ASSOCIATED WITH PREGNANCY AND CHILDBIRTH. FROM THE EXCITING NEWS THAT A WOMAN IS PREGNANT THROUGH BIRTH 9 months later, the entire experience evokes awe and wonder. The events of pregnancy and birth provide the foundation upon which all child development is built. In Module 3.1, we'll trace the events of prenatal development that transform sperm and egg into a living, breathing human being. In Module 3.2, we'll learn about some developmental problems that can occur before birth. In Module 3.3, we'll turn to birth. We'll see what happens during labor and delivery and some problems that can arise. In Module 3.4, we'll discover what newborn babies are like.

FROM CONCEPTION TO BIRTH

Learning Objectives

■ **What happens to a fertilized egg in the first 2 weeks after conception?**

■ **When do body structures and internal organs emerge in prenatal development?**

■ **When do body systems begin to function well enough to support life?**

Eun Jung has just learned that she is pregnant with her first child. Like many other parents-to-be, she and her husband Kinam are ecstatic. But they also soon realize how little they know about "what happens when" during pregnancy. Eun Jung is eager to visit her obstetrician to learn more about the normal timetable of events during pregnancy.

Prenatal development begins when a sperm successfully fertilizes an egg. **The changes that transform the fertilized egg into a newborn human are known as** *prenatal development.* Prenatal development takes an average of 38 weeks, which are divided into three periods: the period of the zygote, the period of the embryo, and the period of the fetus. Each period gets its name from the scientific term used to describe the baby-to-be at that point in prenatal development.

In this module, we'll trace the major developments during each of these periods. As we do, you'll learn the answers to the "what happens when" question that so intrigues Eun Jung.

PERIOD OF THE ZYGOTE (WEEKS 1–2)

This first period of prenatal development begins with fertilization and lasts about 2 weeks. **It ends when the fertilized egg, called a** *zygote,* **implants itself in the wall of the uterus.** During these 2 weeks, the zygote grows rapidly through cell division. The diagram traces the egg cell from the time it is released

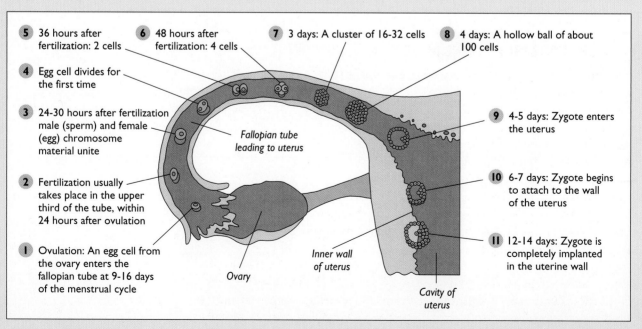

5 36 hours after fertilization: 2 cells

6 48 hours after fertilization: 4 cells

7 3 days: A cluster of 16-32 cells

8 4 days: A hollow ball of about 100 cells

4 Egg cell divides for the first time

3 24-30 hours after fertilization male (sperm) and female (egg) chromosome material unite

2 Fertilization usually takes place in the upper third of the tube, within 24 hours after ovulation

1 Ovulation: An egg cell from the ovary enters the fallopian tube at 9-16 days of the menstrual cycle

Fallopian tube leading to uterus

Ovary

Inner wall of uterus

Cavity of uterus

9 4-5 days: Zygote enters the uterus

10 6-7 days: Zygote begins to attach to the wall of the uterus

11 12-14 days: Zygote is completely implanted in the uterine wall

from the ovary until the zygote becomes implanted in the wall of the uterus. The zygote travels down the fallopian tube toward the uterus. Within hours, the zygote divides for the first time, then division occurs every 12 hours. Occasionally, the zygote separates into two clusters that develop into identical twins. Fraternal twins, which are more common, are created when two eggs are released and each is fertilized by a different sperm cell.

After about 4 days, the zygote consists of about 100 cells and resembles a hollow ball. The inner part of the ball is destined to become the baby. The outer layer of cells will form a number of structures that provide life-support during prenatal development.

By the end of the first week, the zygote reaches the uterus. **The next step is *implantation*: The zygote burrows into the uterine wall and establishes connections with the mother's blood vessels.** Implantation takes about a week to complete and triggers hormonal changes that prevent menstruation, letting the woman know she has conceived.

The implanted zygote, shown in the photograph, is less than a millimeter in diameter. Yet its cells have already begun to differentiate. In the diagram, which shows a cross-section of the zygote and the wall of the uterus, you can see different layers of cells. **A small cluster of cells near the center of the zygote, the *germ disc*, eventually develops into the baby.** The other cells are destined to become structures that support, nourish, and protect the developing organism. **The layer of cells closest to the uterus becomes the *placenta*, a structure through which nutrients and wastes are exchanged between the mother and the developing organism.**

Implantation and differentiation of cells mark the end of the period of the zygote. Comfortably sheltered in the uterus, the zygote is well prepared for the remaining 36 weeks of the marvelous journey to birth.

PERIOD OF THE EMBRYO (WEEKS 3–8)

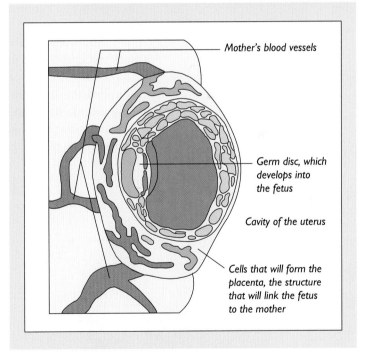

Mother's blood vessels

Germ disc, which develops into the fetus

Cavity of the uterus

Cells that will form the placenta, the structure that will link the fetus to the mother

Once the zygote is completely embedded in the uterine wall, it is called an *embryo.* This new period typically begins the third week after conception and lasts until the end of the eighth week. During the period of the embryo, body structures and internal organs develop. At the beginning of the period, three layers form in the embryo. **The outer layer or *ectoderm* will become hair, the outer layer of skin, and the nervous system; the middle layer or *mesoderm* will form muscles, bones, and the circulatory system; the inner layer or *endoderm* will form the digestive system and the lungs.**

One dramatic way to see the changes that occur during the embryonic period is to compare a 3-week-old embryo with an 8-week-old embryo. The 3-week-old embryo shown in the left photo at the top of page 54 is about 2 millimeters long. Specialization of cells is underway, but the organism looks more like a salamander than a human being. But growth and specialization proceeds so rapidly that an 8-week-old embryo—shown in the photo on the right at the top of page 54—looks very different:

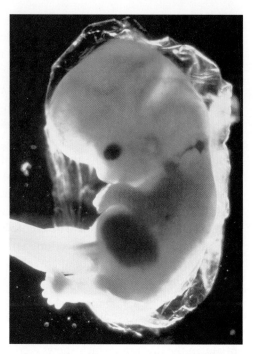

You can see eyes, jaw, arms, and legs. The brain and the nervous system are also developing rapidly, and the heart has been beating for nearly a month. Most of the organs found in a mature human are in place, in some form. (The sex organs are a notable exception). Yet, being only an inch long and weighing a fraction of an ounce, the embryo is much too small for the mother to feel its presence.

The embryo's environment is shown in the diagram below. **The embryo rests in a sac called the *amnion,* which is filled with *amniotic fluid* that cushions the embryo and maintains a constant temperature.** The embryo is linked to the mother by two structures. **The *umbilical cord* houses blood vessels that join the embryo to the placenta.** In the placenta, the blood vessels from the umbilical cord run close

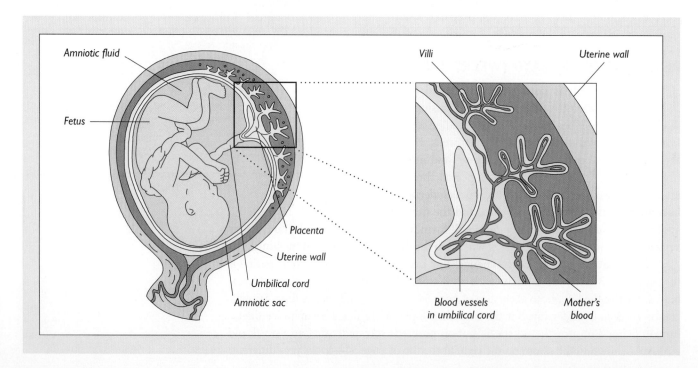

to the mother's blood vessels, but aren't actually connected to them. The close proximity of the blood vessels allows nutrients, oxygen, vitamins, and waste products to be exchanged between mother and embryo.

Growth in the period of the embryo follows two important principles: First, the head develops before the rest of the body. **Such growth from the head to the base of the spine illustrates the *cephalocaudal principle.*** Second, arms and legs develop before hands and feet. **Growth of parts near the center of the body before those that are more distant illustrates the *proximodistal principle.*** Growth after birth also follows these principles.

With body structures and internal organs in place, another major milestone passes in prenatal development. What's left is for these structures and organs to begin working properly. This is accomplished in the final period of prenatal development, as we'll see in the next section.

Body parts and systems are formed in the period of the embryo and begin to work effectively in the period of the fetus.

PERIOD OF THE FETUS (WEEKS 9–38)

The final and longest phase of prenatal development, the *period of the fetus,* extends from the ninth week after conception until birth. During this period, the baby-to-be becomes much larger and its bodily systems begin to work. The increase in size is remarkable. At the beginning of this period, the fetus weighs less than an ounce. At about 4 months, the fetus weighs roughly 4 to 8 ounces, enough for the mother to feel its movements. In the last 5 months of pregnancy, the fetus gains an additional 7 or 8 pounds before birth.

During the fetal period, the finishing touches are placed on the body systems that are essential to human life, such as the nervous system, respiration, and digestion. For example, by the fifth month, the billions of cells that make up the brain are in place and the brain has begun to function. Some simple reflexes like sucking and swallowing are present and mothers can sometimes feel the fetus hiccupping! The chart, which depicts the fetus at one-eighth of its actual size, shows some highlights of the fetal period.

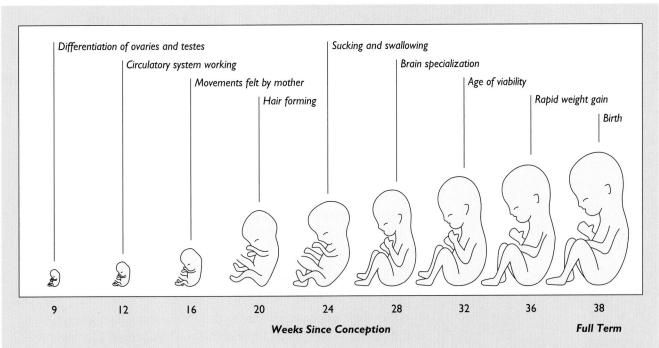

Differentiation of ovaries and testes

Circulatory system working

Movements felt by mother

Hair forming

Sucking and swallowing

Brain specialization

Age of viability

Rapid weight gain

Birth

| 9 | 12 | 16 | 20 | 24 | 28 | 32 | 36 | 38 |

Weeks Since Conception

Full Term

Source: Moore and Persaud, 1993.

By about 7 months, most systems function well enough so that a fetus born at this age has a chance to survive, which is why 7 months is called the *age of viability.* Babies born this early (or earlier) have trouble breathing, because their lungs are not yet mature. Also they cannot regulate their body temperature very well because they lack the insulating layer of fat that appears in the eighth month after conception. With modern neonatal intensive care, infants born this early can survive, but they face other challenges, as I'll describe in Module 3.3.

By the last 2 months of prenatal development, the fetus is so well developed that it registers experiences. Of course, there's not much in the way of "visual experience" in the dark world of the uterus, but sounds abound. Microphones placed in the uterus reveal a noise level of about 75 decibels, which is the volume of normal conversation. Of course, every second or so the noise level increases as the mother's heart beats (Birnholz & Benacerraf, 1983).

By 7 months after conception, body systems can support life and allow the fetus to register some prenatal experiences.

Remarkably, newborns apparently can recognize some of the sounds they hear during prenatal development. DeCasper and Spence (1986) had pregnant women read aloud the famous Dr. Seuss story *The Cat in the Hat* twice a day for the last 1½ months of pregnancy. As newborns, then, these babies had heard *The Cat in the Hat* for more than 3 hours. The newborns were then allowed to suck on a mechanical nipple connected to a tape recorder so that the baby's sucking could turn the tape on or off. The investigators discovered that babies would suck to hear a tape of their mother reading *The Cat in the Hat* but not to hear her reading other stories. Evidently, newborns recognized the familiar, rhythmic quality of *The Cat in the Hat* from their prenatal story-times.

Findings like these tell us that the last few months of prenatal development prepare the fetus remarkably well for independent living as a newborn baby. But these astonishing prenatal changes can only take place when a woman provides a healthy environment for her baby-to-be. The "Making Children's Lives Better" feature describes what pregnant women should do to provide the best foundation for prenatal development.

Making Children's Lives Better: FIVE STEPS TOWARD A HEALTHY BABY

1. Visit a health care provider for regular prenatal checkups. You should have monthly visits until you get close to your due date, when you will have a checkup every other week or maybe even weekly.

2. Eat healthy foods. Be sure your diet includes foods from each of the five major food groups (cereals, fruits, vegetables, dairy products, and meats and beans). Your health care provider may recommend that you supplement your diet with vitamins, minerals, and iron, so that you are assured of providing your baby with all the nutrients it needs.

3. Stop drinking alcohol and caffeinated beverages. Stop smoking. Consult your health care provider before taking *any* over-the-counter medications or prescription drugs.

4. Exercise throughout pregnancy. If you are physically fit, your body is better equipped to handle the needs of the baby.

5. Get enough rest, especially during the last 2 months of pregnancy. Also, attend childbirth education classes so that you'll be prepared for labor, delivery, and your new baby. ▣

As critically important as these steps are, they unfortunately do not guarantee a healthy baby. In Module 3.2, we'll see how prenatal development can sometimes go awry.

Check Your Learning

1. The period of the zygote ends _____.

2. Body structures and internal organs form during the period of the _____.

3. _____ is called the age of viability because this is the age at which most body systems function well enough to support life.

Answers: (1) at 2 weeks after conception (when the zygote is completely implanted in the wall of the uterus), (2) embryo, (3) Seven months

 NFLUENCES ON PRENATAL DEVELOPMENT

Learning Objectives

- **How is prenatal development influenced by a pregnant woman's nutrition, the stress she experiences while pregnant, and her age?**
- **What is a teratogen, and what specific diseases, drugs, and environmental hazards can be teratogens?**
- **How exactly do teratogens affect prenatal development?**
- **How can prenatal development be monitored? Can abnormal prenatal development be corrected?**

MODULE
3.2
Influences on Prenatal Development

General Risk Factors

Teratogens: Diseases, Drugs, and Environmental Hazards

How Teratogens Influence Prenatal Development

Prenatal Diagnosis and Treatment

> *Chloe was barely 2 months pregnant at her first prenatal checkup. As she waited for her appointment, she looked at the list of questions that she wanted to ask her obstetrician. "I spend much of my workday at a computer. Is radiation from the monitor harmful to my baby?" "When my husband and I get home from work, we'll have a glass of wine to help unwind from the stress of the day. Is moderate drinking like this okay?" "I'm 38. I know older women more often give birth to mentally retarded babies. Is there any way I can know if my baby will be mentally retarded?"*

All of Chloe's questions concern potential harm to her baby-to-be. She worries about the safety of her computer monitor, about her nightly glass of wine, and about her age. Chloe's concerns are well founded. Many factors can influence the course of prenatal development, and they are the focus of this module. If you're sure you can answer *all* of Chloe's questions, skip this module and go directly to Module 3.3 on page 68. Otherwise, read on to learn about problems that sometimes arise in pregnancy.

GENERAL RISK FACTORS

As the name implies, general risk factors can have widespread effects on prenatal development. Scientists have identified three general risk factors: nutrition, stress, and a mother's age.

Nutrition. The mother is the developing child's sole source of nutrition, so a balanced diet that includes foods from each of the five major food groups is vital. Most pregnant women need to increase their intake of calories by about 10 to 20 percent to meet the needs of prenatal development. A woman should expect to gain between 25 and 35 pounds during pregnancy, assuming that her weight was normal before pregnancy. A woman who was underweight before becoming pregnant may gain as much as 40 pounds; a woman who was overweight should gain at least 15 pounds (Institute of Medicine, 1990). Of this gain, about one-third reflects the weight of the baby, the placenta, and the fluid in the amniotic sac; another third comes from increases in a woman's fat stores; yet another third comes from the increased volume of blood and increases in the size of her breasts and uterus (Whitney & Hamilton, 1987).

Sheer amount of food is only part of the equation for a healthy pregnancy. *What* a pregnant woman eats is also very important. Proteins, vitamins, and minerals are essential for normal prenatal development. For example, folic acid, one of the B vitamins, is important for the nervous system to develop properly (Shaw et al., 1995). **When mothers do not consume adequate amounts of folic acid, their babies are at risk for *spina bifida,* a disorder in which the embryo's neural tube does not close properly during the first month of pregnancy.** Since the neural tube develops into the brain and spinal cord, when it does not close properly, the result is permanent damage to the spinal cord and the nervous system. Many children with spina bifida need crutches, braces, or wheelchairs. Other prenatal problems have also been traced to inadequate proteins, vitamins, or minerals, so health care providers typically recommend that pregnant women supplement their diet with additional proteins, vitamins, and minerals.

When a pregnant woman does not provide adequate nourishment, the infant is likely to be born prematurely and to be underweight. Inadequate nourishment during the last few months of pregnancy can particularly affect the nervous system, because this is a time of rapid brain growth. Finally, babies who do not receive adequate nourishment are vulnerable to illness (Guttmacher & Kaiser, 1986).

Stress. Does a pregnant woman's mood affect the zygote, embryo, or fetus in her uterus? Is a woman who is happy during pregnancy more likely to give birth to a happy baby? Is a woman who is irritable during pregnancy more likely to give birth to an irritable baby? We can answer these questions with some certainty for nonhumans. When pregnant female animals experience constant stress—such as repeated electric shock or intense overcrowding—their offspring are often smaller than average and prone to other physical and behavioral problems (Schneider, 1992).

The risk of problems during pregnancy depends on a woman's nutrition, the amount of chronic stress that she experiences, and her age.

Deciding the impact of stress on human pregnancy is more difficult because we must rely solely on correlational studies. (It would be unethical to do an experiment in which some pregnant women were assigned to a condition in which they would receive extreme stress.) Studies typically show a moderate relation between the amount of stress that a woman reports during pregnancy and premature birth or low birth weight. That is, women who report greater anxiety during pregnancy more often give birth early or have babies who weigh less than average (Lobel, Dunkel-Schetter, & Scrimshaw, 1992).

Increased stress can harm prenatal development in several ways. First, when a pregnant woman experiences stress, her body secretes hormones that reduce the flow of oxygen to the fetus while increasing its heart rate and activity level. Second, stress can weaken a pregnant woman's immune system, making her more susceptible to illness (Cohen & Williamson, 1991), which can, in turn, damage fetal development. Third, when pregnant women are under stress, they often behave in ways that are not conducive to healthy prenatal development: They are more likely to smoke or drink alcohol and less likely to rest, exercise, and eat properly.

I want to emphasize that the results described here apply to women who experience prolonged, extreme stress. Virtually all women sometimes become anxious or upset while pregnant. But occasional, relatively mild anxiety is not thought to have any harmful consequences for prenatal development.

Mother's Age. For many years, the 20s were thought to be the prime childbearing years. Teenage women as well as women who were 30 or older were thought to be less fit for the rigors of pregnancy. Is being a 20-something really important for a successful pregnancy? Let's answer this question separately for teenage and older women. Compared to women in their 20s, teenage women are more likely to have problems during pregnancy, labor, and delivery, but this is largely because pregnant teenagers do not get good prenatal care, usually because they are unaware of the need and do not seek it out. For example, research done on African American adolescents suggests that when differences in prenatal care are taken into account, teenagers are just as likely as women in their 20s to have problem-free pregnancies and give birth to healthy babies (Goldenberg & Klerman, 1995).

Nevertheless, even when a teenager receives adequate prenatal care and gives birth to a healthy baby, all is not rosy. Children of teenage mothers generally do less well in school and more often have behavioral problems (Dryfoos, 1990). The problems of teenage motherhood—incomplete education, poverty, and marital difficulties—affect the child's later development (Furstenberg, Brooks-Gunn, & Morgan, 1987).

Of course, not *all* teenage mothers and their infants follow this dismal life course. Some teenage mothers finish school, find good jobs, and have happy marriages; their children do well in school, academically and socially. However, teenage pregnancies with "happy endings" are definitely the exception; for most teenage mothers and their children, life is a struggle. For this reason, government and private agencies emphasize the importance of educating teenagers about the true consequences of teen pregnancies.

Are older women better suited for pregnancy? This is an important question because today's American woman is waiting longer than ever to have her first child. Completing an education and beginning a career often delay childbearing. In fact the birthrate in the 1990s among 30- to 34-year-olds is nearly triple what it was in the early 1970s (U.S. Department of Health and Human Services, 1995).

Traditionally, older women like the one in the photo were thought to have more difficult pregnancies and more complicated labor and deliveries. Is this still the case for today's growing number of older pregnant women? Actually, women in their 30s who are in good health before they become pregnant are no more risk-prone during pregnancy, labor, and delivery than women in their 20s (Ales, Druzin, & Santini, 1990). However, older women—especially those in their 40s—remain more liable to give birth to babies with Down syndrome.

In general, then, prenatal development is most likely to proceed normally when women are healthy and eat right, get good health care, and lead lives that are free of chronic stress. But even in these optimal cases, prenatal development can be disrupted as we'll see in the next section.

TERATOGENS: DISEASES, DRUGS, AND ENVIRONMENTAL HAZARDS

In the late 1950s, many pregnant women in Germany took thalidomide, a drug to help them sleep. Soon, however, came reports that many of these women were giving birth to babies with deformed arms, legs, hands, or fingers (Jensen, Benson, & Bobak, 1981). **Thalidomide was a powerful *teratogen,* an agent that causes abnormal prenatal development.** Ultimately, more than 7,000 babies worldwide were harmed before thalidomide was withdrawn from the market (Moore & Persaud, 1993).

Prompted by the thalidomide disaster, scientists began to study teratogens extensively. Today, we know a great deal about many teratogens, which fall into one of three broad categories: diseases, drugs, and environmental hazards. Let's look at each.

Diseases. Sometimes women become ill while pregnant. Most diseases, such as colds and many strains of the flu, do not affect the developing organism. However, several bacterial and viral infections can be very harmful and, in some cases, fatal to the embryo or fetus; five of the most common are listed in the chart.

Teratogenic Diseases and Their Consequences

Disease	Potential Consequences
AIDS	Frequent infections, neurological disorders, death
Cytomegalovirus	Deafness, blindness, abnormally small head, mental retardation
Genital herpes	Encephalitis, enlarged spleen, improper blood clotting
Rubella (German measles)	Mental retardation; damage to eyes, ears, and heart
Syphilis	Damage to the central nervous system, teeth, and bones

Some of these diseases pass from the mother through the placenta to attack the embryo or fetus directly. They include cytomegalovirus, rubella, and syphilis. Other diseases attack at birth: The virus is present in the lining of the birth canal, and the baby is infected as it passes through to be born. Genital herpes is transmitted this way. AIDS is transmitted both ways—through the placenta and during passage through the birth canal.

The only way to guarantee that these diseases do not harm prenatal development is for a woman to not contract the disease before or during her pregnancy. Medication may help the woman, but does not prevent the disease from damaging the developing baby.

Drugs. Thalidomide illustrates the harm that drugs can cause during prenatal development. The chart on page 61 lists other drugs that are known teratogens.

Teratogenic Drugs and Their Consequences

Drug	Potential Consequences
Alcohol	Fetal alcohol syndrome, cognitive deficits, heart damage, retarded growth
Aspirin	Deficits in intelligence, attention and motor skill
Caffeine	Lower birth weight, decreased muscle tone
Cocaine and heroin	Retarded growth, irritability in newborns
Marijuana	Lower birth weight, less motor control
Nicotine	Retarded growth, facial deformities

Notice that most of the drugs in the list are substances that you may use routinely—alcohol, aspirin, caffeine, nicotine. Nevertheless, when consumed by pregnant women, they present special dangers (Behnke & Eyler, 1993). Alcohol is a good example. **Pregnant women who consume large quantities of alcoholic beverages often give birth to babies with** *fetal alcohol syndrome (FAS).* Children with FAS usually grow more slowly than normal and have heart problems and misshapen faces. Like the boy in the photo, youngsters with fetal alcohol syndrome often have a small head, a thin upper lip, a short nose, and widely spaced eyes. They are also often mentally retarded and may have limited motor skills (Niebyl, 1991).

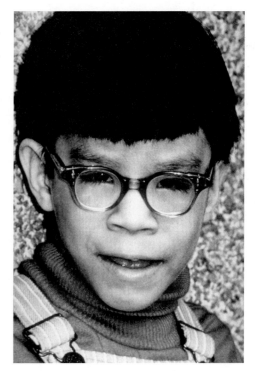

Fetal alcohol syndrome is most likely when pregnant women drink 3 or more ounces of alcohol daily. Does this mean that moderate drinking is safe? No. When women drink moderately throughout pregnancy, their children often have lower scores on tests of attention, memory, and intelligence (Streissguth et al., 1994).

Is there any amount of drinking that's safe during pregnancy? Maybe, but that amount is yet to be determined. This inconclusiveness stems from two factors: First, researchers usually determine the amount a woman drinks by her own responses to interviews or questionnaires. If for some reason she does not accurately report her consumption, it is impossible to accurately estimate the amount of harm associated with drinking. Second, any safe level of consumption is probably not the same for all women. Based on their health and heredity, some women may be able to consume more alcohol more safely than others.

These factors make it impossible to guarantee safe levels of alcohol or any of the other drugs listed in the table at the top of the page. The best policy, therefore, is for woman to avoid all drugs throughout pregnancy.

Environmental Hazards. As a byproduct of life in an industrialized world, people are often exposed to toxins in food they eat, fluids they drink, and air they breathe. Chemicals associated with industrial waste are the most common environmental teratogens, and the quantities involved are usually minute. However, as was true for drugs, amounts that go unnoticed by an adult can cause serious damage to prenatal development. Several environmental hazards that are known teratogens are listed in the table at the top of page 62.

Environmental Teratogens and Their Consequences

Hazard	Potential Consequences
Lead	Mental retardation
Mercury	Retarded growth, mental retardation, cerebral palsy
PCBs	Impaired verbal and memory skill
X-rays	Retarded growth, leukemia, mental retardation

You'll notice that although X-rays are included in this table, radiation associated with computer monitors and video display terminals (VDTs) is not. Several major studies have examined the impact of exposure to the electromagnetic fields that are generated by VDTs, and found no negative results. For example, Schnorr and her colleagues (1991) compared the pregnancies in telephone operators who worked at VDTs at least 25 hours weekly with operators who never used VDTs. For both groups of women, about 15 percent of their pregnancies ended in miscarriages. Other studies have not found a connection between exposure to VDTs and birth defects (Parazzini et al., 1991). Evidently, VDTs can be used safely by pregnant women.

In the "Focus on Research" feature, we look at one of the environmental teratogens in detail.

Focus on Research: IMPACT OF PRENATAL EXPOSURE TO PCBS ON COGNITIVE FUNCTIONING

Who were the investigators and what was the aim of the study? For many years, polychlorinated biphenyls (PCBs) were used in electrical transformers and paints, but the U.S. government banned them in the 1970s. Like many industrial byproducts, they seeped into the waterways where they contaminated fish and wildlife. The amount of PCB in a typical contaminated fish does not affect adults, but Joseph Jacobson, Sandra Jacobson and Harold Humphrey (1990) wanted to determine if this level of exposure was harmful to prenatal development. In particular, they knew from earlier work that substantial prenatal exposure to PCBs affected infants' cognitive skills; they hoped to determine if prenatal exposure similarly affected preschoolers' cognitive skills.

How did the investigators measure the topic of interest? Jacobson and his colleagues needed to measure prenatal exposure to PCBs and cognitive skill. To measure prenatal exposure, they measured concentrations of PCBs in (a) blood obtained from the umbilical cord and (b) breast milk of mothers who were breast-feeding. To measure cognitive skill, they used a standardized test, the McCarthy Scales for Children's Abilities. The McCarthy Scales measure children's abilities in five areas: verbal, perceptual, quantitative, memory, and motor abilities.

Who were the children in the study? The sample included 236 children who were born in western Michigan in 1980–1981. This region was chosen because, at the time, Lake Michigan contained many contaminated salmon and lake trout.

What was the design of the study? The study was correlational because Jacobson and his colleagues were interested in the relation that existed naturally between two variables: exposure to PCB and cognitive skill. The study was longitudinal because children were tested twice: Their exposure to PCBs was measured immediately after birth and their cognitive skill was measured at 4 years of age.

Were there ethical concerns with the study? No. The children had been exposed to PCBs naturally, prior to the start of the study. (Obviously, it would not have been ethical to do an experimental study in which the researchers deliberately asked pregnant women to eat contaminated fish.) The investigators obtained permission from the parents for the children to participate.

What were the results? PCB exposure was unrelated to performance on the perceptual, quantitative, and motor scales of the McCarthy tests. That is, children with high levels of PCB exposure were just as likely to get high scores on these tests as children with low levels of PCB exposure. However, PCB exposure did affect scores on the verbal and memory scales. Looking at the graphs, you can see that verbal and memory scores were highest in children who had the least prenatal exposure to PCBs and lowest for the 4-year-olds who had the greatest prenatal exposure. In other words, as prenatal exposure to PCBs increased, verbal and memory skills decreased.

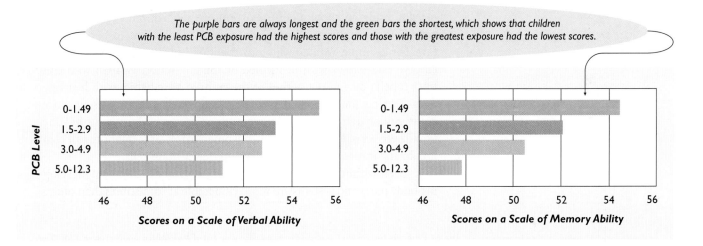

The purple bars are always longest and the green bars the shortest, which shows that children with the least PCB exposure had the highest scores and those with the greatest exposure had the lowest scores.

What did the investigators conclude? Prenatal exposure to PCBs affects at least two aspects of cognitive development—verbal and memory skill. Though children's scores were in the normal range, their reduced verbal and memory skills will probably cause some trouble in school, such as in learning to read.

Environmental teratogens are treacherous because people are unaware of their presence. The mothers of the children in the Jacobson, Jacobson, and Humphrey (1990) study, for example, did not realize they were eating PCB-laden fish. How, then, can a pregnant woman protect herself from hidden environmental teratogens? The best advice is for her to be particularly careful of the food she eats and the air she breathes. Be sure that all foods are cleaned thoroughly to rid them of insecticides. Avoid convenience foods that often contain many chemical additives. Stay away from air that's been contaminated by heavy-duty household cleansers, paint strippers, and fertilizers. Finally, because the number of environmental teratogens continues to increase, check with a health care provider to learn if other materials should be avoided.

HOW TERATOGENS INFLUENCE PRENATAL DEVELOPMENT

By assembling all of the evidence of harm caused by diseases, drugs, and environmental hazards, scientists have identified four important general principles about how teratogens usually work (Hogge, 1990; Vorhees & Mollnow, 1987).

1. *The impact of a teratogen depends upon the genotype of the organism.* A substance may be harmful to one species but not to another. To determine its safety, thalidomide had been tested with pregnant rats and rabbits and their offspring had normal limbs. Yet, when pregnant women took the same drug in comparable doses, many had children with deformed limbs. Thalidomide was harmless to rats and rabbits but not people. Moreover, some women who took thalidomide gave birth to babies with normal limbs while others, taking comparable doses at the same time in their pregnancies, gave birth to babies with deformities. Apparently, heredity makes some individuals more susceptible than others to a teratogen.

2. *The impact of teratogens changes over the course of prenatal development.* The timing of exposure to a teratogen is very important. The chart shows how the consequences of teratogens differ for the periods of the zygote, embryo, and fetus. During the period of the zygote, exposure to teratogens usually results in spontaneous abortion of the fertilized egg. During the period of the embryo, exposure produces major defects in bodily structure. For example, women who took thalidomide during the period of the embryo had babies with ill-formed or missing limbs. Women who contract rubella during the period of the embryo have babies with heart defects. During the period of the fetus, exposure to teratogens produces either minor defects in bodily structure or causes body systems to function improperly. For example, when women drink large quantities of alcohol during this period, the fetus develops fewer brain cells.

Even within the different periods of prenatal development, developing body parts and systems are more vulnerable at some times than others.

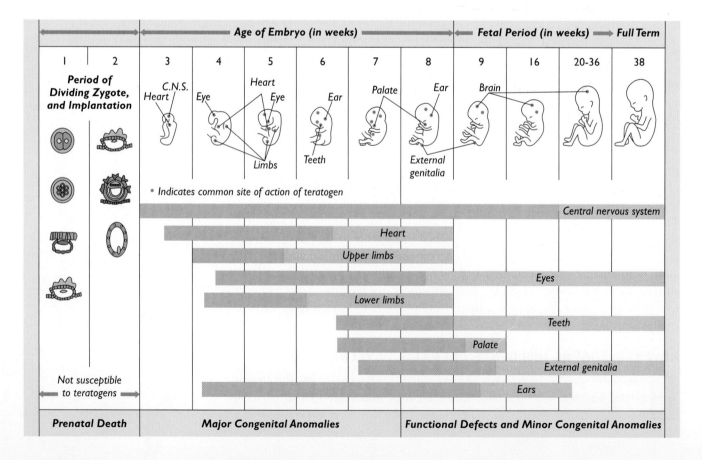

The purple shading in the chart indicates a time of maximum vulnerability; orange shading indicates a time when the developing organism is less vulnerable. The heart, for example, is most sensitive to teratogens during the first two-thirds of the embryonic period. Exposure to teratogens before this time rarely produces heart damage; exposure after results in milder damage.

3. *Each teratogen affects a specific aspect (or aspects) of prenatal development.* Said another way, teratogens do not harm all body systems; instead, damage is selective. If a woman contracts rubella, the baby may have problems with eyes, ears, and heart but limbs will be normal. If a mother consumes PCB-contaminated fish, the baby typically has normal body parts and normal motor skills but below-average verbal and memory skills.

4. *Damage from teratogens is not always evident at birth but may appear later in life.* In the case of malformed limbs or babies born addicted to cocaine, the effects of a teratogen are obvious immediately. A cocaine baby goes through withdrawal—shaking, crying, and being unable to sleep. Sometimes, however, the damage from a teratogen becomes evident only as the child develops. For example, when women ate PCB-contaminated fish, their babies were normal at birth. Their below average cognitive skills were not evident until later.

A dramatic example of the delayed impact of a teratogen involves the drug diethylstilbestrol (DES). Between 1947 and 1971, many pregnant women in North America and Europe took DES to prevent miscarriages. Their babies appeared normal at birth, but as adults, daughters are more likely to have a rare cancer of the vagina and to have difficulty becoming pregnant themselves. Sons of women who took DES may have abnormal seminal fluid and are at risk for cancer of the testes (Meyers, 1983). Here is a case in which the impact of the teratogen is not evident until decades after birth.

The Real World of Prenatal Risk. I have discussed risk factors individually, as if each were the only potential threat to prenatal development. In reality, many infants are exposed to multiple general risks and multiple teratogens. Pregnant women who drink alcohol often smoke and drink coffee (Barr et al., 1990). Pregnant women who are under stress often drink alcohol (Giberson & Weinberg, 1992), and may self-medicate with aspirin or other over-the-counter drugs. Many of these same women may have poor nutrition. When all the risks are combined, prenatal development is rarely optimal.

From what I've said so far in this module, you may think that the developing child has little chance of escaping harm. But most babies *are* born in good health. Of course, a good policy for pregnant women is to avoid diseases, drugs, and environmental hazards that are known teratogens. This, coupled with thorough prenatal medical care and adequate nutrition, is the best recipe for normal prenatal development.

Many infants are exposed to multiple risks because their mothers have poor nutrition and poor prenatal care, and because their mothers smoke and drink.

PRENATAL DIAGNOSIS AND TREATMENT

"I really don't care whether I have a boy or girl, just as long as it's healthy." Legions of parents worldwide have felt this way, but until recently, all they could do was hope for the best. Today, however, advances in technology mean that parents can have a much better idea whether their baby is developing normally.

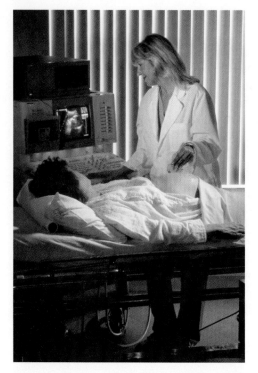

Even before a woman becomes pregnant, a couple may go for genetic counseling, which I described in Module 2.2. A counselor constructs a family tree for each parent to assess the odds of the child inheriting a disorder. If the family tree suggests that a parent is likely to be a carrier of the disorder, further tests can determine the parent's genotype. With this more detailed information, a genetic counselor can advise prospective parents about their choices. A couple might simply go ahead and attempt to conceive a child "naturally." Or, they could decide to use sperm or eggs from other people. Yet another choice would be to adopt a child.

After a woman is pregnant, how can we know if prenatal development is progressing normally? Traditionally, obstetricians gauged development by feeling the size and position of the fetus through a woman's abdomen. This technique was not very precise and, of course, couldn't be done at all until the fetus was large enough to feel. Today, however, new techniques have revolutionized our ability to monitor prenatal growth and development. **A standard part of prenatal care in North America is *ultrasound,* a procedure using sound waves to generate a picture of the fetus.** As the photo shows, an instrument about the size of a hair dryer is rubbed over the woman's abdomen; the image is shown on a nearby TV monitor. The pictures that are generated are hardly portrait quality; they are grainy and it can take an expert's eye to distinguish what's what. Nevertheless, the procedure is painless and parents are thrilled to be able to see their baby and watch it move.

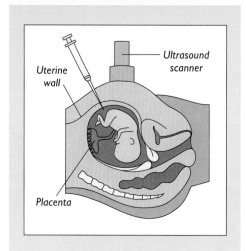

Ultrasound can be used as early as 4 or 5 weeks after conception; before this time the fetus is not large enough to generate an interpretable image. Ultrasound pictures are useful for determining the position of the fetus in the uterus and, at 16 to 20 weeks after conception, its sex. Ultrasound can also help in detecting twins, triplets, or multiple pregnancies. Finally, ultrasound can be used to identify gross physical deformities, such as abnormal growth of the head.

When a genetic disorder is suspected, two other techniques are particularly valuable because they provide a sample of fetal cells that can be analyzed. **In *amniocentesis,* a needle is inserted through the mother's abdomen to obtain a sample of the amniotic fluid that surrounds the fetus.** As you can see in the top diagram, ultrasound is used to guide the needle into the uterus. The fluid contains skin cells that can be grown in a laboratory dish and then analyzed to determine the genotype of the fetus.

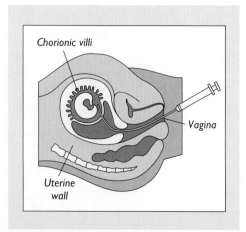

Although amniotic fluid can be extracted about 16 weeks after conception, another 3 weeks must pass for the individual cells to grow sufficiently to allow testing. There is a procedure that can be used within 8 or 9 weeks after conception, and results are available in 24 hours. **In *chorionic villus sampling (CVS),* a sample of tissue is obtained from the chorion, part of the placenta, and analyzed.** The bottom diagram shows that a small tube, inserted through the vagina and into the uterus, is used to collect a small plug of cells from the placenta.

With samples obtained from either amniocentesis or CVS, about 200 different genetic disorders can be detected. These procedures are virtually error-free but at a price: Miscarriages are slightly more likely—1 or 2 percent—after amniocentesis or CVS (Cunningham, MacDonald, & Gant, 1989). A woman must decide if the information gained from amniocentesis or CVS justifies the slight risk of a miscarriage.

Ultrasound, amniocentesis, and chorionic villus sampling have made it much easier to determine if prenatal development is progressing normally. But what happens when it is not? Until recently a woman's options were limited: She could continue the pregnancy or end it. But options are expanding. **A whole new field called** ***fetal medicine*** **is concerned with treating prenatal problems before birth.** One approach in fetal medicine is to treat disorders medically, by administering drugs or hormones to the fetus. In one case, when ultrasound pictures showed a fetus with an enlarged thyroid gland that would have made delivery difficult, a hormone was injected into the amniotic fluid to shrink the thyroid gland, and allow normal delivery (Davidson et al., 1991). In another case, amniocentesis revealed that a fetus had inherited an immune system disorder that would leave the baby highly vulnerable to infections, so healthy immune cells were injected into the umbilical cord (Elmer-DeWitt, 1994).

Ultrasound, amniocentesis, and CVS can detect many problems of prenatal development; fetal medicine can treat some of the problems that are found.

Another approach to correcting prenatal problems is fetal surgery. Doctors partially remove the fetus from the uterus, perform corrective surgery, then return the fetus to the uterus. For example, if the diaphragm, which separates the lungs from other organs in the abdomen, does not develop correctly, babies often die at birth because they cannot breathe properly. But the problem can be corrected with fetal surgery in the seventh or eighth month of pregnancy. Surgeons cut through the mother's abdominal wall to expose the fetus, then cut through the fetal abdominal wall; the diaphragm is repaired and the fetus is returned to the uterus (Kolata, 1990). Fetal surgery has also been used to correct some heart defects and urinary tract blockages (Ohlendorf-Moffat, 1991).

Yet another approach is genetic engineering, replacing defective genes with synthetic normal genes. Take PKU as an example. Remember, from Module 2.2, that if a baby inherits the recessive allele for PKU from both parents, toxins accumulate that cause mental retardation. In theory, it should be possible to take a sample of cells from the fetus, remove the recessive genes from the 12th pair of chromosomes and replace them with the dominant genes. These "repaired" cells could then be injected into the fetus, where they would multiply and cause enough enzyme to be produced to break down phenylalanine, thereby avoiding PKU (Verma, 1990).

Translating this idea into practice has been difficult and there are many problems yet to be solved (Marshall, 1995). Nevertheless, gene therapy has been successful in a few cases. In one, a preschool girl was suffering from a hereditary disease of the immune system that left her unprotected against infection. Doctors took some of the girl's cells and inserted the immune gene into them. The cells were then injected into her bloodstream, where they help to ward off infection.

Fetal medicine may sound like science fiction, but these techniques have been used with humans. Granted, they are highly experimental and failures occur, but just as the end of the 20th century has seen huge progress in prenatal diagnosis, the turn of the century should make prenatal treatment more common.

Answers to Chloe's questions: Return to Chloe's questions in the module-opening vignette (page 57) and answer them for her. If you're not certain, I'll help by giving you the pages in this module where the answers appear:

■ Question about her computer monitor—page 62

■ Question about her nightly glass of wine—page 61

■ Question about giving birth to a baby with mental retardation—page 66

Check Your Learning

1. Important general risk factors in pregnancy include a woman's nutrition, _____, and her age.

2. _____ are some of the most dangerous teratogens because a pregnant woman is often unaware of their presence.

3. During the period of the zygote, exposure to a teratogen typically _____.

4. Two techniques used to determine if a fetus has a hereditary disorder are amnio-centesis and _____.

Answers: (1) the degree of prolonged stress that she experiences, (2) Environmental hazards, (3) results in spontaneous abortion of the fertilized egg, (4) chorionic villus sampling (CVS)

HAPPY BIRTHDAY!

Learning Objectives

- **What are the stages in labor and delivery?**
- **What are "natural" ways of coping with the pain of childbirth? Is childbirth at home safe?**
- **What are some complications that can occur during birth?**

> *Marlena is about to begin classes to prepare for her baby's birth. She is relieved that the classes are finally starting because this means the end of pregnancy is in sight. But all the talk she has heard about "breathing exercises" and "coaching" sounds pretty silly to her. Marlena would prefer to get knocked out for the delivery and wake up when everything is over.*

As women like Marlena near the end of pregnancy, they find that sleeping and breathing become more difficult, they tire more rapidly, they become constipated, and their legs and feet swell. Women look forward to birth, both to relieve their discomfort and, of course, to see their baby. In this module, we'll see the different stages involved in birth, review various approaches to childbirth, and look at problems that can arise. We'll also look at childbirth classes like the one Marlena is taking.

LABOR AND DELIVERY

In a typical pregnancy, a woman goes into labor about 38 weeks after conception. Scientists don't know all the events that initiate labor but one key element seems to be a "ready" signal from an area of the fetal brain that tracks the progress of developing body organs and systems (Palca, 1991).

"Labor" is named appropriately, for it is the most intense, prolonged physical effort that humans experience. Labor is usually divided into the three stages shown in the diagram at the top of page 69. The first stage of labor begins when the muscles of the uterus start to contract. These contractions force amniotic fluid up against the cervix, the opening at the bottom of the uterus that is the entryway to the birth canal. The wavelike motion of the amniotic fluid with each contraction causes the cervix to enlarge gradually. In the early phase of Stage 1, the contractions are weak and spaced irregularly. By the end of the early phase, the cervix is about 5 centimeters (2 inches) in diameter. In the late phase of Stage 1, contractions are stronger and occur at regular intervals. By the end of the late phase, the cervix is about 7 to 8 centimeters (3 inches) in diameter. In the transition phase of Stage 1, contractions are intense and sometimes occur without interruption. Women report that the transition phase is the most painful part of labor. At the end of transition, the cervix is about 10 centimeters (4 inches) in diameter.

Stage 1 lasts from 12 to 24 hours for the birth of a first child, and most of the time is spent in the relative tranquility of the early phase. Stage 1 is usually shorter for subsequent births, with 3 to 8 hours being common. However, as the wide ranges suggest, these times are only rough approximations; the actual times vary greatly among women and are virtually impossible to predict.

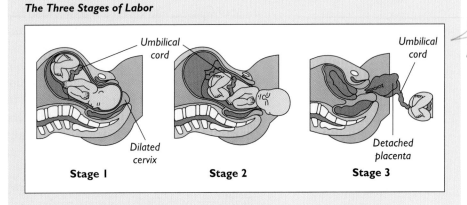

The Three Stages of Labor

Stage 1 — Umbilical cord — Dilated cervix

Stage 2 — Umbilical cord

Stage 3 — Detached placenta

When the cervix is fully enlarged, the second stage of labor begins. Most women feel a strong urge to push the baby out, using their abdominal muscles. This pushing, along with uterine contractions, propels the baby down the birth canal. **Soon the top of the baby's head appears, an event known as** *crowning.* In about an hour for first births and less for later births, the baby passes through the birth canal and emerges from the mother's body. **Most babies arrive headfirst, but a small percentage come out feet- or bottom-first, which is known as a** *breech presentation.* (I was one of these rare bottom-first babies and have been the butt of bad jokes ever since.) The baby's birth marks the end of the second stage of labor.

With the baby born, you might think that labor is over, but it's not. There is a third stage, in which the placenta (also called, appropriately, the afterbirth) is expelled from the uterus. The placenta becomes detached from the wall of the uterus and contractions force it out through the birth canal. This stage is quite brief, typically lasting 10 to 15 minutes.

You can see the growing intensity of labor in this typical account. For Becky, a 27-year-old pregnant for the first time, the early phase of Stage 1 labor lasted 8½ hours. For the first 4 hours, Becky averaged one contraction every 20 minutes. Each contraction lasted approximately 30 seconds. Then the contractions became longer—lasting 45 seconds. They came about every 15 minutes for 3 hours, and then every 8 to 10 minutes for another 1½ hours. At this point, Becky's cervix was 5 centimeters in diameter—the early phase was over.

In the first phase of labor, contractions cause the cervix to expand; in the second, the baby is born; and, in the third, the placenta is expelled.

The late phase of Stage 1 lasted 3 hours. For 2 hours she had one 60-second contraction every 5 minutes. Then for 1 hour she had a 75-second contraction every 3 minutes. At this point, her cervix was 8 centimeters in diameter and she entered the transition phase. For the next 30 minutes she had a 90-second contraction every 2 minutes. Finally, her cervix was a full 10 centimeters and she could push. Thirty minutes later, Randy was born.

APPROACHES TO CHILDBIRTH

When my mother went into labor (with me), she was admitted to a nearby hospital where she soon was administered a general anesthetic. My father went to a waiting room where he and other fathers-to-be anxiously awaited news of their babies. Some time later my mother recovered from anesthesia and learned that she had given birth to a healthy baby boy. My father, who had grown tired of waiting, had gone back to work, so he got the good news in a phone call.

These were standard hospital procedures in 1950 and virtually all American babies were born this way. No longer. Since the 1960s, many women have used more "natural" or prepared approaches to childbirth, viewing labor and delivery as life events to be celebrated, not medical procedures to be endured. One of the fundamental beliefs of all prepared approaches is that birth is more likely to be problem-free and rewarding when mothers and fathers understand what's happening during pregnancy, labor, and delivery. Consequently, prepared childbirth means going to classes to learn basic facts about pregnancy and childbirth (not unlike the material presented in this chapter).

Childbirth classes also spend considerable time showing women how to handle the pain of childbirth. Natural methods of dealing with pain are emphasized over medication. Why? When a woman is anesthetized—either with general anesthesia or local anesthesia (only the lower body is numbed)—she can't use her abdominal muscles to help push the baby through the birth canal. Without this pushing, the obstetrician may have to use mechanical devices to pull the baby through the birth canal, which involves some risk to the baby (Johanson et al., 1993). Also, drugs that reduce the pain of childbirth cross the placenta and affect the baby. Consequently, when a woman receives large doses of pain-relieving medication, her baby is often withdrawn or irritable for days or even weeks (Brazelton, Nugent, & Lester, 1987). These effects are temporary, but they may give the new mother the impression that she has a difficult baby. It is best, therefore, to minimize the use of pain-relieving drugs during birth.

> *Drugs that relieve labor pain make it difficult for the woman to push the baby through the birth canal and they make the newborn withdrawn or irritable.*

Childbirth classes emphasize three strategies to counter birth pain without drugs. First, because pain often feels greater when a person is tense, pregnant women learn ways to relax during labor. One technique is deep breathing. Second, women are taught visual imagery, picturing in detail a reassuring, pleasant scene or experience. Whenever they begin to experience pain during labor, they focus intensely on this image instead of the pain. A third strategy is to involve a supportive "coach." The father-to-be, a relative, or close friend attends childbirth classes with the mother-to-be. The coach learns the techniques for coping with pain and, like the man in the photo, practices them with the pregnant woman. During labor and delivery, the coach is present to help the woman use the techniques she has learned and offer support and encouragement.

Although Marlena, the pregnant woman in the vignette at the beginning of the module, may have her doubts about childbirth classes, research shows that they *are* useful (Hetherington, 1990). Although most mothers who attend childbirth classes use some medication to reduce the pain of labor, they typically use less than mothers who do not attend childbirth classes. Also, mothers and fathers who attend childbirth classes feel more positively about labor and birth compared to mothers and fathers who do not attend classes.

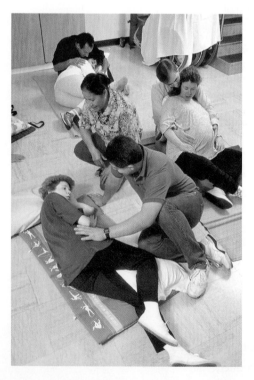

Another basic premise of the trend to natural childbirth is that birth need not always take place in a hospital. Virtually all babies in the United States are born in hospitals—only 1 percent are born at home. However, home birth is a common practice in Europe. In the Netherlands, for example, about one-third of all births take place at home. Advocates note that home delivery is less expensive and that most women are more relaxed during labor in their homes. Advocates also point out that many women enjoy the greater control they have over labor and birth in a home delivery. A health care professional is present for home labor and delivery. Sometimes this is a doctor, but more often, it is a trained nurse-midwife like the one in the photo.

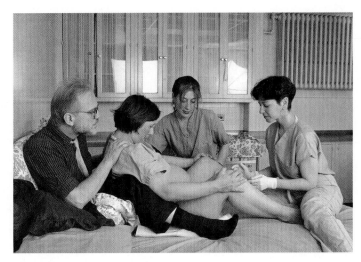

For Americans accustomed to hospital delivery, home delivery can seem like a risky proposition. Is it safe? Yes, but with a very important catch. Birth problems are no more common in babies delivered at home than in babies delivered in a hospital, *if* the woman is healthy, her pregnancy has been problem-free, the labor and delivery are expected to be problem-free, and a trained health care professional is there to assist (Rooks et al., 1989). If there is *any* reason to believe problems requiring medical assistance might occur, labor and delivery should take place in the hospital, not at home.

Another alternative to home or hospital birth is the freestanding birth center. Birthing centers are typically small, independent clinics. A woman, her coach, and other family members and friends are assigned a birthing room that is often decorated to look homelike rather than institutional. A doctor or nurse-midwife assists in labor and delivery, which takes place entirely in the birthing room, where it can be observed by all. Like home deliveries, birthing centers are best for deliveries that are expected to be trouble-free.

BIRTH COMPLICATIONS

Women who are healthy when they become pregnant usually have a normal pregnancy, labor, and delivery. When women are not healthy or don't receive adequate prenatal care, problems can surface during labor and delivery. (Of course, even healthy women face these problems, but not as often.) In this section, we'll look at problems associated with lack of oxygen, being born too early, and being born underweight.

Lack of Oxygen. Until birth, the fetus obtains oxygen from the mother's blood that flows through the placenta and umbilical cord. **If this flow of blood is disrupted, infants do not receive adequate oxygen, a condition known as *anoxia.*** Anoxia sometimes occurs during labor and delivery because the umbilical cord is pinched or squeezed shut, cutting off the flow of blood. **Anoxia may also reflect *placental abruption,* which occurs when the placenta becomes detached from the wall of the uterus, severing the connection to the mother's blood supply.** Anoxia is a very serious condition because it can lead to mental retardation, cerebral palsy, and even death (Petrie, 1991).

To guard against anoxia, fetal heart rate is monitored during labor, either by ultrasound or with a tiny electrode that is passed through the vagina and attached to the scalp of the fetus. An abrupt change in heart rate can be a sign that the fetus is not receiving enough oxygen. If heart rate does change suddenly, a health care professional will try to confirm that the fetus is in distress, perhaps by measuring fetal heart rate with a stethoscope on the mother's abdomen.

When a fetus is in distress, a doctor may decide to remove it from the mother's uterus surgically (Guillemin, 1993). **In a *cesarean section* (or *C-section*) an incision is**

made in the abdomen to remove the baby from the uterus. A C-section poses little risk for babies, although they are often depressed from the anesthesia that the mother receives before the operation. However, for mothers, a C-section is riskier than a vaginal delivery because of increased bleeding and greater danger of infection.

In the United States, about 25 percent of babies are delivered by C-section, up from only 5 percent 30 years ago (Ventura et al., 1994). Many health care professionals believe C-sections are often performed unnecessarily. Since methods for monitoring fetal heart rate are not foolproof, many C-sections are performed when the fetus is not really in distress. C-sections are also frequently used to end a slow or difficult labor. The U.S. Public Health Service has urged doctors to reduce the number of C-sections, saving the procedure only for emergencies that demand immediate delivery (Ventura et al., 1994).

Prematurity and Low Birth Weight. Normally, gestation takes 38 weeks from conception to birth. *Premature infants* **are born less than 38 weeks after conception.** *Small-for-date infants* **are substantially smaller than would be expected based on the length of time since conception.** Sometimes these two complications coincide, but not necessarily. Some, but not all, small-for-date infants are premature. And some, but not all, premature infants are small-for-date. In other words, an infant can go the full 9-month term and be under the average 7- to 8-pound birth weight of newborns; the child is therefore small-for-date but not premature. Similarly, an infant born at 7 months that weighs 3 pounds (the average weight of a 7-month fetus) is only premature. But if the baby born after 7 months weighs less than the average, it is both premature and small-for-date.

Of the two complications, prematurity is the less serious. In the first year or so, premature infants often lag behind full-term infants in many facets of development, but by 2 or 3 years of age, differences have vanished and most premature infants develop normally thereafter (Greenberg & Crnic, 1988). Prospects are usually not so optimistic for small-for-date babies. These infants are most often born to women who smoke or drink alcohol frequently during pregnancy or who do not eat enough nutritious food (Chomitz, Cheung, & Lieberman, 1995). Babies that weigh less than 1,500 grams (3.3 pounds) at birth often do not survive; when they do, they are usually delayed in their cognitive and motor development (Ventura et al., 1994).

Premature babies often develop normally, but small-for-date babies usually do not.

For babies who weigh more than 1,500 grams, the prospects are better, though some reach a higher developmental level than others. (This is also true but to a lesser extent for babies who weigh less than 1,500 grams.) Why? Environmental factors turn out to be critical. Development of small-for-date infants depends upon the quality of care they receive in the hospital and at home. These babies can thrive *if* they receive excellent medical care and their home environment is supportive and stimulating. Unfortunately, not all at-risk babies have these optimal experiences. Many receive inadequate medical care because their families are living in poverty and can't afford it. Others experience stress or disorder in their family life. In these cases, development is usually delayed.

The importance of a supportive environment for at-risk babies was demonstrated dramatically in a longitudinal study of all children born in 1955 on the Hawaiian island of Kauai (Werner, 1994). At-risk newborns who grew up in stable homes were indistinguishable from children born without birth complications. ("Stable family environment" was defined as two supportive, mentally healthy parents present throughout childhood.) When at-risk newborns experienced an unstable family environment due to divorce, parental alcoholism, or mental illness, for example, they lagged behind their peers in intellectual and social development.

The Hawaiian study underscores a point I have made several times in this chapter: Development is best when pregnant women receive good prenatal care and children live in a supportive environment. The "Cultural Influences" feature makes the same point in a different way, by looking at infant mortality around the world.

Cultural Influences: **INFANT MORTALITY**

 In many respects, medical facilities in the United States are the finest in the world. Nevertheless American babies don't fare well when compared to infants from other countries. ***Infant mortality* is the number of infants out of 1,000 births who die before their first birthday.** In the United States, about 9 babies out of 1,000— roughly 1 percent—live less than a year. This figure places the United States near the bottom of the industrialized countries of the world, as you can see in the graph (Wegman, 1994).

One reason so many American babies die is low birth weight. The United States has more babies with low birth weight than any other country listed in the graph and we've already seen that low birth weight places an infant at risk. Low birth weight can usually be prevented if a pregnant woman gets regular prenatal care, but many pregnant women in the United States receive inadequate or no prenatal care. Virtually all the countries that rank ahead of the United States provide complete prenatal care at little or no cost. Many of these countries also provide for paid leaves of absence for pregnant women (Kamerman, 1993).

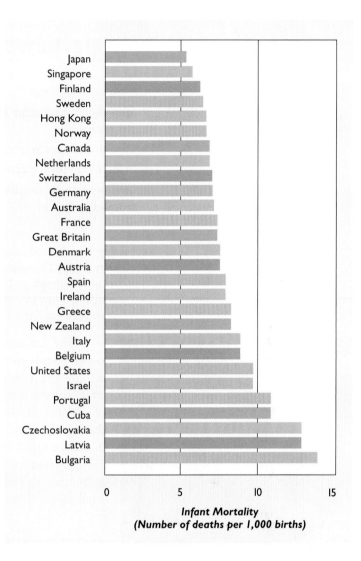

Infant Mortality
(Number of deaths per 1,000 births)

Prenatal development is the foundation of all development, and only with regular prenatal checkups can we know if this foundation is being laid properly. Pregnant women and the children they carry *need* this care, and countries need to be sure that they receive it. ■

Check Your Learning

1. The first (and longest) stage of labor includes early, late, and _____ phases.

2. Two problems with using anesthesia during labor are that a woman can't use her abdominal muscles to help push the baby down the birth canal and _____.

3. Home delivery is safe when the pregnant woman is healthy, has had a problem-free pregnancy, expects to have a problem-free delivery, and _____.

4. The supply of oxygen to the fetus can be disrupted because the umbilical cord is squeezed shut or because _____.

Answers: (1) transition, (2) the pain-relieving medication crosses the placenta and affects the baby, (3) a trained health care professional is present to deliver the baby, (4) the placenta becomes detached from the wall of the uterus (placental abruption)

THE NEWBORN

Learning Objectives

- **How do we determine if a baby is healthy and adjusting to life outside the uterus?**
- **How do reflexes help newborns to interact with the world?**
- **What behavioral states are observable in newborns?**
- **How well do newborns experience the world? Can they learn from experience?**

Lisa and Steve, the proud but exhausted parents, were astonished at how their lives revolved around 10-day-old Dan's eating and sleeping. Lisa felt as if she were feeding Dan around the clock. When Dan napped, Lisa would think of many things she should do but usually napped herself because she was so tired. Steve wondered when Dan would start sleeping through the night, so that he and Lisa could get a good night's sleep themselves.

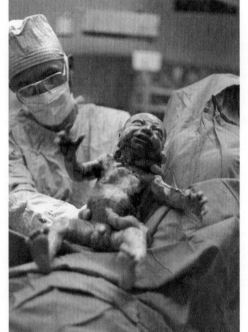

The newborn baby that thrills parents like Lisa and Steve is actually rather homely, as this photo of my son Ben shows. I took it when he was 20 seconds old. Like other newborns, Ben is covered with blood and vernix, a white-colored "grease" that protects the fetus's skin during the many months of prenatal development. His head is temporarily distorted from coming through the birth canal, he has a beer belly, and he is bow-legged. Still, to us he was beautiful, and we were glad he'd finally arrived.

What can newborns like Dan and Ben do? We'll answer that question in this module and, as we do, learn when Lisa and Steve can expect to resume a full night's sleep.

ASSESSING THE NEWBORN

Imagine that a mother has just asked you if her newborn baby is healthy. How would you decide? You would probably check to see if it seemed to be breathing and if its heart seemed to be beating. In fact, breathing and heartbeat are two vital signs that are included in the Apgar score, a measure devised by Virginia Apgar to evaluate the newborn baby's condition. The other vital signs are muscle tone, presence of reflexes such as coughing, and skin tone. Each of the five vital signs receives a score of 0, 1, or 2, with 2 being the optimal score. For example, a newborn whose muscles are completely limp receives a 0; a baby who shows strong movement of arms and legs receives a 2. The five scores are added together, with a score of 7 or more indicating a baby in good physical condition. A score of 4 to 6 means the newborn will need special attention and care. A score of 3 or less signals a life-threatening situation that requires emergency medical care (Apgar, 1953).

The Apgar score provides a quick, approximate assessment of the newborn's status by focusing on the body systems needed to sustain life. For a comprehensive evaluation of the newborn's well-being, pediatricians and child development specialists use the Neonatal Behavioral Assessment Scale, or NBAS for short (Brazelton, 1984). The NBAS evaluates a broad range of newborn abilities and behaviors that the infant needs to adjust to life outside the uterus. It measures reflexes, hearing, vision, alertness, irritability, and consolability (how easily the infant is soothed). The NBAS, along with a thorough physical examination, can determine if the newborn is functioning normally. It is particularly helpful in diagnosing disorders of the central nervous system (Brazelton et al., 1987).

THE NEWBORN'S REFLEXES

Most newborns are well prepared to begin interacting with their world. **The newborn is endowed with a rich set of *reflexes,* unlearned responses that are triggered by a specific form of stimulation.** The chart shows the variety of reflexes commonly found in newborn babies.

Some Major Reflexes Found in Newborns

Name	Response	Significance
Babinski	A baby's toes fan out when the sole of the foot is stroked from heel to toe	Unknown
Blink	A baby's eyes close in response to bright light or loud noise	Protects the eyes
Moro	A baby throws its arms out and then inward (as if embracing) in response to loud noise or when its head falls	May help a baby cling to its mother
Palmar	A baby grasps an object placed in the palm of its hand	Precursor to voluntary grasping
Rooting	When a baby's cheek is stroked, it turns its head toward the stroking and opens its mouth	Helps a baby find the nipple
Stepping	A baby who is held upright by an adult and is then moved forward begins to step rhythmically	Precursor to voluntary walking
Sucking	A baby sucks when an object is placed in its mouth	Permits feeding
Withdrawal	A baby withdraws its foot when the sole is pricked with a pin	Protects a baby from unpleasant stimulation

You can see that some reflexes pave the way for newborns to get the nutrients they need to grow: The rooting and sucking reflexes ensure that the newborn is well prepared to begin a new diet of life-sustaining milk. Other reflexes protect the newborn from danger in the environment. The blink and withdrawal reflexes, for example, help newborns to avoid unpleasant stimulation.

Yet other reflexes serve as the foundation for larger, voluntary patterns of motor activity. For example, the motions of the stepping reflex, shown in the photo, look like a precursor to walking. In fact, we'll see in Module 4.4 that babies who practice the stepping reflex learn to walk earlier (Zelazo, 1983).

Reflexes indicate whether or not the newborn's nervous system is working properly. For example, infants with damage to their sciatic nerve, which is found in the spinal cord, do not show the withdrawal reflex, and infants who have problems with the lower part of the spine do not show the Babinski reflex. If these or other reflexes are weak or missing altogether, a thorough physical and behavioral assessment is called for.

NEWBORN STATES

Newborns spend most of their day alternating among four states (Berg & Berg, 1987; Wolff, 1987):

■ *Alert inactivity.* The baby is calm with eyes open and attentive; the baby looks as if he is deliberately inspecting his environment.

■ *Waking activity.* The baby's eyes are open, but they seem unfocused; the baby moves her arms or legs in bursts of uncoordinated motion.

■ *Crying.* The baby cries vigorously, usually accompanied by agitated but uncoordinated motion.

■ *Sleeping.* The baby's eyes are closed and the baby drifts from periods when breathing is regular and the baby is still to periods when breathing is irregular and the baby gently moves its arms or legs.

Of these states, crying captures the attention of parents and researchers alike. Newborns spend 2 to 3 hours each day crying or on the verge of crying. If you've not spent much time around newborns, you might think that all crying is pretty much alike. In fact, scientists and parents can identify three distinctive types of cries (Holden, 1988). **A *basic cry* starts softly, then gradually becomes more intense and usually occurs when a baby is hungry or tired; a *mad cry* is a more intense version of a basic cry; and a *pain cry* begins with a sudden, long burst of crying, followed by a long pause, and gasping.** Crying actually represents the newborn's first attempts at interpersonal communication. By crying, babies tell their parents that they are hungry or tired, angry, or hurt. By responding, parents encourage their newborn's efforts to communicate.

Parents are naturally concerned when their baby cries, and if they can't quiet a crying baby, their concern mounts and can easily give way to frustration and annoyance. It's no surprise, then, that parents develop little tricks for soothing their babies. The "Real Children" feature shows what one mother did when her baby cried.

Real Children: CALMING DANIEL

Whenever 4-week-old Daniel cried, Debbie's first reaction was to try to figure out why he was crying. Was he hungry? Was his diaper wet? Simply addressing the needs that caused Daniel to cry in the first place usually quieted him. If he continued to cry, she found that the best method was to lift Daniel to her shoulder and rock him or walk with him. The combination of being upright, restrained, in physical contact with her, and moving all helped to calm him. Sometimes Debbie would swaddle Daniel—wrap him tightly in a blanket—and then rock him in a cradle or take him for a ride in a stroller. Another method Debbie used sometimes was to give Daniel a pacifier to suck; sucking seemed to allow Daniel to calm himself. Sometimes, as a last resort, she would use the technique shown in the cartoon on page 77: She'd strap Daniel in his car seat and go on a drive. The motion of the car seemed to soothe him.

Debbie's techniques weren't foolproof. Some would work one day but not another. Sometimes Debbie combined these techniques, for example, taking a swaddled Daniel to her shoulder. Sometimes, nothing seemed to work, so she'd just put Daniel in his crib. And sometimes, as if he were teasing Debbie, Daniel would stop crying spontaneously and go right to sleep! ■

Hi and Lois © 1994. Reprinted with special permission of King Features Syndicate.

Crying gets parents' attention, but sleep is what newborns do more than anything else. They sleep 16 to 18 hours daily. The problem for tired parents like Lisa and Steve is that newborns sleep in naps taken round-the-clock. Newborns typically go through a cycle of wakefulness and sleep about every 4 hours, awake for about an hour, asleep for 3 hours, then awake again. During the hour when newborns are awake, they regularly move between alert inactivity, waking activity, and crying.

As babies grow older, the sleep-wake cycle gradually begins to correspond to the night-day cycle. Most babies begin sleeping through the night at 3 or 4 months, a major milestone for bleary-eyed parents like Lisa and Steve.

Roughly half of newborns' sleep is irregular or *rapid-eye-movement (REM) sleep,* **a time when the body is quite active.** During REM sleep, newborns move their arms and legs, they may grimace, and their eyes may dart beneath their eyelids. Brain waves register fast activity, the heart beats more rapidly, and breathing is more rapid. **In regular or** *non-REM sleep,* **breathing, heart rate, and brain activity are steady and newborns lie quietly without the twitching associated with REM sleep.** REM sleep becomes less frequent as infants grow. By 4 months, only 40 percent of sleep is REM sleep. By the first birthday, REM sleep drops to 25 percent, not far from the adult average of 20 percent (Roffwarg, Muzio, & Dement, 1966).

The function of REM sleep is still debated. Older children and adults dream during REM sleep, and brain waves during REM sleep resemble the brain waves of an alert, awake person. Consequently, many scientists believe that REM sleep stimulates the brain and fosters growth of the nervous system (Roffwarg et al., 1966).

Yet, for many parents of young babies, sleep is sometimes a cause of concern. **In** *sudden infant death syndrome (SIDS),* **a healthy baby dies suddenly, for no apparent reason.** Approximately 1 to 3 of every 1,000 American babies dies from SIDS. Most of them are between 2 and 4 months of age.

Scientists don't know the exact causes of SIDS, but they do know several contributing factors. Babies are more vulnerable to SIDS if they were born prematurely or with low birth weight. They are also more vulnerable if their parents smoke. Furthermore, SIDS is more likely when a baby sleeps on its stomach (face down) than when it sleeps on its back (face up). Finally, SIDS is more likely during winter when babies sometimes become overheated from too many blankets and too heavy sleepwear (Carroll & Loughlin, 1994).

Evidently, SIDS infants, many of whom were born prematurely or with low birth weight, are less able to withstand physiological stresses and imbalances that are brought on by cigarette smoke, breathing that is temporarily interrupted, or by

Premature and low birth weight babies are more vulnerable to SIDS, particularly when they are exposed to physiological stresses.

overheating. The best advice for parents—particularly if their babies were premature or small-for-date—is to keep their babies away from smoke, to place infants on their backs at nap time, and not to overdress them or to wrap them too tightly in blankets (Willinger, 1995).

PERCEPTION AND LEARNING IN THE NEWBORN

Do you believe it is important to talk to newborns and give them fuzzy little toys? Should their rooms be bright and colorful? If you do, you really believe two things about newborns. First, you believe that newborns can perceive experiences—they can see, smell, hear, taste, and feel. Second, you believe that sensory experiences are somehow registered in the newborn—through learning and memory—because unless experiences are registered, they can't influence later behavior. You'll be happy to know that research confirms your beliefs. All the basic perceptual systems are operating at some level at birth. The world outside the uterus can be seen, smelled, heard, tasted, and felt (Aslin, 1987). Moreover, newborns show the capacity to learn and remember. They change their behavior based on their experiences (Rovee-Collier, 1987). We'll discuss these perceptual changes in more detail in Chapter 5 and discuss learning and memory in Chapter 7. For now, the important point is that newborns are remarkably prepared to interact with the world. Adaptive reflexes coupled with perceptual and learning skills provide a solid foundation for the rest of child development.

Check Your Learning

1. The _____ is based on five vital functions and provides a quick indication of a newborn's physical health.

2. Some reflexes help infants get necessary nutrients; other reflexes protect infants from danger; and still other reflexes _____.

3. A baby lying calmly with its eyes open and focused is in a state of _____.

4. Newborns spend more time asleep than awake and about half of this time asleep is spent in _____, a time thought to foster central nervous system growth.

5. At birth, all the basic perceptual systems, such as vision and hearing, are _____.

Answers: (1) Apgar score, (2) serve as the basis for later motor behavior, (3) alert inactivity, (4) REM sleep, (5) working, allowing the newborn to perceive and experience the world

PRENATAL DEVELOPMENT, BIRTH, AND THE NEWBORN IN PERSPECTIVE

Prenatal development sets the stage for a child's life. In Module 3.1, we saw that prenatal development includes the period of the zygote, when the fertilized egg is implanted in the uterine wall; the period of the embryo, when major body parts are formed; and the period of the fetus, when body systems begin to function. In Module 3.2, we discovered that prenatal development can be disrupted by inadequate nutrition, stress, diseases, drugs, and environmental hazards. Advances in prenatal diagnosis make it easier to track prenatal development and advances in fetal medicine are starting to make it possible to correct problems that are detected. In Module 3.3, we traced the three stages of labor and delivery, learned about natural childbirth, and saw the complications associated with lack of oxygen, prematurity, and low birth weight. Finally, in Module 3.4, we found how newborns' health and behavioral development can be assessed and we saw that newborns are born with many reflexes. We also learned about newborn states and discovered that newborns are quite able to perceive experiences and learn from them.

This chapter is a good opportunity to highlight the theme that *early development is related to later development but not perfectly.* Remember the Hawaiian study? This study showed that outcomes for at-risk infants are not uniform. When at-risk infants grow up in a stable, supportive environment, they become quite normal children, but when they grow up in stressful environments, they lag intellectually and socially. Similarly, SIDS is more likely to affect babies born prematurely and with low birth weight, yet, not all of these babies die of SIDS. When premature and low birth weight babies sleep on their backs, are not overheated, and their parents don't smoke, they're unlikely to die from SIDS; when they sleep on their stomachs, are overheated, and their parents smoke, they're definitely at risk for SIDS. Traumatic events early in development, such as being born early or underweight, do not predetermine the rest of a child's life, but they do make some developmental paths easier to follow than others.

THINKING ABOUT DEVELOPMENT

1. For simplicity, obstetricians often divide the 9 months of pregnancy into three 3-month trimesters. Use the material in Module 3.1 to describe the highlights of prenatal development during each trimester.

2. Explain how the impact of teratogens on prenatal development shows that nature *and* nurture both influence development even prior to birth.

3. Suppose that a friend of yours who is pregnant starts her day with a cup of caffeinated coffee, smokes six to eight cigarettes daily, and has a can of beer with dinner each evening. She's convinced that these small amounts of caffeine, nicotine, and alcohol can't possibly hurt her baby. What do you think?

4. Imagine that you are 42 years old and pregnant. Would you want to have amniocentesis or chorionic villus sampling to determine the genotype of the fetus? Why or why not?

5. Do studies on the long-term effects of prematurity and low birth weight provide evidence for continuity in development or for discontinuity in development? Explain your answer.

6. Newborns are remarkably well prepared to interact with their environments. Which of the theories described in Module 1.2 would predict such preparedness? Which would not?

SEE FOR YOURSELF

Words can hardly capture the miracle of a newborn baby. If you have never seen a newborn, you need to see one, or even better, a roomful. Arrange to visit the maternity ward of a local hospital, which will include a nursery for newborns. Through a large viewing window, you will be able to observe a few or as many as 15 to 20 newborns. These babies will no longer be covered with blood or vernix, but you will be able to see how the newborn's head is often distorted by its journey from the uterus. As you watch the babies, look for reflexive behavior and changes in states. Watch while a baby sucks its fingers. Find a baby who seems to be awake and alert, then note how long the baby stays this way. When alertness wanes, watch for the behaviors that replace it. Finally, observe how different the newborns look and act from each other. The wonderful variety and diversity found among human beings is already evident in humans who are hours or days old. See for yourself!

RESOURCES

For more information about...

 *prenatal development,* try Lennart Nilsson and Lars Hamberger's *A Child is Born* (Delacorte, 1990) which is the source of some of the remarkable photographs of the zygote, embryo, and fetus that appear in this chapter

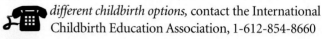 *different childbirth options,* contact the International Childbirth Education Association, 1-612-854-8660

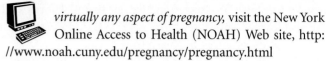 *virtually any aspect of pregnancy,* visit the New York Online Access to Health (NOAH) Web site, http://www.noah.cuny.edu/pregnancy/pregnancy.html

KEY TERMS

SUMMARY

MODULE 3.1:
FROM CONCEPTION TO BIRTH

PERIOD OF THE ZYGOTE
The first period of prenatal development lasts 2 weeks. It begins when the egg is fertilized by the sperm in the fallopian tube and ends when the fertilized egg has implanted in the wall of the uterus. By the end of this period, cells have begun to differentiate.

PERIOD OF THE EMBRYO
The second period of prenatal development begins 2 weeks after conception and ends 8 weeks after. This is a period of rapid growth when most major body structures are formed. Growth in this period is cephalocaudal (the head develops first) and proximodistal (parts near the center of the body develop first).

PERIOD OF THE FETUS
The third period of prenatal development begins 8 weeks after conception and lasts until birth. The highlights of this period are a remarkable increase in the size of the fetus and changes in body systems that are necessary for life. By 7 months, most body systems function well enough to support life.

MODULE 3.2:
INFLUENCES ON PRENATAL DEVELOPMENT

GENERAL RISK FACTORS
Prenatal development can be influenced by several general factors. Prenatal development can be harmed if a pregnant mother does not provide adequate nutrition for the developing organism and when women experience considerable stress during pregnancy.

A mother's age also is a factor in prenatal development. Teenagers often have problem pregnancies because they rarely receive adequate prenatal care. Women in their 30s are likely to have problem-free pregnancies if they are in good health before becoming pregnant.

TERATOGENS: DISEASES, DRUGS, AND ENVIRONMENTAL HAZARDS
Teratogens are agents that can cause abnormal prenatal development. Several diseases are teratogens. Only by avoiding these diseases entirely can a pregnant woman escape their harmful consequences. Many drugs that adults take are teratogens. For most drugs, scientists

have not established amounts that can be consumed safely. Environmental teratogens are particularly dangerous because a pregnant woman may not know when these substances are present.

HOW TERATOGENS INFLUENCE PRENATAL DEVELOPMENT

The impact of teratogens depends upon the genotype of the organism, the period of prenatal development when the organism is exposed to the teratogen, and the amount of exposure. Sometimes the impact of a teratogen is not evident until later in life.

PRENATAL DIAGNOSIS AND TREATMENT

Many techniques are used to track prenatal development. Ultrasound uses sound waves to generate a picture of the fetus. This picture can be used to determine the position of the fetus, its sex, and if there are gross physical deformities. When genetic disorders are suspected, amniocentesis or chorionic villus sampling (CVS) is used to determine the genotype of the fetus. The new field of fetal medicine seeks to correct problems of prenatal development medically, surgically, or through genetic engineering.

MODULE 3.3:
HAPPY BIRTHDAY!

LABOR AND DELIVERY

Labor consists of three stages. In Stage 1, the muscles of the uterus contract. The contractions, which are weak at first and gradually become stronger, cause the cervix to enlarge. In Stage 2, the baby moves through the birth canal. In Stage 3, the placenta is delivered.

APPROACHES TO CHILDBIRTH

Natural or prepared childbirth is based on the assumption that parents should understand what takes place during pregnancy and birth. In natural childbirth, pain-relieving medications are avoided because they prevent women from pushing during labor and because they affect the fetus. Instead, women learn to cope with pain through relaxation, visual imagery, and the help of a supportive coach.

Most American babies are born in hospitals but many European babies are born at home. Home birth is safe when the mother is healthy, labor and birth are expected to be trouble-free, and a health care professional is present to deliver the baby.

BIRTH COMPLICATIONS

During labor and delivery, the flow of blood to the fetus can be disrupted, either because the umbilical cord is squeezed shut or because the placenta becomes detached from the wall of the uterus. Interrupted blood flow causes anoxia, a lack of oxygen to the fetus. If the fetus is endangered, the doctor may do a cesarean section, removing it from the uterus surgically.

Some babies are born prematurely and others are small-for-date. Premature babies develop more slowly at first but catch up by 2 or 3 years of age. Small-for-date babies often do not fare well, particularly if they weigh less than 1,500 grams at birth and if their environment is stressful.

Infant mortality is relatively high in the United States, primarily because of low birth weight and inadequate prenatal care.

MODULE 3.4:
THE NEWBORN

ASSESSING THE NEWBORN

The Apgar score measures five vital signs to determine a newborn baby's physical well being. The Neonatal Behavioral Assessment Scale (NBAS) provides a comprehensive evaluation of a baby's behavioral and physical status.

THE NEWBORN'S REFLEXES

Babies are born with a number of different reflexes. Some help them adjust to life outside of the uterus, some help protect them from danger, and some serve as the basis for later voluntary motor behavior.

NEWBORN STATES

Newborns spend their day in one of four states: alert inactivity, waking activity, crying, and sleeping. A newborn's crying includes a basic cry, a mad cry, and a pain cry. The best way to calm a crying baby is by putting it on your shoulder and walking or rocking.

Newborns spend approximately two-thirds of every day asleep and go through a complete sleep-wake cycle once every 4 hours. By 3 or 4 months, babies sleep through the night. Newborns spend about half their time in REM sleep. REM sleep is characterized by active brain waves and frequent movements of the eyes and limbs. It may stimulate nervous system growth.

Some healthy babies die from sudden infant death syndrome (SIDS). Factors that contribute to SIDS are prematurity and low birth weight. Babies are also vulnerable to SIDS when they sleep on their stomachs, when they are overheated, and when they are exposed to cigarette smoke.

PERCEPTION AND LEARNING IN THE NEWBORN

Newborns' perceptual and learning skills function from very early in life, which make babies well prepared to perceive and experience the world.

Physical and Motor Development

UMANS TAKE LONGER TO BECOME PHYSICALLY MATURE THAN ANY OTHER ANIMAL. WE SPEND ABOUT 20 PERCENT OF OUR LIVES—ALL OF CHILDHOOD AND ADOLESCENCE—GROWING PHYSICALLY. THIS SLOW JOURNEY TO PHYSICAL MATURITY IS NOT only an interesting story in itself, but the basis for cognitive, social, and personality development. As children grow physically, they become less dependent on others for care, they're treated differently by adults, and they come to view themselves as older and more mature.

In this chapter, we'll learn how children grow physically. In Module 4.1, we'll look at different facets of physical growth and some of the reasons why people differ in their physical growth and stature. Then, in Module 4.2, we'll explore problems that can disrupt physical growth. In Module 4.3, we'll look at physical growth that's not so obvious—that which takes place in the brain. Finally, in Module 4.4, we'll see how physical growth is accompanied by greater control of the body, which increases children's ability to explore, understand, and enjoy their world.

PHYSICAL GROWTH

Learning Objectives

- **What are the important features of physical growth during childhood? How do they vary from child to child?**
- **How do heredity, hormones, and nutrition contribute to physical growth?**
- **What are the physical changes associated with puberty and what are their consequences?**
- **Why are some adolescents sexually active? Why do so few use contraceptives?**

Pete just had his 15th birthday, but, as far as he was concerned, there was no reason to celebrate. Although most of his friends have grown about 6 inches in the past year or so, have a much larger penis and larger testicles, and have mounds of pubic hair, Pete looks just as he did when he was 10 years old. He is embarrassed by his appearance, particularly in the locker room, where he looks like a little boy among men. "Won't I ever change?" he wonders.

For parents and children alike, physical growth is a topic of great interest. Parents marvel at the speed with which babies add pounds and inches; 2-year-olds proudly proclaim, "I bigger now!" Many adolescents take great satisfaction in finally becoming taller than a parent; others, like Pete, suffer through their teenage years as they wait for the physical signs of maturity.

In this module, we'll examine some of the basic features of physical growth and variations in growth patterns. We'll also consider the mechanisms responsible for growth. Finally, we'll end the module with a phase of physical growth that is so special it needs to be considered separately—puberty.

FEATURES OF HUMAN GROWTH

Probably the most obvious way to measure physical growth is in terms of sheer size—height and weight. The growth charts show the average changes in height and weight that take place as children grow from birth to age 20. Between birth

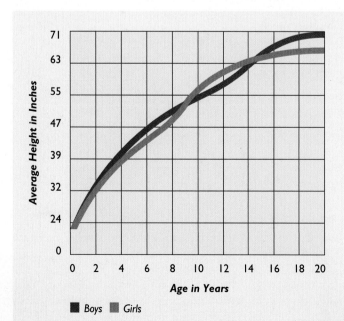

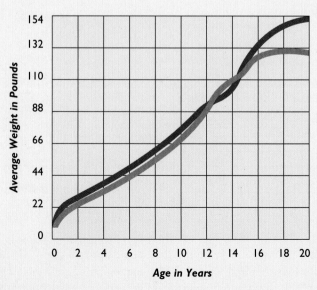

■ Boys ■ Girls

and 2 years, for example, average height increases from 19 to 32 inches; average weight increases from 7 to 22 pounds. (An interesting rule of thumb is that boys achieve half their adult height by 2 years and girls by 18 months.)

What is not so obvious in growth charts is that increases in height and weight are not steady. Looking at the average *increase* in weight and height annually—as opposed to the average weight for each year—gives quite a different picture of the pattern of physical growth. The graphs below show that growth is extraordinarily rapid

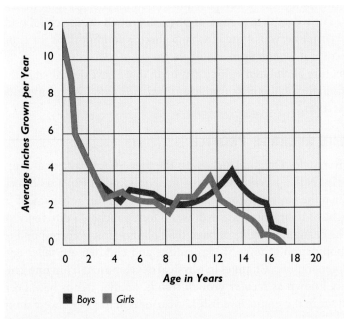
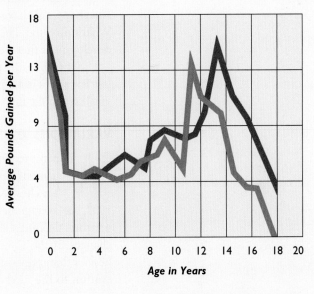

during the first year: The average baby gains about 10 inches and 15 pounds. Growth is fairly steady through the preschool and elementary school years, about 3 inches and 7 to 8 pounds each year. In early adolescence, growth is rapid again. During this growth spurt, which corresponds to the peaks in the middle of the charts, teenagers typically grow 4 inches and 16 to 17 pounds each year. After this spurt, growth again slows as children reach adulthood.

Another important feature of human growth is that it follows the cephalocaudal principle that was introduced in Module 3.1 (p. 55). That is, the head and trunk develop first; infants and young children are not simply scaled-down versions of adults. As you can see in the photo, the toddler has a disproportionately large head and trunk, making him look top-heavy compared to the older boy. As growth of the hips, legs, and feet catches up later in childhood, bodies take on more adult proportions.

A third important feature of physical growth takes place inside the body, with the development of muscle, fat, and bones. Virtually all the body's muscle fibers are present at birth. During childhood, muscles become longer and thicker as individual fibers fuse together. This process accelerates during adolescence, particularly for boys.

A layer of fat first appears under the skin near the end of the fetal period of prenatal development. Fat continues to accumulate rapidly during the first year after birth, producing the familiar look we call baby fat. During the preschool years, children actually become leaner but in the early elementary-school years they begin to acquire more fat again. This happens gradually at

first, then more rapidly during adolescence. The increase in fat in adolescence is more pronounced in girls than in boys.

Bone begins to form during prenatal development. What will become bone starts as cartilage, a soft flexible tissue. During the embryonic period, the center of the tissue turns to bone. **Then, shortly before birth, the ends of the cartilage structures, known as *epiphyses*, turn to bone.** Now the structure is hard at each end and in the center. Working from the center, cartilage turns to bone until finally the enlarging center section reaches the epiphyses, ending skeletal growth.

If you combine the changes in muscle, fat, and bone with changes in body size and shape, you have a fairly complete picture of physical growth during childhood. What's missing? The central nervous system. Change here is so important for child development that we cover it separately in Module 4.3.

Of course, the picture of children's physical growth that I have described in the last few pages is a typical profile; there are important variations on this prototype, as you'll see in the next section.

VARIATIONS ON THE AVERAGE PROFILE

When the University of Oregon Ducks won the first NCAA basketball tournament, in 1939, the average height of their starting lineup was 6 feet, 2 inches. When the University of Arizona Wildcats won the tournament in 1997, the average height of their starting lineup was 6 feet, 6 inches, a difference of 4 inches. Of course, the changing heights of basketball players simply correspond to changes in the U.S. population at large. Today, adults and children are taller and heavier than previous generations. **Changes in physical development from one generation to the next are known as *secular growth trends*.** Secular trends have been quite large, as you can see in the graph. Swedish 12-year-olds in the 1960s were more than 5 inches taller than their counterparts in the 1880s. Put another way, each generation of Swedish 12-year-olds was just over 1 inch taller than its predecessor. (We are using statistics for Swedish children because equally comprehensive data for American children are nowhere to be found).

Not only does "average" physical growth vary from one generation to the next, it varies from one country to another. The graph at the top of page 87 shows the average height of 8-year-old boys and girls in several countries around the world. Youngsters from the United States, western European countries, Japan, and China are about the same height, approximately 49 inches. Children in Africa and India are shorter, averaging just under 46 inches. And 8-year-olds in Polynesia are shorter still, averaging 43 inches.

We also need to remember that "average" and "normal" are not the same. Many children are much taller or shorter than average and perfectly normal, of course. For example, among American 8-year-old boys, normal weights range from approximately 44 pounds to 76 pounds. In other words, an extremely light but normal 8-year-old boy would weigh only slightly more than half as much as his extremely heavy but normal peer. What is "normal" can vary greatly, and this applies not only to height and other aspects of

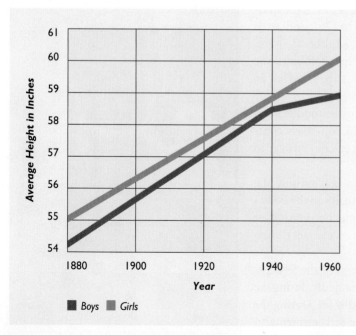

Boys ■ Girls

physical growth but to all aspects of development. Whenever a "typical" or "average" age is given for a developmental milestone, you should remember that the normal range for passing the milestone is much wider. Some children pass the milestone sooner than the stated age and some later, but all are normal.

We've seen that children's heights vary within a culture, across time, and between cultures. What accounts for these differences? To answer this question, we need to look at the mechanisms that are responsible for human growth.

MECHANISMS OF PHYSICAL GROWTH

It's easy to take physical growth for granted. Compared to other milestones of child development, such as learning to read, physical growth seems to come so easily. Children, like weeds, seem to sprout without any effort at all. In reality, of course, physical growth is complicated; to understand it, we need to consider three factors: heredity, hormones, and nutrition.

Heredity. Dave and Doug are identical twins. Throughout childhood, they never differed in height by more than ¼ inch. In contrast, Sam and Max, who are fraternal twins, usually differed by at least ½ inch and sometimes by as much as 1½ inches. These variations are typical for identical and fraternal twins: The correlation between heights of identical twins is usually larger than .9 whereas the correlation for fraternal twins is approximately .5 (Wilson, 1986). This finding indicates that heredity plays a role in determining both a person's adult height as well as the rate at which the person achieves adult height.

Both parents contribute equally to their children's height. The correlation between the average of the two parents' height and their child's is about .7 (Plomin, 1990). Obviously, as a general rule, two tall parents will have tall children; two short parents will have short children; and, one tall parent and one short parent will have average-height offspring.

Hormones. Glands throughout the body release *hormones,* chemicals that travel in the bloodstream to act on other body parts. One of these glands, the pituitary, is located deep in the brain. A few times each day, the pituitary secretes growth hormone (GH). This usually happens during sleep but sometimes after exercise. From the pituitary, GH travels to the liver, where it triggers the release of another hormone, somatomedin, which causes muscles and bones to grow (Tanner, 1990).

Without adequate amounts of GH, a child develops into a dwarf: As adults, dwarfs have normal proportions but they are quite short, measuring about 4 to 4½ feet tall. Dwarfism can be treated with injections of GH, and children grow to normal height.

Another hormone, *thyroxine,* released by the thyroid gland in the neck, is essential for the proper development of nerve cells. Without thyroxine, nerve cells do not develop properly and mental retardation is the result. Thyroxine also seems to be essential for most cells in the body to function properly, so deficiencies in thyroxine can retard physical growth by making the pituitary gland itself ineffective.

Nutrition. The third factor affecting physical growth is nutrition. Nutrition is particularly important during infancy, when physical growth is so rapid. In a 2-month-old, roughly 40 percent of the body's energy is devoted to growth. Most of the remaining energy fuels basic bodily functions, such as digestion and respiration.

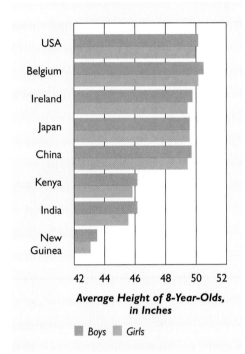

Average Height of 8-Year-Olds, in Inches

■ Boys ■ Girls

Heredity, hormones, and nutrition all play important roles in children's physical growth.

Because growth requires so much high energy, young babies must consume an enormous number of calories in relation to their body weight. While an adult needs to consume only 15 to 20 calories per pound, depending upon level of activity (National Research Council, 1989), a 12-pound 3-month-old should eat about 50 calories per pound of body weight, or 600 calories. What's the best way for babies to receive the calories they need? The "Making Children's Lives Better" feature has some answers.

Making Children's Lives Better: **WHAT'S THE BEST FOOD FOR BABIES?**

 Breast-feeding is the best way to ensure that babies get the nourishment they need. Human milk contains the proper amounts of carbohydrates, fats, protein, vitamins, and minerals for babies. Breast-feeding also has several other advantages compared to bottle-feeding (Shelov, 1993; Sullivan & Birch, 1990). First, breast-fed babies are ill less often because breast milk contains the mother's antibodies. Second, breast-fed babies are less prone to diarrhea and constipation. Third, breast-fed babies typically make the transition to solid foods more easily, apparently because they are accustomed to changes in the taste of breast milk that reflect a mother's diet. Fourth, breast milk cannot be contaminated, which is a significant problem in developing countries when formula is used to bottle-feed babies.

The many benefits of breast-feeding do not mean that bottle-feeding is harmful. Formula, when prepared in sanitary conditions, provides generally the same nutrients as human milk, but infants are more prone to develop allergies from formula and formula does not protect infants from disease. However, bottle-feeding has advantages of its own. A mother who cannot readily breast-feed can still enjoy the intimacy of feeding her baby, and other family members can participate in feeding. In fact, long-term longitudinal studies typically find that breast- and bottle-fed babies are similar in physical and psychological development (Fergusson, Horwood, & Shannon, 1987), so women in industrialized countries can choose either method and know that their babies' dietary needs will be met.

In the United States and Canada, newborns and very young babies are often breast-fed exclusively. Between 3 and 6 months of age, infants are weaned from the breast and given formula. At about the same time, solid foods are introduced into the baby's diet. One suggested "menu" for the first year is shown in the table:

When babies are breast-fed, they get proper nourishment, are ill less often, and adjust to solid food more readily.

Ages When Solid Foods Can Be Introduced into an Infant's Diet

Age (months)	Food
4–6	rice cereal, then other cereals
5–7	strained vegetables, then strained fruits
6–8	protein foods (cheese, yogurt, cooked beans)
9–10	finely chopped meat, toast, crackers
10–12	egg

Source: Whitney, Cataldo, & Rolfes, 1987.

A good rule is to introduce only one food at a time. A 7-month-old having cheese for the first time, for instance, should have no other new foods for a few days. In this way, allergies that may develop—skin rash or diarrhea—can be linked to a particular food, making it easier to prevent reoccurrences. ◼

By 2 years, growth slows, so children need less to eat. This is also a time when many children become picky eaters. Like the little girl in the photo, toddlers and preschool children find foods that they once ate willingly "yucky." As a toddler, my daughter, Laura, loved green beans. When she reached 2, she decided that green beans were awful and adamantly refused to eat them. Though such finickiness can be annoying, it may actually be adaptive for increasingly independent preschoolers. Because preschoolers don't know what is safe to eat and what isn't, eating only familiar foods protects them from potential harm (Birch & Fisher, 1995).

Adolescents need to eat more to provide the nutrition necessary for the adolescent growth spurt. Unfortunately, many adolescents have notoriously poor diets, eating far too many Big Macs and fries. Consequently, many teenagers do not get adequate nutrients, such as iron and calcium (Malina, 1990). Furthermore, their eating habits often lead to obesity, which I'll discuss in Module 4.2.

THE ADOLESCENT GROWTH SPURT AND PUBERTY

Early adolescence is marked by several physical changes known collectively as *puberty.* One obvious part of puberty is the adolescent growth spurt. As I described on page 85, physical growth during the elementary-school years is slow: In an average year, a 6- to 10-year-old girl or boy gains about 5 to 7 pounds and grows 2 to 3 inches. But during the peak of the adolescent growth spurt, a girl may gain as many as 20 pounds in a year and a boy, 25 (Tanner, 1970). This growth spurt lasts a few years, so that girls typically achieve most of their mature stature by age 15 and boys by age 17.

Puberty includes other physical changes, notably maturation of the reproductive system. The chart shows these reproductive changes and the ages when they typically occur for boys and girls. For girls, puberty begins with growth of the breasts and the growth spurt, followed by the appearance of pubic hair. **Menarche, the onset of menstruation, typically occurs at about age 13.** Early menstrual cycles are usually irregular and without ovulation.

For boys, puberty usually commences with the growth of the testes and scrotum, followed by the appearance of pubic hair, the start of the growth spurt, and growth of the penis. At about age 13, most boys have their first spontaneous ejaculation, a discharge of fluid

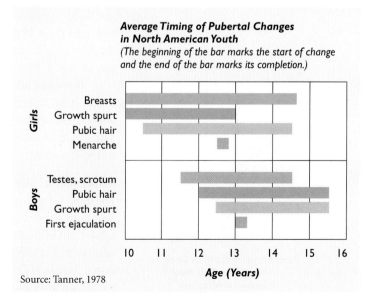

Average Timing of Pubertal Changes in North American Youth
(The beginning of the bar marks the start of change and the end of the bar marks its completion.)

Source: Tanner, 1978

containing sperm. Initial ejaculations often contain relatively few sperm; only months or sometimes years later are there sufficient sperm to fertilize an egg (Chilman, 1983).

Rate of Maturation. Of course, puberty does not always begin at age 10 for girls and age 12 for boys. For many children, puberty begins months or even years before or after these norms. An early-maturing boy might begin puberty at age 11, whereas a late-maturing boy might start at 15 or 16. An early-maturing girl might start puberty at 9, a late-maturing girl, at 14 or 15. For example, the girls shown in the photo are the same age, but only one has reached puberty.

Timing of puberty is regulated, in part, by genetics. However, experience also influences the onset of puberty. For example, puberty occurs earlier in girls who experience a great deal of family conflict (Belsky, Steinberg, & Draper, 1991). The exact mechanism is unknown, but stress apparently influences the levels of hormones that trigger puberty.

Whether children mature early or late does not predict their height as adults, but maturing early or late does have psychological consequences and they differ for boys and girls. In several longitudinal studies, the general pattern is that early maturation benefits boys but not girls. Boys who mature early tend to be more independent and self-confident. They're also more popular with peers. In contrast, girls who mature early often lack self-confidence and are less popular with peers.

The differing consequences of early maturation on boys and girls is shown in the results of an extensive longitudinal study of adolescents growing up in Milwaukee during the 1970s (Simmons & Blyth, 1987). The early-maturing boys in this study dated more often and had more positive feelings about their physical development and athletic abilities. The early-maturing girls had more negative feelings about their physical development, received poorer grades, and were more often in trouble in school.

Why does rate of maturation have such different consequences? Early maturation may benefit boys because others perceive them as more mature and are therefore more willing to give them adultlike responsibilities. In contrast, late-maturing boys, like Pete in the vignette at the beginning of the module, are often frustrated because others treat them like little boys instead of like young men. Early maturation in girls may lead them to associate with older adolescents, who apparently encourage them to engage in age-inappropriate activities, such as drinking, smoking, and sex, for which they are ill-prepared (Brooks-Gunn, 1988).

By young adulthood, most of the effects associated with rate of maturation have vanished. That is, early-maturing, on-time, and late-maturing adolescents cannot be distinguished as adults (Simmons & Blyth, 1987). Thus, rate of maturation may influence the path through adolescence but not necessarily the rest of life.

Adolescent Sexuality. Sexual behavior usually begins in adolescence. For most teens, sex progresses from kissing to petting above the waist to petting below the waist to intercourse (Rodgers & Rowe, 1993). The extent of adolescent sexuality is shown in the graph, which charts the percentage of adolescents at different ages who have experienced sexual intercourse (National Research Council, 1987). Notice that by the end of adolescence, most American boys and girls have had intercourse at least once.

Why are some adolescents sexually active whereas others are not? Parents' and peers' attitudes towards sex play a key role. In one study of high-

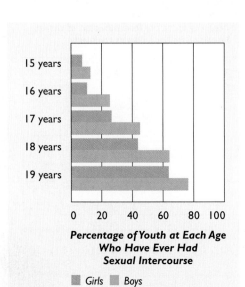

Percentage of Youth at Each Age Who Have Ever Had Sexual Intercourse

■ Girls ■ Boys

school students (Treboux & Busch-Rossnagel, 1990), positive attitudes toward sex by parents and friends were associated with students' positive attitudes, which, in turn, were associated with more frequent and more intense sexual behavior. That is, when parents and friends had positive attitudes toward sexuality in general, students had more open attitudes and were more likely to have sexual intercourse. In another study of junior-high and high-school students (DiBlasio & Benda, 1990), sexually active adolescents believed that their friends were also sexually active. They also thought the rewards of sex (for example, emotional and physical closeness) outweighed the costs (for example, guilt and fear of pregnancy or disease). Thus, sexual activity reflects the influence of parents and peers as well as an individual's beliefs and values.

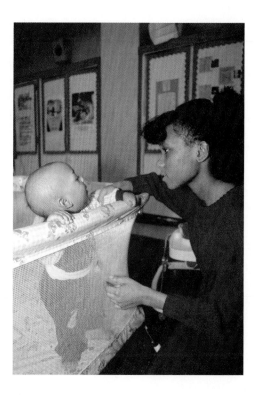

Adolescents' sexual behavior is a cause for concern because approximately 1 in 10 American adolescent girls becomes pregnant. About 60 percent of pregnant teenagers give birth; the remaining 40 percent abort the pregnancy (Henshaw, 1993). The result is that roughly 500,000 babies are born to American teenagers annually. As I described in Module 3.2, teenage mothers and their children like those in the photo usually face bleak futures. If this is the case, why do so many teens become pregnant? The answer is simple: Few sexually active teenagers use birth control. Those who do, often use ineffective methods, such as withdrawal, or practice contraception inconsistently (National Research Council, 1987).

Adolescents' infrequent use of contraceptives can be traced to several factors (Adler, 1994):

- *Ignorance:* Many adolescents are seriously misinformed about the facts of conception. For example, many do not know when conception is most likely to occur during the menstrual cycle.

- *Illusion of invulnerability:* Too many adolescents deny reality. They believe they are invincible—"It couldn't happen to me"—only others become pregnant.

- *Lack of motivation:* For some adolescent girls, becoming pregnant is appealing. They think having a child is a way to break away from their parents, gain status as an independent-living adult, and have "someone to love them."

- *Lack of access:* Some teenagers do not know where to obtain contraceptives. Others may find it awkward to do so. Still others don't know how to use contraceptives.

The best way to deal with adolescent sexual behavior is to give adolescents the facts about sex, teenage pregnancy, and contraception (Boyer & Hein, 1991). Effective programs not only teach the relevant biology, they also emphasize responsible sexual behavior or abstaining from premarital sex altogether (Dryfoos, 1990). For example, in the program called "Postponing Sexual Involvement" (Howard & McCabe, 1990), trained, older adolescents lead student groups in discussions of the pressures to become involved sexually. They discuss common "lines" that teens use to induce others to have sex and strategies for responding to these lines. Along with the discussions, students practice refusal strategies in role-playing sessions. Students who participate in programs like this one are less likely to have intercourse; when they do have intercourse, they are more likely to use contraceptives (Howard & McCabe, 1990).

Adolescents are less likely to become sexually active when they are given information about the biology of sex, the need for responsible sexual behavior, and ways to respond to pressure to become sexually active.

The conclusion: Adolescents need more than catchy sayings like, "True love waits." Love and sex are enormously complicated and emotionally charged issues, even for adults. Effective programs for adolescents recognize this complexity and try to provide adolescents with skills for dealing with the issues involved in their emerging sexuality.

Check Your Learning

1. Physical growth involves increases in height and weight, changes in _____, and changes in bone, muscle, and fat.

2. Changes in physical development from one generation to the next are called _____.

3. Normal physical growth depends upon heredity, hormones, and _____.

4. Early maturation often benefits boys because _____.

5. Sexually active adolescents usually don't use contraceptives due to ignorance, the illusion of invulnerability, lack of motivation, and _____.

Answers: (1) body proportions, (2) secular growth trends, (3) nutrition, (4) others are more likely to give them adult responsibilities, (5) lack of access to contraceptives

ROBLEMS OF PHYSICAL GROWTH

MODULE
4.2

Problems of Physical Growth

⌐ *Malnutrition*

⌐ *Anorexia Nervosa*

⌐ *Obesity*

Learning Objectives

- **What is malnutrition? What are its consequences? What is the solution to malnutrition?**
- **How do nature and nurture lead some adolescent girls to diet excessively?**
- **Why do some children become obese? How can they lose weight permanently?**

> *Ricardo, 12, has been overweight for most of his life. He dislikes the playground games that entertain most of his classmates during recess, preferring to stay indoors. He has relatively few friends and is not particularly happy with his lot in life. Many times Ricardo has lost weight from dieting but he's always regained it quickly. His parents know that being overweight is a health hazard, and they wonder if there is anything that will help their son.*

Two major problems of physical growth concern nutrition. Growth requires enormous reserves of energy, and many children do not eat enough food to provide this energy. Other children and adolescents eat too much. We'll look at these problems in this module, and as we do, we'll understand some of the reasons why Ricardo is overweight and what he can do about it.

MALNUTRITION

An adequate diet is only a dream to many of the world's children. **Children who weigh less than 60 percent of the average body weight for their age are considered severely *malnourished*.** According to the World Health Organization of the United Nations, 10 million children under age 5 years are severely malnourished. Many, like the little girl in the photo at the top of page 93, are from third-world countries. But malnutrition is regrettably common in industrialized countries, too. Many American children growing up homeless and in poverty are malnourished. Approximately 20 percent of American children receive inadequate amounts of iron, and 10 percent go to bed hungry (Children's Defense Fund, 1996; Pollitt, 1994).

Malnourishment is especially damaging during infancy because growth is so rapid during these years. A longitudinal study conducted in Barbados in the West Indies (Galler & Ramsey, 1989; Galler, Ramsey, & Forde, 1986) followed children who were severely malnourished as infants and children from similar family environments who had adequate nutrition as infants. As older children, the two groups were indistinguishable physically: Children who were malnourished as infants were just as tall and weighed just as much as their peers. However, the children with a history of infant malnutrition had much lower scores on intelligence tests. They also had difficulty maintaining attention in school; they were easily distracted. Malnutrition during rapid periods of growth apparently damages the brain, affecting a child's intelligence and ability to pay attention (Morgane et al., 1993).

Malnutrition would seem to have a simple cure—an adequate diet. But, the solution is more complex than that. Malnourished children are frequently listless and inactive (Ricciuti, 1993), behaviors that *are* useful because they conserve energy. At the same time, when children are routinely unresponsive and lethargic, parents may provide fewer and fewer experiences that foster their children's development. For example, parents who start out reading to their children at night may stop because their malnourished children seem uninterested and inattentive. The result is a self-perpetuating cycle in which malnourished children are forsaken by parents who feel that nothing they do gets a response, so they quit trying. A biological influence—lethargy stemming from insufficient nourishment—causes a profound change in the experiences—parental teaching—that shape a child's development.

In addition to improving children's diets, parents must foster their children's development. Programs that combine dietary supplements with parent training are a promising treatment for malnutrition (Super, Herrera, & Mora, 1990).

ANOREXIA NERVOSA

A persistent refusal to eat, accompanied by an irrational fear of being overweight, describes a condition known as *anorexia nervosa*. Anorexia primarily (but not exclusively) affects females and usually begins with the onset of adolescence (Attie, Brooks-Gunn, & Petersen, 1990). Adolescents with anorexia tend to be well-behaved, conscientious, good students, and from middle-class families. But their image of their body is grossly distorted. Like the girl in the photo, girls with anorexia are painfully thin, yet they claim to be overweight (Attie et al., 1990). Anorexia is a very serious disorder, often leading to heart damage. Without treatment, as many as 15 percent of adolescents with anorexia die (Wicks-Nelson & Israel, 1991). The "Real Children" feature describes a teenage girl with anorexia.

Real Children: **LAYLA'S BATTLE WITH ANOREXIA**

Layla had always been a pleasant and obedient child. She was an above-average student in school, though she could never quite make the honor roll as her older brothers always did. At 15, Layla was 5 feet, 4½ inches tall and weighed 120 pounds. Her weight was perfectly normal for her height, but she decided she was fat and began to diet. Over the next year, Layla lost 35 pounds. She looked pale, tired, and wasted, and she no longer menstruated. Layla insisted she looked fine and that nothing was wrong with her, but her parents and family doctor were so concerned they insisted she be hospitalized. Forced to eat regular meals in the hospital, Layla gained some weight and was sent home. But this cycle was repeated several times over the next two years: Layla would diet to the point that she looked like a skeleton draped in skin, and then she would be hospitalized. In her generally weakened condition, Layla developed mononucleosis and hepatitis; ultimately her liver and kidneys failed. Three days before her 18th birthday, Layla had a heart attack and died.

Why do girls like Layla become anorexic? It probably won't surprise you that nature and nurture both play a role. Let's start with nurture and cultural ideals of the female body. In many industrialized cultures—and certainly in the United States—the ideal female body is tall and slender. As girls enter adolescence, these cultural norms becomes particularly important and influential. Also during adolescence, girls experience a "fat spurt" in which they gain about 25 pounds, most of it fat. Though this pattern of growth is normal, some girls unfortunately perceive themselves to be overweight and begin to diet. This is especially the case when the girl's mother is preoccupied with her own weight (Attie et al., 1990). Faced with a cultural value of being thin and a change in their bodies, adolescent girls believe they are fat and try to lose weight.

Family dynamics also contribute to anorexia. Adolescent girls are more prone to anorexia if their parents are autocratic, leaving their adolescent daughters with little sense of self-control. Dieting allows the girls to assert their autonomy and achieve an individual identity (Graber et al., 1994). Layla, for example, who was entering mid-adolescence and seeking greater personal autonomy, enjoyed the sense of control over her weight that dieting gave her.

Cultural emphases on thinness, combined with a regimented home life, can explain many cases of anorexia. Of course, most teenage girls growing up in regimented homes in the United States do *not* become anorexic, which raises the question of biological factors. Identical twins are more likely to both be anorexic than fraternal twins (Fisher & Brone, 1991). This result points to an inherited predisposition for anorexia. Thus, anorexia is most likely to develop in girls who inherit the predisposition, who internalize cultural ideals of thinness, and whose parents grant them little independence.

OBESITY

Ricardo, the boy in the module-opening vignette, is typical of the 5 to 10 percent of American children and adolescents who are obese, at least 20 percent over the ideal body weight for their age and height. Overweight youngsters like the boy in the photo are often unpopular and have low self-esteem. Furthermore, they are at risk for many medical problems, including high blood pressure and diabetes, throughout life because the vast majority of overweight children and adolescents become overweight adults (Epstein & Wing, 1987).

Heredity plays an important role in juvenile obesity. Studies show that adopted children and adolescents' weight is related to the weight of their biological parents, not to the weight of their adoptive parents (Stunkard et al., 1986). Genes may influence obesity by helping to determine a person's activity level. In other words, being genetically more prone to inactivity makes it more difficult to burn off calories and easier to gain weight. **Heredity may also help set *basal metabolic rate*, the speed at which the body consumes calories.** Children and adolescents with a slower basal metabolic rate burn off calories less rapidly, making it easier for them to gain weight (Epstein & Cluss, 1986).

The environment is also influential. Television advertising, for example, encourages youth to eat tasty but fattening foods. Parents play a role, too. They may inadvertently encourage obesity by emphasizing external eating signals rather than internal. Infants eat primarily because of internal signals: They eat when they experience hunger and stop eating when they feel full. During the preschool years, this internal control of eating is often gradually replaced by external signals. Parents who urge their children to "clean their plates" even when they are no longer hungry are teaching their children to ignore internal cues to eating. Thus, obese children and adolescents may overeat because they rely on external cues and disregard internal cues to stop (Birch, 1991).

Childhood obesity can be traced to heredity, ads that promote fatty foods, and reliance upon external cues for eating.

Obese youth *can* lose weight. The most effective way is to involve the entire family. Children and parents first set goals for caloric intake and exercise. They might agree to daily goals of 2,000 calories of food and 20 minutes of exercise. Both children and parents monitor eating and exercise, and children earn rewards from parents when they meet their goal weight (Epstein et al., 1990). The graph shows results of a

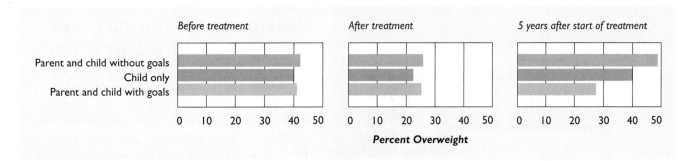

weight-loss study by Epstein and Wing (1987). Notice that young people who participated alone and those who participated with their parents but without joint eating and exercise goals both lost weight while in the program but regained almost all of it in the ensuing years. In contrast, when children and parents pursued goals together, the children maintained their weight at lower levels. Apparently, parental involvement results in a long-lasting lifestyle change—particularly in eating and exercising—that allows children to sustain their initial weight loss. Notice, too, that youth in the parent involvement group are still over their ideal weight 5 years after starting the program, though not by as much as before the program. It is best to establish good eating and exercise habits early in order to *avoid* obesity in the first place.

Check Your Learning

1. Malnourished children need an adequate diet and _____.

2. Cultural ideals of thinness, a regimented home life, and _____ all contribute to anorexia nervosa.

3. The most effective programs for childhood obesity involve _____.

Answers: (1) parents who foster their development, (2) an inherited disposition for the disorder, (3) parents and children in achieving eating and exercise goals

THE DEVELOPING NERVOUS SYSTEM

Learning Objectives

- **What are the parts of a nerve cell? How is the brain organized?**
- **When is the brain formed in prenatal development? When do different regions of the brain begin to function?**

> *While crossing the street, 10-year-old Martin was struck by a passing car. He was in a coma for a week, but then gradually became more alert, and now he seems to be aware of his surroundings. Needless to say, Martin's mother is grateful that he survived the accident, but she wonders what the future holds for her son.*

The physical changes that we see as children grow are impressive, but even more awe-inspiring are the changes we cannot see, those involving the brain and the nervous system. An infant's feelings of hunger, a child's laugh, and an adolescent's efforts to learn algebra all reflect the functioning brain and the rest of the nervous system.

How does the brain accomplish these many tasks? To begin to answer this question, let's look at how the brain is organized in adults.

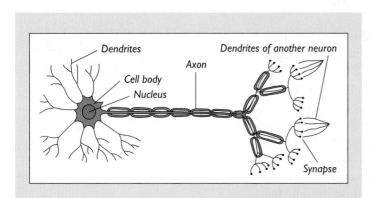

ORGANIZATION OF THE MATURE BRAIN

The basic unit of the brain and the rest of the nervous system is the *neuron,* a cell that specializes in receiving and transmitting information. Neurons have three basic parts, as shown in the top diagram. **The *cell body* at the center of the neuron contains the basic biological machinery that keeps the neuron alive. The receiving end of the neuron, the *dendrite,* looks like a tree with many branches.** The highly branched dendrite allows one neuron to receive input from many thousands of other neurons (Morgan & Gibson, 1991). **The tubelike structure at the other end of the cell body is the *axon,* which sends information to other neurons.**

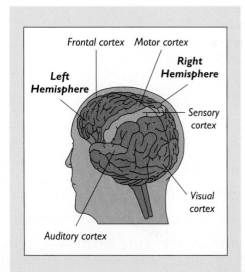

Take 50 to 100 billion neurons like these and you have the beginnings of a human brain. An adult's brain weighs a little less than 3 pounds and it easily fits into your hands. **The wrinkled surface of the brain is the *cerebral cortex;* made up of 10^{10} neurons, the cortex regulates many of the functions that we think of as distinctly human. The cortex consists of left and right halves, called *hemispheres,* that are linked by a thick bundle of neurons called the *corpus callosum.*** The characteristics that you value the most—your engaging personality, your "way with words," your uncanny knack for reading others—are all controlled by specific regions of the cortex, many of which are shown in the bottom diagram. **Personality, and your ability to make and carry out plans are largely functions of an area at the front of the cortex that is called, appropriately, the *frontal cortex.*** Your abilities to produce and understand language, to reason, and to compute are largely due to neurons in the cortex of the left hemisphere. Your artistic and musical abilities, perception of spatial relationships, and ability to recognize faces and emotions come from neurons in the right hemisphere.

Now that we know a bit of the organization of the mature brain, let's look at how the brain develops and begins to function.

MAKING OF THE WORKING BRAIN

The brain weighs only ¾ of a pound (340 grams) at birth, which is roughly 25 percent of the weight of an adult brain. But as you can see from the figure, the brain grows rapidly during infancy and the preschool years. By age 3, for example, the brain has achieved 80 percent of its ultimate weight.

Brain weight doesn't tell us much, however, about the working brain. To understand how changes in brain structure produce increased brain function, we need to move back to prenatal development. **If you were to look at an embryo at roughly 3 weeks after conception, you would see a group of cells that form a flat structure known as the *neural plate.*** At four weeks, the neural plate folds to form a tube that is open at the ends. One end of this tube becomes the spinal cord; the other becomes the brain. Soon after the ends fuse shut, neurons are produced in one small region of the neural tube. Production of neurons begins about 10 weeks after conception, and by 28 weeks, the developing brain has virtually all the neurons it will ever have. During these weeks, neurons form at the incredible rate of more than 4,000 per second (Kolb, 1989).

From the neuron-manufacturing site in the neural tube, neurons migrate to their final positions in the brain. The brain is built in stages, beginning with the innermost layers. Neurons in the deepest layer are positioned first, followed by neurons in the second layer, and so on. This layering process continues until all six layers of the mature brain are in place, which occurs about 7 months after conception (Huttenlocher, 1990).

When neurons reach their final position in the brain, their axons and dendrites grow. Surprisingly, the embryonic brain produces many more neurons than necessary. **Beginning after birth and continuing through childhood and adolescence, rarely used neurons simply disappear, a phenomenon known as *neural pruning.*** The brain goes through its own version of "downsizing" in which unnecessary elements are weeded out (Greenough & Black, 1992).

Another important stage in the making of a working brain is *myelinization,* in which neurons become wrapped in *myelin,* a fatty sheath that allows them to transmit information more rapidly. The boost in speed from myelin is like the difference between driving and flying: from about 6 feet per second to 50 feet per second. Myelinization begins in the fourth month of prenatal development and continues through infancy and into childhood and adolescence (Casaer, 1993). You can see the effect of increased myelinization in improved coordination and reaction times. The older the infant and, later, the child, the more rapid and coordinated his or her reactions. We'll talk more about this phenomenon when we discuss fine-motor skills in Module 4.4.

It probably won't surprise you to learn that, because the brain develops so rapidly, many areas of the cortex begin to function early in life. In fact, it appears that, at birth, the cortex of the left hemisphere is uniquely prepared to process language. Scientists know this from studying the brain's electrical activity. **Metal electrodes placed on an infant's**

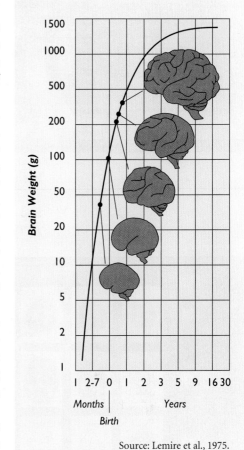

Source: Lemire et al., 1975.

During childhood, some unneeded neurons are pruned; other neurons become wrapped in myelin, allowing them to transmit more rapidly.

scalp, as shown in the top photo, produce an *electroen-cephalogram (EEG),* a pattern of brain waves. Studies show that a newborn infant's left hemisphere generates more electrical activity in response to speech than the right hemisphere (Molfese & Burger-Judisch, 1991), because, apparently, the language center is already functioning. As we'll see in Chapter 9, this specialization allows for language to develop rapidly during infancy.

Is the right hemisphere equally well prepared to function at birth? This is a difficult question to answer, in part because the right hemisphere influences so many nonlinguistic functions. Music does elicit greater electrical activity in the infant's right hemisphere than in the left hemisphere. Other functions, such as understanding spatial relations and recognizing faces, come more gradually but are under the right hemisphere's control by the preschool years (Hahn, 1987).

The frontal cortex, too, begins to function early. **Mapping the areas of activity and energy in the frontal cortex is possible with *positron emission tomography* or *PET-scan.*** The brain gets energy to function from glucose, a form of sugar. Areas of the brain that are particularly active use more glucose than areas that are less active. The brain's use of glucose is measured by injecting a radioactive form of glucose into the bloodstream. Then, the amount of glucose in various parts of the brain is recorded. Higher levels of glucose indicate greater activity in that area. The photo reveals little activity in the frontal cortex of 5-day-old babies. Activity has increased considerably by 11 weeks of age and reaches adult levels by 7 or 8 months after birth (Chugani & Phelps, 1986). Obviously, 8-month-olds cannot plan and function as adults do, but their frontal cortex *has* become very active.

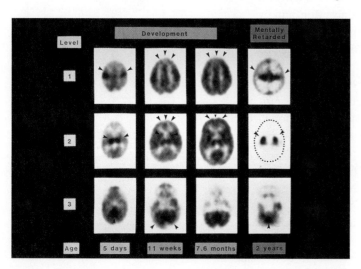

What is the frontal cortex regulating in PET-scans like the ones in the photo? Deliberate, goal-oriented behavior is a good bet. To understand research that leads to this conclusion, think back to a time when you had to make a permanent change in your regular routine. At the start of a new school year, perhaps you were assigned a new locker. For the first few days, you might have turned down the old hallway, reflecting last year's habit, instead of walking on to your new locker. To override your old response, maybe you deliberately reminded yourself to walk past the old hallway and turn at the new one.

Overriding responses that become incorrect or inappropriate is an important part of deliberate, goal-directed behavior. Adults with damage to the frontal cortex often have great difficulty inhibiting responses that are no longer appropriate. The frontal cortex begins to regulate inappropriate responding at about 1 year and gradually achieves greater control throughout the preschool and school-age years (Welsh, Pennington, & Groisser, 1991). Thus, children gradually become better able to regulate their behavior to achieve cognitive and social goals.

Not only does the frontal cortex regulate responses, it also regulates feelings such as happiness, sadness, and fear. Nathan Fox (1991) believes that "emotional experience arises from two opposing innate action tendencies in the organism: approach and exploration of the novel versus freezing, fleeing, or withdrawal from harmful or dangerous stimuli" (p. 865). That is, emotions like happiness and curiosity stem from an organism's desire to approach a stimulus, and emotions like distress, disgust, or fear come from the desire to avoid a stimulus.

Fox and his co-investigators have shown that the left frontal cortex tends to regulate emotions stemming from the tendency to approach, while the right frontal cortex regulates emotions stemming from avoidance. For example, when babies display joy, the EEG reveals more activity in the left frontal area, and when babies like the one in the photo display stress or disgust, the right frontal area is more electrically active.

Babies also differ in their typical patterns of brain activity. These differences in brain activity are the subject of the "Focus on Research" feature.

Focus on Research: **FRONTAL CORTEX ACTIVITY AND REACTIVITY TO NOVEL STIMULI**

Who were the investigators and what was the aim of the study? Previous research had shown that in neutral situations—situations where no stimuli obviously elicit attraction or avoidance—some babies have more spontaneous activity in the left frontal areas, whereas other babies have greater right frontal activity. Infants with greater right frontal activity do not cope as well with stress. For example, they cry more when separated from their mothers than babies who have more spontaneous left frontal activity. Susan Calkins, Nathan Fox, and Timothy Marshall (1996) wanted to know if they could predict differences in brain activity from infants' behavior. Specifically, they wanted to know if there was a connection between infants' responses to novel stimuli at 4 months and their brain activity at 9 months. The investigators expected that infants who responded negatively to the mild stress of a novel stimulus at 4 months (by fussing and crying) would have more right frontal activity at 9 months; infants who responded positively to novelty at 4 months (by smiling and vocalizing) would have more left frontal activity at 9 months.

How did the investigators measure the topic of interest? Calkins and her colleagues needed to measure infants' response to novelty at 4 months. They did this by presenting novel sights (colored toys presented about 12 inches from the infant's face); novel sounds (tape-recorded syllables and sentences presented at increasingly loud volume); and novel odors (different concentrations of diluted alcohol presented on a cotton swab ½ inch from the baby's nose). The infants were videotaped as the stimuli were presented. Later, the investigators determined the degree of positive and negative emotion that babies expressed. Positive emotion was defined as smiling and vocalizing; negative emotion was defined as fussing, fretting, and crying.

The next step was to measure brain activity at 9 months. Calkins and her colleagues attached electrodes to different sites on the infants' scalps, including over the frontal cortex. Then they recorded electrical activity at each site while the infant sat on the mother's lap watching different colored balls move in a container. (The moving balls were simply meant to capture the infants' attention and keep them still for the 2 minutes required to measure brain activity.)

Who were the children in the study? The researchers tested 207 4-month-olds. Of these, the 49 whose responses to novelty were particularly positive or negative were retested as 9-month-olds.

> *The left frontal cortex regulates emotions like happiness and curiosity; the right frontal cortex regulates emotions like distress and fear.*

What was the design of the study? This study was correlational because Calkins and her colleagues were interested in the relation that existed naturally between two variables: response to novelty and electrical activity in the frontal cortex. The study was longitudinal because children were tested twice at different ages: Their response to novelty was measured at 4 months and their brain activity was measured at 9 months.

Were there ethical concerns with the study? No. The novel stimuli were mildly upsetting to some infants, but they were no more fear-provoking than other novel stimuli that young babies encounter in daily life. Measuring brain activity with EEGs is painless and safe. The investigators obtained permission from the parents for the children to participate.

What were the results? The infants were divided in two groups, based on their response to novelty as 4-month-olds: infants who responded positively and infants who responded negatively. Then Calkins and her colleagues looked at patterns of electrical activity in the left and right frontal cortex. They calculated the difference between activity in these two regions: A positive number meant relatively greater activation in the left frontal cortex and a negative number meant relatively greater activation in the right frontal cortex. The graph shows that infants who responded negatively to novelty as 4-month-olds had relatively more right frontal activity as 9-month-olds. In contrast, infants who responded positively to novelty as 4-month-olds had relatively more left frontal activity as 9-month-olds.

What did the investigators conclude? Infants' response to novelty at 4 months predicts their brain activity at 9 months. Babies who respond to novelty by fussing and crying have a more active right frontal cortex, the region that regulates emotions linked to avoidance. Babies who respond to novelty by smiling have a a more active left frontal cortex, the region that regulates emotions linked to approach. These differences provide further evidence that, in the first year, the left frontal cortex regulates infants' tendency to approach or explore stimuli and the right frontal cortex regulates infants' tendency to avoid or elude stimuli. ■

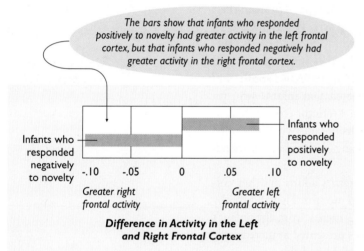

The bars show that infants who responded positively to novelty had greater activity in the left frontal cortex, but that infants who responded negatively had greater activity in the right frontal cortex.

Infants who responded negatively to novelty

Infants who responded positively to novelty

-.10   -.05   0   .05   .10

Greater right frontal activity   *Greater left frontal activity*

Difference in Activity in the Left and Right Frontal Cortex

The "Focus on Research" highlights an important point in this module: The brain begins to specialize early in life. Language processing is associated primarily with the left hemisphere; recognizing nonspeech sounds, emotions, and faces is associated with the right hemisphere; and regulating emotions and intentional behavior is a function of the frontal cortex. Of course, this early specialization does not mean that the brain is functionally mature. Over the remainder of childhood and into adulthood, these and other regions of the brain continue to become more specialized.

One last point: Remember Martin, the 10-year-old in the vignette at the beginning of the module who was struck by a car? The only lasting effect of the accident was on Martin's speech, which is now slow and deliberate. This is not surprising because the left hemisphere of Martin's brain absorbed the force of the collision, and the left hemisphere is specialized for language processing.

Check Your Learning

1. The _____ is the part of the neuron containing the basic machinery that keeps the cells alive.

2. The wrinkled surface of the brain is the _____.

3. During prenatal development, the brain forms from a flat group of cells called the _____.

4. Human speech elicits greater electrical activity from the _____ of an infant's brain.

Answers: (1) cell body, (2) cerebral cortex, (3) neural plate, (4) left hemisphere

 # OTOR DEVELOPMENT

MODULE
4.4
Motor Development

Locomotion ─

Fine-motor Skills ─

Maturation, Experience, ─
and Motor Skill

Learning Objectives

- **What are the component skills involved in learning to walk, and at what age do infants typically master them?**
- **How do infants learn to coordinate the use of their hands? When and why do most children begin to prefer to use one hand?**
- **How do maturation and experience influence children's acquisition of motor skills?**

Nancy is 14 months old and a world-class crawler. Using hands and knees, she can get just about anywhere she wants to go. Nancy does not walk and seems to have no interest in learning how. Nancy's dad wonders whether he should be doing something to help Nancy progress beyond crawling. And down deep, he worries that perhaps he was negligent in not providing more exercise or training for Nancy when she was younger.

Do you remember what it was like to learn to type, to drive a car with a stick shift, to play a musical instrument, or to play a sport? **Each of these activities involves *motor skills*—coordinated movements of the muscles and limbs.** Success demands that each movement be done in a precise way and in a specific sequence. For example, to use a stick shift properly, you need to move the clutch pedal, gas pedal, and the stick shift in specific ways and in exactly the right sequence. If you don't give the car enough gas as you let out the clutch, you'll kill the engine. If you give it too much gas, the engine races and the car lurches forward.

If new activities are demanding for adults, think about the challenges infants face. **Infants must learn *locomotion,* that is, to move about in the world.** Newborns are relatively immobile, but infants soon learn to crawl, stand, and walk. Learning to move through the environment upright leaves the arms and hands free. Taking full advantage of this arrangement, the human hand has fully independent fingers (instead of a paw), with the thumb opposing the remaining four fingers. An opposable thumb makes it possible for humans to grasp and manipulate objects. **Infants must learn the *fine-motor skills* associated with grasping, holding, and manipulating objects.** In the case of feeding, for example, infants progress from being fed by others to holding a bottle, to feeding themselves with their fingers, to eating with a fork and spoon. Each new skill requires incredibly complex physical movements.

Together, locomotion and fine-motor skills give children access to an enormous amount of information about their environment. Let's look at each of these activities more carefully.

LOCOMOTION

In little more than a year, advances in posture and locomotion change the newborn from an almost motionless piece of humanity into an upright standing individual who walks through the environment. The chart shows some of the important milestones in motor development and the age by which most infants achieve them. By about 4 months of age, most babies can sit upright with support. By 7 months, they can sit without support, and by 9 months, can stand if they hold on to an object for support. A typical 14-month-old can stand alone briefly and walk with assistance. **Youngsters at this age are called *toddlers,* after the toddling manner of early walking.** Of course, not all children walk at exactly the same age. Some walk before their first birthday; others, like Nancy, the world-class crawler in the module-opening vignette, take their first steps as late as 17 or 18 months of age. By 24 months, most children can climb steps, walk backwards, and kick a ball.

Source: Based on Shirley, 1931 and Bayley, 1969.

This sequence of milestones fails to do justice to the truly remarkable accomplishment of learning to walk, which reflects the maturity and coalescence of many component skills. For example, the ability to maintain an upright posture is fundamental to walking. But upright posture is virtually impossible for newborns and young infants because of the shape of their body. Cephalocaudal growth means that an infant is top-heavy. Consequently, as soon as a young infant starts to lose her balance, she tumbles over. Only with growth of the legs and muscles can infants maintain an upright posture (Thelen, Ulrich, & Jensen, 1989).

To walk, infants must master distinct skills of standing upright, maintaining their balance, and stepping alternately; then they must integrate these skills into a coherent whole.

A second important aspect of walking is balance: Infants must continuously adjust their posture to avoid falling down. By 4 months of age, infants are able to use cues from their inner ears to help them stay upright. If a 4-month-old is propped in a sitting position and starts to lose his balance, he will nevertheless keep his head upright, using muscles in the back of his neck. This happens even when the infant is blindfolded, which tells us that the essential cues are from the inner ears, not the eyes (Woollacott, Shumway-Cook, & Williams, 1989).

Another essential element of walking is moving the legs alternately, repeatedly transferring the weight of the body from one foot to the other. Children don't step spontaneously until approximately 10 months because they must be able to stand to step. Can younger children step if they are held upright? Thelen and Ulrich (1991) devised a clever procedure to answer this question. Infants were placed on a treadmill and held upright by an adult. When the belt on the treadmill started to move, infants could respond one of several ways. They might simply let both legs be dragged rearward by the belt. Or they might let their legs be dragged briefly, then move them forward together in a hopping motion. Some 3-month-olds, though, and many 6- and 7-month-olds, demonstrated the mature pattern of alternating steps on each leg that is shown in the photo. Even more amazing is that when the treadmill was equipped with separate belts for each leg that moved at different speeds, babies adjusted, stepping more rapidly on the faster belt. Apparently, the alternate stepping motion that is essential for walking is evident long before infants walk alone.

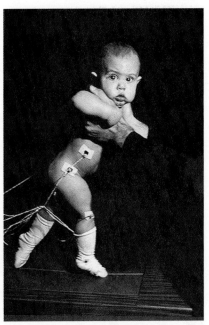

Findings like Thelen and Ulrich's (1991) with the treadmill remind us that each motor milestone—learning to sit or learning to walk—is not a solitary event. Instead, each demands orchestration of many individual skills. Each component skill must first be mastered alone and then integrated with the other skills, which is a general principle of motor development (Werner, 1948). **That is, mastery of intricate motions requires both *differentiation*—mastery of component skills— and their *integration*—combination in proper sequence—into a coherent, working whole.** In the case of walking, not until 12 to 15 months of age has the child mastered the component skills so that they can be coordinated to allow independent, unsupported walking.

The first tentative steps are followed by others that are more skilled. Walking is followed by jumping, hopping, running, and skipping—forms of locomotion that exhilarate children and parents alike. If you can recall the feeling of freedom that accompanied your first driver's license, you can imagine how the world expands for infants and toddlers as they learn to move independently. Much of youngsters' enthusiasm for their growing locomotive skills is because they are so useful (Bertenthal, Campos, & Kermoian, 1994). Now toddlers can get to desired objects like toys, food, and books alone, without depending upon a parent. Of course, once the desired object is reached, another set of motor skills is called to action, which we discuss next.

FINE-MOTOR SKILLS

Soon after birth, infants begin to use their hands to grasp objects (Karniol, 1989). They use only one hand and simply hold an object. Soon, when they hold an object, they move their hand, too. By 3 months, they perform more complicated motions, such as shaking a toy. At about 4 months, infants use both hands. At first these motions are not coordinated, as if each hand has a mind of its own. Infants may hold a toy motionless in one hand while shaking a rattle in the other. Soon, however, infants use both hands together in common actions, such as holding a large toy.

Infants first use one hand at a time, then both hands independently, then both hands in common actions, and, finally, both hands in different actions with a common purpose.

At roughly 5 months of age, infants can coordinate the motions of their hands. The hands can now perform different actions that serve a common goal. So a child might, for example, hold a toy animal in one hand and pet it with the other.

The gradual changes in fine-motor coordination are well illustrated by watching children feed themselves. Parents usually allow their infants to experiment with finger foods such as sliced bananas and green beans at about 6 months. Infants can easily pick up such foods, but getting them into their mouths is another story. The hand grasping the food may be raised to the cheek, then moved to the edge of the lips, and, finally, shoved into the mouth. Mission accomplished, but only with many detours along the way! Eye-hand coordination improves rapidly, so, before long, foods varying in size, shape, and texture reach the mouth directly.

At about the first birthday, many parents allow their children to try eating with a spoon. Youngsters first simply play with the spoon, dipping it in and out of a dish filled with food or sucking on an empty spoon. With a little help, they learn to fill the spoon with food and place it in their mouth, though the motion is awkward because they don't rotate their wrist. Instead, most 1-year-olds fill a spoon by placing it di-

rectly over a dish, and lowering it until the bowl of the spoon is full. Then, like the child in the photo, they raise the spoon to the mouth—all the while keeping the wrist rigid. In contrast, 2-year-olds rotate the hand at the wrist while scooping food from a dish and placing the spoon in the mouth—the same motions that adults use.

Fine-motor skills progress beyond infancy. Most 18-month-olds scribble with a pencil and build with blocks. During the preschool years, youngsters typically learn to draw simple geometric figures and the human body (Frankenburg & Dobbs, 1969). Soon, they master using scissors, buttoning shirts and coats, and tying shoelaces.

Each of these actions illustrates the same principles of differentiation and integration that were introduced in our discussion of locomotion. Complex acts involve many component movements. Each must be performed correctly and in the proper sequence. Development involves first mastering the separate elements and then assembling them to form a smoothly functioning whole.

Handedness. Are you right-handed or left-handed? If you're right-handed, you're in good company. About 90 percent of the people worldwide prefer to use their right hand, although this figure varies in different countries, reflecting cultural influences. Most of the remaining 10 percent are left-handed; a relatively small percentage of people are truly ambidextrous.

A preference for one hand over the other does not seem to emerge until after the first birthday. Most 6- and 9-month-olds, for example, use their left and right hands interchangeably (McCormick & Maurer, 1988). They may shake a rattle with their left hand and, moments later, pick up blocks with their right. In one study, infants and toddlers were videotaped as they played with toys that could be manipulated with two hands, such as a pinwheel (Cornwell, Harris, & Fitzgerald, 1991). The 9-month-olds used their left and right hands equally, but by 13 months, most of the children acted like the child in the photo: They grasped the toy with their right hand, and then used their left hand to steady the toy while the right hand manipulated the object.

This early preference for one hand becomes stronger and more consistent during the preschool years. By the time children are ready to enter kindergarten, handedness is well established and is very difficult to reverse (McManus et al., 1988).

What determines whether children become left- or right-handed? Heredity plays a role. Parents who are both right-handed tend to have right-handed children. Children who are left-handed generally have a parent or grandparent who was also left-handed. But experience also contributes to handedness. Modern industrial cultures favor right-handedness. School desks, scissors, and can openers, for example, are designed for right-handed people and can be used by left-handers only with difficulty. Sometimes cultural values influence handedness. The Islam religion dictates that the left hand is unclean, and so forbids its use in eating and greeting others. Writing with the left hand is a cultural taboo in China, but when children of Chinese parents grow up elsewhere, about 10 percent of them write with their left hand, the typical figure worldwide (Harris, 1983). In the United States, elementary-school teachers used to actively encourage left-handed children to use their right hands. As this practice has diminished in the last 50 years, the percentage of left-handed children has risen steadily (Levy, 1976). Thus, handedness seems to have both hereditary and environmental influences.

MATURATION, EXPERIENCE, AND MOTOR SKILL

For locomotion and fine-motor skill, the big picture is much the same: Progress is rapid during the first year as fundamental skills are mastered and combined to generate even more complex behaviors. Is the progress that we observe due primarily to maturation? That is, do skills gradually unfold, regardless of the child's upbringing? Or does the appearance of these motor skills depend on training, practice, and experience? As you might imagine, maturation and experience both contribute.

Let's begin with the impact of maturation on motor development, which is well documented. The sequence of motor development that we have described for locomotion and fine-motor skill holds for most cultures. That is, despite enormous variation across cultures in child-rearing practices, motor development proceeds in much the same way and at roughly the same rate worldwide. This general point is well illustrated in the "Cultural Influences" feature.

Cultural Influences: **LEARNING TO WALK IN A NATIVE AMERICAN CULTURE**

Traditionally, infants in the Hopi culture are secured to cradle boards, like the one shown in the photo. Cradle boards prevent babies from moving hands or legs, rolling over, or raising their bodies. Infants feed and sleep while secured to the board; they are removed from the cradle board only for a change of clothes. This practice begins the day the infant is born and continues for the first 3 months. Thereafter, infants are allowed time off the boards so they can move around. Time off the cradle board increases gradually, but for most of the first year, infants sleep on the boards and spend some part of their waking time on them as well.

Obviously, the cradle board strictly limits the infant's ability to locomote during much of the first year, a time when most infants are learning to sit, creep, and crawl. Nevertheless, Dennis and Dennis (1940) discovered that infants reared with cradle boards learn to walk at approximately 15 months—about the same age as Hopi children reared by parents who had adopted Western practices and no longer used cradle boards.

Thus, a restrictive environment that massively reduces opportunities for practice has no apparent effect on the age of onset for walking. This suggests that the timing of an infant's first steps is determined more by an underlying genetic timetable than by specific experiences or practice. So, the worried father of Nancy, our world-class crawler in the opening vignette, can be reassured that his daughter's motor development is perfectly normal. ■

When the Dennis and Dennis (1940) study was repeated more than 40 years later, the story remained the same. Chisholm (1983) studied Navajo infants who spent much of their infancy secured to cradle boards. They, too, began to walk at about the same age as infants whose parents did not use cradle boards, confirming the importance of maturation in learning to walk.

Of course, maturation and experience are not mutually exclusive. Just because maturation figures importantly in the development of one motor skill, walking, does not imply that experience plays no role. In fact, practice and training do affect children's mastery of many motor skills. Here, too, studies of other cultures are revealing. In some African countries, young infants are given daily practice walking under the tutelage of a parent or sibling. In addition, infants are commonly carried by their parents in the "piggyback" style shown in the photo, which helps develop muscles in the infants' trunk and legs. These infants walk months earlier than American infants (Super, 1981).

Experience can improve the rate of motor development, but the improvement is limited to the specific muscle groups that are involved. In other words, just as daily practice kicking a soccer ball won't improve your golf game, infants who receive much practice in one motor skill usually don't improve in others. For example, in a study by Zelazo and her colleagues (1993), parents had their 6-week-olds practice stepping. Other parents had their infants practice sitting. After 7 weeks of practice, the two groups of infants, as well as a control group of 6-week-olds who had had no practice of any kind, were tested in their ability to step and sit. The graphs tell the whole story. For both stepping and sitting, infants improved the skill they had practiced. When infants were tested on the skill they had not practiced, they did no better than infants in the control group. Thus, the impact of practice is specific, not widespread.

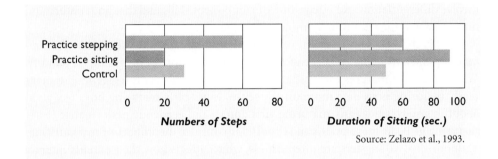

Source: Zelazo et al., 1993.

Experience becomes even more important in complex actions. Mastering discrete skills, connecting them in the correct sequence, and then timing them properly requires more than a few simple repetitions. Observing others, repeated practice, and getting feedback on errors is required. Of course, learning a complex behavior must build upon maturational changes. But with biological readiness and practice, youngsters learn a gamut of complex motor behaviors—from hitting a tennis ball, to playing a violin, to signing to communicate with people who do not hear.

Check Your Learning

1. Skills important in learning to walk include maintaining upright posture and balance and _____.

2. Motor development involves differentiation of individual skills and their _____ into a cohesive whole.

3. Not until age _____ do children rotate their wrists while using a spoon.

4. Handedness is determined by heredity and _____.

5. Compared to infants reared in less restrictive environments, infants reared on cradle boards learn to walk _____.

6. When infants practice motor skills, the impact of this practice is _____.

Answers: (1) moving the legs alternately—transferring weight from one foot to the other; (2) integration; (3) 2 years; (4) environmental influences; (5) at about the same time; (6) limited to the practiced skill—there is no widespread effect

PHYSICAL AND MOTOR DEVELOPMENT IN PERSPECTIVE

Physical growth seems so simple—children just keep getting bigger and bigger. Yet we saw in this chapter that physical and motor development are, in reality, quite intricate. In Module 4.1, we saw that physical growth does not simply refer to height and weight; that physical growth varies considerably within the normal range; and that heredity, hormones, and nutrition are the keys to growth. We also saw that puberty has enormous impact on adolescents. In Module 4.2, we examined some problems of physical growth, including malnutrition, anorexia nervosa, and obesity. In Module 4.3, we looked at a less obvious aspect of physical growth—development of the nervous system. We outlined the organization of the neuron and the brain, and saw that different regions of the brain have specialized functions very soon after birth. Finally, in Module 4.4, we saw that locomotion and fine-motor coordination involve differentiation and integration of component skills and that both nature and nurture play important roles in motor development.

This chapter is an excellent opportunity to highlight the theme that *development in different domains is connected.* Consider the impact of timing of puberty. Whether a child matures early or late has widespread effects on social development (early maturing boys date more often), self-esteem (early maturing boys feel good about themselves but early maturing girls don't), and academic performance (early maturing girls do more poorly in school). Or consider the impact of malnutrition. Malnourished youngsters are often listless, which affects how their parents interact with them (they're less likely to provide stimulating experiences). Less stimulation, in turn, slows the children's intellectual development. Physical, cognitive, social, and personality development are linked: Change in one area almost always leads to change of some kind in the others.

THINKING ABOUT DEVELOPMENT

1. In Chapter 2, you learned that polygenic inheritance is often involved when phenotypes form a continuum. Height is such a phenotype. Propose a simple polygenic model to explain how height might be inherited.

2. How does the pattern of development of the nervous system, described in Module 4.3, compare to the pattern of development for physical growth, described in Module 4.1?

3. How does research on locomotion show the impact of maturation? How does research show the impact of experience?

4. Some children start to walk shortly before their first birthday; others don't start to walk until a few months after. Describe some possible advantages of walking early. Can you think of possible disadvantages? (You might consider the advantages and disadvantages of starting puberty early).

5. Watching a *Larry King Live* interview devoted to obesity, you hear a caller complain that experts always try to make everything so complicated. The caller explains, "Fat people get that way cause they eat too much. Nough said." In your call to Larry, set the record straight.

SEE FOR YOURSELF

How can we decide if a preschooler is left- or right-handed? Adults can simply tell us which hand they use in writing or throwing, but we need a more concrete approach with preschoolers, few of whom even know left from right. With the permission of a local nursery school or day-care center, you could ask several preschoolers of different ages—say 2 to 5—to do the following tasks (from McManus et al., 1988):

1. draw a face with a pen
2. color a square
3. throw a ball
4. thread a bead onto a wire
5. turn over cards placed on a table
6. show how they use a spoon to eat
7. brush their teeth with an imaginary toothbrush
8. comb their hair with an imaginary comb
9. blow their nose with a tissue
10. pick a piece of candy from a bag

You should see that younger preschoolers use their left hand on some tasks and their right on others. However, by the time children are 5 years old, most will do at least eight of these activities with one hand, showing that handedness is now well established. See for yourself!

RESOURCES

For more information about . . .

ways to help children and adolescents stay physically fit, try Kenneth Cooper's *Kid Fitness* (Random House, 1992) which describes a program of diet and exercise developed by the originator of the concept of aerobic fitness

ways to help combat malnutrition and poverty in developing countries, contact Save the Children, 1-800-243-5075

sexual and reproductive health, birth control, sexually transmitted diseases, and sexuality education, visit the Planned Parenthood Federation of America Web site, http://www.ppfa.org/ppfa/index.html

KEY TERMS

anorexia nervosa *93*
axon *96*
basal metabolic rate *95*
cell body *96*
cerebral cortex *96*
corpus callosum *96*
dendrite *96*
differentiation *103*
electroencephalogram (EEG) *98*
epiphyses *86*

fine-motor skills *101*
frontal cortex *96*
hemispheres *96*
hormones *87*
integration *103*
locomotion *101*
malnourished *92*
menarche *89*
motor skills *101*
myelin *97*

myelinization *97*
neural plate *97*
neural pruning *97*
neuron *96*
positron emission tomography (PET-scan) *98*
puberty *89*
secular growth trends *86*
thyroxine *87*
toddlers *102*

SUMMARY

MODULE 4.1:
PHYSICAL GROWTH

FEATURES OF HUMAN GROWTH
Physical growth is particularly rapid during infancy, slows, then accelerates again during adolescence. Growth follows the cephalocaudal principle, with the head and trunk developing before the legs. Consequently, infants and young children have disproportionately larger heads and trunks. Physical growth refers to not only height and weight, but also development of muscle, fat, and bones.

VARIATIONS ON THE AVERAGE PROFILE
Children are taller today than in previous generations. Average heights vary around the world and, within any culture, there is considerable variation in the normal range of height.

MECHANISMS OF PHYSICAL GROWTH
A person's height and weight as an adult are influenced by heredity. Hormones are also important for physical development: Growth hormone (GH) affects bone and muscle growth, and thyroxine affects nerve cells.

Nutrition is particularly important during infancy and adolescence because both are periods of rapid growth. Breast-feeding provides babies with all the nutrients they need and has other advantages as well. Many adolescents do not get adequate nutrients because of poor diets.

THE ADOLESCENT GROWTH SPURT AND PUBERTY
Puberty includes the adolescent growth spurt as well as sexual maturation. Early puberty tends to benefit boys but is often harmful for girls.

Sexual behavior begins in adolescence. Most U.S. teenagers are sexually active, particularly if their parents and peers have positive attitudes toward sex. Few teenagers use contraception because of ignorance, the illusion of invulnerability, lack of motivation, and lack of access.

MODULE 4.2:
PROBLEMS OF PHYSICAL GROWTH

MALNUTRITION
Malnutrition is a problem worldwide—including the United States—that is particularly harmful during infancy, when growth is so rapid.

Malnutrition can cause brain damage, affecting children's intelligence and ability to pay attention. Treating malnutrition requires improving children's diet and training their parents to provide stimulating environments.

ANOREXIA NERVOSA

Anorexia nervosa is a disorder that typically affects adolescent girls; it is characterized by an irrational fear of being overweight. Several factors contribute to anorexia, including cultural standards for thinness, a need for independence within an autocratic family, and heredity.

OBESITY

Many obese children and adolescents are unpopular, have low self-esteem, and are at risk for medical disorders. Obesity reflects both heredity and acquired eating habits. In the most effective programs for treating obesity in youth, both children and their parents set eating and exercise goals and maintain their daily progress.

MODULE 4.3:
THE DEVELOPING NERVOUS SYSTEM

ORGANIZATION OF THE MATURE BRAIN

Nerve cells, called neurons, are composed of a cell body, a dendrite, and an axon. The mature brain consists of billions of neurons organized into nearly identical left and right hemispheres connected by the corpus callosum. The frontal cortex is associated with personality and goal-directed behavior; the cortex in the left hemisphere, with language; and the cortex in the right hemisphere, with nonverbal processes.

MAKING OF THE WORKING BRAIN

Brain structure begins in prenatal development, when neurons form at an incredible rate. Myelinization is an important part of brain development during which neurons become wrapped in myelin, allowing them to transmit information more rapidly.

An infant's brain begins to function early in life, as proven with electroencephalograms (EEGs), which record the brain's electrical activity, and positron emission tomography (PET-scan), which measures the brain's use of glucose. The cortex in the left hemisphere specializes in language processing at (or soon after) birth. The cortex in the right hemisphere controls some nonverbal functions, such as perception of music, very early in infancy; control of other right-hemisphere functions, such as understanding spatial relations, is achieved by the preschool years. The frontal cortex has begun to regulate goal-directed behavior and emotional responding by the first birthday.

MODULE 4.4:
MOTOR DEVELOPMENT

LOCOMOTION

Infants progress through a sequence of motor milestones during the first year, culminating in walking a few months after the first birthday. Like most motor skills, learning to walk involves differentiation of individual skills, such as maintaining balance and stepping on alternate legs, and then integrating these skills into a coherent whole.

FINE-MOTOR SKILLS

Infants first use only one hand at a time, then both hands independently, then both hands in common actions, and, finally, at about 5 months of age, both hands in different actions with a common purpose.

Most people are right-handed, a preference that emerges after the first birthday and that becomes well established during the preschool years. Handedness is determined by heredity but can be influenced by experience and cultural values.

MATURATION, EXPERIENCE, AND MOTOR SKILL

Biology and experience both shape the mastery of motor skills. On the one hand, the basic developmental timetable for passing motor milestones is similar around the world, which emphasizes underlying biological causes. On the other hand, specific experience can accelerate motor development, particularly for complex motor skills.

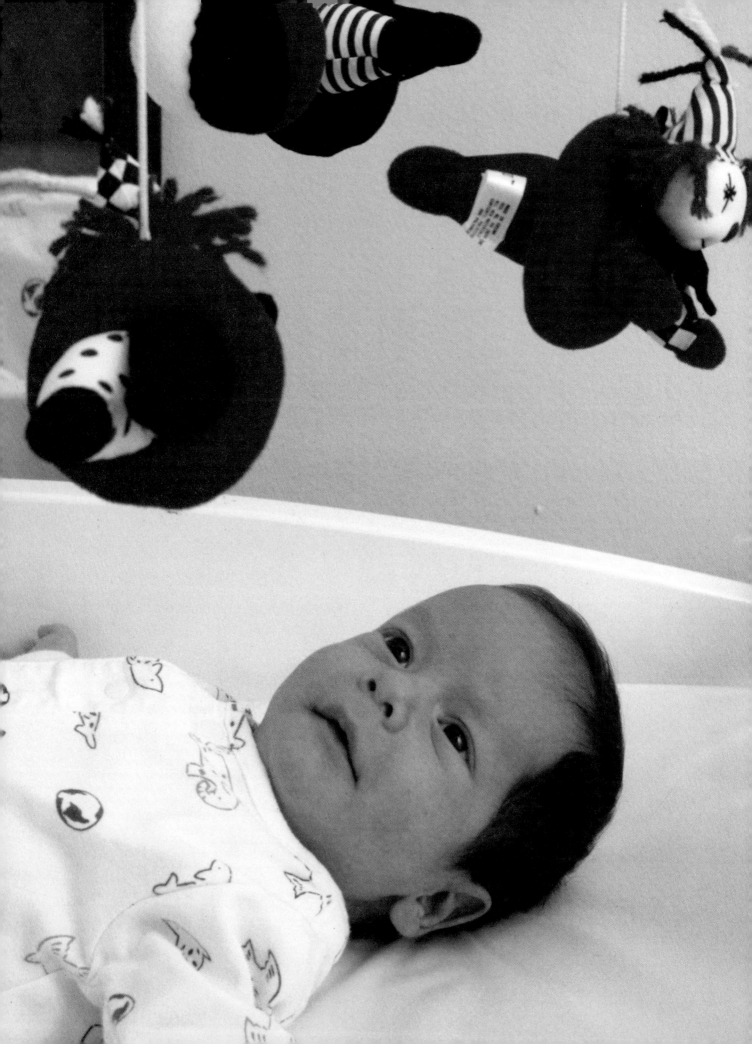

Sensory and Perceptual Development

HEN MY FIRSTBORN, BEN, WAS A PRESCHOOLER, HE LOVED TO WATCH RERUNS OF *CHIPS*. (MAYBE YOU, TOO, REMEMBER ERIK ESTRADA ZOOMING ALONG THE L.A. FREEWAYS ON HIS KAWASAKI?) BEN WAS TOTALLY ABSORBED BY THE SHOW AND OBLIVIOUS to everything else. The house could burn, the family room could flood with dollar bills, and Courtney Love could give a concert in the kitchen, but Ben wouldn't notice. Ben's behavior is a common but powerful example of perception in action. Our systems are assaulted with stimulation, but much of it is ignored. *Sensory and perceptual processes* **are the means by which the nervous system receives, selects, modifies, and organizes stimulation from the world.** Sensory and perceptual processes are the first step in the complex process of accumulating information that eventually results in "knowing." We'll begin our study of sensory and perceptual processes in Module 5.1 by examining different theories of perceptual development. In Module 5.2, we'll look at the origins of sensory processes in infancy; and in Module 5.3, we'll see how more complex sensory and perceptual processes develop throughout childhood.

APPROACHES TO PERCEPTUAL DEVELOPMENT

Learning Objectives

- **What are the essential elements of the empirical approach to perception?**
- **What is the cognitive approach to perception, and how does it differ from the empirical approach?**
- **What features of Gibson's theory distinguish it from the empirical and cognitive views?**

> *Jeff is a frustrated stand-up comic who loves to tell funny stories and play practical jokes. Most people don't think he's very funny, but his 7-month-old daughter, Erin, loves it when Jeff puts on an old top hat and makes silly faces at her. Erin smiles, giggles, and waves her hands in excitement at Jeff's "top-hat routine." In his more serious moments, Jeff wonders why Erin finds him funny when no one else does!*

We can't help Jeff improve his humor, but we can learn how Erin recognizes her dad and his "top-hat routine." Sensory and perceptual skills hold the key. In this first module, you'll learn three general approaches to understanding sensory and perceptual skills like those that Erin uses to recognize her dad and his antics. We'll begin with the empirical approach, then consider the cognitive approach, and end with Eleanor Gibson's theory of perceptual development.

THE EMPIRICAL APPROACH

This approach traces its roots to the great Greek philosopher, Aristole (384–322 B.C.), who was the first empiricist—he believed that experience is the source of all knowledge. The *empirical approach* holds that sensory experience is the building block of all perception and, ultimately, all knowledge. You can think of a sensory experience as a snapshot of sensory input at a particular point in time. As infants have more and more experience in the world, they accumulate more and more of these snapshots. Gradually, they notice that some snapshots occur repeatedly, such as their mother's face during nursing. Infants also notice that other snapshots, though different, resemble each other, such as their mother's face while nursing and while playing with them.

The snapshot analogy is most appropriate for vision, but the same sort of phenomenon occurs with all senses. In hearing, for example, the "snapshot" might consist of segments of sounds. Babies gradually come to recognize the same sound snapshots, such as their mother calling them by name. And they recognize similarities in different sounds, such as a mother's voice. Over time, infants make connections between their speech snapshots and their visual snapshots. These snapshots then become associated with snapshots from other senses, until ultimately they define the concept "mother."

How does the empirical approach explain Erin's recognition of her dad? Erin's initial sensory experiences might be of individual elements of Jeff's face. She notices that many snapshots have white ellipses with a dark circle in the center. Eventually she notices there are two ellipses and they appear side by side. Gradually, other facial features are associated with the eyes, until Erin finally recognizes that this stable configuration of elements is Jeff's face. With even more experience, she recognizes the sound of Jeff's voice and comes to associate it with the configuration of features that makes up his face.

Erin's recognition of Jeff illustrates the fundamental assumptions of the empirical approach to perceptual development. First, experience provides the data necessary for infants (and children and adults) to observe how objects are alike and how they differ, which is the starting point for understanding the world. Erin needs to see and hear Jeff repeatedly to recognize him. Second, the simple sensory experience is the basic unit of perception; over time, sensory experiences are integrated to form perceptions. Each time that Erin sees Jeff, she has a new, unique sensory snapshot that is connected with other similar snapshots. Third, the flow of perceptual processing is one way. Sensory experience influences perception and understanding but not the reverse. That is, even though Erin may have 10, 100, or 1,000 other snapshots of Jeff, every time she sees him the process is the same—another snapshot is created and linked to similar snapshots.

As you'll see in the next few pages, experience is also important in the cognitive approach and Gibson's theory. These other approaches, however, believe that perception involves more than just experience.

> *The empirical and cognitive approaches both emphasize the role of experience in perception, but only the cognitive approach claims that knowledge can influence perception.*

THE COGNITIVE APPROACH

If I were to create a list of my favorite 10 experiments, it would definitely include one by Ballin (cited by Solley, 1966). In the weeks leading up to Christmas, 5- to 7-year-olds were shown a picture of Santa Claus. They were asked to estimate Santa's size by selecting a disk that looked, to them, to be the same size as Santa. Children chose increasingly larger disks as Christmas drew near, but after Christmas had passed, they chose smaller disks. Even though Santa remained the same size, evidently he *looked* larger as Christmas approached. Apparently, children's emotions and values—in this case, their excitement over the upcoming holiday—influence their perception.

The results of Ballin's study would trouble an empiricist. Why? Because it suggests that understanding influences sensory and perceptual processing, counter to the one-way flow of information in the empirical approach. Ballin's experiment supports a second approach to perceptual development—the cognitive. In the cognitive approach to perception, not only does sensory experience influence perception and understanding, but also understanding influences sensory and perceptual processing.

A variety of research shows that understanding influences perception. For example, cross-cultural studies have produced some fascinating demonstrations of perception based on understanding; we'll look at one example in the "Cultural Influences" feature.

Cultural Influences: **CULTURE INFLUENCES HOW WE PERCEIVE THE WORLD**

Are the lines marked A and B the same length? Or is one line longer than the other? Most people think line A is longer, but A and B are really the same length. **The tendency to see a line with inward-facing arrows as longer than the same line with outward-facing arrows is the *Müller-Lyer illusion*.**

Why are people fooled by the Müller-Lyer illusion? One explanation says it's because we mistakenly use our experience with corners of rooms

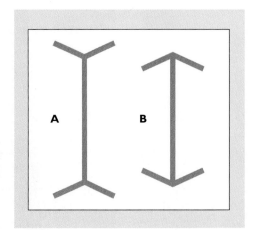

and buildings. You can see in the drawing that corners near us seem to be outward-facing, while corners farther away seem to be inward-facing. Thus, our understanding of the normal appearance of corners leads us to interpret the inward-facing arrows on line A to mean it is farther away than line B, and that line A is therefore longer than line B.

If this explanation is accurate, what should happen if we test people who grow up in environments that don't have the rectangular corners found in urban-industrial countries? Someone who has had little or no experience with corners should not interpret the arrows as clues to the distance of the vertical line and should therefore say that lines A and B are the same length.

In fact, several studies show that individuals who grow up in nonindustrialized cultures are less susceptible to the Müller-Lyer illusion (Pederson & Wheeler, 1983; Segall et al., 1990). For example, the Navajo, Native Americans whose traditional homes are circular, are less prone to the Müller-Lyer illusion. So are people who grow up in parts of Africa, Asia, and Australia that don't have the straight-line and right-angle buildings that come with urbanization and economic development.

Cross-cultural studies of the Müller-Lyer illusion thus show that children and adults interpret sensory information in a particular way based on their experience. Because children growing up in different cultures have different experiences, they may interpret sensory information differently. ■

Laboratory studies also show that understanding influences perception. In one study, children were asked to identify ambiguous pictures like the one shown here. Identifying these pictures is very difficult for children, unless they're given a clue (Potter, 1966). For example, told that this figure is an elephant, children can "see" the picture almost instantly.

Another way to show the impact of context on children's ability to recognize words or pictures is through priming experiments, experiments that somehow prepare the participant to respond. As you can see in the bottom diagram, the task is simple: Children merely read words or name pictures as rapidly as they can. However, they perform much more rapidly when the target word or picture is related to the preceding phrase than when it is not (Morris, 1994; Potter et al., 1993). In this case (as with the ambiguous picture in the previous study), knowledge primes perception: Knowing what to see, children perceive stimuli more accurately and more rapidly.

How does the cognitive approach explain Erin's behavior when Jeff tries to make her laugh? Part of the explanation follows the empirical approach: Erin gradually comes to associate the features—eyes, nose, mouth, and sounds—that go together, and this leads to the knowledge of what Jeff looks and sounds like. But the cognitive approach goes on to say that Erin's

knowledge then influences her perception. If Jeff is out of sight but she hears his voice, this primes her to perceive his face. Similarly, seeing Jeff don his top hat primes Erin to expect his funny faces. The cognitive approach thus goes beyond the empirical approach by saying that Erin's growing understanding of her dad causes her to interpret sensory information in a particular way.

Cognitive theories of perception tend to be more about cognition than perception. (This shouldn't surprise you, knowing that this approach emphasizes the influence of knowledge and understanding on perception.) One of the most important cognitive theorists is Piaget, whose work was introduced in Module 1.2. Piaget emphasized that perception is regulated by cognition; he performed experiments that showed children are less influenced by perceptual illusions as they grow older, because of their growing understanding of the world (Piaget & Albertini, 1950–1952). To use Piaget's own terminology, sensory experiences are assimilated into one's knowledge.

For Piaget and other cognitive theorists, perception and understanding are linked by a two-way street: Perception influences understanding and understanding influences perception.

The empirical and cognitive approaches view perception as a gradual accumulation of sensory experiences, but Gibson's differentiation theory views perception as the extraction of complex information.

GIBSON'S DIFFERENTIATION THEORY

The empirical and cognitive approaches are alike in claiming that, over time, sensory inputs are gradually associated and give rise to perception. An influential theory of perceptual development proposed by Eleanor Gibson, who is pictured here, takes a different tack. According to Gibson (1969), "... the environment is rich in varied and complex potential stimulus information, capable of giving rise to diverse, meaningful, complex perceptions" (p. 75). But, Gibson contends, this complex information is not perceived piece by piece as the empirical and cognitive theorists would have us believe. Instead, complex stimuli are *extracted* from the flow of perceptual information; they are *not assembled* from elementary sensory experiences. In other words, complex patterns can be perceived directly, if you know what to look for. **According to Gibson's *differentiation theory,* perception reflects children's growing ability to identify the features that distinguish complex patterns.**

To understand the idea of differentiation that is central to Gibson's theory, consider the following:

■ To the average adult, all red wines taste pretty much the same; however, a skilled wine taster can differentiate an incredible number of varieties.

■ For most people, an X-ray is simply a meaningless mixture of shades of gray; however, to a skilled radiologist, it provides a wealth of information.

■ For very young children, the letters of the alphabet are simply a jumble of curved and straight lines; however, to older children and adults they are recognizable symbols that can be used to create words.

In each of these cases, a complex pattern of stimulation is present and potentially perceivable by all. However, only those with sufficient experience can identify the critical features that distinguish a burgundy from a Chianti, a healthy lung from one that is diseased, and the letter *b* from the letter *p*.

Applied to Erin's perception of Jeff's face, Gibson's theory holds that, as a newborn, Erin saw Jeff's face in much the same way that a novice sees an X-ray: as a complex but undifferentiated pattern. With repeated exposure to faces, Erin became able to extract some features, such as two eyes separated by a nose, that differentiate faces from other complex stimuli. Eventually Erin differentiated Jeff's features from features of other faces. The process by which Erin came to recognize Jeff demonstrates the basic assumptions of Gibson's differentiation theory. First, infants (and children and adults) are not passive recipients of sensory experience. Instead, they actively try to make sense out of their sensory experiences. Erin did not simply passively register successive snapshots of Jeff; she actively tried to see how the different snapshots related to each other. Second, in the search to understand sensory experience, infants look for features that are constant against the backdrop of ever changing sensory information. Erin noticed, for example, that regardless of Jeff's facial expression, his eyes were always next to each other. Third, with greater and greater experience, infants can make ever sharper distinctions between features. Just as a radiologist distinguishes more features in X-rays with greater experience, Erin distinguished more of Jeff's facial expressions with greater experience.

Gibson's theory, the cognitive approach, and empirical approach are the three major views of perceptual development. One way for you to see the similarities and differences in these views is to think about the role that nature and nuture plays in each. The empirical approach is the simplest to understand. Empiricists claim that heredity provides the sense organs that allow children to perceive. They also believe that perception requires experience; without experience, there is no sensory information to perceive.

The cognitive approach and Gibson's theory include these assumptions, too, but they cast a larger role for nature. Cognitive theorists believe we have a built-in ability to use knowledge to interpret sensory information. As soon as infants acquire knowledge, this knowledge influences their perception. Gibson believes that perception involves actively trying to interpret sensory experience by searching for constant perceptual features. From birth, infants don't simply see and hear, they look and listen, trying to make sense of their experiences (Gibson, 1969).

The three approaches to perception that we have discussed are not only useful in themselves; they have stimulated a great deal of research into sensory and perceptual development. In the next two modules of this chapter, we'll look at some of this research. As we do, ask yourself whether the findings are most consistent with the empirical approach, the cognitive approach, or with Gibson's theory.

Check Your Learning

1. _____ emphasizes that sensory experiences are the basic building blocks from which perception is constructed.

2. According to _____, knowledge influences sensory and perceptual processing.

3. Differentiation of distinctive features is a central element of _____.

Answers: (1) The empirical approach, (2) the cognitive approach, (3) Gibson's differentiation theory

B ASIC SENSORY AND PERCEPTUAL PROCESSES

Learning Objectives

- **Are newborn babies able to smell, taste, and respond to touch?**
- **How well do infants hear? How do they use sounds to understand their world?**
- **How accurate is infants' vision? Do infants perceive color and depth?**

MODULE
5.2
Basic Sensory and Perceptual Processes

Smell, Taste, and Touch ⎤

Hearing ⎦

Seeing ⎦

Darla adores her 3-day-old son. She loves holding him, talking to him, and simply watching him. Darla is certain that her baby is already getting to know her, coming to recognize her face and the sound of her voice. Darla's husband, Steve, thinks she is crazy. He tells her, "Everyone knows that babies are born blind. And they probably can't hear much either." Darla doubts that Steve is right, but she wishes someone would tell her about babies' vision and hearing.

Darla's questions are really about her newborn son's sensory and perceptual skills. To help her, we need to remember that humans have different kinds of sense organs, each receptive to a unique kind of physical energy. The retina at the back of the eye, for example, is sensitive to some types of electromagnetic energy, and sight is the result. The eardrum detects changes in air pressure, and hearing is the result. Cells at the top of the nasal passage detect airborne molecules, and smell is the result. In each case, the sense organ translates the physical stimulation into nerve impulses that are sent to the brain.

The senses begin to function early in life, which explains why this module is devoted entirely to infancy. How can we know what an infant senses? Since infants can't tell us directly what they smell, hear, or see, researchers have had to devise other ways to find out. In many studies, an investigator presents two stimuli to a baby, such as a high-pitched tone and a low-pitched tone or a sweet-tasting substance and a sour-tasting substance. Then the investigator records the baby's physiological responses, such as heart rate, or facial expression or head movements. If the baby consistently responds differently to the two stimuli, the baby must be distinguishing between them.

Another approach is based on the fact that infants usually prefer novel stimuli over familiar stimuli. **When a novel stimulus is presented, babies pay much attention, but they pay less attention as it becomes more familiar, a phenomenon known as *habituation*.** Researchers use habituation to study perception by repeatedly presenting a stimulus such as a low-pitched tone until an infant barely responds. Then they present a second stimulus, such as a higher-pitched tone. If the infant responds strongly, then it can distinguish the two stimuli.

Techniques used to study infants' perception typically involve presenting several distinct stimuli and determining if infants respond the same to all or differently.

In this module, you'll learn what researchers using these techniques have discovered about infants' perception. We begin with smell, taste, and touch because they are among the most mature senses at birth.

SMELL, TASTE, AND TOUCH

Newborns have a keen sense of smell. Infants respond positively to pleasant smells and negatively to unpleasant smells. They have a relaxed, contented-looking facial expression when they smell honey or chocolate but frown, grimace, or turn away when they smell rotten eggs or ammonia (Maurer & Maurer,

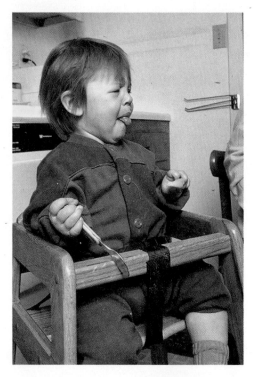

1988). Young babies also use odor to identify their mothers. For example, 2-week-old infants will look in the direction of a pad saturated with the odor of their mother's breast. They will also look in the direction of a pad saturated with their mother's perfume (Porter et al., 1991; Schleidt & Genzel, 1990).

Infants also have a highly developed sense of taste. They readily differentiate salty, sour, bitter, and sweet tastes (Crook, 1987). Most infants seem to have a "sweet tooth." They react to sweet substances by smiling, sucking, and licking their lips. In contrast, you can probably guess what the infant in the photo has tasted! This grimace is typical when infants are fed bitter- or sour-tasting substances (Kaijura, Cowart, & Beauchamp, 1992). Infants are also sensitive to changes in the taste of breast milk that reflect a mother's diet. Infants will nurse more after their mother has consumed a sweet-tasting substance such as vanilla (Mennella & Beauchamp, 1996).

Newborns are sensitive to touch. As I described in Module 3.4, many areas of the newborn's body respond reflexively when touched. Touching an infant's cheek, mouth, hand, or foot produces reflexive movements, documenting that infants perceive touch.

If babies react to touch, does this mean they experience pain? This is difficult to answer because pain has such a subjective element to it. The same pain-eliciting stimulus that leads some adults to complain of mild discomfort causes others to report that they are in agony. Since infants cannot express their pain to us directly, we must use indirect evidence.

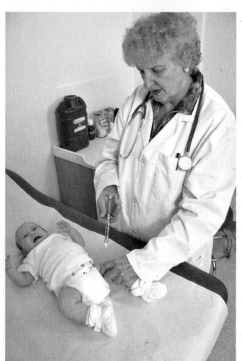

The infant's nervous system definitely is capable of transmitting pain: Receptors for pain in the skin are just as plentiful in infants as they are in adults (Anand & Hickey, 1987). Furthermore, babies' behavior in response to apparent pain-provoking stimuli also suggests that they experience pain. Look, for example, at the baby in the photo who is receiving an inoculation. She lowers her eyebrows, purses her lips, and, of course, opens her mouth to cry. Although we can't hear her, the sound of her cry is probably the unique pattern associated with pain. The pain cry begins suddenly, is high-pitched, and is not easily soothed. This baby is also agitated, moving her hands, arms, and legs (Craig et al., 1993). All together, these signs strongly suggest that babies experience pain.

Perceptual skills are extraordinarily useful to newborns and young babies. Their senses of smell and touch help them recognize their mothers. Infants' senses of smell and taste make it much easier for them to learn to eat. Early development of smell, taste, and touch prepare newborns and young babies to learn about their worlds.

HEARING

Do you remember, from Module 3.1, the study with mothers in late pregnancy who read *The Cat in the Hat* aloud every day? This research showed that the fetus can hear at 7 or 8 months. As you would expect from these results, newborns typically respond to sounds in their surroundings. If a parent is quiet but then coughs, an infant may startle, blink his eyes and move his arms or legs. These responses may seem natural, but they do indeed indicate that infants are sensitive to sound.

Not surprisingly, infants do not hear as well as adults. **Auditory threshold refers to the quietest sound that a person can hear.** An adult's auditory threshold is fairly easy to measure: A tone is presented, and the adult simply tells when he or she hears it. To test auditory thresholds in infants, who obviously cannot report what they hear, researchers have devised a number of clever techniques. One is shown in the diagram (Werner & Bargones, 1992). The infant is seated on a parent's lap. Both parent and baby wear headphones, as does an observer seated in another room who watches the baby through an observation window. When the observer believes the baby is attentive, he signals the experimenter, who sometimes presents a tone over the *baby's* headphones and sometimes does nothing. Neither the observer nor the parent knows when tones are going to be presented, and they can't hear the tones through their headphones. On each trial, the observer simply judges if the baby responds in any fashion, such as turning its head or changing its facial expression or activity level. Afterwards, the experimenter determines how well the observer's judgments match the trials: If a baby can hear the tone, observers should judge that they respond only on trials when a tone was presented.

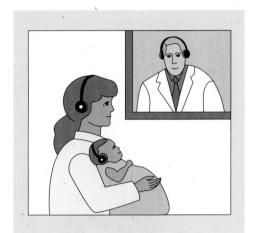

This type of testing reveals that, overall, adults can hear better than infants; adults can hear some very quiet sounds that infants can't. More importantly, this testing shows that infants best hear sounds that have pitches in the range of human speech—neither very high- nor very low-pitched. Infants can differentiate vowels from consonant sounds, and by 4½ months they can recognize their own names (Jusczyk, 1995; Mandel, Jusczyk, & Pisoni, 1995).

Infants also use sound to locate objects, determining whether they are left or right and near or far. In one study (Clifton, Perris, & Bullinger, 1991), 7-month-olds were shown a rattle. Then the experimenters darkened the room and shook the rattle, either 6 inches away from the infant or about 2 feet away. Infants often reached for the rattle in the dark when it was 6 inches away but seldom when it was 2 feet away, as they matched the distant sound with the toy being out of reach. These 7-month-olds were quite capable of using sound to estimate distance, in this case distinguishing a toy they could reach from one they could not.

Infants can distinguish different sounds and they use sound to judge the distance and location of objects.

Thus, by the middle of the first year, most infants respond to much of the information that is provided by sound. However, not all infants are able to do so, which is the topic of the "Making Children's Lives Better" feature.

Making Children's Lives Better: **HEARING IMPAIRMENT IN INFANCY**

Some infants are born with limited hearing. Others are born deaf. (Exact figures are hard to come by because infants' hearing is rarely tested precisely.) African, Asian, European, and Hispanic American babies are equally susceptible. Heredity is the leading cause of hearing impairment in newborns. After birth, the leading cause is meningitis, an inflammation of the membranes surrounding the brain and spinal cord.

What are signs of hearing impairment that a parent should watch for? Obviously, parents should be concerned if a young baby never responds to sudden, loud sounds. They should also be concerned if their baby has repeated ear infections, if it does not turn its head in the direction of sounds by 4 or 5 months, does not respond to its own name by 8 or 9 months, and does not begin to imitate speech sounds and simple words by 12 months.

If parents see these problems, their baby should be examined by a physician, who will check for ear problems, and an audiologist, who will measure the infant's hearing. Parents should never delay checking for possible hearing impairment. The earlier the problem is detected, the more the baby can be helped.

If testing reveals that a baby has impaired hearing, several treatments are possible, depending upon the degree of hearing loss. Some children with partial hearing benefit from mechanical devices, such as hearing aids, and some benefit from training in lipreading. Children with profound hearing loss can learn to communicate with sign language. By mastering language (either oral language or sign language) and communicating effectively, a child's cognitive and social development will be normal. The key is to recognize impairment promptly. ◼

SEEING

I f you've watched infants you've probably noticed that, while awake, they spend a lot of time looking around. Sometimes they seem to be scanning their environment broadly, and sometimes they seem to be focusing on nearby objects. But what do they actually see? Is their visual world a sea of gray blobs? Or do they see the world essentially as adults do? Actually, neither is the case, but the second is closer to the truth.

The various elements of the visual system—the eye, the optic nerve, and the brain—are relatively well developed at birth. Newborns respond to light and can track moving objects with their eyes. But what is the clarity of their vision and how can we measure it? *Visual acuity* **is defined as the smallest pattern that can be distinguished dependably.** You've undoubtedly had your visual acuity measured by trying to read rows of progressively smaller letters or numbers from a chart. The same basic logic is used in tests of infants' acuity, which are based on two premises. First, most infants will look at patterned stimuli instead of plain, nonpatterned stimuli. For example, if we were to show the two stimuli in the top diagram to infants, most would look longer at the striped pattern than the gray pattern. Second, as we make the lines narrower (along with the spaces between them), there comes a point at which the black and white stripes become so fine that they simply blend together and appear gray—just like the all gray pattern.

To estimate an infant's acuity, then, we pair the gray square with squares that differ in the width of their stripes, like those in the bottom diagram: When infants look at the two stimuli equally, it indicates that they are no longer able to distinguish the stripes of the patterned stimulus. By measuring the width of the stripes and their distance from an infant's eye, we can estimate acuity (detecting thinner stripes indicates better acuity).

Measurements of this sort indicate that newborns and 1-month-olds see at 20 feet what normal adults see at 200 to 400 feet. But by the first birthday, infants' acuity is essentially the same as a normal adult's (Banks & Dannemiller, 1987). The photographs at the top of page 123 show how poorly very young babies see the world and how their visual acuity dramatically improves during the first year.

Knowing that infants' acuity improves rapidly during the first year, researchers have investigated two other basic aspects of visual perception: perceiving color and depth.

Color. The first color televisions were primitive, with green-tinted people, furniture, and cars. Nevertheless, television was immensely popular (as were the owners) because adding color makes objects more interesting, more enjoyable, and more

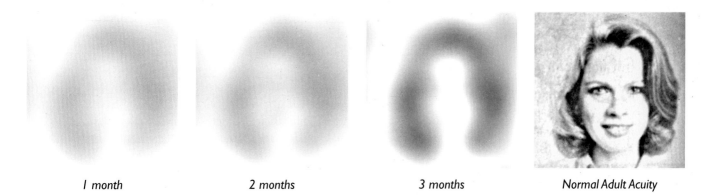

| *1 month* | *2 months* | *3 months* | *Normal Adult Acuity* |

beautiful. But color is more than pleasing; it is functional, too, helping us recognize objects and people and alerting us to danger.

How do we perceive color? The wavelength of light is the source of color perception. The diagram shows that lights we see as red have a relatively long wavelength, whereas violet, at the other end of the color spectrum, has a much shorter wave-

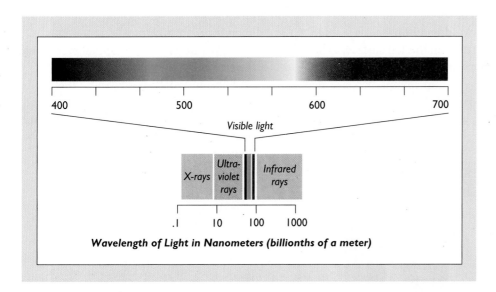

Visible light

X-rays | Ultra-violet rays | Infrared rays

.1   10   100   1000

Wavelength of Light in Nanometers (billionths of a meter)

length. **We detect wavelength—and therefore color—with specialized neurons called *cones* that are in the retina of the eye.** Some cones are particularly sensitive to short-wavelength light (blues and violets), others are sensitive to medium-wavelength light (greens and yellows), and still others to long-wavelength light (reds and oranges). These different kinds of cones are linked in complex circuits, and this circuitry is responsible for our ability to see the world in color.

These circuits gradually begin to function in the first few months after birth (Adams, 1995). Though newborns perceive few colors, 1-month-olds can differentiate blue from gray, which means that the short-wavelength circuit is functioning. One-month-olds can also differentiate red from green, but not yellow from green or yellow from red. Apparently, the medium- and short-wavelength circuits are functioning (because infants discriminate red and green) but not with complete fidelity (because they cannot distinguish yellow).

By 3 to 4 months infants' color perception seems similar to adults' (Adams & Courage, 1995). In particular, infants, like adults, tend to see categories of color. For

Newborns' vision is limited but acuity and color perception improves rapidly during the first year.

example, if a yellow light's wavelength is gradually increased, the infant will suddenly perceive it as a shade of red rather than a shade of yellow. Perception of color as categories has been demonstrated using the habituation technique described on page 119. Typically, infants are shown lights of wavelengths that correspond to what adults see as blue, green, yellow, and red. Infants repeatedly presented with one wavelength habituate to that wavelength. Infants could be habituated to a light with a wavelength of 600 nanometers (billionths of a meter), which adults call yellow. A different light is then presented, but from the same color category as the first light. For example, the second light might have a wavelength of 580 nanometers, which adults also consider yellow. By 3 months of age, infants respond to the second light as if it were a familiar color, looking at it about the same amount as they looked at the 600 nanometer light. If, however, the wavelength of light is changed by the same amount but comes from a new adult color category—to 620 nanometers, which adults call red—infants' looking increases significantly. These responses indicate that infants view the stimuli as adults do—in categories of color (Teller & Bornstein, 1987).

Depth. People see objects as having three dimensions: height, width, and depth. The retina of the eye is flat, so height and width can be represented directly on its two-dimensional surface. But the third dimension, depth, cannot be represented directly on this flat surface, so how do we perceive depth? We use perceptual processing to *infer* depth.

Can infants perceive depth? Eleanor Gibson and Richard Walk (1960) addressed this question using a special apparatus. **The *visual cliff* is a glass-covered platform; on one side a pattern appears directly under the glass, but on the other it appears several feet below the glass.** Consequently, one side looks shallow but the other appears to have a steep drop-off, like a cliff.

As you can see in the photo, in the experiment the baby was placed on the platform and the mother coaxed her infant to come to her. Most babies willingly crawled to their mother when she stood on the shallow side. But almost every baby refused to cross the deep side, even when the mother called the infant by name and tried to lure him or her with an attractive toy. Clearly, infants can perceive depth by the time they are old enough to crawl.

What about babies who cannot yet crawl? When babies as young as 1½ months are simply placed on the deep side of the platform, their heartbeat slows down. Heart rate often decelerates when people notice something interesting, so this would suggest that 1½-month-olds notice that the deep side is different. At 7 months, infants' heart rate accelerates, a sign of fear. Thus, although young babies can detect a difference between the shallow and deep sides of the visual cliff, only older, crawling babies are actually afraid of the deep side (Campos et al., 1978).

How do infants infer depth, on the visual cliff or anywhere? They use several kinds of cues. **One, *retinal disparity,* is based on the fact that when a person views an object, the retinal images in the left and right eyes differ.** When objects are distant, the retinal images are nearly identical; when objects are near, the images differ. Thus, greater disparity in retinal images signifies that an object is close. By 4 to 6 months of age, infants use retinal disparity as a depth cue, correctly inferring that objects are nearby when disparity is great (Yonas & Owsley, 1987).

Other cues for depth depend on the arrangement of objects in the environment.

Linear perspective: **Parallel lines come together at a single point in the distance.** Thus, we use the space between the lines as a cue to distance and, consequently, decide the train in the photo is far away because the parallel tracks look so close together.

Texture gradient: **The texture of objects changes from coarse but distinct for nearby objects to finer and less distinct for distant objects.** In the photo, we judge the distinct flowers to be close and the blurred ones, distant.

Relative size: **Nearby objects look substantially larger than objects in the distance.** Knowing that the runners in the photo are really about the same size, we judge the ones that look smaller to be farther away.

Interposition: **Nearby objects partially obscure more distant objects.** In the photo, the glasses obscure the bottle, so we decide the glass is closer.

By 7 months, infants use most of these cues to judge distance. In one study (Arterberry, Yonas, & Bensen, 1989), for example, babies saw what appeared to be two toys resting on a checkered surface that gave linear perspective and texture gradients as depth cues. In fact, the checkered surface was a flat photograph. Infants were tested with one eye covered so that retinal disparity would not provide a cue to depth. Most 7-month-olds reached for the toy that looked closer, but 5-month-olds reached for the two toys equally often. Evidently, 7-month-olds use linear perspective and texture gradient to infer depth, but 5-month-olds do not.

We've seen throughout this module that infants use their senses to perceive the world. Darla's newborn son, from the opening vignette, can definitely smell, taste, and feel pain. He can distinguish sounds, and in a few months he will use sound to locate objects. His vision is blurry now but will improve rapidly, and in a few months, he'll see the full range of colors and perceive depth. In short, Darla's son, like most infants, is well prepared to make sense out of his environment.

Check Your Learning

1. Babies react to sweet substances by smiling and sucking but grimace when fed substances with a _____ taste.

2. Studies of auditory perception reveal that adults have lower _____ than infants.

3. Infants use sound to judge the distance and _____ of objects.

4. At birth, perception of color is _____.

5. By 7 months of age, infants use a number of cues based on the arrangement of objects to determine depth, including linear perspective, _____, relative size, and interposition.

Answers: (1) bitter or sour, (2) auditory thresholds, (3) location, (4) limited to distinguishing blue from gray, (5) texture gradient

COMPLEX PERCEPTUAL AND ATTENTIONAL PROCESSES

Learning Objectives

- **How do infants perceive objects?**
- **How do infants integrate information from different senses?**
- **How does attention improve as children grow older?**
- **What is attention deficit hyperactivity disorder?**

> *Rosie was only 36 hours old when John and Jean brought her home from the hospital. They quickly noticed that loud noises startled Rosie, and they worried because their apartment was near an entrance ramp to a freeway. Trucks accelerating to enter the freeway made an incredible amount of noise that caused Rosie to "jump" and sometimes to cry. John and Jean wondered if Rosie would get enough sleep. However, within days, the trucks no longer disturbed Rosie; she slept blissfully. Why was a noise that had been so troubling no longer a problem?*

Where we place the dividing line between "basic" and "complex" perceptual processes is quite arbitrary. As you'll see, Module 5.3 is a logical extension of the information presented in Module 5.2. We'll begin by looking at how we perceive objects. Then we'll look at how we integrate information from our different senses. We'll also look at the processes of attention and some children who have attentional problems. By the end of the module, you'll know why Rosie is no longer bothered by noises that once disturbed her.

PERCEIVING OBJECTS

When you look at the pattern, what do you see? If you're like most people, it's almost impossible to not see a square. Of course, there's no specific stimulus that corresponds to the square—the stimuli are four circles with a portion removed. We "see" the square only from the relations between the circles. What this example demonstrates is that people readily perceive relations between stimuli. Of course, we *do* perceive individual stimuli, but at the same time, we spontaneously group them to form familiar patterns.

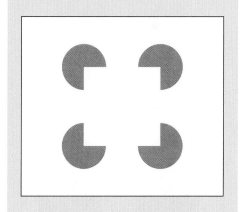

When infants view these circles, would they, too, "see" a square? The answer seems to be yes. In one study (Ghim, 1990), 3-month-olds were shown a simple square. After six presentations of the square, one of the four patterns in the diagram at the top of page 128 was shown. You can see that all consist of four circles, but only Pattern A creates the subjective experience of "seeing" a square. Having seen squares repeatedly, 3-month-olds looked much longer at Patterns B, C, and D than they did at Pattern A. Evidently, Pattern A looked familiar to them, so they looked less. Of course, the only way that Pattern A could be familiar is if infants "saw" a square created by the four circles and interpreted this as yet another presentation of the actual square they had seen previously.

Assembling a pattern from individual elements is an important first step in recognizing objects, but only the first. Perceptual constancies are important, too.

Perceptual Constancies. The scene comes straight out of one of those lousy black-and-white horror movies that Hollywood used to crank out in the 1950s and

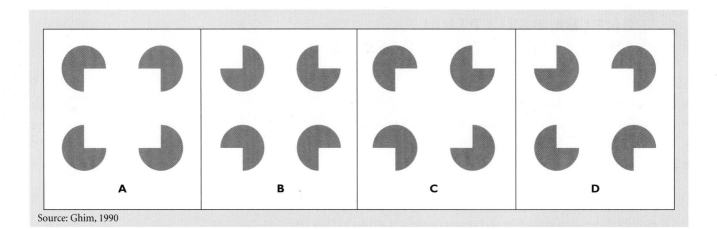

Source: Ghim, 1990

1960s: From its normal size, your mother's head begins to shrink, getting ever smaller until it finally vanishes altogether. Ee-e-e-e-ek!! Actually, for a baby, this scene might be a daily event. After all, any time a mother moves away from her baby, the image that she casts on the retina of her baby's eye gets smaller. Do babies have this nightmare? No. **Infants have mastered *size constancy,* the realization that an object's actual size remains the same despite changes in the size of its retinal image.**

How do we know that infants have a rudimentary sense of size constancy? Suppose we let an infant look at an unfamiliar teddy bear. Then we show the infant the same bear, at a different distance, paired with a larger replica of the bear. If infants lack size constancy, the two bears will be equally novel and babies should respond to each similarly. If, instead, babies have size constancy, they will recognize the first bear as familiar, the larger bear as novel, and be more likely to respond to the novel bear. In fact, by 4 or 5 months, babies treat the bear that they've seen twice—at different distances and therefore with different retinal images—as familiar (Granrud, 1986). This outcome is possible only if infants have size constancy. Thus, infants do *not* believe that mothers (and other people or objects) constantly change size as they move closer or farther away.

Size is just one of several perceptual constancies. Others are brightness and color constancy as well as shape constancy, shown in the diagram. All these constancies are achieved, at least in rudimentary form, by age 4 months (Aslin, 1987; Dannemiller & Hanko, 1987).

If you think about it, the message from the perceptual constancies is that "seeing is not believing," at least not always. A good part of perception, therefore, is knowing how to make sense out of what we see.

Shape Constancy: Even though the door appears to change shape as it opens, we know that it really remains a rectangle.

Object Permanence. As infants master the perceptual constancies, presumably they begin to understand the characteristics of objects. Among the most important is that objects exist independently of oneself and one's actions. You, I, this book, your instructor, and a pencil—to choose some objects at random—all coexist in the world. Each object occupies space in the world, and its existence does not depend on interaction with any other objects. When do infants begin to have these insights? For many years, our best answer to this question came from Piaget (1952) whose research suggested that 1- to 4-month-olds believe objects no longer exist when they disappear from view. For these young babies, out of sight truly means out of mind. According to Piaget, not until 12 months do babies really understand the permanence of objects.

Other investigators, however, doubted that younger infants were so limited in their understanding of objects. Some clever experiments by Renée Baillargeon (1987, 1994) suggested babies understand objects much earlier than Piaget claimed. She assessed object permanence using procedures like those shown in the diagram.

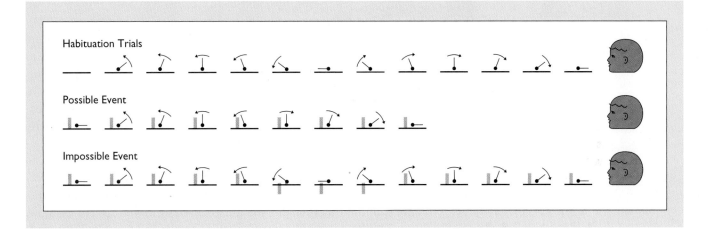

Infants first saw a screen that appeared to be rotating back and forth. When they seemed familiar with this display, one of two new displays was shown. In the *possible event,* an orange box appeared behind the screen, making it impossible for the screen to rotate as far back as it had previously. Instead, the screen rotated until it made contact with the box, then rotated forward. In the *impossible event,* the orange box appeared, but the screen continued to rotate as before. The screen rotated back until it was flat, then rotated forward again, revealing the orange box. The illusion was possible because the box was mounted on a movable platform that allowed it to drop out of the way of the moving screen. However, from the infant's perspective, it appeared as if the box vanished behind the screen, only to reappear.

The disappearance and reappearance of the box violates the idea that objects exist permanently. Consequently, an infant who understands the permanence of objects should find the impossible event a truly novel stimulus and look at it longer than the possible event. Baillargeon (1987) found that 4½-month-olds consistently looked longer at the impossible event than the possible event. Infants apparently thought the impossible event was novel, just as we are surprised when a magician makes an object vanish before our very eyes. Evidently, then, infants have some understanding of object permanence early in the first year of life.

So far in this module, we've seen that young babies use simple relations between stimuli to infer an object, recognize that objects are the same despite changes in appearance, and understand that objects have certain distinctive properties. We can understand infants' perceptual skills from a different perspective by looking at their perception of faces.

By 4 months, infants have begun to master size, brightness, color, and shape constancies, and they have basic understanding of object permanence.

Perceiving Faces. The human face is a particularly important object to infants. Young babies readily look at faces. From the diagram at the top of page 130, which

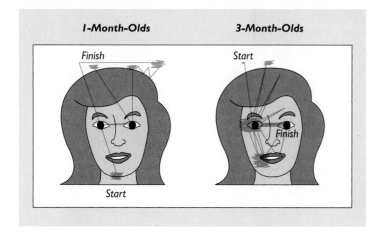

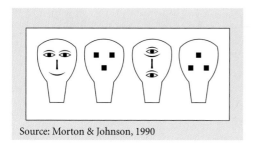

Source: Morton & Johnson, 1990

shows a pattern of eye fixations, you can see that 1-month-olds look mostly at the outer edges of the face. Three-month-olds, however, focus almost entirely on the interior of the face, particularly the eyes and lips.

Some scientists believe that general principles of perception explain how infants perceive faces (Aslin, 1987). They argue that infants are attracted to faces because faces have stimuli that move (the eyes and mouth) and stimuli with dark and light contrast (the eyes, lips, and teeth). Consistent with this viewpoint are results from Dannemiller and Stephens (1988), who found that when face and nonface stimuli are matched for a number of important variables (such as the amount of black/white contrast, the size and number of elements), 1½-month-olds typically look at face and nonface stimuli equally. In other words, infants look at faces because of general perceptual principles (for example, babies like contrasting stimuli), not because faces are intrinsically attractive to infants.

Other theorists, however, argue that babies are innately attracted to stimuli that are facelike. The claim here is that some aspect of the face—perhaps two eyes and a mouth in the correct arrangement—constitutes a distinctive stimulus that is readily recognized, even by newborns. For example, look at the different facelike stimuli in the diagram. In one study (Morton & Johnson, 1991), newborns turned their eyes to follow a moving face (at the left in the diagram) more than they turned their eyes for stimuli that had either facial elements or a facial configuration but not both (the remaining three stimuli in the diagram). Infants preferred faces over facelike stimuli, which supports the view that infants are innately attracted to faces.

More research is needed to decide whether face perception follows general perceptual principles or represents a special case. What is clear, though, is that by 4 months, babies have the perceptual skills that allow them to begin to distinguish individual faces (Carey, 1992). This ability is essential for it provides the basis for social relationships that infants form during the rest of the first year.

INTEGRATING SENSORY INFORMATION

So far, we have discussed infants' sensory systems separately. In reality, of course, most infant experiences are better described as "multimedia events." A nursing mother provides visual and taste cues to her baby. A rattle stimulates vision, hearing, and touch. From experiences like these, infants learn to integrate information from different senses. By 6 months, for example, infants can integrate vision and touch. At this age, if babies feel unfamiliar toys that they cannot see, they will later look at these toys longer than unfamiliar toys they have not felt previously. Thus, infants can come to know objects through touch and later recognize them visually (Rose, 1994).

By the first birthday, infants can integrate sights and sounds. Studies show, for example, that they link the characteristic sounds of male and female voices with the characteristic appearances of male and female faces (Poulin-Dubois et al., 1994). Another example of integrating vision and hearing is the topic of the "Focus on Research" feature.

Focus on Research: DO INFANTS INTEGRATE SIGHT AND SOUND TO ESTIMATE DISTANCE?

Who was the investigator and what was the aim of the study? We already know that older infants use sight and sound independently to judge distance (pages 121, 124–126), but can infants integrate these different sensory systems? That is, do infants know that an approaching object looks larger *and* sounds louder whereas a departing object looks smaller *and* sounds quieter? Jeffrey Pickens (1994) conducted his study to answer these questions.

How did the investigator measure the topic of interest? Pickens created the setup shown in the diagram. He presented pairs of 25-second videotapes on two video monitors placed side by side. In one pair, the first monitor showed a toy train that appeared to be coming toward the viewer; the second monitor showed a train going away from the viewer. These videos were simultaneously shown eight times. The soundtrack in four of the presentations had the engine getting louder; in the other four presentations, the engine became quieter. Research assistants wearing headphones (so that they couldn't hear the soundtrack) recorded which video the infant watched.

What should 5-month-old infants do when they see these videos? If infants know the rules

getting closer = larger and louder

going farther away = smaller and quieter

then they should look at the video that matches the sound: They'll watch the video of the arriving train when the engine gets louder and the video of the departing train when the engine gets quieter. But they might also do just the opposite—look at the mismatching sounds—because they're novel. In either case, there should be a strong link between what they hear and where they look. If, however, infants don't know the rules, then the soundtrack should not influence what they watch: They should watch the videos equally.

Pickens also included another condition with a different pair of videos. One video showed a train moving from the top of the video monitor to the bottom; the other showed a train moving from the bottom to the top. The soundtracks were the same as in the first condition—the sound of an engine getting louder on some trials and getting quieter on others. Neither video corresponded to the soundtrack because the train remained a constant distance from the viewer. Consequently, if infants understood the rules for integrating sight and sound to distance, they should look equally at these two videos.

Infants readily integrate information from different senses, linking seeing to hearing and seeing to touch.

Who were the children in the study? Pickens tested 64 five-month-olds.

What was the design of the study? This study was experimental. The independent variable was the type of video the infants saw. The dependent variable was the amount of time the infants spent watching each video monitor. The study focused on a single age, so it was not developmental (neither longitudinal nor cross-sectional).

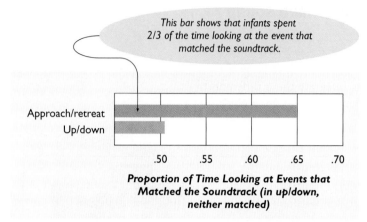

This bar shows that infants spent 2/3 of the time looking at the event that matched the soundtrack.

Approach/retreat
Up/down

.50   .55   .60   .65   .70

Proportion of Time Looking at Events that Matched the Soundtrack (in up/down, neither matched)

Were there ethical concerns with the study? No. Most infants seemed to enjoy watching the videos. All parents agreed to allow their infants to participate.

What were the results? The top bar of the graph, labeled approach/retreat, shows the results for the videos with the trains traveling nearer and farther. The variable shown in the graphs is the percentage of time that the 5-month-olds looked at the video that corresponded to the soundtrack. You can see that infants spent nearly two-thirds of the time watching the video that matched the soundtrack; evidently infants knew the rules for integrating visual and auditory cues to distance. The second bar in the graph, labeled up/down, is from the control condition with the videos showing trains moving from top to bottom and from bottom to top. In this condition, the babies looked at the two videos equally, the expected result since neither video matched the soundtrack.

What did the investigator conclude? By 5 months, infants coordinate sight and sound to determine an object's distance and direction of motion. That is, infants know that as objects get nearer, they look larger and sound louder; as objects move away, they look smaller and sound softer. ■

Skillful integration of sight and sound is yet another variation on the theme that has dominated this chapter: Infants' perceptual skills are impressive. Of course, infants do not integrate sensory information as well as older children, but the more important point is that infants' ability to integrate information acquired from different senses makes them extraordinarily well prepared to learn what goes on about them.

ATTENTION

Have you ever been in a class where you knew you should be listening and taking notes, but the lecture was just *so* boring that you started noticing other things—the construction going on outside or an attractive person seated nearby? After a while, maybe you reminded yourself to "Pay attention!" We get distracted because our perceptual systems are marvelously powerful. They provide us with far more information at any time than we could possible interpret. **Attention is the process by which we select information that will be processed further.** In a class, for example, where the task is to direct your attention to the lecture, it is easy to ignore other stimuli if the lecture is interesting. But if the lecture is not interesting, other stimuli intrude and capture your attention.

The roots of attention can be seen in infancy. Remember Rosie, the newborn in the vignette who jumped when trucks accelerated past her home? Her response was normal not only for infants but also for children and adults. **When presented with a strong or unfamiliar stimulus, an *orienting response* usually occurs: A person startles, fixes the eyes on the stimulus, and shows changes in heart rate and brain-wave patterns.** Collectively, these responses indicate that the infant is attending to this stimulus. Remember, too, that Rosie soon began to ignore the sounds of trucks. After repeated presentations of a stimulus, people become accustomed to it, so their orienting responses diminish and eventually disappear, signs of habituation, which we

Infants orient to a novel stimulus but pay less attention as it becomes more familiar.

discussed on page 119. Habituation indicates that attention is selective: A stimulus that once garnered attention no longer does so.

The orienting response and habituation can both be demonstrated easily in the laboratory. For example, in one study (Zelazo et al., 1989) speech was played through one of two loudspeakers placed at an infant's left or right. Most newborns, on first hearing, turned their heads toward the source of the speech, but after several trials, they no longer responded. Thus, newborns oriented to the novel sound, but then gradually habituated to the sound as it became more familiar.

The orienting response and habituation are both useful to infants. On the one hand, orienting helps the infant be aware of potentially important or dangerous events in the environment. On the other hand, constantly responding to insignificant stimuli is wasteful, so habituation keeps the infant from wasting too much energy on biologically nonsignificant stimuli (Rovee-Collier, 1987). Given the biological significance of being able to habituate, it's not too surprising that infants who habituate more rapidly tend to grow up to be more intelligent children (Rose & Feldman, 1995).

Young children do not direct their attention very effectively compared to older children and adults (Enns, 1990). Preschoolers are readily distracted by extraneous information, as shown in pioneering work by John Hagen and his colleagues (Hagen, 1967; Hagen & Hale, 1973). In their work, children were shown cards like those depicted in the diagram. Children were asked to remember the names of the animals but disregard the household objects. Cards were presented on several trials,

Source: Hagen, 1972

and children were asked to recall the order in which the animals appeared. Then, children were given two sets of cards, one with the eight animals and another with the eight household objects, and were asked to match each animal with the corresponding household object. Doing well on this task measured failure of attention because it meant the child had *not* ignored the household objects as instructed. Compared to preschool and elementary-school children, young adolescents were better able to ignore the household objects that were not important for the task.

Why does attention improve with age? For one thing, older children and adolescents are simply more likely to remind themselves that they need to pay attention. They are also more likely to have mastered some attentional "tricks of the trade." For example, if asked to determine if two objects are the same, older children and adolescents are more likely to compare them feature by feature until they find features that do not match or they run out of features to check (Vurpillot, 1968). Used properly, this strategy guarantees that children will do the task accurately and in the least amount of time possible. Asked if the two houses in the diagram at the top of page 134 are the

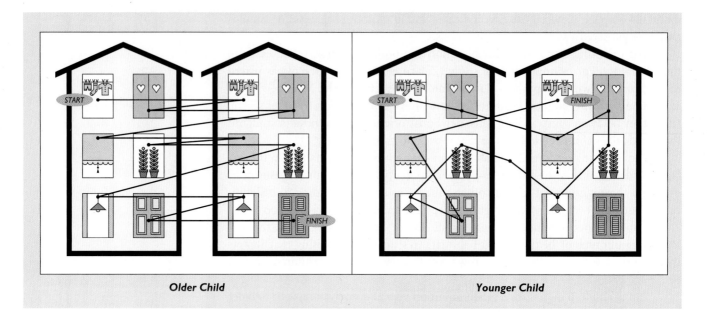

Older Child   **Younger Child**

same, older children typically start by comparing the top windows and work down until they have compared all six pairs of windows. In contrast, younger children perform the task haphazardly—not systematically checking corresponding windows—so they often don't find the differing windows.

Young children need help to pay attention better. One approach is to make relevant information more salient than irrelevant information. For example, closing a classroom door may not eliminate competing sounds and smells entirely, but it will make them less salient. Or, when preschoolers are working at a table or desk, we can remove all objects that are not necessary for the task. It's also very helpful, particularly for young children, to remind them to pay attention only to relevant information and ignore the rest. These techniques improve some but not all children's attention, as we'll see in the next section.

ATTENTION DEFICIT HYPERACTIVITY DISORDER

Children with attention deficit hyperactivity disorder—ADHD for short—have special problems when it comes to paying attention. Roughly 3 to 15 percent of all school-age children are diagnosed with ADHD; boys outnumber girls by a 3:1 ratio (Wicks-Nelson & Israel, 1991). The "Real Children" feature describes one boy with ADHD.

Real Children: WHY CAN'T STEPHEN PAY ATTENTION?

Soon after Stephen entered kindergarten, his teacher remarked that he sometimes seemed to be out of control. Stephen was easily distracted, often moving aimlessly from one activity to another. He also seemed to be impulsive, and compared to other youngsters his age, he had much more difficulty waiting his turn. At first, Stephen's parents just attributed his behavior to boyish energy. But when Stephen progressed to first and second grade, his pattern of behavior continued. He began to fall behind in reading and arithmetic. Also, his classmates were annoyed by his behavior and began to avoid him. Finally, Stephen's parents took him to a psychologist, who determined that Stephen had attention deficit hyperactivity disorder. ∎

Stephen illustrated three symptoms at the heart of ADHD (American Psychiatric Association, 1987):

■ *Overactivity:* Children with ADHD are unusually energetic, fidgety, and unable to keep still, especially in situations like school classrooms where they need to limit their activity.

■ *Inattention:* Youngsters with ADHD skip from one task to another. They do not pay attention in class and seem unable to concentrate on schoolwork.

■ *Impulsivity:* Children with ADHD often act before thinking; they may run into a street before looking for traffic or interrupt others who are speaking.

Not all children show all of these symptoms or to the same degree. Some, like the boy in the photo, may be primarily hyperactive. Others may be primarily impulsive (Barkley, 1990). However, regardless of the exact profile of symptoms, most children with ADHD have problems with conduct and academic performance. Many hyperactive children are aggressive, and consequently are not liked by their peers (Barkley, 1990; McGee, Williams, & Feehan, 1992). Although youngsters with ADHD usually have normal intelligence, their scores on reading, spelling, and arithmetic achievement tests are often below average; they are often considered to be learning disabled (Pennington, Groisser, & Welsh, 1993).

Why are some children afflicted with ADHD? Does too much sugar cause children to become "hyper"? Are food additives the culprit? In fact, except for a few children who are overly sensitive to sugar or allergic to food dyes, research provides no support for a connection between children's diet and ADHD (McGee, Stanton, & Sears, 1993; Wolraich et al., 1994).

The primary causes of ADHD lie elsewhere. Heredity contributes: Identical twins more often both have ADHD than fraternal twins (Gillis et al., 1992). A stressful home environment also contributes: Youngsters with ADHD often come from families with parents in conflict or under great stress themselves (Bernier & Siegel, 1994). Some children evidently inherit a predisposition for the disorder, which can be triggered by stress at home.

ADHD is often treated with stimulant drugs, such as Ritalin. You may be surprised that stimulants are given to children who are already overactive, but these drugs stimulate the parts of the brain that normally inhibit hyperactive and impulsive behavior. Thus, stimulants actually have a calming influence for many youngsters with ADHD, allowing them to focus their attention (Barkley, DuPaul, & Costello, 1993).

By itself, though, medication does not improve children's performance in school because it ignores psychological and social influences on ADHD. Children with ADHD need to learn to regulate their behavior and attention. For example, children can be taught to remind themselves to read instructions before starting assignments. And they need reinforcement from others for inhibiting impulsive and hyperactive behavior (Barkley, 1994).

Children with ADHD are overactive, inattentive, and impulsive; as a consequence, they often do poorly in school and are disliked.

Another approach is to teach parents techniques for encouraging attention and goal-oriented behavior at home. Anastopoulos and his colleagues (1993) arranged for parents of children with ADHD to attend nine training sessions to learn how to use positive reinforcement to foster their children's attention and compliance. Parents also learned effective ways to punish their children for being inattentive. Following training, their children had fewer symptoms of ADHD. Equally important, the parents felt that receiving training gave them a greater sense of competence in parenting. They also reported feeling significantly less parental stress.

For many children with ADHD, the best approach involves all of these techniques—medication, instruction, and parent training. Research shows that comprehensive treatment is the best way to help a child with ADHD become more attentive, less disruptive, and stronger academically (Carlson et al., 1992).

Check Your Learning

1. An infant understands _____ if she knows that her father does not really become larger as he moves closer to her.

2. Research shows that infants can integrate what they see with what they _____ and what they see with what they hear.

3. Older children and adolescents have better attentional skills because they remind themselves to pay attention more often and because _____.

4. The three primary symptoms of ADHD are overactivity, inattention, and _____.

Answers: (1) size constancy, (2) feel, (3) they have mastered more attentional "tricks of the trade," (4) impulsivity

 ENSORY AND PERCEPTUAL DEVELOPMENT IN PERSPECTIVE

Knowledge and understanding begin with sensory and perceptual processes. In Module 5.1, we saw that the empirical approach, the cognitive approach, and Gibson's differentiation theory provide three explanations of the way perceptual processes operate. In Module 5.2, we discovered young babies are perceptually quite skilled—they can smell, taste, touch, hear, and see (though vision is their least developed sense at birth). In Module 5.3, we learned that infants can perceive objects and that they can integrate information from different senses. We also learned that selective attention improves gradually as children develop, and we found some of the reasons why children with ADHD have difficulty paying attention.

Each module in this chapter touched on the theme that *development is always jointly influenced by heredity and environment*. In Gibson's theory, for example, infants are endowed with the basic perceptual abilities that allow them to differentiate their environments. However, the specific stimuli that they differentiate depends on the experiences that they have. We also saw that heredity is the most common reason why children are born with hearing impairment. At the same time, experience is critical in shaping the lives of children with hearing impairment. If their impairment is recognized early, they can learn to communicate very well. Finally, ADHD has its roots in both nature and nurture: Heredity makes some children prone to the disorder but environmental stress may actually trigger it. Heredity and environment are like the Democrats and Republicans of development—sometimes antagonistic, sometimes cooperative, always influential.

THINKING ABOUT DEVELOPMENT

1. What features of infants' sensory and perceptual skill show the influence of nature? What features show the influence of nurture?

2. Psychologists often refer to "perceptual-motor skills," which implies that the skills described in this chapter are related to the motor skills that were the focus of Module 4.4. Based on what you learned in this chapter, how might motor skills influence perception? How could perception influence motor skills?

3. How would a psychologist who takes an empirical approach explain the research findings on sensory integration in Module 5.3? How would the explanations of psychologists from the cognitive and Gibsonian approaches differ?

SEE FOR YOURSELF

If you really want to grasp Piaget's views on infants' understanding of objects, try administering two tasks that Piaget created. For the first, you'll need a 3-month-old baby, an attractive toy, and a cloth large enough to cover the toy. Place the toy within reach of the baby and watch. You should see the baby reach for the toy, and play with it. After a minute or so, take the toy and hide it under the cloth, well within the infant's reach. The infant will almost certainly not look for the toy, even though its shape is clearly visible under the cloth and within reach!

If you try this with 4- or 5-month-olds, however, they will readily reach for the hidden object. Nevertheless, Piaget argued that understanding of objects is far from complete at this age, which leads us to the second task. This time you need a 9-month-old, an attractive toy, and two opaque containers that are large enough to hold the toy. (The plastic tubs in which margarine is sold work fine.) Place the containers upside down, side by side. Then give the baby the toy to play with. In a little while, take the toy and hide it under one of the containers. A typical 9-month-old will quickly reach for the toy. Do this a few more times, always hiding the toy in the same container. The 9-month-old will continue to reach for the toy, enjoying the game that the two of you are playing. Now for the grand finale: As the baby is watching, place the toy under the *other* container. The baby will reach for the toy in the original container, where it has been hidden previously! Piaget claimed that this outcome shows the fragmentary nature of object understanding at about 9 months of age. See for yourself!

RESOURCES

For more information about . . .

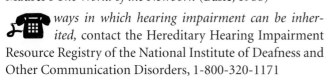 *infant development in general, including perceptual development,* try Charles Maurer and Daphne Maurer's *The World of the Newborn* (Basic, 1988)

ways in which hearing impairment can be inherited, contact the Hereditary Hearing Impairment Resource Registry of the National Institute of Deafness and Other Communication Disorders, 1-800-320-1171

 ADHD, visit this Web site maintained by the U.S. National Institute of Mental Health, http://www.nimh.nih.gov/publicat/adhd.htm

KEY TERMS

attention *132*
auditory threshold *120*
cones *123*
differentiation theory *117*
empirical approach *114*
habituation *119*

interposition *126*
linear perspective *125*
Müller-Lyer illusion *115*
orienting response *132*
relative size *125*
retinal disparity *124*

sensory and perceptual processes *113*
size constancy *128*
texture gradient *125*
visual acuity *122*
visual cliff *124*

UMMARY

MODULE 5.1:
APPROACHES TO PERCEPTUAL DEVELOPMENT

THE EMPIRICAL APPROACH

According to the empirical tradition, perception and, ultimately, knowledge are based upon sensory experience. Over time, sensory experiences accumulate and are linked together, giving rise to perceptions and knowledge. This tradition emphasizes experience and a one-way flow of sensory and perceptual processing.

THE COGNITIVE APPROACH

This approach shares the basic assumptions of the empirical tradition, but it goes beyond to say that knowledge influences perception. In other words, sensory and perceptual processing flows in two directions. Piaget's theory represents a cognitive approach to sensory and perceptual processing.

GIBSON'S DIFFERENTIATION THEORY

According to Eleanor Gibson, perception is not a process of gradual accumulation and integration of basic sensory experiences. Instead,

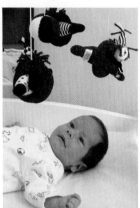

complex stimuli are actively *extracted* from the flow of perceptual information and can be perceived directly, if the child recognizes the features that distinguish complex patterns.

MODULE 5.2:
BASIC SENSORY AND PERCEPTUAL PROCESSES

SMELL, TASTE, AND TOUCH

Newborns are able to smell, and can recognize their mother's odor; they also taste, preferring sweet substances and responding negatively to bitter and sour tastes. Infants respond to touch. Judging from their responses to painful stimuli, which are similar to older children's, we can say they experience pain.

HEARING

Babies can hear, although they are less sensitive to higher- and lower-pitched sounds than adults. Babies can distinguish different sounds and use sound to locate objects in space.

SEEING

A newborn's visual acuity is relatively poor, but 1-year-olds can see as well as an adult with normal vision. Color vision develops as different sets of cones begin to function; by 3 or 4 months, children can see color as well as adults. Infants perceive depth by means of retinal disparity and other cues such as linear perspective, texture gradient, relative size, and interposition.

MODULE 5.3:
COMPLEX PERCEPTUAL AND ATTENTIONAL PROCESSES

PERCEIVING OBJECTS

Infants, like adults, spontaneously group stimuli into patterns. By about 4 months, infants have begun to master size, brightness, shape, and color constancy. At about this same age, they also have an early understanding of object permanence, the idea that objects exist independent of oneself.

Infants perceive faces early in the first year. However, it is not clear whether perception of faces involves specific perceptual mechanisms or whether it is based on the same processes used to perceive other objects.

INTEGRATING SENSORY INFORMATION

Infants coordinate information from different senses. They can recognize by sight an object that they've felt previously. And infants will look at a woman's face when they hear a woman's voice and look at an object that is becoming more distant when a sound becomes softer.

ATTENTION

Attention helps select information for further processing. Infants orient to a novel stimulus, but as it becomes more familiar, they habituate, meaning that they respond less.

Compared to older children, preschoolers are less able to pay attention to a task. Older children are better able to pay attention because they have developed strategies for maintaining attention. Younger children's attention can be improved by making irrelevant stimuli less salient.

ATTENTION DEFICIT HYPERACTIVITY DISORDER

Children with ADHD are typically overactive, inattentive, and impulsive. They sometimes have conduct problems and do poorly in school. ADHD is due to heredity and to environmental factors, particularly a stressful home environment. A comprehensive approach to treatment, involving medication, instruction, and parent training, produces best results.

FORCE OUT

Piaget's Theory of Cognitive Development

IN THE MOVIE, *LOOK WHO'S TALKING,* WE ARE PRIVY TO AN INFANT'S THOUGHTS ON EVERYTHING FROM HIS BIRTH AND DIAPER CHANGES TO HIS MOTHER'S BOYFRIENDS. THE HUMOR, OF COURSE, TURNS ON THE IDEA THAT BABIES ARE CAPABLE OF sophisticated thinking—they just can't express it. But what thoughts do lurk in the mind of an infant who is not yet speaking? And how do an infant's fledgling thoughts blossom into the powerful reasoning skills that older children, adolescents, and adults use daily? In other words, how does thinking change as children develop and why do these changes take place?

For many years, the best answers to these questions came from the theory proposed by Jean Piaget that is the focus of this chapter. We begin, in Module 6.1, with some background on Piaget's theory. In Module 6.2, we look at the four stages of cognitive development that are the hallmark of Piaget's theory. In Module 6.3, we examine some criticisms of the theory and look at alternate theories.

GENERAL PRINCIPLES OF PIAGET'S THEORY

Learning Objectives

- **What are schemes?**
- **How do assimilation and accommodation help children understand experience?**
- **What is equilibration and how does it explain changes in how children think?**

When John, an energetic 2½-year-old, saw a monarch butterfly for the first time, his mother, Patrice, told him, "Butterfly, butterfly; that's a butterfly, John." A few minutes later, a zebra swallowtail landed on a nearby bush and John shouted in excitement, "Butterfly, Mama, butterfly!" A bit later, a moth flew out of another bush; with even greater excitement in his voice, John shouted, "Butterfly, Mama, more butterfly!" As Patrice was telling John, "No, honey, that's a moth, not a butterfly," she marveled at how rapidly John seemed to grasp new concepts with so little direction from her. How was this possible?

For many years, our best answer to Patrice's question came from Jean Piaget, who began work on his theory of mental development in the 1920s. Piaget was trained as a biologist but he developed a keen interest in the branch of philosophy dealing with the nature and origins of knowledge. He decided to investigate the origins of knowledge not as philosophers had—through discussion and debate—but by doing experiments with children.

We'll begin our study of Piaget's work by looking at some key principles of his theory and, as we do, discover why John understands as quickly as he does.

SCHEMES

Piaget believed that children are naturally curious. They constantly want to make sense out of their experience and, in the process, construct their understanding of the world. For Piaget, children at all ages are like scientists in that they create theories about how the world works. Of course, children's theories are often incomplete. Nevertheless, children's theories are valuable because they make the world seem more predictable.

According to Piaget, children come to understand the world by using *schemes,* **psychological structures that organize experience.** That is, schemes are mental categories of related events, objects, and knowledge. During infancy, most schemes are based on actions. Infants group objects based on the actions they can perform on them. For example, infants suck and grasp, and they use these actions to create categories of objects that can be sucked and objects that can be grasped.

Schemes are mental categories that organize experience, based on actions in infancy and progressing to abstract properties in adolescence.

Schemes are just as important after infancy, but then they are based primarily on functional or conceptual relationships, not action. For example, preschoolers learn that forks, knives, and spoons form a functional category of "things I use to eat." Or they learn that dogs, cats, and goldfish form a conceptual category of "pets."

Like preschoolers, older children and adolescents use schemes based on functional and conceptual schemes, but they also have schemes that are based on increasingly abstract properties. For example, an adolescent might put fascism, racism, and sexism in a category of "ideologies that I despise."

Thus, children use schemes of related objects, events, and ideas throughout development. But as children develop, their basis for creating schemes shifts from physical activity to functional, conceptual, and later, abstract properties of objects, events, and ideas.

ASSIMILATION AND ACCOMMODATION

Schemes change constantly, adapting to children's experiences. In fact, intellectual adaptation involves two processes working together: assimilation and accommodation. *Assimilation* **occurs when new experiences are readily incorporated into existing schemes.** Imagine a baby who is familiar with the grasping scheme. Like the baby in the photograph, she will soon discover that the grasping scheme works not only on toys, but also on blocks, balls, and other small objects. Extending the existing grasping scheme to new objects illustrates assimilation. *Accommodation* **occurs when schemes are modified based on experience.** Soon the infant learns that some objects can only be lifted with two hands and that some can't be lifted at all. Changing the scheme so that it works for new objects (for example, using two hands to grasp a big stuffed animal) illustrates accommodation.

Assimilation and accommodation are easy to understand if you remember Piaget's belief that infants, children, and adolescents create theories to understand the world around them. The infant whose theory is that objects can be lifted with one hand finds that her theory is confirmed when she tries to pick up small objects, but she's in for a surprise when she tries to pick up a big stuffed animal. The unexpected result forces the infant, like a good scientist, to revise her theory to include this new finding.

Assimilation and accommodation are illustrated in the vignette at the beginning of the module. Piaget would say that when Patrice named the monarch butterfly for John, he formed a scheme something like, "butterflies are bugs with big wings." The second butterfly differed in color but was still a bug with big wings, so it was readily *assimilated* into John's new scheme for butterflies. However, when John referred to the moth as a butterfly, Patrice corrected him. Presumably, John was forced to *accommodate* to this new experience; the result was that he changed his scheme for butterflies to make it more precise; the new scheme might be something like "butterflies are bugs with thin bodies and big, colorful wings." He also created a new scheme, something like "a moth is a bug with a bigger body and plain wings."

EQUILIBRATION AND STAGES OF COGNITIVE DEVELOPMENT

Assimilation and accommodation are usually in balance, or equilibrium. That is, children find they can readily assimilate most experiences into their existing schemes, but occasionally they need to accommodate their schemes to adjust to new experiences. This balance between assimilation and accommodation was illustrated both by the baby grasping larger objects and John's understanding of butterflies. Periodically, however, the balance is upset and a state of disequilibrium results. Children discover that their current schemes are not adequate because they are spending much more time accommodating than assimilating. **When disequilibrium occurs, children reorganize their schemes to return to a state of equilibrium, a process that Piaget called *equilibration*.** To restore the balance, current but now-outmoded ways of thinking are replaced by a qualitatively different, more advanced set of schemes.

One way to understand equilibration is to return to the metaphor of the child as a scientist. As discussed in Module 1.2, good scientific theories readily explain some phenomena but usually must be revised to explain others. Children's theories allow them to understand many experiences by predicting, for example, what will happen ("It's morning, so it's time for breakfast") or who will do what ("Mom's gone to work, so Dad will take me to school"), but they too must be modified when predictions go awry ("Dad thinks I'm old enough to walk to school, so he won't take me").

Sometimes scientists find that their theories contain critical flaws, so they can't simply revise; they must create a new theory that draws upon the older theory but is fundamentally different. For example, when Copernicus realized that the earth-centered theory of the solar system was wrong, he retained the concept of a central object but proposed that it was the sun, a fundamental change in the theory. In much the same way, children periodically reach a point when their current theories seem to be wrong much of the time, so they abandon these theories in favor of more advanced ways of thinking about their physical and social worlds.

According to Piaget, these revolutionary changes in thought occur three times over the life span, at approximately 2, 7, and 11 years of age. This divides cognitive development into the following four stages:

Stage of Development	Age Range
Sensorimotor stage	Infancy (0 to 2 years)
Preoperational stage	Preschool and early elementary school years (2 to 6 years)
Concrete operational stage	Middle and late elementary school years (7 to 11 years)
Formal operational stage	Adolescence and adulthood (11 years and older)

Each of these stages is marked by a distinctive way of thinking about and understanding the world. The ages listed are only approximate: Some youngsters move through the stages more rapidly than others, depending on their ability and their experience. However, Piaget held that all children go through all four stages and in exactly this sequence. Sensorimotor thinking *always* gives rise to preoperational thinking; a child cannot "skip" preoperational thinking and move directly from sensorimotor to concrete operational thought.

All children progress through all four of Piaget's stages in the same order, though the ages may vary.

In the next module, we will look at each of the four stages of cognitive development in detail.

Check Your Learning

1. In Piaget's theory, a _____ is a mental structure that is used to organize information.

2. _____ takes place when a scheme is modified based on experience.

3. Piaget believed that when _____ occurs, children reorganize their schemes so that assimilation and accommodation are again in balance.

Answers: (1) scheme, (2) Accommodation, (3) disequilibrium

PIAGET'S FOUR STAGES OF COGNITIVE DEVELOPMENT

Learning Objectives

- How do schemes become more advanced as infants progress through the six substages of the sensorimotor stage?
- What are the distinguishing features of thinking during the preoperational stage?
- What are the strengths and weaknesses of concrete operational thinking?
- What types of reasoning skills define formal operational thinking?

> Three-year-old Jamila loves talking to Grandma Powell on the telephone, but sometimes these conversations get derailed: When Grandma Powell asks a question, Jamila often replies by nodding her head. Jamila's dad has explained that Grandma Powell (and others on the phone) can't see her nodding, that she needs to say "yes" or "no." But, no luck. Jamila invariably returns to head-nodding. Her dad can't understand why such a bright and talkative child doesn't realize that nodding is meaningless over the phone.

If Piaget were here, he would reassure Jamila's dad that her behavior is perfectly normal—children between the ages of 2 and 7 generally believe that others see the world as they do. Piaget would also emphasize the extraordinary amount of cognitive development that has taken place in Jamila's 3 years, development that begins with the sensorimotor period, the first topic in this module.

THE SENSORIMOTOR STAGE

Before we begin our discussion of Piaget's first stage of cognitive development, let's review some of the facts of infancy that we've already learned.

- Infants' locomotor skills improve rapidly during the first year, culminating in walking at 14 or 15 months of age (Module 4.4).

- Fine-motor skills develop rapidly during this same period, so that by the middle of the first year, infants coordinate both hands to grasp and manipulate objects (Module 4.4).

- Perceptual skills function early in infancy and improve quickly throughout the first year (Modules 5.2 and 5.3).

Piaget proposed that rapidly changing perceptual and motor skills in the first 2 years of life form a distinct phase in human development: **The *sensorimotor stage*, which spans birth to 2 years, consists of six substages during which the infant progresses from simple reflex actions to symbolic processing.** All infants move through the six substages in the same order. However, they progress at different rates, so the ages listed here are only approximations.

Substage 1: Exercising reflexes (roughly birth to 1 month). You know from Module 3.4 that newborns respond reflexively to many stimuli. As infants use their reflexes during the first month, they become more coordinated. Just as major-league players swing a bat with greater power and strength than Little Leaguers, 1-month-olds suck more vigorously and steadily than newborns.

Substage 2: Learning to adapt (roughly 1 to 4 months). During these months, reflexes become modified by experience. **The chief mechanism for change is the *primary circular reaction,* in which an infant accidentally produces some pleasing event and then tries to recreate the event.** For example, an infant may inadvertently touch her lips with her thumb, thereby initiating sucking and the pleasing sensations associated with sucking. Later, the infant tries to recreate these sensations by guiding her thumb to her mouth. Sucking no longer occurs only reflexively when a mother places a nipple at the infant's mouth; instead, the infant has found a way to initiate sucking herself.

Substage 3: Making interesting events (roughly 4 to 8 months). Primary circular reactions are centered on the infant's own body, typically involving reflexes like sucking or grasping. However, beginning in Substage 3, the infant begins to show greater interest in the world; now objects are more often the focus of circular reactions. For example, the infant shown in the photo accidentally shook a new rattle. Hearing the interesting noise, the infant grasped the rattle again, tried to shake it, and expressed great pleasure at the noise. This sequence was repeated several times.

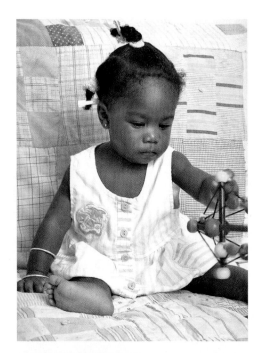

Novel actions like these that are repeated with objects define the *secondary circular reaction.* Secondary circular reactions are significant because they represent an infant's first efforts to learn about the objects in their environments, to explore their properties and their actions. No longer are infants grasping objects "mindlessly," simply because something is in contact with their hands. Instead, they are learning about the sights and sounds associated with objects.

Substage 4: Using means to achieve ends (roughly 8 to 12 months). This substage marks the onset of deliberate, intentional behavior. For the first time, the "means" and "end" of activities are distinct. If, for example, a father places his hand in front of a toy, an infant will move his hand to be able to play with the toy. "The moving the hand" scheme is the means to achieve the goal of "grasping the toy." Using one action as a means to achieve another end is the first indication of purposeful, goal-directed behavior during infancy.

Substage 5: Experimenting (roughly 12 to 18 months). The infant at this stage is an active experimentalist. **An infant will repeat old schemes with novel objects, what Piaget called a *tertiary circular reaction,* as if she is trying to understand why different objects yield different outcomes.** An infant in Substage 5 may deliberately shake a number of different objects trying to discover which produce sounds and which do not. Or an infant may decide to drop different objects to see what happens. An infant in a crib will discover that stuffed animals land quietly whereas bigger toys often make a more satisfying "clunk" when they hit the ground.

Tertiary circular reactions represent a significant extension of the intentional behavior that emerged in Substage 4. Now babies repeat actions with different objects *solely* for the purpose of seeing what will happen.

Substage 6: Using symbols (roughly 18 to 24 months). By 18 months, most infants have begun to talk and gesture, evidence of the emerging capacity to use symbols. Words and gestures are symbols that stand for something else. When the baby in the photo waves, it is just as effective and symbolic as saying "goodbye" to bid farewell. Children also begin to engage in pretend play, another use of symbols. A 20-month-old may move her hand back and forth in front of her mouth, pretending to brush her teeth.

Once infants can use symbols, they can begin to anticipate the consequences of actions mentally, instead of having to perform them. Imagine that an infant and parent have constructed a tower of blocks next to an open door. Leaving the room, a baby in Substage 5 might close the door, knocking over the tower, because he cannot foresee the outcome of closing the door. But a baby in Substage 6 can anticipate the consequence of closing the door and move the tower beforehand.

Sensorimotor thinking begins with reflexive responding and ends with symbolic processing.

Using symbols is the crowning achievement of the sensorimotor period. In just 2 years, the infant has progressed from reflexive responding to symbolic processing. A summary of these changes looks like this:

Six Substages of Sensorimotor Development

Substage	Age (months)	Accomplishment	Example
1	0–1	Reflexes become coordinated	Sucking a nipple
2	1–4	Primary circular reactions appear—an infant's first learned adaptations to the world	Thumb sucking
3	4–8	Secondary circular reactions emerge, allowing infants to learn about objects	Shaking a toy to hear it rattle
4	8–12	Means-end sequencing develops, marking the onset of intentional behavior	Moving an obstacle to reach a toy
5	12–18	Tertiary circular reactions appear, allowing children to experiment	Shaking different toys to hear the sounds they make
6	18–24	Symbolic processing is revealed in language, gestures, and pretend play	Eating pretend food with a pretend fork

The ability to use mental symbols marks the end of sensorimotor thinking and the beginning of preoperational thought, which we'll examine next.

THE PREOPERATIONAL STAGE

With the magic power of symbols, the child crosses the hurdle into preoperational thinking. **The *preoperational stage,* which spans ages 2 to 7, is marked by the child's use of symbols to represent objects and events.** Of course, mastering use of symbols is a lifelong process; the preoperational child's efforts are tentative and sometimes incorrect. For example, suppose you are the adult seated at the table in the drawing. You ask the child, a preschooler, to select the photograph that shows how the objects on the table look to you. Photo 2 shows the objects as they would actually look to you; photo 1 shows the objects as they appear to the child; photo 3 shows them as they would appear to an adult seated at the child's right. Which photograph do you think the preschooler will pick? Surprisingly, many preschoolers pick photo 1, which shows how the objects look to them! Why do children do this? To answer this question, we need to look at some characteristics of preschoolers' fledgling symbolic skills.

Egocentrism. Preoperational children typically believe that others see the world—both literally and figuratively—exactly as they do. *Egocentrism* **refers to young children's difficulty in seeing the world from another's outlook.** When youngsters stubbornly cling to their own way, they are not simply being contrary. Instead, preoperational children do not comprehend that other people have different ideas and feelings. In the problem shown in the drawing at the bottom of page 147, known as the three-mountains problem, preoperational youngsters evidently suppose that the mountains are seen the same way by all; they presume that theirs is the only view, not one of many conceivable views (Piaget & Inhelder, 1956, chapter 8). Similarly, egocentrism explains why Jamila, the 3-year-old in the vignette, nods her head when talking on the phone. Jamila assumes that because she is aware that her head is moving up and down (or side to side!), her grandmother must be aware of it, too.

Their egocentrism sometimes leads preoperational youngsters to attribute their own thoughts and feelings to others. **Preoperational children sometimes credit inanimate objects with life and lifelike properties, a phenomenon known as** *animism* (Piaget, 1929). A 3½-year-old I know, Christine, illustrated preoperational animism in a conversation we had on a rainy day:

RK:	Is the sun happy today?
Christine:	No. It's sad today.
RK:	Why?
Christine:	Because it's cloudy. He can't shine. And he can't see me!
RK:	What about your trike? Is it happy?
Christine:	No, he's very sad, too.
RK:	Why is that?
Christine:	Because I can't ride him. And because he's all alone in the garage, where it's dark.

Caught up in her egocentrism, Christine believes that objects like the sun and her tricycle think and feel as she does.

Centration. Children in the preoperational stage often have a psychological equivalent of tunnel vision: They concentrate on one aspect of a problem but totally ignore other equally relevant aspects. *Centration* **is Piaget's term for this narrowly focused thought that characterizes preoperational youngsters.** Piaget demonstrated centration in his best-known experiments, those involving conservation. In the conservation experiments, Piaget wanted to determine when children realize that important characteristics of objects (or sets of objects) stay the same despite changes in their physical appearance. Some tasks that Piaget used to study conservation are shown in the diagram on page 149. Each begins with identical objects (or sets of objects). Then one of the objects (or sets) is transformed and children are asked if the objects are the same in terms of some important feature. For example, in the conservation of liquid problem in the photo, children are shown identical beakers filled with the same amount of juice. After children agree that the juice in the two beakers is the same, juice is poured from one beaker into a taller, thinner beaker. The juice looks different in the tall, thin beaker—it rises higher—but of course the amount is unchanged. Nevertheless, preoperational children claim that the tall, thin beaker has more juice than the original beaker. (And, if the juice were poured into a wider beaker, they would believe it has less.)

Type of Conservation	Starting Configuration	Transformation	Final Configuration
Liquid quantity	*Is there the same amount of water in each glass?*	Pour water from one glass into a shorter, wider glass.	*Now is there the same amount of water in each glass, or does one have more?*
Number	*Are there the same number of pennies in each row?*	Stretch out the top row of pennies, push together the bottom row.	*Now are there the same number of pennies in each row, or does one row have more?*
Length	*Are these sticks the same length?*	Move one stick to the left and the other to the right.	*Now are the sticks the same length, or is one longer?*
Mass	*Does each ball have the same amount of clay?*	Roll one ball so that it looks like a sausage.	*Now does each piece have the same amount of clay, or does one have more?*
Area	*Does each cow have the same amount of grass to eat?*	Spread out the squares in one field.	*Now does each cow have the same amount to eat, or does one cow have more?*

What is happening here? According to Piaget, preoperational children center on the level of the juice in the beaker. If the juice is higher after it is poured, preoperational children believe that there must be more juice now than before. Because preoperational thinking is centered, these youngsters ignore the fact that the change in the level of the juice is always accompanied by a change in the diameter of the beaker.

In other conservation problems, preoperational children also tend to focus on only one aspect of the problem. In conservation of number, for example, preoperational children concentrate on the fact that, after the transformation, one row of objects is now longer than the other. In conservation of length, preoperational children concentrate on the fact that, after the transformation, the end of one stick is farther to the right than the end of the other. Preoperational children's centered thinking means that they overlook other parts of the problems that would tell them the quantity is unchanged.

Preoperational children often overlook others' perspectives and focus on one aspect of a problem.

Appearance as Reality. Preschool children believe an object's appearance tells what the object is really like. For instance, many a 3-year-old has watched with quiet

fascination as an older brother or sister put on a ghoulish costume only to erupt in frightened tears when their sibling put on scary make-up. For the youngster in the photo, the scary made-up face is reality, not just something that looks frightening but really isn't.

Confusion between appearance and reality is not limited to costumes and masks. It is a general characteristic of preoperational thinking. Consider the following cases where appearances and reality conflict:

- a boy is angry because a friend is being mean but smiles because he's afraid the friend will leave if he reveals his anger

- a glass of milk looks brown when seen through sunglasses

- a piece of hard rubber looks like food (for example, like a piece of pizza)

Older children and adults know that the boy *looks* happy, the milk *looks* brown, and the object *looks* like food but that the boy is *really* angry, the milk is *really* white, and the object is *really* rubber. Preoperational children, however, confuse appearance and reality, thinking the boy is happy, the milk is brown, and the piece of rubber is edible.

Preoperational children's confusion of appearance and reality was demonstrated in a study by Friend and Davis (1993). Stories were presented to 4- and 7-year-olds in which a person's outward appearance conflicted with his or her underlying feelings. For example, children were told about Sally, a school-age child who was sad because her uncle gave her a baby rattle for her birthday. Sally didn't want to hurt her uncle's feelings, so she smiled as she took the gift out of the box. A photograph showed Sally smiling at her uncle. Children in the study were asked if Sally *looks* happy or sad and if she *really is* happy or sad.

The graph shows how accurately children answered the questions. Questions about Sally's appearance were easy for all children; 4- and 7-year-olds readily judged that Sally looked happy. Questions about her real feelings were much more difficult: Most 4-year-olds and even some 7-year-olds answered the questions incorrectly. Thus, when presented with stories about people who feel sad but look happy, preoperational youngsters cannot distinguish between appearance and reality and so think that if people look happy, they are really and truly happy! In contrast, 7-year-olds, who are more likely to have progressed to concrete operational thinking, respond much more accurately.

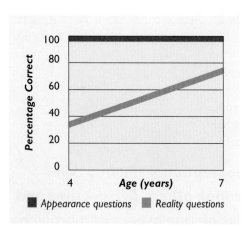

Are you skeptical that young children can be this confused? Many researchers shared your skepticism when these findings were first reported and they went to great lengths to show that young children were somehow being misled by some minor aspects of the experiment. But most of the follow-up experiments failed; rewording the instructions, using different materials, or even training children all had relatively little effect (Flavell, Green, & Flavell, 1986). Confusion about appearance and reality is a deep-seated characteristic of preoperational thinking (especially in the early years of this stage) as are egocentrism and centration.

THE CONCRETE OPERATIONAL STAGE

During the early elementary school years, children enter a new stage of cognitive development that is distinctly more adultlike and much less childlike. **In the** *concrete operational stage,* **which spans ages 7 to 11, children first use mental operations to solve problems and to reason.** What are the mental operations that are so essential to concrete operational thinking? *Mental operations* **are strategies and rules that make thinking more systematic and more powerful.** Some mental operations apply to numbers. For example, addition, subtraction, multiplication, and division are all familiar arithmetic operations that concrete operational children use. Other mental operations apply to categories of objects. For example, classes can be added (mothers + fathers = parents) and subtracted (parents − mothers = fathers). Still other mental operations apply to spatial relations among objects. For example, if point A is near points B and C, then points B and C must be close to each other.

Mental operations give concrete operational thinking a rule-oriented, logical flavor that is missing in preoperational thought. Applied properly, mental operations should yield consistent results. Taking the familiar case of arithmetic operations, 4 + 2 is always 6, not just usually or only on weekends.

Another important property of mental operations is that they can be reversed. Each operation has an inverse that can "undo" or reverse the effect of an operation. If you start with 5 and add 3, you get 8; by subtracting 3 from 8, you reverse your steps and return to 5. For Piaget, reversibility of this sort applied to mental operations. Concrete operational children are able to reverse their thinking in a way that preoperational youngsters cannot. In fact, reversible mental operations is part of why concrete operational children pass the conservation tasks described on page 149: Concrete operational thinkers understand that if the transformation were reversed (for example, the water was poured back into the original container), the objects would be identical.

> *Concrete operational thinking is based on mental operations that yield consistent results and that can be reversed.*

Concrete operational thinking is much more powerful than preoperational thinking. Remember that preoperational children are egocentric, believing that others see the world as they do; are centered in their thinking; and confuse appearances with reality. None of these limitations applies to children in the concrete-operational stage. Egocentrism wanes as youngsters have more experiences with friends and siblings who assert their own perspectives on the world (LeMare & Rubin, 1987). Learning that events can be interpreted in different ways leads children to realize that many problems have different facets that must be considered (thereby avoiding centration) and that appearances can be deceiving.

Concrete operational thinking is a major cognitive advance, but it has its own limits. As the name implies, concrete operational thinking is limited to the tangible and real, to the here and now. The concrete operational youngster takes "an earthbound, concrete, practical-minded sort of problem-solving approach, one that persistently fixates on the perceptible and inferable reality right there in front of him" (Flavell, 1985, p. 98). That is, thinking abstractly and hypothetically is beyond the ability of concrete operational thinkers.

THE FORMAL OPERATIONAL STAGE

In the *formal operational stage,* **which extends from roughly age 11 into adulthood, children and adolescents apply mental operations to abstract entities, allowing them to think hypothetically and reason deductively.** Freed from the concrete and the real, adolescents explore the possible—what might be and what could be. Unlike reality-oriented concrete operational children, formal operational thinkers understand that reality is not the only possibility. They can envision alternative realities and examine their consequences. For example, ask a concrete operational child, "What would happen if gravity meant that objects 'floated up'?" or "What would happen if men gave birth?" and you're likely to get a confused or even irritated look and comment like, "It doesn't—they fall" or "They don't—women have babies." Reality is the foundation of concrete operational thinking. In contrast, formal operational adolescents use hypothetical reasoning to probe the implications of fundamental change in physical or biological laws.

Formal operations also allow adolescents to take a different, more sophisticated approach to problem solving than concrete operational children. Formal operational thinkers can solve problems by creating hypotheses (sets of possibilities) and testing them. Piaget (Inhelder & Piaget, 1958) showed this aspect of adolescent thinking by presenting children and adolescents with several flasks, each containing what appeared to be the same clear liquid. They were told that one combination of the clear liquids would produce a blue liquid and were asked to determine the necessary combination.

A typical concrete operational youngster, like the ones in the photograph, plunges right in, mixing liquids from different flasks in a haphazard way. But formal operational adolescents understand that setting up the problem in abstract, hypothethical terms is the key. The problem is not really about pouring liquids but about forming hypotheses about different combinations of liquids and testing them systematically. A teenager might mix liquid from the first flask with liquids from each of the other flasks. If none of those combinations produces a blue liquid, the adolescent would conclude that the liquid in the first flask is not an essential part of the mixture. Next, he or she would mix the liquid in the second flask with each of the remaining liquids. A formal operational thinker would continue in this manner until he or she finds the critical pair that produces the blue liquid. For adolescents, the problem is not one of concrete acts of pouring and mixing; rather, they understand that the problem consists of identifying possible hypotheses (in this case, combinations of liquids) and then evaluating each one. The adolescent's approach to problem solving is also illustrated in the "Real Children" feature.

Real Children: HYPOTHETICAL REASONING GOES TO THE RACES

As a 15-year-old, I delivered the Indianapolis *Star*. In the spring of 1966, the newspaper announced a contest for all newspaper carriers. The person who created the most words from the letters contained in the words "SAFE RACE" would win two tickets to the Indianapolis 500 auto race.

I realized that this was a problem in hypothetical reasoning. All I needed to do was create all possible combinations of letters, then look them up. Following this procedure I had to win (or, at worst, tie). So, I created endless lists of possible words, beginning with each of the letters individually, then all possible combinations of two letters, and working my way up to possible combinations of all eight letters (e.g., SCAREEFA, SCAREEAF). This was monotonous enough, but no more than looking up all these possible words in a dictionary. (Remember, this was in the days before computerized spell checkers.) Weeks later, I had generated a list of 126 words. And, a few months later, I learned that I had won the contest. Hypothetical reasoning has its payoffs! ■

Because adolescents' thinking is not concerned solely with reality, they are also better able to reason logically from premises and draw appropriate conclusions. **Adolescents' more sophisticated reasoning is shown in their ability to make appropriate conclusions from information, what is known as *deductive reasoning*.** Suppose we tell a person the following two facts:

1. If you hit a glass with a hammer, the glass will break.

2. Don hit a glass with a hammer.

The correct conclusion, of course, is that "the glass broke," a conclusion that formal operational adolescents will reach. Concrete operational youngsters, too, will sometimes reach this conclusion, but based on their experience and *not* because the conclusion is logically necessary. To see the difference, imagine that the two facts are now:

1. If you hit a glass with a feather, the glass will break.

2. Don hit a glass with a feather.

The conclusion "the glass broke" follows from these two statements just as *logically* as it did from the first pair. In this instance, however, the conclusion is counterfactual—it goes against what experience tells us is really true. Concrete operational 10-year-olds resist reaching conclusions that are counter to known facts; they reach conclusions based on their knowledge of the world. In contrast, formal operational 15-year-olds often reach counterfactual conclusions (Markovits & Vachon, 1989). They understand that these problems are about abstract entities that need not correspond to real-world relations.

Formal operational adolescents think hypothetically and reason deductively.

Hypothetical and deductive reasoning are powerful tools for formal operational thinkers. In fact, we can characterize this power by paraphrasing the quotation about concrete operational thinking that appears on page 151: "Formal operational youth take an abstract, hypothetical approach to problem solving; they are not constrained by the reality that is staring them in the face but are open to different possibilities and alternatives." The ability to ponder different alternatives makes possible the experimentation of lifestyles and values that are common in adolescence, topics that we'll encounter on several occasions later in this book.

With the achievement of formal operations, cognitive development is over in Piaget's theory. Of course, adolescents and adults acquire more knowledge as they grow older, but their fundamental way of thinking remains unchanged, in Piaget's view. The table at the top of page 154, which you first saw in Module 1.2, summarizes the cognitive changes between birth and adulthood that Piaget described.

Check Your Learning

1. Sensorimotor thought begins with reflexive responding and ends with _____ .

2. An important characteristic of preoperational thought is _____, which refers to children's inability to see the world as others do.

3. Unlike preoperational children, concrete operational children are capable of _____, which are actions that can be performed on objects or ideas.

Piaget's Four Stages of Cognitive Development

Stage	Approximate Age	Characteristics
Sensorimotor	Birth to 2 years	Infant's knowledge of the world is based on senses and motor skills. By the end of the period, infant uses mental representations.
Preoperational thought	2 to 6 years	Child learns how to use symbols such as words and numbers to represent aspects of the world, but relates to the world only through his or her perspective.
Concrete operational thought	7 to 11 years	Child understands and applies logical operations to experiences, provided they are focused on the here and now.
Formal operational thought	Adolescence and beyond	Adolescent or adult thinks abstractly, speculates on hypothetical situations, and reasons deductively.

4. The formal operational period marks the onset of ＿＿＿＿＿＿＿reasoning and deductive reasoning.

Answers: (1) symbolic processing, (2) egocentrism, (3) mental operations, (4) hypothetical

 EYOND PIAGET'S THEORY

Learning Objectives

■ **What are some criticisms of Piaget's theory?**

■ **How do neo-Piagetian theories differ from Piaget's original theory?**

■ **How does Vygotsky's theory compare to Piaget's theory and to neo-Piagetian theories?**

Chris, a 14-year-old boy, was a bit of an enigma to his mother, Terri. On the one hand, Chris's growing reasoning skills impressed and sometimes even surprised her. He not only readily grasped technical discussions of her medical work, but he was becoming adept at finding loopholes in her explanations of why he wasn't allowed to do some things with his friends. On the other hand, sometimes Chris was a real teenage "space cadet." Simple problem solving stumped him, or he made silly mistakes and got the wrong answer. Chris didn't correspond to Terri's image of the formal operational thinker that she remembered from her college child psych class.

Like Terri, developmental psychologists have observed that adolescents' thinking is not always as sophisticated as Piaget's theory predicts. This is one of several criticisms we'll examine in the first part of this module. In the second part, we'll look at theories based on Piaget's work that attempt to address some of the criticisms. Finally, we'll look at a unique theory proposed by a contemporary of Piaget.

EVALUATING PIAGET'S THEORY

Because Piaget's theory is so comprehensive, it has stimulated a great deal of research. Much of this work supports Piaget's view that children actively try to understand the world around them and organize their knowledge, and that cognitive development includes major qualitative changes (Brainerd, 1996; Flavell, 1996). Also, many teachers and parents have found Piaget's theory a rich source of ideas for fostering children's development. Some of these ideas are described in the "Making Children's Lives Better" feature.

Making Children's Lives Better: **FOSTERING COGNITIVE GROWTH**

Piaget's view of cognitive development has some straightforward implications for teaching practices that promote cognitive growth:

1. Cognitive growth occurs as children construct their *own* understanding of the world, so the teacher's role is to create environments where children can discover *for themselves* how the world works. A teacher shouldn't simply try to tell children how addition and subtraction are complementary but instead should provide children with materials that allow them to discover the complementarity themselves.

2. Children profit from experience only when they can interpret this experience with their current cognitive structures, so the best teaching experiences are those that are slightly ahead of the children's current level of thinking. As a youngster begins to master basic addition, don't jump right to subtraction but go to slightly more difficult addition problems.

3. Cognitive growth is often particularly rapid when children discover inconsistencies and errors in their own thinking, so teachers need to encourage children to look at the consistency of their thinking but then let children take the lead in sorting out the inconsistencies. If a child is making mistakes in borrowing on subtraction problems, a teacher shouldn't correct the error directly but should encourage the child to look at a large number of these errors to discover what he or she is doing wrong. ■

Although later research supports many general features of Piaget's theory, some specific elements of his theory have held up better than others. Let's look at some of the criticisms that have been raised.

Alternative Explanations of Performance. As we have seen, Piaget explained cognitive development with constructs like accommodation, assimilation, and equilibration. Subsequent researchers, however, have found other ways to explain age differences in children's performance on Piaget's tasks. For example, preoperational children's performance on the conservation task appears to reflect, at least in part, their growing sensitivity to language, not purely their centration. In fact, it is the questions concerning the amount of water that turn out to be critical (Winer, Craig, & Weinbaum, 1992). Remember that in this procedure, youngsters are twice asked if the amount of water in the two beakers is the same—once before the water is poured and once after. In everyday conversation, a question is usually repeated like this because the answer was wrong the first time. Or it may be repeated because the answer was correct at first but something has changed so that it is now wrong. Both of these rules about questions would lead young children who had answered "yes"

One criticism of Piaget's theory is that researchers have discovered better ways to explain children's performance on tasks like conservation and object permanence.

to the first question to wonder if they were wrong or if a different answer is expected and perhaps say "no" the second time. In fact, when the procedure is changed (for example, by asking the question only once) preschoolers are more likely to conserve. Thus, children's performance on conservation problems is based partly on language development, not just the processes that Piaget described.

Researchers have also found an alternative explanation for infants' performance on object permanence tasks. This time, success may be a matter of memory rather than an understanding of objects. According to Piaget, one of the milestones of infancy is understanding that objects exist independently of oneself and one's actions. He claimed that 1- to 4-months-olds—who are in sensorimotor substage 2—believe that objects no longer exist when they disappear from view—out of sight means out of mind. If you take a favorite toy from a 3-month-old and hide it under a cloth directly in front of her, she will not look for it even though the shape of the toy is clearly visible under the cloth and within reach! At 8 months, infants search for objects, but their understanding of object permanence is far from complete. If 8- to 10-month-olds see an object hidden under one container, then see it hidden under a second container, they routinely look for the toy under the *first* container. Piaget claimed that this behavior showed only a fragmentary understanding of objects because the infants did not distinguish the object from the actions they used to locate it, such as lifting a particular container. Not until approximately 18 months do infants apparently have full understanding of object permanence.

Investigators have since questioned Piaget's conclusions. Some fairly minor changes in procedures can affect 8- to 10-month-olds' success on the hidden object task. An infant is more likely to look under the correct container if, for example, the interval between hiding and looking is brief and if the containers are easily distinguished from each other. Therefore, 8- to 10-month-olds who are not successful at this task may be showing poor memory rather than inadequate understanding of the nature of objects (Wellman, Cross, & Bartsch, 1986). Recall, too, Baillargeon's work (1987, 1994), which was described in Module 5.3. She found that 4½-month-olds were surprised by objects that seemed to vanish, suggesting that infants have some understanding of object permanence at a much younger age than Piaget's theory predicts.

Alternative explanations for children's performance on object permanence and conservation tasks do not mean that Piaget's theory is fundamentally wrong. They merely mean that the theory needs some revision to include important constructs that Piaget overlooked.

Consistency in Performance. In Piaget's view, each stage of intellectual development has unique characteristics that leave their mark on everything a child does. Just as you can recognize McDonald's by its golden arches, you can recognize preoperational thinking by its egocentrism and formal operational thinking by its abstractness. Consequently, children's performance on different tasks should be very consistent. On the conservation and the three-mountains tasks, for instance, a 4-year-old should always respond in a preoperational way: He should say the water is not the same after pouring and the other person sees the mountains in the same way he does.

Contrary to Piaget's theory, children's performance often varies across tasks that have the same logical structure.

What does research tell us about the consistency of children's performance on different tasks? There is some consistency, but exceptions are common, too. A good illustration comes from research by Siegler (1981), who tested children on the three tasks illustrated in the diagram at top of page 157. In the balance scale task, children are shown a balance scale with weights placed at various distances on either side of a fulcrum. Children must decide

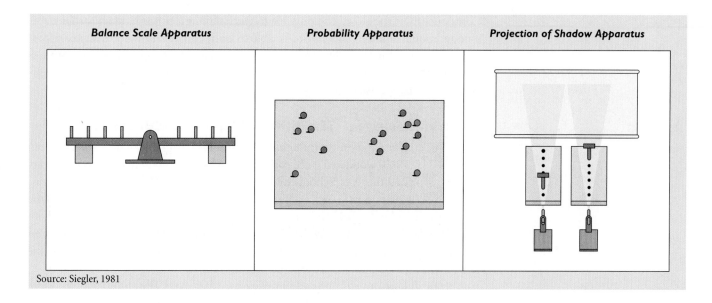

| Balance Scale Apparatus | Probability Apparatus | Projection of Shadow Apparatus |

Source: Siegler, 1981

which side of the balance scale will go down, if either, when the supporting blocks are removed. In the probability task, children are shown two piles of marbles, each containing red and blue marbles. They decide which pile would be more likely to produce a red marble if they must choose a marble with their eyes closed. Finally, on the projected shadows task, the T-shaped bars are placed at various distances from the light source, and the length of the horizontal part of the T varies. Children are asked to judge which of the two bars will cast a longer horizontal shadow.

Although the tasks *look* different, the underlying structure is the same for each, involving a comparison of ratios.

- *Balance scale:* The scale will balance when the ratio of weight to distance is the same on the two sides of the scale.

- *Projection of shadows:* The shadows will be the same when the ratio of the length of the horizontal part of the T-bar to the distance of the bar from the light is the same for both bars.

- *Probability task:* The probability of selecting a red marble will be the same when the ratio of the red marbles to the total number of marbles is the same in both piles.

Because the tasks have fundamentally the same underlying structure, Piaget's theory predicts consistency in children's performance across the three tasks. Yet, Siegler (1981) discovered that only one-third of the children performed at the same level on all three tasks. The remainder were inconsistent, sometimes differing considerably from one task to the next. For example, all 11 children who performed at the formal operational level on the balance scale only performed at the concrete operational level on the shadows task. This inconsistent performance on different tasks does not support Piaget's view that children's thinking should always reflect the distinctive imprint of their current stage of cognitive development.

Training Piagetian Concepts. According to Piaget, children master different concepts as they move from one stage to the next. Children master conservation as they move from preoperational to concrete operational thinking, and they master hypothetical reasoning as they move from concrete to formal operational thinking.

Consequently, it should not be possible to teach children concepts at an earlier stage; preoperational children should not be able to learn conservation, for instance. However, many investigators have shown that children can be taught Piagetian concepts ahead of schedule. The "Focus on Research" feature describes one example of teaching preschoolers conservation.

Focus on Research: TEACHING CHILDREN TO CONSERVE

Who was the investigator and what was the aim of the study? Rochel Gelman (1969) wondered if she could teach preschool children to conserve. She argued that a preschool child's attention is drawn to many cues in the conservation task, such as the size, height, and diameter of the beakers and the level of the liquid in the beakers. Most of these cues change as the liquid is poured from one beaker to another, which probably prompts youngsters to believe that the amount of liquid has changed. Gelman wondered if, by teaching children that quantities are the same despite looking different, they could learn to conserve.

How did the investigator measure the topic of interest? The study involved three phases: pretest, training, and post-test. First, Gelman administered four conservation tasks (length, number, liquid, and mass, shown on page 149), so that she could exclude children who already understood conservation. Next, the training phase included nearly 200 problems in which two quantities were the same but a third differed; the task was to select the two quantities that were the same. For example, in the problem on the left in the figure, the child would be asked to select the two rows that had the same number of dots. In the problem on the right, the child would select the two lines that were the same length. To answer correctly, children had to pay attention only to the number of

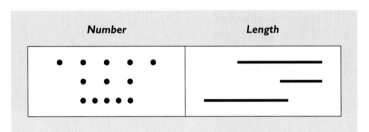

dots and the lengths of the lines and ignore other distracting cues, such as the length of the rows of dots or the position of the lines. Finally, in the post-test, Gelman readministered the four conservation tasks.

Who were the children in the study? Gelman tested 110 kindergarten children; 70 failed the conservation tasks during the pretest and received training. Their average age was 5½ years.

What was the design of the study? This study was experimental because Gelman compared children's performance before and after training. That is, the independent variable was the presence or absence of training. The dependent variable was the number of correct answers on the conservation tasks. The study was not developmental (neither cross-sectional nor longitudinal) because Gelman tested only 5½-year-olds and they were tested only once.

Were there ethical concerns with the study? No. Children usually enjoy Piaget's conservation tasks, and the training phase of the experiment was easy.

What were the results? Children were only included in the study if they were wrong on all of the conservation tasks during the pretest. Nevertheless, the graph at the top of page 159 shows that after training, children were quite successful on the conservation of length and number tasks that resembled the problems used in training. More impressive, however, is that after training children were also much more successful on the conservation of liquid and mass tasks, which did *not* resemble the training problems.

What did the investigator conclude? By training children to focus strictly on one cue and providing many different examples, children learned to ignore misleading cues

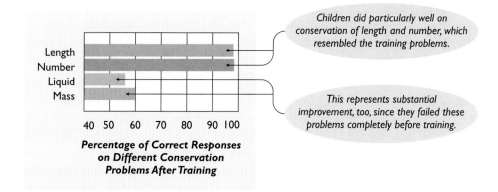

Percentage of Correct Responses on Different Conservation Problems After Training

Children did particularly well on conservation of length and number, which resembled the training problems.

This represents substantial improvement, too, since they failed these problems completely before training.

and came to recognize that quantity does not change in the conservation task. Contrary to Piaget's prediction, preoperational children can be taught to conserve. ■

Training procedures like Gelman's, although successful, may seem artificial because children don't ordinarily experience such a structured set of problems. However, children can learn to conserve another way—through discussion with peers. When nonconservers solve conservation problems together with children who can conserve, their joint answer is likely to be a conservation response. More importantly, when nonconservers are later tested alone, they conserve. These children are not simply parroting the conservers' answers because they explain the conservation response correctly and the training generalizes to new conservation tasks (Ames & Murray, 1982; Miller & Brownell, 1975).

A Theory of Actual Thinking or Possible Thinking? Simply because children and adolescents attain a particular level of reasoning in Piaget's theory does not mean that they always reason at that level. Children who are in the concrete operational period often revert to preoperational thinking. Adolescents often fail to reason logically, even when they are capable and when it would be beneficial. For example, adolescents typically show more sophisticated reasoning when the problems are relevant to them personally than when they are not (Ward & Overton, 1990). Thus, Terri, the mother in the opening vignette, should not be so perplexed by her son's seemingly erratic thinking: Adolescents (and adults, for that matter) simply do not always use the most powerful levels of thinking that they possess. Piaget's account of intellectual development is really a description of how children and adolescents *can* think, not how they always or even usually think.

Children's and adolescents' reasoning is often less sophisticated than predicted by Piaget's theory.

Because of the many criticisms of Piaget's theory, researchers have taken several different paths in studying cognitive development. Some have based their work directly on his. We'll look at these neo-Piagetian approaches next. Still others have used very different theoretical perspectives. Lev Vygotsky, a contemporary of Piaget's, proposed his own theory that we'll examine at the end of this module. Still other researchers have taken an information-processing approach to understanding cognitive development; we'll look at their findings in the next chapter.

NEO-PIAGETIAN APPROACHES TO COGNITIVE DEVELOPMENT

Beginning in the late 1960s, several researchers (e.g., Fischer & Farrar, 1987; Halford, 1988) proposed theories that elaborated and updated Piaget's theory. **As a group, these are called *neo-Piagetian theories* because they are modern theories rooted in Piaget's basic assumptions about cognitive development.** The neo-Piagetian theorists generally retain Piaget's belief that important qualitative changes occur in thinking as children develop, but their theories reflect the new research findings we have just been discussing and thus allow for much greater variation in performance from task to task. Let's look at one of the most elaborate of the neo-Piagetian theories, one proposed by Robbie Case (1985, 1992).

Case's Theory. The basic features of Case's theory are strikingly Piagetian: There are four qualitatively different stages of development; transitions between stages typically occur at roughly the same ages that Piaget proposed, 2, 5, and 11 years; and all individuals progress through all four stages. Where Case's theory diverges from Piaget's is in the means by which thinking progresses from one stage to the next. Recall that Piaget believed that cognitive development occurs by means of accommodation and assimilation. That is, schemes grow and change through assimilation and accommodation. Case, in contrast, believes that cognitive development occurs when two distinct schemes become integrated, with one subordinate to the other. For example, suppose a child is asked to decide which side of a balance beam is heavier. The child might count the weights on the two sides. Finding that this method works (at least on some problems) the child integrates the "weight-determining scheme" with the "counting scheme." The "weight-determining scheme" is dominant in that it triggers the "counting scheme" not vice versa.

> *Neo-Piagetian theories include four qualitatively different stages of thought, but also include a mechanism to explain why children's performance varies across tasks.*

Integrating schemes in this manner explains how the age at which children master specific tasks can vary. By exploring their environments, imitating peers or adults, or getting specific instruction, children may become proficient at some tasks earlier than others. To explain why there is some consistency in the ages at which children master skills, Case proposes that only a limited number of schemes can be kept in mind at once, and that this number increases with age. **Specifically, schemes are kept in a *short-term storage space* whose size increases with age.** Thus, even though the specific integrations that occur at a particular age differ from one child to the next, the complexity should be similar, reflecting the limit imposed by the available short-term storage space. That is, regardless of the task, older children and adolescents can maintain more schemes in short-term storage space, which explains why they usually perform better than younger children.

Case's theory typifies the neo-Piagetian approach in allowing for both general developmental changes as well as the development of specific individual skills. That is, neo-Piagetian theories share Piaget's effort to provide a general account of cognitive development, one that has at its core the idea that thinking changes qualitatively with development. However, neo-Piagetian theories also incorporate a mechanism to explain why a child's thinking may mature more rapidly in some areas than others.

Piaget's and neo-Piagetian theories are also alike in claiming that the four periods of cognitive development apply to children and adolescents everywhere, regardless of the culture in which they live. Although children's thinking is influenced by parents, siblings, school, and other elements of their culture, progression through the stages is largely the child's own doing. As you'll see in the next section, though, not all theorists share this view that culture has little impact on cognitive development.

VYGOTSKY'S THEORY OF COGNITIVE DEVELOPMENT

Like many authors, I often refer to child development as a journey that can proceed along many different paths. For Piaget and neo-Piagetian theorists, children make the journey alone. Other people (and culture in general) certainly influence the direction that children take, but the child is seen as a solitary adventurer-explorer boldly forging ahead. Lev Vygotsky (1896–1934), a Russian psychologist, proposed a very different account. Vygotsky, shown in the photo, saw development as an apprenticeship in which children advance when they collaborate with others who are more skilled. According to Vygotsky (1978), children rarely make much headway on the developmental path when they walk alone; they progress when they walk hand in hand with an expert partner.

Vygotsky died of tuberculosis when he was only 37 years old, so he never had the opportunity to formulate a complete theory of cognitive development as Piaget did. Nevertheless, his ideas are influential because they fill some gaps in the Piagetian and neo-Piagetian accounts. Three of Vygotsky's most important contributions are the zone of proximal development, scaffolding, and private speech.

The Zone of Proximal Development. Four-year-old Ian and his dad often work on puzzles together. Ian does most of the work; like the father in the photo, his dad sometimes finds a piece that Ian needs or correctly orients a piece. When Ian tries to do the same puzzles himself, he rarely can complete them. **The difference between what Ian can do with assistance and what he can do alone defines the *zone of proximal development.*** That is, the zone refers to the *difference* between the level of performance a child can achieve when working independently and the higher level of performance that is possible when working under the guidance of more skilled adults or peers (Wertsch & Tulviste, 1992). Think, for example, about preschoolers who are asked to clean their bedroom. Few succeed because they simply don't know where to begin. By structuring the task for children—"start by putting away your books, then your toys, then your dirty clothes"—adults help children accomplish what they cannot do by themselves. Just as training wheels help children learn to ride a bike by allowing them to concentrate on other aspects of bicycling, collaborators help children perform effectively by providing structure, hints, and reminders.

The idea of a zone of proximal development follows naturally from Vygotsky's basic premise that cognition develops first in a social setting and only gradually comes under the child's independent control. Understanding how the shift from social to individual learning occurs brings us to the second of Vygotsky's key contributions.

Scaffolding. Have you ever had the good fortune to work with a master teacher, one who seemed to know exactly when to say something to help you over an obstacle but otherwise let you work uninterrupted? *Scaffolding* **refers to a teaching style that matches the amount of assistance to the learner's needs.** Early in learning a new task, when a child knows little, the teacher provides a lot of direct instruction. But, as the child begins to catch on to the task, the teacher provides less instruction and only occasional reminders (McNaughton & Leyland, 1990). We saw earlier how a parent helping a preschooler clean her room must provide detailed structure. But as the child does the task more often, the parent needs to provide less structure. Similarly, when high-school students first try to do proofs in geometry, the teacher must lead them through each step; as the students begin to understand how proofs are done and can do more on their own, the teacher gradually provides less help.

Do parents worldwide scaffold their children's learning? If so, do they use similar methods? The "Cultural Influences" feature answers these questions.

Cultural Influences: **HOW DO PARENTS IN DIFFERENT CULTURES SCAFFOLD THEIR CHILDREN'S LEARNING?**

Cross-cultural research by Barbara Rogoff and her colleagues (1993) suggests that parents and other adults in many cultures scaffold learning, but they do it in different ways. These researchers studied parents and 1- to 2-year-olds in four different settings: a medium-sized U.S. city, a small tribal village in India, a large city in Turkey, and a town in the highlands of Guatemala. In one part of the study, parents tried to get their toddlers to operate a novel toy (for example, a wooden doll that danced when a string was pulled). No ground rules or guidelines concerning teaching were given; parents were free to be as direct or uninvolved as they cared.

What did parents do? In all four cultural settings, the vast majority attempted to scaffold their children's learning, either by dividing a difficult task into easier subtasks or by doing parts of the task themselves, particularly the more complicated parts. However, as the graphs show, parents in different cultures scaffold in different ways. Turkish parents give the most verbal instruction and use some gestures (point-

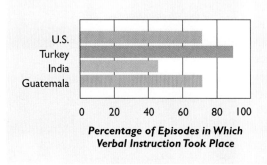

*Percentage of Episodes in Which
Verbal Instruction Took Place*

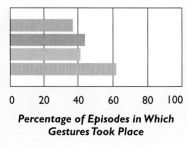

*Percentage of Episodes in Which
Gestures Took Place*

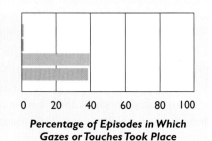

*Percentage of Episodes in Which
Gazes or Touches Took Place*

ing, nodding, shrugging). U.S. parents also use these methods but to slightly lesser degrees. Turkish and U.S. parents almost never touch (such as nudging a child's elbow) or gaze (eye contact, such as winking or staring). Indian parents seem to use roughly equal amounts of speech, gesture, and touch or gaze to scaffold. Guatemalan parents also use all three techniques, and overall, Guatemalan parents give the most scaffolding of the four cultures. Evidently, parents worldwide try to simplify learning tasks for their children, but the methods that they use to scaffold learning vary across cultures.

The defining characteristic of scaffolding—giving help but not more than is needed—clearly promotes learning. Youngsters do not learn readily when they are constantly told what to do or when they are simply left to struggle through a problem unaided. However, when teachers collaborate with them—allowing children to take on more and more of a task as they master its different elements—they learn more effectively (Pacifici & Bearison, 1991). Scaffolding is an important technique for transferring the control of cognitive skills from others to the child.

Private Speech. Like the little girl in the photo, many children talk to themselves as they play or perform various tasks. **This behavior demonstrates *private speech,* comments not intended for others but intended to help children regulate their own behavior.** Vygotsky (1934/1986) viewed private speech as an intermediate step toward self-regulation of cognitive skills. At first, children's behavior is regulated by speech from other people that is directed towards them. When youngsters first try to control their own behavior and thoughts, without others present, they instruct themselves by speaking aloud. Finally, as children gain ever greater skill, private speech becomes *inner speech,* Vygotsky's term for thought.

If children use private speech to help control their behavior, when do you suppose a child would be most likely to use it? We should see children using private speech more often on difficult tasks than on easy tasks, and more often after a mistake than after a correct response. These predictions are generally supported in research (Berk, 1992), documenting the power of language in helping children learn to control their own behavior and thinking.

Vygotsky's view of cognitive development as an apprenticeship, a collaboration between expert and novice, complements Piaget's (and the neo-Piagetians') view of qualitatively different stages of cognitive development. Contributing further to our understanding of cognitive development is information processing, which is the topic of Chapter 7.

Check Your Learning

1. One criticism of Piaget's theory is that children's performance on tasks like conservation and object permanence is _____.

2. Neo-Piagetian theories typically retain Piaget's claim that _____.

3. The _____ refers to the difference between what children can do alone and what they can do with skilled help.

Answers: (1) better explained by ideas that are not part of Piaget's theory, (2) cognitive development includes four qualitatively different stages, (3) zone of proximal development

PIAGET'S THEORY OF COGNITIVE DEVELOPMENT IN PERSPECTIVE

We know, of course, that infants do not have mature thoughts like the infant in *Look Who's Talking.* Instead, adultlike cognition is achieved gradually during infancy and childhood. In Module 6.1, we saw that Piaget's account of cognitive development is based on the idea that children actively try to understand their worlds. In Module 6.2, we discovered that children's search for understanding takes them through four distinct stages of thinking, beginning with sensorimotor thinking in infancy and ending with formal operational thinking in adolescence. In Module 6.3, we learned that although many researchers agree with Piaget's general view of cognitive development, others (including Case and Vygotsky) have proposed theories to fill in some of the gaps in Piaget's theory.

This chapter emphasizes that *children help determine their own development.* This idea is the cornerstone of Piaget's theory. Beginning in infancy and continuing through childhood and adolescence, children are constantly trying to make sense out of what goes on around them. Their understanding—and the shortcomings therein—is what propels cognitive development to more sophisticated levels. Experiences matter for cognitive development but primarily because they provide intellectual food for children to digest. Parents, teachers, and peers are important in cognitive development, not so much for what they teach directly as for the guidance and challenges they provide. Thus, as children take their developmental journeys, Piaget's child is a busy navigator, trying to understand the routes available and decide among them.

THINKING ABOUT DEVELOPMENT

1. Describe how nature and nurture seem to be involved in an infant's progression through the six stages of sensorimotor development.

2. One of the criticisms of Piaget's theory (mentioned on page 159) is that children's reasoning is often *not* as sophisticated as it should be according to the theory. That is, children and adolescents revert to simpler forms of reasoning, even though they are capable of more advanced forms. How might neo-Piagetian theorists explain this gap between what children can do and what they actually do?

3. Compare the role of sociocultural influences in Piaget's theory, neo-Piagetian theories, and Vygotsky's theory.

SEE FOR YOURSELF

The best way to see some of the developmental changes that Piaget described is to test some children with the same tasks that Piaget used. The conservation tasks shown on page 149 are good because they're simple to set up and children usually enjoy them. For each task, ask a 3- or 4-year-old and a 7- or 8-year-old to confirm that the two amounts are the same. Then, transform one quantity as illustrated in the diagram on page 149 and ask children if the quantities are still the same and to explain their answers. The differences between 3- and 7-year-olds' answers are truly remarkable. See for yourself!

RESOURCES

For more information about . . .

 activities for babies that promote cognitive development, read S. H. Jacobs's *Your baby's mind* (Bob Adams, 1992), which describes learning games and exercises for babies that are derived from Piaget's view of sensorimotor intelligence

 ways for teaching math and science that are based on Piaget's view that children actively construct their understanding of the world, contact the North Central Regional Educational Laboratory, 1-800-356-2735

Piaget's life, his theory, and his research (as well as related research on cognitive development), visit the Web site of the Jean Piaget Archives, http://www.unige.ch/piaget/PiagetGB.html

KEY TERMS

accommodation *143*
animism *148*
assimilation *143*
centration *148*
concrete operational stage *151*
deductive reasoning *153*
egocentrism *148*

equilibration *143*
formal operational stage *151*
mental operations *151*
neo-Piagetian theories *159*
preoperational stage *147*
primary circular reaction *146*
private speech *162*

scaffolding *161*
scheme *142*
secondary circular reaction *146*
sensorimotor stage *145*
short-term storage space *160*
tertiary circular reaction *146*
zone of proximal development *161*

 SUMMARY

MODULE 6.1:
GENERAL PRINCIPLES OF PIAGET'S THEORY

SCHEMES

In Piaget's view, children construct their understanding of the world by creating schemes—mental categories of related events, objects, and knowledge. Infants' schemes are based on actions, but older children's and adolescents' schemes are based on functional, conceptual, and abstract properties.

ASSIMILATION AND ACCOMMODATION

Schemes change constantly. In assimilation, experiences are readily incorporated into existing schemes. In accommodation, experiences cause schemes to be modified.

EQUILIBRATION AND STAGES OF COGNITIVE DEVELOPMENT

When accommodation becomes much more frequent than assimilation, it is a sign that children's schemes are inadequate, so children reorganize them. This reorganization produces four different stages of mental development from infancy through adulthood. All individuals go through all four phases, but not necessarily at the same rate.

MODULE 6.2:
PIAGET'S FOUR STAGES OF COGNITIVE DEVELOPMENT

THE SENSORIMOTOR STAGE

The first 2 years of life constitute Piaget's sensorimotor stage, which is divided into six substages. As infants progress through the substages, schemes become more sophisticated. By 8 to 12 months, one scheme is used in the service of another; by 12 to 18 months, infants experiment with schemes; and by 18 to 24 months, infants begin to engage in symbolic processing.

THE PREOPERATIONAL STAGE

From 2 to 7 years of age, children are in Piaget's preoperational stage. Although now capable of using symbols, their thinking is limited by egocentrism, the inability to see the world from another's point of view. Preoperational children also are centered in their thinking and sometimes confuse appearance with reality.

THE CONCRETE OPERATIONAL STAGE

Between ages 7 and 11 children begin to use and can reverse mental operations to solve perspective-taking and conservation problems. The main limit to thinking at this stage is that it is focused on the concrete and real.

THE FORMAL OPERATIONAL STAGE

With the onset of formal operational thinking, adolescents can think hypothetically and reason abstractly. In deductive reasoning, they understand that conclusions are based on logic, not experience.

MODULE 6.3:
BEYOND PIAGET'S THEORY

EVALUATING PIAGET'S THEORY

Piaget's theory has been faulted because children's performance on tasks is sometimes better explained by ideas that are not part of his theory. A second shortcoming is that children's performance from one task to the next is not as consistent as the theory predicts. A third is that, with training, children can readily grasp ideas that should be too advanced for them based on their Piagetian stage. A fourth shortcoming is that children and adolescents often use simpler forms of reasoning than they should based on the theory.

Despite the criticisms, Piaget's theory has stimulated considerable research, much of which supports his basic premises. The theory is also a rich source of ideas for fostering children's cognitive growth.

NEO-PIAGETIAN APPROACHES TO COGNITIVE DEVELOPMENT

Neo-Piagetian theorists adhere to many of the basic premises of Piaget's theory but differ in their explanations of the specifics of cognitive development. Case, for example, says cognitive change occurs when schemes become integrated. Schemes are kept in a short-term storage space, which increases in size with age. This increase in size means that older children are able to integrate more and more complex schemes.

VYGOTSKY'S THEORY OF COGNITIVE DEVELOPMENT

Vygotsky believed that cognition develops first in a social setting and only gradually comes under the child's independent control. The difference between what children can do with assistance and what they can do alone defines the zone of proximal development.

Control of cognitive skills is most readily transferred from others to the child through scaffolding, a teaching style that allows children to take on more and more of a task as they master its different components.

Children often talk to themselves, particularly when the task is difficult or after they have made a mistake. Such private speech is one way that children regulate their behavior, and it represents an intermediate step in the transfer of control of thinking from others to the self.

Information-Processing Approaches to Cognitive Development

PERHAPS YOU'VE SEEN THE CLASSIC SCIENCE FICTION FILM *2001: A SPACE ODYSSEY.* THE PLOT INVOLVES A COMPUTER—HAL*—WHO BECOMES UPSET AND THEN DIABOLICAL WHEN HE LEARNS THAT HE IS TO BE DISCONNECTED IN ORDER TO SOLVE A PROBLEM on board his spaceship. When Arthur Clarke wrote *2001* in 1968, "living, feeling computers" must have seemed like wild stuff. Even today, the question of whether computers can think (or feel) stimulates heated debate. What is not arguable, however, is the fact that many psychologists have borrowed heavily from computer science to formulate their ideas about human thinking and how it develops. Their approach is called information processing and it is the focus of this chapter. We'll begin, in Module 7.1, by talking about some general characteristics of the information-processing approach. In Module 7.2, we look at children's memory, an aspect of development that information processing has illuminated well. In Module 7.3, we'll consider information-processing research on academic skills like reading and arithmetic.

*Part of the trivia associated with *2001* is that Clarke created the name HAL by moving backwards in the alphabet by one letter from IBM.

AN INTRODUCTION TO INFORMATION PROCESSING

Learning Objectives

■ **What are the basic characteristics of the information-processing approach?**

■ **According to information-processing psychologists, how does children's thinking change as they develop?**

■ **How does information processing differ from Piaget's theory?**

> *Phung, a 15-year-old girl, has just completed driver's ed and loves getting behind the wheel. Most of the time, her parents are okay when she drives; they don't scream or get hysterical if she goes a little fast or hits the brakes too hard. But every time Phung asks to turn on the radio, they go ballistic. "No, no, no, you need to pay attention to your driving, not listen to music," they say. Phung thinks this is stupid. What does listening to music have to do with how well she drives?*

Phung's question is a good one, and later in this module we'll see that information-processing researchers have an answer for her. But first, let's learn more about information processing as a theoretical approach.

BASIC FEATURES OF THE INFORMATION-PROCESSING APPROACH

A few weeks ago, a friend of mine, Jim, bought a new computer for his office. In a few hours (and after some oaths that aren't fit to print in a G-rated textbook), Jim finally had the hardware—computer, keyboard, monitor, and printer—connected properly. He turned on the power, fully expecting the computer was ready to handle his correspondence, prepare graphs for sales meetings, and when his boss wasn't looking, play a few games. Jim, who is quite naive about personal computers, was shocked to discover that, fresh out of the box, his computer could do none of the tasks for which he had purchased it. Instead, he needed to make another trip to the local computer store and fork over several hundred more dollars for software to make his computer function as he had intended.

This simple distinction between computer hardware and computer software is the basis of an approach to human thinking known as *information processing.* The information-processing approach arose in the 1960s and is now one of the principal approaches to cognitive development (Kail & Bisanz, 1992). You remember, from Module 1.2, that information-processing theorists believe human thinking is based on both mental hardware and mental software. Mental hardware refers to mental and neural structures that are built-in and that allow the mind to operate. If the hardware in a personal computer refers to random-access memory, the central processor, and the like, what does mental hardware refer to? Information-processing theorists generally agree that mental hardware has three components: sensory memory, working memory, and long-term memory. The diagram shows how they are related.

***Sensory memory* is where information is held in raw, unanalyzed form very briefly (no longer than a few seconds).** For example, look at your hand as you clench

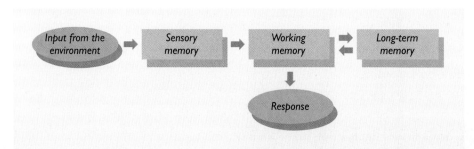

your fist, then rapidly open your hand (so that your fingers are extended) and then rapidly reclench your fist. If you watch your fingers, you'll see an image of your fingers that lasts momentarily after you reclench your hand. What you're seeing is an image stored in sensory memory.

***Working memory* is the site of ongoing cognitive activity.** Some theorists liken working memory to a carpenter's workbench that includes space for storing the materials for a current project as well as space for the carpenter to do the sawing, nailing, and painting involved in the project (Klatzky, 1980). In much the same way, working memory includes both ongoing cognitive processes and the information that they require (Baddeley, 1996). For example, as you read these sentences, part of working memory is allocated to the cognitive processes responsible for determining the meanings of individual words; working memory also stores the results of these analyses briefly while they are used by other cognitive processes to give meaning to sequences of words.

In the information processing view, mental hardware includes sensory, working, and long-term memories.

This description of working memory probably has a familiar ring to it. That's because working memory is essentially synonymous with Robbie Case's short-term storage space, described in Module 6.3. Working memory is the more common term, which is why I've used it here.

***Long-term memory* is a limitless, permanent storehouse of knowledge of the world.** Information rarely is forgotten from long-term memory, though it is sometimes hard to access. For example, do you remember the name of the African-American agricultural chemist who pioneered crop-rotation methods and invented peanut butter? If his name doesn't come to mind, look at this list:

Marconi   Carver   Fulton   Luther

Now do you know the answer? (If not, it appears before "Check Your Learning," on page 172.) Just as books are sometimes misplaced in a library, you sometimes can not find a fact in long-term memory. Given a list of names, though, you can go directly to the location in long-term memory associated with each name and determine which is the famed chemist.

If you're familiar with personal computers, you'll recognize that working memory resembles random-access memory (RAM) because that's where we load programs we want to run and temporarily store the data those programs are using. In contrast, long-term memory is like a computer's hard drive, a fairly permanent storehouse of programs and data.

Mental hardware allows us to "run" mental software, so the next question is what is mental software? To answer this question, think about personal computer software you've used, such as programs for word processing, spreadsheets, or graphing. In each case, the software was designed to accomplish a specific function. In much the same way, mental software refers to mental programs that are the basis for performing particular tasks. According to information-processing psychologists, children have special mental software that allows them to accomplish particular tasks, such as reading, doing arithmetic, or finding their way to and from school. For example, suppose a mother asks her son to make his bed, brush his teeth, and take out the trash. A bit later, the mother wonders if she asked her son about the trash, so she says, "Did I ask you to take out the trash?" Almost immediately, he says, "Yes." Despite the speed of the boy's reply, information-processing theorists believe that his mental software has gone through four general steps to answer the question, shown in the diagram at the top of page 170. First, the mental software must understand the

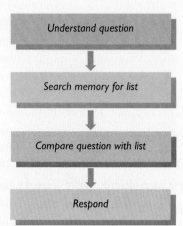

mother's question. That is, the software must decode the sounds of the mother's speech and give them meaning. Next, the software searches working memory and long-term memory for the mother's earlier requests. When that list is located and retrieved, the software compares "take out the trash" with each of the items on the list. Finding a match, the software selects "yes" as the appropriate answer to the question. Thus, the processes of understanding, searching, comparing, and responding create a mental program that allows the boy to answer his mother.

In the next section, we'll see how developmental psychologists use these ideas to understand how children's thinking changes as they grow older.

HOW INFORMATION PROCESSING CHANGES WITH DEVELOPMENT

All theories of cognitive development try to explain how experiences and mental structures interact to produce cognitive growth. You may recall from Module 6.1 that Piaget's explanation of cognitive development emphasized equilibration—the process by which mental structures are massively reorganized so that schemes can assimilate information more readily. Information-processing theorists believe that developmental change comes in several important forms, rather than a single mechanism like equilibration (Kail & Bisanz, 1992; Siegler, 1989). Let's look at four of them.

As children develop, they use more efficient strategies, have more working memory, more automatic processes, and more rapid processing.

More Efficient Strategies. Older children rely upon more efficient strategies to solve problems (Crowley & Siegler, 1993; Schneider & Bjork-lund, 1997). That is, as children develop they use strategies that are faster, more accurate, and easier. Having lost a hat on the way to school, a younger child might search the entire route; an older child might recall taking off the hat midway to school and so only search the last half of the route (Sophian & Wellman, 1987). Both children will probably find the missing hat, but the older child's approach is more efficient.

How do children learn more effective strategies? Of course, parents and teachers often show youngsters more effective strategies. However, youngsters also learn new strategies by watching more skilled children. For example, children and adolescents at an arcade watch others play in order to learn good game strategies. Children also discover new strategies on their own (Siegler & Jenkins, 1989). For example, I once watched my 5-year-old daughter match words with their antonyms in a language workbook. The pages always had an equal number of words and antonyms, so she quickly learned to connect the last word with the one remaining antonym, without thinking about the meaning of either. Thus, with input from parents, teachers, peers, and their own observations, children's mental software becomes more powerful and more efficient.

Increased Capacity of Working Memory. Remember that working memory is the part of mental hardware responsible for ongoing mental activity. What would happen if this work space became larger as children grew? To answer this question, think about technological change in personal computers in the 1990s: Today's personal computers run much more impressive software, in part, because they have much more random-access memory available than their counterparts from the 1980s. If you apply this technological change to children's development, the implication is clear. The diagram at the top of page 171 shows that, compared to younger children, older children have more working memory to allocate to mental software and to storing information (Case, 1992; Kail, 1995). Consequently, older children usually outperform younger children on tasks where working memory is important for performance, such as reading or solving complicated problems.

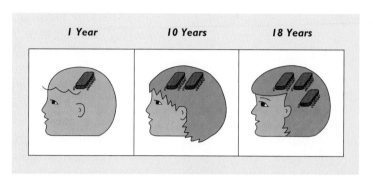

Increased Automatic Processing. Think back to the days when you were learning a brand new skill, like how to type. In the beginning, you had to think about every single step in the process. If, as a fledgling typist, you were asked to type "child," you probably started like the child in the photograph, by trying to remember the location of "c" on the keyboard and then deciding which finger to use to reach that key. You had to repeat this process for each of the remaining four letters. As your skill grew, each step became easier until, if you are now a skilled typist, you could type "child" without even thinking about it; your fingers seem to move automatically to the right locations, in the right sequence. **Cognitive activities that require virtually no effort are known as *automatic processes.***

To understand how automatic processes affect developmental change, we need to return to working memory. In the early phases of learning a skill, each individual step (such as finding a "c" on the keyboard) must be stored in working memory. Because there are so many steps, an unmastered skill can easily occupy much of the capacity of working memory. In contrast, when a skill has been mastered, individual steps are no longer stored in working memory, which means that more capacity is available for other activities. Thus, beginning drivers like Phung are told to keep the music turned off because listening would consume capacity of working memory that is needed for driving. However, with more experience behind the wheel, many driving skills become automatic, freeing capacity that can be used to listen to the radio. (Patience, Phung, your time will come!)

Compared to adolescents and adults, children have limited experience in most tasks, so they perform few processes automatically. Instead, like Phung, their processing requires substantial working memory capacity. As children gain experience, however, some processes become automatic, freeing working memory capacity for other processes (Kail & Park, 1990). Thus, when faced with complex tasks involving many processes, older children are more likely to succeed because they can perform some of the processes automatically. In contrast, younger children must think about all or most of the processes, taxing or even exceeding the capacity of their working memory.

Increased Speed of Processing. As children develop, they complete most mental processes at an ever-faster rate (Cerella & Hale, 1994). Improved speed is obvious when we measure how fast children of different ages respond on tasks. Across a wide range of cognitive tasks such as deciding which of two numbers is greater, determining the name of a pictured object, and searching memory, 4- and 5-year-olds are generally one-third as fast as adults whereas 8- and 9-year-olds are one-half as fast as adults (Kail, 1991).

Age differences in processing speed are critical when a specified number of actions must be completed in a fixed period of time. For example, perhaps you've had the unfortunate experience of trying to understand a professor who lectures at warp speed. The instructor's speech was so rapid that your cognitive processes couldn't keep up, which meant that you didn't get much out of the lecture. The problem is even more serious for children, who process information much more slowly than adults.

The four types of developmental change—more efficient strategies, more working memory, more automatic processing, and more rapid processing—occur throughout infancy, childhood, adolescence, and adulthood. Furthermore, sometimes the different types of change interact with each other. To see this interaction, think back to the analogy of working memory as a workbench. A carpenter who quickly finds the tools she needs can complete the project on her workbench promptly and move on to other projects. A carpenter who must search endlessly for tools will complete the project much more slowly. In much the same way, as children process information more rapidly, they use working memory more efficiently. With the four types of change interacting in this fashion (and functioning independently), information processing provides a very detailed account of cognitive development.

COMPARING INFORMATION PROCESSING AND PIAGET'S THEORY

Piaget's theory is so influential that it has long been the standard by which other approaches to cognitive development are measured. By comparing information processing with Piaget's theory, you can see some of the strengths and weaknesses of each (Kail & Bisanz, 1992). One important difference is that Piaget's work is a single comprehensive theory, whereas information processing represents a general approach encompassing many different theories to describe specific components of cognitive development. Thus, the advantage of Piaget's work is that it is comprehensive—all the links between different facets of cognitive development are included in his theory. But the advantage of the information-processing approach is that specific components of cognition are described with incredible precision. In essence, Piaget emphasized the "whole" of cognitive development, whereas information processing emphasizes the "parts." Both the whole and the parts are important for complete understanding of cognitive development, so Piaget's theory and information processing complement each other.

> *Piaget emphasized the "whole" of cognitive development and abrupt change; information processing psychologists emphasize the "parts" of cognitive development and gradual change.*

A second difference is that Piaget emphasized periodic, qualitative change in cognition: Children's thinking remains at one stage for years, then changes abruptly as equilibration propels thinking into the next, qualitatively different stage. In contrast, the four types of change in information processing—more efficient strategies, more working memory, more automatic processing, and more rapid processing—occur as steady age-related increases in cognitive skill. Unlike Piaget's account, there are no abrupt or qualitative changes that create distinct cognitive stages. Instead, cognitive change is constant and gradual. Since both types of change play a role in development, here, too, Piaget's theory and information processing may complement each other.

Keep these differences in mind as you read about the development of memory (Module 7.2) and academic skills (Module 7.3). Think about the need to balance the "whole" with the "parts," and think about the role of abrupt change versus gradual change in cognitive development.

Response to question on page 169: The agricultural chemist who pioneered crop-rotation while on the faculty of Tuskegee Institute of Technology is George Washington Carver.

Check Your Learning

1. Information-processing psychologists believe that mental hardware includes sensory memory, working memory, and _____.

2. _____ refers to specialized processes that allow children to complete particular tasks, such as reading or arithmetic.

3. According to the information-processing view, the older child's greater cognitive skill can be traced to more efficient strategies, _____, increased automatic processing, and more rapid speed of processing.

4. Piaget emphasizes distinct stages in cognitive development, while information processing emphasizes _____.

Answers: (1) long-term memory, (2) Mental software, (3) increased working memory capacity, (4) steady, gradual change

MEMORY

Learning Objectives

- **How well do infants remember?**
- **How do strategies help children to remember?**
- **How does children's knowledge influence what they remember?**

> One afternoon 4-year-old Cheryl came home sobbing and reported that Mr. Johnson, a neighbor and long-time family friend, had taken down her pants and touched her "private parts." Her mother was shocked. Mr. Johnson had always seemed an honest, decent man, which made her wonder if Cheryl's imagination had simply run wild. Yet, at times, he did seem a bit peculiar, so her daughter's claim had a ring of truth.

Regrettably, episodes like this are all too common in America today. When child abuse is suspected, and the child is the sole eyewitness, the child must testify to prosecute the alleged abuser. But can preschool children like Cheryl be trusted to recall events accurately on the witness stand? To answer this question, we need to understand more about how memory functions in infancy and childhood.

ORIGINS OF MEMORY

Roots of memory are laid down in the first few months after birth. Young babies remember events for days or even weeks at a time. Some of the studies that opened our eyes to the infant's ability to remember were conducted by Carolyn Rovee-Collier (1987; Rovee-Collier, Evancio, & Earley, 1995). The method used in her studies is shown in the photo. A ribbon from a mobile is attached to a 2- or 3-month old's leg; within a few minutes, the babies learn to kick to make the mobile move. When Rovee-Collier brought the mobile to the infants' homes several days or a few weeks later, babies would still kick to make the mobile move. If Rovee-Collier waited several weeks to return, most babies forgot that kicking moved the mobile. When that happened, she gave them a reminder—she moved the mobile herself without attaching the ribbon to their foot. Then she would return the next day, hook up the apparatus, and the babies would kick to move the mobile. Rovee-Collier's experiments show that three important features of memory exist as early as 2 and 3 months of age: (1) an event from the past is

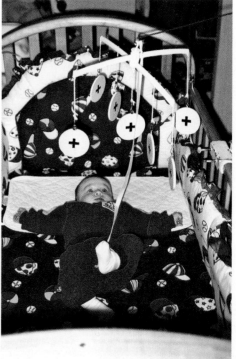

remembered, (2) over time, the event can no longer be recalled, and (3) a cue can serve to dredge up a memory that seems to have been forgotten.

Once youngsters begin to talk, we can study their memory skills using most of the same methods we use with older children and adults. Research using these methods has linked age-related improvement in memory to two factors (Kail, 1990, 1992). First, as children grow, they use more effective strategies for remembering. Second, children's growing factual knowledge of the world allows them to organize information more thoroughly and, therefore, remember better. We'll discuss each of these factors in the next few pages.

STRATEGIES FOR REMEMBERING

Last week, I wrote four pages for this book that would have made Tom Clancy green with envy, when the unthinkable happened—a power failure knocked out my computer and all those wonderful words were lost. If I had only saved the text to the hard drive . . . but I hadn't.

This tale of woe sets the stage for understanding how strategies aid memory. Recall that working memory is used for briefly storing a small amount of information, such as the words in these sentences. However, as you read additional sentences, they displace words read earlier from working memory. For you to learn this information, it must be transferred to long-term memory. Anything not transferred from working memory to long-term memory is lost, just as my words vanished from the computer's memory with the power failure.

As children develop, they are better able to identify the goals of memory tasks and select appropriate strategies.

Memory strategies are activities that improve remembering. Some strategies help maintain information in working memory. Others help transfer information to long-term memory. Still others help retrieve information from long-term memory. Obviously, there are many kinds of memory strategies.

Children begin to use memory strategies early. Preschool children look at or touch objects that they've been told to remember (DeLoache, 1984). Looking and touching aren't very effective, but they tell us that preschoolers understand that they should be doing something to try to remember; remembering doesn't happen automatically!

During the elementary school years, children begin to use more powerful strategies. For example, 7- and 8-year-olds use rehearsal, a strategy of repetitively naming information that is to be remembered. As children get older, they learn other memory strategies and they learn when it is best to use them. That is, children and adolescents begin to identify the unique characteristics of different memory problems and which memory strategies are most appropriate. For example, when reading a textbook or watching a television newscast, the aim is to remember the main points, not the individual words or sentences. Rehearsal is ineffective for this task, but outlining or writing a summary are good strategies because they identify the main points *and* organize them (Kail, 1990). Like the student in the photo, older children and adolescents often use outlines to help them remember information in textbooks. Also, as children grow, they are more likely to write down information on calendars, so that, like the boy in the photo, they won't forget future events.

Thus, successful learning and remembering involves identifying the goals of memory problems and choosing suitable strategies. As you might expect, younger children sometimes misjudge the objectives of a memory task, which causes them to choose an inappropriate strategy. For example, young children may believe that they are supposed to remember a textbook passage verbatim whereas they really only need to remember its gist. Or, they may understand the memory task, but not pick the best strategy. For example, to remember the gist of a textbook paragraph, a younger child might re-hearse it (a bad choice) while an older child would outline it (a good choice). Children gradually become more skilled at identifying task goals and select-ing appropriate strategies, but even high-school students do not always use effective learning strategies when they should (Lovett & Pillow, 1996; Slate, Jones, & Dawson, 1993).

After children choose a memory strategy, they need to monitor its ef-fectiveness. That is, they need to decide if the strategy is working. If it's not, they need to begin anew—reanalyzing the memory task to select a better ap-proach. If the strategy is working, they should determine the portion of the material that they have not yet mastered and concentrate their efforts there.

Monitoring improves gradually with age. For example, elementary-school children can accurately identify which material they have not yet learned, but they do not consistently focus their study efforts on this material (Kail, 1990).

The diagram summarizes the sequence of steps in monitoring. Perhaps this di-agram looks familiar? It should. Analyzing, strategizing, and monitoring are the key elements of productive studying. Study goals may change when you move from this book to your math text to a novel that you are reading for English, but the basic se-quence still holds. Studying should always begin with a clear understanding of what goal you are trying to achieve, because this sets the stage for all the events that follow. Too often, students just read a text, without any clear idea of what they should be getting out of the material. Always plan a study session with a well-defined goal, such as "Become familiar with the basic contents of Module 7.2 in my child development book." With this goal, you would start by carefully reading the outline, learning objectives, and vignette that begin the mod-ule. Then, skim the module, paying close attention to headings, summary boxes, and topic sentences of para-graphs. Now—before even reading the module—write an outline of its main topics. If you can't, then you need to skim again and try writing—you don't yet understand the overall structure of the module. If you can write an outline, then you know you are familiar with the basic contents of the chapter, and you're ready to go on to reading the module carefully to master its details.

know 5 steps to becoming an efficient studying person.

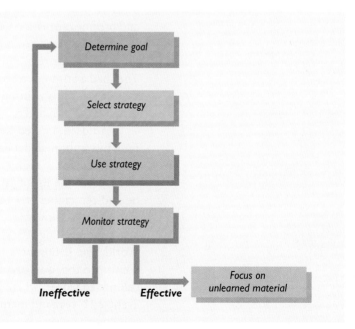

Skilled use of strategies is one aspect of effective remembering; as you'll see in the next few pages, knowledge is also an aid to memory.

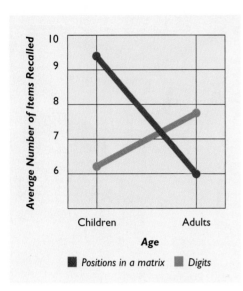

Average Number of Items Recalled

10
9
8
7
6

Children   Adults

Age

■ Positions in a matrix ■ Digits

KNOWLEDGE AND MEMORY

Let's start our examination of how knowledge influences memory by looking at a study by Michelene Chi (1978), who asked 10-year-olds and adults to remember sequences of numbers and positions of objects. In the graph, you can see that adults remembered more numbers than children did. However, when asked to remember the positions of objects in a matrix, 10-year-olds' recall was much better than adults'. What was responsible for this unusual reversal of the expected age difference? Actually, the objects were chess pieces on a chessboard, and the children were skilled chess players but the adults were novices. The positions of the pieces were taken from actual games, so they were familiar configurations for the child chess players. For the adults, who lacked knowledge of chess, the patterns seemed arbitrary. But the children had the knowledge to organize and give meaning to the patterns, so they could recognize and then recall the whole configuration instead of many isolated pieces. It was as if the adults were seeing this meaningless pattern

n n c c b a s b c c b n

while the children were seeing this

n b c   c b s   a b c   c n n.

The link between knowledge and memory is also illustrated in the "Real Children" feature.

Real Children: KEITH VISITS THE AIR FORCE MUSEUM

A few years ago, I went with a troop of Boy Scouts to visit the U.S. Air Force Museum in Dayton, Ohio. On the drive home, I asked James, a 12-year-old who likes computers and basketball but not airplanes, what he had seen in the museum. "Uh, lotsa planes. Some jets and prop jobs. Oh, and some rockets, too," was his reply. I posed the same question to Keith, another 12-year-old, whose father is a pilot and aeronautical engineer and who lives and breathes airplanes. Keith began, "This was so incredibly cool. I started in the Air Power Gallery and saw a Lightning, a Mustang, a Thunderbolt, a Mitchell, a Liberator, a Flying Fortress, and a Super Fort. Then we went to the Modern Flight hangar. They had a Stratojet, a Stratofort, and a Hustler. There was a Sabre and a Super Sabre there, too." Keith went on like this for another 5 minutes. When he was done, I estimated that Keith had remembered the names of 40 to 50 airplanes.

Amused, I asked Keith to try to remember the following words: table, green, rain, bus, spoon, dad, coal, doll, salt, doctor, hill, tennis, shirt, piano, nickel, robin. He paused for a moment, then began to remember words. He finished with 6 words from the list of 16. How could Keith recall so few words from my list when he had remembered 7 or 8 times that many planes? The key is Keith's extensive aeronautical knowledge, which allowed him to organize his recall of planes. He began by recalling World War II fighters (Lightning, Mustang, Thunderbolt), then World War II bombers (Mitchell, Liberator, Flying Fortress, Super Fortress). He continued this way, organizing his recall by category. However, when asked to recall my 16 words, where his knowledge of airplanes was useless, Keith was just an average 12-year-old memory-wise. For Keith, as for Chi's chess experts, knowledge is memory power. ■

Usually, of course, the knowledge that allows a child to organize information and give it meaning increases gradually with age. Psychologists often depict knowledge as a network like this one, depicting part of a 13-year-old's knowledge of animals. The entries in the network are linked by different types of associations. Some of the links denote membership in categories (dalmatian *is a* dog), and others denote properties (elephant *has a* trunk). **Still others denote a *script*, a memory structure used to describe the sequence in which events occur.** For example, the list of events in walking the dog is a script.

A network diagram like this for a younger child would have fewer entries and fewer and weaker connecting links. Consequently, the youngster could not organize information as extensively, which would make remembering more difficult than for an older child. Nevertheless, the knowledge that young children have *is* organized, and this turns out to be a powerful asset. In the case of events that fit scripts, for example, they needn't try to remember each individual activity; instead, they simply remember the script. When the preschooler in the photo wants to tell his dad about baking cookies, he can simply retrieve the "baking cookies" script and use it to organize his recall of the different events.

Source: Kail, 1990

Though knowledge can improve memory, it can also distort memory. If a specific experience does not correspond to children's knowledge, the experience is likely to be forgotten or distorted so that it conforms to the child's knowledge. For example, told a story about a female helicopter pilot, many youngsters will remember the pilot as a man because their network specifies that pilots are men (Levy & Boston, 1994).

Scripts, too, can distort memory because children cannot distinguish what they experienced from what is specified in the script. For example, the boy baking cookies may remember greasing the cookie sheet simply because this is part of the baking cookie script, not because he actually did the greasing (Hudson, 1988). Of course, an inaccurate memory for greasing a cookie sheet usually has relatively minor consequences. However, memory distortions can be pivotal when children are asked to testify in court.

Eyewitness Testimony. Remember Cheryl, the 4-year-old in the module-opening vignette who claimed that a neighbor had touched her "private parts"? If Cheryl's comments lead to a police investigation, Cheryl's testimony will be critical. But can her recall of events be trusted? This question is difficult to answer. In legal proceedings, children are often interviewed repeatedly, sometimes as many as 10 to 15 times. Over the course of repeated questioning, they may confuse what actually happened with what others suggest may have happened. When, as in the situation in the

photo, the questioner is an adult in a position of authority, children often believe that what is suggested by the adult actually happened (Lampinen & Smith, 1995). As you'll see in the "Focus on Research" feature, preschoolers are particularly prone to confusion of this sort (Ceci & Bruck, 1983).

Focus on Research: **DO STEREOTYPES AND SUGGESTIONS INFLUENCE PRESCHOOLERS' REPORTS?**

Who were the investigators and what was the aim of the study? During legal proceedings, children are often interviewed repeatedly. In the process, interviewers sometimes suggest that certain events took place. Cheryl might be asked, "When Mr. Johnson touched your private parts, was anyone else around?"—a question implying that Mr. Johnson definitely touched Cheryl. Furthermore, interviewers may suggest to children that the accused is a "bad person," which may make suggestions of abuse more plausible to children. Michelle D. Leichtman and Stephen J. Ceci (1995) wanted to know if repeated questioning and hints about an adult's "nature" would influence preschool children's recall of events.

How did the investigators measure the topic of interest? Leichtman and Ceci had a man named Sam Stone briefly visit classes of 3- and 4-year-olds and 5- and 6-year-olds at a day-care center. During his visit, Sam greeted the teacher, who introduced him to the class. Sam mentioned that the story being read by the teacher was one of his favorites, then waved goodbye and left the room. Leichtman and Ceci created four different conditions, shown in the diagram, that differed in what children were told before and after Sam's visit. Children in the *control* condition were interviewed once a week for 4 weeks. In these interviews, youngsters were simply asked to describe Sam's visit.

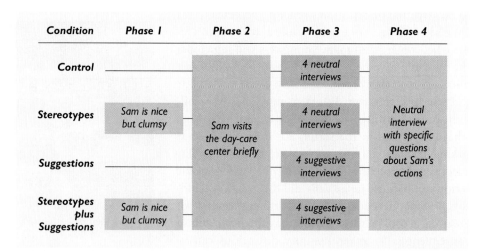

Condition	Phase 1	Phase 2	Phase 3	Phase 4
Control		Sam visits the day-care center briefly	4 neutral interviews	Neutral interview with specific questions about Sam's actions
Stereotypes	Sam is nice but clumsy		4 neutral interviews	
Suggestions			4 suggestive interviews	
Stereotypes plus Suggestions	Sam is nice but clumsy		4 suggestive interviews	

The *stereotype* condition differed from the control condition in one way: Three times prior to Sam's visit, teachers described Sam as a nice but clumsy man, thereby implying that children should expect Sam to be clumsy. The *suggestions* condition also differed from the control condition: During each of the four weekly interviews that followed Sam's visit, the interviewer made misleading suggestions that Sam had ripped a book and soiled a teddy bear, such as "Remember when Sam Stone ripped the book? Did he rip it on purpose or by accident?" (p. 577). Of course, he had done neither. In the fourth condition, *stereotypes plus suggestions,* teachers told children about Sam's clumsiness before the visit and interviewers made misleading suggestions afterward.

Finally, 10 weeks after Sam had visited the classroom, a different interviewer, one not present during Sam's visit or the previous interviews, asked children several questions about what had happened when Sam visited, including whether Sam had ripped a book or soiled a teddy bear.

Who were the children in the study? A total of 176 preschool children participated. Half were 3- and 4-year-olds and half were 5- and 6-year-olds.

What was the design of the study? This study was experimental. There were three independent variables: (a) the age of the child, (b) whether the child was given information before Sam's visit that he was clumsy, and (c) whether the child received misleading suggestions after Sam's visit. The dependent variable was the child's answer to questions corresponding to the interviewers' misleading suggestions in the suggestions conditions. That is, Leichtman and Ceci counted the percentage of time that children said they had actually seen Sam rip a book or soil the teddy bear, events that never happened. The study was also cross-sectional because it included a group of younger children (3- and 4-year-olds) and a group of older children (5- and 6-year-olds).

Were there ethical concerns with the study? No. Sam's visit, the teachers' comments about Sam beforehand, and the interviews afterward posed no special risks to children.

What were the results? Children's answers to the misleading questions are shown in the graph, separately for the four different conditions. For simplicity, I've shown only the data for 3- and 4-year-olds. The data for 5- and 6-year-olds were similar but the effects were smaller. (That is, the older children were less suggestible than the younger children.) Almost no children in the control condition claimed to have seen Sam rip the book or soil the bear. However, some children in the stereotyped condition claimed to have seen Sam rip a book or soil the bear, and more than one-third of the children in the suggestions condition claimed he did one or the other. When stereotypes and suggestions were combined, almost half the children said that they had seen events that never took place. Although the 5- and 6-year-olds described events much more accurately, even 15 percent of these youngsters claimed to have seen Sam rip a book or soil the bear.

What did the investigators conclude? Leichtman and Ceci believe that whether preschoolers are suggestible depends entirely upon the way in which their memory for events is probed. The results from their control condition suggest that, without stereotypes and suggestions, preschoolers are unlikely to report events that never happened. However, when adults suggest that a person is likely to behave in a particular way and later imply that some events actually did happen, many preschoolers will go along. From their results, since Cheryl's report was spontaneous, not elicited by repeated questions, it is probably bonafide.

Unless misled by others, preschoolers rarely "recall" events that didn't happen.

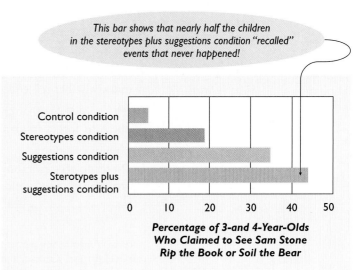

This bar shows that nearly half the children in the stereotypes plus suggestions condition "recalled" events that never happened!

Percentage of 3-and 4-Year-Olds Who Claimed to See Sam Stone Rip the Book or Soil the Bear

But, you say, surely it must be possible to tell when a young child is describing events that never happened? In fact, law-enforcement officials and child-protection workers *believe* that they can usually tell if children are telling the truth (Brigham & Spier, 1992). But research points to a different conclusion. Later in their study, Leichtman and Ceci (1995) asked experts to watch videotapes of preschoolers who were telling the truth as well as other preschoolers who were describing events that had not happened, such as Sam's ripping the book. Law-enforcement officials, caseworkers, and developmental psychologists could *not* distinguish the truthful children from the fabricators.

So what conclusions can we finally draw about preschoolers on the witness stand? If Cheryl's parents press charges against Mr. Johnson, can Cheryl's testimony be trusted? Preschoolers *can* provide reliable testimony, but many commonly used legal procedures can undermine their credibility. Here are several guidelines for improving the reliability of child witnesses:

- Warn children that interviewers may sometimes try to trick them or suggest things that didn't happen.

- Interviewers' questions should evaluate alternative explanations of what happened and who was involved.

- Children should not be questioned repeatedly on a single issue.

Following these guidelines will foster the conditions under which preschoolers (and older children, too) are more likely to provide accurate testimony.

Check Your Learning

1. Four-month-old Tanya has forgotten that kicking moves a mobile. To remind her of the link between kicking and the mobile's movement, we could _____.

2. Children and adolescents often select a memory strategy after they _____.

3. The term _____ refers to periodic evaluation of a strategy to determine whether it is effective.

4. The knowledge that children acquire can distort their recall, either by causing them to forget information that does not conform to their knowledge or by _____.

5. Preschoolers' testimony is more likely to be reliable if interviewers test alternate hypotheses and avoid repeated questioning, and if we warn children that _____.

Answers: (1) show her a moving mobile, (2) determine the goal of a memory task, (3) monitoring, (4) causing them to recall events that are part of a script but did not actually take place, (5) interviewers may try to trick them

ACADEMIC SKILLS

Learning Objectives

- **What are the components of skilled reading?**
- **When and how do children first discriminate quantity?**
- **How do children count, add, and subtract?**
- **Do American children learn math as well as children from other countries?**

When Harriett, a bubbly 3-year-old, is asked how old she'll be on her next birthday, she proudly says, "Four!" while holding up five fingers. If Harriett is asked to count four objects—whether they're candies, toys, or socks—she almost always

MODULE
7.3
Academic Skills

├─ *Reading*

└─ *Knowing and Using Numbers*

says, "1, 2, 6, 7 . . . SEVEN!" Harriett's older brothers find all of this very funny, but her mother thinks that, the obvious mistakes notwithstanding, Harriett's behavior shows that she knows a lot about numbers and counting. But what, exactly, does Harriett understand? That question has her mother stumped!

According to information-processing psychologists, cognitive development consists of the acquisition of mental software that is specific to particular domains. Some of the mental software that children must acquire for success in school is in the domains of reading and quantitative skill. Information-processing psychologists have studied these domains extensively, as you'll see in this module. We'll start with reading, then study number, where you'll learn why Harriett counts as she does.

READING

Try reading the following sentence:

Sumisu-san wa nawa o naifu de kirimashita.

You probably didn't make much headway, did you? (Unless you know Japanese.) Now try this one:

Snore secretary green plastic sleep trucks.

These are English words and you probably read them quite easily, but did you get anything more out of this sentence than the one in Japanese? These examples show two important processes involved in skilled reading. ***Word recognition* is the process of identifying a unique pattern of letters.** Unless you know Japanese, your word recognition was not successful in the first sentence. You did not know that *nawa* means rope or that *kirimashita* is the past tense of the English verb *cut*. Furthermore, because you could not recognize individual words, you had no idea of the meaning of this sentence. ***Comprehension* is the process of extracting meaning from a sequence of words.** In the second sentence, your word recognition was perfect, but comprehension was still impossible because the words were presented in a random sequence. These examples remind us just how difficult learning to read can be.

In the next few pages, we'll look at some of the skills that children must acquire if they are to learn to read and to read well. We'll start with prereading skills, then move to word recognition and comprehension.

Prereading Skills. English words are made up of individual letters, so children need to know their letters before they can learn to read. Consequently, it's not surprising that kindergarten children who know most of their letters tend to learn to read more easily than their peers who don't know their letters (Stevenson et al., 1976).

Prereading skills include knowing letters and the sounds they make.

Letters have distinctive sounds and readers need to be able to hear these different sounds, a skill known as *phonological awareness*. Children who can readily distinguish these sounds learn to read more readily than children who do not. For example, Wagner, Torgesen, and Rashotte (1994) measured kindergarten children's phonological awareness in a number of ways. In one task, the experimenter presented four words—*fun, pin, bun, gun*—and asked the child to pick the word that didn't rhyme with the others. In another task, children were asked to say the first, last, or middle sound of a word: "What's the first sound in *cat?*" After these children entered first grade, the experimenters measured their ability to read individual words. The investigators found that the correlation between children's performance on phonological awareness tasks in kindergarten and their reading score in first grade was .82. That is, kindergarten children who were aware of letter sounds tended to be skilled readers in first grade whereas kindergarten children who were unaware of letter sounds tended to be unskilled readers in first grade. The "Making Children's Lives Better" feature describes one easy way adults can help children to learn about word sounds.

Making Children's Lives Better: RHYME IS SUBLIME BECAUSE SOUNDS ABOUNDS

The Cat in the Hat and *Green Eggs and Ham* are two books in the famous Dr. Seuss series. You probably know these stories for their zany plots and extensive use of rhyme. When parents frequently read rhymes—not just Dr. Seuss, but also Mother Goose and other nursery rhymes—their children become more aware of word sounds. Passages like this draw children's attention to the different sounds that make up words:

> *I do not like them in a house. I do not like them with a mouse. I do not like them here or there. I do not like them anywhere. I do not like green eggs and ham. I do not like them, Sam-I-am (Geisel, 1960, p. 20).*

The more parents read rhymes to their children, the greater their children's phonological awareness, which makes learning to read much easier (Bradley & Bryant, 1983; Goswami & Bryant, 1990).

So, the message is clear. Read to children—the more, the better. As the photo shows, children love it when adults read to them—and learning more about word sounds is icing on the cake! ▣

Recognizing Words. The first step in actual reading is identifying individual words. One way to do this is to say the sounds associated with each letter, and then blend the sounds to produce a recognizable word. Such "sounding out" is a common technique among beginning readers. Older children sometimes sound out words, but only when they are unfamiliar, which points to another common way of recognizing words. Words are recognized through direct retrieval from long-term memory: As the individual letters in a word are identified, long-term memory is searched to see if there is a matching sequence of letters. Knowing that the letters are, in sequence, *c-a-t*, long-term memory is searched for a match and the child recognizes the word as *cat*.

Readers recognize words by sounding them out or by retrieving them directly from long-term memory.

So far, word recognition may seem like a one-way street in which readers first recognize letters and then recognize words. In reality, we know that information flows both ways, as described in the cognitive approach to perception (Module 5.1). Readers constantly use context to help them recognize letters and words. For example, readers typically recognize *t* faster in *cast* than in *asct*. That is, readers recognize letters faster when they appear in words than in nonwords. How do the nearby letters in *cast* help readers to recognize the *t*? As children recognize the first letters in the word as *c*, *a*, and *s*, the possibilities for the last letter become more limited. Because English only includes four 4-letter words that start with *cas* (well, five if you include *Cass*), the last letter can only be *e*, *h*, *k*, or *t*. In contrast, there are no four-letter words (in English) that begin with *acs,* so all 26 letters must be checked, which takes more time than just checking four letters. In this way, a reader's knowledge of words simplifies the task of recognizing letters, which, in turn makes it easier to recognize words (Rumelhart & McClelland, 1981).

Readers also use the sentence context to speed word recognition. Read these two sentences:

> *The last word in this sentence is cat.*
> *The little girl's pet dog chased the cat.*

Most readers recognize *cat* more rapidly in the second sentence. The reason is that the first seven words put severe limits on the last word: It must be something "chaseable," and because the "chaser" is a *dog, cat* is a very likely candidate. In contrast, the first seven words in the first sentence put no limits on the last word; virtually any word could end the sentence. Beginning and skilled readers both use sentence context like this to help them recognize words (Kim & Goetz, 1994).

As you can imagine, most beginning readers, like the child in the photo, rely more heavily on "sounding out" because they know fewer words. As they gain more reading experience, they are more likely to be able to retrieve a word directly from long-term memory. You might be tempted to summarize this as, "Beginning readers sound out and more advanced readers retrieve directly." Don't! From their very first efforts to read, most children use direct retrieval for a few words. From that point on, the general strategy is to try retrieval first and, if that fails, then children sound out the word or ask a more skilled reader for help (Siegler, 1986). For example, when my daughter Laura was just beginning to read, she knew *the, Laura,* and several one-syllable words that ended in *at,* such as *bat, cat,* and *fat.* Shown a sentence like

> *Laura saw the fat cat run,*

she would say, "Laura s-s-s . . ah-h . . wuh . . . saw the fat cat er-r-r . . uh-h-h . . n-n-n . . . run." Familiar words were retrieved rapidly but the unfamiliar ones were slowly sounded out. With more experience, fewer words are sounded out and more are retrieved (Siegler, 1986), but even skilled readers sometimes fall back on sounding out when they confront unfamiliar words. Try reading

> *The rock star rode to the concert in a palanquin.*

You may well need to do some sounding out, then consult a dictionary (or look in the answers prior to "Check Your Learning") for the correct meaning.

Comprehension. Once individual words are recognized, reading begins to have a lot in common with understanding speech. That is, the means by which people understand a sequence of words is much the same whether the source of words is printed text or speech or, for that matter, Braille or sign language (Crowder, 1982). **In all of these cases, children derive meaning by combining words to form *propositions* or ideas and then combining propositions.** For example, as you read

> *The tall boy rode his bike,*

you spontaneously derive a number of propositions, including "There is a boy," "The boy is tall," and "The boy was riding." If this sentence were part of a larger body of text, you would derive propositions for each sentence, then link the propositions together to derive meaning for the passage as a whole (Perfetti & Curtis, 1986).

As children get older and more experienced, they are better able to comprehend what they read. Several factors contribute to this improved comprehension (Siegler, 1991):

- *Working memory capacity increases, which means that older children can store more of a sentence in memory as they try to identify the propositions it contains* (Engle, Carullo, & Collins, 1991; Siegel, 1994): This extra capacity is handy when readers move from sentences like, "Kevin hit the ball" to "In the bottom of the ninth, with the bases loaded and the Cardinals down 7–4, Kevin put a line drive into the left-field bleachers, his fourth home run of the Series."

- *Children acquire more general knowledge of their physical, social, and psychological worlds, which allows them to understand more of what they read* (Bisanz et al., 1992): For example, even if a 6-year-old could recognize all of the words in the longer sentence about Kevin's home run, the child would not fully comprehend the meaning of the passage because he or she lacks the necessary knowledge of baseball.

- *With experience, children better monitor their comprehension:* When readers don't grasp the meaning of a passage—because it is difficult or confusing—they read it again (Baker & Brown, 1984). Try this sentence (adapted from Carpenter & Daneman, 1981): "The Midwest State Fishing Contest would draw fishermen from all around the region, including some of the best bass guitarists in Michigan." When you first encountered "bass guitarists" you probably interpreted "bass" as a fish. This didn't make much sense, so you reread the phrase to determine that "bass" refers to a type of guitar. Older readers are better able to realize that their understanding is not complete and take corrective action.

- *With experience, children use more appropriate reading strategies:* The goal of reading and the nature of the text dictate how you read. When reading a novel, for example, do you often skip sentences (or perhaps paragraphs or entire pages) to get to "the good parts"? This approach makes sense for pleasure reading but not for reading textbooks or recipes or how-to manuals. Reading a textbook requires attention to both the overall organization and the relation of details to that organization. Older, more experienced readers are better able to select a reading strategy that suits the material being read.

> *Greater working memory capacity, greater world knowledge, greater monitoring skill, and use of more appropriate reading strategies allow more experienced readers to gain more meaning from what they read.*

Greater working memory capacity, greater world knowledge, greater monitoring skill, and use of more appropriate reading strategies are all part of the information-processing explanation of how older and more experienced readers get more meaning from what they read. In the last part of this module, you'll see how information-processing psychologists explain children's developing understanding of numbers.

KNOWING AND USING NUMBERS

The origins of basic number skills can be traced to infancy, long before babies have learned names of numbers. Many babies experience daily variation in quantity. They play with two blocks and see that another baby has three; they watch as a father sorts laundry and finds two black socks but only one blue sock, and they eat one hot dog for lunch while an older brother eats three.

From these experiences, babies apparently come to appreciate that quantity or amount is one of the ways in which objects in the world can differ. This conclusion is based on research in which babies are shown pictures like these. The actual objects in the pictures differ, as do their size, color, and position in the picture. The only common element is that each picture always depicts two of something. When the first of these pictures is shown, an infant will look at it for several seconds. After several have been shown, an infant habituates (Module 5.3); he or she will glance at the picture briefly, then look away, as if saying, "Enough of these pictures of two things—let's

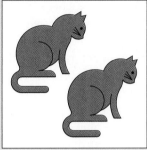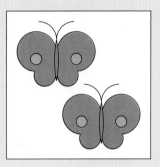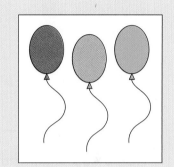

move on to something else." And, in fact, if a picture of a single object or of three objects is then shown, infants will again look for several seconds, their interest apparently renewed. Because the only systematic change is the number of objects depicted in the picture, this result tells us that babies can distinguish stimuli on the basis of number. Typically, 5-month-olds can distinguish two objects from three and, less often, three objects from four (Canfield & Smith, 1996; Wynn, 1996).

How do infants distinguish differences in quantity? Older children might count, but, of course, infants have not yet learned names of numbers. Instead, the process is probably more perceptual in nature. As we saw in Module 5.2, the infant's perceptual system is sensitive to characteristics such as shape and color (Bornstein, 1981). Quantity may well be another characteristic of stimuli to which infants are sensitive. That is, just as colors (reds, blues) and shapes (triangles, squares) are basic perceptual properties, small quantities ("twoness" and "threeness") may be perceptually obvious (Strauss & Curtis, 1984).

Names of numbers are not among most babies' first words, but by 2 years, youngsters know some number words and they have begun to count. Usually, their counting is full of mistakes. In Harriett's counting sequence that was described in the vignette—"1, 2, 6, 7"—she skips 3, 4, and 5. But if we ignore her mistakes momentarily, the counting sequence reveals that she does understand a great deal.

Gelman and Meck (1986) have charted preschoolers' understanding of counting. They simply placed several objects in front of a child and asked, "How many?" By analyzing children's answers to many of these questions, Gelman and Meck discovered that by age 3 most children have mastered three basic principles of counting, at least when it comes to counting up to five objects.

■ ***One-to-one principle*: There must be one and only one number name for each object that is counted.** A child who counts three objects as "1, 2, a" understands this principle because the number of number words matches the number of objects to be counted.

- *Stable-order principle:* **Number names must be counted in the same order.** A child who counts in the same sequence—for example, consistently counting four objects as "1, 2, 4, 5"—shows understanding of this principle.

- *Cardinality principle:* **The last number name differs from the previous ones in a counting sequence by denoting the number of objects.** Typically, 3-year-olds reveal their understanding of this principle by repeating the last number name, often with emphasis: "1, 2, 4, 8 . . . EIGHT!"

During the preschool years, children master these basic principles and apply them to ever larger sets of objects. By age 5, most youngsters apply these counting principles to as many as nine objects. Of course, children's understanding of these principles does not mean that they always count accurately. To the contrary, children can apply all these principles consistently while counting incorrectly. They must master the conventional sequence of the number names and the counting principles to learn to count accurately. (To see if you understand the counting principles, go back to Harriett's counting in the vignette and decide which principles she has mastered; my answer is given before "Check Your Learning" on page 190.)

By 3 years, children begin to apply the one-to-one, stable-order, and cardinality principles when counting small sets of objects.

Learning the number names beyond 9 is easier because the counting words can be generated based on rules for combining decade number names (20, 30, 40) with unit names (1, 2, 3, 4). And later, similar rules are used for hundreds, thousands, and so on. By 4 years of age, most youngsters know the numbers to 20 and some can count to 99. Usually, they stop counting at a number ending in 9 (29, 59), apparently because they don't know the next decade name (Siegler & Robinson, 1982).

Learning to count beyond 10 is more complicated in English than in other languages. For example, *eleven,* and *twelve* are completely irregular names, following no rules. Also, the remaining "teen" number names differ from the 20s, 30s, and the rest in that the decade number name comes after the unit (*thirteen,* four-*teen*) rather than before (*twenty*-three, *thirty*-four). Also, some decade names only loosely correspond to the unit names on which they are based: *twenty, thirty,* and *fifty* resemble *two, three,* and *five* but are not the same. In contrast, the Chinese, Japanese, and Korean number systems are almost perfectly regular. *Eleven* and *twelve* are expressed as *ten-one* and *ten-two.* There are no special names for the decades: *Two-ten* and *two-ten-one* are names for 20 and 21. These simplified number names help explain why youngsters growing up in Asian countries count more accurately than U.S. preschool children of the same age (Miller et al., 1995). Furthermore, the direct correspondence between the number names and the base-ten system makes it easier for Asian youngsters to learn base-ten concepts (Miura et al., 1988).

Adding and Subtracting. Counting is the starting point for children as they learn to add. For instance, suppose you ask a preschooler to solve the following problem: "John had four oranges. Then Mary gave him two more oranges. How many oranges does John have now?" Like the child in the photo, many 6-year-old children solve the problem by counting. They first count out four fingers on one hand, then count out two more on the other. Finally, they count all six fingers on both hands. To subtract, they do the same procedure in reverse (Siegler & Jenkins, 1989; Siegler & Shrager, 1984).

Youngsters soon abandon this approach for a slightly more efficient method. Instead of counting the fingers on the first hand, they simultane-

ously extend the number of fingers on the first hand corresponding to the larger of the two numbers to be added. Next, they count out the smaller number, with fingers on the second hand. Finally, they count all of the fingers to determine the sum (Groen & Resnick, 1977).

After children begin to receive formal arithmetic instruction in first grade, addition problems are less often solved by counting aloud or by counting fingers. Instead, children add and subtract by counting mentally. That is, children act as if they are counting silently, beginning with the larger number, and adding on. By 8 or 9 years of age, children have learned the addition tables so well that sums of the single-digit integers (from 0 to 9) are facts that are simply retrieved from memory (Ashcraft, 1982).

These counting strategies do not occur in a rigid developmental sequence. Individual children use many or all of these strategies, depending upon the problem. Children usually begin by trying to retrieve an answer from memory. If they are not reasonably confident that the retrieved answer is correct, then they resort to counting aloud or on fingers (Siegler, 1988). Retrieval is most likely for problems with small addends (e.g., 1 + 2, 2 + 4) because these problems are presented frequently in textbooks and by teachers. Consequently, the sum is highly associated with the problem, which makes the child confident that the retrieved answer is correct. In contrast, problems with larger addends, such as 9 + 8, are presented less often. The result is a weaker link between the addends and the sum and, consequently, a greater chance that children will need to determine an answer by counting.

Of course, arithmetic skills continue to improve as children move through elementary school. They become more proficient in addition and subtraction, learn multiplication and division, and move on to the more sophisticated mathematical concepts involved in algebra, geometry, trigonometry, and calculus.

Comparing U.S. Students with Students in Other Countries.

Let's return to the issue of cultural differences in mathematical competence. The graph shows math achievement of college-bound high-school seniors in countries worldwide (Salganik et al., 1993). U.S. students don't fare well—they're near the bottom of the list, scoring substantially lower than students from many other countries. We can phrase these results another way: The very best U.S. students perform at the level of average students in countries such as Taiwan and Korea.

Are you skeptical of these findings? Maybe you believe these comparisons are flawed because American high schools educate all students, not just a select few as in some other countries. If you're right, comparisons among elementary-school children should be revealing because elementary schools are not selective. But in fact, the results are virtually the same: American students trail students in other countries. The most comprehensive evidence comes from studies conducted by Stevenson and Lee (1990) of first- and fifth-graders in the United States, Japan, and Taiwan. Their findings, shown in the graph at the top of page 188, are sobering and raise serious concerns about American schools. American students lag behind their peers in Taiwan and Japan, in both math operations and math problem solving.

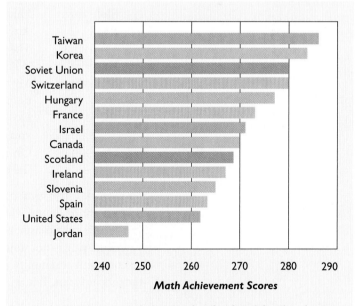

Source: Based on data from Salganik et al., 1993.

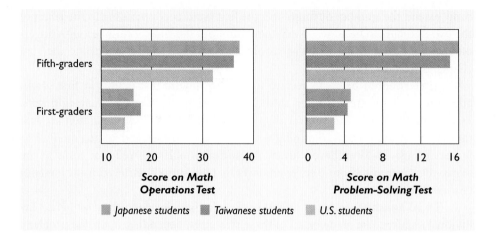

Fifth-graders

First-graders

10   20   30   40
*Score on Math
Operations Test*

0   4   8   12   16
*Score on Math
Problem-Solving Test*

■ *Japanese students*   ■ *Taiwanese students*   ■ *U.S. students*

Why do American students rate so poorly? The "Cultural Influences" feature gives some answers.

Cultural Influences: FIFTH GRADE IN TAIWAN

 Shin-ying is an 11-year-old attending school in Taipei, the largest city in Taiwan. Like most fifth-graders, Shin-ying is in school from 8 A.M. until 4 P.M. daily. Most evenings, she spends 2 to 3 hours doing homework. This academic routine is grueling by U.S. standards, where fifth-graders typically spend 6 to 7 hours in school each day and less than an hour doing homework. I asked Shin-ying what she thought of school and schoolwork. Her answers surprised me.

RK:	Why do you go to school?
Shin-ying:	I like what we study.
RK:	Any other reasons?
Shin-ying:	The things that I learn in school are useful.
RK:	What about homework? Why do you do it?
Shin-ying:	My teacher and my parents think its important. And I like doing it.
RK:	Do you think that you would do nearly as well in school if you didn't work so hard?
Shin-ying:	Oh no. The best students are always the ones who work the hardest.

Schoolwork is the focal point of Shin-ying's life. Although many American schoolchildren are unhappy when schoolwork intrudes on time for play and television, Shin-ying is enthusiastic about school and school-related activities.

Shin-ying is not unusual among Chinese elementary-school students. Many of her comments exemplify Stevenson and Lee's findings (1990) in a study comparing students in Japan, Taiwan, and the United States:

■ *Time in school and how it is used.* By fifth grade, students in Japan and Taiwan spend 50 percent more time than American students in school, and more of this time is devoted to academic activities than in the U.S.

■ *Time spent in homework and attitudes towards it.* Students in Taiwan and Japan spend more time on homework and value homework more than American students.

■ *Parents' attitudes.* American parents are more often satisfied with their children's performance in school; in contrast, Japanese and Taiwanese parents set much higher standards for their children.

■ *Parents' beliefs about effort and ability.* Japanese and Taiwanese parents believe more strongly than American parents that effort, not native ability, is the key factor in school success.

Thus, students in Japan and Taiwan excel because they spend more time both in and out of school on academic tasks. Furthermore, their parents (and teachers) set loftier scholastic goals and believe that students can attain these goals with hard work. Japanese classrooms even post a motto describing ideal students—*gambaru kodomo*—they who strive the hardest. Parents underscore the importance of schoolwork in many ways to their children. For example, even though homes and apartments in Japan and China are very small by U.S. standards, Asian youngsters, like the child in the photo, typically have a desk in a quiet area where they can study undisturbed (Stevenson & Lee, 1990). For Japanese and Taiwanese teachers and parents, academic excellence is paramount and it shows in their children's success. ■

What can Americans learn from Japanese and Taiwanese educational systems? From their experiences with Asian students, teachers, and schools, Stevenson and Stigler (1992) suggest several ways American schools could be improved:

■ Give teachers more free time to prepare lessons and correct students' work.

■ Improve teachers' training by allowing them to work closely with older, more experienced teachers.

■ Organize instruction around sound principles of learning such as providing multiple examples of concepts and giving students adequate opportunities to practice newly acquired skills.

■ Set higher standards for children, who need to spend more time and effort in school-related activities in order to achieve those standards.

By changing teaching practices and attitudes toward achievement, we can begin to reduce the gap between American students and students in other industrialized countries, particularly Asian countries. Ignoring the problem will mean an increasingly undereducated work force and citizenry in a more complex world—an alarming prospect for the 21st century.

Definition on page 183: A *palanquin* is a covered couch resting on two horizontal poles that are carried by four people, one at each end of the poles.

American schools could be improved by giving teachers better training and more time to prepare lessons, basing instruction on sound principles of learning, and setting higher standards for education.

Response to question about Harriett's counting on page 186: Since Harriett uses four number names to count four objects ("1, 2, 6, 7 . . . SEVEN!"), we can credit her with understanding the one-to-one principle. The four number names are always used in the same order, so we can credit her with the stable-order principle. And, finally, she repeats the last number name with emphasis, so we can credit her with the cardinality principle.

Check Your Learning

1. Important prereading skills include knowing letters and _____.

2. Beginning readers typically recognize words by sounding them out; with greater experience, readers are more likely able to _____.

3. Older and more experienced readers understand more of what they read because the capacity of working memory increases, they have more general knowledge of the world, _____, and they are more likely to use appropriate reading strategies.

4. By 3 years of age, most children have mastered the _____, stable-order, and cardinality principles of counting.

5. The simplest way of solving addition problems is to _____; the most advanced way is to retrieve sums from long-term memory.

6. Compared to students in U.S. elementary schools, students in Japan and Taiwan spend more time in school, and a greater proportion of that time is _____.

Answers: (1) sounds associated with each letter, (2) retrieve words from long-term memory, (3) they monitor their comprehension more effectively, (4) one-to-one, (5) count on one's fingers, (6) devoted to academic activities

INFORMATION-PROCESSING APPROACHES TO COGNITIVE DEVELOPMENT IN PERSPECTIVE

The information-processing approach to cognitive development is derived from computer science. We saw, in Module 7.1, that information processing distinguishes mental hardware from mental software. Furthermore, information-processing psychologists propose that cognitive development can be linked to changes in strategies, working memory, automatic processing, and processing speed. In Module 7.2, we looked at the development of memory. Memory is evident in infancy and improves rapidly as children begin to use memory strategies and acquire more knowledge of the world. In Module 7.3, we examined information processing accounts of reading and saw the skills involved in reading individual words and comprehending text. We also outlined developmental change in quantitative skill, which begins with infants' awareness of number and rapidly leads to counting and arithmetic operations.

This chapter highlights the theme that *children help determine their own development:* Japanese and Chinese elementary-school children typically like homework (attitudes fostered by their parents), and this makes them quite willing to do homework for 2 or 3 hours nightly. This, in turn, contributes to their high levels of scholastic achievement. American schoolchildren usually abhor homework and do as little of it as possible, which contributes to their relatively lower level of scholastic achievement. Thus, children's attitudes help to determine how they behave, which determines how much they will achieve over the course of childhood and adolescence.

THINKING ABOUT DEVELOPMENT

1. In Module 3.3, you learned that infants with low birth weight often lag behind their peers. Use the information-processing approach to propose some specific ways in which these children's development might be delayed.

2. An "expert" on a talk radio show says, "It's a waste of time to have preschool children testify in court. They can never be trusted because once the seed of abuse is planted their imaginations run wild." Defend or refute this claim.

3. One of the perennial debates in education is whether reading should be taught with phonics (sounding out words) or with whole-word methods (recognizing entire words). Does the research described in Module 7.3 provide evidence that one method rather than the other would be more effective?

SEE FOR YOURSELF

Create several small sets of objects that vary in number. You might have two pennies, three candies, four buttons, five pencils, six erasers, seven paper clips, and so on. Place each set of objects on a paper plate. Then find some preschool children—4- and 5-year-olds would be ideal. Put a plate in front of each child and ask, "How many?" Then watch to see what the child does. If possible, tape record the children's counting, so that you can analyze it later. If this is impossible, try to write down exactly what each child says as he or she counts. Later, go back through your notes and determine if the children follow the counting principles described on pages 185-186. You should see that children, particularly younger ones, more often follow the principles while counting small sets of objects than larger sets. See for yourself!

RESOURCES

For more information about . . .

cultural differences in scholastic achievement, try Harold W. Stevenson and James W. Stigler's *The Learning Gap* (Summit Books, 1992) which describes research comparing schooling in the United States and in Asia

ways to help children learn math (and enjoy it!), contact the National Council of Teachers of Mathematics, 1-800-235-7566

tips and exercises to help develop better study skills for college, visit the Web site of the University Counseling Center of the Virginia Polytechnic Institute and State University, http://www.ucc.vt.edu/stdysk/stdyhlp.html

KEY TERMS

automatic processes *171*	memory strategies *174*	sensory memory *168*
cardinality principle *186*	one-to-one principle *185*	stable-order principle *186*
comprehension *181*	phonological awareness *181*	word recognition *181*
information processing *168*	propositions *183*	working memory *169*
long-term memory *169*	script *177*	

UMMARY

AN INTRODUCTION TO INFORMATION PROCESSING

BASIC FEATURES OF THE INFORMATION-PROCESSING APPROACH

According to the information-processing approach, cognitive development involves changes in mental hardware and mental software. Mental hardware refers to mental processes that are built-in and allow the mind to function, including sensory, working, and long-term memories. Mental software refers to mental programs that allow people to perform specific tasks.

HOW INFORMATION PROCESSING CHANGES WITH DEVELOPMENT

Information-processing psychologists believe that cognitive development reflects changes involving more effective strategies, increased capacity of working memory, increased automatic processing, and increased speed of processing.

COMPARING INFORMATION PROCESSING AND PIAGET'S THEORY

Piaget's theory is a single, comprehensive theory whereas information processing represents a general approach encompassing many spe-

cific theories. In addition, Piaget's theory emphasizes qualitative change in development whereas information processing emphasizes quantitative change.

MODULE 7.2:
MEMORY

ORIGINS OF MEMORY

Rovee-Collier's studies of kicking show that infants can remember, forget, and be reminded of events that occurred in the past.

STRATEGIES FOR REMEMBERING

Beginning in the preschool years, children use strategies to help them remember. With age, children use more powerful strategies, such as rehearsal and outlining. Using memory strategies successfully depends, first, upon analyzing the goal of a memory task and, second, upon monitoring the effectiveness of the chosen strategy, skills that are mastered during childhood and adolescence.

KNOWLEDGE AND MEMORY

A child's knowledge of the world can be used to organize information that is to be remembered. When several events occur in a specific order, they are remembered as a single script. Knowledge improves memory for children and adolescents, although older individuals often reap more benefit because they have more knowledge. Knowledge can also distort memory by causing children and adolescents to forget information that does not conform to their knowledge or to remember events that are part of their knowledge but that did not actually take place.

Young children's memory in court cases is often inaccurate because children are questioned repeatedly, which makes it hard for them to distinguish what actually occurred from what adults suggest may have occurred. Children's testimony would be more reliable if interviewers tested alternate hypotheses during their questioning, avoided repeated questioning, and warned children that they may try to trick them.

MODULE 7.3:
ACADEMIC SKILLS

READING

Information-processing psychologists divide reading into a number of component skills. Prereading skills include knowing letters and the sounds associated with them. Word recognition is the process of identifying a word. Beginning readers more often accomplish this by sounding out words; advanced readers more often retrieve a word from long-term memory. Comprehension, the act of extracting meaning from text, improves with age due to several factors: working memory capacity increases, readers gain more world knowledge, and readers are better able to monitor what they read and to match their reading strategies to the goals of the reading task.

KNOWING AND USING NUMBERS

Infants can distinguish quantities, probably by means of basic perceptual processes. Children begin to count by about age 2, and by 3 years, most children have mastered the one-to-one, stable-order, and cardinality principles, at least when counting small sets of objects. Counting is how children first add, but it is replaced by more effective strategies such as retrieving sums directly from memory.

In mathematics, American students lag behind students in most other industrialized nations, chiefly because of cultural differences in the time spent on schoolwork and homework and in parents' attitudes towards school, effort, and ability.

EIGHT

Intelligence and Individual Differences in Cognition

HAVE YOU EVER STOPPED TO THINK HOW MANY STANDARDIZED TESTS YOU'VE TAKEN IN YOUR STUDENT CAREER? YOU PROBABLY TOOK EITHER THE SAT OR THE ACT TO ENTER COLLEGE. BEFORE THAT YOU TOOK COUNTLESS ACHIEVEMENT AND APTITUDE tests during elementary school and high school. Psychological testing is an integral part of American education and has been for most of the 20th century.

Of all standardized tests, none attracts more attention—and generates more controversy—than tests designed to measure intelligence. Intelligence tests have been hailed by some as one of psychology's greatest contributions to society and cursed by others. Intelligence tests and what they measure are the focus of Chapter 8. We'll start, in Module 8.1, by looking at different definitions of intelligence. In Module 8.2, we'll see how intelligence tests work and examine some influences on test scores. Finally, in Module 8.3, we'll look at special children—youngsters whose intelligence sets them apart from their peers.

WHAT IS INTELLIGENCE?

Learning Objectives

- **What is the psychometric view of the nature of intelligence?**
- **How does Gardner's theory of multiple intelligences differ from the psychometric approach?**
- **What are the three components of Sternberg's triarchic theory of intelligence?**

> *Max is 22 years old and is moderately mentally retarded. That is, he performs most tasks at the level of a nonretarded 5- or 6-year-old. For example, he can't do many of Piaget's conservation tasks and he reads very slowly and with much effort. Nevertheless, if Max hears a song on the radio, he can immediately sit down at the piano and play the melody flawlessly, despite having had no musical training. Everyone who sees Max do this is astonished. How can a person who is otherwise so limited intellectually perform such an amazing feat?*

Before you read further, how would you answer the question that is the title of this module? What is *your* definition of intelligence? If you're typical of most Americans, your definition probably includes the ability to reason logically, connect ideas, and solve real problems. You might mention verbal ability, meaning the ability to speak clearly and articulately. You might also mention social competence, referring, for example, to an interest in the world at large and an ability to admit when you make a mistake (Sternberg, 1987).

As you'll see in this module, many of your ideas about intelligence are included in psychological theories of intelligence. We'll begin by considering the oldest theories of intelligence, those associated with the psychometric tradition. Then we'll look at two newer approaches and, along the way, get some insights into Max's uncanny musical skill.

PSYCHOMETRIC THEORIES

Psychometricians are psychologists who specialize in the measurement of psychological characteristics such as intelligence and personality. When psychometricians want to research a particular question, they usually begin by administering a large number of tests to many individuals. Then they look for patterns in performance across the different tests. The basic logic underlying this technique is similar to the logic a jungle hunter uses to decide whether some dark blobs in a river are three separate rotting logs or a single alligator (Cattell, 1965). If the blobs move together, the hunter decides they are part of the same structure, an alligator. If they do not move together, they are three different structures, three logs. Similarly, if changes in performance on one test are accompanied by changes in performance on a second test—that is, they move together—one could assume that the tests are measuring the same attribute or factor.

Suppose, for example, that you believe there is such a thing as general intelligence. That is, you believe that some people are smart regardless of the situation, task, or problem, whereas others are not so smart. According to this view, children's performance should be very consistent across tasks. Smart children should always receive high scores, and the less smart youngsters should always get lower scores. As early as 1904, Charles Spearman reported findings supporting the idea that a general

When psychometricians have examined patterns of performance on intelligence tests, they have found evidence for a general intelligence as well as for specific abilities.

factor for intelligence, or *g,* is responsible for performance on all mental tests. Other researchers, however, have found that intelligence consists of distinct abilities. For example, Thurstone and Thurstone (1941) analyzed performance on a wide range of tasks and identified seven distinct patterns, each reflecting a unique ability: perceptual speed, word comprehension, word fluency, space, number, memory, and induction. Thurstone and Thurstone also acknowledged a general factor that operated in all tasks, but they emphasized that the specific factors were more useful in assessing and understanding intellectual ability.

These conflicting findings have led many psychometric theorists to propose hierarchical theories of intelligence that include both general and specific components. John Carroll (1993), for example, proposed the hierarchical theory with three levels that's shown in the diagram. At the top of the hierarchy is *g,* general intelli-

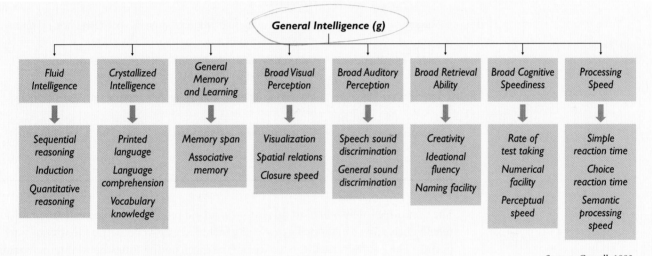

Source: Carroll, 1993.

gence. In the level underneath *g* are eight broad categories of intellectual skill, ranging from fluid intelligence to processing speed. Each of the abilities in the second level is further divided into the skills listed in the third and most specific level. Crystallized intelligence, for example, includes understanding printed language, comprehending language, and knowing vocabulary.

Carroll's hierarchical theory is, in essence, a compromise between the two views of intelligence—general versus distinct abilities. But some critics find it unsatisfactory because it ignores the research and theory on cognitive development described in Chapters 6 and 7. They believe we need to look beyond the psychometric approach to understand intelligence. In the remainder of this module, then, we'll look at two newer theories that have gained a following.

GARDNER'S THEORY OF MULTIPLE INTELLIGENCES

Only recently have developmental psychologists viewed intelligence from the perspective of Piaget's theory and information-processing psychology. These new theories present a much broader theory of intelligence and how it develops. Among the most ambitious is Howard Gardner's (1983, 1993) theory of multiple intelligences. Rather than using test scores as the basis for his theory, Gardner draws on research in child development, studies of brain-damaged persons, and studies of exceptionally talented people to propose the seven distinct intelligences that are shown in the table.

Seven Intelligences in Gardner's Theory of Multiple Intelligences

Type of Intelligence	Definition
Linguistic	Knowing the meaning of words, having the ability to use words to understand new ideas, and using language to convey ideas to others
Logical-mathematical	Understanding relations that can exist among objects, actions, and ideas, as well as the logical or mathematical relations that can be performed on them
Spatial	Perceiving objects accurately and imagining in the "mind's eye" the appearance of an object before and after it has been transformed
Musical	Comprehending and producing sounds varying in pitch, rhythm, and emotional tone
Bodily-kinesthetic	Using one's body in highly differentiated ways, as dancers, craftspeople, and athletes do
Interpersonal	Identifying different feelings, moods, motivations, and intentions in others
Intrapersonal	Understanding one's emotions and knowing one's strengths and weaknesses

Source: Gardner, 1983, 1993

The first three intelligences in this list—linguistic intelligence, logical-mathematical intelligence, and spatial intelligence—are included in psychometric theories of intelligence. The last four intelligences are not: musical, bodily-kinesthetic, interpersonal, and intrapersonal intelligences are unique to Gardner's theory. According to Gardner, a gifted athlete, a talented dancer, and a sensitive, caring child are showing intelligence as is the child who writes well or is skilled at math.

How did Gardner arrive at these seven distinct intelligences? First, each has a unique developmental history. Linguistic intelligence, for example, develops much earlier than the other six. Second, each intelligence is regulated by distinct regions of the brain, as shown in studies of brain-damaged persons. Spatial intelligence, for example, is regulated by particular regions in the brain's right hemisphere. Third, each has special cases of talented individuals. **Musical intelligence is often shown by *savants*, individuals with mental retardation who are extremely talented in one domain.** Max, the 22-year-old in the module-opening vignette, is a savant whose special talent is music. Like Max, Eddie B., the 10-year-old savant in the photo, can play a tune correctly after a single hearing and without ever having had formal musical training (Shuter-Dyson, 1982).

Gardner (1993) argues that his theory has important implications for education. He believes that schools should foster all intelligences, not just the linguistic and logical-mathematical intelligences that have been important traditionally. Teachers should capitalize on the strongest intelligences of individual children. Some students may best understand unfamiliar cultures, for example, by studying their dance, while other students may understand these cultures by studying their music.

Some American schools have enthusiastically embraced Gardner's ideas (Gardner, 1993). Are these schools better? We don't really know because school performance is usually evaluated with tests and there aren't acceptable tests to evaluate progress in all the areas covered by Gardner's theory. At this point, researchers are still evaluating the theory and the educational reforms it has inspired. However, there is no doubt that Gardner's work *has* helped liberate researchers from narrow psychometric-based views of intelligence. A comparably broad, but different view of intelligence comes from another new theory that we'll look at in the next section.

STERNBERG'S TRIARCHIC THEORY

Robert Sternberg's (1977) early work included a theory explaining how adults solve problems on intelligence tests. **He later elaborated this theory into what he called the** *triarchic theory* **because it includes three parts or subtheories** (Sternberg, 1985).

According to the *contextual subtheory,* **intelligent behavior involves skillfully adapting to an environment.** That is, intelligence is always partly defined by the demands of an environment or cultural context. What are intelligent behaviors for children growing up in cities in North America may not be intelligent for children growing up in the Sahara desert, the Australian outback, or on a remote island in the Pacific Ocean. Moreover, what is intelligent behavior at home may not be intelligent behavior in the neighborhood. The "Cultural Influences" feature illustrates how intelligent behavior is always defined by the context.

Cultural Influences: **HOW CULTURE DEFINES WHAT IS INTELLIGENT**

 In Brazil, many elementary-school-age boys like the two in the top photo sell candy and fruit to bus passengers and pedestrians. These children often cannot identify the numbers on paper money, yet they know how to purchase their goods from wholesale stores, make change for customers, and keep track of their sales (Saxe, 1988).

Adolescents who live on Pacific Ocean Islands near New Guinea learn to sail boats like the one in the bottom photo hundreds of miles across open seas to get from one small island to the next. They have no formal training in mathematics, yet they are able to use a complex navigational system based on the positions of stars and estimates of the boat's speed (Hutchins, 1983).

If either the Brazilian vendors or the island navigators were given the tests that measure intelligence in

American students, they would fare poorly. Does this mean they are less intelligent than American children? Of course not. The skills that are important to American conceptions of intelligence and assessed on our intelligence tests are less valued in these other cultures and so are not cultivated in the young. Each culture defines what it means to be intelligent, and the specialized computing skills of vendors and navigators are just as intelligent in their cultural settings as verbal skills are in American culture. ▨

In addition to the contextual subtheory, the triarchic theory includes two other subtheories. **According to the *experiential subtheory,* intelligence is revealed in both novel and familiar tasks.** For novel tasks, intelligence is associated with the ability to apply existing knowledge to a new situation. At the start of a new school year, for example, readily adjusting to new tasks is a sign of intelligence. Bright children learning multiplication readily draw upon relevant math knowledge to grasp what's involved in multiplication.

For familiar tasks, intelligence is associated with the automatic processing that was described in Module 7.1. Completing a task automatically means using few mental resources. At the end of a school year, performing now-familiar school tasks automatically rather than with effort is a sign of intelligence. Bright children now solve multiplication problems automatically, without thinking about the intermediate steps involved.

Finally, according to the *componential subtheory,* intelligence depends on basic cognitive processes called *components.* A component is really nothing more than Sternberg's term for the different information-processing skills described in Chapter 7, such as monitoring and retrieval. Whether the task is solving an item on an intelligence test, reading a newspaper, or understanding a conversation with a friend, components must be selected and organized in the proper sequence to complete the task successfully. In this subtheory, intelligence is associated with more efficient organization and use of components.

In contrast to the psychometric approach and to Gardner's theory, the triarchic theory does not identify specific contents of intelligence. Instead, Sternberg defines intelligence in terms of processes: the strategies people use to complete tasks (componential subtheory), the familiarity of those tasks (experiential subtheory), and the relevance of the tasks to personal and cultural goals (contextual subtheory).

In Sternberg's triarchic theory, intelligence is defined in terms of the strategies that children use to complete tasks, the familiarity of the tasks, and the relevance of the tasks.

Sternberg's theory also underscores the dangers of comparing test scores of different cultural, ethnic, or racial groups. Comparisons are usually invalid because the test items are not equally relevant in different cultures. In addition, test items will typically not be equally novel in different cultures. A vocabulary test, for example, is useful in assessing intelligence in cultures where formal education is essential to skilled adaptations (because skilled use of language is important for success in schools). In cultures where schooling is not a key to success, a vocabulary test would not provide useful information because it would be irrelevant to cultural goals and much too novel.

As with Gardner's theory, researchers are still evaluating Sternberg's theory. And, as you can see in the table at the top of page 201 that summarizes the different approaches, theorists are still debating the question of what intelligence is. But, however it is defined, the fact is that individuals differ substantially in intellectual ability, and numerous tests have been devised to measure these differences. The construction, properties, and limitations of these tests are the focus of the next module.

Features of Major Perspectives on Intelligence

Approach to Intelligence	Distinguishing Features
Psychometric	Intelligence is a hierarchy of general and specific skills
Gardner's theory of multiple intelligences	Seven distinct intelligences—linguistic, logical-mathematical, spatial, musical, bodily-kinesthetic, interpersonal, and intrapersonal intelligences
Sternberg's triarchic theory	Intelligence is defined by context, experience, and information-processing components

Check Your Learning

1. According to _____ theories, intelligence includes both general intelligence as well as more specific abilities, such as verbal and spatial skill.

2. Gardner's theory of multiple intelligences includes linguistic, logical-mathematical, and spatial intelligences, which are included in psychometric theories, as well as musical, _____, interpersonal, and intrapersonal intelligences, which are ignored in psychometric theories.

3. According to Sternberg's _____ subtheory, intelligence refers to adapting to an environment to achieve goals.

Answers: (1) hierarchical, (2) bodily-kinesthetic, (3) contextual

EASURING INTELLIGENCE

Learning Objectives

- **Why were intelligence tests devised initially? What are modern tests like?**
- **How well do modern intelligence tests work?**
- **What are the roles of heredity and environment in determining intelligence?**
- **How do ethnicity and social class influence intelligence test scores?**

MODULE
8.2
Measuring Intelligence

Binet and the Development of Intelligence Testing

Do Tests Work?

Hereditary and Environmental Factors

Impact of Ethnicity and Social Class

> *Charlene, an African American third grader, received a score of 75 on an intelligence test administered by a school psychologist. Based on the test score, the psychologist believes that Charlene is mildly mentally retarded and should receive special education. Charlene's parents are indignant; they believe that the tests are biased against African Americans and that the score is meaningless.*

American schools faced a crisis at the beginning of the 20th century. Between 1890 and 1915, school enrollment nearly doubled nationally as great numbers of immigrants arrived and reforms restricted child labor and emphasized education (Chapman, 1988). Increased enrollment meant that teachers now had larger numbers of students who did not learn as readily as the "select few" students who had populated their classes previously. How to deal with these less capable children was one of the pressing issues of the day. In this module, you'll see how intelligence tests were devised initially to address a changed school population. Then we'll look at a simple question: "How well do modern tests work?" Finally, we'll examine how race, ethnicity, social class, environment, and heredity influence intelligence and we'll learn how to interpret Charlene's test score.

BINET AND THE DEVELOPMENT OF INTELLIGENCE TESTING

The problems facing educators at the beginning of the 20th century were not unique to the United States. In 1904, the Minister of Public Instruction in France asked two noted psychologists, Alfred Binet and Theophile Simon, to formulate a way to recognize children who needed special instruction in school. Binet and Simon's approach was to select simple tasks that French children of different ages ought to be able to do, such as naming colors, counting backwards, and remembering numbers in order. Based on preliminary testing, Binet and Simon determined problems that normal 3-year-olds could solve, that normal 4-year-olds could solve, and so on. **Children's *mental age* or *MA* referred to the difficulty of the problems that they could solve correctly.** A child who solved problems that the average 7-year-old could pass would have an MA of 7.

Binet and Simon created the first intelligence test by using simple tasks to distinguish children who would do well in school from children who wouldn't.

Binet and Simon used mental age to distinguish "bright" from "dull" children. A "bright" child would have the MA of an older child; for example, a 6-year-old with an MA of 9 was considered bright. A "dull" child would have the MA of a younger child; for example, a 6-year-old with an MA of 4. Binet and Simon confirmed that "bright" children did better in school than "dull" children. Voilá—the first objective measure of intelligence!

The Stanford-Binet. Lewis Terman, of Stanford University, revised Binet and Simon's test and published a version known as the Stanford-Binet in 1916. **Terman described performance as an *intelligence quotient*, or *IQ*, which was simply the ratio of mental age to chronological age, multiplied by 100:**

$$IQ = MA/CA \times 100$$

At any age, children who are perfectly average will have an IQ of 100 because their mental age equals their chronological age. The figure shows the typical distribution of test scores in the population. You can see that roughly two-thirds of children taking a test will have IQ scores between 85 and 115 and that 95 percent will have scores between 70 and 130.

The IQ score can also be used to compare intelligence in children of different ages. A 4-year-old with an MA of 5 has an IQ of 125 ($5/4 \times 100$), the same as an 8-year-old with an MA of 10 ($10/8 \times 100$). Although IQ scores are no longer computed this way, the concept of intelligence as the ratio of MA to CA helped popularize the Stanford-Binet test.

By the 1920s, the Stanford-Binet had been joined by many other intelligence tests. Educators enthusiastically embraced the tests as an efficient and objective way to assess a student's chances of succeeding in school (Chapman, 1988).

Today, more than 75 years later, the Stanford-Binet remains a popular test. It was last revised in 1986. Like the earlier versions, today's Stanford-Binet consists of many cognitive and motor tasks, ranging from the extremely easy to the extremely difficult. The test may be administered to individuals ranging in age from ap-

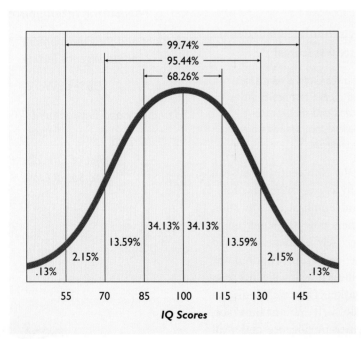

IQ Scores

proximately 2 years to adulthood, but not every individual is given every question. For example, preschool children like the youngster in the photo may be asked to name pictures of familiar objects, string beads, answer questions about everyday life, or fold paper into shapes. Older individuals may be asked to define vocabulary words, solve an abstract problem, or decipher an unfamiliar code. The examiner determines, according to specific guidelines, the appropriate starting place on the test and administers progressively more difficult questions until the child fails all the questions at a particular level. An IQ score is assigned on the basis of how many questions the child passed compared with the average number passed by children of the same age.

The Stanford-Binet is administered to one person at a time, rather than to a group. Group tests of intelligence have the advantage of providing information about many individuals quickly and inexpensively, often without the need of highly trained psychologists. But individual testing optimizes the motivation and attention of the examinee and provides an opportunity for a sensitive examiner to assess factors that may influence test performance. The examiner may notice that the examinee is relaxed and that test performance is therefore a reasonable sample of the individual's talents. Or the examiner may observe that intense anxiety is interfering with performance. Such determinations are not possible with group tests. Consequently, most psychologists prefer individualized tests of intelligence over group tests.

Let's look briefly at two other types of individualized tests, the Wechsler Intelligence Scale for Children-III (WISC-III) and the Kaufman Assessment Battery for Children (K-ABC).

The Wechsler Scales. A set of intelligence scales widely used in assessment and research with children is based on the work of David Wechsler. The original Wechsler scale, the Wechsler-Bellevue, was published in 1939 and designed specifically to measure adult intelligence for clinical (medical, not school) use. Later revisions produced tests for adults (Wechsler Adult Intelligence Scale, or WAIS), for schoolchildren (Wechsler Intelligence Scale for Children-III), and for children 4 to 6 years of age (Wechsler Preschool and Primary Scale of Intelligence-Revised, or WPPSI-R). All these tests follow a similar format.

The WISC-III, unlike the Stanford-Binet, includes subtests for verbal and performance skills, some of which are shown in the figure on page 204. Children thus are assessed on verbal IQ, performance IQ, and a combination of the two, the full-scale IQ. A second major difference between the WISC-III and the Stanford-Binet is that each child receives the same subtests, with some adjustment for either age level or competence or both.

The Kaufman Assessment Battery for Children. Alan Kaufman directed the 1974 revision of the WISC and wrote a well-known book on the proper use of the WISC (Kaufman, 1979). From these experiences, he and Nadeen Kaufman developed a new test of intelligence for 2- through 12-year-olds, the Kaufman Assessment Battery for Children, or K-ABC (Kaufman & Kaufman, 1983a, b). **One scale of the K-ABC measures *simultaneous processing,* how well a child integrates different**

Items Like Those Appearing on Different Subtests of the WISC-III

Verbal Scale	*Information: The child is asked questions that tap his or her factual knowledge of the world.* 1. *How many wings does a bird have?* 2. *What is steam made of?*
	Comprehension: The child is asked questions that measure his or her judgment and common sense. 1. *What should you do if you see someone forgot his book when he leaves a restaurant?* 2. *What is the advantage of keeping money in a bank?*
	Similarities: The child is asked to describe how words are related. 1. *In what way are a lion and a tiger alike?* 2. *In what way are a saw and a hammer alike?*
Performance Scale	*Picture arrangement: Pictures are shown and the child is asked to place them in order to tell a story.*
	Picture completion: The child is asked to identify the part that is missing from the picture.

Source: Simulated items similar to those in the Wechsler Intelligence Scales for Adults and Children. Copyright 1949, 1955, 1974, 1981, and 1990 by the Psychological Corporation. Reproduced by permission. All rights reserved.

information at the same time. We use such "mental synthesis" to understand pictures, in which many elements must be integrated to form a cohesive whole. **Another scale assesses** *sequential processing,* **how well a child integrates information over time.** We integrate in sequence to comprehend language, where meaning hinges on the particular order of words. A third scale measures academic achievement.

The Stanford-Binet, WISC-III, and K-ABC typify individualized tests used today to assess children's intelligence. The basic approach of each is similar—asking children to solve simple tasks, some of which are novel and some of which are relatively familiar—but they provide different results. The Stanford-Binet reports a single IQ score, the WISC-III provides verbal, performance, and overall IQ scores, and the K-ABC provides simultaneous and sequential processing scores along with academic achievement.

Infant Tests. The Stanford-Binet, WISC-III, and K-ABC cannot be used to test intelligence in infants. For this purpose, many psychologists use the Bayley Scales of Infant Development (Bayley, 1970). Designed for 2- to 30-month-olds, the Bayley

Scales consist of mental and motor scales. The mental scale assesses adaptive behavior, such as attending to visual and auditory stimuli, following directions, looking for a fallen toy, and imitating. The motor scale assesses an infant's control of its body, its coordination, and its ability to manipulate objects. For example, 6-month-olds should turn their head toward an object that the examiner drops on the floor, 12-month-olds should imitate the examiner's actions, and 16-month-olds should build a tower from three blocks.

The Bayley Scales were revised recently (Bayley, 1993). They can now be used with children as old as 42 months, and they assess additional abilities, including habituation, memory, and problem solving.

DO TESTS WORK?

To determine whether intelligence tests work, we need to consider two separate issues, reliability and validity. **A test is *reliable* if it yields scores that are consistent.** Reliability is often measured by administering similar forms of a test on two occasions. If the test is reliable, a person will have similar scores both times. Today's intelligence tests are very reliable. If a child takes an intelligence test and then retakes it days or a few weeks later, the two scores are usually quite similar (Wechsler, 1991).

Reliability over the long term is more complex. In general, scores from infant intelligence tests are not related to IQ scores obtained later in childhood, adolescence, or adulthood (McCall, 1989). Apparently, children must be at least 18 to 24 months old before their Bayley scores, or scores from similar scales, can predict later IQ scores on the Wechsler or Stanford-Binet scales (Kopp & McCall, 1982).

Why don't scores on infant intelligence tests predict childhood or adult IQ more accurately? One reason is that infant tests measure different abilities than tests administered to children and adolescents: Infant tests place more emphasis on sensorimotor skills and less on tasks involving cognitive processes such as language, thinking, and problem solving.

According to this reasoning, a measure of infant cognitive processing might yield more accurate predictions of later IQ. In fact, habituation, a measure of information processing described in Module 5.2, does predict later IQ more effectively than scores from the Bayley. The average correlation between habituation and later IQ is approximately –.5 (Bornstein, 1997). That is, 1- to 6-month-olds who habituate to visual stimuli more rapidly—they look less—tend to have higher IQs as children.

Infant IQ scores do not predict childhood IQ scores but habituation does: Infants who habituate rapidly have higher IQs as children.

If scores on the Bayley Scales do not predict later IQs, why are these tests used at all? The answer is that they are important diagnostic tools: They can be used to determine if development is progressing normally. For example, the Bayley mental scale can detect the impact of prenatal exposure to teratogens (Bellinger et al., 1987). It can also assess whether the infant's home environment provides sufficient stimulation for mental development (Bradley et al., 1987).

Although infant test scores don't reliably predict IQ later in life, scores obtained in childhood do. The top graph on page 206 shows the results from several longitudinal studies that correlated IQ scores obtained at different points in childhood or adolescence and at maturity. (Each line in the graph represents a different study.) You can see that the correlation between IQ at 5 years and maturity is approximately .5 and that the correlations get steadily larger as children get older.

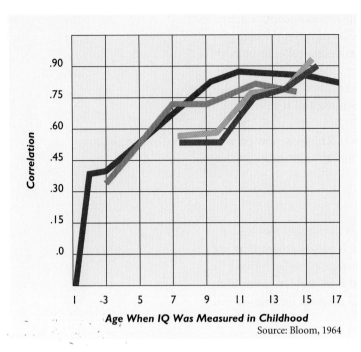

Age When IQ Was Measured in Childhood

Source: Bloom, 1964

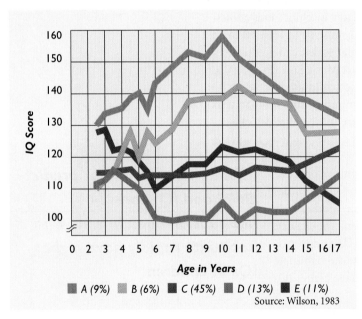

Age in Years

■ A (9%) ■ B (6%) ■ C (45%) ■ D (13%) ■ E (11%)

Source: Wilson, 1983

These correlations appear to support the idea that intelligence is relatively stable from early childhood on. However, when individual performance over time is examined, stability is not a hard-and-fast rule. McCall, Appelbaum, and Hogarty (1973) conducted a longitudinal study in which 80 individuals typically had their intelligence tested 14 times between ages 2 and 17. A complex statistical analysis revealed the five different patterns of change that are shown in the bottom graph. The numbers in parentheses indicate the percentage of individuals showing each pattern of change. The most common pattern—C—was for little change in IQ from 2 to 17 years of age. However, children in groups A and B had IQ scores that first increased, then decreased with age. Children in group D had the opposite pattern. Group E had many ups and downs, but the overall trend was for lower scores as children developed.

McCall and his colleagues (1973) also found that children were most likely to have increasing IQ scores when their parents deliberately trained their intellectual and motor skills. When parents did not train their youngsters' intellectual and motor development (or, in some cases, actively discouraged it), IQ scores were likely to decline as children got older.

Thus, although IQ is often relatively stable throughout childhood and adolescence, this is definitely not the only pattern. For many children, IQ will change—both up and down—as they develop. As we shall see later in this module, heredity and environment are both implicated in these patterns.

Are Tests Valid? Reliability of tests—whether short- or long-term—is not the only criterion for evaluating a test. What do test scores *mean*? Are they really measuring intelligence? **These questions raise the issue of *validity,* which refers to the extent that a test really measures what it claims to measure.** Validity is usually measured by determining the relation between test scores and other independent measures of the construct that the test is thought to measure. For example, to measure the validity of a test of extroversion, we would have children take the test, then observe them in a social setting, such as a school recess, and record who is outgoing and who is shy. The test would be valid if scores correlated highly with our independent observations of extroverted behavior.

How would we extend this approach to intelligence tests? Ideally, we would administer the intelligence tests and then correlate the scores with other independent estimates of intelligence. Therein lies the problem. There are *no* other independent ways to estimate intelligence; the only way to measure intelligence is with tests. Consequently, many follow Binet's lead and obtain measures of performance in school, such as grades or teachers' ratings of their students. Correlations between these measures and scores on intelligence tests typically fall somewhere between .4 and .6 (Brody, 1992). For example, the correlation between scores on the WISC-III and grade point average is .47 (Wechsler, 1991). This correlation is positive but far from 1. Obviously, some youngsters with high test scores do not excel in school, whereas others with low scores get good grades. In general, however, tests do a reasonable job of predicting school success.

> *Most test developers claim that their tests are valid—actually measure intelligence—by showing that test scores have moderate correlations with children's performance in school.*

Does this mean that intelligence tests are synonymous with intelligence? Probably not. Tests measure intellectual skills, like verbal ability and abstract reasoning, that are important for success in school. However, tests are less effective in predicting success outside of school (Sternberg et al., 1995). Why? They were not designed to assess skills important for on-the-job success, such as practical problem-solving ability and interpersonal skills. Consequently, it is fair to conclude that current intelligence tests are reasonably valid primarily for measuring the components of intelligence related to achievement in school.

HEREDITARY AND ENVIRONMENTAL FACTORS

Joanna, a 5-year-old girl, was administered the WISC-III and obtained a score of 112. Ted, a 5-year-old boy, took the same test and received a score of 92. What can account for the 20-point difference in scores by these youngsters? Heredity and experience both matter. Some of the evidence for hereditary factors is shown in the graph. If genes influence intelligence, then siblings' test scores should become more alike as siblings become more similar genetically (Bouchard & McGue, 1981). Identical twins are identical genetically and they typically have virtually identical test scores, which would be a correlation of 1. Fraternal twins have about 50 percent of their genes in common, just like nontwins of the same biological parents. Consequently, their test scores should be (a) less similar than scores for identical twins, (b) as similar as other siblings who have the same biological parents, and (c) more similar than scores of children and their adopted siblings. You can see in the graph that each of these predictions is supported.

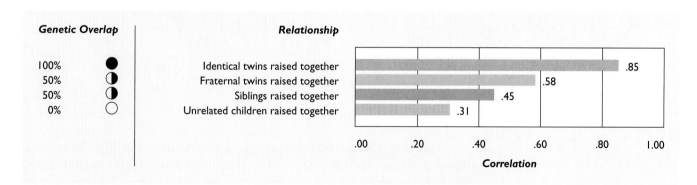

Heredity also influences developmental profiles for IQ scores. IQ profiles are more alike for identical twins than for fraternal twins. The set of graphs on page 208 shows typical profiles of IQ scores for four pairs of twins. The identical twins in graphs A and B develop more similarly than the fraternal twins shown in graphs C and D. Thus, identical twins are not only more alike in overall IQ, but in developmental change in IQ as well.

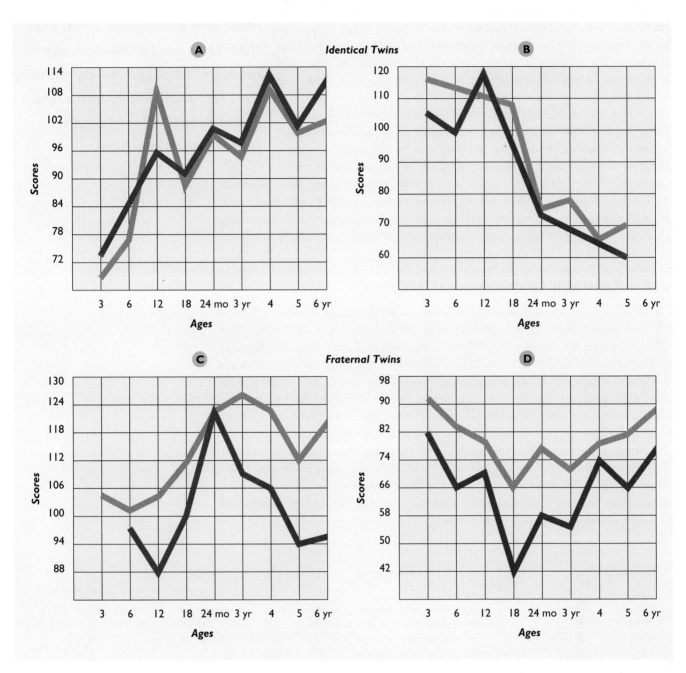

Studies of adopted children also suggest that the impact of heredity increases during childhood and adolescence: If heredity helps determine IQ, then children's IQs should be more like their biological parents' IQs than their adoptive parents' IQs. These correlations were computed in the Colorado Adoption Project (Fulker, DeFries, & Plomin, 1988), which included 245 adopted children as well as their biological and adoptive parents. At age 3, children's IQs resembled both sets of parents equally. However, by age 7, the correlation was higher for biological parents than for adoptive parents. In other words, by the time adopted children like the ones in the photograph are in elementary school, their test scores resemble their biological parents' scores more than their adoptive parents' scores. Youngsters with high test scores have biological parents with high test scores but not necessarily adoptive parents with high test scores. These results are evidence for greater impact of inheritance on IQ as a child grows.

Do these results mean that heredity is the sole determiner of intelligence? No. Two areas of research show the importance of environment on intelligence. The first is research on characteristics of families and homes. The second is research on the impact of preschool intervention or enrichment programs.

If intelligence were solely due to heredity, environment should have little or no impact on children's intelligence. But we know that many characteristics of parents' behavior and home environments *are* related to children's intelligence. Bettye Caldwell and Robert Bradley (1994) developed the Home Observation for Measurement of the Environment (HOME), an inventory for assessing parents' behavior as well as the quality and organization of the child's home environment. Research with the HOME indicates that children with high test scores typically have parents who are stimulating, responsive, and involved (Bradley, Caldwell, & Rock, 1988). In addition, among European American children, an environment that includes plenty of variety and appropriate play materials is linked to high test scores; among African American children, a well-organized home environment is associated with higher scores (Bradley et al., 1989).

Identical twins' IQ scores are more alike than fraternal twins' and adopted children's IQ scores gradually become more similar to their biological parents' scores—two results that show the influence of heredity on intelligence.

The importance of a stimulating environment for intelligence is also demonstrated by intervention programs designed to prepare economically disadvantaged children for school. When children grow up in never-ending poverty, the cycle is predictable and tragic: Youngsters have few of the intellectual skills to succeed in school, so they fail; lacking an education, they find minimal jobs (if they can work at all), guaranteeing that their children, too, are destined to grow up in poverty. Since Project Head Start was begun in 1965 by President Lyndon Johnson as part of his War on Poverty, massive educational intervention has been an important tool in the effort to break this repeated cycle of poverty. Intervention programs for preschool youngsters typically include an elaborate, structured curriculum for both children and their parents (Ramey & Ramey, 1990). When children participate in these enrichment programs, their test scores increase by about 10 points (Clarke & Clarke, 1989). In the "Focus on Research" feature, we look at one of these success stories in detail.

Focus on Research: **THE CAROLINA ABECEDARIAN PROJECT**

Who were the investigators and what was the aim of the study? Since the 1960s, many intervention programs have demonstrated that young children's intelligence test scores can be raised with enrichment, but the improvement is often short-lived. That is, within a few years after completing the intervention program, test scores are at the same level as before the program. Frances Campbell and Craig Ramey (1994; Ramey & Campbell, 1991)

[handwritten margin note:] weether preschool helps kids become smarter or not.

designed the Carolina Abecedarian Project to see if massive and sustained intervention could produce more long-lasting changes.

How did the investigators measure the topic of interest? Some children did not participate in any intervention program. Other children attended a special day-care facility daily from 4 months until 5 years of age. The curriculum emphasized mental, linguistic, and social development for infants, and prereading skills for preschoolers. Some children also participated in another intervention program during their first 3 years of elementary school. During this phase, a teacher visited the home a few times each month, bringing materials for improving reading and math. The teachers taught parents how to use the materials with their child and also acted as facilitators between home and school.

When children receive massive, long-term intervention, their scores improve substantially on intelligence and achievement tests.

Campbell and Ramey measured the impact of intervention in several ways, including scores on intelligence tests, scores on achievement tests, and children's need for special services in school.

Who were the children in the study? At the start, the project included 111 children; most were born to African American mothers who had less than a high-school education, an average IQ score of 85, and on average, no income. Over the course of the study, 21 children dropped out of the project, leaving 90 children at the end.

What was the design of the study? This study was experimental because children were randomly assigned to an intervention condition (preschool intervention, elementary-school intervention, both, or no intervention). The independent variable was the intervention condition. The dependent variables included performance on intelligence and achievement tests. The study was longitudinal because children were tested repeatedly over an 8-year period.

Were there ethical concerns with the study? No. The nature of the study was explained fully to parents, including the assignment of their child to a specific intervention condition.

What were the results? The graph shows children's performance on three achievement tests that they took as 12-year-olds, 4 years after the school-age intervention had ended. In all three areas that were tested—written language, math, and reading—performance clearly reflects the amount of intervention. Youngsters who had a full 8 years of intervention generally have the highest scores; children with no intervention have the lowest scores.

What did the investigators conclude? Massive, continued intervention works. An improvement of 7 to 10 points may not strike you as very much, but it *is* a substantial improvement from a practical standpoint. For example, the written language scores of the youngsters with 8 years of intervention place them near the 50th percentile, meaning that their scores are greater than about half of the children taking the test. In contrast, children with no intervention have scores at the 20th percentile, making their scores greater than only 20 percent of the children taking the test. Thus, after intervention, children moved from being substantially below average to average, quite an accomplishment.

Of course, massive intervention over 8 years is expensive. But so are the economic consequences of poverty, unemployment, and their byproducts. Pro-

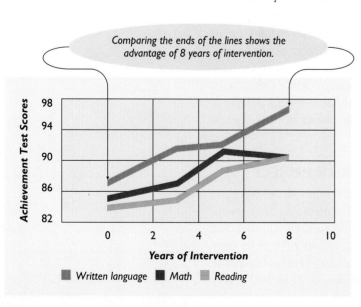

Comparing the ends of the lines shows the advantage of 8 years of intervention.

■ Written language ■ Math ■ Reading

grams like the Abecedarian Project show that the repetitive cycle of school failure and education can be broken. And, in the process, they show that intelligence is fostered by an environment that is stimulating and responsive. ▨

IMPACT OF ETHNICITY AND SOCIAL CLASS

On many intelligence tests, the average score of African Americans is about 15 points lower than that of European Americans (Brody, 1992). What accounts for this difference? Some of the difference is due to social class. Typically, children from lower social classes have lower scores on intelligence tests, and African American children are more likely than European American children to live in lower-class homes. When European American and African American children of comparable social class are compared, the difference in IQ test scores is reduced but not eliminated (Brooks-Gunn, Klebanov, & Duncan, 1996). So social class explains some but not all of the difference between European American and African American children's IQ scores.

Some critics contend that the difference in test scores reflects bias in the tests themselves. They argue that test items reflect the cultural heritage of the test creators—most of whom are middle-class European Americans—and so tests are biased against lower-class and African American children. They point to test items like this one:

A conductor is to an orchestra as a teacher is to what?

book   school   class   eraser

Children whose background includes exposure to orchestras are more likely to answer this question correctly than children who lack this exposure.

The problem of bias has led to the development of *culture-fair intelligence tests,* **which include test items based on experiences common to many cultures.** An example is Raven's Progressive Matrices, which consists solely of items like the one shown here. Examinees are asked to select the piece that would complete the design correctly (6, in this case). Culture-fair tests predict achievement in school, but

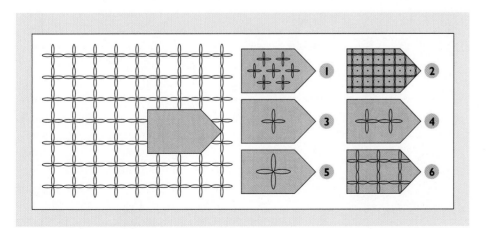

do not eliminate group differences in test scores: European and African Americans still differ (Anastasi, 1988; Herrnstein & Murray, 1994). Why? Culture can influence a child's familiarity with the entire testing situation, not simply familiarity with particular items. A culture-fair test will underestimate a child's intelligence if, for example, the child's culture encourages children to solve problems in collaboration with others and discourages them from excelling as individuals.

Moreover, because of their wariness of questions posed by unfamiliar adults, many African American and other economically disadvantaged children often answer test questions by saying, "I don't know." Obviously, this strategy guarantees an artificially low test score. When these children are given extra time to become at ease with the examiner, they often abandon the "I don't know" approach and their test scores improve considerably (Zigler & Finn-Stevenson, 1992).

A low score on an intelligence test means that a child currently lacks some skills needed to succeed in school, not that the child will forever fail in school or is just plain stupid.

If all tests reflect cultural influences, at least to some degree, how should we interpret test scores? Remember that tests assess successful adaptation to a particular cultural context. Most intelligence tests predict success in a school environment, which usually espouses middle-class values. Regardless of ethnic group—African American, Hispanic American, or European American—a child with a high test score has the intellectual skills needed for academic work based on middle-class values. A child with a low test score, like Charlene in the module-opening vignette, lacks those skills.

Does a low score mean Charlene is destined to fail in school? No. It simply means that, based on her current skills, she's unlikely to do well. As we saw in the "Focus on Research" feature about the Abecedarian Project, improving Charlene's skills will improve her school performance. Does a low score mean that Charlene is just plain stupid? No. Intelligence tests measure abilities important to school. As the cartoon suggests, many other abilities are important for intelligent adaptation outside of school, and these abilities are generally not evaluated on intelligence tests. When one group has higher average scores than another it simply means that one

"You're wise, but you lack tree smarts."

Drawing by D. Reilly; © 1988 The New Yorker Magazine, Inc.

group has more of the specific skills that are critical for success in the middle-class school environment, *not* that its members have more of some pervasive general-purpose ability called intelligence.

Check Your Learning

1. The WISC-III provides a verbal IQ score and a _____ .

2. Modern intelligence tests are typically validated by _____ .

3. As identical twins develop, their IQ scores _____ .

4. The problem of cultural bias on intelligence tests led to the development of _____ .

Answers: (1) performance IQ score, (2) showing that test scores are correlated with measures of performance in school, (3) follow the same developmental profile, (4) culture-fair intelligence tests, which have test items common to many cultures

SPECIAL CHILDREN, SPECIAL NEEDS

Learning Objectives

- **What are the characteristics of gifted and creative children?**
- **What are the different forms of mental retardation?**
- **What are learning disabilities?**

MODULE
8.3
Special Children, Special Needs

Gifted and Creative Children

Children with Mental Retardation

Children with Learning Disabilities

> *Sanjit, a second grader, has taken two separate intelligence tests and both times he had above-average scores. Nevertheless, Sanjit absolutely cannot read. Letters and words are as mysterious to him as Metallica's music would be to Mozart. His parents took him to an ophthalmologist who determined that his vision was 20-30; nothing is wrong with his eyes. What is wrong?*

Throughout history, societies have recognized children with limited mental abilities as well as those with extraordinary talents. Today, we know much about the extremes of human talents. We'll begin this module with a look at gifted and creative children. Then we'll look at children with mental retardation and learning disabilities and discover why Sanjit can't read.

GIFTED AND CREATIVE CHILDREN

In many respects the boy in the photo, Bernie, is an ordinary middle-class 12-year-old: He is the goalie on his soccer team, takes piano lessons on Saturday mornings, sings in his church youth choir, and likes to go roller blading. However, when it comes to intelligence and academic prowess, Bernie leaves the ranks of the ordinary. He received a score of 175 on an intelligence test and is taking a college calculus course. **Bernie is *gifted,* which traditionally has referred to individuals with scores of 130 or greater on intelligence tests** (Horowitz & O'Brien, 1986).

Bernie doesn't fit the stereotype of gifted children, who are often thought to be emotionally troubled and unable to get along with their peers (Halpern & Luria, 1989). In fact, research shows that gifted youngsters tend to be more mature than their peers and have fewer emotional problems

(Luthar, Zigler, & Goldstein, 1992). Gifted children's thinking seems to develop in the same sequence as nongifted children's thinking, just more rapidly. Gifted children simply think like older nongifted children (Jackson & Butterfield, 1986).

Traditionally, the definition of giftedness was in terms of IQ scores, so exceptional ability was associated exclusively with scholastic skills. But modern definitions of giftedness are broader and include exceptional talent in an assortment of areas, including art, music, creative writing, and dance (Ramos-Ford & Gardner, 1991).

Whether the domain is music or math, though, exceptional talent seems to have several prerequisites (Feldman & Goldsmith, 1991; Rathunde & Csikszentmihalyi, 1993):

- The child loves the subject and has an almost overwhelming desire to master it.

- Instruction to develop the child's special talent usually begins at an early age with inspiring and talented teachers.

- Parents are committed to promoting their child's talent.

The message here is that exceptional talent must be nurtured. Without encouragement and support from parents and stimulating and challenging mentors, a youngster's talents will wither, not flourish.

Creativity. If you've seen the movie *Amadeus,* you know the difference between being talented and being creative. Mozart and Salieri were rival composers in Europe during the 18th century. Both were talented, ambitious musicians. Yet, more than 200 years later, Mozart is revered and Salieri is all but forgotten. Why? Then and now, Mozart was considered creative but Salieri was not.

What is creativity and how does it differ from intelligence? **Intelligence is associated with *convergent thinking,* using information that is provided to determine a standard, correct answer. In contrast, creativity is associated with *divergent thinking,* where the aim is not a single correct answer (often there isn't one) but novel and unusual lines of thought** (Guilford, 1967).

Divergent thinking is often measured by asking children to produce many ideas in response to some specific stimulus (Kogan, 1983). For example, children might be asked to name different uses for a common object, such as a coat hanger. Or they might be shown a page filled with circles and asked to draw as many different pictures as they can, as shown in the figure. Both the number of responses and the originality of the responses are used to measure creativity.

Creativity, like giftedness, must be cultivated. The "Making Children's Lives Better" feature gives some guidelines for fostering children's creativity.

Making Children's Lives Better: **FOSTERING CREATIVITY**

Here are some guidelines for helping children to be more creative.

1. Encourage children to take risks. Not all novel ideas bear fruit. Some won't work and some are silly. But only by repeatedly thinking in novel and unusual ways are children likely to produce something truly original.

2. Encourage children to think of alternatives to conventional wisdom. Have them think what would happen if accepted practices were changed. For example, "What would life be like without cars?" or "Why not eat breakfast in the evening and dinner in the morning?"

3. Praise children for working hard. As the saying goes, creativity is one part inspiration and nine parts perspiration. The raw creative insight must be polished to gain the luster of a finished product.

4. Help children get over the "I'm not creative" hurdle. Too often they believe that only others are creative. Assure children that anyone who follows these guidelines will become more creative. ▣

Gifted and creative children represent one extreme of human ability. Who is at the other extreme? Youngsters with mental retardation, the topic of the next section.

CHILDREN WITH MENTAL RETARDATION

"Little David" was the oldest of four children. He learned to sit only days before his first birthday, he began to walk at 2, and said his first words as a 3-year-old. By age 5, David was far behind his agemates developmentally. David had Down syndrome, described in Module 2.2. An extra 21st chromosome caused David's retarded mental development.

Mental retardation **refers to substantially below average intelligence and problems adapting to an environment that emerge before the age of 18.** Below-average intelligence is defined as a score of 70 or less on an intelligence test such as the Stanford-Binet. Adaptive behavior is usually evaluated from interviews with a parent or other caregiver and refers to the daily living skills needed to live, work, and play in the community—skills for caring for oneself and social skills. Only individuals who are under 18 and have problems in these areas *and* IQ scores of 70 or less are considered mentally retarded (American Association on Mental Retardation, 1992).

Types of Mental Retardation. Your image of a mentally retarded child may be someone with Down syndrome, like the child shown on page 42. In reality, mentally retarded individuals are just as varied as nonretarded people. How, then, can we describe this variety? One approach is to distinguish the causes of mental retardation. **Some cases of mental retardation—no more than 25 percent—can be traced to a specific biological or physical problem and are known as** *organic mental retardation.* Down syndrome is the most common organic form of mental retardation. Other types of mental retardation apparently do not involve biological damage. *Familial mental retardation* **simply represents the lower end of the normal distribution of intelligence.**

Organic mental retardation has a specific biological cause and is usually more severe than familial mental retardation, which represents the lower end of the normal distribution of intelligence.

AAMR	Profound	Severe	Moderate		Mild	
IQ Level	10 20	30	40 50		60 70	
Educators	Custodial		Trainable		Educable	

Organic mental retardation is usually substantial, and familial mental retardation is usually less pronounced. The American Association on Mental Retardation identifies four levels of retardation. The levels, along with the range of IQ scores associated with each level, are shown in the chart. Also shown are the three levels of retardation typically used by educators in the United States (Cipani, 1991).

The most severe forms of mental retardation are, fortunately, relatively uncommon. Profound, severe, and moderate retardation together make up only 10 percent of all cases. Profoundly and severely retarded individuals usually have so few skills that they must be supervised constantly. Consequently, they usually live in institutions for retarded persons, where they can sometimes be taught self-help skills such as dressing, feeding, and toileting (Reid, Wilson, & Faw, 1991).

Moderately retarded persons may develop the intellectual skills of a nonretarded 7- or 8-year-old. With this level of functioning, they can sometimes support themselves, typically at a sheltered workshop, where they perform simple tasks under close supervision.

The remaining 90 percent of individuals with mental retardation are classified as mildly or educable mentally retarded. These individuals go to school and can master many academic skills, but at an older age than a nonretarded child. Individuals with mild mental retardation can lead independent lives. Like the man in the photograph, many mildly retarded people work. Some marry. Comprehensive training programs that focus on vocational and social skills help individuals with mild mental retardation be productive citizens and satisfied human beings (Ellis & Rusch, 1991), as you can see by learning more about "little David" in the "Real Children" feature.

Real Children: **LITTLE DAVID, THE REST OF THE STORY**

"Little David," so named because his father was also named David, was the oldest of four children; none of his siblings was mentally retarded. As the children grew up, they interacted the way most siblings do— laughing and playing together and sometimes fighting and arguing. Beginning as a teenager and continuing into adulthood, each day David took a city bus from home to his job at a sheltered workshop. He worked 6 hours at such tasks as making bows for packages and stuffing envelopes. He saved his earnings to buy what became his prized possessions—a camera, a color TV, and a VCR. As David's siblings entered adulthood, they began their own families. David relished his new role as "Uncle David" and looked forward to visits from his nieces and nephews. As David entered his 40s, he began to suffer memory loss and was often confused. When he died, at age 47, family and friends grieved over their loss. Yet they all marveled at the richness of David's life. By any standards, David had led a full and satisfying life. ▨

Little David's mental retardation represents one end of the intelligence spectrum; Bernie's precocity represents the other. Falling between these two extremes are other special children, those with learning disabilities.

CHILDREN WITH LEARNING DISABILITIES

For some children with normal intelligence, learning is a struggle. **These young-sters have a *learning disability,* which refers to a child who (a) has difficulty mastering an academic subject, (b) has normal intelligence, and (c) is not suffering from other conditions that could explain poor performance, such as sensory impairment or inadequate instruction** (Hammill, 1990).

In the United States, about 5 percent of school-age children are classified as learning disabled, which translates into roughly 2 million youngsters (Moats & Lyon, 1993). The number of distinct disabilities and the degree of overlap among them is still debated (Stanovich, 1993). However, one common classification scheme distinguishes disability in language (including listening, speaking, and writing), in reading, and in arithmetic (Dockrell & McShane, 1993).

The variety of learning disabilities complicates the task for teachers and researchers because it suggests that each type of learning disability may have its own cause and treatment. Take reading, the most common area of learning disability, as an example. Many children with a reading disability have problems in phonological awareness (described in Module 7.3), which refers to understanding and using the sounds in written and oral language. For a reading-disabled child like Sanjit, the child in the vignette at the beginning of the module, all vowels sound alike. Thus *pin* sounds like *pen* which sounds like *pan.* These youngsters benefit from explicit, extensive instruction on the connections between letters and their sounds (Lovett et al., 1994). In the case of arithmetic disability, children often have difficulty recognizing what operations are needed and how to perform them. Here, instruction emphasizes determining the goal of arithmetic problems, using goals to select correct arithmetic operations, and using operations accurately (Goldman, 1989).

Learning disabilities occur in language, reading, and arithmetic, with each type of disability having its own cause and treatment.

The key to helping these children is to move beyond the generic label "learning disability" to pinpoint specific cognitive and academic deficits that hamper an individual child's performance in school. Then instruction can be specifically tailored to improve the child's skills (Moats & Lyon, 1993).

Planning effective instruction for children with learning disabilities is much easier said than done, however, because diagnosing learning disability is very difficult. Some children have both reading and language disabilities; other children have reading and arithmetic disabilities; still others have a learning disability and another problem, attention deficit hyperactivity disorder, described in Module 5.3.

Check Your Learning

1. Creativity is associated with _____ thinking, in which the goal is to think in novel and unusual directions.

2. Cases of _____ mental retardation can be linked to specific biological or physical problems.

3. Children with a learning disability are unable to master an academic subject, have _____, and have no other condition, such as sensory impairment, that could explain their poor performance.

Answers: (1) divergent, (2) organic, (3) normal intelligence

INTELLIGENCE AND INDIVIDUAL DIFFERENCES IN COGNITION
IN PERSPECTIVE

Navigating to a distant island, running a business selling candy, and speaking fluently—so different yet all just a few manifestations of this marvelous thing called human intelligence. In Module 8.1, we found that human intelligence does indeed come in many varieties but that researchers have yet to agree on how many and what they are. In Module 8.2, we saw that several tests can be used to assess children's intelligence reliably and validly, but the aspects of intelligence that most of today's tests measure are those involved in school success. In Module 8.3, we saw that the extremes of intelligence include gifted and creative children as well as children with mental retardation and learning disabilities.

In this chapter, I want to underscore the theme that *development is always jointly influenced by heredity and environment.* In no other area of child development is this theme as important, because the implications for social policy are so profound. If intelligence were completely determined by heredity, for example, intervention programs would be a waste of time and tax dollars because no amount of experience would change nature's prescription for intelligence. But we've seen several times in this chapter that neither heredity nor environment is all-powerful when it comes to intelligence. Studies of twins, for example, remind us that heredity clearly has substantial impact on IQ scores. Identical twins' IQs are consistently more alike than fraternal twins', a result that documents heredity's influence on intelligence. Yet, at the same time, intervention studies like the Carolina Abecedarian Project show that intelligence is malleable. Children's intelligence can be enhanced by intensely stimulating environments.

Thus, heredity imposes some limits on how a child's intelligence will develop, but the limits are fairly modest. We can nurture all children's intelligence considerably if we are willing to invest the time and effort.

THINKING ABOUT DEVELOPMENT

1. If Jean Piaget were asked to create an intelligence test, how might it differ from the type of test that Binet created? How would a test devised by Howard Gardner differ from Binet's test?

2. How might our definitions of giftedness and mental retardation change if they were based on Robert Sternberg's triarchic theory?

3. IQ scores from the Stanford-Binet, WISC-III, and K-ABC tests tend to be highly related. That is, a child who has a high score on the Stanford-Binet usually has a high score on the WISC-III and the K-ABC. What does this tell us about the tests and the nature of intelli-

gence? What does this tell us about the general and specific factors in intelligence described in Module 8.1?

4. IQ scores of identical twins are similar throughout childhood and adolescence whereas IQ scores of fraternal twins often differ. How could niche-picking (described in Module 2.3) be used to explain this phenomenon?

5. Module 8.3 described three types of special children: gifted, mentally retarded, and learning disabled. How does the existence (and nature) of these varying abilities bear on the debate that intelligence reflects a general ability or specific abilities in different domains?

SEE FOR YOURSELF

We've seen that the definition of intelligence differs across cultural settings. See how parents define intelligence by

asking them to rate the importance of four common elements of intelligence:

- problem-solving skill (thinking before acting, seeing different sides to a problem)

- verbal skill (speaking clearly, having a large vocabulary)

- creative skill (asking many questions, trying new things)

- social skill (playing and working well with other people, respecting and caring for others)

Ask parents to rate the importance of each element on a 6-point scale, where 1 means extremely unimportant to intelligence and 6 means extremely important. Try to ask parents from different ethnic groups; then compare your results with other students' to see if parents' views of intelligence are similar or different and if cultural background affects parents' definitions. See for yourself!

RESOURCES

For more information about . . .

 *the lives of brilliant and creative people,* read Howard Gardner's *Creating Minds* (Basic Books, 1993) which illustrates each different intelligence in Gardner's theory by tracing its development in the life of an extraordinary person, such as Albert Einstein, Pablo Picasso, and Igor Stravinsky

mental retardation, contact the American Association on Mental Retardation, 1-800-424-3688

different psychological tests, including those that measure intelligence and creativity, visit the Web site of the library of the Psychology Department, Macquarie University, http://www.bhs.mq.edu.au/lib/testref.html

KEY TERMS

componential subtheory *200*
components *200*
contextual subtheory *199*
convergent thinking *214*
culture-fair intelligence tests *211*
divergent thinking *214*
experiential subtheory *200*

familial mental retardation *215*
gifted *213*
intelligence quotient (IQ) *202*
learning disability *217*
mental age (MA) *202*
mental retardation *215*
organic mental retardation *215*

psychometricians *196*
reliable *205*
savants *198*
sequential processing *204*
simultaneous processing *203*
triarchic theory *199*
validity *206*

SUMMARY

MODULE 8.1:
WHAT IS INTELLIGENCE?

PSYCHOMETRIC THEORIES
Psychometric approaches to intelligence include theories that describe intelligence as a general factor as well as theories that include specific factors. Hierarchical theories include both general intelligence as well as various specific skills, such as verbal and spatial ability.

GARDNER'S THEORY OF MULTIPLE INTELLIGENCES
Gardner's theory of multiple intelligences proposes seven distinct intelligences. Three are found in psychometric theories (linguistic, logical-mathematical, and spatial intelligence), but four are new (musical,

bodily-kinesthetic, interpersonal, and intrapersonal intelligence). Gardner's theory suggests that schools should adjust teaching to each child's unique intellectual strengths.

STERNBERG'S TRIARCHIC THEORY
Robert Sternberg's triarchic theory includes (a) the contextual subtheory, which specifies that intelligent behavior must always be considered in relation to the individual's culture, (b) the experiential subtheory, which specifies that intelligence is associated with the familiarity of the task, and (c) the componential subtheory, which specifies that intelligent behavior involves organizing basic cognitive processes into an efficient strategy for completing a task.

MODULE 8.2:
MEASURING INTELLIGENCE

BINET AND THE DEVELOPMENT OF INTELLIGENCE TESTING

Binet created the first intelligence test to identify students who would have difficulty in school. Using this work, Terman created the Stanford-Binet, which introduced the concept of the intelligence quotient (IQ). Other widely used tests are the WISC-III and K-ABC. These tests provide IQs based on subtests (e.g., the verbal subscale of the WISC-III). Infant tests, such as the Bayley Scales, typically assess mental and motor development.

DO TESTS WORK?

In the short-term, intelligence tests are reliable, which means that people usually get consistent scores on the tests. In the longer-term, scores on infant intelligence tests do not predict adult IQ scores, but infant habituation predicts childhood IQs, and preschool IQ scores predict adult IQs. Intelligence tests are reasonably valid measures of achievement in school but are less valid in measuring aspects of intelligence that are important outside of school.

HEREDITARY AND ENVIRONMENTAL FACTORS

Evidence for the impact of heredity on IQ comes from the finding that siblings' IQ scores become more alike as siblings become more similar genetically. Evidence for the impact of the environment comes from the finding that children who live in responsive, well-organized home environments tend to have higher IQ scores, as do children who participate in intervention programs.

IMPACT OF ETHNICITY AND SOCIAL CLASS

The average IQ scores for African Americans is lower than the average score for European Americans, a difference attributed to the fact that more African American children live in poverty and that the test assesses knowledge based on middle-class experiences. IQ scores remain valid predictors of school success because middle-class experience is often a prerequisite for school success.

MODULE 8.3:
SPECIAL CHILDREN, SPECIAL NEEDS

GIFTED AND CREATIVE CHILDREN
Traditionally, gifted children have been those with high scores on IQ tests. Contrary to folklore, gifted children are socially mature and emotionally stable. Modern definitions of giftedness are broader and include exceptional talent in, for example, the arts.

Creativity is associated with divergent thinking, thinking in novel and unusual directions. Tests of divergent thinking can predict which children are most likely to be creative when they are older. Creativity can be fostered by experiences that encourage children to think flexibly and explore alternatives.

CHILDREN WITH MENTAL RETARDATION
Individuals with mental retardation have IQ scores of 70 or lower and deficits in adaptive behavior. Organic mental retardation can be linked to specific biological or physical causes; familial mental retardation reflects the lower end of the normal distribution of intelligence. Most retarded persons are classified as mildly or educably retarded; they attend school, work, and have families.

CHILDREN WITH LEARNING DISABILITIES
Children with a learning disability have normal intelligence but have difficulty mastering specific academic subjects. The most common is reading disability, which often can be traced to inadequate understanding and use of language sounds.

Language and Communication

AMY TAN, A CONTEMPORARY AMERICAN WRITER, ONCE SAID, "I AM FASCINATED BY LANGUAGE IN DAILY LIFE . . . THE WAY IT CAN EVOKE AN EMOTION, A VISUAL IMAGE, A COMPLEX IDEA, OR A SIMPLE TRUTH." LANGUAGE IS A REMARKABLE HUMAN TOOL. Speech allows us to express thoughts and feelings to others. Through written language, we preserve our ideas and benefit from the accomplishments of the past.

At first glance, acquiring language may seem like nothing more than learning words. But this is far from accurate and underestimates the complexity of the task. In fact, children must master four different aspects of language, and each is the focus of a module in this chapter. Distinguishing speech sounds is the essential first step in acquiring language. In Module 9.1, we'll see when infants can first hear and produce speech sounds. Module 9.2 concerns how children learn to speak and how they learn new words thereafter. Soon after children begin to speak, they start to form simple sentences. Even these earliest sentences follow simple rules; what these rules are and how children learn them is the focus of Module 9.3. Finally, in Module 9.4, we'll learn how children use language to communicate with others.

HE ROAD TO SPEECH

Learning Objectives

- **What are phonemes and how well can infants distinguish them?**
- **How does infant-directed speech help children learn about language?**
- **What is babbling and how does it become more complex in older infants?**

When Kathy moved from Atlanta to Montreal, she enrolled her 8-month-old son, Richard, in a day-care center where everyone spoke French. Richard did not yet talk but he did make many sounds that resembled words, like "gah-gah" and "beh-beh." What surprised Kathy was that, after just a few weeks in the day-care center, Richard's speech started to sound like French to her, even though he was still not talking. Was this possible or was her imagination just getting the best of her?

From birth, infants make sounds—they laugh, cry, and, like Kathy's son Richard, produce sounds that resemble speech. Yet, for most of their first year, infants do not talk. This contrast raises two important questions about infants as nonspeaking creatures. First, can babies who are unable to speak understand any of the speech that is directed to them? Second, how do infants progress from crying to more effective methods of oral communication, such as speech? Let's begin this module by answering the first question.

PERCEIVING SPEECH

We learned in Module 5.2 that even newborn infants hear remarkably well. But can babies distinguish speech sounds? To answer this question, we first need to know more about the elements of speech. **The basic building blocks of language are *phonemes,* unique sounds that can be joined to create words.** Phonemes include consonant sounds such as the sound of *t* in *toe* and *tap* along with vowel sounds such as the sound of *e* in *get* and *bed*. Infants can distinguish many of these sounds, some of them by as early as 1 month after birth.

How do we know that infants can distinguish different vowels and consonants? Researchers have devised a number of clever techniques to determine if babies respond differently to distinct sounds. One approach is illustrated in the diagram. A rubber nipple is connected to a tape recorder so that sucking turns on the tape and sound comes out a loudspeaker. In just a few minutes, 1-month-olds learn the relation between their sucking and the sound: They suck rapidly to hear a tape that consists of nothing more than the sound of *p* as in *pin, pet,* and *pat* (pronounced "puh"). After a few more minutes, infants seemingly tire of this repetitive sound and they suck less often, which represents the habituation phenomenon described in Module 5.2. But, if the tape is changed to a different sound—such as the sound of *b* in *bed, bat,* or *bird* (pronounced "buh")—babies begin sucking rapidly again. Evidently, they recognize that the sound of *b* is different from *p* because they suck more often to hear the new sound (Jusczyk, 1995).

"puh"

Infants can even discriminate speech sounds that they have never heard before. Not all languages use the same set of phonemes; a distinction that is important in one language may be ignored in another. For example, unlike English, French and Polish differentiate between nasal and nonnasal vowels. To hear the difference, say the word *rod*. Now repeat it, but holding your nose. The subtle difference between the two sounds illustrates a nonnasal vowel (the first version of *rod*) and a nasal one (the second). Babies growing up in homes where English is spoken have no systematic experience with nasal versus nonnasal vowels, but they can still hear differences like this one. Interestingly, towards their first birthday, infants apparently lose this competence and no longer readily distinguish sounds that are not part of their own language environment. For example, Werker and Lalonde (1988) found that 6- to 8-month-old infants of English-speaking parents could distinguish speech sounds that are used in Hindi but not in English. By 11 to 13 months of age, the infants, like their parents, could no longer tell the difference.

Findings like these suggest that newborns are biologically capable of hearing the entire range of phonemes in all languages worldwide. But as babies grow and are more exposed to a particular language, they only notice the linguistic distinctions that are meaningful in that environment. For example, the Japanese youngster in the photo will learn language sounds used in Japanese but will have difficulty hearing sounds used in other languages, such as English. Specialization in one language apparently comes at a cost; the potential to hear other language sounds easily is lost (Kuhl, 1993).

Of course, hearing individual phonemes is only the first step in perceiving speech. One of the biggest challenges for infants is identifying recurring patterns of sounds—words. Imagine, for example, an infant overhearing this conversation between a parent and an older sibling:

Sibling: Jerry got a new *bike.*
Parent: Was his old *bike* broken?
Sibling: No. He'd saved his allowance to buy a new mountain *bike.*

An infant listening to this conversation hears *bike* three times. Can the infant learn from this experience? Yes. When 7- to 8-month-olds hear a word repeatedly in different sentences, they later pay more attention to this word than to words they haven't heard previously. Evidently, 7- and 8-month-olds can listen to sentences and recognize the sound patterns that they hear repeatedly (Juscyzk & Aslin, 1995; Saffran, Aslin, & Newport, 1996). (Of course, they don't yet understand the meanings of these words; they just recognize a word as a distinct configuration of sounds.)

Parents (and other adults) often help infants master language sounds by talking in a distinctive style. **In *infant-directed speech,* adults speak slowly and with exaggerated changes in pitch and loudness.** If you could hear the mother in the photo talking to her baby, you would notice that she alternates between speaking softly and loudly and between high and low pitches. (Infant-directed speech was once known as *motherese* until it became clear that most caregivers, not just mothers, talk this way to infants.) Infant-directed speech attracts infants'

attention more than adult-directed speech (Kaplan et al., 1995), perhaps because its slower pace and accentuated changes provide infants with more, and more salient, language clues, just as understanding a person speaking a foreign language is easier when that person talks slowly and carefully.

Infant-directed speech, then, helps infants perceive the sounds that are fundamental to their language. But how do infants accomplish the next step, producing speech? We answer this question in the next section of this module.

PUBLIC SPEAKING IN A FEW EASY STEPS

As any new parent can testify, newborns and young babies use sound to communicate—they cry to indicate discomfort or distress. At 2 months, though, babies begin to make sounds that are language-based. **They begin to produce vowel-like sounds, such as "ooooooo" or "ahhhhhh," a phenomenon known as** *cooing.* Sometimes infants become quite excited as they coo, perhaps reflecting the joy of simply playing with sounds.

After cooing comes *babbling,* speechlike sound that has no meaning. A typical 5- or 6-month-old might say "dah" or "bah," utterances that sound like a single syllable consisting of a consonant and a vowel. Over the next few months, babbling becomes more elaborate as babies apparently experiment with more complex speech sounds. Older infants sometimes repeat a sound as in "bahbahbah" and begin to combine different sounds, "dahmahbah" (Oller, 1986).

At roughly 7 months, infants' babbling includes *intonation,* **a pattern of rising or falling pitch.** In English declarative sentences, for example, pitch first rises, then falls towards the end of the sentence. In questions, however, the pitch is level, then rises towards the end of the question. Older babies' babbling reflects these patterns: Babies who are brought up by English-speaking parents have both the declarative and question patterns of intonation in their babbling. Babies exposed to a language with different patterns of intonation, such as Japanese or French, reflect their language's intonation in their babbling (Levitt & Utman, 1992). Richard, the baby in the vignette who hears French at his day-care center, will definitely babble with French intonation!

The appearance of intonation in babbling indicates a strong link between perception and production of speech: Infants' babbling is influenced by the characteristics of the speech that they hear. If hearing is crucial for the development of babbling, then can deaf children babble? The "Real Children" feature has the answer.

> *Babbling appears at 5 or 6 months with a single consonant and vowel, then combines different speech sounds and, even later, includes intonation.*

Real Children: LORRAINE LEARNS TO BABBLE

Lorraine, now 22 months old, has been deaf since birth. She has worn a hearing aid since she was 7 months old and receives language therapy weekly from a speech-language therapist. At 11 months, Lorraine occasionally made simple sounds consisting of a consonant and a vowel, such as "bah." Her babbling remained very simple until about 15 months of age, when she began uttering longer, repetitive sequences of syllables. Thus, compared to children with normal hearing, Lorraine's babbling was delayed by several months.

In another respect, Lorraine's language skills developed right on schedule: As soon as Lorraine's parents learned of her deafness, they began using American Sign Language to communicate with her. They noticed that, at about 8 months, Lorraine began to imitate parts of the signs they used with her. At 13 months, she began to produce sequences of signs that were meaningless but matched the tempo and duration of real signing. In other words, Lorraine was going through different phases of babbling with her signing. ■

Lorraine is typical of deaf children: Compared to children with normal hearing, her babbling was much delayed as spoken language but right on schedule as sign language (Oller & Eilers, 1988; Pettito & Marentette, 1991). Evidently, in the middle of the first year, infants try to reproduce the sounds of language that others use in trying to communicate with them (or, in the case of deaf infants, the signs that others use). Hearing "dog," an infant may first say "dod," then "gog" before finally saying "dog" correctly. In the same way that beginning typists gradually link movements of their fingers with particular keys, through babbling, infants learn to use their lips, tongue, and teeth to produce specific sounds, gradually making sounds that approximate real words (Poulson et al., 1991). Fortunately, learning to produce language sounds is easier for most babies than the cartoon suggests!

Reprinted by permission of Johnny Hart and Creators Syndicate, Inc.

The ability to produce sound, coupled with the 1-year-old's advanced ability to perceive speech sounds, sets the stage for the infant's first true words. In Module 9.2, we'll see how this happens.

Check Your Learning

1. Young infants can distinguish many language sounds, but older infants are more likely to notice only _____.

2. Adults using infant-directed speech speak slowly and exaggerate the loudness and _____ of their speech.

3. At about 7 months, most infants' babbling includes phrases that sound like questions, which shows infants are learning about patterns of _____.

Answers: (1) sounds that they hear in their language environment, (2) pitch, (3) intonation

EARNING THE MEANINGS OF WORDS

Learning Objectives

- **How do children make the transition from babbling to talking?**
- **What different styles of language learning do young children use?**
- **What rules do children follow to learn new words?**
- **What conditions foster children's learning of new words?**

Nabina is 2 years old and just loves to talk. What amazes her parents is how quickly she adds words to her vocabulary. For example, the day her parents brought home a computer, Nabina watched as they set it up. The next day, she spontaneously pointed to the computer and said, "puter." This happens all the time—Nabina hears a word once or twice, then uses it correctly herself. Nabina's parents wonder how she does this, particularly because learning vocabulary in a foreign language is so difficult for them!

At about their first birthday, most youngsters say their first words. Typically, these words are an extension of advanced babbling, consisting of a consonant-vowel pair that may be repeated. *Mama* and *dada* are probably the most common first words that stem from advanced babbling. Other common words in early vocabularies denote animals, food, and toys (Nelson, 1973). Also common are words that denote actions (for example, *go*). By age 2, most youngsters have a vocabulary of a few hundred words; and by age 6, a typical child's vocabulary includes over 10,000 words (Anglin, 1993).

Like Nabina, most children learn new words with extraordinary ease and speed. How they do it? We'll answer that question in this module.

UNDERSTANDING WORDS AS SYMBOLS

When my daughter, Laura, was 9 months old she sometimes babbled "bay-bay." A few months later, she still said "bay-bay" but with an important difference. As a 9-month-old, "bay-bay" was simply an interesting set of sounds that she made for no reason (at least, none that was obvious to us). As a 13-month-old, "bay-bay" was her way of saying "baby." What had happened between 9 and 13 months? Laura had begun to understand that speech is more than just entertaining sound. She realized that sounds form words that refer to objects, actions, and properties. Put another way, Laura recognized that words are symbols, entities that stand for other entities. She already had formed concepts such as "round, bouncy things" and "furry things that bark" and "little humans that adults carry" based on her own experiences. With the insight that speech sounds can denote these concepts, she began to match words and concepts (Reich, 1986).

If this argument is correct, we should find that children use symbols in other areas, not just in language. They do. Gestures are symbols, and like the baby in the photo, infants begin to gesture shortly before their first birthday (Goodwyn & Acredolo, 1993). Young children may smack their lips to indicate hunger or wave "bye-bye" when leaving. In these cases, gestures and words convey a message equally well. Both reflect the child's developing ability to use symbols to represent actions and objects, which is one of the grand achievements of human development.

STYLES OF LEARNING LANGUAGE

As youngsters expand their vocabulary, they often adopt a distinctive style of learning language (Bates, Bretherton, & Snyder, 1988). **Some children have a** *referential style;* **their vocabularies tend to be dominated by words that are the names of objects, persons, or actions. Other children have an** *expressive style;* **their vocabularies include some names but also many social phrases that are used like a single word, such as "go away," "what'd you want?," and "I want it."**

Katherine Nelson (1973) was the investigator who discovered these two basic styles of learning language. She studied 18 children for about a year, starting at approximately their first birthdays, a period during which the children's vocabularies increased from fewer than 10 words to nearly 200. She visited each child monthly for about an hour to tape record samples of spontaneous speech and test language development.

By the time children had 50-word vocabularies—typically at about 1½ years—two distinct groups had emerged. Children in the referential group had vocabularies dominated by words that were the names of objects, persons, or actions, such as *milk, Jo-Jo,* and *up.* Other children, the expressive group, also learned some names but knew a much higher percentage of words that were used in social interactions *(go away, I want it)* and question words *(what, where).* For example, Rachel, a referential child, had 41 name words in her 50-word vocabulary but only 2 words for social interaction or questions; Elizabeth, an expressive child, had a more balanced vocabulary: 24 name words and 14 for social interactions and questions.

Language is primarily an intellectual tool for referential children and primarily a social tool for expressive children.

Children with the referential style primarily use language as an intellectual tool—a means of talking about objects. In contrast, children with an expressive style use language as more of a social tool—a way of enhancing interactions with others. Of course, both of these functions—intellectual and social—are important functions of language, and as you might expect, most children blend the referential and expressive styles of learning language.

FAST MAPPING MEANINGS TO WORDS

Having the insight that a word can symbolize an object or action, the young talker now faces a formidable task. Matching a word with its exact referent is challenging because most words have many plausible but incorrect referents. To illustrate, imagine what's going through the mind of the child in the photo. The mother has just pointed to her glasses and said, "Glasses. These are glasses. See the glasses." To the mother (and you), this all seems crystal clear and incredibly straightforward. But what might a child learn from this episode? Perhaps the correct referent for "glasses." But a youngster could, just as reasonably, conclude that "glasses" refers to the lens, to the color of the frames, or to the mother's actions in pointing to the glasses.

Surprisingly, though, most youngsters learn the proper meanings of simple words in just a few presentations. ***Fast mapping* refers to children's**

ability to make connections between new words and referents so rapidly that they cannot be considering all possible meanings for the new word. Fast mapping of meaning onto new words means that children must use rules to link words with their meanings (Carey, 1978).

What are the rules that guide children to discover a word's meaning? How can we identify them? A study by Au and Glusman (1990) answers both questions. Au and Glusman presented preschoolers with a stuffed animal with pink horns that otherwise resembled a monkey and called it a *mido*. *Mido* was then repeated several times, always referring to the monkeylike stuffed animal with pink horns. Later, these youngsters were asked to find a *theri* in a set of stuffed animals that included several *mido*. Never having heard of a *theri*, what did the children do? They never picked a *mido*; instead, they selected other stuffed animals. Knowing that *mido* referred to monkeylike animals with pink horns, evidently they decided that *theri* had to refer to one of the other stuffed animals.

Apparently children were following this simple but effective rule for learning new words:

■ If an unfamiliar word is heard in the presence of objects that already have names and objects that don't, the word refers to one of the objects that doesn't have a name.

Can you think of other simple rules that might help children match words with the correct referent? Here are two more that child development researchers have discovered (Taylor & Gelman, 1989):

> *Children use simple rules to help them simplify the process of associating names to new objects and actions.*

■ A name refers to a whole object, not its parts or its relation to other objects, and refers not just to this particular object but to all objects of the same type. For example, when a grandparent points to a stuffed animal on a shelf and says "dinosaur," children conclude that *dinosaur* refers to the entire dinosaur, not just its ears or nose, not to the fact that the dinosaur is on a shelf, and not to this specific dinosaur but to all dinosaurlike objects.

■ If an object already has a name and another name is presented, the new name denotes a subcategory of the original name. If the child who knows the meaning of *dinosaur* sees a brother point to another dinosaur and hears the brother say "T-rex," the child will conclude that T-rex is a special type of dinosaur.

Rules like these make it possible for children like Nabina, the child in the vignette, to learn words rapidly because they reduce the number of possible referents.

Of course, these rules for learning new words are not foolproof. **A common mistake is *underextension*, defining a word too narrowly.** Using *car* to refer only to the family car and *ball* to a favorite toy ball are examples of underextension. **Between 1 and 3 years, children sometimes make the opposite error, *overextension*, defining a word too broadly.** Children may use *car* to also refer to buses and trucks or, like the boy in the photo, use *doggie* to refer to all four-legged animals.

The overextension error occurs more frequently when children are producing words than when they are comprehending words. Two-year-old Jason may say "doggie" to refer to a goat but nevertheless correctly point to a picture of a goat when asked. Because overextension is more common in word production, it may actually reflect another fast-mapping rule that children follow: "If you can't remember the name for an object, say the name of a related object" (Naigles & Gelman, 1995).

Both underextension and overextension disappear gradually as youngsters refine their meanings for words based on feedback they receive from parents and others.

ENCOURAGING WORD LEARNING

How can parents and other adults help children learn words? For children to expand their vocabularies, they need to hear others speak. Not surprisingly, then, children learn words more rapidly if their parents speak to them frequently (Huttenlocher et al., 1991). Of course, sheer quantity of parental speech is not all that matters. Parents can foster word learning by naming objects that are the focus of a child's attention (Dunham, Dunham, & Curwin, 1993). Parents can name different products on store shelves as they point to them. During a walk, parents can label the objects—birds, plants, vehicles—that the child sees.

Parents can also help children learn words by asking them questions. For example, do you remember your parents reading stories to you at bedtime? Bedtime stories are often fun for parents and children alike, and they provide opportunities for children to learn new words. However, the way that parents read makes a difference. In a study of 4-year-olds (Sénéchal, Thomas, & Monker, 1995), one group of parents simply read the story and children listened. Parents in another group read the story and questioned their children. After specific words, parents stopped and asked a "what" or "where" question that the child could answer with the target word. Afterwards, Sénéchal and her colleagues measured children's abilities to recognize the target words and produce them. The graph shows that children who just listened recognized about one-third of the target words but children who answered questions recognized nearly half. Children who answered questions were also much more likely to produce the target words.

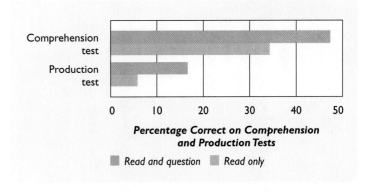

Percentage Correct on Comprehension and Production Tests

■ Read and question ■ Read only

Why is questioning effective? Think about what happens when an adult reads a sentence (e.g., "Arthur is angling") and then asks a question about the new word (e.g., "What is Arthur doing?"). A child must actively match the new word *(angling)* with the pictured activity *(fishing)* and then say the word aloud. When parents read without questioning, children can ignore the words they don't understand. Questioning, however, forces them to identify the meanings of new words and practice saying them.

Viewing television can also help word learning under some circumstances. For example, preschool children who regularly watch *Sesame Street* often have larger vocabularies by the time they enter kindergarten than preschoolers who watch *Sesame Street* only occasionally (Rice et al., 1990). Other television programs, notably cartoons, do not have this positive influence. What accounts for the difference? *Sesame*

Helps u or hurts in school

Street involves children in language activities to help them learn words (in the photo, words with *E*). Cartoons, however, require no interaction at all.

For school-age children, reading is one of the best ways to learn new words. Written material—books, magazines, textbooks—almost always contains more unfamiliar words than conversational language, so reading is rich in opportunities to expand vocabulary (Hayes, 1988). Not surprisingly, children who read a lot tend to have larger vocabularies than children who read less often (Allen, Cipielewski, & Stanovich, 1992).

Research on reading, along with research on television and parents' influence, points to a simple but powerful conclusion: Children are most likely to learn new words when they participate in activities that force them to understand the meanings of new words and use those new words. Is learning new words (and other aspects of language) more difficult for children learning two languages? The "Cultural Influences" feature has the answer.

Cultural Influences: **GROWING UP BILINGUAL**

About 6 million American schoolchildren come from homes where English is not the primary language. In some states, 25 percent or more of the children are bilingual, and the percentages are even higher in some urban areas (U.S. Bureau of the Census, 1995b). These youngsters usually speak English and another language, such as Spanish or, like the children in the photo, Chinese.

Is learning two languages easier or harder than learning just one language? For much of the 20th century, the general view was that bilingualism harmed children's development. One child psychology text published in 1952 surveyed the research and concluded, "There can be no doubt that the child reared in a bilingual environment is handicapped in his language growth. One can debate the issue as to whether speech facility in two languages is worth the consequent retardation. . . ." (Thompson, 1952, p. 367). Today, we know that this conclusion is wrong because it was based on studies of poor, immigrant children's scores on intelligence tests. In retrospect, immigrant children's test scores had more to do with their poverty and unfamiliarity with a new culture than with their bilingualism.

In fact, modern studies lead to a different picture. When 1- and 2-year-olds learn two languages simultaneously, they often progress somewhat slowly at first because they mix words from the two languages. By age 3 or 4, however, children separate the languages; and by the time they begin elementary school, most are as proficient as monolinguals in both languages (Baker, 1993; Lanza, 1992). During elementary school, bilingual children actually *surpass* monolingual children on some measures of language skill. Bilingual children better understand fine points of grammar. Bilingual children also better understand that words are simply arbitrary symbols. For example, bilingual youngsters are more likely than monolingual children to understand that, as long as all English speakers agreed, *dog* could refer to cats and *cat* could refer to dogs (Bialystok, 1988; Campbell & Sais, 1995).

Of course, many children in America can't speak English at the time when they should begin school. How to teach these children has prompted much national debate. One view is that all Americans should speak English and so all teaching should be in English. Another view is that children learn more effectively in their native tongue and so all teaching should be done in that language.

Bilingual children learn language as rapidly as monolingual children and they better understand grammar and the symbolic nature of words.

Much of the debate over the proper language of instruction is political, reflecting people's desire for a society with a universal cultural heritage and language rather than a society with pluralistic heritages and languages. Ignoring the political aspects, research shows that the best method uses the child's native language *and* English (Padilla et al., 1991; Wong-Fillmore et al., 1985). Initially, children receive basic English-language teaching while they are taught other subjects in their native language. Gradually, more instruction is in English, in step with children's growing proficiency in the second language. When instruction is in children's native language and English, they are most likely to master academic content and English, outcomes that are less likely when instruction is solely in the native language or English. ▨

Check Your Learning

1. Children begin to _____ at about the same age that they begin to talk, and both apparently reflect children's growing understanding of symbols.

2. Children with a(n) _____ style of language learning typically have many social phrases (e.g., *go away*) in their vocabularies.

3. When young children hear an unfamiliar word in the presence of a novel object, they _____.

4. Children are most likely to learn new words when parents _____, when they watch TV programs like *Sesame Street,* and when they read.

Answers: (1) gesture, (2) expressive, (3) infer that the word refers to the novel object, (4) label objects that children play with or ask questions as they read to them

S PEAKING IN SENTENCES

Learning Objectives

- **How do children progress from speaking single words to complicated sentences?**
- **How do children acquire the grammar of their native language?**

MODULE
9.3
Speaking in Sentences

From Two-word Speech
to Complex Sentences

How Children Acquire
Grammar

Jaime's daughter, Luisa, is a curious 2½-year-old who bombards her father with questions. Jaime enjoys Luisa's questioning but he is bothered by the way she phrases her questions. Luisa will say, "What you are doing?" and "Why not she sleep?" Obviously, Jaime doesn't talk this way, so he wonders where Luisa learned to ask questions like this. Is it normal, or is it a symptom of some type of language disorder?

Not long after children begin to talk, they start combining words to form simple sentences. **These simple sentences are the first step in a new area of language** learning, mastering *grammar,* **a language's rules for combining words to create sentences.** We'll begin this module by tracing the stages in children's acquisition of grammar and, along the way, see that Luisa's way of asking questions is quite normal for youngsters learning English. Then we'll examine different factors that influence children's mastery of grammar.

FROM TWO-WORD SPEECH TO COMPLEX SENTENCES

At about 1½ years, children begin to combine individual words to create two-word sentences, like *more juice, gimme cookie, truck go, my truck, Daddy go, Daddy bike.* **Researchers call this kind of talk** *telegraphic speech* **because, like telegrams of days gone by, it consists of only words directly relevant to meaning.** Before phones and e-mail, people sent urgent messages by telegraph, and the charge was based on the number of words. Consequently, telegrams were brief and to the point, containing only the important nouns, verbs, adjectives, and adverbs, much like children's two-word speech.

In their two-word speech, children follow rules to express different meanings. For example, the sentences *truck go* and *Daddy eat* are both about agents—people or objects that do something—and the actions they perform. Here the rule is "agent + action." In contrast, *my truck* is about a possessor and a possession; the rule for creating these sentences is "possessor + possession."

When English-speaking children are in the two-word stage, they use about eight basic rules to express meaning (Brown, 1973). These are listed in the table.

Rules Used to Express Meaning During the Two-word Stage

Rule	Example
agent + action	"Daddy eat"
possessor + possession	"my truck"
action + object	"gimme cookie"
agent + object	"boy car" (meaning the boy is pushing the car)
action + location	"put chair" (meaning put the object in the chair)
entity + location	"truck chair" (meaning the truck is on the chair)
attribute + entity	"big car"
demonstrative + entity	"that cup"

Based on Brown, 1973

Of course, not all children use all eight rules, but most do. And this is true of children around the world (Tager-Flusberg, 1993). Regardless of the language they learn, children's two-word sentences follow a common set of rules that are very useful in describing ideas concerning people and objects, their actions and their properties.

Children around the world use a common set of eight rules to create two-word sentences that describe people and objects, their actions, and their properties.

When children move beyond two-word sentences, they quickly begin to use much longer sentences. For example, at 1½ years, my daughter Laura would say, "gimme juice" or "bye-bye Mom." As a 2½-year-old, she had progressed to "When I finish my ice cream, I'll take a shower, okay?" and "Don't turn the light out—I can't see better!" Her improvement was characteristic of most children. At about the second birthday, children move to three-word and even longer sentences. **Their longer sentences are filled with *grammatical morphemes*, words or endings of words (such as -ing, -ed, or -s) that make a sentence grammatical.** To illustrate, a 1½-year-old might say, "kick ball," but a 3-year-old would be more likely to say, "I am kicking the ball." Compared to the 1½-year-old's telegraphic speech, the 3-year-old has added several elements including a pronoun, *I*, to serve as the subject of the sentence, the auxiliary verb *am*, *-ing* to the verb *kick*, and an article, *the*, before *ball*. Each of these grammatical morphemes makes the older child's sentence slightly more meaningful and much more grammatical by adult standards.

How do children learn all of these subtle nuances of grammar? Conceivably, a child might learn that *kicking* describes kicking that is ongoing and that *kicked* describes kicking that occurred in the past. Later, the child might learn that *raining* describes current weather and *rained* describes past weather. But learning different tenses for individual verbs—one by one— would be remarkably slow going. More effective would be to learn the general rules that "verb + *-ing*" denotes an ongoing activity and "verb + *-ed*" denotes a past activity. In fact, this is what children do: They learn general rules about grammatical morphemes. Jean Berko (1958) conducted one of the first studies showing that children's use of grammatical morphemes is based on their growing knowledge of grammatical rules, not simply memory for individual words. She showed preschoolers pictures of nonsense objects like the one in the diagram. The experimenter labeled it, saying, "This is a wug." Then youngsters were shown pictures of two of the objects while the experimenter said, "Now there is another one. There are two of them. There are two . . . " Most children spontaneously said, "Wugs." Because *wug* is a novel word, children could answer correctly only by applying the rule of adding *-s* to indicate plural.

This is a wug.

Now there is another one.
There are two of them.
There are two_____ .

Sometimes, of course, applying the general rule can lead to very creative communication. For example, as a 2- and 3-year-old, my daughter would say, "unvelcro it," meaning detach the Velcro. She had never heard *unvelcro*, but she created this word from the rule that "*un-* + verb" means to reverse or stop the action of a verb. Creating such novel words is, in fact, evidence that children learn grammar by applying rules, not learning individual words.

Additional evidence that children master grammar by learning rules comes from preschoolers' *overregularization*, applying rules to words that are exceptions to the rule. Youngsters learning English may incorrectly add an *s* instead of using an irregular plural—*two mans* instead of *two men* or *two foots* instead of *two feet*. With the past tense, children may add *ed* instead of using an irregular past tense—*I goed* instead of *I went* or *she runned* instead of *she ran* (Marcus et al., 1992). Children apparently know the general rule but not all the words that are exceptions.

The rules governing grammatical morphemes range from fairly simple to very complex. The rule for plurals, add *-s*, is simple to apply and, as you might expect, it's one of the first grammatical morphemes that children master. Adding *-ing* to denote ongoing action is also simple and it, too, is mastered early. More complex forms, such as the various forms of the verb *to be* are mastered later; but, remarkably, by the end of the preschool years, most children have mastered most of the rules that govern grammatical morphemes.

At the same time that preschoolers are mastering grammatical morphemes, they extend their speech beyond the subject-verb-object construction that is basic in English. You can see these changes in the way children ask questions. Children's questions during two-word speech are marked by intonation alone. Soon after a child can declare, "My ball," he or she can also ask "My ball?" Children quickly discover *wh* words *(who, what, when, where, why)*, but they don't use them correctly. Like Luisa, the 2½-year-old in the module-opening vignette, many youngsters merely attach the *wh* word to the beginning of a sentence without changing the rest of the sentence: *What he eating? What we see?* But by 3 or 3½ years, youngsters insert the required auxiliary verb before the subject, creating *What is he eating?* or *What did we see?* (deVilliers & deVilliers, 1985).

Between ages 3 and 6 years, children also learn to use negation ("That isn't a butterfly") and embedded sentences ("Maya thinks that Sam is ugly."). They begin to comprehend passive voice ("The ball was kicked by the girl.") as opposed to the active voice ("The girl kicked the ball."), although full understanding of this form continues into the elementary-school years (Tager-Flusberg, 1993). In short, by the time most children enter kindergarten, they use most of the grammatical forms of their native language with great skill.

Ponder these accomplishments for a moment, particularly in light of what else you know about 5-year-old children. Most can neither read nor do arithmetic and some don't know the letters of the alphabet, but virtually all have mastered the grammar of their native tongue. How do they do it? Some answers to this question are in the next section.

HOW CHILDREN ACQUIRE GRAMMAR

If you were asked to explain how children master grammar, where would you begin? You might propose that children learn to speak grammatically by listening to and then copying adult sentences. In much the same way that Richard, the English-speaking baby at the beginning of Module 9.1, imitated the French language sounds that he heard, children might simply copy the grammatical forms they hear. In fact, B. F. Skinner (1957) and other learning theorists once claimed that all aspects of language—sounds, words, grammar, and communication—could be learned through imitation and reinforcement (Whitehurst & Vasta, 1975).

Critics were quick to point to some flaws in the learning explanation of grammar, however. One problem is that children produce many more sentences than they have ever heard. In fact, most of children's sentences are novel, which is difficult to explain in terms of simple imitation of adults' speech. For example, when children create questions by inserting a *wh* word at the beginning of a sentence ("What she doing?"), who are they imitating? Also troublesome for the learning view is that even when children imitate adult sentences, they do not imitate adult grammar. In simply trying to repeat "I am drawing a picture," young children will say "I draw picture." Furthermore, linguists, particularly Noam Chomsky (1957), argued that grammatical rules are far too complex for toddlers and preschoolers to infer them solely on the basis of speech that they hear.

If grammatical rules are not acquired through imitation and reinforcement, what is the mechanism? Perhaps children are born with mechanisms that simplify the task of learning grammar (Slobin, 1985). According to this view, children are born with neural circuits in the brain that allow them to infer the grammar of the language that they hear. That is, grammar itself is not built into the child's nervous system, but processes that guide the learning of grammar are.

This proposal that inborn mechanisms help children to learn grammar might not be as intuitively appealing as imitation, but there is much evidence supporting it:

1. *Specific regions of the brain are known to be involved in language processing.* If children are born with a "grammar-learning processor," it should be possible to locate a specific region or regions of the brain that are involved in learning grammar. In fact, you may remember from Module 4.3 that for most people the left hemisphere of the brain plays a critical role in understanding language. Some functions of language have been located even more precisely. For example, the shaded area in the diagram is Broca's area: a region in the left frontal cortex that is necessary for combining words into meaningful sentences. The fact that specific areas in the brain, such as Broca's area, have well-defined functions for language make it plausible that children have specialized neural circuits that help them learn grammar.

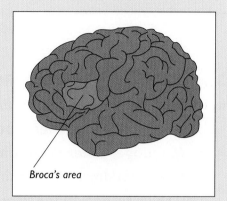

Broca's area

2. *Only humans learn grammar readily.* If grammar is learned solely through imitation and reinforcement, then it should be possible to teach rudimentary grammar to nonhumans. If, instead, learning grammar depends upon specialized neural mechanisms that are present only in humans, then efforts to teach grammar to nonhumans should fail. This prediction has been tested many times by trying to teach grammar to chimpanzees, the species closest to humans on the evolutionary ladder. Chimpanzees like the one in the photo have been taught to communicate using gestures taken from sign language or with plastic chips to stand for words. The result? Chimps master only the simplest of grammatical rules and, even then, do so only with massive effort that is completely unlike the preschool child's learning of grammar (Savage-Rumbaugh et al., 1993). Since numerous efforts to teach grammar to chimps have failed, this suggests that children rely upon some type of inborn mechanism that is unique to humans to master grammar.

3. *There is a critical period for learning language.* You recall, from Module 1.2, that a critical period refers to a time in development when children master skills or behaviors readily. Apparently, the period from birth to about 12 years is critical to acquiring language generally and mastering grammar particularly. If children do not acquire language in this period, they will never truly master language later. Evidence of a critical period for language comes from studies of isolated children. In one tragic instance, a baby girl named Genie was restrained by a harness during the day and in a straightjacket-like device at night. No one was permitted to talk to Genie, and she was beaten when she made any noises. When Genie was discovered, at age 13, her language was very primitive. After several years of language training, her mastery of grammar remains limited, resembling the telegraphic speech of a 2-year-old (Curtiss, 1989; Rymer, 1993).

Further evidence for a critical period for language comes from studies of individuals learning second languages. Individuals master the grammar of a foreign language at the level of a native speaker only if they are exposed to the language prior to adolescence (Newport, 1991). Why is it that one period of time can be so much more influential for language than others? Why can't missed language experiences be made up after age 12? A critical period for language answers these questions. That is, just as females ovulate for only a limited portion of the life span, the neural mechanisms involved in learning grammar may function only during infancy and childhood.

Some researchers believe built-in neural circuits help children infer the grammar of their native language; other researchers believe children use cognitive skills to determine regular patterns in the speech they hear.

The evidence in favor of an inborn grammar-learning device is impressive but only indirect. As yet, there is no definitive finding that makes an airtight case for the existence of a grammar-learning device. Consequently, scientists have continued to look for other explanations. Some theorists believe that children learn grammar using the same cognitive skills that allow them to learn other rules and regularities in their environments. **According to the *semantic bootstrapping hypothesis*, children rely upon their knowledge of the meanings of words to discover grammatical rules** (Bates & MacWhinney, 1987). That is, children notice that some words (nouns) typically refer to objects, and others (verbs) to actions. They also notice that nouns and verbs have distinct functions in sentences. By detecting such regularities in speech, children gradually infer the grammatical rules that provide structure for their language.

Both the grammar-learning device and the bootstrapping hypothesis could be correct: Children may learn grammar using some mechanisms that are specific to language as well as some that are not. And both views agree that language experience is important because it provides the information from which grammatical rules are inferred. After all, children growing up in a home where Japanese is spoken master Japanese grammar, not Russian or English grammar. For many children, parents' speech is the prime source of information about language. Parents fine-tune their speech so that it includes examples of the speech that their children are attempting to master (Hoff-Ginsberg, 1990). For example, when 2- and 3-year-olds begin to experiment with pronouns like *you, I, she,* and *he,* their parents provide many examples of how to use pronouns correctly. Similarly, as these children begin to use auxiliary verbs such as *have, has, was,* and *did,* parents use speech that is especially rich in these verbs (Sokolov, 1993). By providing extra instances of the parts of speech that children are mastering, parents make it easier for children to unearth new grammatical rules.

Parents also provide feedback to help children evaluate their tentative grammatical rules. Most of the feedback is indirect. When a child's speech is incorrect or incomplete, parents don't say, "That's wrong!" or "How ungrammatical!" Instead, they rephrase or elaborate the child's remark. For example, if a child were to say, "Sara eating cookie," a parent might reply, "Yes, Sara is eating a cookie." "Doggie go" might lead to "Yes, the doggie left." A parent's reply captures the meaning of the child's remark while demonstrating correct grammatical forms (Bohannon, MacWhinney, & Snow, 1990). At the same time, when a child's grammar is accurate, a parent will often simply repeat it or continue the conversation. Thus, when parents rephrase their children's speech, it means that some aspect of the remark was ungrammatical; if they continue the conversation, it means that the remark was grammatical.

Parents don't provide feedback for all utterances; in fact, a majority of children's errors go uncorrected. However, the amount of feedback is sufficient for children to reject incorrect hypotheses about grammatical rules and retain correct ones (Bohannon et al., 1990).

How can we evaluate these different ideas about how children learn grammar? As yet, there is no single, comprehensive theory of how grammar is mastered; but there is general agreement that such a theory will include some mechanisms that are specific to learning grammar, a child actively seeking to identify regularities in his or her environment, and an environment that is rich in language. All three factors keep children on the trail that leads to mastering grammar.

The "Making Children's Lives Better" feature suggests some ways parents and other adults can help children master grammar and other aspects of language.

Making Children's Lives Better: PROMOTING LANGUAGE DEVELOPMENT

Parents help children learn grammar by providing extra examples of parts of speech their children are trying to master and by providing feedback for ungrammatical speech.

Adults eager to promote children's language development can follow a few guidelines:

1. Talk with children frequently and treat them as partners in conversation. That is, try talking with children interactively, not directively.

2. Use a child's speech to show new language forms. Expand a child's remark to introduce new vocabulary or new grammatical forms. Rephrase a child's ungrammatical remark to show the correct grammar.

3. Encourage children to go beyond minimal use of language. Have them answer questions in phrases and sentences, not single words. Have them replace vague words such as "stuff" or "somebody" with more descriptive ones.

4. Listen. This guideline has two parts. First, because children often talk slowly, it's tempting for adults to complete their sentences for them. Don't; let children express themselves. Second, pay attention to what children are saying and respond appropriately. Let children learn that language works.

5. Make language fun. Use books, rhymes, songs, jokes, and foreign words to increase a child's interest in learning language. ■

Of course, as children's language improves during the preschool years, others can understand it more readily, which means that children become better at communicating. The emergence and growth of communication skills is the topic of the next module.

Check Your Learning

1. Children's first sentences are referred to as telegraphic speech because _____.

2. As children move beyond two-word sentences, _____ appear in their speech, beginning with those that follow simple rules.

3. Findings supporting the idea that children are born with specialized neural circuits for learning grammar include the facts that specific brain regions are associated with language processing, _____, and there is a critical period for learning language.

4. Parents help their children learn grammar by _____ and by providing them with feedback.

Answers: (1) they include only words that are essential to meaning, (2) grammatical morphemes, (3) only humans learn grammar, (4) providing extra examples of the parts of speech that children are trying to master

U SING LANGUAGE TO COMMUNICATE

Learning Objectives

■ **When and how do children learn to take turns in conversations?**

■ **What are the skills required to be an effective speaker? When do children master them?**

■ **What is involved in becoming a good listener?**

Morgan and Brittany, both 5-year-olds, usually are good friends, but right now they're boiling mad at each other. Morgan was going to the mall with her dad to buy some new markers. Brittany found out and gave Morgan money to buy some markers for her, too. Morgan returned with the markers, but they weren't the kind that Brittany liked, so she was angry. Morgan was angry because she didn't think Brittany had any right to be upset; after all, it was Brittany's fault for not telling her what kind to buy. Meanwhile, Morgan's dad hopes they come to some understanding soon and cut out all the racket.

Listening to these girls arguing is an excellent way to learn what is needed for effective communication. Both talk at the same time, their remarks are rambling or incoherent, and neither bothers to listen to the other. In other words, for effective oral communication, don't do what they do. Follow these guidelines instead:

■ People should take turns, alternating as speaker and listener.

■ A speaker's remarks should relate to the topic and be clear to the listener.

■ A listener should pay attention and let the speaker know if his or her remarks don't make sense.

Complete mastery of these communication skills is a lifelong pursuit; after all, even adults often miscommunicate with one another because they don't observe one or more of these rules. However, youngsters grasp many of the basics of communication early in life. Let's see.

TAKING TURNS

Many parents begin to encourage turn taking long before infants say their first words (Field & Widmayer, 1982):

Parent:	Can you see the bird?
Infant (cooing):	ooooh
Parent:	It *is* a pretty bird.
Infant:	ooooh
Parent:	You're right, it's a cardinal.

Soon after 1-year-olds begin to speak, parents like the father in the photo encourage their youngsters to participate in conversational turn taking. To help children along, parents often carry both sides of a conversation to demonstrate how the roles of speaker and listener alternate (Ervin-Tripp, 1970):

Parent (initiating conversation):	What's Amy eating?
Parent (illustrating reply for child):	She's eating a cookie.

By age 2, spontaneous turn taking is common in conversations between youngsters and adults (Barton & Tomasello, 1991). And by 3 years of age, children have progressed to the point that if a listener fails to reply promptly, the child repeats his or her remark in order to elicit a response (Garvey & Berninger, 1981). A 3-year-old might say, "Hi, Paul" to an older sibling who's busy reading. If Paul doesn't answer in a few seconds, the 3-year-old might say, "Hi, Paul" again. When Paul remains unresponsive, the 3-year-old is likely to shout, "PAUL!"—showing that by this age children understand the norm that a comment deserves a response.

SPEAKING EFFECTIVELY

You've probably endured at least one boring conversation that left you wondering afterwards, "What was the point?" The moral of this experience is that every message—whether an informal conversation or a formal lecture—should have a clear meaning. However, clarity can only be judged by considering the listener's age, experience, knowledge of the topic, and the context of the conversation. For example, think about the simple request "Please hand me the Phillips-head screwdriver." This message may be clear to older listeners familiar with different types of screwdrivers, but it won't mean much to younger listeners who think all screwdrivers are alike. And, if the tool box is filled with Phillips-head screwdrivers of assorted sizes, the message won't be clear even to a knowledgeable listener.

Constructing clear messages is a fine art, but, amazingly, by the preschool years, youngsters begin to adjust their messages to match the listener and the context. For example, as you'll see in the "Focus on Research" feature, 4-year-olds use simpler grammar and avoid complex topics when talking to 2-year-olds.

Focus on Research: PRESCHOOLERS SPEAK DIFFERENTLY TO YOUNGER CHILDREN

Who were the investigators and what was the aim of the study? A good general rule for effective communication is that speakers should consider their listeners' level of ability. Thus, college professors should teach at a different level to graduate students than to undergraduates, physicians should discuss diseases at a different level with other medical personnel than with patients, and parents should speak at a different level to one another than to their children. Do preschool children know this important communicative rule? Do they take the listener's ability level into account? These were the questions that Marilyn Shatz and Rochel Gelman (1973) wanted to answer.

How did the investigators measure the topic of interest? Shatz and Gelman asked 4-year-olds to explain how a toy worked, once to a 2-year-old and once to an adult. Shatz and Gelman tape-recorded these explanations so that they could measure the complexity of the 4-year-olds' speech.

Who were the children in the study? Shatz and Gelman tested sixteen 3- to 5-year-olds; the average age was 4 years, 4 months.

What was the design of the study? This study was experimental: The independent variable was the age of the person to whom the 4-year-old explained the toy—either a 2-year-old or an adult. Shatz and Gelman had many dependent variables, including the total amount of speech and the average length of each remark. The study was not developmental (only 4-year-olds participated and they were tested just once), so it was neither cross-sectional nor longitudinal.

Were there ethical concerns with the study? No. The task—describing a toy to a younger child and an adult—posed no danger to the children. Mothers were present during testing.

What were the results? The graphs show the impact of the age of the listener (2-year-old versus adult) on the length and complexity of the 4-year-olds' talk.

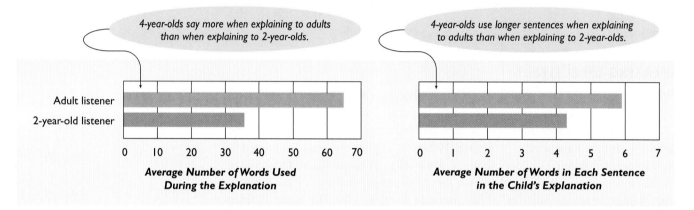

You can see that 4-year-olds talked more overall to adults than to 2-year-olds. Also, 4-year-olds' sentences were longer to adult listeners than to 2-year-old listeners. Shatz and Gelman also analyzed the grammatical structures of all sentences of at least four words and found that children used simpler grammar and more attention-getting words, such as *see, look, watch,* and *hey,* when speaking with 2-year-olds. Here, for example, is how one 4-year-old child explained the toy to her two different listeners. (By the way, the toy is a garage with drivers and trucks that carry marbles to a dumping station):

> Adult listener: *You're supposed to put one of these persons in, see? Then one goes with the other little girl. And then the little boy. He's the little boy and he drives. And then they back up.... And then the little girl falls out and then it goes backwards.*

> 2-year-old listener: *Watch, Perry. Watch this. He's back in here. Now he drives up. Look, Perry. Look here, Perry. Those are marbles, Perry. Put the men in here. Now I'll do it (Shatz & Gelman, 1973, p. 13).*

What did the investigators conclude? By changing how much they say, their grammar, and their use of attentional words, 4-year-olds create messages that are more appropriate for 2-year-old listeners. ■

Shatz and Gelman's findings show that preschoolers are already sensitive to the importance of the listener's skill in formulating a clear message. More recent findings also show that children consider the listener and setting in devising clear messages:

■ School-age children give more elaborate messages to listeners who are unfamiliar with a topic than to listeners who are familiar with it (Sonnenschein, 1988). For example, a child describing where to find a toy store in a mall will give more detailed directions to a listener who has never been to the mall.

■ School-age children speak differently to adults and peers. They are more likely to speak politely with adults and be more demanding with peers (Warren-Leubecker & Bohannon, 1989). A child might ask a parent, "May I have one of your cookies?" but say to a peer, "Give me one of your cookies."

■ **Some African Americans speak** *Black English,* **a dialect of standard English that has slightly different grammatical rules.** For example, "He be tired" in Black English is synonymous with "He is tired" in standard English. Many African American children learn both Black English and standard English, and they switch dialects depending on the situation (Warren & McCloskey, 1993). They use standard English more often in school and when talking with European Americans but use Black English more often at home and when talking with African American peers.

All of these findings show that school-age children (and, sometimes, preschoolers) are well on their way to understanding the factors that must be considered in creating clear messages. In the next section, we'll see if children are as skilled at listening.

LISTENING WELL

If a message is vague or confusing, the listener should ask the speaker to clarify the message. This seems obvious enough, but young children do not always realize when a message is ambiguous. Told to find "the red toy," they may promptly select the red ball from a pile that includes a red toy car, a red block, and a red toy hammer. Instead of asking the speaker which *specific* red toy, young listeners often assume that they know which toy the speaker had in mind (Beal & Belgrad, 1990). Only when messages almost defy comprehension—they are too soft to be heard or give obviously ambiguous or even conflicting information—are youngsters likely to detect the shortcomings of messages. Because young children's remarks often contain ambiguities and because, as listeners, they often do not detect ambiguities, young children often miscommunicate, just like Morgan and Brittany in the opening vignette. Brittany probably didn't communicate exactly what kind of markers she wanted, and Morgan didn't understand that the directions were unclear. Throughout the elementary-school years, youngsters gradually master the many skills involved in determining if a message is consistent and clear (Ackerman, 1993).

Young listeners often ignore ambiguities in messages and sometimes interpret metaphor and sarcasm literally.

Sometimes listeners must go beyond the words to understand the real meaning of a message. Metaphor is one example. When I tell my teenage sons, "Your bedroom is a junk yard," you (and they) know that this remark is not to be taken literally. Instead, the metaphor highlights the fact that the bedroom is a mess and filled with things that could be thrown away.

As you might expect, understanding nonliteral meanings of messages develops slowly. In the case of metaphor, young children easily understand simple metaphors in which the nonliteral meaning is based on references to concrete objects and their properties. For example, a parent might say to a 5-year-old, "You're a fish," referring to how well the child swims and enjoys the water, and the child will likely understand.

More complex metaphors require children to make connections based upon abstract relations. For example, in Shakespeare's *Romeo and Juliet*, Romeo proclaims that "Juliet is the sun." You might interpret this line to mean that Juliet is the center of Romeo's universe or that without Juliet, Romeo will die. The first interpretation depends upon your knowledge of astronomy; the second, on your knowledge of biology. Younger children lack this sort of knowledge to comprehend metaphors, so they try to interpret them literally. Only when children gain the necessary knowledge and formal operational abstract reasoning do they understand metaphors based on abstract relations (Winner, 1988).

Sarcasm is another form of communication that is not to be interpreted literally. When a soccer player misses the ball entirely and a teammate says, "Nice kick," the literal meaning of the remark is the opposite of the intended meaning. Understanding of sarcasm develops in much the same way as understanding of metaphor. When people emphasize their sarcasm by speaking in mocking or overly enthusiastic tones, school-age children can detect their meaning. However, if sarcasm must be detected solely from the context—by realizing that the comment is the opposite of what would be expected—only adolescents and adults are likely to understand the real meaning of the remark (Capelli, Nakagawa, & Madden, 1990).

This discussion of listening skills completes our catalog of the important accomplishments that take place in communication during childhood. As children enter kindergarten, they have mastered many of the fundamental rules of communication; and as they grow older, they acquire even greater proficiency.

Check Your Learning

1. If a listener doesn't respond promptly, a 3-year-old speaker will _____.

2. One example of the way that children adjust their speech to consider listeners is that many African American children _____.

3. Young children often ignore ambiguities in messages because _____.

Answers: (1) repeat his or her remarks, in an effort to elicit a reply, (2) use Black English more often than at home in school, (3) they assume that they know what the speaker means

ANGUAGE AND COMMUNICATION
IN PERSPECTIVE

Helen Keller, an American lecturer and writer who was blind and deaf from a childhood illness, once described language development as a " . . . vast distance between our first stammered syllable and the sweep of thought in a line of Shakespeare." The distance is indeed vast, yet children cover it with remarkable speed. We saw, in Module 9.1, that infants hear language sounds from very early in life but take much longer to produce language sounds correctly. In Module 9.2, we discovered that babies' first words at about age 1 reflect their ability to use symbols. We also learned that although children use different language learning styles, they all use rules to help them learn word meanings and they learn words best from activities that make them think about the meanings of new words. In Module 9.3, we saw that although children's sentences become more complex during the preschool years, children always follow simple rules to organize words into sentences. Mastery of grammar probably involves a combination of built-in mechanisms and language experience. Finally, in Module 9.4, we found that, as speakers, young children often communicate unclearly and, as listeners, they don't recognize lack of clarity in others' messages.

This chapter is an appropriate occasion to stress the theme that *development in different domains is connected:* Language has important connections to biological, cognitive, and social development. A link to biological development would be children's mastery of grammar: In ways that we don't yet fully understand, children seem to be endowed with a mechanism that smooths the path to mastering grammar. A link to cognitive development would be children's first words: Speaking words reflects the cognitive insight that speech sounds are symbols. A link to social development would be the communication skills that enable children to interact with peers and adults.

THINKING ABOUT DEVELOPMENT

1. According to Piaget's theory, preschoolers are egocentric. How do you think this egocentrism influences their communication skill? Are the findings on communication described in Module 9.4 consistent with Piaget's view?

2. Generate a list of the basic features of Piaget's, Vygotsky's, and the information-processing approaches to cognitive development. Then compare the emphasis each puts on the role of language in intellectual development.

3. Compare the role of experience in each aspect of language development that we examined in this chapter: learning to talk, learning words, learning grammar, and communicating skillfully.

4. A local hospital has hired you to write a pamphlet for new parents. The title of the pamphlet is supposed to be "What you can do to help your child learn language." What would you include in the pamphlet?

SEE FOR YOURSELF

Berko's (1958) "wugs" task is fun to try with preschool children. Photocopy the drawing on page 235 and show it to a preschooler, repeating the instructions that appear on that page. You should find that the child quite predictably says, "two wugs." Create some pictures of your own to examine other grammatical morphemes, such as adding *-ing* to denote ongoing activity or adding *-ed* to indicate past tense. See for yourself!

RESOURCES

For more information about . . .

Genie, the girl whose tragic childhood provided some fascinating insights into the critical period for language development, read Russ Rymer's *Genie* (Harper-Collins, 1993), which describes Genie's childhood and the debates about how best to rehabilitate her

bilingual education in America, contact the U.S. Department of Education, Office of Bilingual Education and Minority Languages Affairs, 1-800-872-5327

American Sign Language (ASL), visit the Animated American Sign Language Dictionary Web site, http://www.feist.com/~randys

KEY TERMS

babbling *226*
Black English *243*
cooing *226*
expressive style *229*
fast mapping *229*
grammar *234*

grammatical morphemes *235*
infant-directed speech *225*
intonation *226*
overextension *230*
overregularization *235*
phonemes *224*

referential style *229*
semantic bootstrapping hypothesis *238*
telegraphic speech *234*
underextension *230*

SUMMARY

MODULE 9.1:
THE ROAD TO SPEECH

PERCEIVING SPEECH

Phonemes are the basic units of sound that make up words. Infants can hear phonemes soon after birth. They can even hear phonemes that are not used in their native language, but this ability is lost by the first birthday.

Infant-directed speech refers to adults' speech to infants that is slower and has greater variation in pitch and loudness. Infants prefer infant-directed speech, perhaps because it provides them additional language clues.

PUBLIC SPEAKING IN A FEW EASY STEPS

Newborns are limited to crying, but at about 3 months of age, babies coo. Babbling soon follows, consisting of a single syllable; over several months, infants' babbling includes longer syllables and intonation. Deaf children babble later than children with normal hearing, but if adults use sign language with them they can learn to make partial signs that are thought to be analogous to babbling.

MODULE 9.2:
LEARNING THE MEANINGS OF WORDS

UNDERSTANDING WORDS AS SYMBOLS

Children's first words represent a cognitive accomplishment that is not specific to language. Instead, the onset of language is due to a child's ability to interpret and use symbols. Consistent with this view, there are parallel developments in the use of gestures.

STYLES OF LEARNING LANGUAGE

Some youngsters use a referential style in learning words that emphasizes words as names and that views language as an intellectual tool. Other children use an expressive style that emphasizes phrases and that views language as a social tool.

FAST MAPPING MEANINGS TO WORDS

Most children learn the meanings of words too rapidly for them to consider all plausible meanings systematically. Instead, children use a number of rules to determine probable meanings of new words. The rules do not always lead to the correct meaning. An underextension denotes a child's meaning that is narrower than an adult's meaning; an overextension denotes a child's meaning that is broader.

ENCOURAGING WORD LEARNING

Children's word learning is fostered by experience, including being read to, watching television, and for school-age children, reading to themselves. The key ingredient is making children think about the meanings of new words.

MODULE 9.3:
SPEAKING IN SENTENCES

FROM TWO-WORD SPEECH TO COMPLEX SENTENCES

Not long after their first birthday, children produce two-word sentences that are based on simple rules for expressing ideas or needs. These sentences are sometimes called telegraphic because they focus solely on meaning. Moving from two-word to more complex sentences involves adding grammatical morphemes. Children first master grammatical morphemes that express simple relations, then those that denote complex relations.

As children acquire grammatical morphemes they also extend their speech to other sentence forms, such as questions, and, later, to more complex constructions, such as passive sentences.

HOW CHILDREN ACQUIRE GRAMMAR

Some researchers claim that grammar is too complex for children to learn solely from their experience; instead, the brain must be prewired to simplify the task. Findings consistent with this argument are specialized regions in the brain for processing language, the inability of chimpanzees to master grammar, and critical periods in language acquisition. Other researchers believe that children use general cognitive skills to infer grammatical rules from regularities in the speech that they hear.

Language experience is important for learning grammar. Parents provide examples of the rules of speech that their children are trying to master and they provide children with feedback concerning grammatical rules.

MODULE 9.4:
USING LANGUAGE TO COMMUNICATE

TAKING TURNS

Parents encourage turn taking even before infants talk and, later, demonstrate both the speaker and listener roles for their children. By age 3, children spontaneously take turns and prompt one another to speak.

SPEAKING EFFECTIVELY

During the preschool years, children gradually become more skilled at constructing clear messages, in part by adjusting their speech to fit the listener's needs.

LISTENING WELL

Preschoolers are unlikely to identify ambiguities in another's speech. Also, they sometimes have difficulty understanding messages that are not to be taken literally, such as those that rely upon metaphor and sarcasm.

Emotional Development

IF YOU'RE A FAN OF *STAR TREK,* YOU KNOW THAT MR. SPOCK FEELS LITTLE EMOTION BECAUSE HE'S HALF VULCAN AND PEOPLE FROM THE PLANET VULCAN DON'T FEEL EMOTIONS. WOULD YOU LIKE TO LIVE AN EMOTIONLESS LIFE LIKE MR. SPOCK? Probably not. For most of us, feelings enrich our lives. As partial testimony to their importance, the English language has more than 500 words that refer to emotions (Averill, 1980). Joy, happiness, satisfaction, and, yes, anger, guilt, and humiliation are just a few of the feelings that give life meaning.

In this chapter, we'll see how emotions emerge and how they affect development. In Module 10.1, we'll discuss when children first express different emotions and recognize emotions in others. Next, in Module 10.2, we'll see that children have different behavioral styles and that these styles are rooted, in part, in emotions. Finally, in Module 10.3, we'll examine the infant's first emotional relationship, the one that develops with the primary caregiver.

EMERGING EMOTIONS

Learning Objectives

■ **At what ages do children begin to express basic emotions?**

■ **What are complex emotions and when do they develop?**

■ **When do children begin to understand other people's emotions? How do they use this information to guide their own behavior?**

> Nicole was ecstatic that she was finally going to see her 7-month-old nephew, Claude. She rushed into the house and, seeing Claude playing on the floor with blocks, swept him up in a big hug. After a brief, puzzled look, Claude burst into angry tears and began thrashing around, as if saying to Nicole, "Who are you? What do you want? Put me down! Now!" Nicole quickly handed Claude to his mother, who was surprised by her baby's outburst and even more surprised that he continued to sob while she rocked him.

Nicole's initial happiness, Claude's anger, and his mother's surprise illustrate three basic human emotions. Happiness, anger, and surprise, along with fear, disgust, and sadness are considered basic emotions because people worldwide experience them and because each consists of three elements: a subjective feeling, a physiological change, and an overt behavior (Izard, 1991). For example, suppose you wake to the sound of a thunderstorm and then discover your roommate has left for class with your umbrella. Subjectively, you might feel ready to explode with anger; physiologically, your heart would beat faster; and behaviorally, you would probably be scowling.

In addition to basic emotions, people feel complex emotions such as pride, guilt, and embarrassment. Unlike basic emotions, complex emotions have an evaluative component to them. For example, a 2-year-old who has spilled juice all over the floor may hang his head in shame; another 2-year-old who has, for the first time, finished a difficult puzzle by herself will smile in a way that radiates pride. Also, in contrast to basic emotions, complex emotions are not experienced the same way in all cultures.

In this module, we look at when children first express basic and complex emotions, then discover how children come to understand emotions in others.

BASIC EMOTIONS

Facial expressions probably reflect an infant's emotions because expressions are associated with specific physiological changes, they are similar around the world, and they change predictably in response to infants' experiences.

Is there a time when infants are like Mr. Spock—relatively free of emotion? No; emotions are with us from the first few months of life. To see for yourself, look at the photos of young babies at the top of page 251. Which one is angry? Which are the sad and happy babies? The facial expressions are so revealing that I'm sure you guessed that the babies are, in order, sad, happy, and angry. But, do these distinctive facial expressions mean the infants are actually experiencing these emotions? Not necessarily. Remember that facial expressions are only one component of emotion—the behavioral manifestation. Emotion also involves physiological responses and subjective feelings. Of course, infants can't express their feelings to us verbally, so we don't know much about their subjective experiences. We're on firmer ground with the physiological

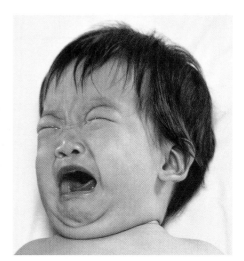

element. At least some of the physiological responses that accompany facial expressions are the same in infants and adults. For example, when infants and adults smile—which suggests they're happy—the left frontal cortex of the brain tends to have more electrical activity than the right frontal cortex (Fox, Kimmerly, & Schaffer, 1991).

Many scientists use this and similar findings to argue that facial expressions are reliable clues to an infant's emotional state. For example, research also shows that infants and adults worldwide express basic emotions in much the same way (Izard, 1991). The child in the photo on the right shows the universal signs of fear. Her eyes are open wide, her eyebrows are raised, and her mouth is relaxed but slightly open. The universality of emotional expression suggests that humans are biologically programmed to express emotions in a specific way; it's simply in our genes to smile when we're happy and scowl when we're unhappy.

Another finding linking infants' facial expressions to emotions is that, by 5 to 6 months, infants' facial expressions change predictably and meaningfully in response to events. When a happy mother greets her baby, the baby usually smiles in return; when a tired, distracted mother picks up her baby roughly, the baby usually frowns at her. These findings suggest that by the middle of the first year (and maybe earlier) facial expressions are fairly reliable indicators of an infant's emotional state (Weinberg & Tronick, 1994).

If facial expressions provide a window on a baby's emotions, what do they tell us about the early phases of emotional development? Let's start with happiness. During the first few weeks after birth, infants begin to smile, but this seems to be related to internal physiological states. An infant may smile after feeding or while asleep, for example. **At about 2 months of age, *social smiles* first appear: Infants smile when they see another human face.** Sometimes social smiling is accompanied by cooing, the early form of vocalization described in Module 9.1 (Sroufe & Waters, 1976). Smiling and cooing seem to be the infant's way of expressing pleasure at seeing another person.

At about 4 months, smiling is joined by laughter, which usually occurs when a baby experiences vigorous physical stimulation (Sroufe & Wunsch, 1972). Tickling 4-month-olds or bouncing them on your knee is a good way to prompt a laugh.

Toward the end of the first year, infants often laugh when familiar events take a novel turn. For example, a 1-year-old will laugh when her mother pretends to drink from a baby bottle or her father drapes a diaper around his waist. Laughter is now a response to psychological stimulation as well as physical stimulation.

The early stages of positive feelings, like happiness, are fairly clear: An infant's experience of happiness is first linked primarily to physical states, such as feeling full after a meal or being tickled. Later, feelings of happiness reflect psychological states, such as the pleasure of seeing another person or an unusual event.

We know much less about the development of negative emotions such as fear, anger, and sadness. Certainly, newborns express distress, but specific negative emotions are hard to verify. Anger emerges gradually, with distinct displays appearing between 4 and 6 months of age. Infants will become angry, for example, if a favorite food or toy is taken away (Sternberg & Campos, 1990). Reflecting their growing understanding of goal-directed behavior (see Module 6.2), infants also become angry when their attempts to achieve a goal are frustrated. For example, if a parent restrains an infant trying to pick up a toy, the guaranteed result is a very angry baby.

Like anger, fear seems to be rare in newborns and young infants. **The first distinct signs of fear emerge at about 6 months when infants become wary in the presence of an unfamiliar adult, a reaction known as *stranger anxiety*.** When a stranger approaches, a 6-month-old typically looks away and begins to fuss (Mangelsdorf, Shapiro, & Marzolf, 1995). The baby in the photo is showing the signs of stranger anxiety. The grandmother has picked him up without giving him a chance to warm up to her, and the outcome is as predictable as it was with Claude, the baby boy in the vignette who was frightened by his aunt: He cries, looks frightened, and reaches with arms outstretched in the direction of someone familiar.

How anxious an infant feels around strangers depends on a number of factors (Thompson & Limber, 1991). First, infants tend to be less fearful of strangers when the environment is familiar and more fearful when it is not. Many parents know this firsthand from traveling with their infants: Enter a friend's house for the first time and the baby clings tightly to its mother. Second, the amount of anxiety depends on the stranger's behavior. Instead of rushing to greet or pick up the baby, as Nicole did in the vignette, a stranger should talk with other adults and, in a while, perhaps offer the baby a toy (Mangelsdorf, 1992). Handled this way, many infants will soon be curious about the stranger instead of afraid.

Fear of strangers is adaptive because it emerges at the same time that children begin to master creeping and crawling (described in Module 4.4). Like Curious George, the monkey in a famous series of children's books, babies are inquisitive and want to use their new locomotor skills to explore their worlds. Fear of strangers provides a natural restraint against the tendency to wander away from familiar caregivers.

An infant is more likely to fear strangers in an unfamiliar environment and when strangers don't give the infant ample time to warm up to them.

Fear of strangers gradually declines as infants learn to interpret facial expressions and recognize when a stranger is friendly and not hostile, but then other fears develop. Many preschoolers are afraid of the dark and of imaginary creatures. These fears typically diminish during the elementary-school years as children grow cognitively and better understand the difference between appearance and reality (see Module 6.2). Fears of specific objects or events, such as snakes or storms, often arise in childhood and remain into adulthood. Such fears are considered normal unless they become so extreme they overwhelm the child (Rutter &

Garmezy, 1983). For example, a 7-year-old's fear of spiders would not be unusual unless her fear grew to the point that she refused to go outside at all. In the "Making Children's Lives Better" feature, we'll look at one form of excessive fear and how it can be treated.

Making Children's Lives Better: "BUT I DON'T WANT TO GO TO SCHOOL!"

 Many youngsters plead, argue, and fight with their parents daily over going to school. **An overwhelming fear of going to school and active resistance to attending school constitutes** *school phobia.* For example, every school day, 9-year-old Keegan would cling to his mother and start to sob as soon as he finished his breakfast. When it was time to leave the house to catch the bus, he would drop to the floor and start kicking.

Children may develop school phobia because they are overanxious generally and school is full of situations that can cause anxiety, such as reading aloud, taking tests, or learning new activities with competitive classmates. **School-phobic children can be helped with** *systematic desensitization,* **a technique that associates deep relaxation with progressively more anxiety-provoking situations.** First the therapist asks the child to generate a list of school-related situations, from pleasant ("I got the highest grade on my math test") to neutral ("We say the pledge of allegiance every morning") to very anxiety-provoking ("I got home and realized that I'd left my assignments in my locker"). Setting the list aside, the therapist then teaches the child how to reduce tension by relaxing different muscle groups. When the child masters the relaxation techniques, the therapist asks the child to relax and imagine the pleasant school-related situations. Over several sessions, the child imagines progressively more anxiety-provoking situations while relaxed, so that the anxiety the child used to feel is replaced by feelings of calm relaxation. Children taught this technique report feeling much less anxious, and their school attendance improves (Kearney & Silverman, 1995). ■

COMPLEX EMOTIONS

Basic emotions emerge early in infancy but complex emotions such as feelings of guilt, embarrassment, and pride don't surface until 18 to 24 months of age (Lewis, 1992). Complex emotions depend on the child having some understanding of the self, which typically occurs between 15 and 18 months (see Module 11.1). Children feel guilty or embarrassed, for example, when they've done something that they know they shouldn't have done: A child who breaks a toy is thinking, "You told me to be careful. But I wasn't!" Similarly, children feel pride when they've done something that was challenging: A little girl catching a ball for the first time thinks, "This was hard, but I did it, all by myself!" For children to experience complex emotions, they need to be more advanced cognitively, which explains why complex emotions don't appear until the very end of infancy (Lewis, Alessandri, & Sullivan, 1992).

Complex emotions also depend upon the cultural setting: Situations that evoke pride in one culture may evoke embarrassment or shame in another. For example, American elementary-school children often show pride at personal achievement, such as getting the highest grade on a test or, as shown in the photo, coming in first place in a county fair. In contrast, Asian

elementary-school children are embarrassed by a public display of individual achievement but show great pride when their entire class is honored for its achievement (Stevenson & Stigler, 1992). Thus, the conditions that trigger complex emotions such as pride, envy, and shame depend upon the culture, so children have to learn when these emotions are appropriate.

In sum, complex emotions like guilt and pride require more sophisticated understanding and are more culturally specific than basic emotions like happiness and fear, which are more biologically based and culturally universal. By age 2, however, children express both basic and complex emotions. Of course, expressing emotions is only part of the developmental story. Children must also learn to recognize others' emotions, which is our next topic.

RECOGNIZING AND USING OTHERS' EMOTIONS

Imagine you are broke (only temporarily, of course) and plan to borrow $20 from your roommate when she returns from class. Shortly, she storms into your apartment, slams the door, and throws her backpack on the floor. Immediately, you change your plans, realizing that now is hardly a good time to ask for a loan. This example reminds us that we often need to recognize others' emotions and sometimes change our behavior as a consequence.

When can infants first identify emotions in others? By 6 or 7 months, infants begin to distinguish facial expressions associated with different emotions. A 6-month-old can, for example, distinguish a happy, smiling face from a sad, frowning face (Ludemann, 1991; Ludemann & Nelson, 1988). Strictly speaking, these studies tell us only that infants can discriminate facial expressions, not emotions per se. Other research, however, indicates that 6-month-olds have indeed begun to recognize the emotions themselves. The best evidence is that infants often match their own emotions to other people's emotions. When happy mothers smile and talk in a pleasant voice, infants express happiness themselves. If mothers are angry or sad, infants become distressed, too (Haviland & Lelwica, 1987).

Also like adults, infants use others' emotions to direct their behavior. **Infants in an unfamiliar or ambiguous environment often look at their mother or father, as if searching for cues to help them interpret the situation, a phenomenon known as *social referencing.*** For example, in a study by Hirshberg and Svejda (1990), 12-month-olds were shown novel toys that made sounds, such as a stuffed alligator that hissed. For some toys, parents were told to look happy; for others, parents were to look afraid. When parents looked afraid, their infants, too, appeared distressed and moved away from the toys. Thus, social referencing shows that infants rely on their parents' emotions to help them regulate their own behavior.

By the first birthday, infants can recognize others' emotions and use these emotions to direct their own behavior.

As their cognitive skills grow, children become more adept at identifying others' emotions and modifying their behavior accordingly (Dunn, Brown, & Maguire, 1995). They begin to understand why people feel as they do and how emotions can influence a person's behavior. Preschool children, for example, understand that an angry child is more likely to hurt someone than a happy child (Russell & Paris, 1994).

During the elementary school years, children begin to comprehend that people sometimes experience "mixed feelings." Wintre and Vallance (1994) read sentences describing emotionally evocative situations to 4- through 8-year-olds and asked them how happy, angry, sad, scared, or loving they would feel in each situation. A sentence describing a fear-provoking situation was "You are home all alone" and one describing a sad situation was "Your best friend moves away." You can see in the results, shown in the figure, that by about 8 years of age, children realize how people

Stages in the Development of Children's Understanding That People Can Experience Multiple Emotions Simultaneously

Stage	Age	Understanding	Example
1	5 years	A situation can cause a person to experience two different emotions.	A child could be sad and angry that a best friend is moving away. 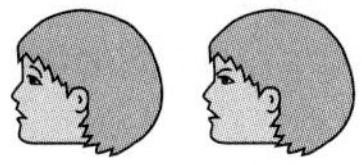
2	6 1/2 years	A situation can cause a person to experience two different emotions that differ in intensity.	A child could be very sad and a little angry that a best friend is moving away. 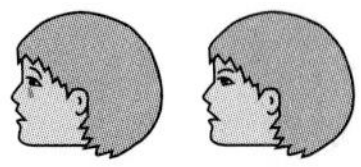
3	8 years	A situation can cause a person to feel positively and negatively at the same time.	A child could be happy and scared about staying home alone. 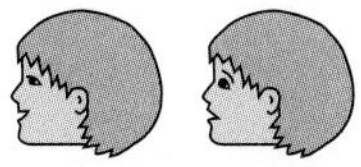

Based on Wintre and Vallance, 1994.

can feel good and bad at the same time. The increased ability to see multiple, differing emotions coincides with the decentered thinking that characterizes the concrete operational stage (Module 6.2).

Children's growing understanding of emotions in others contributes in turn to a growing ability to help others. They are more likely to recognize the emotions that signal a person's need. Better understanding of emotions in others also contributes to children's growing ability to play easily with peers because they can see the impact of their behavior on others. We'll cover empathy and social interaction in detail later in the book; for now, the important point is that recognizing emotions in others is an important prerequisite for successful, satisfying interactions.

Check Your Learning

1. The first detectable form of fear is _____, which emerges at about 6 months.

2. Complex emotions, such as guilt and shame, emerge later than basic emotions because _____.

3. In social referencing, infants use a parent's facial expression _____.

Answers: (1) stranger anxiety, (2) complex emotions require more advanced cognitive skills, (3) to direct their own behavior (for example, deciding if an unfamiliar situation is safe or frightening)

TEMPERAMENT

Learning Objectives

- **What are the different features of temperament?**
- **How stable is a child's temperament across childhood?**
- **What are the consequences of different temperaments?**

Soon after Sueko arrived in the United States from Japan to begin graduate studies, she enrolled her 5-month-old son in day care. She was struck by the fact that, compared to her son, the European American babies in the day-care center were "wimps" (slang she had learned from American television). The other babies cried often and with minimal provocation. Sueko wondered whether her son was unusually "tough" or whether he was just a typical Japanese baby.

When you've seen young babies—perhaps as part of "See for Yourself" in Chapter 3—did you notice some babies who, like Sueko's, were quiet most of the time while others cried often and impatiently? Maybe you saw some infants who responded warmly to strangers and others who seemed very shy? **An infant's consistent mood and style of behavior is referred to as** *temperament.* Temperament does not refer so much to *what* babies do as to *how* they do what they do. For example, all babies become upset occasionally and cry. However, some, like Sueko's son, recover quickly while others are very hard to console. These differences in emotion and style of behavior are evident in the first few weeks after birth and are important throughout life.

Let's start this module by looking at different ways that scientists define temperament.

WHAT IS TEMPERAMENT?

The pioneering work on temperament was done by Alexander Thomas and Stella Chess (Chess & Thomas, 1986; Thomas, Chess, & Birch, 1968). In 1956, they began the New York Longitudinal Study, tracing the lives of 141 individuals from infancy through adulthood. Thomas and Chess gathered their initial data by interviewing the babies' parents and asking individuals unfamiliar with the children to observe them at home. Based on these interviews and observations, Thomas and Chess evaluated the behavior of the 141 infants along the nine temperamental dimensions listed in the table at the top of page 257.

Using these nine dimensions, Thomas and Chess could place most infants into one of three groups. About 40 percent of the babies were categorized as "easy" babies. These infants were usually happy and cheerful, tended to adjust well to new situations, and had regular routines for eating, sleeping, and toileting. About 10 percent of the babies were categorized as "difficult." As you might imagine, they were in many respects the opposite of the easy babies: Difficult babies were often unhappy, did not adjust well to new situations, and their routines for eating and sleeping were irregular. In addition, difficult babies tended to withdraw from novel experiences and they responded intensely to novel stimulation. About 15 percent of the babies were categorized as "slow-to-warm-up." Like difficult babies, slow-to-warm-up babies tended to be unhappy and did not adjust well when placed in new situations. But unlike difficult babies, slow-to-

Thomas and Chess discovered that about two-thirds of the infants in their New York Longitudinal Study could be placed in one of three temperamental categories: easy, difficult, and slow-to-warm-up.

Dimensions of Temperament in the New York Longitudinal Study

Dimension	Description
Activity level	Amount of physical and motor activity in daily situations
Rhythmicity	Regularity in eating, sleeping, toileting
Approach/withdrawal	Response to a novel object (accepting vs. rejecting)
Distractibility	Ease with which ongoing activity is disrupted by competing stimuli
Adaptability	Ease with which the child adjusts to changes in the environment
Intensity of reaction	Energy level of the child's responses
Mood	Balance between happy and unhappy behavior
Threshold	Level of stimulation needed for the child to respond
Attention span and persistence	Amount of time devoted to an activity, particularly with obstacles or distractions present

warm-up babies did not respond intensely and they tended to be relatively inactive. The remaining babies—roughly one-third—did not fit any of the groups; in general, they were average on most of the nine dimensions.

The New York Longitudinal Study launched the modern study of infant temperament. However, as you might suspect, not all investigators agree with Thomas and Chess's nine dimensions and three groups. For example, Arnold Buss and Robert Plomin (1975, 1984) propose that temperament involves three primary dimensions—emotionality, activity, and sociability. *Emotionality* **refers to the strength of the infant's emotional response to a situation, the ease with which that response is triggered, and the ease with which the infant can be returned to a nonemotional state.** At one extreme are infants whose emotional responses are strong, easily triggered, and not easily calmed; at the other are infants whose responses are subdued, relatively difficult to elicit, and readily soothed. *Activity* **refers to the tempo and vigor of a child's activity.** Active infants are always busy, like to explore their environment, and enjoy vigorous play. Inactive infants have a more controlled behavioral tempo and are more likely to enjoy quiet play. *Sociability* **refers to a preference for being with other people.** Some infants relish contact with others, seek their attention, and prefer play that involves other people. Other infants, like the girl in the photo, enjoy solitude and are quite content to play alone with toys.

If you compare these three dimensions with the nine listed in the table above, you'll see a great deal of overlap. For example, Buss and Plomin's emotionality dimension combines the intensity and threshold dimensions of the New York Longitudinal Study. In fact, the major theories of temperament include most of the same elements; what is still undecided is the best way to assemble these elements into a cohesive theory of temperament.

Theories of temperament also agree that temperament reflects both heredity and experience. The influence of heredity is shown in twin studies: Identical twins are more alike in most aspects of temperament than fraternal twins (Braungart et al., 1992). Like the youngsters in the photo at the top of page 258, if one identical twin is temperamentally active, the other usually is, too. The influence of experience is

shown by studies of mother-child interaction: When mothers interact easily and confidently with infants, their infants are less likely to develop intense, difficult temperaments (Belsky, Fish, & Isabella, 1991). Heredity and experience may also explain why Sueko, the Japanese mother in the vignette, has such a hardy son. The "Cultural Influences" feature tells the story.

Cultural Influences: WHY IS SUEKO'S SON SO TOUGH?

 If you've ever watched an infant getting a shot, you know the inevitable response. After the syringe is removed, the infant's eyes open wide, as if saying, "Wow, that hurt!" and then the baby begins to cry. Infants differ in how intensely they cry and in how readily they are soothed, reflecting differences in the emotionality dimension of temperament. But virtually all European American babies cry. It's easy to suppose that crying is a universal response to the pain from the inoculation, but that's not true. In stressful situations like getting a shot, Japanese and Chinese infants are less likely to become upset (Kagan et al., 1994). Lewis, Ramsay, and Kawakami (1993) found that most European American 4-month-olds cried loudly within 5 seconds of an injection; only half the Japanese babies in their study cried. Furthermore, when Japanese and Chinese babies become upset, they are soothed more readily than European American babies. Lewis and his colleagues found that about three-fourths of the Japanese babies were no longer crying 90 seconds after the injection compared to fewer than half of the European American babies. The conclusion seems clear: Sueko's son appears to be a typical Japanese baby in crying less often and less intensely than the European American babies at his day-care center.

Why are Asian infants less emotional than their European American counterparts? Heredity may be involved. Perhaps the genes that contribute to emotionality are less common among Asians than among European Americans. But we can't overlook experience. Compared to European American mothers, Japanese mothers spend more time in close physical contact with their babies, constantly and gently soothing them; this may reduce the tendency to respond emotionally. ■

There's no question that heredity and experience cause babies' temperaments to differ, but do calm, easygoing babies grow up to be calm, easygoing children, adolescents, and adults? In other words, how stable is temperament across childhood and adolescence? We'll find out in the next section.

STABILITY OF TEMPERAMENT

Temperament *is* somewhat stable; calm, easygoing babies are more likely to grow up to be calm, easygoing children, adolescents, and adults. Let's look first at research on stability from infancy to the preschool years.

Many investigators have found that temperament measured in the first few months of life is related to temperament measured later in infancy or in the preschool years. For example, Worobey and Blajda (1989) assessed infants' temperament at 2 and 12 months of age by having mothers complete questionnaires.

Most measures of temperament obtained at 2 months were related to measures of the same dimensions obtained at 12 months. For example, the correlation between mothers' assessments of activity level at 2 and 12 months was .40. However, these data are not very convincing because mothers were the source on both occasions, and a mother's initial impression of her infant's temperament may color her later perceptions and bias her ratings toward stability. That is, a mother's impression of her baby's temperament may be more stable than the baby's actual temperament.

Temperament is moderately stable during infancy: Active or emotional newborns often but not always become active or emotional 1-year-olds.

One way to avoid the problem of mothers' biased perceptions is to have independent observers evaluate an infant's behavior. Stifter and Fox (1990) did this in studying infants' responses in two moderately stressful situations. First, newborns were allowed to suck briefly on a pacifier, which was then taken away from them. Stifter and Fox then recorded whether the baby cried or not. When the babies were 5 months old, Stifter and Fox asked the babies' mothers to gently restrain their infants. As you can see in the photo, the babies couldn't move, which makes most babies unhappy. Again, the researchers looked for crying. They discovered that 53 percent of the newborns who cried when the pacifier was removed cried as 5-month-olds, and 72 percent who did not cry when the pacifier was removed did not cry when they were restrained. In other words, emotional reactivity, as indicated by crying, was fairly consistent from birth to 5 months of age. Similar evidence suggests that other dimensions of temperament are moderately stable throughout infancy (Bates, 1987).

Does temperament remain stable beyond infancy and the preschool years? Are emotional preschoolers likely to be emotional adults? Here, too, the evidence suggests moderate consistency. Most investigators report that measures of temperament obtained during the preschool years are related to measures obtained later in childhood and adolescence, but the correlations are not very strong. Exactly this pattern is described in the "Focus on Research" feature.

Focus on Research: ONCE A DIFFICULT CHILD, ALWAYS A DIFFICULT CHILD?

Who were the investigators and what was the aim of the study? The overall aim of the Dunedin Multidisciplinary Health and Development Study is to trace health and behavior of children in New Zealand through infancy, childhood, and adolescence. Every two years, individuals participating in the ongoing study are assessed with medical, psychological, and sociological measures. In one part of the study, Avshalom Caspi and his colleagues, Bill Henry, Rob McGee, Terrie Moffitt, and Phil Silva (1995), examined the stability of children's temperament between ages 3 and 9.

How did the investigators measure the topic of interest? An observer watched as children performed several cognitive and motor tasks. The observer rated 22 specific behaviors, such as fear, self-confidence, impulsivity, restlessness, and self-criticism. These measures were then combined to determine children's scores on four dimensions of temperament:

- *Irritability:* Children with high scores on this dimension were unstable emotionally, often overreactive, impulsive, and very aggressive.

- *Distractibility:* Children with high scores on this dimension were unable to concentrate on tasks and often refused to continue when tasks became difficult.

- *Sluggishness:* Children with high scores on this dimension tended to be placid, shy, apprehensive, and emotionally flat.

- *Approach:* Children with high scores on this dimension adjusted readily to new situations and were friendly and self-confident.

Who were the children in the study? The Dunedin Study involved children born in Dunedin, New Zealand, within 12 months during 1972 and 1973. The study began with 1,037 three-year-olds. Of these, 991 were tested as 5-year-olds, 954 as 7-year-olds, and 955 as 9-year-olds.

What was the design of the study? This study was correlational because Caspi and his colleagues were interested in the relation that existed naturally between measures of temperament early and later in development. The study was longitudinal because children were tested many times, at ages 3, 5, 7, and 9 years.

Were there ethical concerns with the study? No. The cognitive and motor tasks that children performed were similar to tasks that they might do in school.

What were the results? Caspi and his colleagues reported correlations for all pairs of years between 3 and 9. For simplicity, the graph shows some typical correlations between scores at 5 and 9 years. The most remarkable aspect of the Dunedin data is that the correlations are not very large, which suggests that temperament is only moderately stable. This is true for both boys and girls. Irritability, an element of difficult temperament, is the most stable dimension overall.

What did the investigators conclude? There is continuity in temperament: A young child's temperament does give clues to that child's temperament later in childhood. However, early temperament predicts later temperament only roughly, not precisely. To put this concretely, we can contrast two hypothetical children: John, a difficult 5-year-old, has high scores on irritability and distractibility but a low score on the approach dimension. Jerry, an easy 5-year-old, has low scores on irritability and distractibility but a high score on the approach dimension. What does the future hold for these boys? John is certainly more likely than Jerry to become a difficult 9-year-old, but it is far from certain that John will remain difficult. ▣

The bars show that the largest correlation is not even .40, which shows only modest stability in temperament.

Correlations Between Temperament Scores at 5 and 9 Years

Irritability
Distractability
Sluggishness
Approach

.10   .20   .30   .40
Size of the Correlation (r)

■ Boys   ■ Girls

Though temperament is only moderately consistent over the years, it can still shape development in important ways. For example, an infant's temperament may determine the experiences that parents provide. Parents may read more to quiet babies but, like the parent in the photo, play more physical games with their active babies. These different experiences, driven by the infants' temperaments, contribute to each infant's development, despite the fact that the infants' temperaments may change over the years. In the next section, we'll see some of the connections between temperament and other aspects of development.

TEMPERAMENT AND OTHER ASPECTS OF DEVELOPMENT

One of the goals of Thomas and Chess's New York Longitudinal Study was to discover temperamental features of infants that would predict later psychological adjustment. In fact, the researchers discovered that about two-thirds of the preschoolers with difficult temperaments had developed behavioral problems by the time they entered school. In contrast, fewer than one-fifth of the children with easy temperaments had behavioral problems (Thomas et al., 1968).

Other scientists have followed the lead of the New York Longitudinal Study in looking for links between temperament and outcomes of development and they've found that temperament is an important influence on development. Here are some illustrative examples:

■ Persistent children are likely to succeed in school whereas active and distractible children are less likely to succeed (Martin, Olejnik, & Gaddis, 1994).

■ Shy, inhibited children often have difficulties interacting with their peers, particularly in unfamiliar situations (Asendorpf, 1991; Kochanska & Radke-Yarrow, 1992).

■ Anxious, fearful children are more likely to comply with a parent's rules and requests, even when the parent is not present (Kochanska, 1995).

In some of these areas, the connection probably reflects the direct impact of temperament. For example, persistence is a definite asset in school: Children who keep plugging along definitely do better than youngsters who falter when tasks become difficult or tedious. In other cases, the impact of temperament is indirect. That is, temperament does not cause a particular outcome but makes children more susceptible to certain developmental influences. Why, for example, are anxious children more compliant? When young children transgress, most feel at least some distress; anxious children are particularly uncomfortable with this distress and rapidly learn that the best way to reduce their discomfort is to comply with parents. In this instance, anxious temperament makes children more susceptible to parental influence than children who are less anxious.

Children's temperament is related to their success in school, to difficulties in peer interactions, and to compliance with parents' wishes.

Other studies show that temperament is a factor in the emotional relationship between an infant and its primary caregiver. In Module 10.3, we look at how this first emotional relationship is formed.

Check Your Learning

1. Buss and Plomin's theory has three temperamental dimensions, including emotionality, _____, and sociability.

2. Compared to European American infants, Asian infants are calmer and _____.

3. Research on the stability of temperament from the preschool years to adolescence and beyond typically finds that _____.

4. Thomas and Chess found that by the time difficult babies had entered school, many had _____.

Answers: (1) activity, (2) are soothed more readily when upset, (3) temperament is only moderately stable, (4) developed behavioral problems

TTACHMENT

Learning Objectives

- **How does an attachment relationship develop between an infant and primary caregiver?**
- **What different types of attachment relationships are there? What are the consequences of different types of relationships?**
- **Is the attachment relationship affected if a mother works outside the home?**

Kendra's son Roosevelt was a happy, affectionate 18-month-old and Kendra so loved spending time with him that she kept avoiding the decision. She wanted to return to her job as a loan officer at the local bank. Kendra knew a woman in the neighborhood who had cared for some of her friends' children and they all thought she was wonderful. But Kendra still had a nagging feeling that going back to work wasn't a "motherly" thing to do, that being away during the day might hamper Roosevelt's development.

The social-emotional relationship that develops between an infant and a parent (usually, but not necessarily, the mother) is special. This is a baby's first social-emotional relationship, so theorists and parents alike believe it should be satisfying and trouble-free to set the stage for later relationships. In this module, we'll look at the steps involved in creating the baby's first emotional relationship. Along the way, we'll see how this relationship is affected by the separation that sometimes comes when a parent like Kendra works full time.

THE GROWTH OF ATTACHMENT

Sigmund Freud was the first modern theorist to emphasize the importance of emotional ties to the mother for psychological development. Today, however, the dominant view of early human relationships comes from John Bowlby (1969). His work originated in ethology, a branch of biology (described in Module 1.2) concerned with adaptive behaviors of different species. **According to Bowlby, children who form an *attachment* to an adult—that is, an enduring social-emotional relationship—are more likely to survive.** This person is usually the mother, but need not be; the key is a strong emotional relationship with a responsive, caring person—so attachments can form with fathers, grandparents, or someone else.

Bowlby (1969) argued that evolutionary pressure favored behaviors likely to elicit caregiving from an adult, such as clinging, sucking, crying, and smiling. That is, over the course of human evolution, these behaviors have become a standard part of the human infant's biological heritage, and the responses they evoke in adults create an interactive system that leads to the formation of attachment relationships.

Bowlby theorizes that many infant behaviors, such as clinging, crying, and smiling, are designed to elicit caregiving from a parent and thus promote the development of an emotional relationship between infant and parent.

The attachment relationship develops gradually over the first several months after birth, reflecting the baby's growing perceptual and cognitive skills described in Chapters 5 and 6. The first step is for the infant to learn the difference between people and other objects. Typically, in the first few months, babies begin to respond differently to people and to objects—for example, smiling more and vocalizing more to people—suggesting that they have begun to identify members of the social world.

During these months, mother and infant begin to synchronize their interactions. Remember from Module 3.4 that young babies' behaviors go through cycles. Infants move between states of alertness and attentiveness to states of distress and inattentiveness. Caregivers begin to recognize these states of behavior and adjust their own behavior accordingly. A mother who notices that her baby is awake and alert will begin to smile at and talk to her baby. These interactions often continue until the baby's state changes, which prompts the mother to stop. In fact, by 3 months of age, if a mother does not interact with her alert baby (but, instead, stares silently), babies become at least moderately distressed, looking away from her and sometimes crying (Toda & Fogel, 1993).

Thus, mothers and infants gradually calibrate their behaviors so that they are both "on" at the same time (Gable & Isabella, 1992). These interactions provide the foundation for more sophisticated communication and foster the infant's trust that the mother will respond predictably and reassuringly.

By approximately 6 or 7 months, most infants have singled out the attachment figure—usually the mother—as a special individual. An infant will smile at the mother and cling to her more than to other people. The attachment figure is now the infant's stable social-emotional base. For example, a 7-month-old like the one in the photo will explore a novel environment but periodically look towards his mother, as if seeking reassurance that all is well. The behavior suggests the infant trusts his mother and indicates the attachment relationship has been established.

Attachment typically first develops between infants and their mothers because mothers are usually the primary caregivers of American infants. Most babies soon become attached to their fathers, too, but they interact differently with fathers. Fathers typically spend much more time playing with their babies than taking care of them. In countries around the world—Australia, India, Israel, Italy, Japan, and the United States—"playmate" is the customary role for fathers (Roopnarine, 1992). Fathers even play with infants differently than mothers. Physical play is the norm for fathers, particularly with sons, whereas mothers spend more time reading and talking to babies, showing them toys, and playing games like patty-cake (Parke, 1990). Given the opportunity to play with mothers or fathers, infants more often choose their fathers. However, when infants are distressed, mothers are preferred (Field, 1990). Thus, although most infants become attached to both parents, mothers and fathers typically have distinctive roles in their children's early social development.

QUALITY OF ATTACHMENT

Attachment between infant and mother usually occurs by 8 or 9 months of age, but the attachment can take on different forms. Mary Ainsworth (1978, 1993) pioneered the study of attachment relationships using a procedure that has come to be known as the Strange Situation. You can see in the diagram on page 264 that the Strange Situation involves a series of episodes, each about 3 minutes long. The mother and infant enter an unfamiliar room filled with interesting toys. The mother leaves briefly, then mother and baby are reunited. Meanwhile, the experimenter observes the baby, recording its response to both events.

Based on how the infant reacts to separation from the mother and then reunion, Ainsworth (1993) and other researchers (Main & Cassidy, 1988) have discovered four primary types of attachment relationships. One is a secure attachment and three are insecure attachments (avoidant, resistant, disorganized):

1. Observer shows the experimental room to mother and infant, then leaves the room.

2. Infant is allowed to explore the playroom for 3 minutes; mother watches but does not participate.

3. A stranger enters the room and remains silent for 1 minute, then talks to the baby for a minute, and then approaches the baby. Mother leaves unobtrusively.

4. The stranger does not play with the baby but attempts to comfort it if necessary.

5. After 3 minutes, the mother returns, greets, and consoles the baby.

6. When the baby has returned to play, the mother leaves again, this time saying "bye-bye" as she leaves.

7. Stranger attempts to calm and play with the baby.

8. After 3 minutes, the mother returns and the stranger leaves.

■ *Secure attachment:* **The baby may or may not cry when the mother leaves, but when she returns, the baby wants to be with her and if the baby is crying, it stops.** Babies in this group seem to be saying, "I missed you terribly, I'm delighted to see you, but now that all is well, I'll get back to what I was doing." Approximately 60 to 65 percent of American babies have secure attachment relationships.

■ *Avoidant attachment:* **The baby is not upset when the mother leaves and, when she returns, may ignore her by looking or turning away.** Infants with an avoidant attachment look as if they're saying, "You left me *again*. I always have to take care of myself!" About 20 percent of American infants have avoidant attachment relationships, which is one of the three forms of insecure attachment.

■ *Resistant attachment:* **The baby is upset when the mother leaves and remains upset or even angry when she returns, and is difficult to console.** Like the baby in the photo, these babies seem to be telling the mother, "Why do you do this? I need you desperately and yet you just leave me without warning. I get so angry when you're like this." About 10 to 15 percent of American babies have this resistant attachment relationship, which is another form of insecure attachment.

■ *Disorganized (disoriented) attachment:* **The baby seems confused when the mother leaves and, when she returns, seems as if it doesn't really understand what's happening.** The baby often has a dazed look on its face as if wondering, "What's going on here? I want you to be here, but you left and now you're back. I don't know whether to laugh or cry!" About 5 to 10 percent of American babies have this disorganized attachment relationship, the last of the three kinds of insecure attachment.

Secure attachments and the different forms of insecure attachments are observed worldwide. As you can see in the graph, secure attachments are the most common throughout the world (van IJzendoorn & Kroonenberg, 1988). This is fortunate because, as we'll see, a secure attachment provides a solid base for later social development.

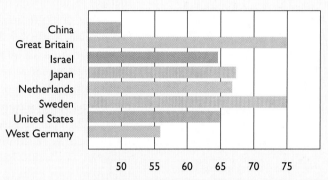

Percentage of Babies Who Are Securely Attached

Consequences of Quality of Attachment.

Erikson, Bowlby, and other theorists (Sroufe & Fleeson, 1986) believe that attachment, as the first social relationship, lays the foundation for all of an infant's later social relationships. In this view, infants who experience the trust and compassion of a secure attachment should develop into preschool children who interact confidently and successfully with their peers. In contrast, infants who do not experience a successful, satisfying first relationship should be more prone to problems in their social interactions as preschoolers.

Both of these predictions are supported by research, as the following findings demonstrate:

■ Interactions between 3- and 4-year-olds were relatively tranquil and satisfying when both friends had been securely attached as infants; in contrast, disagreements were common and not resolved readily when one of the youngsters had been attached insecurely as an infant (Park & Waters, 1989).

■ Preschool children were much more likely to exhibit abnormal levels of hostility if they had had a disorganized attachment as an infant (Lyons-Ruth, Alpern, & Repacholi, 1993).

■ At a summer camp, 11-year-olds who'd had secure attachment relationships as infants interacted more skillfully with their peers and had more close friends than 11-year-olds who'd had insecure attachment relationships (Elicker, Englund, & Sroufe, 1992).

The conclusion seems inescapable: As infants who have secure attachment relationships develop, their social interactions tend to be more satisfying. Why? Secure attachment evidently promotes trust and confidence in other humans, which leads to more skilled social interactions later in childhood. Of course, attachment is only one step along the long road of social development. Infants with insecure attachments are not doomed, but this initial misstep *can* interfere with their social development.

Factors Determining Quality of Attachment.

Because secure attachment is so important to a child's later development, researchers have tried to identify the factors involved. Undoubtedly the most important is the interaction between parents and their babies (van IJzendoorn et al., 1992). A secure attachment is most likely when parents respond to infants predictably and appropriately. For example, the mother in the photo has promptly responded to her baby's crying and is trying to reassure the baby. The mother's behavior evidently conveys that social interactions are predictable and satisfying and, apparently this behavior instills in infants the trust and confidence that are the hallmark of secure attachment.

Why does predictable and responsive parenting promote secure attachment relationships? To answer this question, think about your own friendships and romantic relationships. These relationships are usually most satisfying when we believe we can trust the other people and depend on them in times of need. The same formula seems to hold for infants. **Infants develop an *internal working model,* a set of expectations about parents' availability and responsivity, generally and in times of stress.** When parents are dependable and caring, babies come to trust them, knowing they can be relied upon for comfort. That is, babies develop an internal working model in which they believe that their parents are concerned about their needs and will try to meet them (Bretherton, 1992).

Many research findings attest to the importance of a caregiver's sensitivity for quality of attachment:

- In a longitudinal study, infants were more likely to have a secure attachment relationship at 12 months when their parents were sensitive, responding quickly and appropriately to their infant at 3 months (Cox et al., 1992).

- In a study conducted in Israel, infants were less likely to develop secure attachment when they slept in dormitories with other children under 12, where they received inconsistent (if any) attention when they became upset overnight (Sagi et al., 1994).

- In a study conducted in The Netherlands, infants were more likely to form a secure attachment when their mother had 3 months of training that emphasized monitoring an infant's signals and responding appropriately and promptly (van den Boom, 1994).

Thus, secure attachment is most likely when parents are sensitive and responsive. Of course, not all caregivers react to babies in a reliable and reassuring manner. Some respond intermittently or only after the infant has cried long and hard. And when these caregivers finally respond, they are sometimes annoyed by the infant's demands and may misinterpret the infant's intent. Over time, these babies tend to see social relationships as inconsistent and often frustrating, conditions that do little to foster trust and confidence.

A secure attachment relationship is most likely to develop between infant and parent when the parent responds to the infant's needs reliably and sensitively.

Another factor that contributes to quality of attachment is the baby's temperament. Babies with difficult temperaments are somewhat less likely to form secure attachment relationships (Goldsmith & Harman, 1994; Seifer et al., 1996). That is, babies who fuss often and are difficult to console are more prone to insecure attachment. This may be more likely when a difficult, emotional infant has a mother whose personality is rigid and traditional than when the mother is accepting and flexible (Mangelsdorf et al., 1990). Rigid mothers do not adjust well to the often erratic demands of their difficult babies; instead, they want the baby to adjust to them. This means that rigid mothers less often provide the responsive, sensitive care that leads to secure attachment.

Is the trust that is the basis of secure attachment disrupted when both parents work outside of the home full time? We'll see in the next section.

ATTACHMENT, WORK, AND ALTERNATE CAREGIVING

Each day, approximately 10 million U.S. children age 5 and under are cared for by someone other than their mother, a phenomenon linked to the increased number of dual-earner couples and single-parent households in the United States in the 1990s. Who is caring for America's children? The pie charts have the answer and

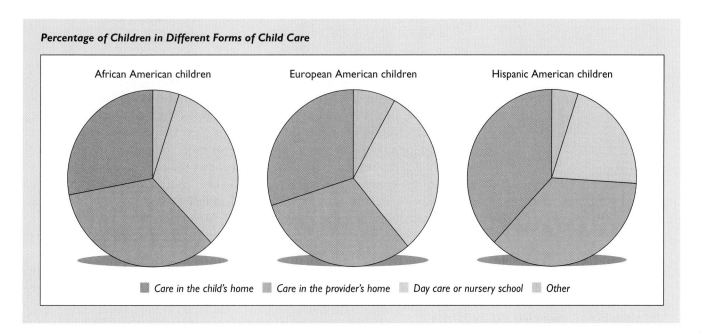

Percentage of Children in Different Forms of Child Care

African American children European American children Hispanic American children

■ *Care in the child's home* ■ *Care in the provider's home* □ *Day care or nursery school* ■ *Other*

reveal that patterns are very similar for European American, African American, and Hispanic American infants and preschoolers (U.S. Bureau of the Census, 1995a). About one-third of preschoolers are cared for in the home, typically by the father or a grandparent. Another third receive care in the provider's home (the provider is often but not always a relative). Finally, another third attend day-care or nursery-school programs.

Many parents, particularly women who have traditionally been sole caregivers, have misgivings about their children spending so much time in the care of others. Should parents worry? Does nonmaternal care disrupt the development of parent-child relationships? The answer depends, in part, on the child's age. Let's start by looking at infants.

When infants receive full-time parental care until their first birthday, about 70 percent typically form secure attachments. However, when parents work full time, so that before their first birthday babies spend roughly 40 hours each week with alternative caregivers, approximately 60 to 65 percent form secure attachments (Lamb, Sternberg, & Prodromidis, 1992). Thus, although secure attachments are the norm for both working and nonworking parents, odds of secure attachments *are* somewhat less for infants when they are placed in full-time day care before their first birthday (Clarke-Stewart, 1989).

Several factors are known to increase the odds of an insecure attachment for infants of working parents (Jaeger & Weinraub, 1990; Lamb et al., 1992):

■ *Hours that the infant spends in alternative care:* Insecure attachments are more likely when infants spend more than 20 hours per week with an alternate caregiver.

■ *Gender:* Boys in alternative care are more likely to form insecure attachment relationships than girls.

■ *Birth order:* First-born children in alternative care are more likely to form insecure attachment relationships than later-born children.

■ *Quality of parenting:* Employment can cause the quality of a parent's interactions with an infant to deteriorate. Stress, fatigue, guilt, or marital conflict can contribute to less responsive caregiving, which often leads to insecure attachment.

When children begin full-time day care after their first birthday, day care actually has a number of *beneficial* effects on them and relatively few harmful effects. Overall, children who attend day care are more mature intellectually and socially than their counterparts who stay at home full time with a parent. Children who attend early childhood programs are more self-confident, more outgoing, and more self-sufficient (Clarke-Stewart & Fein, 1983). Sometimes these youngsters are less agreeable and less compliant, but this difference can be traced to greater maturity: Assertive, self-confident day-care youngsters may be more insistent in pursuing their own interests and less inclined to go along with parental requests.

Quality day care has few children for each well-trained caregiver, provides a socially and educationally stimulating environment, and communicates well with parents.

On balance, parents like Kendra, the mother in the vignette at the beginning of the module, can work outside of the home without fearing harmful consequences for their children, as long as they follow some simple guidelines. First, if possible, wait until the baby's first birthday to begin full-time day care. Try to limit the amount of time spent in alternate care to no more than 20 hours weekly until the baby's first birthday. Second, be sure that work does not reduce the quality of parenting. If parents experience too much stress, they should seek help from a counselor. Perhaps parents can rearrange work schedules to better allow work and parenting. Or perhaps one parent should consider working part time, taking a leave of absence, or not working. Third, obtain *quality* child care. Some factors to look for in a first-rate day-care facility are: (a) a low ratio of children to caregivers (four infants and toddlers to one caregiver; six or eight 2- to 4-year-olds to one caregiver), (b) caregivers trained in child development and safety, (c) a plentiful supply of appropriate play materials, (d) a well-planned daily routine that includes ample opportunity for educational and social stimulation, and (e) effective communication between parents and day-care workers on the general aims and daily routines of the day-care program.

For American couples, juggling two full-time jobs and parenthood is often easier said than done. Other industrialized countries with many dual-earner families, such as Sweden, Denmark, and Finland, provide inexpensive but high-quality day care. In contrast, in the United States, arranging for child care is left to parents. Fortunately, employers have begun to do their part, realizing that convenient, high-quality child care means a more productive employee. In Flint, Michigan, for example, child care was negotiated into the contract between the United Auto Workers and General Motors. The child-care center is open from 5:30 A.M. until 1:00 A.M. to accommodate workers' schedules, and part of the tuition is paid by General Motors. Many cities, such as Pittsburgh, have revised their zoning codes so that new shopping complexes and office buildings must have child-care facilities, like those in the photo. Businesses are realizing that the availability of excellent child care helps attract and retain a skilled labor force. As Sophie Masloff, mayor of Pittsburgh noted when her city revised its zoning code, "With more women in the work force, more so than ever before, we just knew [providing adequate child care] was a necessity."

With effort, organization, and help from business and the community, full-time employment and quality caregiving *can* be compatible. The "Real Children" feature provides one example of a successful case of a father who stays home to care for his daughter while the mother works full time.

Real Children: JULIE, BILL, AND LYNNE

Julie and Bill had been married nearly 4 years when Julie gave birth to Lynne. Julie had worked in advertising and returned to work full time 4 months after Lynne was born. Bill, who had been an editor of college textbooks, became a full-time househusband. Bill does the cooking and takes care of Lynne during the day. Most days, Julie comes home from work at noon so that the family can eat lunch together. Three afternoons a week, Bill and Lynne go to the Y. Lynne stays in the child-care center while Bill jogs with a group of mothers whose children are also in the child-care center. By all accounts, Lynne looks to be a healthy, happy, outgoing 9-month-old. Is this arrangement nontraditional? Clearly. Is it effective for Julie, Bill, and Lynne? Definitely. Lynne receives the nurturing care that she needs, Julie goes to work assured that Lynne is in Bill's knowing and caring hands, and Bill relishes being the primary caregiver. ■

Check Your Learning

1. By approximately _____ months of age, most infants have identified a special individual—typically, but not always, the mother—as the attachment figure.

2. Joan, a 12-month-old, was separated from her mother for about 15 minutes. When they were reunited, Joan would not let her mother pick her up. When her mother approached, Joan looked the other way and toddled to another part of the room. This behavior suggests that Joan has a(n) _____ attachment relationship.

3. The single most important factor in fostering a secure attachment relationship is _____.

4. To reduce the chance that their infant forms an insecure attachment, working parents should wait until the child's first birthday to begin full-time day care, try to have their infant in alternative care for no more than 20 hours each week during the first year, and _____.

Answers: (1) 6 or 7 (2) avoidant, (3) responsive parenting that fosters an infant's trust and confidence, (4) be sure that work does not reduce the quality of parenting

EMOTIONAL DEVELOPMENT IN PERSPECTIVE

Most of us would find life on Mr. Spock's emotionless home planet very unsatisfying because emotions are so central to our daily lives. In this chapter, we've seen that emotions take center stage very early in development. In Module 10.1, we learned that children express basic emotions like happiness before age 1 and complex emotions like guilt before age 2. Infants use others' emotions to guide their behavior and this skill improves as children grow cognitively. In Module 10.2, we discovered that emotion is a defining characteristic of temperament, a consistent mood and style of behavior that is moderately stable as children develop. In Module 10.3, we traced the development of the emotion-filled attachment relationship between infant and parents. We saw that secure attachment reflects the infant's trust in the parent, which is rooted in responsive caregiving.

Temperament is one of the best examples in the entire book of the theme that *children help determine their own development.* Temperament helps determine how parents, peers, and other adults respond to children. Parents and peers, for example, usually respond positively to temperamentally easy children. Parents find it more straightforward to establish a secure attachment with an easy child than with a difficult child. Peers get along better with easy children than with shy, inhibited children. Children's temperament does not alone dictate the direction of their development, but it makes some directions much easier to follow than others.

THINKING ABOUT DEVELOPMENT

1. The different approaches to cognitive development described in Chapters 6 and 7 (Piaget's theory, Vygotsky's theory, the information-processing approach) don't explicitly consider emotion. How might emotion affect thinking? Which of these approaches could most readily include emotion?

2. Buss and Plomin's emotionality dimension of temperament includes the New York Longitudinal Study's intensity and threshold dimensions (see page 257). Which dimensions of the New York Longitudinal Study are comparable to Buss and Plomin's activity and sociability dimensions of temperament?

3. According to Piaget's theory, what cognitive-developmental changes in infancy might be important prerequisites for the formation of an attachment relationship?

4. A political candidate says that a woman's place is in the home because when women work children don't get the love they need and this plants the seed for a disordered family. Do you agree? Why or why not?

5. Each of the three modules in this chapter deals with emotions, but in very different ways. Compare and contrast emotion as it is presented in each module.

SEE FOR YOURSELF

Arrange to visit a local day-care center where you can unobtrusively observe preschoolers for several days. As you watch the children, see if you can detect the temperamental differences that are described in Module 10.2. Can you identify an emotional child, an active child, and a social child? Also, decide how the day-care center fares against the quality criteria listed on page 268. Are the children in this center receiving high-quality care? If not, what changes would be the most important? See for yourself!

RESOURCES

For more information about . . .

the development of the attachment relationship, read T. Berry Brazelton and Bertrand Cramer's *The Earliest Relationship* (Addison-Wesley, 1990), which illustrates the drama of attachment through lively case studies

programs for preschool children, contact the National Association for the Education of Young Children (NAEYC), an organization dedicated to improving early childhood education programs, 1-800-424-2460

temperament, visit the Web site of temperament. com, maintained by a publisher of questionnaires and software used to measure temperament, at http://www. temperament.com

SUMMARY

MODULE 10.1:
EMERGING EMOTIONS

BASIC EMOTIONS

Scientists often use infants' facial expressions to judge when different emotional states emerge in development. The earliest indicator of happiness is the social smile, which emerges at about 2 months. Laughter appears at 4 months. Anger and fear are both evident by about 6 months of age. Fear first appears in infancy as stranger anxiety; fears of specific objects develop later in childhood.

COMPLEX EMOTIONS

Complex emotions have an evaluative component and include guilt, embarrassment, and pride. They appear between 18 and 24 months, requiring more sophisticated cognitive skills than basic emotions like happiness and fear.

RECOGNIZING AND USING OTHERS' EMOTIONS

By 6 months, infants have begun to recognize the emotions associated with different facial expressions. They use this information to help them evaluate unfamiliar situations. Beyond infancy, children understand the causes and consequences of different emotions and that people can feel multiple emotions simultaneously.

MODULE 10.2:
TEMPERAMENT

WHAT IS TEMPERAMENT?

Temperament refers to stable patterns of behavior that are evident soon after birth. The New York Longitudinal Study suggests three temperamental patterns: easy, difficult, and slow-to-warm-up; other research suggests that the dimensions of temperament are emotionality, activity, and sociability. The major theories of temperament include many of the same elements, organized differently. The major theories also agree that both heredity and environment contribute to temperament.

STABILITY OF TEMPERAMENT

Temperament is moderately stable from infancy to the preschool years and into childhood and adolescence. The correlations are not very strong, which means that, for many children, temperament does change as they develop.

TEMPERAMENT AND OTHER ASPECTS OF DEVELOPMENT

Many investigators have shown that temperament is related to other aspects of development. Difficult babies are more likely to have be-

havioral problems by the time they are old enough to attend school. Persistent children are more successful in school, shy children sometimes have problems with peers, and anxious children are more compliant with parents.

MODULE 10.3:
ATTACHMENT

THE GROWTH OF ATTACHMENT

Attachment is an enduring social-emotional relationship between infant and parent. Many of the behaviors that contribute to the formation of attachment are biologically programmed. Attachment develops gradually over the first year of life; by about 6 or 7 months, infants have identified an attachment figure, typically the mother. In the ensuing months, infants often become attached to other family members, including fathers, whose usual role is playmate.

QUALITY OF ATTACHMENT

Research with the Strange Situation, in which infant and mother are separated briefly, reveals four primary forms of attachment. Most common is a secure attachment, in which infants have complete trust in the mother. Less common are three types of insecure attachment relationships that lack this trust. In avoidant relationships, infants deal with the lack of trust by ignoring the mother; in resistant relationships, infants often seem angry with her; in disorganized (disoriented) relationships, infants seem to not understand the mother's absence.

Children who have had secure attachment relationships during infancy often interact with their peers more readily and more skillfully. Secure attachment is most likely to occur when mothers respond sensitively and consistently to their infants' needs.

ATTACHMENT, WORK, AND ALTERNATE CAREGIVING

The impact of parental employment on children depends upon the child's age. Children who are 1 year or older actually benefit from exposure to other children and caregivers in day care; they are often more advanced intellectually and socially. Insecure attachments are slightly more likely when infants are placed in full-time day care before their first birthday. Other factors affecting attachment include the amount of time spent with alternative caregivers, the quality of parenting provided, and the child's gender and position in the birth order.

Understanding Self and Others

EARLY 100 YEARS AGO, G. STANLEY HALL, AN INFLUENTIAL AMERICAN DEVELOPMENTAL PSYCHOLOGIST, WROTE THAT ADOLESCENCE WAS " . . . STREWN WITH WRECKAGE OF MIND, BODY, AND MORALS" (1904, P. XIV). JUDGING BY TODAY'S MOVIES AND MEDIA, Hall's analysis would seem to have stood the test of time: When teens aren't presented as runaways, drug addicts, and shoplifters, they're moody and withdrawn or manic. But how accurate is this picture? What does current research show about adolescence and the process of developing independence and identity?

In Module 11.1, we'll look at the mechanisms that give rise to a person's identity and we'll see if storm and stress is a necessary step in achieving an identity. Of course, people are often happier with some aspects of themselves than with others. These evaluative aspects of identity are the focus of Module 11.2. Finally, in Module 11.3, we'll look at how we develop an understanding of others, because as we learn more about ourselves, we learn more about other people, too.

HO AM I? SELF-CONCEPT

Learning Objectives

- **When do infants first acquire a sense of self?**
- **What is theory of mind and how does it develop during the preschool years?**
- **How does self-concept become more elaborate as children grow?**
- **How do adolescents achieve an identity?**

> *Dea was born in Seoul of Korean parents but was adopted by a Dutch couple in Michigan when she was 3 months old. Growing up, she considered herself a red-blooded American. In high school, however, Dea realized that others saw her as an Asian American, an identity about which she had never given much thought. She began to wonder, who am I really? American? Dutch American? Asian American?*

Like Dea, do you sometimes wonder who you are? **Answers to "Who am I?" reflect a person's** *self-concept,* **which refers to the attitudes, behaviors, and values that a person believes make him or her a unique individual.** Part of one teenage girl's self-concept is evident in her answer to "Who am I?"

> *I'm sensitive, friendly, outgoing, popular, and tolerant, though I can also be shy, self-conscious, and even obnoxious! I'd like to be friendly and tolerant all of the time. That's the kind of person I want to be, and I'm disappointed when I'm not. I'm responsible, even studious now and then, but on the other hand, I'm a goof-off, too, because if you're too studious, you won't be popular (Harter, 1990, p. 352).*

As an adult, your answer is probably even more complex because, after all, most people are complex creatures. But how did you acquire this complex self-concept? We'll answer that question in this module, beginning with the origins of an infant's sense of self.

ORIGINS OF SELF-RECOGNITION

What is the starting point for self-concept? Following the lead of the 19th century philosopher and psychologist, William James, modern researchers believe that the foundation of self-concept is the child's awareness that he or she exists. At some point early in life, children must realize that they exist independently of other people and objects in the environment and that their existence continues over time.

Measuring the onset of this awareness is not easy. Obviously, we can't simply ask a 3-year-old, "So, tell me, when did you first realize that you existed and that you weren't simply part of the furniture?" A less direct approach is needed, and the photo shows one route that many investigators have taken. Like many babies his age, the 9-month-old in the photo is smiling at the face he sees in the mirror. Babies at this age sometimes touch the face in the mirror or wave at it, but none of their behaviors indicates that they recognize themselves in the mirror. Instead, babies act as if the face in the mirror is simply a very interesting stimulus.

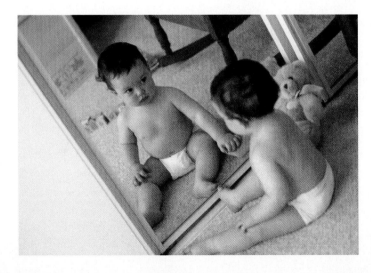

How would we know that infants recognize themselves in a mirror? One clever approach is to have the mother place a red mark on her infant's nose; she does this surreptitiously, while wiping the baby's face. Then the infant is returned to the mirror. Many 1-year-olds touch the red mark on the mirror, showing that they notice the mark on the face in the mirror. By 15 months, however, an important change occurs: Babies see the red mark in the mirror, then reach up and touch *their own* noses. By age 2, virtually all children do this (Bullock & Lütkenhaus, 1990; Lewis & Brooks-Gunn, 1979). When these older children notice the red mark in the mirror, they understand that the funny-looking nose in the mirror is their own.

Do you doubt that the mirror task shows an infant's emerging sense of self? Perhaps you think it tells more about an infant's growing understanding of mirrors than the baby's self-awareness? One way to examine this possibility would be to test infants who have never seen mirrors previously. Priel and deSchonen (1986) took this approach, testing infants from Israeli desert communities. These babies had never seen mirrors or, for that matter, virtually any reflective surfaces because they lived in tents. Nevertheless, the same developmental trend appeared in the desert infants as in a comparison group of infants living in a nearby city. No 6- to 12-month-olds in either group touched their noses after they saw the mark, a few 13- to 19-month-olds did, and nearly all the 20- to 26-month-olds did.

Most children are self aware by age two because they recognize themselves in mirrors and photos, and refer to themselves by name or with "I" and "me."

We don't need to rely solely on the mirror task to know that self-awareness emerges between 18 and 24 months. During this same period, toddlers look more at photographs of themselves than at photos of other children. They also refer to themselves by name or with a personal pronoun, such as "I" or "me," and sometimes they know their age and their gender. These changes suggest that self-awareness is well established in most children by age 2 (Lewis, 1987).

Once self-awareness is established, children soon have more insights into themselves as thinking human beings. In the next section, we'll look at the nature of these insights.

THEORY OF MIND

The French philosopher René Descartes is well known for his statement, "I think, therefore I am." When do children have this insight? That is, when do children come to understand that they (and other people) have thoughts, beliefs, and intentions? And, when do children understand that thoughts, beliefs, and intentions often cause people to behave as they do?

Collectively, a person's ideas about connections between thoughts, beliefs, intentions, and behavior form a *theory of mind,* an intuitive understanding of the relations between mind and behavior. One of the leading researchers on theory of mind, Henry Wellman (1990, 1992), believes that children's theory of mind moves through three phases during the preschool years. In the earliest phase, common in 2-year-olds, children are aware of desires and they often speak of their wants and likes, as in "Lemme see" or "I wanna sit." And they often link their desires to their behavior, such "I happy there's more cookies" (Wellman, 1990). Thus, by age 2, children understand that they and other people have desires and that desires can cause behavior.

By about age 3, an important change takes place. Now children clearly distinguish the mental world from the physical world. For example, if told about one girl who has a cookie and another girl who is thinking about a cookie, 3-year-olds know that only the first girl's cookie can be seen, touched, and eaten (Harris et al., 1991). And, most 3-year-olds use "mental verbs" like "think," "believe," "remember," and "forget," which suggests that they have a beginning understanding of different mental states (Bartsch & Wellman, 1995). Although 3-year-olds talk about thoughts and beliefs, they nevertheless emphasize desires when trying to explain why people act as they do.

Not until 4 years of age do mental states really take center stage in children's understanding of their and other's actions. That is, by age 4, children understand that their and others' behavior is based on their beliefs about events and situations, even when those beliefs are wrong. This developmental transformation is particularly evident when children are tested on false belief tasks like the one shown in the figure. In all false belief tasks, a situation is set up so that the child being tested has accurate information, but someone else does not. For example, in the story in the figure, the child being tested knows that the marble is really in the box, but Sally, the girl in the story, believes that the marble is still in the basket. Remarkably, although 4-year-olds correctly say that Sally will look for the marble in the basket (acting on her false belief), most 3-year-olds claim that she will look for the marble in the box. The 4-year-olds understand that Sally's behavior is based on her beliefs, despite the fact that her beliefs are incorrect (Frye, 1993). As Bartsch and Wellman (1995) phrase it, 4-year-olds ". . . realize that people not only have thoughts and beliefs, but also that thoughts and beliefs are crucial to explaining why people do things; that is, actors' pursuits of their desires are inevitably shaped by their beliefs about the world" (p. 144).

As children's theory of mind becomes more elaborate, children begin to acquire a self-concept. To paraphrase Descarte's saying, it's as if many preschoolers say, "I am, so who am I?" That is, once children fully understand that they exist and that they have a unique mental life, they begin to wonder who they are. They want to define themselves. In the next section, we'll see how this self-concept becomes more complex as children develop.

THE EVOLVING SELF-CONCEPT

Before you go any further, return to the quotation on page 274 from the teenager. In describing herself, this girl relies heavily on psychological traits. The first sentence alone includes eight adjectives referring to psychological traits: sensitive, friendly, outgoing, popular, tolerant, shy, self-conscious, and obnoxious.

How do children develop such a complex view of themselves? Some of the most intriguing research on this question comes from Levine (1983), who studied 20- to 28-month-olds. This is the period when children are just beginning to become self-aware. Children were tested on several measures of self-awareness, including the mirror recognition task. They were also

This is Sally. Sally has a basket.

This is Anne. Anne has a box.

Sally has a marble.

She puts the marble into her basket.

Sally goes out for a walk.

Anne takes the marble out of the basket and puts it into the box.

Now Sally comes back. She wants to play with her marble. Where will she look for her marble?

observed as they interacted with an unfamiliar peer in a playroom filled with toys. The key finding was that children who were self-aware were much more likely to say, "Mine!" while playing with toys than children who were not yet self-aware. Maybe you think these self-aware children were being confrontational in saying, "Mine" as in, "This car is mine and don't even think about taking it." But they weren't. Actually, self-aware children were more likely to say positive things during their interactions with peers. Levine argued that "[C]laiming toys was not simply a negative or aggressive behavior, but appeared to be an important part of the child's definition of herself within her social world" (p. 547). In other words, the girl in the photo saying, "Mine!" is not trying to deny the doll to the other girl; she is simply saying that playing with dolls is part of who she is.

Throughout the preschool years, possessions continue to be one of the ways that children define themselves. Preschoolers are also likely to mention physical characteristics ("I have blue eyes"), their preferences ("I like spaghetti"), and their competencies ("I can count to 50"). What these features have in common is a focus on a child's characteristics that are observable and concrete (Damon & Hart, 1988).

Sometime between 6 and 8 years of age, children's self-descriptions begin to change (Harter, 1994). Children are more likely to mention emotions ("Sometimes I get angry"). They are also more likely to mention the social groups to which they belong ("I'm on the soccer team"). Finally, in contrast to preschool children, who simple mention their competencies, elementary-school children describe their level of skill in relation to their peers ("I'm the best speller in my whole class").

Self-concepts change again as children enter adolescence (Harter & Monsour, 1992). They now include attitudes ("I love algebra") and personality traits ("I'm usually a very happy person"). Adolescents also begin to make religious and political beliefs a part of their self-concept ("I'm a Catholic" or "I'm a conservative Republican"). Another change is that adolescents' self concepts often vary with the setting. A teenager might say "I'm really shy around people that I don't know, but I let loose when I'm with my friends and family."

Yet another change is that adolescents' self-concepts are often future oriented: Adolescents often describe themselves in terms of what they will be when they reach adulthood (Harter, 1990). These descriptions may include occupational goals ("I'm going to be an English teacher"), educational plans ("I plan to go to a community college to learn about computers"), or social roles ("I want to get married as soon as I finish high school").

The gradual elaboration of self-concept from the preschool years to adolescence is summarized in the diagram at the top of page 278. Two general changes are evident in the diagram. First, self-concept becomes richer as children grow; adolescents simply know much more about themselves than preschoolers do. Second, the type of knowledge that children have of themselves changes. Preschoolers' understanding is linked to the concrete, the real, and the here and now. Adolescents' understanding, in contrast, is more abstract, more psychological, and sees the self as evolving over time. The change in children's knowledge of themselves should not surprise you because it's exactly the type of change that Piaget described.

A preschooler's self-concept is linked to the concrete and real but an adolescent's self-concept is more abstract and more psychological.

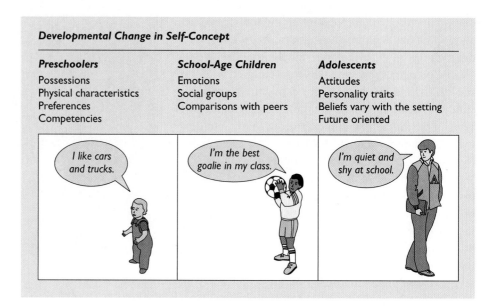

Developmental Change in Self-Concept

Preschoolers	School-Age Children	Adolescents
Possessions	Emotions	Attitudes
Physical characteristics	Social groups	Personality traits
Preferences	Comparisons with peers	Beliefs vary with the setting
Competencies		Future oriented

I like cars and trucks.

I'm the best goalie in my class.

I'm quiet and shy at school.

Concrete operational children's focus on the real and tangible extends to their thoughts about themselves, just as formal operational adolescents' focus on the abstract and hypothetical applies to their thoughts about themselves.

Adolescence is also a time of increasing self-reflection. Adolescents look for an identity to integrate the many different and sometimes conflicting elements of the self (Marcia, 1991). We'll look at this search for identity in detail in the next section.

THE SEARCH FOR IDENTITY

Erik Erikson (1968) believed that adolescents struggle to achieve an identity that will allow them to participate in the adult world. How exactly do they accomplish this? Adolescents use the hypothetical reasoning skills of the formal operational stage to experiment with different selves to learn more about possible identities. Adolescents' advanced cognitive skills allow them to imagine themselves in different roles.

Much of the testing and experimentation is career oriented. Some adolescents, like the ones shown in the photo, may envision themselves as rock stars; others may imagine being a professional athlete, a Peace Corps worker, or a best-selling novelist. Other testing is romantically oriented. Teens may fall in love and imagine living with the loved one. Still other exploration involves religious and political beliefs. Teens

give different identities a trial run just as you might test drive different cars before selecting one. By fantasizing about their future, adolescents begin to discover who they will be.

The self-absorption that marks the teen-age search for identity is referred to as *adolescent egocentrism* (Elkind, 1978). Unlike preschoolers, adolescents *know* that others have different perspectives on the world. At the same time, many adolescents believe, wrongly, that they are the focus of others' thinking. A teen eating lunch with friends who spills catsup on herself may imagine that *all* of her friends are thinking only about the stain on her blouse and how sloppy she is. **The feeling of many adolescents is that they are, in effect, actors whose performance is watched constantly by their peers, a phenomenon known as the** *imaginary audience.*

A related feature of adolescent self-absorption is the *personal fable,* **which refers to teenagers' tendency to believe that their experiences and feelings are unique, that no one has ever felt or thought as they do.** Whether the excitement of first love, the despair of a broken relationship, or the confusion of planning for the future, adolescents often believe that they are the first to experience these feelings and that no one else could possibly understand the power of their emotions (Elkind & Bowen, 1979). **Adolescents' belief in their uniqueness also contributes to an *illusion of invulnerability*—the belief that misfortune only happens to others.** They think they can have sex without becoming pregnant and they can drive recklessly without being in an auto accident. Those misfortunes only happen to other people.

Adolescent egocentrism, imaginary audiences, personal fables, and the illusion of invulnerability become less common as adolescents make progress toward achieving an identity. What are the steps involved in achieving an identity? Most adolescents progress through different phases or statuses, though not necessarily in strict sequence (Marcia, 1980, 1991):

- *Diffusion:* **Individuals in this status are confused or overwhelmed by the task of achieving an identity and are doing little to achieve one.**

- *Foreclosure:* **Individuals in this status have an identity determined largely by adults, rather than from personal exploration of alternatives.**

- *Moratorium:* **Individuals in this status are still examining different alternatives and have yet to find a satisfactory identity.**

- *Achievement:* **Individuals in this status have explored alternatives and have deliberately chosen a specific identity.**

Unlike Piaget's stages, these four phases do not necessarily occur in sequence. Most young adolescents are in a state of diffusion or foreclosure. The common element in these phases is that teens are not exploring alternative identities. They are avoiding the crisis altogether or have resolved it by taking on an identity based on suggestions from parents or other adults. However, as individuals move beyond adolescence and into young adulthood, they have more opportunity to explore alternative identities, and so diffusion and foreclosure become less common, and as the pie charts show, achievement and moratorium become more common (Meilman, 1979).

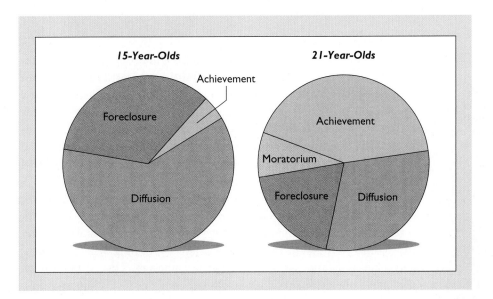

Sometimes youth reach the achievement status for some aspects of identity but not others. Dellas and Jernigan (1990), for example, found that 39 percent of the college students in their sample were in the achievement status for careers, but only 22 percent were in this status for religion and 13 percent for politics. Furthermore, only 3 percent of students in their sample were in the same status across all three content areas. Evidently, adolescents and young adults do not achieve a sense of identity all at once; instead, the crisis of identity is first resolved in some areas and then in others.

One element of identity that has been examined in some detail is career development. According to a theory proposed by Donald Super (1976, 1980), identity is a primary force in an adolescent's choice of a career. **At about age 13 or 14, adolescents use their emerging identities as a source of ideas about careers, a process called** *crystallization.* Teenagers use their ideas about their own talents and interests to limit potential career prospects. A teenager who is extroverted and sociable may decide that working with people would be the career for him. Another who excels in math and science may decide she'd like to teach math. Decisions are provisional, and adolescents experiment with hypothetical careers, trying to envision what each might be like. Rarely, however, are careers as hypothetical as the one imagined by the teenager in the cartoon!

"Your son has made a career choice, Mildred. He's going to win the lottery and travel a lot."

By permission of Bunny Hoest, Wm. Hoest Enterprises, Inc.

The next phase usually begins at about age 18 and is an extension of the activities associated with crystallization. **During** *specification,* **individuals further limit their career possibilities by learning more about specific lines of work and starting to obtain the training required for a specific job.** Our extroverted teenager who wants to work with people may decide that a career in sales would be a good match for his abilities and interests. The teen who likes math may have learned more about careers and decided she'd like to be an accountant. Some teens, like the young man in the photo, may begin an apprenticeship as a way to learn a trade.

The end of the teenage years or the early 20s marks the beginning of the third phase. **During** *implementation,* **individuals enter the work force and learn firsthand about jobs.** This is a time of learning about responsibility and productivity, of learning to get along with coworkers, and of altering one's lifestyle to accommodate work. This period is often unstable; individuals may change jobs frequently as they adjust to the reality of life in the workplace.

In each of the three phases of career development, there is continuous give-and-take between an individual's identity and career choice. A person's self-concept makes some careers more attractive than others; occupational experiences, in turn, refine and shape a person's identity.

What circumstances help adolescents decide on a career and achieve identity? Parents are influential (Marcia, 1980). When parents encourage discussion and recognize their children's autonomy, their children are more likely to reach the achievement status. Apparently these youth feel encouraged to undertake the personal experimentation that leads to identity. In contrast, when parents set rules with little justification and enforce them without explanation, children are more likely to be in the foreclosure status. These teens are discouraged from experimenting personally; instead, their parents simply tell them what identity to adopt. Overall, adolescents are most likely to establish a well-defined identity in a family atmosphere where parents encourage children to explore alternatives on their own but do not pressure or provide explicit direction (Harter, 1990).

For many adolescents growing up in North America today, achieving an identity is even more challenging because they are members of ethnic minority groups. The "Cultural Influences" feature describes one example.

Cultural Influences: **DEA'S ETHNIC IDENTITY**

 Dea, the adolescent in the opening vignette, belongs to the one-third of the adolescents and young adults living in the United States who are members of ethnic minority groups. They include African Americans, Asian Americans, Hispanic Americans, and Native Americans. These individuals typically develop an ethnic identity: They feel a part of their ethnic group and learn the special customs and traditions of their group's culture and heritage (Phinney, 1996).

Achieving an ethnic identity seems to occur in three phases. Initially, adolescents have not examined their ethnic roots. A teenage African American girl in this phase remarked, "Why do I need to learn about who was the first Black woman to do this or that? I'm just not too interested" (Phinney, 1989, p. 44). For this girl, ethnic identity is not yet an important personal issue. In the second phase, however, adolescents begin to explore the personal impact of their ethnic heritage. The curiosity and questioning that is characteristic of this stage is captured in the comments of a teenage Mexican American girl who said, "I want to know what we do and how our culture is different from others. Going to festivals and cultural events helps me to learn more about my own culture and about myself" (Phinney, 1989, p. 44). Part of this phase involves learning cultural traditions; for example, like the girl in the photo, many adolescents learn to prepare ethnic food.

In the third phase, individuals achieve a distinct ethnic self-concept. One Asian American adolescent explained his ethnic identification like this: "I have been born Filipino and am born to be Filipino.... I'm here in America, and people of many different cultures are here, too. So I don't consider myself only Filipino, but also American" (Phinney, 1989, p. 44).

To see if you understand the differences between these stages of ethnic identity, reread the vignette on page 274 about Dea and decide which stage applies to her. The answer appears on page 283, just before "Check Your Learning."

Older adolescents are more likely than younger ones to have achieved an ethnic identity, because they are more likely to have had opportunities to explore their

Adolescents are most likely to establish an identity when parents encourage discussion and recognize their children's autonomy.

cultural heritage (Phinney & Chavira, 1992). Also, as is the case with overall identity, adolescents are most likely to achieve an ethnic self-concept when their parents encourage them to explore alternatives instead of pressuring them to adopt a particular ethnic identity (Rosenthal & Feldman, 1992).

Do adolescents benefit from a strong ethnic identity? Yes. Adolescents who have achieved an ethnic identity tend to have higher self-esteem and find their interactions with family and friends more satisfying (Blash & Unger, 1995). In addition, many investigators have found that adolescents with a strong ethnic identity do better in school than adolescents whose ethnic identities are weaker (Stalikas & Gavaki, 1995; Taylor et al., 1994).

Some individuals achieve a well-defined ethnic self-concept and, at the same time, identify strongly with the mainstream culture. In the United States, for example, many Chinese Americans embrace both Chinese and American culture; in England, many Indians identify with both Indian and British cultures. For other individuals, the cost of strong ethnic identification is a weakened tie to mainstream culture. Some investigators report that, for Hispanic Americans, strong identification with American culture is associated with a weaker ethnic self-concept (Phinney, 1990).

We shouldn't be too surprised that identifying with mainstream culture weakens ethnic identity in some groups but not others (Berry, 1993). Racial and ethnic groups living in the United States are diverse. African American, Asian American, Hispanic American, and Native American cultures and heritages differ, and so we should expect that the nature and consequences of a strong ethnic self-concept will differ across these and other ethnic groups. Even within any particular group, the nature and consequences of ethnic identity may change over successive generations (Montgomery, 1992). ■

Does the search for identity always make adolescence a time of storm and stress? In reality, the rebellious teen is largely a myth. Think about the following conclusions derived from research findings (Steinberg, 1990). Most adolescents

■ admire and love their parents,

■ rely upon their parents for advice,

■ embrace many of their parents' values,

■ feel loved by their parents.

Not exactly the image of the rebel, is it? Furthermore, cross-cultural evidence underscores the view that adolescence is not necessarily a time of turmoil and conflict. Offer and his colleagues (1988) interviewed adolescents from 10 different countries: the United States, Australia, Germany, Italy, Israel, Hungary, Turkey, Japan, Taiwan, and Bangladesh. These investigators found most adolescents moving confidently and happily towards adulthood. As the graphs show, most adolescents around the world reported that they were usually happy, and few avoided their homes.

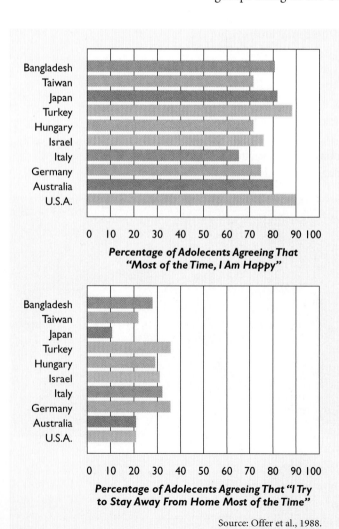

Percentage of Adolescents Agreeing That "Most of the Time, I Am Happy"

Percentage of Adolescents Agreeing That "I Try to Stay Away From Home Most of the Time"

Source: Offer et al., 1988.

Of course, parent-child relations do change during adolescence. As teens become more independent, their relationships with their parents become more egalitarian. Parents must adjust to their children's growing sense of autonomy, treating them more like equals (Laursen & Collins, 1994). Greater autonomy means, too, that teens spend less time with their parents, show them less affection, and more often disagree with them about matters of style, taste, and freedom. However, these changes are not about storm and stress; they are natural byproducts of a changing parent-child relationship in which the "child" is nearly a fully independent young adult (Steinberg, 1990). Adolescence is an interesting and challenging time for youth and their parents, but it is not inherently tempestuous as the myth would have us believe.

Adolescence is not inherently a period of storm and stress—most teens report that they love and rely upon their parents—but it is a time when parent-child relationships become more egalitarian.

Response to question on page 281 about Dea's ethnic identity: Dea, the Dutch Asian American college student, doesn't know how to integrate the Korean heritage of her biological parents with the Dutch American culture in which she was reared. This would put her in the second phase of acquiring an ethnic identity. On the one hand, she is examining her ethnic roots, which means she's progressed beyond the initial stages. On the other hand, she has not yet integrated her Asian and European roots, and so has not reached the third and final phase.

Check Your Learning

1. Apparently children become self-aware by age 2 because at this age they recognize themselves in a mirror and in photographs and they _____.

2. By age 2, children know that their and other people's behavior is often caused by _____.

3. Children's self-concepts begin to include emotions, membership in social groups, and comparisons with peers during _____.

4. The _____ phase or status would describe an adolescent who has attained an identity based almost entirely on her parents' advice and urging.

5. Children's relations with their parents change in adolescence, reflecting adolescents' growing independence and a _____ parent-child relationship.

Answers: (1) refer to themselves by name or with the pronouns "I" and "me," (2) desire (3) the elementary-school years, (4) foreclosure (5) more egalitarian

SELF-ESTEEM

Learning Objectives

- **What is self-esteem? How is it measured?**
- **How does self-esteem change as children develop?**
- **What factors influence the development of self-esteem?**

Darnel, age 10, loves school and for good reason: Every year, he is always one of the best students in his class. Darnel's mother, Karen, wants to enroll him in a program for gifted children, where she believes the pace will be more appropriate for her talented son. Darnel's dad, Jon, doesn't think this is such a great idea. He's afraid that if Darnel doesn't do well against all of those other bright kids, his son will begin to doubt his academic ability.

MODULE
11.2
Self-Esteem

Measuring Self-Esteem

Developmental Changes
in Self-Esteem

Sources of Self-Esteem

Jon is concerned about Darnel's *self-esteem*, which refers to a person's judgment and feelings about his or her own worth. Children with high self-esteem judge themselves favorably and feel positively about themselves. In contrast, children with low self-esteem judge themselves negatively, are unhappy with themselves, and often would rather be someone else. In this module, we'll see how self-esteem is measured, how it changes as children develop, and what forces shape it.

MEASURING SELF-ESTEEM

Think about your own self-esteem. Do you think you have high self-esteem or low self-esteem? To help you answer this question, read each of these sentences and decide how well each applies to you:

I'm very good at schoolwork.

I find it very easy to make friends.

I do very well at all kinds of different sports.

I'm happy with the way I look.

If you agreed strongly with each of these statements, you definitely have high self-esteem. Usually, however, people agree with some of these statements more strongly than others. This tells us that, in addition to an overall sense of self-worth, people evaluate themselves in different areas. That is, people have multiple self-esteems, each linked to a specific content area. This phenomenon should seem familiar because it's like intelligence: In Module 8.1, we saw that hierarchical theories of intelligence begin with a general intelligence that is divided into more specific abilities, such as verbal ability and spatial ability.

How can we measure different aspects of self-esteem? The method depends upon the age of the child. With 4- to 7-year-olds, an approach devised by Harter and Pike (1984) uses pairs of pictures. The sample pictures show a girl either solving a

puzzle easily or having difficulty. During testing, children are first asked to point to the pictured child who is most like them. Then they point to the larger circle if they believe that they are "a lot" like the child in that picture or the smaller one if they believe that are "a little" like the child in that picture. Harter and Pike used 24 pairs of pictures like these to measure children's self-worth in four areas: cognitive competence, physical competence, acceptance by peers, and acceptance by mother.

Self-esteem in older children and adolescents can be measured with a questionnaire. The child reads statements like the ones at the beginning of this section. The most widely used self-esteem questionnaire of this sort is the *Self-Perception Profile for Children* (SPPC for short) devised by Susan Harter (1985, 1988). The SPPC is designed to evaluate self-worth in children age 8 and older in five domains (Harter, 1988, p. 62):

- *Scholastic competence:* How competent or smart the child feels in doing schoolwork.

- *Athletic competence:* How competent the child feels at sports and games requiring physical skill or athletic ability.

- *Social acceptance:* How popular or accepted the child feels in social interactions with peers.

- *Behavioral conduct:* How adequate the child feels about behaving the way one is supposed to.

- *Physical appearance:* How good-looking the child feels and how much the child likes his or her physical characteristics, such as height, weight, face, and hair.

The SPPC includes six statements for each domain. For example, the figure at the top of page 286 lists two of the statements used to evaluate scholastic competence, shown as they actually appear on the SPPC. In both statements, the child has checked the response that indicates the highest level of self-esteem. A child's answers to all six statements are used to create an average level of self-esteem in that domain. The averages for each of the five domains are then used to generate a self-perception profile for each child. Two profiles are illustrated in the figure on page 286. Allison's self-esteem is high across all five domains; Colleen's self-esteem is much more varied. She feels positive about her social acceptance and physical appearance and, to a lesser extent, about her conduct. However, she feels negative about her scholastic and athletic competence.

Notice that each profile ends with a bar graph depicting the child's overall self-worth. Overall self-worth is measured on the SPPC with six more items, such as "Some kids like the way they are leading their life" and "Some kids like the kind of person they are." Children's responses to these statements are then averaged to create a measure of overall self-worth.

Are you surprised that overall self-worth is measured separately? Why not simply average children's ratings on the five dimensions? The reason is that children's overall self-worth is usually not simply the average of their self-worth in specific domains. You can see that this is true in the profiles for Allison and Colleen. Both girls feel very positive about themselves overall. This isn't surprising for Allison based on her ratings in the individual domains. But it is hardly what we would expect for Colleen if overall self-worth were simply the sum of self-worth in specific domains. Evidently, overall feelings of self-worth somehow transcend feelings of self-worth in specific domains.

The Self-Perception Profile for Children (SPPC) measures children's overall self-worth and their self-evaluation in five areas: scholastic and athletic competence, social acceptance, behavioral conduct, and physical appearance.

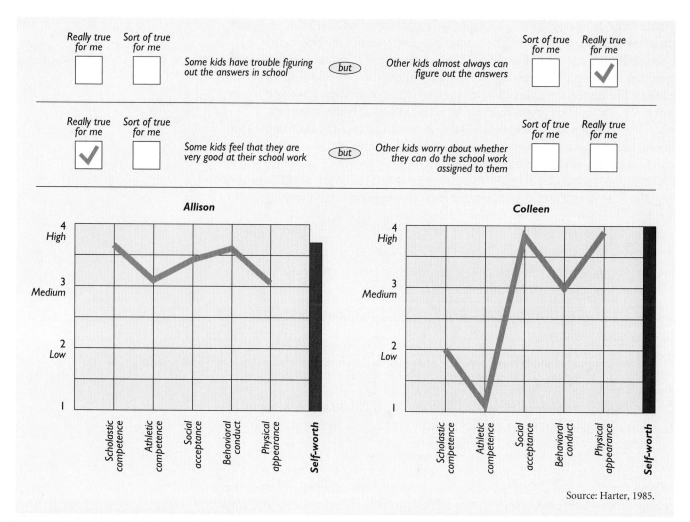

Source: Harter, 1985.

The SPPC is intended for use with children and young adolescents. For assessing self-esteem in older adolescents and young adults, Harter (1990) created a more extensive scale. This scale includes the five domains in the SPPC, along with job competence, close friendships, and romantic appeal. These additional domains were included because self-esteem becomes more differentiated during adolescence. That is, older adolescents judge themselves in more areas than children and younger adolescents.

In the next section, we'll see that greater differentiation is only one of several important developmental changes in self-esteem.

DEVELOPMENTAL CHANGES IN SELF-ESTEEM

At what age is self-esteem greatest? The answer may surprise you—it's during the preschool years. Most preschool children have very positive views of themselves across many different domains. For example, when Harter and Pike (1984) used the pictures shown on page 284 to estimate kindergarten children's cognitive competence, the average score was 3.6 out of a possible 4. In other words, virtually all the children said they were either a little or a lot like the competent child. Like the youngster in the photo, most preschool children are full of self-confidence and eager to take on new tasks.

As children progress through the elementary-school years, self-esteem usually drops somewhat. Why? Unlike in Garrison Keillor's mythical *Lake Wobegon,* all children are *not* above average. During the elementary-school years, children begin to compare themselves with peers (Ruble et al., 1980). When they do, they discover that they are not necessarily the best reader or the fastest runner. They may realize, instead, that they are only an average reader. Or, like the girl in the background of the photo, they come to understand that they are one of the slowest runners in the class. This realization often produces a modest drop in those dimensions of self-esteem in which the child compares less favorably to peers.

By the time most children enter adolescence, their self-esteem has usually stabilized (Harter, Whitesell, & Kowalski, 1992). That is, during the late elementary-school years, children's self-esteem neither increases nor decreases. Evidently, children learn their place in the "pecking order" of different domains and adjust their self-esteem accordingly.

Some studies indicate that self-esteem changes when children move from elementary school to middle school or junior high (Seidman et al., 1994). Apparently, when students from different elementary schools enter the same middle school or junior high, they know where they stand relative to their old elementary-school classmates but not to students from other elementary schools. Thus, peer comparisons begin anew, and self-esteem often suffers. The "Focus on Research" feature highlights a study that shows this drop in self-esteem that often accompanies school transitions.

Focus on Research: **HOW SCHOOL TRANSITIONS AFFECT SELF-ESTEEM**

Who were the investigators and what was the aim of the study? Many psychologists have claimed that the transition to middle or junior high school is stressful for young adolescents and that their self-esteem drops during this transition. Allan Wigfield and his colleagues, Jacquelynne S. Eccles, Douglas Mac Iver, David A. Reuman, and Carol Midgley, (1991) wanted to determine if, in fact, the transition to junior high school affected self-esteem. They were particularly interested in the possibility that the transition to junior high school might affect some aspects of self-esteem more than others.

How did the investigators measure the topic of interest? The researchers measured overall self-esteem as well as children's self-ratings in four specific domains: math, English, sports, and social interactions. To measure overall self-esteem, they used the overall self-worth items from the SPPC (described on page 285); children answered using a 4-point scale. For math, English, and sports, children answered two questions: "How good at math [or English or sports] are you?" and "If you were to rank all of the students in your class from the worst to the best in math [or English or sports] where would you put yourself?" Children answered two similar questions for social interactions: "How good are you at making friends?" and "How popular are you at school?" On each of these domain-specific questions, children answered on a 7-point scale with higher scores indicating more positive self-evaluations.

Who were the children in the study? The sample included nearly 2,000 students living in low- and middle-income communities in the greater Detroit area. Approximately 90 percent of the children participating were European Americans.

Overall self-esteem often declines as children move from elementary school to junior high or middle school because children don't know where they stand relative to their new classmates.

What was the design of the study? This study was correlational because Wigfield and his colleagues were interested in the relation of self-esteem before and after the transition to junior high school. The study was longitudinal because subjects were tested four times: They were tested in the fall and spring of sixth grade and then again in junior high in the fall and spring of seventh grade.

Were there ethical concerns with the study? No. Students answered the questions privately in their math classrooms; the data were confidential. The investigators obtained permission from the parents for the children to participate.

What were the results? The graphs show the average scores for overall self-esteem and in the four domains. In every case, scores decline slightly between sixth

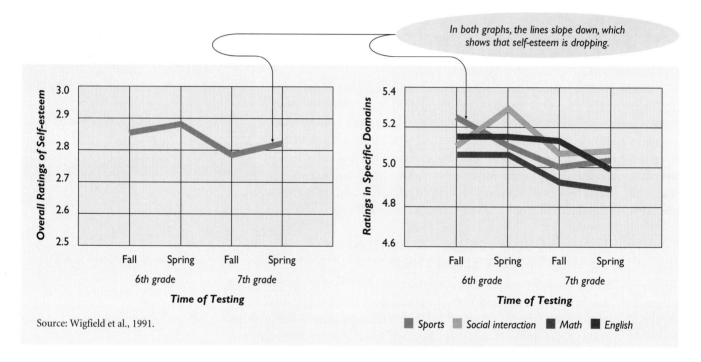

Source: Wigfield et al., 1991.

and seventh grade. That is, children's self-esteem was slightly lower after leaving elementary school for junior high. On four of the five measures, boys' and girls' self-esteem dropped by the same amount. The exception was social interaction, where boys' self-esteem dropped slightly more than girls'.

What did the investigators conclude? Self-esteem drops during the transition to junior high. Why? According to the investigators,

> *In the sixth grade, the students were the oldest students in their schools, and, as such, were likely to have the most status. They knew their school routines well, and the school was familiar to them.... In the seventh grade, the students were the youngest children in the school and were adjusting to their new environment (p. 559).*

In other words, self-esteem falls when children move from the top of the pecking order to the bottom and from the familiar to the unfamiliar. ▪

The drop in self-esteem associated with the transition to junior high is usually temporary. As children enter middle and late adolescence, self-esteem frequently increases (Savin-Williams & Demo, 1984). New schools become familiar and students gradually adjust to the new pecking order. In addition, adolescents begin to compare themselves to adults. They see themselves acquiring more and more adult skills, such as driving a car or having a job. Also, they see themselves acquiring many of the signs of adult status, such as greater independence and greater responsibility for their decisions. These changes apparently foster self-esteem.

The overall pattern, then, is for self-esteem to start out very high during the preschool years, to decline during the elementary-school years, to level off during adolescence, and to increase toward the end of adolescence. These changes in overall level of self-esteem are accompanied by the change that I mentioned earlier: Self-esteem becomes more differentiated as children become older (Boivin, Vitaro, & Gagnon, 1992). Children are able to evaluate themselves in more domains as they develop, and their evaluations in each domain are increasingly independent. That is, younger children's ratings of self-esteem are often like Allison's (on page 286): The ratings are consistent across the different dimensions. In contrast, older children's and adolescents' ratings more often resemble Colleen's, with self-esteem varying from one domain to another.

Sadly, many children do not view themselves very positively. Some children are ambivalent about who they are; others actually feel negative about themselves. The graph shows that roughly 25 percent of 9- and 10-year-olds in one study (Cole, 1991) had negative self-esteem on three scales of the SPPC. Why do these children have so little self-worth compared to their peers? We'll answer this question in the next section.

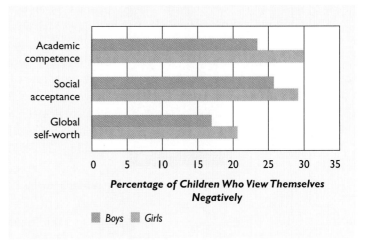

Percentage of Children Who View Themselves Negatively

Boys   Girls

SOURCES OF SELF-ESTEEM

Think back to Allison and Colleen, the two girls whose self-perceptions are graphed on page 286. Both girls evaluated their overall self-worth very positively. In general, they were happy with themselves and with their lives. Why do these girls feel so positive while some children feel so negative about themselves? You won't be surprised to learn that parenting plays a key role. Children are more likely to view themselves positively when their parents are affectionate toward them and involved with them (Lord, Eccles, & McCarthy, 1994). Around the world, children have higher self-esteem when families live in harmony and parents nurture their children (Scott, Scott, & McCabe, 1991). A father who routinely hugs his daughter and gladly coaches her soccer team is saying to her, "You *are* important to me." When children hear this regularly from parents, they evidently internalize the message and come to see themselves positively.

Parents' discipline also is related to self-esteem. Children with high self-esteem generally have parents who aren't afraid to set rules, but are also willing to discuss rules and discipline with their children (Coopersmith, 1967). Parents who fail to set rules are, in effect, telling their children that they don't care—they don't value them enough to go to the trouble of creating rules and enforcing them. In much the same way, parents who refuse to discuss discipline with their children are saying, "Your opinions don't matter to me." Not surprisingly, when children internalize these messages, the result is lower overall self-worth.

Children with positive self-esteem often have parents who are warm and involved and who set and discuss rules with them.

Allison's and Colleen's positive self-worth can therefore be credited, at least in part, to their parents for being warm and involved, for establishing rules, and for discussing these rules with them. But how can we account for the fact that Allison views herself positively in all domains whereas Colleen's self-perceptions are more varied? As I've suggested before, social comparisons are important (Butler, 1992).

Both girls have many opportunities during each day to compare themselves with peers. Allison is almost always the first to finish assignments, usually gets one of the highest grades in the class on exams, and is often asked by her teacher to help classmates on math and science problems. Meanwhile, Colleen is usually among the last to finish assignments, typically gets low grades on tests, and is one of the students that Allison helps with math and science. Daily classroom routines give every student ample opportunities to discover everyone's academic standing within the room. Soon, everyone knows that Allison is one of the most capable students and Colleen, one of the least capable. Allison understands that her classmates see her as talented academically, so her academic self-esteem is quite high. Like the boy in the photo, Colleen knows that her classmates see her as not very talented academically, so her academic self-esteem is low.

The basic idea, then, is that children's self-esteem is based, in part, on how they are viewed by those around them. Children's self-esteem is high when others view them positively and low when others view them negatively (Hoge, Smit, & Hanson, 1990). This explanation has implications for academically talented youngsters, like Darnel in the opening vignette, who might be placed in classes for gifted children. We'll look at these implications in the "Making Children's Lives Better" feature.

Making Children's Lives Better: SELF-ESTEEM IN GIFTED CLASSES

 In a traditional classroom of students with a wide range of ability, talented youngsters compare themselves with other students and develop positive academic self-esteem. But in classes for gifted students, many talented youngsters are only average and some are below average. The resulting social comparisons cause these children's academic self-esteem to drop (Marsh et al., 1995).

There is a clear lesson here for parents and teachers: When parents like Karen and Jon (from the module-opening vignette) think about enrolling their child in classes for gifted children, they should understand that accelerated academic progress often comes at a price: Children's academic self-esteem often declines somewhat, even though their actual skills are improving.

What can parents do? First, they should look honestly at their child and decide whether her or she values learning per se versus being at the top of his or her class. Students who value being at the top of the class will be more affected by social comparisons in a gifted class than students who are more intent on mastering challenging academic material. Second, parents should find out whether common assignments and comparative evaluations are made, as in typical classrooms, or whether the gifted class emphasizes individualized work. The latter is more conducive to self-esteem. Carefully considering these factors can help parents decide if a gifted program is likely to lower their child's self-esteem, a very unwelcome side effect. ■

Children have greater self-esteem when they work hard in school, get along with peers, avoid disciplinary problems, participate in extracurricular activities, and feel that teachers care about them.

In examining sources of self-esteem—not just for children in gifted classes, but for all children—several characteristics of teachers and schools should also be taken into account (Hoge et al., 1990). In general, self-esteem is greater when students work hard in school, get along with their peers, and avoid disciplinary problems. In addition, self-esteem is greater when students participate in extracurricular activities, such as music, student council, sports, and clubs. Finally, students' self-esteem is enhanced when the overall climate of the school is nurturing—when students believe that teachers care about them and listen to them. Grades matter, too, but good grades affect a students' self-esteem in specific disciplines—in math or English—not their overall self-esteem (Hoge et al., 1990).

By encouraging students to work to the best of their ability and by being genuinely interested in their progress, teachers can enhance the self-esteem of all students, regardless of their talent. Parents can do the same and, by encouraging their children to participate in extracurricular activities that match their talents, further promote self-esteem.

It is important that parents and teachers make an effort to enhance children's self-esteem because children with low self-esteem are at risk for many developmental problems. Children with low self-esteem are more likely to have problems with peers (Hymel et al., 1990), and they are more prone to psychological disorders such as depression (Block, Gjerde, & Block, 1991; Button et al., 1996). *All* children have some talents that can be nurtured. Taking the time to recognize each child creates the feelings of "being special" that promote self-esteem.

Check Your Learning

1. Harter's *Self-Perception Profile for Children* (SPPC) is used to assess a child's self-esteem in five domains (scholastic competence, athletic competence, social acceptance, behavioral conduct, physical appearance) and the child's _____.

2. Self-esteem is usually at its peak during the _____ years.

3. Children are more likely to have positive self-worth when parents are affectionate and involved with them and when parents _____.

 NDERSTANDING OTHERS

Learning Objectives

- **As children develop, how do they describe others differently?**
- **How does understanding of others' thinking change as children develop?**
- **When do children develop prejudice toward others?**

MODULE
11.3
Understanding Others

Describing Others ─┐

Understanding What ─┤
Others Think

Prejudice ─┘

> *When 12-year-old Ian agreed to baby-sit for his 5-year-old brother, Kyle, his mother reminded him to keep Kyle out of the basement because Kyle's birthday presents were there, unwrapped. But as soon as their mother left, Kyle wanted to go to the basement to ride his tricycle. When Ian told him no, Kyle burst into angry tears and shouted, "I'm gonna tell Mom that you were mean to me!" Ian wished he could explain to Kyle, but he knew that would just cause more trouble!*

We know from Modules 11.1 and 11.2 that Ian, as a young adolescent, has a growing understanding of himself. This vignette suggests that his understanding of other people is also growing. He understands why Kyle is angry, and he also knows that if he gives in to Kyle, his mother will be angry when she returns. Children's growing understanding of others is the focus of this module. We'll begin by looking at how children describe others, then examine their understanding of how others think. We'll also see how children's recognition of different social groups can lead to prejudices.

DESCRIBING OTHERS

As children develop, their self-descriptions become richer, more abstract, and more psychological. These same changes occur in children's descriptions of others. Children begin by describing other people in terms of concrete features, such as behavior and appearance, and progress to describing them in terms of abstract traits (Barenboim, 1981; Livesley & Bromley, 1973). The "Real Children" feature shows this progression in one child.

Real Children: TELL ME ABOUT A GIRL YOU LIKE

 Every few years, Tamsen was asked to describe a girl that she liked a lot. Each time, she described a different girl. More importantly, the contents of her descriptions changed, focusing less on behavior and emphasizing psychological properties. Let's start with the description she gave as a 7-year-old:

> *Vanessa is short. She has black hair and brown eyes. She uses a wheelchair because she can't walk. She's in my class. She has dolls just like mine. She likes to sing and read.*

Tamsen's description of Vanessa is probably not too different from the way she would have described herself: The emphasis is on concrete characteristics, such as Vanessa's appearance, possessions, and preferences. Contrast this with the following description, which Tamsen gave as a 10-year-old:

> *Kate lives in my apartment building. She is a very good reader and is also good at math and science. She's nice to everyone in our class. And she's very funny. Sometimes her jokes make me laugh so-o-o hard! She takes piano lessons and likes to play soccer.*

Tamsen's account still includes concrete features, such as where Kate lives and what she likes to do. However, psychological traits are also evident: Tamsen describes Kate as nice and funny. By age 10, children move beyond the purely concrete and observable in describing others. During adolescence, descriptions become even more complex, as you can see in the following, from Tamsen as a 16-year-old:

> *Jeannie is very understanding. Whenever someone is upset, she's there to give a helping hand. Yet, in private, Jeannie can be so sarcastic. She can say some really nasty things about people. But I know she'd never say that stuff if she thought people would hear it because she wouldn't want to hurt their feelings.*

This description is more abstract: Tamsen now focuses on psychological traits like understanding and concern for others' feelings. It's also more integrated: Tamsen tries to explain how Jeannie can be both understanding and sarcastic. ■

Each of Tamsen's three descriptions is very typical. As a 7-year-old, she emphasized concrete characteristics; as a 10-year-old, she began to include psychological traits; and as a 16-year-old, she tried to integrate traits to form a cohesive account.

The progression in how children perceive others was illustrated vividly in a classic study by Livesley and Bromley (1973). They interviewed 320 7- to 15-year-olds attending school in Merseyside, England (near Liverpool, home of the Beatles). All participants were asked to describe eight people that they knew: two boys, two girls, two men, and two women. The examiner told the participants, "...I want you to describe what sort of person they are. I want you to tell me what you think about them and what they are like" (p. 97).

The participants at different ages typically produced descriptions much like Tamsen's at different ages. Livesley and Bromley then categorized the contents of the descriptions. Some of their results appear in the graph. Descriptions referring to appearances or possessions become less common as children grow older, as do descriptions giving general information, such as the person's age, gender, religion, or school. In contrast, descriptions of personality traits (for example, "friendly" or "conceited") increase between 8 and 14 years of age. This pattern of changes in children's descriptions of others resembles children's changing understanding of the self, which I explained on pages 276–278 of Module 11.1.

Children's descriptions of others first focus on concrete characteristics, then on psychological traits, and, finally, on providing a comprehensive description that integrates the different aspects of a person.

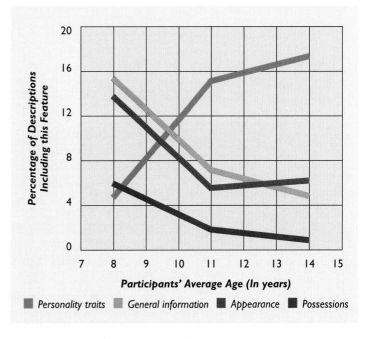

UNDERSTANDING WHAT OTHERS THINK

One trademark of the preschool child's thinking is difficulty in seeing the world from another's view. Piaget's term for this was egocentrism and it was a defining characteristic of his preoperational stage of development (see Module 6.2). In much the same way, preschool children's communication is often ineffective because they don't consider the listener's perspective when they talk (see Module 9.4). As children move beyond the preschool years, though, they realize that others see the world differently, both literally and figuratively. For example, in the module-opening vignette, 12-year-old Ian knows why his little brother, Kyle, is angry: Kyle thinks that Ian is being bossy and mean. Ian understands that Kyle doesn't know there is a good reason why he can't go to the basement.

Sophisticated understanding of how others think is achieved gradually throughout childhood and adolescence. Robert Selman (1980, 1981) has proposed a theory of how understanding others' thinking—perspective-taking, for short—occurs. Selman's theory is based on two of Piaget's key assumptions, namely, that understanding of others occurs in stages and that movement from one stage to the next is based on cognitive development. The table at the top of page 294 shows Selman's five stages of perspective-taking.

A good way to appreciate the progression from stage to stage is to look at one of the social dilemmas that was used to explore children's perspective-taking.

Holly is an 8-year-old girl who likes to climb trees. She is the best tree climber in the neighborhood. One day while climbing down from a tall tree she falls off the bottom branch but does not hurt herself. Her father sees her fall. He is upset and asks her to promise not to climb trees anymore. Holly promises.

Selman's Stages of Perspective-Taking

Stage	Approximate Ages	Description
Undifferentiated	3–6 years	Children know that self and others can have different thoughts and feelings, but often confuse the two
Social-informational	4–9 years	Children know that perspectives differ because people have access to different information
Self-reflective	7–12 years	Children can step into another's shoes and view themselves as others do; they know that others can do the same
Third-person	10–15 years	Children can step outside of the immediate situation to see how they and another person are viewed by a third person
Societal	14 years to adult	Adolescents realize that a third person's perspective is influenced by broader personal, social, and cultural contexts

Later that day, Holly and her friends meet Sean. Sean's kitten is caught up in a tree and cannot get down. Something has to be done right away or the kitten may fall. Holly is the only one who climbs well enough to reach the kitten and get it down, but she remembers her promise to her father (Selman & Byrne, 1974, p. 805).

This dilemma is typical in that it includes people who don't share the same knowledge about the events taking place. After hearing the story, children are asked questions to investigate their ability to take on each character's view and predict what Holly does.

As children grow, their answers reflect ever more sophisticated understanding of who is thinking what and why in these dilemmas (Selman, 1980, 1981; Selman & Byrne, 1974). The youngest children, those in the undifferentiated stage, might reply, "Holly's father will be happy if she gets the kitten because he likes kittens." This answer confuses the child's own feelings with the father's and ignores Holly's promise. Children in the social-informational stage might say, "If Holly's father knew why she climbed the tree, he probably wouldn't be angry." This answer indicates that the child thinks the father's response depends upon whether or not he knows the reason for Holly's behavior.

In the self-reflective stage, a child might say, "Holly's father would understand that she thought saving the kitten's life was really important, so he wouldn't be mad. He'd probably be proud." This comment shows Holly's father stepping into Holly's shoes, the defining characteristic of the self-reflective stage.

At the next level, the third-person stage, a child might respond, "Holly remembers the promise, but she doesn't think her father will be angry when she explains that she wouldn't have climbed the tree except to save the kitten's life. Her father might wish that Holly had asked an adult for help, but he'd also understand why it was important to Holly to save the kitten." This child simultaneously considers both Holly's and her father's perspectives on the dilemma. That is, in answering, the child has

In Selman's theory, children's thinking about others begins with a stage in which children often confuse their own and another's view, but progresses to a stage in which children can view their and another's view from a third person's perspective.

stepped outside the immediate situation to take the perspective of a neutral third party who can look at both Holly's and her father's views.

At the most advanced level, the societal stage, an adolescent might reply, "Holly and her father both know that she almost always obeys him. So, they'd both know that if she disobeyed him to climb the tree, there would have to be an awfully good reason. So, they'd talk about it." This child's answer, like the previous one, considers Holly's and her father's perspectives simultaneously. The difference is that this comment puts the issue in the broader context of the history of their father-daughter relationship.

As predicted by Selman's theory, research shows that as children develop, their reasoning moves through each stage, in sequence. In addition, regardless of age, children at more advanced cognitive levels tend to be at more advanced stages in perspective-taking (Gurucharri & Selman, 1982; Krebs & Gillmore, 1982).

Additional support for Selman's theory comes from studies on perspective-taking and social behavior. In the photo, the children with the soccer ball apparently recognize that the girl on the sideline wants to play, so they're inviting her to join the game. Children who can anticipate what others are thinking should get along better with their peers, and research indicates that they do. For example, children with good perspective-taking skills are typically well liked by their peers (LeMare & Rubin, 1987). Of course, mere understanding does not guarantee good social behavior; sometimes children who understand what another child is thinking take advantage of that child. But, in general, greater understanding of others seems to promote positive interactions, a topic that we'll discuss further in Chapter 12 on moral understanding and behavior.

PREJUDICE

As children learn more about others, they discover that people belong to different social groups, based on variables such as gender, ethnicity, and social class. By the preschool years, most children can distinguish males from females and can identify people from different ethnic groups (Aboud, 1993). Once children learn their membership in a specific group—"I'm a Vietnamese American boy"—they typically show prejudice. ***Prejudice* is a negative view of others based on their membership in a specific group.** At the same time, children view their own group more favorably. Preschool and kindergarten children more often attribute positive traits (being friendly and smart) to their own group and negative traits (being mean and fighting a lot) to other groups (Black-Gutman & Hickson, 1996).

As children move into the elementary-school years, prejudice usually declines somewhat (Powlishta et al., 1994). Why? Cognitive development holds the answer. Preschool and kindergarten children usually view people in social groups as much more homogeneous than they really are. People from other groups are seen as all alike and, typically, not as good as people from the child's own group. Older children understand that people in social groups are heterogeneous—they know that individual European Americans, girls, and obese children, for example, are not all alike. And they have learned that people from different groups may be more alike than people from the same group. Gary, an African American whose passion is

computers, finds that he enjoys being with Vic, an Italian American who shares his love of computers, but not Curtis, another African American whose passion is music. As children realize that social groups consist of all kinds of different people, prejudice lessens.

Prejudice may be less pronounced in older children, but it does not vanish. Older children and adolescents remain biased positively toward their own group and negatively toward others (Powlishta et al., 1994). Of course, many adults have these same biases, and children and adolescents simply reflect the attitudes of those around them. The best way to rid children of lingering prejudice is through additional contact with individuals from other social groups (Ramsey, 1995). For example, as Gary spends more time with Vic, he starts to realize that Vic acts, thinks, and feels as he does simply because he's Vic, not because he's an Italian American. When, as shown in the photo, children and adolescents have experience with individuals from other groups, they discover for themselves that a person's membership in a social group tell us very little about that person.

Check Your Learning

1. When adolescents describe others, they usually _____.

2. In Selman's theory, at the most advanced stage of perspective-taking, adolescents _____.

3. Prejudice declines somewhat as children get older because _____.

Answers: (1) try to provide a cohesive, integrated account, (2) take a third person's perspective and recognize the influence of context on this perspective, (3) with cognitive development, children realize that social groups are not homogeneous.

 **NDERSTANDING SELF AND OTHERS IN PERSPECTIVE**

The cognitive growth that we examined in Chapters 6 and 7 allows children to understand themselves and other people with greater breadth and depth as they develop. In Module 11.1, we saw that 15-month-olds typically recognize themselves in a mirror, one of the first signs of the complex process of self-definition that reaches its peak in adolescence, when individuals achieve an identity. In Module 11.2, we discovered how children's self-esteem is measured and learned that self-esteem is highest during the preschool years, then declines until adolescence when it begins to increase again. We also saw that children's self-esteem is greatest when parents and teachers support and encourage them. In Module 11.3, we learned that children's descriptions of others parallel their descriptions of themselves and that children's understanding of others becomes more complex with age. We also learned that prejudice declines with age, but positive steps can be taken to rid children of any lingering bias towards other social groups.

This chapter is a good occasion to feature the theme that *development is always jointly influenced by heredity and environment:* The emergence of self-awareness between 15 and 24 months of age is primarily due to biological forces. Regardless of circumstances, children become self-aware between ages 1 and 2 years. However, the elaboration of self-awareness into a specific self-concept depends largely upon a child's experiences at home and in school. The specific direction that children take in establishing an identity is strongly influenced by those around them, particularly their parents and teachers.

THINKING ABOUT DEVELOPMENT

1. Self-awareness emerges at about 15 months and is well established by 24 months. What important changes occur during this same period in cognition and language? How might these changes in cognition and language relate to the emergence of self-awareness?

2. Although Piaget's theory was not concerned with identity formation, how might his theory explain why identity is a central issue in adolescence?

3. Your local newspaper has just done a feature on the "storm and stress" associated with adolescence. Write a letter to the editor in which you set the record straight.

4. When gifted children are put in special classes, their intellectual development can be accelerated but sometimes at the expense of self-esteem. Do you believe the intellectual gain is worth the drop in self-esteem? Why or why not?

5. How might an information-processing theorist describe the stages of Selman's perspective-taking theory?

SEE FOR YOURSELF

The mirror recognition task, described on pages 274–275, is great fun to do, and you'll be astonished by the rapid change in children's responses between 1 and 2 years. For this task, you simply need a mirror, some tissue, rouge, and a few cooperative parents of 12- to 18-month-olds. Have the parents play with their toddler near the mirror, and, in the process, wipe the toddler's nose with a tissue that has rouge on it. Then see how the toddler responds to the now red nose. Some 12-month-olds will do nothing; others will touch the red nose in the mirror. When the 15- or 18-month-olds see themselves, though, they should stop, get a curious expression on their faces, and then reach up to touch their nose. See for yourself!

RESOURCES

For more information about . . .

adolescent search for identity, read Erik Erikson's *Gandhi* (Norton, 1969), a Pulitzer Prize–winning book in which Erikson shows how the adolescent search for identity influenced the development of this great leader of India

materials to promote children's understanding of people from other races, creeds, and ethnic groups, contact the Anti-Defamation League, 1-800-343-5540

deciding on a career or finding a job that's right for you, visit the Northwestern University Career Services Web site: http://www.stuaff.nwu.edu/ucs/internet

KEY TERMS

achievement status *279*
adolescent egocentrism *278*
crystallization *280*
diffusion status *279*
foreclosure status *279*

illusion of invulnerability *279*
imaginary audience *278*
implementation *280*
moratorium status *279*
personal fable *278*

prejudice *295*
self-concept *274*
self-esteem *284*
specification *280*
theory of mind *275*

UMMARY

MODULE 11.1:
WHO AM I? SELF-CONCEPT

ORIGINS OF SELF-RECOGNITION
Beginning at about 15 months, infants begin to recognize themselves in the mirror, one of the first signs of self-recognition. They also begin to prefer to look at pictures of themselves, to refer to themselves by name and with personal pronouns, and sometimes to know their age and gender. Evidently, by 2 years, most children are self-aware.

THEORY OF MIND
Theory of mind, which refers to a person's ideas about connections between thoughts, beliefs, intentions, and behavior, develops rapidly during the preschool years. Most 2-year-olds understand that people have desires and that desires can cause behavior. By age 3, children distinguish the mental world from the physical world, but still emphasize desire in explaining others' actions. By age 4, however, children understand behavior is based on beliefs about the world, even when those beliefs are wrong.

THE EVOLVING SELF-CONCEPT
Preschoolers often define themselves in terms of observable characteristics, such as possessions, physical characteristics, preferences, and competencies. During the elementary-school years, self-concept begins to include emotions, a child's membership in social groups, and

comparisons with peers. During adolescence, self-concept includes attitudes, personality traits, beliefs, and future plans. In general, adolescents' self-concepts are more abstract, more psychological, and more future oriented than self-concepts in younger children.

THE SEARCH FOR IDENTITY
The search for identity typically involves four statuses. Diffusion and foreclosure are more common in early adolescence; moratorium and achievement are more common in late adolescence and young adulthood. Adolescents are most likely to achieve an identity when parents encourage discussion and recognize their autonomy; they are least likely to achieve an identity when parents set rules and enforce them without explanation.

According to Super's theory, an adolescent's developing identity is a primary influence on his or her career aspirations. Super proposes three phases of vocational development during adolescence and young adulthood: crystallization, in which basic ideas about careers are identified, based on the person's identity; specification, in which lines of work associated with interests are identified; and implementation, which marks entry into the work force.

Adolescents from ethnic groups often progress through three phases in acquiring an ethnic identity: initial disinterest, exploration, and identity achievement. Achieving an ethnic identity usually results in higher self-esteem but is not consistently related to the strength of one's identification with mainstream culture.

Contrary to myth, adolescence is not usually a period of storm and stress. Most adolescents love their parents, feel loved by them, rely upon them for advice, and adopt their values. The parent-child relationship becomes more egalitarian during the adolescent years, reflecting adolescents' growing independence.

MODULE 11.2:
SELF-ESTEEM

MEASURING SELF-ESTEEM
Most tasks assess self-esteem in different areas. One of the most common measures is Harter's *Self-Perception Profile for Children* (SPPC), which is designed for children as young as 8 years. It assesses self-esteem in five areas: scholastic competence, athletic competence, social acceptance, behavioral conduct, and physical appearance. It also measures overall self-worth. For measuring self-esteem in older adolescents, job competence, close friendships, and romantic appeal are added.

DEVELOPMENTAL CHANGES IN SELF-ESTEEM
Self-esteem is very high during the preschool years but declines somewhat during the elementary-school years as children compare themselves to peers. Self-esteem begins to rise in adolescence as teenagers see themselves acquiring more adult skills and responsibilities. Self-esteem becomes more differentiated in older children and adolescents as they evaluate themselves on more aspects of self-esteem.

SOURCES OF SELF-ESTEEM
Children's self-esteem is greater when parents are affectionate and involved with them and when parents set rules and discuss discipline with their children. Self-esteem also depends on peer comparisons. Self-esteem is usually greater when children know that others view them positively.

MODULE 11.3:
UNDERSTANDING OTHERS

DESCRIBING OTHERS
Children's descriptions of others change in much the same way that their descriptions of themselves change. During the early elementary-school years, descriptions emphasize concrete characteristics. In the late elementary-school years, they emphasize personality traits. In adolescence, they emphasize an integrated picture of a person.

UNDERSTANDING WHAT OTHERS THINK
According to Selman's perspective-taking theory, children's understanding of how others think progresses through five stages. In the first, the undifferentiated stage, children often confuse their own and another's view. In the last, the societal stage, adolescents take a third-person's perspective and understand that this perspective is influenced by context.

PREJUDICE
Prejudice emerges in the preschool years, soon after children recognize different social groups. Prejudice declines during childhood, as children's cognitive growth helps them understand that social groups are heterogenous, not homogeneous. However, older children and adolescents still show prejudice, which is best reduced by additional exposure to individuals from other social groups.

Moral Understanding and Behavior

CONSIDER THE FOLLOWING HYPOTHETICAL SITUATION. YOU ENTER A NURSERY FILLED WITH 2-DAY-OLDS. THE BABIES LOOK LIKE BABIES IN ANY NURSERY— SOME ARE ASLEEP, SOME ARE CRYING, OTHERS ARE SIMPLY LYING QUIETLY. HOWEVER, THE NURSE tells you that the newborns include Mother Teresa, Adolf Hitler, Mohandas Gandhi, and Martin Luther King Jr. Although seemingly identical now, three of the newborns will rank among the 20th century's greatest figures and one will be guilty of unspeakable horrors. Why? What determines whether children act morally or immorally? Whether they care about others or take from others? Whether they become Samaritans or follow a path of evil? The four modules in this chapter provide some answers to these questions. In Module 12.1, we'll see how children learn to control their behavior. In Module 12.2, we'll look at how children and adolescents reason about moral issues, and in Module 12.3, we'll look at factors that encourage children to be kind to others. Finally, in Module 12.4, we'll see why children act aggressively toward others.

SELF-CONTROL

Learning Objectives

- **When does self-control begin and how does it change as children develop?**
- **How do parents influence their children's ability to maintain self-control?**
- **What strategies can children use to improve their self-control?**

> *Shirley returned from a long day at work tired but eager to celebrate her son Chris's second birthday. Her excitement quickly turned to dismay when she discovered that Chris had taken a huge bite of icing from the birthday cake while the baby sitter fixed lunch. Before she had left for work that morning, Shirley had explicitly told Chris not to touch the cake. Why couldn't Chris wait? Why did he give in to temptation? What could she do to help Chris control himself better in the future?*

In this vignette, Shirley wishes that Chris had greater *self-control,* the ability to rise above immediate pressures and not give in to impulse. A child who saves her allowance to buy a much-desired object instead of spending it immediately on candy is showing self-control, as is an adolescent who studies for an exam instead of going to the mall with his friends, knowing that tomorrow he can enjoy the mall *and* a good grade on his exam.

Self-control is one of the first steps toward moral behavior because children must learn that they cannot constantly do whatever tempts them at the moment. Instead, society has rules for behavior in certain situations, and children must learn to restrain themselves.

In this module, we'll first see how self-control emerges during the preschool years. Then we'll learn some of the factors that determine how well children control themselves. Finally, we'll look at strategies that children use to improve their self-control.

BEGINNINGS OF SELF-CONTROL

In this cartoon, Calvin shows little self-control. Is he typical for his age? Thankfully, no. Self-control begins during infancy and the preschool years. Claire Kopp (1982, 1987) believes that self-control develops in three phases:

Calvin and Hobbes   by Bill Watterson

CALVIN AND HOBBES © 1993 Watterson. Dist. by UNIVERSAL PRESS SYNDICATE. Reprinted with permission. All rights reserved.

■ At approximately the first birthday, infants become aware that people impose demands on them and they must react accordingly. They learn that they are *not* entirely free to behave as they wish; instead, others set limits on what they can do. These limits reflect both concern for their safety ("Don't touch! It's hot.") as well as early socialization efforts ("Don't grab Ravisha's toy.").

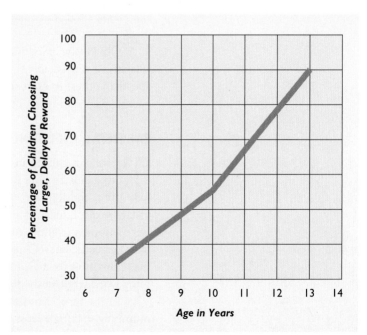

■ At about 2 years, toddlers have internalized some of the controls imposed by others and they are capable of some self-control in parents' absence. For example, although the boy on the left in the photo certainly looks as if he wants to play with the toy that the other toddler has, so far he has inhibited his desire to grab the toy, perhaps because he remembers that his parents have told him not to take things from others.

■ At about 3 years, children become capable of self-regulation, which "involves flexible and adaptive control processes that can meet quickly changing situational demands" (Kopp, 1987, p. 38). Children can devise ways to regulate their own behavior. To return to the example of a playmate's interesting toy, children might tell themselves that they really don't want to play with it, or they might turn to another activity that removes the temptation to grab it.

By age 3, children are capable of self-regulation, largely because they can formulate plans for dealing with the demands of different situations.

Of course, preschoolers have much to learn about regulating impulsive behavior, and control is achieved only gradually throughout the elementary-school years. For example, in a study by Rotenberg and Mayer (1990), after children had completed a task, they were offered the choice of a relatively small reward immediately or a much larger reward if they waited one day. The graph depicts a definite shift in responding as children grow. Only about one-third of the 6- to 8-year-olds and about half the 9- to 11-year-olds opted to wait for the larger reward. But by 12 to 15 years, nearly everyone waited a day to obtain the larger reward. Thus, although self-control may be evident in toddlers, mastery occurs gradually throughout childhood.

At any age, individuals differ tremendously in their self-control. Think of your peers and how they spend their money. You probably know some people who spend money as fast as they earn it. Others steadily save their pennies for some long-range goal. Individual differences are evident in research that examines consistency in self-control. Vaughn, Kopp, and Krakow (1984), for example, examined preschoolers' self-control on three different tasks. The correlations between children's performance on the different tasks ranged from .29 to .47. These correlations mean that, although children were far from perfectly consistent, in general a child who had good self-control on one task tended to have good control on other tasks, too.

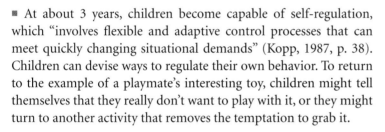

Longitudinal studies of the long-term consistency of self-control have produced some astonishing findings. Shoda, Mischel, and Peake (1990) tracked down nearly two hundred 15- to 18-year-olds who had participated in delay-of-gratification experiments as 4-year-olds. In the original experiments, 4-year-olds were told that if they waited alone in a room until the experimenter returned, they would receive a big prize. If they rang a bell to signal the experimenter to return, they would receive a much smaller prize. Then the researchers simply recorded the length of time children waited until the experimenter returned. You may be surprised to learn that the length of time that 4-year-olds waited was related to a host of characteristics some 11 to 14 years later. The table shows some of the significant correlations between the 4-year-olds' ability to delay gratification and their coping skills, personality characteristics, and SAT scores as adolescents. In general, 4-year-olds who waited the longest before calling the experimenter were still, as 15- to 18-year-olds, better able to exert self-control, more attentive and able to plan, and had higher SAT scores.

Preschoolers who are better able to resist temptation often grow up to be adolescents who have better self-control, are more planful, and have higher SAT scores.

Correlations between Preschoolers' Delayed Gratification and Measures of Coping, Personality, and Academic Achievement in Adolescence

Measure	r
Coping	
Is likely to yield to temptation	−.50
Distractibility when trying to concentrate	−.41
Personality	
Is planful, thinks ahead	.36
Tends to go to pieces under stress, becomes rattled and disorganized	−.34
SAT scores	
Verbal scale	.42
Quantitative scale	.57
Source: Shoda, Mischel, and Peake, 1990	

Obviously, individuals differ in their ability to resist temptation, and this characteristic is remarkably stable over time. But *why* are some children and adults better able than others to exert self-control? As you'll see in the next section of this module, parents play an important role in determining children's self-control.

PARENTAL INFLUENCES

There is a county in Nova Scotia, Canada, where conflicting subcultures have lived side by side for generations (Bandura & Walters, 1963). In one subculture, children are expected to control immediate impulses and work toward distant goals. Educational and vocational achievement is stressed and parents spend large amounts of time with their children and transmit the patterns of their culture with great efficiency. Children growing up in this subculture are unlikely to give in to the temptation to take an immediate small pleasure when it means forfeiting something worthwhile in the future.

In the same Nova Scotian county lives another group of people whose community is strikingly lacking in cohesion: There is a great deal of fighting, drunkenness, theft, and other antisocial behavior. Adults here believe that "it's best to escape one's problems as quickly as possible." Their children are exposed to models that overwhelmingly prefer immediate gratification.

What would happen if a child from the second subculture were adopted by parents from the first subculture and a child from the first subculture were adopted by parents from the second, which prefers immediate gratification? Would the children behave like their biological parents or be influenced by their new models? We'll see in the "Focus on Research" feature.

Focus on Research: IS CHILDREN'S SELF-CONTROL INFLUENCED BY ADULTS' SELF-CONTROL?

 Who were the investigators and what was the aim of the study? Albert Bandura and Walter Mischel (1965) wanted to determine if children's self-control would be changed by watching adult models. Specifically, would children who showed little self-control have better control after watching an adult demonstrate self-control? Would children who had self-control abandon it after watching an adult demonstrate little self-control?

How did the investigators measure the topic of interest? Bandura and Mischel's study included two phases. In the first phase, fourth- and fifth-graders made a series of choices between a small immediate reward and a larger delayed outcome. For instance, they could have a small candy bar immediately or a larger one in a week. The children who most preferred immediate reward and the ones who most preferred delayed reward then participated in the second phase. They observed an adult model make a series of choices between a less valuable item, which could be obtained immediately, and a more valuable item that required delay. For children who preferred waiting for a larger reward, the adult always chose the immediate reward. For children who had preferred immediate but small rewards, the adult always chose the delayed reward item. In both cases, the adult also briefly explained his behavior. For example, when the choice was between getting a plastic chess set immediately and a more expensive wooden set in two weeks, the adult commented, "Chess figures are chess figures. I can get much use out of the plastic ones right away" (p. 701). Later, the adult summarized his choices by saying, "One can spend so much time in life waiting that one never gets around to really living. I find that it is better to make the most of each moment or life will pass you by" (p. 701). Immediately after watching the model, children had the opportunity to choose between immediate but small rewards or delayed but larger rewards.

Who were the children in the study? Approximately 250 fourth- and fifth-graders participated in the first phase and 40 participated in the second.

What was the design of the study? This study was experimental because Bandura and Mischel compared children's choices before and after they watched the model choose. Thus, the independent variable was whether the child had yet observed the model. The dependent variable was the number of choices that matched the model's choices. The study included only fourth- and fifth-graders and was neither longitudinal nor cross-sectional.

Were there ethical concerns with the study? Helping impulsive children improve their self-control poses no problem, but is it ethical to encourage children with self-control to abandon it in favor of "living-for-the-moment" as the model touted? Apparently the panel that reviewed Bandura and Mischel's study did not object. What do you think?

What were the results? The graph at the top of page 306 shows children's choices before and after viewing the model. The results are clear: Children exposed to a

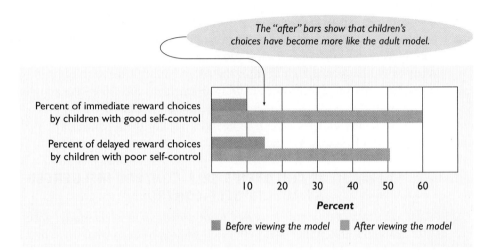

The "after" bars show that children's choices have become more like the adult model.

Percent of immediate reward choices by children with good self-control

Percent of delayed reward choices by children with poor self-control

10   20   30   40   50   60

Percent

■ Before viewing the model   ■ After viewing the model

model who delayed gratification shifted their own preferences so that on post-test about 50 percent also delayed their choices. Similarly, most of the children exposed to models who showed little self-control were easily swayed and abandoned their own self-control.

What did the investigators conclude? Children often imitate many adult behaviors, including self-control (and lack of it). Apparently, children can show self-restraint *or* be incredibly impulsive, simply depending upon how they observe others behave in similar situations. ■

Are you skeptical of Bandura and Mischel's (1965) results, maybe because the setting seems artificial? Perhaps children's self-control can't be so easily influenced outside of the laboratory, in a normal home setting? In fact, correlational studies show that parents' behavior is related to their children's self-control, but not in a way that they may expect. Self-control is lower in children whose parents are very strict with them (Feldman & Wentzel, 1990). One interpretation of this finding is that strict parents "overcontrol" their children: By constantly directing them to do one thing but not another, parents do not give their children either the opportunity or the incentive to internalize control. Consistent with this argument is the finding that children have greater self-control when parents encourage them to be independent and make their own decisions (Silverman & Ragusa, 1990).

Parents can best foster their children's self-control by not being overly strict, but instead allowing their children opportunities to regulate their own behavior.

The message here is clear: For children to gain self-control, parents must relinquish control. By gradually giving children more opportunities to regulate their own behavior and see the consequences of their choices, parents foster self-control. For example, instead of insisting that elementary-school children follow a set after-dinner routine, parents can allow children to decide how to balance entertainment, homework, and household chores. Of course, children are not perfectly consistent in their self-control. Children who are able to resist temptation on one occasion may give in the next time. Why do children show self-control on some tasks but not others? As we'll see in the next section, the answer lies in children's plans for resisting temptation.

IMPROVING SELF-CONTROL

Imagine it's one of the first nice days of spring. You have two major exams that you should study for, but it's so-o-o-o tempting to spend the entire day in the sun, relaxing and ridding yourself of winter blues. What do you do to resist this temptation and stick to studying? You might remind yourself that these exams are very important. You might also move to a windowless room to keep your mind off the tempting weather. Stated more generally, effective ways to resist temptation include (a) reminding yourself of the importance of long-term goals over short-term temptations and (b) reducing the attraction of the tempting event.

During the preschool years, some youngsters begin to use both of these methods spontaneously. In an experiment by Mischel and Ebbesen (1970), 3- to 5-year-olds were asked to sit alone in a room for 15 minutes. If they waited the entire time, they would receive a desirable reward. Children could call the experimenter back to the room at any time by a prearranged signal; in this case, they would receive a much less desirable reward.

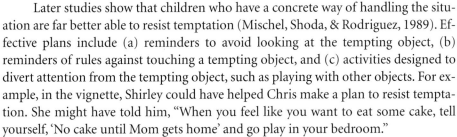

Some children, of course, were better able than others to wait the full 15 minutes. How did they do it? Some children talked to themselves: "I've gotta wait to get the best prize!" As Vygotsky described (Module 6.3), these youngsters were using private speech to control their own behavior. Others, like the child in the photograph, sang. Still others invented games. All were effective techniques for enduring 15 boring minutes to receive a desired prize.

Later studies show that children who have a concrete way of handling the situation are far better able to resist temptation (Mischel, Shoda, & Rodriguez, 1989). Effective plans include (a) reminders to avoid looking at the tempting object, (b) reminders of rules against touching a tempting object, and (c) activities designed to divert attention from the tempting object, such as playing with other objects. For example, in the vignette, Shirley could have helped Chris make a plan to resist temptation. She might have told him, "When you feel like you want to eat some cake, tell yourself, 'No cake until Mom gets home' and go play in your bedroom."

Overall, then, how children think about tempting objects or outcomes makes all the difference. Even among preschoolers, self-control can be gained by making plans that include appropriate self-instruction. As children learn to regulate their own behavior, they also begin to learn about moral rules—cultural rights and wrongs—which are described in the next module.

Check Your Learning

1. At approximately _____ year(s) of age, children first learn that other people make demands of them.

2. Fifteen- to 18-year-olds who were better able to resist temptation as preschoolers still have better self-control, are more attentive and planful, and have _____.

3. Bandura and Mischel's classic study of adults' influence on children's self-control revealed that, after viewing adults who showed little self-control, children _____.

4. When parents are very controlling, their children tend to _____.

5. Children can maintain self-control more effectively when they remind themselves of the need to resist temptation and _____.

Answers: (1) 1, (2) higher SAT scores, (3) imitated the adults' poor self-control, (4) have poor self-control, (5) they divert their attention from the tempting object or event

REASONING ABOUT MORAL ISSUES

Learning Objectives

- **How does reasoning about moral issues change during childhood and adolescence?**
- **How do concern for justice and caring for other people contribute to moral reasoning?**
- **What factors help promote more sophisticated reasoning about moral issues?**

Howard, the least popular boy in the entire fourth grade, had been wrongly accused of throwing food at lunch. Min-shen, another fourth-grader, knew that Howard was innocent but said nothing to the lunchroom supervisor for fear of what his friends would say about siding with Howard. A few days later, when Min-shen's father heard about the incident, he was upset that his son apparently had so little "moral fiber." Why hadn't Min-shen acted in the face of an injustice?

On one of the days when I was writing this module, my local paper had two articles about youth from the area. One article was about a 14-year-girl who was badly burned while saving her younger brothers from a fire in their apartment. Her mother said she wasn't surprised by her daughter's actions because she had always been an extraordinarily caring person. The other article was about two 17-year-old boys who had beaten an elderly man to death. They had only planned to steal his wallet, but when he insulted them and tried to punch them, they became enraged.

Reading articles like these, you can't help but question why some people act in ways that earn our deepest respect and admiration, whereas others earn our utter contempt as well as our pity. And, at a more mundane level, we wonder why Min-shen didn't tell the truth about the food fight to the lunchroom supervisor. In this module, we'll begin our exploration of moral understanding and behavior by looking at children's thinking about moral issues: How do children judge what is "good" and what is "bad"? Let's start by looking at Jean Piaget's ideas about the development of moral reasoning.

PIAGET'S VIEWS

Once, when my son Matt was about 6, we were playing Chutes and Ladders®. This is a board game in which you can advance rapidly when you land on a space that has a ladder but must go backward if you land on a chute. To speed up the game, I suggested to Matt that we be allowed to advance if we landed on a chute as well as a ladder. I reminded him that he liked to climb up slides at playgrounds, so my suggestion had some logic to it. Matt would have none of this. He told me, "It's a *rule* that you *have* to go backward when you land on a chute. You can't go forward. The people who made Chutes and Ladders® say so. Just read the instructions, Daddy." I tried again to persuade him (because, in my humble opinion, Chutes and Ladders® gives new meaning to "bored" game), but he was adamant.

Matt's inflexibility is typical of 6-year-olds and illustrates Jean Piaget's first stage of moral development. Based on children's play and their responses to stories about children who misbehave, Piaget proposed one of the first theories of moral development. According to his observa-

In Piaget's view, from 5 to 7 years, children are moral realists who believe that rules are absolute; by age 8, children understand that rules are relative and created by people to help them get along.

tions, preschool children have no well-defined ideas about morality. **But, beginning at about 5 years and continuing through age 7, children are in a stage of *moral realism*; they believe that rules are created by wise adults and, therefore, must be followed and cannot be changed. Another characteristic of the stage of moral realism is that children believe in *immanent justice*, the idea that breaking a rule always leads to punishment.** Suppose I had forced Matt to use my new rules for Chutes and Ladders® and that, the next day, he had tripped on his way to school, scraping his knee. Believing in immanent justice, he would have seen the scraped knee as the inevitable consequence of breaking the rule the previous day.

At about age 8, children progress to the stage of *moral relativism*, the understanding that rules are created by people to help them get along. Children progress to this more advanced level of moral reasoning in part because advances in cognitive development allow them to understand the reasons for rules. Furthermore, from interactions with their peers, children come to understand the need for rules and how they are created. For example, as the boys in the photograph decide where to ride their skateboards, they might follow a rule that everybody can suggest some place and then they'll vote. The boys understand that this rule isn't absolute; they follow it because it's reasonably fair and, by using this rule, they spend more time skating and less time arguing.

Children in the stage of moral relativism also understand that because people agree to set rules in the first place, they can also change them if they see the need. If the skateboarding boys decided another rule would be fairer and help them get along better, they could adopt the new rule.

Some of Piaget's ideas about moral reasoning have stood the test of time better than others. Research shows that preschool children believe adults' authority is limited. For example, preschoolers believe that pushing a child or damaging another child's possession are wrong even when an adult says that it's okay (Tisak, 1993). Thus, in contrast to Piaget's theory, children's early moral reasoning does not consider adult authority final and absolute. A lasting contribution of Piaget's work, however, is the idea that moral reasoning progresses through a sequence of stages, driven by cognitive development and interactions with peers. One modern theory that builds on Piaget's stage approach is Lawrence Kohlberg's; it is the focus of the next section.

KOHLBERG'S THEORY

To begin, I'd like you to read this story:

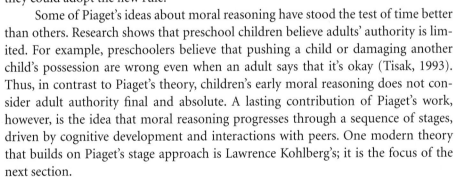

In Europe, a woman was near death from cancer. One drug might save her, a form of radium that a druggist in the same town had recently discovered. The druggist was charging $2,000, ten times what the drug cost him to make. The sick woman's husband, Heinz, went to everyone he knew to borrow the money, but he could only get together about half of what it cost. He told the druggist that his wife was dying and asked him to sell it cheaper or let him pay later. But the druggist said, "No." The husband got desperate and broke into the man's store to steal the drug for his wife (Kohlberg, 1969, p. 379).

STOP! Before reading any further, contemplate the problem in this story. What do you think? Should Heinz have stolen the drug to save his wife? How do you explain your decision?

Kohlberg created this story and others like it to study how people reason about moral dilemmas. He made it very difficult to reach a decision in his stories because every alternative involved some undesirable consequences. In fact, there is no "correct" answer—that's why the stories are referred to as moral "dilemmas." Kohlberg was more interested in the reasoning used to justify a decision than the decision itself.

Kohlberg analyzed children's, adolescents', and adults' responses to a large number of dilemmas and identified three levels of moral reasoning, each divided into two stages. Across the six stages, the basis for moral reasoning shifts. In the earliest stages, moral reasoning is based on external forces, such as the promise of reward or the threat of punishment. At the most advanced levels, moral reasoning is based on a personal, internal moral code and is unaffected by others' views or society's expectations. You can clearly see this gradual shift in the three levels:

> *In Kohlberg's theory, moral reasoning is first based on external forces such as reward and punishment, but ultimately is based on a personal moral code.*

- *Preconventional level:* **For most children, many adolescents, and some adults, moral reasoning is controlled almost solely by obedience to authority and by rewards and punishments.**

  Stage 1: Obedience orientation. People believe that adults know what is right and wrong. Consequently, a person should do what adults say is right to avoid being punished. A person at this stage would argue that Heinz should not steal the drug because it is against the law (which was set by adults).

  Stage 2: Instrumental orientation. People look out for their own needs. They often are nice to others because they expect the favor to be returned in the future. A person at this stage would say it was all right for Heinz to steal the drug because his wife might do something nice for him in return (that is, she will reward him).

- *Conventional level:* **For most adolescents and most adults, moral decision making is based on social norms—what is expected by others.**

  Stage 3: Interpersonal norms. Adolescents and adults believe that they should act according to others' expectations. The aim is to win the approval of others by behaving like "good boys" and "good girls." An adolescent or adult at this stage would argue that Heinz should not steal the drug because then others would see him as a honest citizen who obeys the law.

  Stage 4: Social system morality. Adolescents and adults believe that social roles, expectations, and laws exist to maintain order within society and promote the good of all people. An adolescent or adult in this stage would reason that Heinz should steal the drug because a husband is obligated to do all that he possibly can to save his wife's life. Or a person in this stage would reason that Heinz should not steal the drug because stealing is against the law and society must prohibit theft.

- *Postconventional level:* **For some adults, typically those older than 25, moral decisions are based on personal, moral principles.**

  Stage 5: Social contract orientation. Adults agree that members of cultural groups adhere to a "social contract" because a common set of expectations and laws benefits all group members. However, if these expectations and laws no longer promote the welfare of individuals, they become invalid.

Consequently, an adult in this stage would reason that Heinz should steal the drug because social rules about property rights are no longer benefiting individuals' welfare.

Stage 6: Universal ethical principles. Abstract principles like justice, compassion, and equality form the basis of a personal moral code that may sometimes conflict with society's expectations and laws. An adult at this stage would argue that Heinz should steal the drug because life is paramount and preserving life takes precedence over all other rights.

Putting all of the stages together, this is what Kohlberg's theory looks like:

Preconventional Level: Punishment and Reward

Stage 1: obedience to authority

Stage 2: nice behavior in exchange for future favors

Conventional Level: Social Norms

Stage 3: live up to others' expectations

Stage 4: follow rules to maintain social order

Postconventional Level: Moral Codes

Stage 5: adhere to a social contract when it is valid

Stage 6: personal morality based on abstract principles

Support for Kohlberg's Theory. Kohlberg proposed that his stages form an invariant sequence. That is, individuals move through the six stages in the order listed and in only that order. If his stage theory is right, then level of moral reasoning should be strongly associated with age and level of cognitive development: Older and more advanced thinkers should, on the average, be more advanced in their moral development, and indeed, they usually are (Stewart & Pascual-Leone, 1992). For example, the graph shows developmental change in the percentage of individuals who reason at Kohlberg's different stages. Stages 1 and 2 are common among children and young adolescents but not older adolescents and adults. Stages 3 and 4 are common among older adolescents and adults. The graph also shows that most individuals do not progress to the final stages. Most adults' moral reasoning is at Stages 3 and 4.

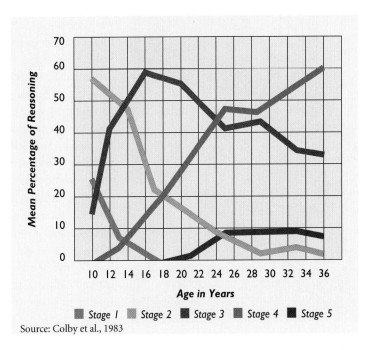

Source: Colby et al., 1983

Support for Kohlberg's invariant sequence of stages also comes from longitudinal studies measuring individuals' level of reasoning over several years. Individuals do progress through each stage in sequence and virtually no individuals skip any stages (Colby et al., 1983). Longitudinal studies also show that, over time, individuals become more advanced in their level of moral reasoning or remain at the same level. They do not regress to a lower level (Walker & Taylor, 1991).

Additional support for Kohlberg's theory comes from research on the link between moral reasoning and moral behavior. In general, level of moral reasoning should be linked to moral behavior. Remember that less advanced moral reasoning reflects the influence of external forces such as rewards and social norms whereas more advanced reasoning is based on a personal moral code. Therefore, individuals at the preconventional and conventional levels would act morally when external forces demand, but otherwise they may not. In contrast, individuals at the postconventional level, where reasoning is based on personal principles, should be compelled to moral action even when external forces may not favor it.

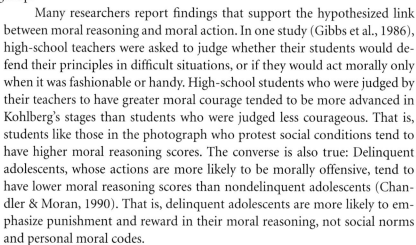

As predicted by Kohlberg, students who have greater moral courage tend to have more sophisticated moral reasoning.

Let's consider a hypothetical example. Suppose you're one of the most popular students in the ninth grade. You learn that one of the least popular students has been wrongly accused of putting graffiti on a school wall; you know that some friends in your group are actually responsible. What would you do? Speaking out on behalf of the unpopular student is unlikely to lead to reward. Furthermore, there are strong social norms against "squealing" on friends. So if you are in the preconventional or conventional level of moral reasoning—like Min-shen, the boy in the vignette at the beginning of the module—you would probably let the unpopular student be punished unfairly. But if you are at the postconventional level and see the situation in terms of principles of justice and fairness, you would be more likely to identify the real perpetrators, despite the price to be paid in rejection by the group.

Many researchers report findings that support the hypothesized link between moral reasoning and moral action. In one study (Gibbs et al., 1986), high-school teachers were asked to judge whether their students would defend their principles in difficult situations, or if they would act morally only when it was fashionable or handy. High-school students who were judged by their teachers to have greater moral courage tended to be more advanced in Kohlberg's stages than students who were judged less courageous. That is, students like those in the photograph who protest social conditions tend to have higher moral reasoning scores. The converse is also true: Delinquent adolescents, whose actions are more likely to be morally offensive, tend to have lower moral reasoning scores than nondelinquent adolescents (Chandler & Moran, 1990). That is, delinquent adolescents are more likely to emphasize punishment and reward in their moral reasoning, not social norms and personal moral codes.

On another point of Kohlberg's theory, support is mixed. Kohlberg claimed his sequence of stages is universal: All people in all cultures progress through the six-stage sequence. Some research shows that children and adolescents in cultures worldwide reason about moral dilemmas at Stages 2 or 3, just like North American children and adolescents. But as we'll see in the "Cultural Influences" feature, beyond the earliest stages, moral reasoning in other cultures is often *not* described well by Kohlberg's theory (Snarey, 1985).

Cultural Influences: **MORAL REASONING IN INDIA**

Many critics note that Kohlberg's emphasis on individual rights and justice reflects traditional American culture and Judeo-Christian theology. Not all cultures and religions share this emphasis; consequently, moral reasoning might be based on different values in other cultures. The

Hindu religion, for example, emphasizes duty and responsibility to others, not individual rights and justice (Simpson, 1974). Accordingly, children and adults reared with traditional Hindu beliefs might emphasize caring for others in their moral reasoning more than individuals brought up in the Judeo-Christian tradition.

Miller and Bersoff (1992) tested the hypothesis of cultural differences in moral reasoning by constructing dilemmas with both justice- and care-based solutions. For example:

> *Ben planned to travel to San Francisco in order to attend the wedding of his best friend. He needed to catch the very next train if he was to be on time for the ceremony, as he had to deliver the wedding rings. However, Ben's wallet was stolen in the train station. He lost all of his money as well as his ticket to San Francisco.*
>
> *Ben approached several officials as well as passengers ... and asked them to loan him money to buy a new ticket. But, because he was a stranger, no one was willing to lend him the money he needed.*
>
> *While Ben ... was trying to decide what to do next, a well-dressed man sitting next to him walked away.... Ben noticed that the man had left his coat unattended. Sticking out of the man's coat pocket was a train ticket to San Francisco.... He also saw that the man had more than enough money in his coat pocket to buy another train ticket (p. 545).*

One solution emphasized individual rights and justice:

> *Ben should not take the ticket from the man's coat pocket—even though it means not getting to San Francisco in time to deliver the wedding rings to his best friend (p. 545).*

The other solution placed a priority on caring for others:

> *Ben should go to San Francisco to deliver the wedding rings to his best friend—even if it means taking the train ticket from the other man's coat pocket (p. 545).*

When children and adults living in the United States read dilemmas like the one about Ben, a slight majority selected the justice-based alternative. In contrast, when Hindu children and adults living in India, like the mother and son in the photo, read the same dilemmas, the overwhelming majority selected the care-based alternative. Clearly, moral reasoning reflects the emphases of the culture in which one is reared. Consistent with Kohlberg's theory, judgments by American children and adults reflect their culture's priority on individual rights and justice. But judgments by Indian children and adults reflect their culture's priority on caring for other people. The bases of moral reasoning are not universal as Kohlberg claimed; instead, they reflect cultural values. ■

BEYOND KOHLBERG'S THEORY

Kohlberg's theory obviously is not the final word on moral development. Much about his theory seems valid, but investigators have addressed some of its shortcomings. The next few pages describe some work that helps complete our picture of the development of moral thinking.

Gilligan's Ethic of Caring. Findings of cultural differences in moral reasoning like those described in the "Cultural Influences" feature indicate that Kohlberg's theory is not universal but applies primarily to cultures with Western philosophical and religious traditions. Researcher Carol Gilligan (1982; Gilligan & Attanucci, 1988) questions how applicable Kohlberg's theory is even within the Western tradition. Gilligan argues that Kohlberg's emphasis on justice applies more to men than to women, whose reasoning about moral issues is often rooted in concern for others. Gilligan writes, "The moral imperative that emerges repeatedly in interviews with women is an injunction to care, a responsibility to discern and alleviate the 'real and recognizable trouble' of this world" (1982, p. 100). Gilligan therefore proposes a developmental progression in which individuals gain greater understanding of caring and responsibility. In the first stage, children are preoccupied with their own needs. In the second stage, people care for others, particularly those who are less able to care for themselves, like infants and the aged. The third stage unites caring for others and for oneself by emphasizing caring in all human relationships.

Gilligan proposed that moral reasoning is sometimes based on concern for others, not based solely on justice and individual rights as Kohlberg had claimed.

Like Kohlberg, Gilligan also believes that moral reasoning becomes qualitatively more sophisticated as individuals develop, progressing through a number of distinct stages. However, Gilligan emphasizes care (helping people in need) instead of justice (treating people fairly).

What does research tell us about the importance of justice and care in moral reasoning? Gilligan's claim that females and males differ in the bases of their moral reasoning is not supported. Girls and boys as well as men and women reason about moral issues similarly (Walker, 1995). Both females *and* males often think about moral issues in terms of care and interpersonal relationships. Justice and care *both* serve as the basis for moral reasoning. It is the nature of the moral problem that largely determines whether justice, care, or both will be the basis for moral reasoning (Smetana, Killen, & Turiel, 1991).

Distinguishing Moral Rules from Social Conventions. Neither Piaget nor Kohlberg nor Gilligan had much to say about moral reasoning during the preschool years. For example, according to Piaget, children have no real understanding of moral issues until they enter the stage of moral realism at about age 5. In fact, research shows that an understanding of moral rules emerges during the preschool years. Moral rules are designed to protect people. Thus, prohibitions against theft and murder are moral rules. **In contrast, *social conventions* are arbitrary standards of behavior agreed to by a cultural group to facilitate interactions within the group.** Thus social convention says that we can eat French fries but not green beans with our fingers and that we can address peers but not teachers by their first names. By age 3, most children distinguish moral rules from social conventions. They judge that hurting other people and taking their possessions are more serious transgressions than eating ice cream with one's fingers and not paying attention to a story (Smetana & Braeges, 1990).

Eisenberg's Levels of Prosocial Reasoning. Nancy Eisenberg (1982; Eisenberg et al., 1995) argues that Kohlberg's theory is flawed because the dilemmas are unrealistic. They involve breaking a law or disobeying a person in authority. In real life, says Eisenberg, most children's moral dilemmas involve choosing between self-interest and helping others. For example, in one of Eisenberg's moral dilemmas, a child walking to a party comes upon a child injured from a fall. The first child must decide whether to continue to the party or help the second child and miss the party.

Like Kohlberg, Eisenberg focuses on how children explain their choices. **Most preschool and many elementary-school children have a *hedonistic orientation*: they pursue their own pleasure.** Children with this orientation would not help the injured child because they would miss the party. Or they might help because they expect that the injured child would return the favor in the future. In either case, self-interest is the basis of their decision.

Some preschool and many elementary-school children have a *needs-oriented orientation*: They are concerned about others' needs and want to help. Children at this stage have learned a simple rule, to help others. They often explain their desire to help as a straightforward, "He needs my help." Their desire to help is not based on imagining how the injured child feels or on a personal moral code.

Many elementary-school children and adolescents have a *stereotyped, approval-focused orientation*, behaving as they think society expects "good people" to behave. The helpful child in the photo would explain her behavior by saying that the person she's helping will like her more because she's helping.

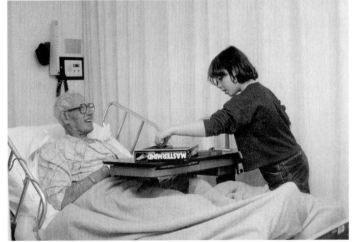

Finally, some children and many adolescents develop an *empathic orientation*; they consider the injured child's perspective and how their own actions will make them feel. An adolescent with this orientation might say, "He'd be in pain, so I'd feel bad if I didn't help."

The same kinds of evidence that support Kohlberg's theory support Eisenberg's. For example, longitudinal studies indicate that children in many countries move through Eisenberg's different orientations in sequence (Eisenberg, 1986; Eisenberg et al., 1995). Moreover, children who reason at the more advanced levels are more likely to actually help others than children who reason at the less advanced levels (Miller et al., 1996).

Eisenberg's theory is like Kohlberg's in emphasizing that moral development involves a developmental shift away from self-centered thinking to social norms and moral principles. Her theory is like Gilligan's in emphasizing that caring for others is an important element in everyday moral reasoning. The net result of Eisenberg's studies, Gilligan's work, and research on the emergence of moral rules is a broader view of moral reasoning. As Kohlberg claimed, moral reasoning becomes progressively more sophisticated as children develop. However, contrary to Kohlberg's original claims, moral reasoning is not always based on justice and rights. Concern for others is sometimes the basis. And, although Kohlberg had little to say about the preschool years, this is when children begin to understand that moral rules are more important than social conventions.

Making Children's Lives Better: PROMOTING MORE ADVANCED MORAL REASONING

How do individuals develop more mature forms of moral reasoning? Kohlberg's answer to this question is based on an idea from Piaget. Kohlberg proposed that change occurs when people notice that their current level of moral reasoning is inadequate; either it leads to

contradictions or it does not always lead to a clear course of action. Seeing that their thinking is inadequate, they abandon it in favor of more advanced forms.

Sometimes, too, simply being exposed to more advanced moral reasoning is sufficient to promote developmental change (Walker, 1980). A child may notice, for example, that older friends do not wait to be rewarded to help others. An adolescent may notice that respected peers take courageous positions regardless of the social consequences. Such experiences apparently cause youngsters to re-evaluate their reasoning on moral issues and propel them towards more sophisticated thinking.

Discussion can be particularly effective in revealing shortcomings in moral reasoning. When people, like the adolescents in the photo, reason about moral issues with others whose reasoning is at a higher level, the usual result is that individuals reasoning at lower levels improve (Berkowitz & Gibbs, 1985). Imagine, for example, two 9-year-olds discussing the Heinz dilemma. Suppose one takes the position that Heinz should not steal the drug because he might get caught—reasoning at the preconventional level. The other argues that Heinz should steal the drug because a husband should do anything to save his wife's life—reasoning at the conventional level. During conversations of this sort, 9- and 10-year-old children at the preconventional level usually adopt the logic of the children arguing at the higher conventional level.

Children move to more advanced levels of moral reasoning by noticing contradictions in their current level of reasoning, by observing others, and by discussing moral issues with others.

Research findings such as these have an important message for parents: Discussion is probably the best way for parents to help their children think about moral issues in more mature terms. Research consistently shows that mature moral reasoning comes about when children are free to express their opinions on moral issues to their parents, who are expressing their own opinions on these issues and, consequently, exposing their children to more mature moral reasoning (Hoffman, 1988).

Discussion and modeling, then, help children become more advanced in their moral reasoning. More advanced moral reasoning should, in turn, lead to moral behavior, an "other" rather than "self" orientation. We'll look at the development of other-oriented, helpful behavior in the next module. ■

Check Your Learning

1. Kohlberg's theory includes the preconventional, conventional, and _____ stages of moral reasoning.

2. For children in the preconventional level, moral reasoning is strongly influenced by _____.

3. Gilligan's views of morality emphasize _____ instead of justice.

4. When boys' and girls' moral reasoning is compared, the typical result is that _____.

5. If parents wish to foster their children's moral development, they should _____ with them.

Answers: (1) postconventional, (2) reward or punishment, (3) caring for others, (4) they do not differ, (5) discuss moral issues

ELPING OTHERS

Learning Objectives

- **At what age do children begin to act prosocially? How does prosocial behavior change with age?**
- **What skills do children need to behave prosocially?**
- **What situations influence children's prosocial behavior?**
- **How can parents foster prosocial behavior in their children?**

> *Six-year-old Juan got his finger trapped in the VCR when he tried to remove a tape. While he cried and cried, his 3-year-old brother, Antonio, and his 2-year-old sister, Carla, watched but did not help. Later, when their mother had soothed Juan and decided that his finger was not injured, she worried about her younger children's reactions. In the face of their brother's obvious distress, why had Antonio and Carla done nothing?*

Most parents, most teachers, and most religions try to teach children to act in cooperative, helping, giving ways—at least most of the time and in most situations. **Actions that benefit others are known as *prosocial behavior.*** Of course, cooperation often "works" because individuals gain more than they would by not cooperating. ***Altruism* is a particular kind of prosocial behavior; it is behavior that helps another with no direct benefit to the individual.** Altruism is driven by feelings of responsibility towards other people. Two youngsters pooling their funds to buy a candy bar to share demonstrates cooperative behavior. One youngster giving half her lunch to a friend who forgot his demonstrates altruism.

But, as the story of Juan and his siblings shows, children (and adults, for that matter) are not always helpful or cooperative. In this module, you'll learn how prosocial behavior changes with age and some of the factors that promote prosocial behavior.

DEVELOPMENT OF PROSOCIAL BEHAVIOR

Simple acts of altruism can be seen by 18 months of age. When toddlers and preschoolers see other people who are obviously hurt or upset, they appear concerned, like the child in the photo. They try to comfort the person by hugging them or patting them, and they try to determine why the person is upset (Zahn-Waxler et al., 1992). Apparently, at this early age, children recognize signs of distress.

During the preschool years, children gradually begin to understand others' needs and learn appropriate altruistic responses (Farver & Branstetter, 1994). Their early attempts at altruistic behavior are limited because their knowledge of what they can do to help is modest. As youngsters acquire more strategies to help others, their preferred strategies become more adultlike (Strayer & Schroeder, 1989).

Thus, as a general rule, intentions to act prosocially increase with age, as do children's strategies for helping. Of course, not all children respond to the needs of others, either in toddlerhood or at later ages. Some children attach greater priority to looking out for their own interests. What makes some children more likely than others to help? We'll answer this question in the next section.

SKILLS UNDERLYING PROSOCIAL BEHAVIOR

Think back to an occasion when you helped someone. How did you know that the person needed help? Why did you decide to help? Although you didn't realize it at the time, your decision to help was probably based on several skills:

■ *Perspective-taking.* In Module 6.2, you learned about Piaget's concept of egocentrism, the preoperational youngster's inability to see things from another's point of view. Egocentrism limits children's ability to share or help because they simply do not realize the need for prosocial behavior. They have only one perspective—their own. For example, young children might not help someone carrying many packages because they cannot envision that carrying lots of bulky things is a burden. Older children, however, can take the perspective of others, so they recognize the burden and are more inclined to help. In general, the better children understand the thoughts and feelings of other people, the more willing they are to share and help others (Eisenberg, 1988).

■ *Empathy.* **The ability to experience another person's emotions is** *empathy.* Children who deeply feel another person's fear, disappointment, sorrow, or loneliness are more inclined to help that person than children who do not feel these emotions (Eisenberg & Miller, 1987). In other words, youngsters like the one in the photo, who is obviously distressed by what he is seeing, are most likely to help others.

■ *Moral reasoning.* In Module 12.2, you learned that reward and punishment influence young children's moral reasoning, whereas a concern for moral principles characterizes adolescents' and adults' moral decision making. Therefore, as you would expect, prosocial behavior in young children is usually determined by the chance of reward or punishment. It also follows that as children mature and begin to make moral decisions on the basis of fairness and justice, they become more prosocial, which is what the research shows (Eisenberg & Shell, 1986).

In sum, children who help others tend to be better able to take another's view, to feel another's emotions, and to act on the basis of principles, not rewards, punishments, or social norms. For example, a 15-year-old who spontaneously loans his favorite video game to a friend sees that the friend would like to play the game, feels the friend's disappointment at not owning the game, and believes that friends should share with others.

Of course, perspective-taking, empathy, and moral reasoning skills do not guarantee that children always act altruistically. Even though children have the skills needed to act altruistically, they may not because of the particular situation, as we'll see in the next section.

SITUATIONAL INFLUENCES

Kind children occasionally disappoint us by being cruel, and children who are usually stingy sometimes surprise us by their generosity. Why? The setting helps determine whether children act altruistically or not.

■ *Feelings of responsibility:* Children act altruistically when they feel responsible to the person in need. They are more likely to help siblings and friends than strangers, simply because they feel a direct responsibility to people that they know well (Costin & Jones, 1992).

■ *Feelings of competence:* Children act altruistically when they feel that they have the skills necessary to help the person in need. Suppose, for example, that a preschooler is growing more and more upset because she can't figure out how to work a computer game. A classmate who knows little about computer games is not likely to help because he doesn't know what to do to help. By helping, he could end up looking foolish (Peterson, 1983).

■ *Mood:* Children act altruistically when they are happy or feeling successful but not when they are sad or feeling as if they have failed. In other words, a preschooler who has just spent an exciting morning as the "leader" in nursery school is more inclined to share treats with siblings than a preschooler who was punished by the teacher (Moore, Underwood, & Rosenhan, 1973).

■ *Cost of altruism:* Children act altruistically when it entails few or modest sacrifices. A preschooler who has received a snack that she doesn't particularly like is more inclined to share it than one who has received her very favorite snack (Eisenberg & Shell, 1986).

Thus, when are children most likely to help? When they feel responsible to the person in need, have the skills that are needed, are happy, and do not think they have to give up a lot by helping. When are children least likely to help? When they feel neither responsible nor capable of helping, are in a bad mood, and believe that helping will entail a large personal sacrifice.

Using these guidelines, how do you explain why Antonio and Carla, the children in the vignette, watched idly as their older brother cried? Hint: the last two factors—mood and cost—are not likely to be involved. However, the first two factors may explain Antonio and Carla's failure to help their older brother. My explanation appears on page 321, just before "Check Your Learning."

So far, we've seen that altruistic behavior is determined by children's skills (such as perspective-taking) and by characteristics of situations (such as whether children feel competent to help in a particular situation). Whether children are altruistic is also determined by socialization, the topic of the next section.

Children are most likely to help when they feel responsible, have the needed skills, are happy, and believe that they will lose little by helping.

SOCIALIZING PROSOCIAL BEHAVIOR

Dr. Martin Luther King Jr. said that his pursuit of civil rights for African Americans was particularly influenced by three people: Henry David Thoreau (a 19th-century American philosopher), Mohandas Gandhi (the leader of the Indian movement for independence from England), and his father. As is true of many humanitarians, Dr. King's prosocial behavior started in childhood, at home. But how do parents foster altruism in their children? The key factors are reasoning, modeling, and praise.

Parents whose favored disciplinary strategy is reasoning tend to have children who behave prosocially (Hoffman, 1988). The "Real Children" feature shows an example of this approach in action.

Real Children: **USING REASONING TO PROMOTE PROSOCIAL BEHAVIOR**

Jim's 4-year-old daughter, Annie, was playing with a friend, Maurice. Annie asked Maurice if she could borrow his crayons. When Maurice refused, Annie pushed him aside and grabbed the crayons, which caused Maurice to cry. At this point, Jim returned the crayons to Maurice and had the following conversation with Annie:

Jim:	Why did you take the crayons away from Maurice?
Annie:	Because I wanted them.
Jim:	How do you think he felt? Happy or sad?
Annie:	I dunno.
Jim:	I think that you know.
Annie:	Okay. He was sad.
Jim:	Would you like it if I took the crayons away from you? How would *you* feel?
Annie:	I'd be mad. And sad, too.
Jim:	Well, that's how Maurice felt and that's why you shouldn't just grab things away from people. It makes them angry and unhappy. Ask first, and if they say "no," then you mustn't take them.

Jim's approach to discipline is to reason with Annie to help her see how her actions affect others. He emphasizes the rights and needs of others as well as the impact of one child's misbehavior on others. Repeated exposure to reasoning during discipline seems to promote children's ability to take the perspective of other people (Hoffman, 1988). ■

Reasoning is one way that parents can influence prosocial behavior; modeling is another. Children imitate others' behavior, including prosocial behavior. In laboratory studies, children imitate the altruistic behaviors of their peers (Wilson, Piazza, & Nagle, 1990). For example, children are more likely to donate toys to hospitalized children or help older adults with household chores when they see other children doing so.

Of course, parents are the models to whom children are most continuously exposed, so they exert a powerful influence. For example, parents who report frequent feelings of warmth and concern for others tend to have children who experience stronger feelings of empathy (Eisenberg et al., 1991). When a mother is helpful and responsive, her children often imitate her by being cooperative, helpful, sharing, and less critical of others (Bryant & Crockenberg, 1980).

Perhaps the most obvious way to foster sharing and other altruistic behavior in children is to reward them directly for acts of generosity. Many parents use praise to reward their children's prosocial acts. **Particularly effective is *dispositional praise,* in which parents link the child's altruistic behavior to an underlying altruistic disposition.** A parent might say, "Thanks for helping me make breakfast; I knew I could count on you because you are such a helpful person." When children like the one in the photo repeatedly hear remarks like this, their self-concept apparently changes to include these characteris-

Parents can foster altruism by using reasoning to discipline their children, by behaving altruistically themselves, and by praising their children's altruism.

tics. Children begin to believe that they *really are* helpful (or nice or friendly). Consequently, when they encounter a situation in which prosocial behavior is appropriate, their self-concept prompts them to act prosocially (Mills & Grusec, 1989).

Thus, parents can foster altruism in their youngsters by using reasoning to discipline them, by behaving altruistically themselves, and by praising their youngsters' altruistic acts. Remember, too, that altruism requires skills like perspective-taking, empathy, and advanced moral reasoning and that the setting influences when children behave altruistically. Combining all these ingredients, we can give a general account of children's altruistic behavior. As children get older, their perspective-taking and empathic skills develop, which enables them to see and feel another's needs. Nonetheless, children are never invariably altruistic (or, fortunately, invariably nonaltruistic) because properties of situations dictate altruistic behavior, too.

As parents and other adults try to encourage children's prosocial behavior, one of the biggest obstacles is aggressive behavior, which is common throughout childhood and adolescence. In the next module, we'll look at some of the forces that contribute to children's aggression.

Answer to question on page 319 about why Antonio and Carla didn't help: Here are two explanations: First, neither Antonio nor Carla may have felt sufficiently responsible to help because (a) with two children who could help, each child's feeling of individual responsibility is reduced, and (b) younger children are less likely to feel responsible for an older brother. Second, it's my guess that neither child has had many opportunities to use the VCR. In fact, it's likely they both have been strongly discouraged from venturing near it! Consequently, they don't feel competent to help because they don't know how it works or what they should do to help Juan remove his finger.

Check Your Learning

1. Preschool children often want to act prosocially but may not because _____.

2. The skills that help children behave prosocially include _____, empathy, and moral reasoning.

3. Children are more likely to behave prosocially when they feel responsible, competent, happy, and when _____.

4. Parents can encourage prosocial behavior by using reasoning when they discipline their children, _____, and praising them for behaving prosocially.

Answers: (1) their knowledge of appropriate prosocial behaviors is limited, (2) perspective-taking, (3) the costs of prosocial behavior are minimal, (4) modeling prosocial behavior

GGRESSION

Learning Objectives

- **When does aggressive behavior first emerge? How stable is aggression across childhood, adolescence, and adulthood?**
- **How do families, television, and the child's own thoughts contribute to aggression?**

Every day, 7-year-old Roberto follows the same routine when he gets home from school: He watches one action-adventure cartoon on TV after another until

MODULE
12.4
Aggression

Change and Stability ─┐

Roots of Aggressive Behavior ─┘

it's time for dinner. Roberto's mother is disturbed by her son's constant TV-viewing, particularly because of the amount of violence in the shows that he likes. Her husband tells her to stop worrying: "Let him watch what he wants to. It won't hurt him and, besides, it keeps him out of your hair."

If you think back to your years in elementary school, you can probably remember a class "bully"—a child who was always teasing classmates and picking fights. **Such acts typify** *aggression,* **behavior meant to harm others.** Aggressiveness is not the same as assertiveness, even though laypeople often use these words interchangeably. You've probably heard praise for an "aggressive businessperson" or a ballplayer who was "aggressive at running the bases." Psychologists and other behavioral scientists, however, would call these behaviors assertive. Assertive behaviors are goal-directed actions to further the legitimate interests of individuals or the groups they represent, while respecting the rights of other persons. In contrast, aggressive behavior, which may be physical or verbal, is intended to harm, damage, or injure and is carried out without regard for the rights of others.

In this module, we will examine aggressive behavior in children and see how it changes with age. Then we'll examine some causes of children's aggression, and, in the process, learn more about the impact of Roberto's TV-watching on his behavior.

CHANGE AND STABILITY

By the time youngsters are old enough to play with one another, they show aggression. When 1- and 2-year-olds play, conflicts frequently arise—often over contested playthings—and youngsters often use aggression to resolve their conflicts (Cummings, Iannotti, & Zahn-Waxler, 1989). Aggressive behaviors included hitting,

kicking, pushing, or biting the other child, or as shown in the photo, trying to grab a toy from another child. Physical aggression declines as children learn other ways to resolve disputes, but it still occurs during childhood and early adolescence, particularly among boys. For example, in one study, fourth- and seventh-grade boys reported that nearly 50 percent of their conflicts with other boys involved physical aggression (Cairns et al., 1989). Physical aggression occurred in less than 20 percent of conflicts between girls, but girls often resort to verbal aggression, making remarks meant to hurt others, such as "You're the dumbest, ugliest kid in third grade and *everyone* hates you!" (Eisenberg, 1988). Girls also often try to hurt one another by telling friends to avoid a particular classmate or by spreading malicious gossip (Crick & Grotpeter, 1995).

Although forms of aggression change with development, individual children's tendencies to behave aggressively are moderately stable, especially among boys. Kupersmidt and Coie (1990) measured aggressiveness in a group of 11-year-olds by having children list the names of classmates who frequently started fights. Seven years later, more than half the aggressive children had police records, compared to less than 10 percent of the nonaggressive children. In another study, conducted in Sweden by Stattin and Magnusson (1989), teachers rated the aggressive behavior of more than one thousand 10-year-olds. Their results, shown in the graph at the top of page 323, indicate that teachers' ratings accurately predicted subsequent criminal activity. Boys in the least aggressive group committed relatively few criminal offenses of any sort, while two-thirds of the most aggressive boys had committed offenses and nearly half had committed major offenses such as assault, theft, or robbery. Overall, girls committed far fewer offenses, but teachers' ratings of aggressive behavior still predicted which girls were more likely to have criminal records.

Findings from these and similar studies show that aggression is not simply a case of playful pushing and shoving that most children outgrow. To the contrary, a small minority of children who are highly aggressive develop into young adults who create havoc in society. What causes children to behave aggressively? Let's look at some of the roots of aggressive behavior.

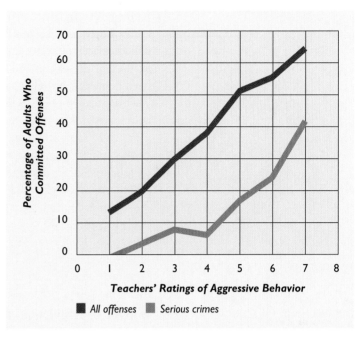

ROOTS OF AGGRESSIVE BEHAVIOR

For many years, psychologists believed that aggression was caused by frustration. The idea was that when children or adults were blocked in their efforts to achieve a goal, they became frustrated and aggressed, often against the interfering person or object. Although frustration can lead to aggression (Berkowitz, 1989), researchers no longer believe that it's the sole cause of aggression, and therefore investigators have looked to other causes, including the family, television, and the child's own thoughts.

Impact of Parents. Early family experiences are a prime training ground for learning patterns of aggression. The pioneering work in this area was conducted by Gerald Patterson (1984), whose findings were based almost entirely on careful, systematic observation of aggressive children in their home environments. One fact that comes through clearly in Patterson's work is that parents and siblings play an enormous role in cultivating aggressive behavior in children, and in ways that are subtle as well as obvious. Many parents and older siblings, for example, use physical punishment or threats to stop aggressive behavior. Although the immediate effect may be to suppress aggression, physical punishment also serves as a model, vividly demonstrating that physical force "works" as a means of controlling others. A parent like the one in the photo is saying, in effect, "You were right. The best way to get people to do what you want, or to stop them from doing what you don't want, is to hit them hard enough."

Not surprisingly, parents' use of harsh physical punishment is associated with aggressive behavior in children. Dodge, Bates, and Pettit (1990) studied children who were so harshly punished physically that bruises resulted or the children needed medical treatment. These children were rated twice as aggressive—by both teachers and peers—as children who had not experienced such harsh punishment.

But strong or aggressive parental responses are not essential in making a child aggressive. Even low-key anger and unfair accusations by parents can pave the way for later aggressiveness. Children are more likely to be aggressive, for example, when parents constantly express irritation at their children's behavior.

In many families with aggressive children, a vicious circle seems to develop. Compared to families with nonaggressive children, both aggressive children and their parents are more likely to respond to neutral behavior

Physical aggression becomes less frequent as children develop, but verbal aggression becomes more frequent.

with aggression. Furthermore, once an aggressive exchange has begun, both parents and children are likely to escalate the exchange, rather than break it off. And once a child has been labeled aggressive by parents and others, that child is more likely to be accused of aggression and to be singled out for punishment, even when the child has been behaving entirely appropriately on the occasion in question (Patterson, 1984). The "aggressive child" will be accused of all things that go wrong—from missing cookies to broken appliances—and other children's misbehaviors will be ignored.

Patterson's work emphasizes the point that hitting a child for aggression does not usually inhibit aggression for very long, because aggression is often a natural response to being the target of aggression, regardless of the other person's motives. What is the best response to a child's aggression? Discourage it—either by ignoring it or punishing it—while encouraging and rewarding other forms of nonaggressive social behavior. An older brother who simply grabs the remote control from a younger sister should be punished ("No TV for 3 days!"), then shown a better way to resolve the conflict ("Wait until your sister finishes her program, then ask if you can change the channel. If she says, 'no,' come see me.") and praised for cooperating rather than aggressing ("Thanks for asking your sister instead of just grabbing the remote control.").

Impact of Television. Most children today watch television regularly by the age of 3, and by the time they are 15, they have spent more time watching television than going to school. In fact, throughout childhood they will have spent more time watching television than in any other activity except sleep (Liebert & Sprafkin, 1988).

What do children see when they watch all this television? The answer varies somewhat from child to child, but most American children spend considerable time watching action-adventure programs that contain a heavy dose of modeled aggression. Heroes and "good guys" on these shows almost invariably end up in a fight with the "bad guys." The good guys always win, of course, and are typically rewarded with praise, admiration, and sometimes more tangible rewards (such as a vacation in the sun).

What are the effects of watching all these rewarded aggressive models for so long? This question first attracted attention in the mid-1950s. At that time, only about half the households in the United States had television sets, yet the public was already aware of the frequent portrayal of violence in TV programs and worried about its effects on viewers, especially young ones. Anecdotal evidence suggested a link. One 6-year-old fan of Hopalong Cassidy (a TV cowboy of the 1950s) asked his father for real bullets for his toy gun because his toy bullets didn't kill people the way Hopalong's did (Schramm, Lyle, & Parker, 1961).

More than 40 years later, citizens remain concerned about violence on TV—with good reason. Children's cartoons like the one shown in the photo typically show one violent act every 3 minutes ("violence" meaning use of physical force against another person). And the average American youngster will see several *thousand* murders on TV before reaching adolescence (Waters, 1993). (If you find these numbers hard to believe, try the activities described in "See for Yourself" at the end of the chapter.)

What does research tell us about this steady diet of televised mayhem and violence? According to Bandura's (1986) social cognitive theory, children learn by observing others; so if they watch violent behavior (either real or televised), they will act violently. In fact, laboratory studies conducted in the 1960s by Bandura, Ross, and Ross (1963) made just this point. Children watched specially created TV programs in which an adult behaved violently toward a plastic "Bobo" doll. The adult kicked and hit the doll. When children were given the opportunity to play with the doll, those who had seen the TV program were much more likely to behave aggressively toward the doll than children who had not seen the program.

Critics thought the laboratory setting of this and other early studies affected the results, and they doubted that viewing TV violence in more realistic settings would have such pronounced effects on children (Klapper, 1968). Today, however, we know that viewing TV violence "hardens" children, making them more accepting of interpersonal violence. Suppose, for example, a teen is baby-sitting two youngsters who begin to argue and then fight. Baby sitters who are frequent viewers of TV violence are more inclined to let them "slug it out" because they see this as a normal, acceptable way of resolving conflicts (Drabman & Thomas, 1976).

Experimental and correlational studies both link children's viewing of television violence to increased aggression.

Is this increased tolerance for aggression reflected in children's behavior? Will Roberto, the avid cartoon-watcher in the vignette at the beginning of the module, become more aggressive? Or, as his father believes, is his TV-watching simply "fun" without consequence? The answer from research is clear: Roberto's father is wrong. Frequent exposure to TV violence causes children to be more aggressive. One of the most compelling studies examined the impact of children's TV-viewing at age 8 on criminal activity at age 30 (Huesmann, 1986). The graph shows clearly that 8-year-old boys who watched large doses of TV violence had the most extensive criminal records as 30-year-olds. This is true for both males and females, even though females' overall level of criminal activity is much lower.

Seriousness of Criminal Activity at Age 30
(Large numbers indicate more serious offenses)

These findings are correlational, which complicates conclusions about cause and effect. But because experimental studies demonstrate that viewing televised violence breeds aggression, it is reasonable to conclude that children who are frequent viewers of TV violence learn to resort to aggression in interacting with others. For some, their aggression eventually puts them behind bars. Of course, TV violence is not the sole cause of aggression in children. But it is an important factor in a highly complex process to which parents and peers also contribute.

Cognitive Processes. The perceptual and cognitive skills described in Chapters 5 through 7 also play a role in aggression. Dodge, Bates, and Pettit (1990) were the first to explore the cognitive aspects of aggression. They discovered that aggressive boys often respond aggressively because they are not skilled at interpreting other people's intentions and, without a clear interpretation in mind, they respond aggressively by default. That is, aggressive boys far too often think, "I don't know what you're up to and, when in doubt, attack."

From findings like these, Crick and Dodge (1994; Dodge & Crick, 1990) formulated the information-processing model of children's thinking that is shown in the figure on page 326. According to the model, responding to a social stimulus involves several steps. First, children selectively attend to certain features of the social stimulus but not others, in the manner described on pages 132–134 of Module 5.3. Second, children try to interpret the features that they have processed; that is, they try to give meaning to the social stimulus. Third, children evaluate their goals for the situation. Fourth, children retrieve from memory a behavioral response that is associated with

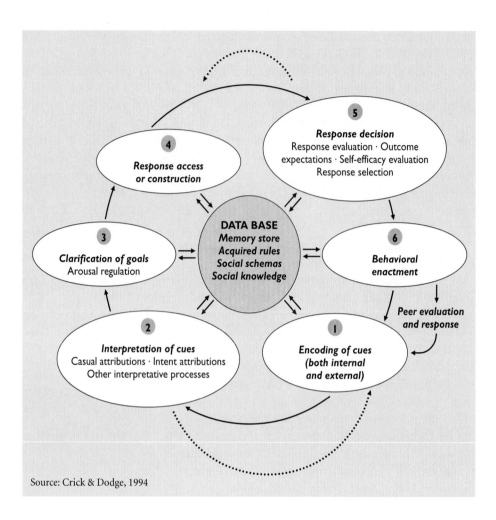

Source: Crick & Dodge, 1994

the interpretation and goals of the situation. Fifth, children evaluate this response to determine if it is appropriate. Finally, the child proceeds with the behavior.

Crick and Dodge (1994) have shown that aggressive children's processing is biased and restricted in many of these steps. For example, aggressive children are less likely to attend to features that would signal nonhostile motives. A surprised, chagrined look that suggests a negative event was an accident is often not processed by aggressive children. And, as we have already seen, when the features of a social situation do not lead to an obvious interpretation, aggressive youngsters *assume* the intent is hostile.

If aggressive children are unskilled at interpreting and responding to others' actions, would training in these skills improve their social behavior? The answer seems to be "yes" (Dodge & Crick, 1990). One approach is to teach aggressive children that aggression is painful and does not solve problems, that intentions can be understood by attending to relevant cues, and that there are more effective, prosocial ways to solve interpersonal disputes. In a study by Guerra and Slaby (1990), adolescents incarcerated for committing violent acts received training designed to increase their understanding of social situations. For example, they were taught to pay attention to nonhostile cues in a social situation, to think of alternative ways of responding to social problems, and to evaluate responses in terms of their consequences. Supervisors at the correctional facility judged that the adolescents were better adjusted following training than before. They were less aggressive, less impulsive, and more flexible in their solutions. Thus, training in social skills can reduce aggressive behavior and increase positive interactions with peers.

> **Aggressive children are unskilled at interpreting others' actions, often assuming hostile intent when none is present.**

To sum up, the vicious cycle of aggression usually begins early. Once youngsters are labeled aggressive, environmental factors may lead them quite unwittingly along an aggressive path. The punishments that parents and teachers dole out may increase the child's hostility and serve as evidence that aggression "works." The child may then choose aggressive companions who further encourage aggressive behavior.

Of course, families are not the sole causes of aggression and violence. Poverty, unemployment, racism, and terrorism create a culture of aggression and violence. But individual parents can be careful to not set the cycle of aggression in motion. Parents can deal with misbehavior with reasoning instead of physical punishment. And, children prone to aggressive responding can be taught equally effective but more prosocial ways to deal with conflict.

Check Your Learning

1. During the elementary-school years, physical aggression becomes less common but _____ becomes more common, especially among girls.

2. Highly aggressive children are more likely to _____ as adults.

3. Aggressive behavior in children is linked to parents' use of _____.

4. Children who regularly watch televised violence are more likely to behave aggressively, and they also _____.

5. Aggressive children often interpret neutral stimuli in _____ terms.

Answers: (1) verbal aggression, (2) engage in criminal activity, (3) harsh physical punishment, (4) become hardened to violence, (5) hostile or aggressive

ORAL UNDERSTANDING AND BEHAVIOR IN PERSPECTIVE

Think back to the nursery filled with the newborn Mother Teresa, Adolf Hitler, Mohandas Gandhi, and Martin Luther King Jr. The material in this chapter doesn't tell us exactly why those newborns developed as they did, following paths of good or evil, but it does help us understand some of the general features involved in the development of moral reasoning and behavior. In Module 12.1, we saw that self-control emerges gradually between 1 and 3 years and is enhanced when parents don't over-control their children but give children opportunities to regulate their own behavior. In Module 12.2, we learned that moral reasoning progresses through stages and includes children's developing understanding of justice, social conventions, and caring for others. In Module 12.3, we saw that prosocial behavior depends upon specific skills, characteristics of the situation, and parenting practices. Finally, in Module 12.4, we found that aggression takes on different forms as children develop and can be fostered by parents, television-viewing, and children's cognitive processes.

This chapter has some nice illustrations of the theme that *early development is related to later development but not perfectly.* For example, look at the table on page 304, which shows correlations between preschoolers' delayed gratification and several measures in adolescence. Preschoolers who were best able to delay gratification were, as adolescents, less likely to yield to temptation and to be distractible. Yet the correlations were far from 1, which shows that many preschoolers who quickly gave into temptation became adolescents who were *not* distractible.

The same conclusion is evident in the results in the graph on page 323. Among children who were rated by their teachers as the most aggressive, about 40 percent had committed serious crimes by age 30, yet 60 percent had not. Among the children who were rated least aggressive, more than 90 percent were crime-free as adults, but 5 percent had committed serious crimes. Behaving aggressively in childhood definitely increases the odds of adult criminal activity, but it does not guarantee it.

THINKING ABOUT DEVELOPMENT

1. Compare and contrast the view of self-control presented in Module 12.1 with Vygotsky's views, which were presented in Module 6.3.

2. In Kohlberg's stage theory of moral reasoning, most children are thought to reason at the preconventional level, whereas adolescents typically reason at the conventional level. According to Piaget, school-age children reason at the concrete operational level and adolescents at the formal operational level. How similar are preconventional moral reasoning and concrete operational thinking? How similar are conventional moral reasoning and formal operational thinking?

3. Suppose some kindergarten children want to raise money for a gift for one of their classmates who is in the hospital. Based on what you know about the factors that influence children to be altruistic, how would you help the kindergartners plan their fund-raising?

4. Crick and Dodge's model of decision making draws upon the information-processing approach to cognitive development that was presented in Chapter 7. Use that approach to suggest other possible causes and remedies for children's aggressive behavior.

SEE FOR YOURSELF

This assignment may seem like a dream come true—you are being *required* to watch TV. Pick an evening when you can watch network television programming from 8 until 10 P.M. (prime time). Your job is to count each instance of (a) physical force by one person against another and (b) threats of harm to compel another to act against his or her will. Select one network randomly and watch the program for 10 minutes. Then turn to another network and watch that program for 10 minutes. Continue changing the channels every 10 minutes until the 2 hours are over. Of course, it won't be easy to follow the plots of all these programs, but you will end up with a wider sample of programming this way. Repeat this procedure on a Saturday morning when you can watch 2 hours of children's cartoons. (Not *Beavis and Butt-head*!)

Now simply divide the total number of aggressive acts by four to estimate the amount of aggression per hour. Then multiple this figure by 11,688 to estimate the number of aggressive acts seen by an average adolescent by age 19. (Why 11,688? Two hours of daily TV viewing—a very conservative number—multiplied by 365¼ days and 16 years.) Then ponder the possible results of that very large number. If your parents told you, nearly 12,000 times, that stealing was okay, would you be more likely to steal? Probably. Then what are the consequences of massive exposure to the televised message, "Solve conflicts with aggression"? See for yourself!

RESOURCES

For more information about . . .

people who have devoted their lives to helping others, read Anne Colby and William Damon's *Some Who Do Care: Contemporary Lives of Moral Commitment* (The Free Press, 1992) in which the authors, two developmental psychologists interested in moral development, use the biographies of humanitarians to identify the important forces that make some people commit their lives to helping others

ways to encourage young people to serve others in their community through volunteerism, contact the Points of Light Foundation at 1-800-879-5400

about the impact of media violence on children, visit the Web site of the University of Oregon's Media Literacy On-Line Project, http://interact.uoregon.edu/MediaLit/FA/MLmediaviolence

KEY TERMS

aggression *322*
altruism *317*

conventional level *310*
dispositional praise *320*

empathic orientation *315*
empathy *318*

SUMMARY

MODULE 12.1:
SELF-CONTROL

BEGINNINGS OF SELF-CONTROL

At 1 year, infants are first aware that others impose demands on them; by 3 years, youngsters can devise plans to regulate their behavior. During the school-age years, children become better able to control their behavior.

Children differ in their self-control, but individuals are fairly consistent across tasks and over time: Preschoolers who have good self-control tend to become adolescents with good self-control.

PARENTAL INFLUENCES

When children observe adults who delay gratification, they are more likely to delay gratification themselves. Similarly, when children observe adults who show little self-control, they are likely to show little self-control themselves. Children who have the best self-control tend to have parents who do not use harsh punishment and who encourage their children to be independent and make their own decisions.

IMPROVING SELF-CONTROL

Children are better able to regulate their own behavior when they have plans to help them remember the importance of the goal and something to distract them from tempting objects.

MODULE 12.2:
REASONING ABOUT MORAL ISSUES

PIAGET'S VIEWS

Piaget theorized that 5- to 7-year-olds are in a stage of moral realism. They believe that rules are created by wise adults; therefore, rules must be followed and cannot be changed. Beginning at about 8 years, children enter a stage of moral relativism, believing that rules are created by people to help them get along.

KOHLBERG'S THEORY

Kohlberg proposed that moral reasoning includes preconventional, conventional, and postconventional levels. Each level has two stages, creating a six-stage developmental sequence. In the early stages, moral reasoning is based on rewards and punishments; in the latter stages, on personal moral codes.

As predicted by Kohlberg's theory, people progress through the stages in sequence and do not regress, and morally advanced reasoning is associated with more frequent moral behavior. However, few people attain the most advanced levels of reasoning, and cultures differ in the bases for moral reasoning.

BEYOND KOHLBERG'S THEORY

Gilligan proposed that females' moral reasoning is based on caring and responsibility for others, not justice. Research does not support

consistent sex differences, but has found that males and females both consider caring as well as justice in their moral judgments, depending upon the situation. Also, the roots of moral reasoning emerge in the preschool years, when children distinguish moral rules from social conventions. According to Eisenberg, children's reasoning about prosocial dilemmas shifts from a self-interested, hedonistic orientation to concern for others based on empathy.

MODULE 12.3:
HELPING OTHERS

DEVELOPMENT OF PROSOCIAL BEHAVIOR

Even toddlers are aware when others are upset, and they will try to offer comfort. As children grow older, they more often see the need to act prosocially and are more likely to have the skills to do so.

SKILLS UNDERLYING PROSOCIAL BEHAVIOR

Children are more likely to behave prosocially when they are able to take others' perspectives, are empathic, and have more advanced moral reasoning.

SITUATIONAL INFLUENCES

Children's prosocial behavior is often influenced by situational characteristics. Children more often behave prosocially when they feel that they should and can help, when they are in a good mood, and when they believe that they have little to lose by helping.

SOCIALIZING PROSOCIAL BEHAVIOR

Parenting approaches that promote prosocial behavior include using reasoning in discipline, modeling prosocial behavior, and praising children for prosocial behavior.

MODULE 12.4:
AGGRESSION

CHANGE AND STABILITY

As children grow older, physical aggression becomes less common but verbal aggression becomes more common. Overall levels of aggression are fairly stable, which means that very aggressive young children often become involved in criminal activities as adolescents and adults.

ROOTS OF AGGRESSIVE BEHAVIOR

Children's aggressive behavior has been linked to their parents' use of harsh physical punishment. Other factors that contribute to children's aggression are excessive viewing of televised violence and lack of skill at interpreting others' actions and intentions.

Gender Roles

YOU BARELY HAVE THE PHONE TO YOUR EAR BEFORE YOUR BROTHER-IN-LAW SHOUTS, "JEANNIE HAD THE BABY!" "THAT'S GREAT," YOU SAY. "A BOY OR A GIRL?" WHY IS THIS ALWAYS THE FIRST QUESTION PEOPLE ASK NEW PARENTS? WHY ARE PEOPLE *SO* interested in a baby's sex? The answer is that being a *boy* or *girl* is not simply a biological distinction. Instead, these terms are associated with distinct social roles. **Like a role in a play, a *social role* is a set of cultural guidelines for how a person should behave.** The social roles associated with gender are among the first that children learn, starting in infancy. As youngsters learn the behaviors assigned to males and females, they begin to identify with one of these groups. As they do, they take on an identity as a boy or girl.

In this chapter, we will see how children acquire a gender role. We'll begin, in Module 13.1, by considering cultural stereotypes of males and females. In Module 13.2, we will examine actual psychological differences between boys and girls. In Module 13.3, we'll focus on how children come to identify with one sex. Finally, in Module 13.4, we'll discuss recent changes in gender roles. Throughout this chapter, I'll use *sex* to refer to aspects of males and females that are clearly biological (such as differences in anatomy) and *gender* to refer all other characteristics that relate to maleness and femaleness.

G ENDER STEREOTYPES

Learning Objectives

- **What are gender stereotypes and how do they differ for males and females?**
- **How do gender stereotypes influence behavior?**
- **When do children learn their culture's stoereotypes for males and females?**

> When Nancy was 7 months pregnant, her 11-year-old son Clark announced that he really wanted a brother, not a sister. Clark explained, "A sister would drive me crazy. Girls never make up their minds about stuff, and they get all worked up over nothin'." "Where did Clark get these ideas?" Nancy wondered. "Is this typical for 11-year-olds?"

All cultures have *gender stereotypes*—beliefs about how males and females differ in personality traits, interests, and behaviors. Of course, because stereotypes are beliefs, they may or may not be true. In this module, we'll look at the features associated with gender stereotypes and discover when children like Clark learn about gender stereotypes.

HOW DO WE VIEW MEN AND WOMEN?

"Terry is active, independent, competitive, and aggressive." As you were reading this sentence, you probably assumed that Terry was a male. Why? Although Terry is a common name for both males and females, the adjectives used to describe Terry are more commonly associated with men than women. The table lists traits that college students typically associate with males and females.

Features Judged to be Characteristically Male or Female by College Students

Male	Female
Independent	Emotional
Aggressive	Home-oriented
Not excitable	Kind
Skilled in business	Cries easily
Mechanical aptitude	Creative
Outspoken	Considerate
Acts as a leader	Devotes self to others
Self-confident	Needs approval
Ambitious	Gentle
Not easily influenced	Aware of others' feelings
Dominant	Excitable

Based on T. L. Ruble, 1983

The traits associated with males are called *instrumental* because they describe individuals who act on the world and influence it. In contrast, the traits associated with females are called *expressive,* because they describe emotional functioning and individuals who value interpersonal relationships.

American men and women both believe that instrumental traits typify males whereas expressive traits typify females (D. N. Ruble, 1988; T. L. Ruble, 1983; Williams & Best, 1990). But are these views shared by adults worldwide? The "Cultural Influences" feature has the answer.

Cultural Influences: AROUND THE WORLD WITH FOUR GENDER STEREOTYPES

Are men seen as aggressive and independent worldwide? And are women seen as emotional and gentle worldwide? Or are these stereotypes of men and women unique to the United States? John Williams and Deborah Best (1990) addressed these questions in an ambitious project involving 300 different traits and participants in 30 countries. The graphs show the results for just four traits and seven countries. You can see that each trait

Compared to people in many other countries, Americans have more extreme stereotypes of men and women.

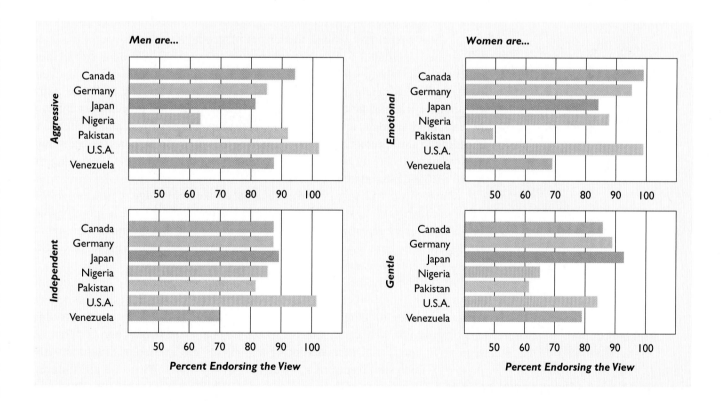

shows considerable cultural variation. For example, virtually all American subjects consider men aggressive, but only a slight majority of Nigerian subjects do. Thus, American views of men and women are not shared worldwide. In fact, what's notable about the research results is that Americans' gender stereotypes are more extreme than any other country listed. Keep this in mind as you think about

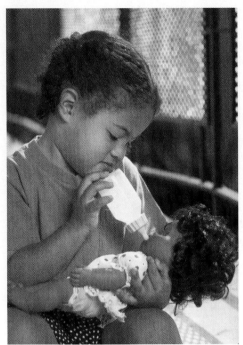

what men and women can and cannot do and what they should and should not do. Your ideas about gender are shaped by your culture's beliefs, which are not held universally. ■

It's important to understand our tendency to stereotype gender behavior because stereotypes are very limiting. If we have stereotyped views, we expect males to act in particular ways and females to act in other ways, and we respond to males and females solely on the basis of gender, not as individuals. For example, do you assume the youngster in the photo is a girl based on her taste in toys? Assuming the child is a girl, would, in turn, probably lead you to think she plays more quietly and is more easily frightened than if you had assumed the child was a boy (Stern & Karraker, 1989). Making stereotyped assumptions about gender leads to a whole host of inferences about behavior and personality that may not be true.

When do children begin to learn their culture's stereotypes for males and females? We'll answer this question in the next section.

LEARNING GENDER STEREOTYPES

By the time children enter elementary school, they are well on their way to forming gender stereotypes; and by the time they have completed elementary school, their ideas of gender stereotypes are virtually as well formed as adults'. Children's growing understanding of gender stereotypes was demonstrated in a study by Deborah Best and her colleagues (1977). Children were asked if 16 stereotypically masculine and 16 stereotypically feminine traits were more typical of boys or girls. At age 5, boys and girls judged one-third of the traits the way adults would; by age 11, they judged about 90 percent of the traits according to adult stereotypes. The table at the top of page 335 shows the traits that children judged stereotypically at ages 5 and 11. A check means that boys and girls agreed with the listed stereotype.

Obviously, by 11 years, children have adultlike knowledge of gender stereotypes; in this regard, Clark's view of girls in the opening vignette is quite typical for his age. Recent research confirms that children understand gender stereotypes by the time they enter kindergarten and that their understanding grows throughout the elementary-school years (Etaugh & Liss, 1992).

As children develop, they begin to understand that gender stereotypes do not always apply; older children are more willing than younger children to ignore stereotypes when judging other children. Martin (1989) told 4- and 8-year-olds about hypothetical children, some of whom had same-sex friends and gender-role appropriate interests. Others had other-sex friends and gender-role inappropriate interests: "Tommy is a 5-year-old boy whose best friend is a girl. Tommy likes to iron with an ironing board." Children were asked how much the hypothetical child would like to play with masculine and feminine toys. The key result was that 4-year-olds based their judgments solely on the hypothetical child's sex: The hypothetical boys would like masculine toys, the hypothetical girls, the feminine ones. Even though Tommy likes to play with a girl and pretend to iron, 4-year-olds thought he would want to play with masculine toys. In contrast, the 8-year-olds considered the hypothetical child's stated interests. They believed, for

By the end of elementary school, children are very familiar with adults' stereotypes of males and females and they understand that these stereotypes are not binding on individuals.

Boys are...			Girls are...		
	5-year-olds	11-year-olds		5-year-olds	11-year-olds
strong	✓	✓	emotional	✓	✓
aggressive	✓	✓	gentle	✓	✓
disorderly	✓	✓	soft-hearted	✓	✓
cruel	✓	✓	affectionate	✓	✓
coarse	✓	✓	weak	✓	✓
ambitious	✓	✓	appreciative		✓
dominant	✓	✓	excitable		✓
adventurous		✓	sophisticated		✓
independent		✓	fickle		✓
loud		✓	meek		✓
boastful		✓	submissive		✓
jolly		✓	whiny		✓
steady		✓	talkative		✓
confident		✓	frivolous		✓

Based on Best et al., 1977

example, that a boy whose interests were not stereotypic would be more interested in feminine toys. They believed Tommy would want to play with a doll because he likes to iron clothes.

Thus, although older children are more familiar with gender stereotypes, they see these stereotypes as general guidelines for behavior that are not necessarily binding for all boys and girls (Signorella, Bigler, & Liben, 1993). In fact, older children consider gender stereotypes less binding than many social conventions and moral rules (Serbin, Powlishta, & Gulko, 1993). You can observe older children's understanding of gender stereotypes and their more flexible attitudes by doing the "See for Yourself" activity at the end of the chapter.

At this point, you're probably wondering whether there's any truth to gender stereotypes. For example, are boys really more dominant than girls? Are girls really more excitable than boys? For answers to these questions, let's go to Module 13.2.

Check Your Learning

1. Male gender stereotypes include instrumental traits while female gender stereotypes emphasize _____ traits.

2. Gender stereotypes are harmful because they lead people to make inferences about a child's behavior or personality based solely on the child's _____, not on individual characteristics.

3. Compared to younger children, older children know more of the contents of gender stereotypes and they know that _____.

Answers: (1) expressive, (2) sex, (3) gender stereotypes are not binding on all boys and girls

DIFFERENCES RELATED TO GENDER

Learning Objectives

■ **How do boys and girls differ in physical development, intellectual abilities, and social behavior?**

■ **What factors are responsible for these gender differences?**

■ **What are the implications of these gender differences for boys' and girls' development?**

> *All through elementary and middle school, Darlene was one of the best students. When she moved into high school, she was particularly proud that she always got the highest grades in her math classes. But she noticed that as each year went by, even though she got the best grades in math, the boys got higher scores on the standardized tests given every spring.*

Is Darlene's experience typical? Do girls usually get higher grades than boys in math class but lower scores on standardized tests? Some of the first answers to these questions came in *The Psychology of Sex Differences,* a book by Eleanor Maccoby and Carol Jacklin published in 1974. Maccoby and Jacklin did no new research; rather, they summarized results from approximately 1,500 research studies that had been done over the years on gender differences. According to Maccoby and Jacklin:

> *. . . physical differences between the sexes are obvious and universal. The psychological differences are not. The folklore that has grown up about them is often vague and inconsistent. We believe there is a great deal of myth in the popular view about sex differences. There is also some substance. . . . we hope to be able to identify the generalizations that may be relied upon with some confidence (p. 3).*

Maccoby and Jacklin's methodology was quite simple: First they searched psychological journals for studies on gender differences. Then they categorized the studies according to the behaviors that were studied and the ages of the children. Finally, they examined the results for gender differences. For example, girls are thought to be more sensitive to touch, but Maccoby and Jacklin found that in six studies of touch sensitivity, infant boys and girls were equally sensitive. In three other studies, girls were more sensitive. In 11 studies of older children and adults, nine found no differences and two found that females were more sensitive. Maccoby and Jacklin concluded that "If a sex difference exists in touch sensitivity . . . our survey has revealed only hints of it" (1974, p. 23).

Maccoby and Jacklin examined numerous studies of cognition, achievement, and social behavior, and concluded that gender differences had been established in only four areas: Girls have greater verbal ability whereas boys have greater mathematical and visual-spatial ability, and boys are more aggressive than girls. Maccoby and Jacklin did not find research evidence to support the beliefs that girls are more social and suggestible than boys, have lower self-esteem, are less analytic in thinking, and lack achievement motivation.

Maccoby and Jacklin were challenged on the grounds that they had included some weak studies and had defined behaviors in ways that

Maccoby and Jacklin concluded that girls have greater verbal ability than boys, but that boys have greater mathematical and spatial abilities and are more aggressive.

other researchers might not (Block, 1976). Some critics questioned outright findings about some specific behaviors. The debate stimulated more research, some applying new statistical techniques that allowed finer analysis (Eagly, 1995). Many developmentalists now believe that gender differences are more extensive than Maccoby and Jacklin suggested, but their book remains a classic because its comprehensiveness provided an excellent starting point for further research.

In the remainder of this module, we'll see what we've discovered about gender differences since Maccoby and Jacklin did their analysis. We'll focus on differences in physical development, cognitive processes, and social behavior.

DIFFERENCES IN PHYSICAL DEVELOPMENT AND BEHAVIOR

Of course, differences in the reproductive system are what differentiate boys and girls, along with differences in secondary sex characteristics such as lower voices and facial hair in boys and breast development and wider hips in girls. Boys are usually larger and stronger than girls, which means that they outperform girls on many measures of physical ability. If you've attended a high school track meet that included both boys' and girls' teams, you've seen the differences: Boys can usually run faster, jump higher, and throw objects farther and more accurately. Outside of sports, on tasks that involve fine-motor coordination, such as tracing and drawing, girls do better than boys (Thomas & French, 1985).

As infants, boys are more active than girls, and this difference increases during childhood (Eaton & Enns, 1986). For example, in a classroom, boys are more likely than girls to have a hard time sitting still. On a playground like the one in the photos, boys are more likely than girls to be involved in vigorous play. And, recall from Module 5.3 that boys are three times more likely than girls to be diagnosed with attention deficit hyperactivity disorder.

Girls tend to be healthier than boys. Female embryos are more likely than male embryos to survive prenatal development. This trend continues after birth: Infant boys are more prone to birth complications; and throughout life, boys are more prone to many diseases and dysfunctions (Jacklin, 1989). Finally, females live longer than males. Typical of this trend, when my father entered an assisted-living center at age 79, he was one of 13 single males compared to 73 single females.

To summarize, boys tend to be bigger, stronger, and more active; girls tend to have better fine-motor coordination and to be healthier. In the next section, which concerns intellectual skills, you'll again see that gender differences vary from one skill to the next.

DIFFERENCES IN INTELLECTUAL ABILITIES AND ACHIEVEMENT

Of the four gender-based differences discovered by Maccoby and Jacklin (1974), three concern intellectual skills: Girls tend to have greater verbal skill but boys tend to have greater mathematical and visual-spatial skill. Since Maccoby and Jacklin's work, we've learned much about the nature of gender differences in these areas.

Verbal Ability. When Janet Hyde and Marcia Linn (1988) updated Maccoby and Jacklin's summary of research, they found that females had greater verbal ability in 75 percent of the 165 studies that they analyzed. The difference was usually small, but was larger for general measures of verbal ability, unscrambling scrambled words, and quality of speech production. Girls also read, write, and spell better than boys (Feingold, 1993; Hedges & Nowell, 1995), and more boys have reading and other language-related problems such as stuttering (Halpern, 1986).

Why are girls more talented verbally than boys? Part of the explanation may lie in biology. The left hemisphere of the brain, which is central to language (see Module 4.3), may mature more rapidly in girls than in boys (Diamond et al., 1983). But experience also contributes. Reading, for instance, is often stereotyped as an activity for girls (Huston, 1983). Consequently, girls are more willing than boys to invest time and effort in mastering verbal skills like reading.

Mathematics. Gender differences in math skill are complex. Let's start with performance on standardized math achievement tests. Standardized tests emphasize computational skills during the elementary- and middle-school years, and girls usually have higher scores than boys. Problem solving and applying math concepts are emphasized in high school and college; here boys' scores are more often higher than girls'. Understanding of math concepts is assessed at all ages, and males and females do not differ. Thus, initially girls excel in math computation, but later boys excel in math problem solving (Hyde, Fennema, & Lamon, 1990). The gender difference remains even when boys and girls are equated for the number of math courses they have taken (Kimball, 1989).

Girls often get higher grades than boys in math courses, but boys typically get higher scores on standardized tests of math achievement.

Paradoxically, the results are different for grades in math courses. Often no differences are detected in boys' and girls' grades, but when a difference occurs, it invariably favors girls. This is even true for courses in high school and college—precisely the time when males are getting higher scores on achievement tests (Kimball, 1989). Darlene's experience, described in the module-opening vignette, is common: Girls get better grades in math courses but lower scores on standardized tests of math achievement.

Why is this so? One idea is that girls are confident when dealing with relatively familiar math problems on classroom tests. However, when girls like the ones in the photo take standardized achievement tests that have many novel problems, they are less confident and don't do as well. Boys are confident in their math skills and like the challenge of novel problems on standardized tests (Kimball, 1989). Girls' lack of confidence in their math ability may be because math is stereotyped as a masculine pursuit and girls are therefore less likely than boys to be encouraged to succeed in math (Jacobs, 1991).

This argument probably sounds familiar to you because the explanation is basically the same one used to explain gender differences in verbal skill: Boys succeed in math and girls succeed in language because these activities are consistent with gender stereotypes.

Some writers (e.g., Feingold, 1993) argue that gender differences in verbal and math skills have become smaller in recent years, reflecting less stereotyped views of reading, language, and math. Is this really the case? The "Focus on Research" feature describes evidence that will help you to decide.

Focus on Research: **ARE GENDER DIFFERENCES IN VERBAL AND MATH SKILLS BECOMING SMALLER?**

Who were the investigators and what was the aim of the study? The National Assessment of Educational Progress (NAEP) was mandated by the U.S. Congress in 1971 to evaluate academic achievement of U.S. schoolchildren. In addition to providing a long-term record of academic achievement, the NAEP data are particularly valuable because the samples are large and representative of the nation's schoolchildren. Larry Hedges and Amy Nowell (1995) wanted to use the NAEP data to determine whether gender differences in academic achievement have become smaller in recent years.

How did the investigators measure the topic of interest? The NAEP includes standardized tests in several areas. Hedges and Nowell examined the data from the reading, mathematics, and writing tests.

Who were the children in the study? Approximately 70,000 to 100,000 American students in grades 3, 7, and 11 participated in the NAEP. Hedges and Nowell examined the data for 11th graders.

What was the design of the study? This study was correlational because Hedges and Nowell were interested in the relation that existed naturally between two variables: the year in which testing took place and students' scores on the achievement tests. The NAEP is a cross-sectional study (because it includes students in grades 3, 7, and 11), but Hedges and Nowell's analysis was not because it included only 11th graders.

Were there ethical concerns with the study? No. Hedges and Nowell did not actually test any children. They used data collected previously by the NAEP. (And the tests themselves were very similar to tests that these children had taken before.)

What were the results? The graph shows the size of the difference between boys and girls in reading, writing, and math. The differences are expressed in standard deviation units, a way of measuring how much a typical child differs from the group average.* A positive value means that the girls' average is greater than the boys' average, and a negative value means that boys' scores are greater. For reading, the difference between boys and girls has been remarkably constant across 20 years: Girls' averages are almost always one-fourth of a standard deviation greater than boys' averages. This means that girls typically differ from boys by about 0.25 standard deviation units, which, in turn, means that the difference is about one-fourth the amount by which boys typically differ from the group average for boys. Obviously, this is not a very large difference. Here's another way to put this difference in perspective: If you gave a test of verbal ability to 100 boys and 100 girls, a difference of one-fourth of a

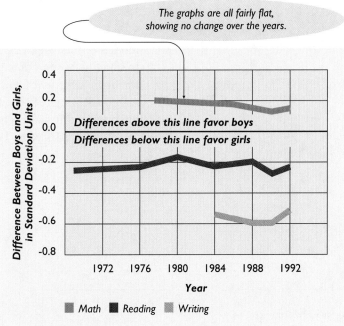

The graphs are all fairly flat, showing no change over the years.

Differences above this line favor boys

Differences below this line favor girls

Difference Between Boys and Girls, in Standard Deviation Units

■ Math ■ Reading ■ Writing

* Here's an example that should help you understand standard deviation units. Suppose you gave a quiz to 10 students and the group's average score was 8. Of course, not all children get 8s; some get 7s, 9s, and other scores. The standard deviation tells you how much a typical child deviates from the group average. If the standard deviation for the 10 quizzes was 1.0, this would tell you that scores of 7 and 9 (which differ from the average by 1.0) were probably common but that scores of 5 and 15 (which differ from the average by 5.0) were not.

standard deviation would lead you to expect 56 girls to be above average on the test but only 44 boys.

The story is much the same for writing skill, which has been assessed in the NAEP since 1984. Here, the differences in the graph are larger: Girls' scores are higher than boys' by approximately one-half of a standard deviation. However, the trend has changed little over time.

Finally, look at the results for math. Hedges and Nowell found that, since 1978, boys' scores have been larger than girls' scores by 0.15 to 0.2 of a standard deviation, with no obvious historical changes.

What did the investigators conclude? Have gender differences become smaller since the 1970s? Hedges and Nowell concluded, "no," at least not for reading, writing, and math skills as they are measured on the NAEP. ■

If gender differences in language and math reflect the fact that boys pursue masculine-stereotyped activities and girls pursue feminine-stereotyped activities, then efforts to reduce stereotypes surrounding reading and math should reduce gender differences. However, Hedges and Nowell's (1995) results show that gender differences are just as large in the 1990s as they were in the 1970s. What does this mean? Perhaps stereotypes for language and math have not changed as much as we thought. Maybe math remains stereotyped as "a guy thing" in the 1990s, despite decades of efforts to show girls that math is just as appropriate and interesting a subject for them and that girls can be just as successful in math as boys. An alternative explanation is that biological factors play a role. If, as some scientists believe, gender differences in verbal ability can be traced to gender differences in brain maturation, perhaps gender differences in math may similarly be due to gender differences in brain function. In the next section, you'll see how biological factors may be involved in another gender difference.

Spatial Ability. In Module 8.1, you saw that spatial ability is a component of most models of intelligence. **One aspect of spatial ability is *mental rotation,* the ability to imagine how an object will look after it has been moved in space.** The items in the figure test mental rotation: The task is to determine which of the figures labeled A through E are rotated versions of the figure in the box on the left. From childhood on, boys tend to have better mental rotation skill than girls (Linn & Peterson, 1985; Voyer, Voyer, & Bryden, 1995). (The correct answers are C and D.)

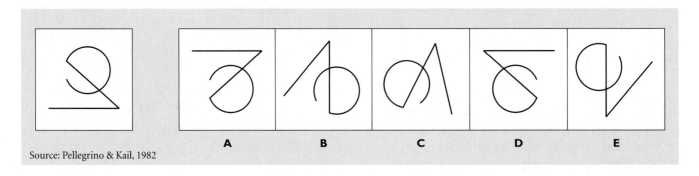

Source: Pellegrino & Kail, 1982

Another element of spatial ability is determining relations between objects in space while ignoring distracting information. For example, which of the tilted bottles of water in the figure on page 341 has the waterline drawn correctly? In an upright bottle, the waterline is at right angles to the sides of the bottle, but selecting the correct answer for the tilted bottle (A, in this case) requires that you ignore the conflicting perceptual information provided by the sides of the bottle. From adoles-

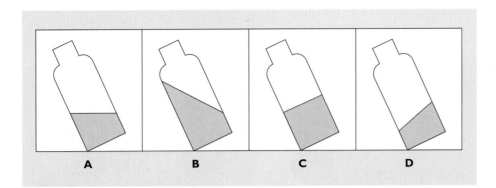

cence on, boys are more accurate than girls on these kinds of spatial tasks (Voyer, Voyer, & Bryden, 1995).

Explanations for gender differences in spatial ability abound:

■ A recessive gene on the X chromosome may promote spatial ability (Thomas & Kail, 1991). In this type of inheritance, males only have to inherit a recessive gene from their mother to have high spatial ability, but females must inherit the recessive gene from both parents.

■ The right hemisphere of the brain may be more specialized for spatial processing in males than in females, perhaps because boys mature more slowly than girls (Waber, 1977).

■ Boys are more likely than girls to participate in activities that foster spatial skill, such as estimating the trajectory of an object moving through space (e.g., a baseball) or, like the boy in the photo, using two-dimensional plans to assemble an object such as a scale model (Baenninger & Newcombe, 1989).

Each of these possible explanations of gender differences in spatial ability is supported by some studies but not by others. And, of course, the explanations are not necessarily mutually exclusive. Biological and experiential forces may both contribute to gender differences in spatial ability, just as both contribute to gender differences in verbal and math ability. Thus, parents and others can foster verbal, math, and spatial abilities in boys and girls because each is influenced considerably by experience.

As we'll see in the next section, nature and nurture also contribute to gender differences in personality and social behavior.

DIFFERENCES IN PERSONALITY AND SOCIAL BEHAVIOR

Maccoby and Jacklin (1974) only found convincing evidence of one gender difference in personality and social behavior: Boys were more aggressive than girls. In this section, we'll see what research in the 20-plus years since has found.

Aggressive Behavior. No one doubts Maccoby and Jacklin's conclusion that boys are more aggressive than girls. As mentioned in Module 12.4 and as you can see in

the photos, the gender difference in aggression is widespread; it is readily observed in laboratory and natural settings and holds across a range of specific types of aggressive behavior. No matter how you slice it, boys *are* more aggressive than girls (Collaer & Hines, 1995; Hyde, 1984.) Of course, some qualifications apply. Boys are not always aggressive. They are, for example, more likely to be aggressive toward other boys than toward girls (Maccoby & Jacklin, 1980). Girls can be aggressive, too, particularly during adolescence when aggression takes nonphysical forms such as spreading rumors or malicious gossip (Cairns et al., 1989).

Because boys and men are more aggressive in virtually all cultures and because males in nonhuman species are also more aggressive, scientists are convinced that biology contributes heavily to this gender difference. **Aggressive behavior has been linked to *androgens*, hormones secreted by the testes.** Androgens do not lead to aggression directly. Instead, androgens make it more likely that boys will be aggressive by making boys more excited or angry and by making boys stronger (e.g., Marcus et al., 1985). Apparently, boys are more likely than girls to respond to provocation with aggression, because the situation makes them angrier and because their greater strength means that they are better equipped to fight.

Just because hormones are involved, though, we can't ignore experience. The media is filled with aggressive male models who are rewarded for their behavior. Furthermore, parents are more likely to use physical punishment with sons than with daughters and are more tolerant of aggressive behavior in sons than in daughters (Block, 1978; Condry & Ross, 1985). As we saw in Module 12.4, these are just the sort of experiences that precipitate a vicious cycle of increasing aggression, and this cycle is much more common for boys than girls. Although androgens may make boys more prone to aggression, experiences are more likely to encourage boys than girls to express their aggression.

Emotional Sensitivity. According to the stereotypes listed on pages 332 and 335, girls are better able to express their emotions and interpret others' emotions. In fact, this is a gender difference supported by research (Hall & Halberstadt, 1981). But does greater emotional sensitivity mean that girls are more empathic? Are they better able to experience another person's emotions? Girls are more willing to *admit* to feelings, but generally boys and girls are equally able to feel what others are feeling (Zahn-Waxler et al., 1992), just as the boys and girls in the photo are all concerned by the distressed child.

Most developmentalists believe that the gender difference in emotional sensitivity is largely due to experience. Parents are more "feeling-oriented" with daughters than with sons. They are more likely to talk about emotions with daughters than with sons and to emphasize the importance of considering others' feelings (Fivush, 1991; Zahn-Waxler, Cole, & Barrett, 1991).

Social Influence. Another gender stereotype is that females are more easily influenced by others, more persuadable. In fact, young girls are more likely than young boys to comply with an adult's request and they are more likely to seek an adult's help (Jacklin & Maccoby, 1978). Girls and women are also influenced more than boys and men by persuasive messages and others' behavior, especially when they are under group pressure (Becker, 1986). However, these gender differences may stem from the fact that females may value group harmony more than boys and thus *seem* to give in to others (Miller, Danaher, & Forbes, 1986). For instance, at a meeting to plan a school function, girls are just as likely as boys to recognize the flaws in a bad idea, but girls are more willing to go along simply because they don't want the group to start arguing.

Girls are more easily influenced by others, perhaps because they value group harmony more than boys.

FRANK TALK ABOUT GENDER DIFFERENCES

Let's review the gender differences we've discussed in this module. Research conducted in the 20 years since Maccoby and Jacklin's (1974) landmark work indicates that boys are bigger, stronger, and more active but that girls are healthier; girls excel in verbal ability but boys excel in math and spatial ability; boys are more aggressive but girls understand emotions better and are more readily influenced by others. What should we make of these differences? What do they tell us about the experience of growing up male versus growing up female?

First, remember that the gender differences described in this module represent differences in the *averages* for boys and girls. These differences are all relatively small and are illustrated in the figure. You can see that small differences in group averages mean that boys' and girls' abilities overlap substantially. For example, many girls

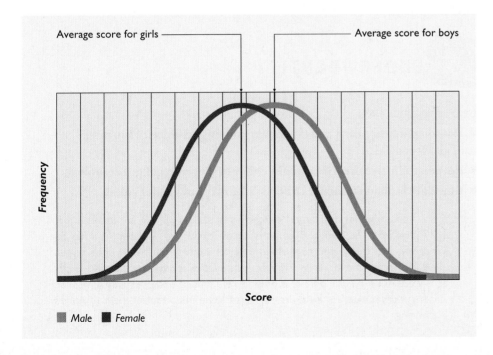

Average score for girls ⎯⎯⎯⎯ | ⎯⎯⎯⎯ Average score for boys

Frequency

Score

■ Male ■ Female

have greater spatial skill than boys; many boys are more susceptible to social influence than girls. A boy who wants to become a writer or a girl who wants to become a mathematician should not be deterred because of small differences in average scores for boys and girls.

At the same time, even small differences in group averages produce substantial differences at the extremes of ability, at the ends of distributions like those shown in the diagram on page 343. Thus, for example, even though the average gender difference in verbal ability is small, there are many more boys with very low ability, which explains why boys are far more likely to have reading or language disabilities.

Second, think about the huge number of abilities, behaviors, and traits that do *not* appear in this module. Boys and girls do not differ in many, many aspects of cognition, personality, and social behavior, a point that is easily lost when focusing on gender differences. In reality, a list of ways that boys and girls are similar is much longer than a list of differences. In cognitive processing, memory, and understanding people—to name just a few areas—boys and girls are much more alike than different. If development is a journey, both boys and girls have many choices as they travel; few if any routes have signs that say, "for girls only" or "for boys only."

Check Your Learning

1. Maccoby and Jacklin found that girls had greater verbal skill, that boys excelled in math and visual-spatial ability, and that boys _____.

2. In physical development and behavior, boys are bigger, stronger, and _____.

3. In math, girls get higher grades but boys _____.

4. Males are more aggressive in laboratory and natural settings, in virtually all cultures and _____.

5. A small average gender difference can still produce large differences in _____.

Answers: (1) were more aggressive, (2) more active, (3) get higher scores on standardized tests, (4) in nonhuman species, (5) the number of boys and girls at the ends of distributions

GENDER IDENTITY

Learning Objectives

- **How do parents, peers, and the media influence children's learning of gender roles?**
- **How do cognitive theories explain children's learning of gender roles?**
- **How does biology influence children's learning of gender roles?**

Anna, who has just turned 4, knows that she's a girl but is convinced that she'll grow up to be a man. Anna plays almost exclusively with boys and her favorite toys are trucks and cars. Anna tells her parents that when she's bigger, she'll grow a beard and will be a daddy. Anna's father is confident that his daughter's ideas are a natural part of a preschoolers' limited understanding of gender, but her mother wonders if they've neglected some important element of Anna's upbringing.

According to the old saying, "Boys will be boys and girls will be girls . . ." but how, in fact, do boys become boys and girls become girls, when it comes to gender roles? That is, how do children acquire their culture's roles for males and females? And how do children develop a sense of identity as a male or female? We'll answer these questions in this module and, as we do, learn whether Anna's wish to grow up to be a man is typical for youngsters her age.

THE SOCIALIZING INFLUENCES OF PEOPLE AND THE MEDIA

Folklore holds that parents and other adults—teachers and television characters, for example—directly shape children's behavior towards the roles associated with their sex. Boys are rewarded for boyish behavior and punished for girlish behavior. The folklore even has a theoretical basis: According to social learning theorists like Albert Bandura (1977, 1986) and Walter Mischel (1970), children learn gender roles in much the same way they learn other social behaviors: through reinforcement and observational learning. Parents and others thus shape appropriate gender roles in children, and children learn what their culture considers appropriate behavior for males and females by simply watching how adults and peers act.

How well does research support social learning theory? The best answer to this question comes from an extensive analysis of 172 studies involving 27,836 children (Lytton & Romney, 1991). The researchers found that parents tend to treat sons and daughters similarly except when it comes to gender-related behavior. That is, parents interact equally with sons and daughters, are equally warm to both, and encourage both sons and daughters to achieve and be independent. But in behavior related to gender roles, parents respond differently to sons and daughters. Activities such as playing with dolls, dressing up, or helping an adult are more often encouraged in daughters than in sons; rough-and-tumble play and playing with blocks are more encouraged in sons than in daughters. Parents also assign sons and daughters different household chores. Daughters tend to be assigned stereotypically female chores such as washing dishes or housecleaning, whereas sons are assigned stereotypically male chores such as taking out the garbage or mowing the lawn (McHale et al., 1990).

Parents treat sons and daughters similarly, except for gender-related behavior.

Fathers are more likely than mothers to treat sons and daughters differently. More than mothers, fathers like the one in the photo often encourage gender-related play. Fathers push their sons more but accept dependence in their daughters (Snow, Jacklin, & Maccoby, 1983). A father, for example, may urge his frightened young son to jump off the diving board ("Be a man!") but not be so insistent with his daughter ("That's okay, honey"). Apparently mothers are more likely to respond based on their knowledge of the individual child's needs, but fathers respond based on gender stereotypes. A mother responds to her son knowing that he's smart but unsure of himself; a father may respond based on what he thinks boys should be like.

After parents, teachers may be the most influential adults in children's lives. Yet we know surprisingly little about the manner in which teachers influence children's learning of gender roles. Two facts do stand out. First, most teachers favor behaviors that are considered feminine—being task oriented, nondisruptive, and perhaps dependent—believing that they contribute to a classroom atmosphere that is more conducive to effective teaching and learning. Teachers encourage both boys and girls to be obedient rather than assertive (Minuchin & Shapiro, 1983). Second, teachers spend more time interacting with boys than girls. Teachers praise boys more for their schoolwork and spend more time scolding them for disruptive classroom behavior (Block, 1983). Teachers' emphasis on obedience and spending more time with boys may promote gender role learning, but researchers have not yet determined how this happens.

Peers. By 3 years, most children's play is gender appropriate—boys prefer blocks and trucks while girls prefer tea sets and dolls—and youngsters are critical of peers who engage in cross-gender play (Langlois & Downs, 1980). This is particularly true of boys who like feminine toys or play at feminine activities. A boy who plays with dolls and a girl like the one in the photo who plays with trucks will both be ignored, teased, or ridiculed by their peers, but the boy more harshly than the girl (Levy, Taylor, & Gelman, 1995). Once children learn rules about gender-typical play, they severely punish peers who violate those rules.

Peers influence gender roles in another way: Between 2 and 3 years of age, children begin to prefer playing with same-sex peers. Little boys play together with cars, and little girls play together with dolls. This preference increases during childhood, reaching a peak in preadolescence. Then the tide begins to turn, but even in adulthood, time spent at work and at leisure is, quite commonly, segregated by gender (Hartup, 1983). Men play sports or cards together; women shop or have lunch together. This tendency for boys to play with boys and girls with girls has several distinctive features (Maccoby, 1990):

- In some cultures, adults select playmates for children. However, in cultures in which children choose playmates, boys select boys as playmates and girls select girls.

- Children spontaneously select same-sex playmates. Adult pressure ("James, why don't you play with John, not Amy") is not necessary.

- Children resist parents' efforts to get them to play with members of the opposite sex. Girls are often unhappy when parents encourage them to play with boys, and boys are unhappy when parents urge them to play with girls.

- Children's reluctance to play with members of the opposite sex is not restricted to gender-typed games, such as playing house or playing with cars. Boys and girls prefer same-sex playmates even in gender-neutral activities such as playing tag or doing puzzles.

Why do boys and girls seem so attracted to same-sex play partners? Eleanor Maccoby (1988, 1990) believes that two factors are critical. First, boys specifically prefer rough-and-tumble play and generally are more competitive and dominating in their interactions. Girls' play is not as rough and is less competitive, so Maccoby argues that boys' style of play may be aversive to girls. Second, when girls and boys play together, girls do not readily influence boys. **Girls' interactions with one another are typically** *enabling*—**their actions and remarks tend to support others and sustain the interaction. In contrast, boy's interactions are often** *constricting*—**one partner tries to emerge as the victor by threatening or contradicting the other, by exaggerating, and so on.** When these styles are brought together, girls find their enabling style is ineffective with boys. The same subtle overtures that work with other girls have no impact on boys. Boys ignore girls' polite suggestions about what to do and ignore girls' efforts to resolve conflicts with discussion.

Regardless of the exact cause, early segregation of playmates by style of play means that boys learn primarily from boys and girls from girls. This helps solidify a youngster's emerging sense of membership in a particular gender group and sharpens the contrast between own gender and other gender.

Boys and girls don't play together often because girls don't like boys' style of play and because girls find that their enabling interaction style is ineffective with boys.

Television. A final source of influence on gender-role learning is television, which often portrays males and females in a stereotyped manner. Women on television tend to be cast in romantic, marital, or family roles; they are depicted as emotional, passive, and weak. Men are more often cast in leadership or professional roles and are depicted as rational, active, and strong (Huston et al., 1992).

What is the impact of these stereotyped portrayals? As you can imagine, children who watch a lot of TV end up with more stereotyped views of males and females. For example, Kimball (1986) studied gender-role stereotypes in a small Canadian town that was located in a valley and could not receive TV programs until a transmitter was installed in 1974. Children's views of personality traits, behaviors, occupations, and peer relations were measured before and after TV was introduced. The graphs show changes in boys' and girls' views on these issues; positive numbers

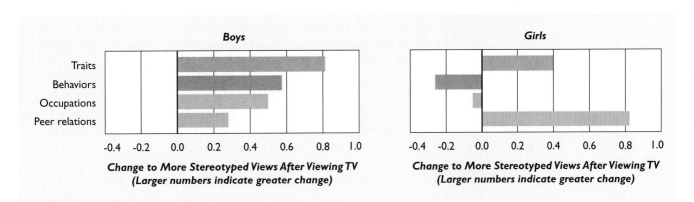

Change to More Stereotyped Views After Viewing TV
(Larger numbers indicate greater change)

indicate a change toward more stereotyped views. Boys' views were more stereotyped on all four dimensions. For example, in their more stereotyped views of occupations, boys now believed that girls could be teachers and cooks whereas boys could be physicians and judges. Girls' views were more stereotyped only for traits and peer relations. After TV was introduced, girls believed that boasting and swearing were characteristic of boys and sharing and helping were characteristic of girls.

Findings like these indicate that TV-viewing causes children to adopt many of the stereotypes that dominate television programming (Signorielli & Lears, 1992). Moreover, the work presented throughout this module on parents, teachers, and peers makes it clear that children learn much about gender roles simply by observing males and females. But simple observation—of real life models or television characters—cannot be the entire explanation. You can see why if you think about young boys growing up. They traditionally have far more opportunities to observe their mother's behavior than their father's, yet boys are more likely to imitate their father (for example, by using hammer and saw) than their mother (for example, by cooking). Thus, an important element in learning about gender is identifying with one gender and then actively seeking out activities that are typical for this gender. This aspect of gender role learning is the focus of cognitive theories, which we'll examine in the next section.

COGNITIVE THEORIES OF GENDER IDENTITY

According to Lawrence Kohlberg (1966; Kohlberg & Ullian, 1974), full understanding of gender develops gradually and involves three elements:

- *Gender labeling:* **By age 2 or 3, children understand that they are either boys or girls and label themselves accordingly.**

- *Gender stability:* **During the preschool years, children begin to understand that gender is stable: Boys become men and girls become women.** However, children in this stage believe that a girl who wears her hair like a boy will become a boy and that a boy who plays with dolls will become a girl (Fagot, 1985).

- *Gender consistency:* **Between 4 and 7 years, most children understand that maleness and femaleness do not change over situations or according to personal wishes.** They understand that a child's sex is unaffected by the clothing that a child wears or the toys that a child likes.

Anna, the 4-year-old in the opening vignette, is in the first stage—she knows that she's a girl. However, she has yet to develop a sense of gender stability or gender consistency. **When children understand labels, stability, and consistency, they have mastered** *gender constancy.*

According to Kohlberg's theory, only children who understand gender constancy should have extensive knowledge of sex-stereotyped activities (Newman, Cooper, & Ruble, 1995). That is, not until children understand that gender is constant do they begin to learn what is appropriate and possible for their gender and what is not, as you'll see in the "Real Children" feature.

Real Children: **LAURA TRADES HER PENIS FOR POMPOMS**

 When my daughter Laura was 2½, she knew that she was a girl but she also insisted that she would grow up to be a daddy. She also claimed that she had a penis, which she would show by pulling her labia away from her body until they were extended about an inch. I have no idea why she did these things, but they clearly document her limited understanding of gender! At about the same time, my son Ben was on a school wrestling team. Laura often went with me to watch Ben wrestle. Afterwards, she thought it was great fun to wrestle on the living room floor, slapping her hand down on the carpet when she pinned me. Never did she comment on the fact that all the wrestlers were boys; evidently this was irrelevant.

By the time she turned 4, Laura's understanding of gender was much better. She knew that she would become a woman and that she did not have a penis. At this age, I remember vividly taking her to watch Ben play football. I wondered if she would become so bored and restless that we'd need to leave. Wrong. Laura immediately discovered the cheerleaders (all girls) and insisted we sit right in front of them. Throughout the game (and the rest of the season), Laura's eyes were riveted to the cheerleaders' every move and when we'd get home, she'd imitate their routines. According to Kohlberg's theory, 4-year-old Laura knew that cheerleading was for girls and that because she was a girl, cheerleading was for her. ■

According to cognitive theories, after children understand that gender is constant, they try to learn more about activities and behaviors typically associated with their gender.

Laura's interest in gender-typical behavior emerged only after she understood gender constancy. You can see this same pattern in findings from research. For example, Martin and Little (1990) measured preschool children's understanding of gender and their knowledge of gender-typed activities (for example, that girls play with dolls and that boys play with airplanes). The youngest children in their study—3½- to 4-year-olds—did not understand gender constancy and they knew little of gender-stereotyped activities. By age 4, children understood gender constancy but still knew little of gender-stereotyped activities. By 4½ years, many children understood gender constancy *and* knew gender-typical and gender-atypical activities. Importantly, there were no children who lacked gender constancy but knew about gender stereotyped activities, a combination that is impossible according to Kohlberg's theory.

Kohlberg's theory specifies *when* children should begin learning about gender-appropriate behavior and activities (once they understand gender constancy) but not *how* such learning takes place. A theory proposed by Martin and Halverson (1987) addresses how children learn about gender. **In *gender-schema theory*, children first decide if an object, activity, or behavior is female or male, then use this information to decide whether or not they should learn more about the object, activity, or behavior.** That is, once children know their gender, they pay attention primarily to experiences and events that are gender-appropriate (Martin & Halverson, 1987). The diagram below illustrates the process: According to gender-schema theory, the preschool boy in the photo who is watching a group of girls playing in sand will decide that playing in sand is for girls and that, because he is a boy, playing in sand is not for him. Seeing a group of older boys playing football, he will decide that football is for boys and, because he is a boy, football is acceptable and he should learn more about it.

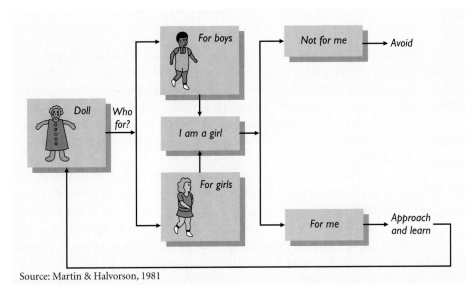

Source: Martin & Halverson, 1981

According to gender-schema theory, after children understand gender, it's as if they see the world through special glasses that allow only gender-typical activities to be in focus (Liben & Signorella, 1993). This selective viewing of the world explains a great deal about children's learning of gender roles, but as we'll see in the next section, there is one final important element that needs to be considered.

BIOLOGICAL INFLUENCES

A fertilized human egg has 23 pairs of chromosomes. If the 23rd pair includes an X and a Y chromosome, then testes develop about 6 weeks after conception; if the 23rd pair includes two X chromosomes, then ovaries appear about 10 weeks after conception. During prenatal development, the testes and ovaries secrete hormones that regulate the formation of male and female genitals and some features of the central nervous system. This raises an obvious question: Do these hormones also contribute to gender differences in behavior and, in turn, social roles? As you can imagine, this question is not easy to answer because scientists cannot experiment directly with hormones as they are secreted during prenatal development. We do know that hormones are a factor in gender differences in aggressive behavior; however, their role in other gender-based differences in behavior is less clear.

Let's look at some evidence that supports a role for biological influence:

■ On questionnaires that measure instrumental traits associated with males (such as being independent, self-confident, aggressive) and expressive traits associated with females (such as being emotional, creative, considerate), identical twins' answers are more similar than fraternal twins' answers (Mitchell, Baker, & Jacklin, 1989). This result suggests that how expressive or instrumental a child is depends, in part, on heredity.

■ During prenatal development the adrenal glands sometimes malfunction and, as a result, some females are inadvertently exposed to unusually large amounts of male hormones, such as androgen. In growing up, some of these girls prefer masculine activities (such as playing with cars instead of dolls) and male playmates to a much greater extent than girls not exposed to these amounts of androgen (Berenbaum & Snyder, 1995; Collaer & Hines, 1995), which suggests that androgen influences the development of masculine traits.

Neither of these findings provides ironclad evidence that biology promotes children's learning of gender roles. The studies of twins, at best, suggest hereditary influence but don't tell how biology promotes learning of gender roles. The studies of prenatal exposure to androgen are not completely convincing because the levels of hormone are so much greater than normal that it's risky to extrapolate from these higher-than-normal amounts to make judgments about normal hormone levels.

During prenatal development, the testes and ovaries secrete hormones that affect the development of the nervous system and, perhaps, sex differences in behavior.

Perhaps the most accurate conclusion to draw is that biology, the socializing influence of people and media, and the child's own efforts to understand gender-typical behavior all contribute to gender roles and differences. Recognizing the interactive nature of these influences on gender learning also enables us to better understand how gender roles are changing today, which is the focus of the next module.

Check Your Learning

1. Parents treat sons and daughters similarly except when it comes to _____.

2. Same-sex play is common because most girls don't enjoy boys' rough-and-tumble play and because _____.

3. According to cognitive theories, children want to learn about gender-typical activities only after _____.

4. Some girls exposed to large amounts of male hormones during prenatal development _____.

Answers: (1) gender-related behavior, (2) girls find that their enabling style of interaction is ineffective with boys, (3) they have learned that gender is constant, (4) prefer masculine activities and male playmates

GENDER ROLES IN TRANSITION

Learning Objectives

- **What is androgyny and how is it related to traditional conceptions of masculinity and femininity?**
- **Can parents rear gender-neutral children?**

Meda and Perry have lived together since the early 1970s when both were active in protests against the war in Vietnam. Their daughter, Hope, is now 6 years old. True to their countercultural roots, both Meda and Perry want their daughter to pick activities, friends, and, ultimately, a career, based on her interests and abilities, not on her gender. They have done their best to encourage gender-neutral values and behavior. Both are therefore astonished that Hope seems to be totally indistinguishable from other 6-year-olds reared by conventional parents. Hope's close friends are all girls. When Hope is together with her friends, they play house or play with dolls. What seems to be going wrong with Meda and Perry's plans for a gender-neutral girl?

Gender roles are not etched in stone; they change with the times. In the United States, the range of acceptable roles for girls and boys and women and men has never been greater than today. For example, fathers like the man in the photo stay home to be the primary caregivers for children, and some women work full time as sole support for the family. What is the impact of these changes on children? In this module, we'll answer this question by looking at new gender roles and at efforts by parents like Meda and Perry to rear gender-neutral children.

EMERGING GENDER ROLES

Traditionally, masculinity and femininity were seen as ends of a continuum: Children possessing many of the traits associated with males were considered highly masculine, and youngsters possessing many of the traits associated with females were considered highly feminine. A newer view of gender roles is based on the independent dimensions of instrumentality and expressiveness that were described in Module 13.1 (Bem, 1984). In this view, traditional males are rated high on instrumentality but low on expressiveness whereas traditional females are low on instrumentality but high on expressiveness. In other words, this approach recognizes that other combinations of traits are possible. ***Androgynous* persons are rated high on both the instrumental and expressive dimensions.** (The term *androgyny* originated from the Greek words for male, *andro,* and female, *gyn.*) That is, androgynous individuals combine many of the traits listed in the table on page 332: They can be both independent and emotional, self-confident and considerate, ambitious and creative.

Many theorists (e.g., Bem, 1984) argue that the ability to react with both instrumental and expressive behaviors is psychologically healthier than reacting primarily with one or the other. In fact, androgynous children often have higher self-esteem than children whose gender roles are highly stereotyped (Markstrom-Adams, 1989). However, the benefits of androgyny are greater for girls than for boys. Androgynous girls have higher self-esteem than expressive girls. For example, a girl like the one in the photo, who is independent and ambitious as well as considerate and creative, is more likely to feel positive about herself than a girl who embodies only the expressive traits traditionally associated with females. However, highly instrumental boys have nearly as high self-esteem as androgynous boys (Lau, 1989).

Evidently, a balance of expressiveness and instrumentality may be especially adaptive across life's many tasks. Being independent and confident has benefits at home and work but so does being kind and considerate. However, teaching children to adopt nontraditional views of gender is no simple task, as we'll see in the next section.

BEYOND TRADITIONAL GENDER ROLES

Many researchers (e.g., Bem, 1989; Eagly, 1995) believe gender is overemphasized to children. They think gender should be linked strictly to reproductive function instead of, as now, to traits, behaviors, and abilities. Is this possible? Apparently children can learn less stereotyped views of gender, at least in the short run. In one study (Bigler & Liben, 1990), some 6- to 11-year-olds were taught how to decide if a person can perform a particular job or occupation. They were told that the person's gender was not relevant; instead, they should decide if the person would like to do at least some of the activities that are part of the job and if

Children can be taught to have fewer stereotypes about males and females, but it's more difficult to change boys' and girls' style of play and their preference for same-sex playmates.

the person has some of the skills necessary for the job. For example, to be a construction worker, a person should like to build things and should know how to drive heavy machinery. When tested later on their attitudes toward household activities and occupations, these children had significantly fewer stereotyped responses than children who had not been taught to think of occupations in terms of interests and skills.

Short-term interventions like the one just described show that more balanced attitudes and behaviors *are* possible (Gash & Morgan, 1993). But accomplishing change over the long-term in a natural setting may be more complicated, based on some results of the Family Lifestyles Project (Weisner & Wilson-Mitchell, 1990). This research examined families whose adults were members of the 1960s and 1970s counterculture and deeply committed to rearing their children without traditional gender stereotypes. In these families, men and women shared the household, financial, and child-care tasks.

According to results from the Family Lifestyle Project, parents like Meda and Perry in the opening vignette can influence some aspects of gender stereotyping more readily than others. The children studied in the Family Lifestyles Project have few stereotypes about occupations: They agree that girls can be president of the United States and drive trucks and that boys can be nurses and secretaries. They also have fewer stereotyped attitudes about use of objects: They claim that boys and girls are equally likely to use an iron, a shovel, hammer and nails, and needle and thread. Nevertheless, children in these families tend to have same-sex friends, and they like gender-stereotyped activities: The boys enjoy physical play and the girls enjoy drawing and reading.

It should not surprise you that some features of gender roles and identities are more readily influenced by experience than others. For 250,000 years, homo sapiens have existed in small groups of families, hunting animals and gathering vegetation. Women have borne the children and cared for them. Over the course of human history, it has been adaptive for women to be caring and nurturing because, as we saw in Module 10.3, this increases the odds of a secure attachment and, ultimately, the survival of the infant. Men's responsibilities included protecting the family unit from predators and hunting with other males, roles for which physical strength and aggressiveness were crucial.

Circumstances of life at the end of the 20th century are, of course, substantially different. Nevertheless, the cultural changes of the past few decades cannot erase hundreds of thousands of years of evolutionary history (Kenrick, 1987). It should not be surprising, then, that boys and girls have different styles of play, that girls tend to be more supportive in their interactions with others, and that boys are usually more aggressive.

The "Making Children's Lives Better" feature suggests ways children can be helped to go beyond traditional gender roles and learn the best from both roles.

Making Children's Lives Better: ENCOURAGING VALUABLE TRAITS—NOT GENDER TRAITS

 Parents and other adults can encourage children to learn the best from both of the traditional gender roles. Being independent, confident, caring, and considerate are valuable traits for all people, not just boys or girls. Here are some guidelines to help achieve these aims:

1. Since children learn gender roles from those around them, parents should be sure that they themselves are not gender-bound. Mothers and fathers can mow lawns, make repairs, and work outside the home. Mothers and fathers can prepare meals, do laundry, and care for the young.

2. Don't base decisions about children's toys, activities, and chores on the child's sex. Decide if a toy, activity, or chore is appropriate for the child as an individual (based on age, talent, and interests), not because the child is a boy or girl.

3. Forces outside the home, such as media and teachers, often work against parents who want their children to go beyond traditional gender roles. It's neither feasible nor wise to shelter children from these influences, but you can encourage them to think critically about others' gender-based decisions. When teachers have boys and girls form separate lines to go to lunch, ask children why this segregation by gender makes sense. When a TV program shows a man coming to aid the stereotypic damsel in distress, ask the child why the woman simply didn't get herself out of her predicament. ▣

Check Your Learning

1. Androgynous children tend to have higher self-esteem than children with highly stereotyped gender roles, but this difference is found primarily among _____ .

2. In the Family Lifestyles Project, parents' efforts to rear gender-neutral children have been most successful when it comes to _____ .

Answers: (1) girls, (2) children's views of occupations and objects

GENDER ROLES IN PERSPECTIVE

People play many roles in their lives but few are cast as early or are as significant as gender. We saw, in Module 13.1, that Americans have well-defined stereotypes for males and females and that children learn these stereotypes early. Yet, we discovered in Module 13.2 that in terms of cognition, personality, and social behavior, boys and girls are generally more alike than different. In Module 13.3, we found that children learn gender roles through a combination of social forces (parents, for example), self-study, and biology. Finally, in Module 13.4, we found that efforts to rear children without traditional gender roles have been moderately successful.

Research on gender illustrates the theme that *development in different domains is connected.* Think about how children learn gender roles. According to conventional wisdom, children acquire masculine or feminine traits and behaviors through a process of socialization by parents and other knowledgeable persons in the child's culture. These processes are important, but we saw that learning gender roles is not simply a social phenomenon: Cognitive processes are essential. Kohlberg's theory shows that children don't really begin to learn about gender until they understand that they will remain a boy or girl for life; once they understand gender constancy, gender-schema theory shows how children use this information to decide which experiences are relevant to them. Biology apparently contributes, too, although we still don't really understand how. Biology, cognition, and social forces all shape the unique gender role that individual boys or girls play.

THINKING ABOUT DEVELOPMENT

1. Examine the traits listed in the table on page 335. How might Piaget have explained the differences between 5- and 11-year-olds' responses?

2. According to Hedges and Nowell's (1995) results, described in the "Focus on Research" feature on pages 339–340, gender differences in reading, writing, and math have not become smaller in the past quarter century. One interpretation of this finding is that gender stereotypes have not changed much over this period of time. What could be done to encourage boys towards more reading and writing and girls towards more math?

3. Television depicts men and women in stereotyped roles that do not accurately reflect the real range of roles that men and women fill in American society. What could you do to help children understand that television's portrayal of men and women is distorted?

4. The women's liberation movement became a powerful social force in America during the 1960s. Describe how you might do research to determine if and how the movement has changed the gender roles that young children learn.

SEE FOR YOURSELF

To see that older children know more about gender stereotypes and understand that stereotypes are not binding, you'll need to create some simple stories that illustrate stereotyped traits. You could create stories for any of the traits listed in the tables on pages 332 and 335, but I suggest that you use "independent," "confident," "appreciative," and "gentle." Each story should include two to three sentences that describe a child. Be sure that your stories contain no other clues that would hint that the child in the story is a boy or a girl. For example, this story illustrates "independent":

> *I know a child who likes to do things without help from adults. This child likes to do homework without help and enjoys traveling alone to visit cousins who live in another city.*

Read your stories to some 11- and 12-year-olds. After you've read each story, ask, "Is this child a boy, a girl, or could it be either?" Record the reply, then ask, "Would most people think that the child is a boy or would most think that the child is a girl?"

In the first question, you're measuring children's understanding that gender stereotypes are flexible. You should find that children answer with "either one" about half of the time, indicating that they believe in some, but not total, flexibility in gender stereotypes. In the second question, you're measuring children's awareness of gender stereotypes. You should find that most children always answer the second question stereotypically: that people would identify the independent and confident children as boys and the appreciative and gentle children as girls. See for yourself!

RESOURCES

For more information about . . .

gender stereotypes and gender differences, try Carol Tavris's *The Mismeasure of Women* (Simon and Schuster, 1992) in which the author argues that women are constantly being measured according to standards developed for men

resources for women in education and in the workplace, contact the American Association of University Women, 1-800-225-9998

ways to encourage girls and young women to pursue interests in science, math, and technology, visit the Web site of the Advocates for Women in Science, Engineering, and Mathematics (AWSEM), http://wwide.com/awsem.html

KEY TERMS

androgens *342*	**gender consistency** *348*	**gender stereotypes** *332*
androgynous *352*	**gender constancy** *348*	**instrumental traits** *333*
constricting *347*	**gender labeling** *348*	**mental rotation** *340*
enabling *347*	**gender-schema theory** *349*	**social role** *331*
expressive traits *333*	**gender stability** *348*	

UMMARY

MODULE 13.1:
GENDER STEREOTYPES

HOW DO WE VIEW MEN AND WOMEN?
Instrumental traits describe individuals acting on the world and are usually associated with males. Expressive traits describe individuals who value interpersonal relationships and are usually associated with females.

LEARNING GENDER STEREOTYPES
By age 5, children have begun to learn some of the traits typically associated with males and females; by 11 years, children's knowledge of these traits is very similar to adults' knowledge. Older children also understand that stereotypes are not necessarily binding.

MODULE 13.2:
DIFFERENCES RELATED TO GENDER

In *The Psychology of Sex Differences,* published in 1974, Eleanor Maccoby and Carol Jacklin concluded that males and females differed

in only four areas—verbal ability, spatial ability, math achievement, and aggression. Subsequent investigators have used their work as the starting point for analyses of gender differences.

DIFFERENCES IN PHYSICAL DEVELOPMENT AND BEHAVIOR
Boys tend to be bigger, stronger, and more active than girls, who tend to have better fine-motor coordination and to be healthier.

DIFFERENCES IN INTELLECTUAL ABILITIES AND ACHIEVEMENT
Girls excel in verbal skills whereas boys excel in mathematics, and the size of these differences has remained the same over the past few decades. Boys have better spatial skill than girls. Each of these differences is thought to reflect some combination of hereditary and environmental factors.

DIFFERENCES IN PERSONALITY AND SOCIAL BEHAVIOR
Boys are more aggressive than girls, and biology probably contributes heavily to this difference. Girls are more sensitive to others' feelings

and are more influenced by others; both differences are probably due to experience.

FRANK TALK ABOUT GENDER DIFFERENCES

Most gender differences are fairly small, which means that abilities for boys and girls overlap considerably. Nevertheless, small differences in average performance can mean fairly large differences at the extremes of ability. Also, despite the emphasis on gender differences, boys and girls are quite similar in many aspects of cognition, personality, and social behavior.

MODULE 13.3:
GENDER IDENTITY

THE SOCIALIZING INFLUENCES OF PEOPLE AND THE MEDIA

Parents treat sons and daughters similarly, except in gender-related behavior. Fathers may be particularly important in teaching about gender, because they are more likely to treat sons and daughters differently. Teachers value feminine behaviors but devote more time to boys.

By the preschool years, peers discourage cross-gender play by ridiculing peers who do it. Peers also influence gender roles because children play almost exclusively with same-sex peers.

Television depicts men and women in stereotyped fashion, and children who watch a lot of television are likely to have very stereotyped views of men and women.

COGNITIVE THEORIES OF GENDER IDENTITY

According to Kohlberg's theory, children gradually learn that gender is constant over time and cannot be changed according to personal wishes. After children understand gender constancy, they begin to learn gender-typical behavior. According to gender-schema theory, children learn about gender by paying attention to behaviors of members of their own sex and ignoring behaviors of members of the other sex.

BIOLOGICAL INFLUENCES

The idea that biology influences some aspects of gender roles is supported by twin studies and by research on females exposed to male hormones during prenatal development.

MODULE 13.4:
GENDER ROLES IN TRANSITION

EMERGING GENDER ROLES

Androgynous persons embody both instrumental and expressive traits. Androgynous girls have higher self-esteem than traditional girls; androgynous boys have about the same level of self-esteem as traditional boys.

BEYOND TRADITIONAL GENDER ROLES

Training studies show that children can learn less stereotyped views of gender, but studies of parents trying to rear gender-neutral children suggest that many stereotyped behaviors are difficult to change.

Family Relationships

AMILY. THE TERM IS AS SACRED TO MOST AMERICANS AS BASEBALL, APPLE PIE, AND CHEVROLET. BUT WHAT COMES TO MIND WHEN YOU THINK OF FAMILY? TELEVISION GIVES US ONE ANSWER—FROM *LEAVE IT TO BEAVER* TO *FAMILY TIES* TO *MARRIED WITH Children,* the American family is portrayed as a mother, father, and 2 or 3 children. In reality, of course, American families are as diverse as the people in them. Some families consist of a single parent and an only child. Others include two parents, many children, and grandparents or other relatives.

All of these family configurations, however, have a common goal: nurturing children and helping them become full-fledged adult members of their culture. To learn how families achieve these goals, we'll begin, in Module 14.1, by looking at relationships between parents and children. Next, in Module 14.2, we'll look at relationships between siblings. Then, in Module 14.3, we'll consider how children are influenced by divorce and remarriage. Finally, in Module 14.4, we'll examine the forces that can cause parents to abuse their children.

PARENTING

Learning Objectives

■ **What are the primary dimensions of parenting?**

■ **What parental behaviors affect children's development?**

■ **What role do culture and family configuration play in children's development?**

■ **How do children help determine how parents rear them?**

> *Tanya and Sheila, both sixth graders, wanted to go to a Smashing Pumpkins concert with two boys from their school. When Tanya asked if she could go, her mom said, "No way!" Tanya responded defiantly, "Why not?" In return, her mother exploded, "Because I say so. That's why. Stop pestering me." Sheila wasn't allowed to go either. When she asked why, her mom said, "I just think you're still too young to be dating. I don't mind your going to the concert. If you want to go just with Tanya, that would be fine. What do you think of that?"*

Were your parents like Tanya's, strict and controlling? Or did they encourage discussion, like Sheila's? Did your parents hug and kiss you often? Or were they more reserved? Did your parents often tell you exactly what to do? Or did they let you do what you wanted to do? Your answers to these questions give a glimpse of your parents' child-rearing style. We'll begin this module by describing different parenting styles that researchers have discovered.

DIMENSIONS AND STYLES

Parenting can be described in terms of general dimensions that are like personality traits in that they represent stable aspects of parental behavior—aspects that hold across different situations. One general dimension of parental behavior is the degree of warmth and responsiveness that parents show their children. Another is the amount of control parents exert over their children.

Let's look first at warmth and responsiveness. At one end of the spectrum are parents who are openly warm and affectionate with their children. They are involved with them, respond to their emotional needs, and spend considerable time with them. At the other end of the spectrum are parents who are relatively uninvolved with and sometimes even hostile towards their children. These parents often seem more focused on their own needs and interests than their children's. Warm parents enjoy hearing their children describe the day's activities; uninvolved or hostile parents aren't interested, considering it a waste of their time. Warm parents see when their children are upset and try to comfort them; uninvolved or hostile parents pay little attention to their children's emotional states and invest little effort comforting them when they're upset.

As you might expect, children benefit from warm and responsive parenting. When parents are warm towards them, children typically feel secure, happy, and are better behaved. In contrast, when parents are uninvolved or hostile, their children are often anxious and less controlled. And, as we saw in Module 11.2, children often have low self-esteem when their parents are uninvolved (Rothbaum & Weisz, 1994).

A second general dimension of parental behavior concerns the control that parents exercise over their children's behavior. At one end of this spectrum are controlling, demanding parents. These parents virtually run

Children benefit from warm, responsive parenting and from a moderate amount of parental control.

their children's lives. Overcontrol is shown by parents who always want to know where their teenagers are and what they are doing. At the other end of the spectrum are parents who make few demands and rarely exert control. Their children are free to do almost anything without fear of parental reproach. Undercontrol is illustrated by parents who never want to know where their teenagers are or what they are doing.

Neither of these extremes is desirable. Overcontrol is unsatisfactory because it deprives children of the opportunity to meet behavioral standards on their own, which is the ultimate goal of socialization. Teenagers who constantly "report in" never learn to make decisions for themselves (e.g., "Should I go to this party with people that I don't know really well?"). Parenting without any control fails because children aren't shown the behavioral standards that their culture has for them. Teenagers who never "report in" believe that they need not account for their behavior, which is definitely not true in the long run.

Parents need to strike a balance, maintaining adequate control while still allowing children freedom to make some decisions for themselves. This is often easier said than done, but a good starting point is setting standards that are appropriate for the child's age, then showing the child how to meet them, and, finally, rewarding him or her for complying (Powers & Roberts, 1995; Rotto & Kratochwill, 1994). Suppose a mother wants her preschooler to fold and put away her socks. This is a reasonable request because the child is physically capable of this simple task and she knows where the socks should be stored. Like the mother in the photo, she should show her daughter how to complete the task, and then praise her when she does.

Once standards are set, they should be enforced consistently. Time and time again, research has shown that children and adolescents are more compliant when parents enforce rules regularly. For example, a mother should insist that her son pick up his toys every night, not just occasionally. When parents enforce rules erratically, children come to see rules as optional instead of obligatory and they try to avoid complying with them (Conger, Patterson, & Ge, 1995).

Another element of effective control is communication. Parents should explain why they've set standards and why they reward or punish as they do. The mother should explain to her son that a messy room is unsafe, makes it difficult to find toys that he wants, and makes it difficult for her to clean. Parents can also encourage children to ask questions if they don't understand or disagree with standards. If the son feels that his mother's standards for orderliness are so high that it's impossible to play in his room, he should feel free to raise the issue with his mother without fear of making her angry.

A balanced approach to control—based on age-appropriate standards, consistency, and communication—avoids the problems associated with overcontrol because the expectations more likely reflect the child's level of maturity and they are open to discussion. A balanced approach also avoids the problems of undercontrol because standards are set and parents expect children to meet those standards consistently.

Parenting Styles. Combining the dimensions of warmth and control results in four prototypic styles of parenting, as shown in the graph (Baumrind, 1975, 1991).

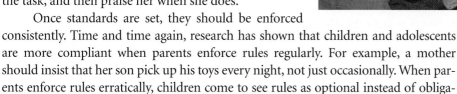

Parental Control

	High	Low
High	Authoritative	Indulgent-Permissive
Low	Authoritarian	Indifferent-Uninvolved

Parental Involvement

- *Authoritarian parenting* **combines high control with little warmth.** These parents lay down the rules and expect them to be followed without discussion or argument. Hard work, respect, and obedience are what authoritarian parents wish to cultivate in their children. There is little give-and-take between parent and child because authoritarian parents do not balance their demands in light of children's needs or wishes. This style is illustrated by Tanya's mother in the opening vignette. Like the mother in the photo, Tanya's mother felt no obligation whatsoever to explain why she would not allow Tanya to attend the concert.

- *Authoritative parenting* **combines a fair degree of parental control with being warm and responsive to children.** Authoritative parents give explanations for rules and encourage discussion. This style is exemplified by Sheila's mother in the opening vignette. She explained why she did not want Sheila going to the concert and encouraged her daughter to discuss the issue with her.

- *Indulgent-permissive parenting* **offers warmth and caring but little parental control.** These parents tend to accept their children's behavior and punish them infrequently. An indulgent-permissive parent would readily agree to Tanya or Sheila's request to go to the concert, simply because it is something the child wants to do.

- *Indifferent-uninvolved parenting* **provides neither warmth nor control.** Indifferent-uninvolved parents provide for their children's basic physical and emotional needs but little else. They try to minimize the amount of time spent with their children and avoid becoming emotionally involved with them. If Tanya or Sheila had parents with this style, she might have simply gone to the concert without asking, knowing that her parents wouldn't care and would rather not be bothered.

Parenting style is fairly stable over time. Parents who are authoritative with their school-age children tend to be authoritative when their children are adolescents (McNally, Eisenberg, & Harris, 1991). Given this stability, you shouldn't be surprised to learn that parenting style influences children's development (Baumrind, 1991; Maccoby & Martin, 1983):

- Children with authoritarian parents typically have lower grades in school, lower self-esteem, and are less skilled socially.

- Children with authoritative parents tend to have higher grades and be responsible, self-reliant, and friendly.

- Children with indulgent-permissive parents have lower grades and are often impulsive and easily frustrated.

- Children with indifferent-uninvolved parents have low self-esteem and are impulsive, aggressive, and moody.

Many of these outcomes are illustrated in a study by Lamborn and her colleagues (1991) that examined the influence of parenting style on high-school students' psychosocial development and school performance. The graphs show very consistent patterns: Adolescents with authoritative parents have the best scores on all measures:

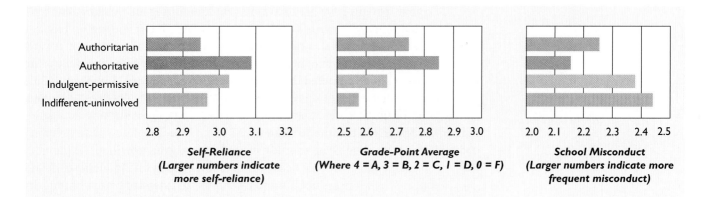

They are the most self-reliant, have the best grades, and misbehave the least in school. Adolescents with indifferent-uninvolved parents tend to be at the other extreme: They are lower in self-reliance, have the lowest grades, and are the most likely to be involved in school misconduct.

Adolescents with either authoritarian or indulgent-permissive parents are in between the other groups on most measures. Adolescents with authoritarian parents were the least self-reliant of all four groups; but in grades and school misconduct, they ranked behind adolescents with authoritative parents. Adolescents with indulgent-permissive parents were nearly as self-reliant as children of authoritative parents, but their grades were lower and they were more likely to be involved in school misconduct.

Authoritative parenting fosters children's school achievement, self-reliance, and conduct.

The links between parenting style and self-reliance, grades, and school misconduct are similar for African, Asian, European, and Hispanic Americans and are similar for boys and girls. Authoritative parenting is consistently associated with positive outcomes for all groups. In short, a parenting style that combines control, warmth, and affection seems to be best for children and adolescents (Lamborn et al., 1991; Steinberg et al., 1992).

As important as these different dimensions and styles are for understanding parenting, there is more to effective child rearing, as we'll see in the next section.

PARENTAL BEHAVIOR

Dimensions and styles are general characterizations of how parents typically behave. If, for example, I describe a parent as warm or controlling, you immediately have a sense of that parent's usual style in dealing with his or her children. Nevertheless, the price for such a broad description is that it tells us little about how parents behave in specific situations and how these parental behaviors influence children's development. Put another way, what specific behaviors can parents use to influence their children? Social cognitive theorists name two: feedback and modeling.

Feedback. By providing feedback to their children, parents can indicate whether a behavior is appropriate and should continue or is inappropriate and should stop. Feedback comes in two general forms. *Reinforcement* **is any action that increases**

the likelihood of the response that it follows. Parents may use praise to reinforce a child's studying or give a reward for completing household chores. ***Punishment* is any action that discourages the reoccurrence of the response that it follows.** Parents may forbid children to watch television when they get poor grades in school or make children go to bed early for neglecting household chores.

Of course, parents have been rewarding and punishing their children for centuries, so what do psychologists know that parents don't know already? In fact, researchers have made some surprising discoveries concerning the nature of reward and punishment. **Parents often unwittingly reinforce the very behaviors they want to discourage, a situation called the *negative reinforcement trap*** (Patterson, 1980). The negative reinforcement trap occurs in three steps, most often between a mother and her son. In the first step, the mother tells her son to do something he doesn't want to do. She might tell him to clean up his room, to come inside while he's outdoors playing with friends, or to study instead of watching television. In the next step, the son responds with some behavior that most parents find intolerable: He argues, complains, or whines—not just briefly, but for an extended period of time. In the last step, the mother gives in—saying that the son needn't do as she told him initially—simply to get the son to stop the behavior that is so intolerable.

The feedback to the son is that arguing (or complaining or whining) works; the mother rewards that behavior by withdrawing the request that the son did not like. That is, although we usually think a behavior is strengthened when it is followed by the presentation of something that is valued, behavior is also strengthened when it is followed by the removal of something that is disliked.

Most forms of punishment are ineffective because they only suppress behavior temporarily and have undesirable side effects.

As for punishment, research shows that it is not very effective in changing children's behavior. Why? Punishment is primarily suppressive: Punished responses are stopped, but only temporarily if children do not learn new behaviors to replace those that were punished. For example, denying TV to brothers who are fighting stops the undesirable behavior, but fighting is likely to recur unless the boys learn new ways of solving their disputes.

Punishment can also have undesirable side effects. Children become upset as they are being punished, which makes it unlikely that they will understand the feedback punishment is meant to convey. A child denied TV for misbehaving may become angry over the punishment per se and ignore *why* he's being punished. Furthermore, as we saw in Module 12.4, when children are punished physically, they often imitate this behavior with others, including peers and younger siblings (Whitehurst & Vasta, 1977). Children who are spanked often use aggression to resolve their disputes with others.

However, at least one form of punishment is relatively effective. **In *time-out*, a child who misbehaves must briefly sit alone in a quiet, unstimulating location.** Some parents have children sit alone in a bathroom; others have children sit in a corner of a room, as shown in the photo. Time-out is punishing because it interrupts the child's ongoing activity and isolates the child from other family members, toys, books, and, generally, all forms of rewarding stimulation. The period is sufficiently brief—usually just a few minutes—for a parent to use the method consistently. During time-out, both parent and child typically calm down. Then, when time-out is over, a parent can talk with the child and explain why the punished behavior was objectionable and what the child should do instead. "Reasoning" like this—even with preschool children—is effective because it emphasizes why a parent punished initially and how punishment can be avoided in the future.

Learning by Observing. Children learn a great deal from parents simply by watching them. For example, in Module 12.4 we saw that youngsters often learn how to interact with others by watching how their parents interact. The parents' modeling and the youngsters' observational learning thus leads to imitation, so children's behavior resembles the behavior they observe. **Observational learning can also produce** *counterimitation,* **learning what should not be done.** If an older sibling kicks a friend and parents punish the older sibling, the younger child may learn not to kick others.

Sometimes observational learning leads to *disinhibition,* **an increase in all behaviors like those observed.** Children who watch their parents shouting angrily, for example, are more likely to yell at or push a younger sibling. In other words, observation can lead to a general increase in aggression, or put still another way, aggressive responses became disinhibited. **The opposite effect, in which an entire class of behaviors is made less likely, is known as** *inhibition.* Returning to an earlier example, the child who sees parents punish an older sibling for kicking may be less likely to hit or push a friend. Aggressive responses in general become inhibited.

In sum, parents can influence children by giving feedback (rewards and punishments), by modeling behavior that they value and *not* modeling what they don't want their children to learn, and through the parenting styles that we examined in the first section of this module. In the next section, we'll see how these general principles are influenced by culture.

CULTURAL INFLUENCES AND FAMILY CONFIGURATION

The general aim of child rearing—helping children become contributing members of their cultures—is much the same worldwide (Whiting & Child, 1953). However, cultures differ in their views of the best ways to achieve this goal. And, within cultures, families do not always consist of a mother, father, and their children; different family configurations can influence child-rearing practices. We'll look at some of these variations in values and practices in this section.

Cultural Differences in Warmth and Control. Warmth and control are universal aspects of parents' behavior, but views about the "proper" amount of warmth and the "proper" amount of control are specific to particular cultures. European Americans want their children to be happy and self-reliant individuals, and they believe these goals can best be achieved when parents are warm and exert moderate control (Goodnow, 1992; Spence, 1985). In many Asian and Latin American countries, however, individualism is less important than cooperation and collaboration (Okagaki & Sternberg, 1993). In China, for example, Confucian principles dictate that parents are always right and that emotional restraint is the key to family harmony (Chao, 1994). Accordingly, we would expect to find that Chinese parents are not as warm towards their children and are more controlling than their American counterparts. Lin and Fu (1990) found exactly this pattern, as shown in the graphs on page 366. Compared to mothers and fathers in the United States, mothers and fathers in China were more likely to emphasize parental control and less likely to express their affection.

Also shown in the graphs on page 366 are the results for a third group studied by Lin and Fu—Chinese parents who emigrated from Taiwan to live in the United States, where their children were born. The findings for this group were between the

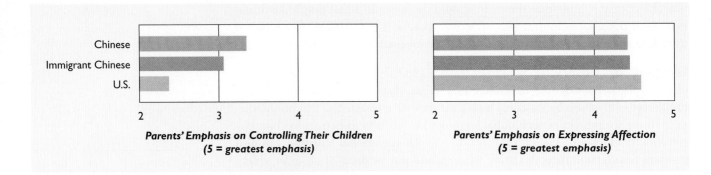

other groups on both warmth and control. That is, immigrant Chinese parents were less controlling than Taiwanese parents but more controlling than U.S. parents. They were also warmer towards their children than Taiwanese parents but not as warm as U.S. parents. Both results suggest that the immigrant group was gradually becoming assimilated into U.S. culture.

Thus, Lin and Fu's study shows that Chinese parents' behavior is consistent with the Confucian principles that are central to traditional Chinese culture, and European American parents' behavior reflects long-standing American beliefs in the importance of individualism and self-reliance. Cultural values help specify appropriate ways for parents to interact with their offspring.

The Role of Grandparents. In many cultures around the world, grandparents play important roles in children's lives. One influential analysis suggested five specific styles of grandparenting (Neugarten & Weinstein, 1964):

- *Formal grandparents* express strong interest in the grandchild but maintain a hands-off attitude toward child rearing.

- *Fun-seeking grandparents* see themselves as a primary source of fun for their grandchildren but avoid more serious interactions.

- *Distant grandparents* have little contact with children, except as part of holidays or other family celebrations.

- *Dispensing-family-wisdom grandparents* provide information and advice to parents and child alike.

- *Surrogate-parent grandparents* assume many of the normal roles and responsibilities of a parent.

Of these different styles, we know the most about the surrogate-parent style because it is particularly common in African American families. The "Cultural Influences" feature describes the important role of grandmothers in African American family life.

Cultural Influences: GRANDMOTHERS IN AFRICAN AMERICAN FAMILIES

Approximately 1 in 8 African American children live with their grandmothers, compared to only 1 in 25 European American children (U.S. Bureau of the Census, 1994). Why? A quarter of all African American children grow up in chronic poverty and living with relatives is one way of sharing—and thereby reducing—the costs associated with housing and child care.

African American grandmothers who live with their daughter and her children frequently become involved in rearing their grandchildren, adopting the surrogate-parent style (Pearson et al., 1990). When the daughter is a teenage mother, the grandmother may be the child's primary caregiver, an arrangement that benefits both the adolescent mother and the child. Freed from the obligations of child rearing, the adolescent mother is able to improve her situation by, for example, finishing school. The child benefits because grandmothers are often more effective mothers than teenage mothers: Grandmothers are less punitive and, like the grandmother in the photo, very responsive to their grandchildren (Chase-Lansdale, Brooks-Gunn, & Zamsky, 1994; Wilson, 1989).

This family arrangement works well for children. In terms of achievement and adjustment, children living with their mothers and grandmothers resemble children living in two-parent families, and they tend to be better off than children in single-parent families (Wilson, 1989). Even when grandmothers are not living in the house, children benefit when their mothers receive social and emotional support from grandmothers and other relatives: Children are more self-reliant and less likely to become involved in delinquent activities such as drug use and vandalism (Taylor & Roberts, 1995).

Thus, grandmothers and other relatives can ease the burden of child rearing in African American families living in poverty, and not surprisingly, children benefit from the added warmth, support, and guidance of an extended family. ■

Children of Gay and Lesbian Parents. More than a million youngsters in the United States have a gay or lesbian parent. In most of these situations, children were born in a heterosexual marriage that ended in divorce when one parent revealed his or her homosexuality. Less frequent, but becoming more common, are children born to single lesbians or to lesbian couples.

Research on gay and lesbian parents and their children is scarce, and most has involved children who were born to a heterosexual marriage that ended in divorce when the mother came out as a lesbian. Most of these lesbian mothers are European American and well-educated.

As parents, gay and lesbian couples are more similar to heterosexual couples than different. There is no indication that gay and lesbian parents are less effective than heterosexual parents. In fact, some evidence suggests that gay men may be especially responsive to children's needs, perhaps because their self-concepts include emotional sensitivity that is traditionally associated with the female gender role (Bigner & Jacobsen, 1989).

In many areas, including gender roles, self-concept, and social skill, children of gay and lesbian parents resemble children of heterosexual parents.

Children reared by gay and lesbian parents seem to develop much like children reared by heterosexual couples (Patterson, 1992). Preschool boys and girls apparently identify with their own gender and acquire the usual accompaniment of gender-based preferences, interests, activities, and friends. As adolescents and young adults, the vast majority are heterosexual (Bailey et al., 1995). In other dimensions, such as self-concept, social skill, moral reasoning, and intelligence—children of lesbian mothers resemble children of heterosexual parents. For example, in one study of 15 lesbian couples and

15 heterosexual couples, the children were comparably intelligent and well-adjusted psychologically (Flaks et al., 1995).

Research on children reared by gay and lesbian couples, along with findings concerning African American grandmothers and warmth and control in Asian parents, remind us that "good parenting" takes on somewhat different meanings in different cultures. These research results also challenge the conventional wisdom that a two-parent family with mother and father both present necessarily provides the best circumstances for development. Multiple adults *are* important (a fact that will become even clearer in Module 14.3 on divorce), but who the adults are seems to matter less than what they do. Children benefit from good parenting skills, whether it's a mother and father or grandparents or two women or two men doing the parenting.

CHILDREN'S CONTRIBUTIONS

From the discussion so far, parent-child relations may seem like a one-way street: Parents influence their children's behavior but not vice versa. Actually, nothing could be further from the truth. Beginning at birth, children influence the way their parents treat them. The family is a dynamic, interactive system with parents and children influencing each other.

The family is a dynamic, interactive system in which parents influence children's development and children influence how parents treat them.

One way to see the influence of children on parents is by looking at how parenting changes as children grow. The same parenting that is marvelously effective with infants and toddlers is inappropriate for adolescents. Let's look again at the two basic dimensions of parental behavior—warmth and control. Warmth is beneficial throughout development—toddlers and teens alike enjoy knowing that others care about them. But the manifestation of parental affection changes, becoming more reserved as children develop. The enthusiastic hugging and kissing that delights toddlers embarrasses adolescents.

Parental control also changes gradually as children develop (Maccoby, 1984). As children develop cognitively and are better able to make their own decisions, parents gradually relinquish control and expect children to be responsible for themselves. For instance, parents of elementary-school children often keep track of their children's progress on school assignments, but parents of adolescents don't, expecting their children to do this themselves.

Not only do parents change their expressions of warmth and control as children develop, parents behave differently depending upon a child's specific behavior. To illustrate the reciprocal influence of parents and children, imagine two children responding to a parent's authoritative style. The first child readily complies with parental requests and responds well to family discussions about parental expectations. These parent-child relations are a textbook example of successful authoritative parenting. But suppose, like the child in the photo, the second child complies reluctantly and sometimes defies requests altogether. Over time, the parent becomes more controlling and less affectionate. The child in turn complies even less in the future, leading the parent to adopt an authoritarian parenting style.

As this example illustrates, parenting style often evolves as a consequence of the child's behavior. With a young child who is eager to please adults and less active, a parent may discover a modest amount of control is adequate. But for a child who is not as eager to please and very active, a parent may need to be more controlling and directive (Dumas, LaFreniere, & Serketich, 1995). Influence is reciprocal: Children's behavior helps determine how parents treat them and the resulting parental behavior influences children's behavior, which in turn causes parents to again change their behavior (Stice & Barrera, 1995).

Reciprocal parent-child relationships greatly affect a child's development, but other relationships within the family are also influential, including siblings, as we'll see in the next module.

Check Your Learning

1. Children who have low self-esteem and are impulsive, aggressive, and moody often have parents who rely on an _____ style of parenting.

2. In a _____, parents unwittingly reinforce undesirable behaviors.

3. _____ grandparents are very interested in their grandchildren but avoid becoming involved in child rearing.

4. The family is an interactive system in which parents influence their children's development and _____.

Answers: (1) indifferent-uninvolved, (2) negative reinforcement trap, (3) Formal, (4) children influence how parents treat them

BROTHERS AND SISTERS

Learning Objectives

- **How do firstborn, laterborn, and only children differ?**
- **How do sibling relationships change as children grow? What determines how well siblings get along?**

> *Bob and Alice adored their 2-year-old son, Robbie, who was friendly, playful, and always eager to learn new things. In fact, Bob thought Robbie was nearly perfect and saw no reason to tempt fate by having another child. However, Alice had heard stories about only children—they were conceited, spoiled, and unfriendly. Alice was sure that Robbie would grow up like this unless she and Bob had another child. What to do?*

For most of a year, all firstborn children are only children like Robbie. Some children remain "onlies" forever, but most get brothers and sisters. Some firstborns are joined by many siblings in rapid succession; others are simply joined by a single brother or sister. As the family acquires these new members, parent-child relationships become more complex. Parents can no longer focus on a single child but must adjust to the needs of multiple children. Just as important, siblings influence each other's development, not just during childhood but, as the cartoon on page 370 reminds us, throughout life. To understand sibling influence, let's look at differences between firstborns, laterborns, and only children.

FIRSTBORN, LATERBORN, AND ONLY CHILDREN

Firstborn children are often "guinea pigs" for most parents, who have lots of enthusiasm but little practical experience rearing children. Parents typically have high expectations for their firstborns and are both more affectionate and more punitive with them. As more children arrive, parents become more adept at their

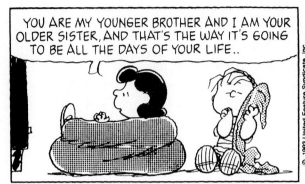

PEANUTS © 1993. Reprinted with permission of United Feature Syndicate.

roles, having learned "the tricks of the parent trade" with earlier children. With later-born children, parents have more realistic expectations and are more relaxed in their discipline (e.g., Baskett, 1985).

The different approaches that parents take with their firstborns and laterborns help explain differences that are commonly observed between these children. First-born children generally have higher scores on intelligence tests and are more likely to go to college. They are also more willing to conform to parents' and adults' requests. In contrast, perhaps because laterborn children are less concerned about pleasing parents and adults but need to get along with older siblings, laterborns are more pop-ular with their peers and more innovative (Eaton, Chipperfield, & Singbeil, 1989).

And what about only children? Alice, the mother in the opening vi-gnette, was well acquainted with the conventional wisdom which says that parents like the ones in the photo dote on "onlies," with the result that they are selfish and egotistical. Is the folklore correct? From a comprehensive analysis of more than 100 studies, the answer is "no." In fact, only children were found more likely to succeed in school than other children and to have higher levels of intelligence, leadership, autonomy, and maturity (Falbo & Polit, 1986).

This general pattern is not limited to only children growing up in the United States and Canada. In China, only children are the norm because governmental policy limits population growth. There, too, comparisons be-tween only and non-only children often find no differences; when differ-ences are found, the advantage usually goes to the only child (Falbo & Poston, 1993). Thus, contrary to the popular stereotype, only children are not "spoiled brats" (or, in China, "little emperors") who boss around par-ents, peers, and teachers. Instead, only children are, for the most part, much like children who grow up with siblings. Alice and Bob needn't have another child just to guarantee that Robbie will grow up to be generous and sensitive to others instead of selfish and egotistical.

In discussing firstborn, laterborn, and only children, we have ignored relationships that exist between siblings. These can be powerful forces on de-velopment, as we'll see in the next section.

QUALITIES OF SIBLING RELATIONSHIPS

From the very beginning, sibling relationships are complicated. On the one hand, most expectant parents are excited by the prospect of another child and their enthusiasm is contagious: Their children, too, eagerly await the arrival of the newest family member. On the other hand, the birth of a sibling is often distressing for older children, who may become withdrawn or return to more childish behavior because of the changes that occur in their lives with a sibling's birth, particularly the need to share parental attention and affection (Gottlieb & Mendelson, 1990). However, distress can be avoided if parents remain responsive to their older children's needs (Howe & Ross, 1990). In fact, one of the benefits of a sibling's birth is that fathers become more involved with their older children (Stewart et al., 1987).

To reduce the stress associated with a sibling's birth, parents should remain responsive to their older children's needs.

Many older siblings enjoy helping their parents take care of newborns (Wagner, Schubert, & Schubert, 1985). Like the sibling in the photo, older children play with the baby, console it, feed it, or change its diapers. As the infant grows, interactions between siblings become more frequent and more complicated. For example, toddlers tend to talk more to parents than to older siblings. But, by the time the younger sibling is 4 years old, the situation is reversed: Now young siblings talk more to older siblings than to their mother (Brown & Dunn, 1992). Older siblings become a source of care and comfort for younger siblings when they are distressed or upset (Garner, Jones, & Palmer, 1994).

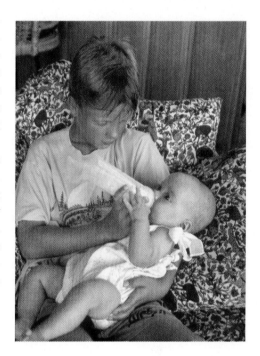

As time goes by, some siblings grow close, becoming best friends in ways that nonsiblings can never be. Other siblings constantly argue, compete, and, overall, simply do not get along with each other. The basic pattern of sibling interaction seems to be established early in development and remains fairly stable. Dunn, Slomkowski, and Beardsall (1994), for example, interviewed mothers twice about their children's interaction, first when the children were 3- and 5-year-olds and again 7 years later, when the children were 10- and 12-year-olds. Dunn and her colleagues found that siblings who got along as preschoolers often continued to get along as young adolescents whereas siblings who quarreled as preschoolers often quarreled as young adolescents.

The "Real Children" feature presents two sibling relationships that, although very different in quality, reveal the stability that Dunn and her colleagues (1994) discovered.

Real Children: **A TALE OF TWO SIBLING RELATIONSHIPS**

When Calvin, age 4, learned that his mother was going to have a baby, he cried uncontrollably and refused to talk to his mother for the rest of the day. After Hope was born, Calvin tried to ignore her, which was impossible because he wanted to be near his mother, and Hope, of course, was there, too. He couldn't see why his mother liked this new baby so much and seemed to have so little time for him. As Hope grew older, Calvin argued with her over just about everything and continued to compete with her for their parents' attention. When Hope entered adolescence and boyfriends entered the scene, Calvin teased her and hassled them. Over the years, Hope was too nice to give Calvin the treatment he deserved but she was glad when he left for college and only came home for vacations.

In contrast, Hillary and Elizabeth were always close. Beginning in the preschool years, the two girls played together constantly. When Elizabeth was upset, Hillary was quick to console her. When Hillary had special activities—a piano recital or a soccer match—Elizabeth always wanted to be there, and she was very proud of her sister's accomplishments. When Hillary and Elizabeth were both in high school, they remained as close as ever, sharing clothes and intimate secrets about their love lives. Hillary still played soccer and Elizabeth remained her biggest fan. Elizabeth had become the family's pianist and was quite talented; she won several state competitions, and Hillary never missed a performance.

Calvin and Hope's relationship is remarkable for Calvin's jealousy and hostility toward his sister; Hillary and Elizabeth's relationship is remarkable for its enduring intimacy, love, and mutual respect. What the relationships have in common is stability: The quality of relationship that was established early in childhood was maintained. ▨

Why was Hillary and Elizabeth's relationship so filled with love and respect whereas Calvin and Hope's was dominated by jealousy and resentment? Put more simply, what factors contribute to the quality of sibling relationships? First, children's sex and temperament matter. Sibling relations are more likely to be warm and harmonious between siblings of the same sex than between siblings of the opposite sex (Dunn & Kendrick, 1981) and when neither sibling is temperamentally emotional (Brody, Stoneman, & McCoy, 1994). Age is also important: Sibling relationships generally improve as the younger child approaches adolescence because siblings begin to perceive one another as equals (Buhrmester & Furman, 1990).

> **When parents fight, they no longer treat their children similarly, which increases conflicts between siblings.**

Parents contribute to the quality of sibling relationships, both directly and indirectly. The direct influence stems from parents' treatment. Siblings more often get along when they believe that parents have no "favorites" but treat all siblings similarly (Kowal & Kramer, 1997). When parents lavishly praise one child's accomplishments while ignoring another's, children notice the difference and their sibling relationship suffers.

The indirect influence of parents on sibling relationships stems from the quality of the parents' relationship with each other: A warm, harmonious relationship between parents often makes for positive sibling relationships; conflict between parents is associated with conflict between siblings (Volling & Belsky, 1992). When parents don't get along, they no longer treat their children the same, leading to conflict among siblings (Brody et al., 1994).

One practical implication of these findings is that in their pursuit of family harmony (otherwise known as peace and quiet), parents can influence some of the factors affecting sibling relationships but not others. Parents *can* help reduce friction between siblings by being equally affectionate, responsive, and caring with all of their children and by caring for one another. At the same time, some dissension is natural in families, especially those with young boys and girls: Children's different interests lead to arguments, like the one in the photo. Faced with common simple conflicts—Who decides which TV show to watch? Who gets to eat the last cookie? Who gets to hold the new puppy?—a 3-year-old brother and a 5-year-old sister *will* argue because they lack the social and cognitive skills that would allow them to find mutually satisfying compromises.

Regardless of the quality of their sibling relationships, American children are more likely than children in other countries to have their family relationships disrupted by divorce. What is the impact of divorce on children and adolescents? Module 14.3 has the answer.

Check Your Learning

1. Compared to firstborn children, laterborn children are more innovative and more _____.

2. Siblings are more likely to get along when they are of the same sex, are not temperamentally emotional, and when the younger child _____.

Answers: (1) popular; (2) enters adolescence

D IVORCE AND REMARRIAGE

Learning Objectives

- **How does family life change for children following divorce?**
- **What are some of the effects of divorce on children?**
- **How do children adjust to a parent's remarriage?**

Jack has lived with his dad for the 4 years since his parents' divorce; he visits his mother every other weekend. Although Jack was confused and depressed when his parents divorced, he has come to terms with the new situation. He's excelling in school, where he is well liked by peers and teachers. One of Jack's friends is Troy. Troy's parents are married but bicker constantly since his dad lost his job. His parents are unable to agree on anything; the pettiest event or remark triggers an argument. Troy's grades have fallen, and while he was once a leader among the boys in his class, now he prefers to be alone.

Like Jack, many American youngsters' parents divorce. As the following statistics show, divorce has become a common part of childhood, at least in America (Burns & Scott, 1994; Hernandez, 1997; Stevenson & Black, 1995):

- The divorce rate in the United States tripled between 1960 and 1980 but has remained fairly stable since 1980.

- The United States has, by far, the highest divorce rate in the entire world.

- Roughly one American child in three will, before age 18, see his or her parents divorce.

- Annually, approximately one million American children have parents who divorce.

According to all theories of child development, divorce is distressing for children because it involves conflict between parents and, usually, separation from one of them. But what aspects of children's development are most affected by divorce? Are these effects long-lasting, or are at least some of them temporary (as seems to be true for Jack)? To begin to answer these questions, let's start with a profile of life after divorce.

FAMILY LIFE AFTER DIVORCE

After divorce, children usually live with their mothers, though fathers are more likely to get custody today than in previous generations. About 15 percent of children live with their fathers after divorce (Meyer & Garasky, 1993). Not much is known about family life in homes headed by single fathers, so the description on the next few pages is based entirely on research done on children living with their mothers.

The best portrait of family life after divorce comes from the Virginia Longitudinal Study of Divorce and Remarriage conducted by Mavis Hetherington (1988, 1989; Hetherington, Cox, & Cox, 1982). The Virginia Study traced the lives of families for several years after divorce along with a comparison sample of families with parents who did not divorce. The findings showed that in the first few months after divorce, mothers were often less affectionate toward their children. They also accepted less mature behavior from their children than they would have before the divorce and, at the same time, had a harder time controlling their children. The overall picture seems to be that both mothers and children showed the distress of a major change in life circumstances: Children regressed to less mature forms of behavior, and mothers were less able to parent effectively. Fathers, too, were less able to control their children, but this was probably because they were often extremely indulgent with them.

Two years after the divorce, mother-child relationships had improved, particularly for daughters. Mothers were more affectionate. They were more likely to expect age-appropriate behavior from their children and discipline their children effectively. Fathers also demanded more mature behavior of their children, but fathers had often become relatively uninvolved with their children.

When children living with their divorced mothers enter adolescence, mothers and daughters are often quite close, but mothers and sons often fight.

Six years after divorce, the children in the study were entering adolescence. Family life continued to improve for mothers with daughters; many mothers and daughters grew extremely close over the years following divorce. In contrast, family life was often problematic for mothers with sons. These mothers often complained about their sons, who resisted maternal efforts at discipline. The negative reinforcement trap described in Module 14.1 was common. Mothers and sons were frequently in conflict, and overall, neither was very happy with the other or with the general quality of family life. Of course, conflict between mothers and adolescent sons is common when parents are married, but it was more intense with single moms, perhaps because adolescent sons are more willing to confront their single mothers concerning standards for their behavior.

Results like these from the Virginia Study underscore that divorce changes family life for parents and children alike. In the next section, we'll look at the effects of these changes on children's development.

IMPACT OF DIVORCE ON CHILDREN

Do the disruptions, conflict, and stress associated with divorce affect children? Of course, they do. Having answered this easy question, however, a host of more difficult questions remain: Are all aspects of children's lives affected equally by divorce? Are there factors that make divorce more stressful for some children and less so for others? Finally, *how* does divorce influence development? Some of the first steps toward answering these questions came from the study that is the subject of the "Focus on Research" feature.

Focus on Research: IMPACT OF A FATHER'S ABSENCE ON DAUGHTERS' DEVELOPMENT

Who was the investigator and what was the aim of the study? Divorce rates in the United States began to skyrocket in the late 1960s and early 1970s. By that time, research had already established that a father's absence was harmful to sons. Mavis Hetherington (1972) decided to study the impact of a father's absence on daughters. Because she was primarily interested in the impact of father absence, she studied daughters whose fathers were absent due to divorce as well as daughters whose fathers had died.

How did the investigator measure the topic of interest? Hetherington was interested in daughters' attitudes and behaviors toward males, particular toward their father and toward boys their own age. She measured this in two ways: by creating an interview that included questions about girls' attitudes toward gender roles and by observing the girls during a dance at a local recreation center.

Who were the children in the study? Hetherington studied 72 girls, ages 13 to 17. Among them were 24 girls from families in which the fathers were present, 24 girls whose fathers had died, and 24 girls whose fathers were absent due to divorce. For the latter 48 girls, there were no males (siblings or adults) living at home.

What was the design of the study? This study was correlational because Hetherington was interested in the relation that existed naturally between the presence or absence of a father (and the reasons for his absence) and different aspects of daughters' attitudes and behaviors. Adolescents were tested only once, so the study was neither longitudinal nor cross-sectional.

Were there ethical concerns with the study? No. The questions in the interview were not threatening and, of course, the daughters enjoyed attending the dance.

What were the results? Hetherington found no differences whatsoever among the three groups of girls in terms of gender roles. That is, they all had friendships with other girls, feelings of warmth toward their mothers, and comparable interest in gender-typical activity. However, striking differences were found on the questions dealing with men. As the first two sets of bars on the graph show, daughters from intact families felt much more secure around males than did daughters of widows or divorced mothers.

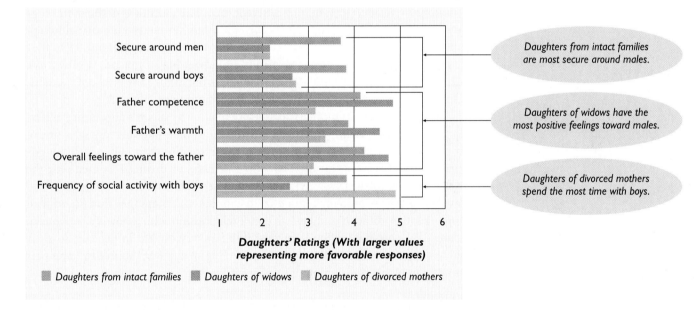

Daughters' Ratings (With larger values representing more favorable responses)

■ Daughters from intact families ■ Daughters of widows ■ Daughters of divorced mothers

Daughters from intact families are most secure around males.

Daughters of widows have the most positive feelings toward males.

Daughters of divorced mothers spend the most time with boys.

The next three sets of bars in the graph concern attitudes towards the father. In each case daughters of widows had the most positive views of the father, followed by daughters from intact families, and then daughters of divorced mothers.

Perhaps the most intriguing finding is shown by the last set of bars: Daughters of divorced mothers—despite feeling relatively less secure around males and having the most negative views of their fathers—report spending the most time with boys.

Hetherington confirmed this last result during her observations of the girls at the dance. As the graph on page 376 shows, daughters of divorced mothers were more likely to seek the attention of the male chaperones, more likely to initiate contact with boys, and more likely to spend time in the boys' areas of the recreation center.

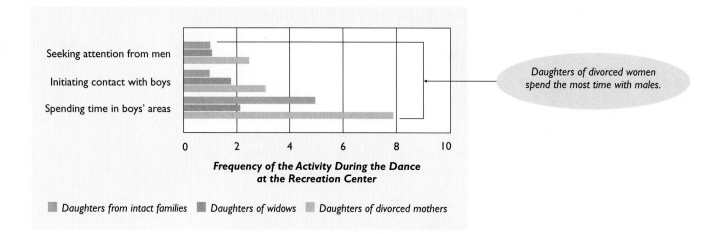

Seeking attention from men

Initiating contact with boys

Spending time in boys' areas

*Frequency of the Activity During the Dance
at the Recreation Center*

0   2   4   6   8   10

*Daughters of divorced women
spend the most time with males.*

■ *Daughters from intact families* ■ *Daughters of widows* ▨ *Daughters of divorced mothers*

What did the investigator conclude? When a father is absent—either because of death or divorce—girls have no trouble acquiring feminine interests and a feminine identity. However, when the father is absent, " . . . the lack of opportunity for constructive interaction with a loving, attentive father [results] in apprehension and inadequate skills in relating to males" (p. 324). This explains why father-absent girls may differ from girls whose fathers are present, but it doesn't explain why divorce and death seem to affect girls in such different ways. Here, attitudes of the mother are important. Hetherington interviewed all the girls' mothers and found that although the divorced mothers described their relationship with their daughter positively, they were negative about their former husbands and about life in general. Widows, too, reported strong relationships with their daughters but, unlike the divorced mothers, had fond views of their husband and generally positive views about life.

Thus, differences in mothers' attitudes explain why divorce affects girls differently than a father's death. Daughters of divorced women undoubtedly see some of their mother's hostility toward their father, which explains their own negative views toward men and fathers. But then why do daughters of divorced women seek the company of males so aggressively? Perhaps they see their mother's unhappiness and believe that a male's company is essential to happiness. Perhaps they find life with an unhappy mother difficult and believe that a relationship with a boy is a way out of the house. In contrast, widows are relatively happy with life in general, so their daughters have less reason to seek males, either as an apparent source of happiness or as a means of avoiding a mother's unhappiness. ■

Hetherington's (1972) study shows that divorce affects children through multiple routes. Some effects of divorce are linked directly to the father's absence. When a father is absent, girls have fewer opportunities to learn how to interact with males. But other effects of divorce depend upon the mother's attitudes and feelings. Many of the divorced mothers in Hetherington's study were unhappy and bitter (in part because divorce was less common and less accepted in the early '70s), and the mothers' unhappiness and bitterness affected their daughters.

By 1990, nearly 20 years after Hetherington's (1972) pioneering study, there were almost 100 studies of the impact of divorce, involving more than 13,000 preschool- through college-age children. Amato and Keith (1991) integrated the results of these studies; their results are shown in the graph on page 377, expressed in the standard deviation units that were described on page 339. In all areas—from school achievement to adjustment to parent-child relations—children whose parents had divorced fared poorly compared to children from intact families.

Not shown in the graph are three other important findings from Amato and Keith's (1991) work. First, overall, the impact of divorce is the same for boys and girls. Second, divorce is more harmful when it occurs during the childhood and adolescent years than during the preschool or college years. Third, as divorce became more frequent (and thus more familiar) in the 1980s, the consequences associated with divorce became smaller. School achievement, conduct, adjustment, and the like are still affected by divorce but not as much as before the 1980s.

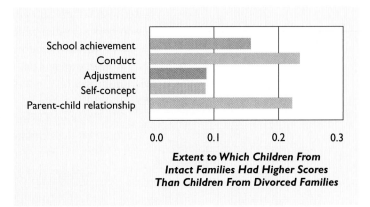

Extent to Which Children From Intact Families Had Higher Scores Than Children From Divorced Families

When children of divorced parents become adults, the effects of divorce persist. As adults, children of divorce are more likely to become teenage parents and to become divorced themselves. Also, they report less satisfaction with life and are more likely to become depressed (Furstenberg & Teitler, 1994; Kiernan, 1992). For example, in one study (Chase-Lansdale, Cherlin, & Kiernan, 1995), 11 percent of children of divorce had serious emotional problems as adults compared to 8 percent of children from intact families. The difference is small—11 percent versus 8 percent—but divorce does increase the risk of emotional disorders in adulthood.

How does divorce influence development? Several factors have been identified (Amato & Keith, 1991). First, the absence of one parent means that children lose a role model, a source of parental help and emotional support, and a supervisor. For instance, a single parent may have to choose between helping one child complete an important paper or watching another child perform in a school play. She *can't* do both and one child will miss out.

Second, single-parent families experience economic hardship, which creates stress and often means that opportunities once taken for granted are no longer available. When a single parent worries about having enough money for food and rent, she has less energy and effort to devote to parenting. Moreover, the drop in income means that a family can no longer afford books for pleasure reading, music lessons, and other activities that promote child development.

Divorce usually means that children lose a role model, experience economic hardship, and are exposed to parental conflict.

Third, conflict between parents is extremely distressing to children. In fact, many of the problems that are ascribed to divorce are really caused by marital conflict occurring before the divorce (Cherlin et al., 1991; Erel & Burman, 1995). Children like Troy, the boy in the opening vignette whose parents are married but fight constantly, often show many of the same effects associated with divorce.

Life for children after divorce is *not* all gloom and doom. Children can adjust to their new life circumstances (Chase-Lansdale & Hetherington, 1990). However, certain factors can ease the transition for children. Children adjust to divorce more readily if their divorced parents cooperate with each other, especially on disciplinary matters (Hetherington, 1989). **In *joint custody*, both parents retain legal custody of the children.** Children benefit from joint custody, if their parents get along (Maccoby et al., 1993).

Of course, many parents do not get along after a divorce, which eliminates joint custody as an option. Traditionally, mothers have been awarded custody; but in recent years fathers have been given custody, especially of sons, more often than in the past. This practice coincides with findings that children like Jack, the other boy in the opening vignette, often adjust better when they live with same-sex parents: Boys fare better with fathers and girls fare better with mothers (Camara & Resnick, 1988). One reason boys are often better off with their fathers is that boys are likely to become involved in negative reinforcement traps (described in Module 14.1) with their mothers. Another explanation is that both boys and girls may forge stronger emotional relationships with same-sex parents than with other-sex parents (Zimiles & Lee, 1991).

The "Making Children's Lives Better" feature shows how parents can make divorce easier on their children, regardless of the child's sex and the living arrangements.

Making Children's Lives Better: **HELPING CHILDREN ADJUST AFTER DIVORCE**

Divorce causes major changes in children's lives, and these changes are stressful for children. Here are some ways parents can reduce stress and help children adjust to their new life circumstances.
Parents should:

■ explain together to children why they are divorcing and what their children can expect to happen to them.

■ reassure children that they will always love them and always be their parents; parents must back up these words with actions by remaining involved in their children's lives, despite the increased difficulty of doing so.

■ expect that their children will sometimes be angry or sad about the divorce, and they should encourage children to discuss these feelings with them.

Parents should not:

■ compete with each other for their children's love and attention; children adjust to divorce best when they maintain good relationships with both parents.

■ take out their anger with each other on their children.

■ criticize their ex-spouse in front of the children.

■ ask children to mediate disputes; parents should work out problems without putting the children in the middle.

Following all these rules all the time is not easy: After all, divorce is stressful and painful for adults, too. But parents owe it to their children to try to follow most of these rules most of the time in order to minimize the disruptive effects of their divorce on their children's development. ■

BLENDED FAMILIES

Following divorce, most children live in a single-parent household for about 5 years. However, like the adults in the photo on page 379, more than two-thirds of men and women eventually remarry (Glick, 1989; Glick & Lin, 1986). **The resulting unit, consisting of a biological parent, stepparent, and children is known as a *blended family*.** Because mothers are more often granted custody of children, the most common form of blended family is a mother, her children, and a stepfather. Preadolescent boys typically benefit from the presence of a stepfather, particularly when he is warm and involved. Preadolescent girls, however, do not adjust readily to their mother's remarriage, apparently because it disrupts the intimate relationship they have established with her. Nevertheless, as boys and girls enter adolescence, both benefit from the presence of a caring stepfather (Hetherington, 1993).

The best strategy for stepfathers is to be interested in their new stepchildren but avoid encroaching on established relationships. Newly remarried mothers must be careful that their enthusiasm for their new spouse does not come at the expense of time and affection for their children. And both parents and children need to have realistic expectations. The blended family *can* be successful but it takes effort because of the many complicated relationships, conflicting loyalties, and jealousies that usually exist.

Much less is known about blended families consisting of a father, his children, and a stepmother, though several factors make a father's remarriage difficult for his children (Brand, Clingempeel, & Bowen-Woodward, 1988). First, fathers are often awarded custody when judges believe that children are unruly and will profit from a father's "firm hand." Consequently, many children living with their fathers do not adjust well to many of life's challenges, which certainly includes a father's remarriage. Second, fathers are sometimes granted custody because they have a particularly close relationship with their children, especially their sons. When this is the case, children sometimes fear that their father's remarriage will disturb their relationship. Finally, noncustodial mothers are more likely than noncustodial fathers to maintain close and frequent contact with their children (Maccoby et al., 1993). The constant presence of the noncustodial mother may interfere with a stepmother's efforts to establish close relationships with her stepchildren, particularly with her stepdaughters.

Over time, children adjust to the blended family. If the marriage is happy, most children profit from the presence of two caring adults. Unfortunately, second marriages are slightly more likely than first marriages to end in divorce, so many children relive the trauma. As you can imagine, another divorce—and possibly another remarriage—severely disrupts children's development, accentuating the problems that followed the initial divorce (Capaldi & Patterson, 1991).

Children in blended families often fear that remarriage will disrupt the close relationship they have with their parent.

Regrettably, divorce is not the only way that parents can disturb their children's development. As we'll see in the next module, some parents harm their children more directly, by abusing them.

Check Your Learning

1. As children approach adolescence, mother- _____ relationships after a divorce remain positive.

2. Children are most likely to be affected by divorce during the _____ years.

3. One difficulty for custodial fathers and stepmothers is that the children's biological mother _____ .

Answers: (1) daughter, (2) school-age and adolescent, (3) may remain very close to the children, making it hard for stepmothers to establish relationships with her stepchildren

PARENT-CHILD RELATIONSHIPS GONE AWRY

Learning Objectives

- **What are the consequences of child maltreatment?**
- **What factors cause parents to mistreat their children?**
- **How can maltreatment be prevented?**

The first time 7-year-old Max came to school with bruises on his face, he said he'd fallen down the basement steps. When Max had similar bruises a few weeks later, his teacher spoke with the school principal, who contacted local authorities. They discovered that Max's mother hit him with a paddle for even minor misconduct; for serious transgressions, she beat Max and made him sleep alone in an unheated, unlighted basement.

Unfortunately, cases like Max's occur far too often in modern America. Maltreatment comes in many forms (Zuraivin, 1991). The two that often first come to mind are physical abuse involving assault that leads to injuries and sexual abuse involving fondling, intercourse, or other sexual behaviors. However, as the poster reminds us, children can also be harmed by psychological abuse—ridicule, rejection, and humiliation. Another form of maltreatment is neglect, in which children do not receive adequate food, clothing, or medical care.

The frequency of these various forms of child maltreatment is difficult to estimate because so many cases go unreported. However, most experts agree that somewhere between 500,000 and 2½ million American children are maltreated annually (Widom, 1989). We'll begin this module by looking at the consequences of maltreatment, then look at some causes, and, finally, examine ways to prevent maltreatment.

CONSEQUENCES OF MALTREATMENT

You probably aren't surprised to learn that the prognosis for youngsters like Max is not very good. Some, of course, suffer permanent physical damage. Even when there is no lasting physical damage, the children's social and emotional development is often disrupted. They tend to have poor relationships with peers, often because they are too aggressive. Their cognitive development and academic performance is also disturbed. Abused youngsters tend to get lower grades in school, have lower scores on standardized achievement tests, and be retained in a grade rather than promoted. Also, school-related behavior problems are common, such as being disruptive in class (Trickett & McBride-

Chang, 1995). Adults who were abused as children often experience emotional problems such as depression or anxiety, are more prone to think about or attempt suicide, and are more likely to be violent to spouses and to their own children (Malinosky-Rummell & Hansen, 1993). In short, when children are maltreated, virtually all aspects of their development are affected and these effects do not vanish with time.

CAUSES OF MALTREATMENT

Why would a parent abuse a child? Maybe you think parents would have to be severely disturbed or deranged to harm their own flesh and blood? Not really. Today, we know that the vast majority of abusing parents cannot be distinguished from nonabusing parents in terms of standard psychiatric criteria (Wolfe, 1985). That is, adults who mistreat their children are not suffering from any specific mental or psychological disorder and they have no distinctive personality profile.

Modern accounts of child abuse no longer look to a single or even a small number of causes. Instead, a host of factors put some children at risk for abuse and protect others; the number and combination of factors determine if the child is a likely target for abuse (Belsky, 1993). Let's look at three of the most important factors: cultural context, the parents, and the children themselves.

The most general category of contributing factors has to do with cultural values and the social conditions in which parents rear their children. For example, a culture's view of physical punishment contributes to child maltreatment. The scene in the photo, a mother spanking her child, is common in the United States. In contrast, many countries in Europe and Asia have strong cultural prohibitions against physical punishment, including spanking. It simply isn't done and would be viewed in much the same way we would view an American parent who punished by not feeding the child for a few days. Countries that do not condone physical punishment tend to have lower rates of child maltreatment than the United States (Zigler & Hall, 1989).

What social conditions seem to foster maltreatment? Poverty is one: Maltreatment is more common in families living in poverty, in part because lack of money increases the stress of daily life (Straus & Kantor, 1987). When parents are worrying if they can buy groceries or pay the rent, they are more likely to resort to punishing their children physically instead of making the extra effort to reason with them.

Social isolation is a second force. Abuse is more likely when families are socially isolated from other relatives or neighbors. When a family, like the one in the photo, lives in relative isolation, it deprives the children of adults who could protect them and deprives parents of social support that would help them better deal with life stresses (Garbarino & Kostelny, 1992; Korbin, 1987).

Work by Claudia Coulton and her colleagues (1995) shows the influence of poverty and isolation on child maltreatment. They obtained data from 177 U.S. census tracts in Cleveland, Ohio. (A typical census tract includes about 2,000 residents.) Child maltreatment was more common in census tracts that were poorer, as indicated by more people living in poverty, higher unemployment, more vacant housing, and greater population loss. In addition, maltreatment was more common in census tracts that had fewer elderly residents, a greater ratio of children to adults, and fewer males. Thus, maltreatment is more common in neighborhoods that are poor and that have few other adults to help with child rearing. Apparently, maltreatment often occurs when parents are unable to cope with the financial and psychological burdens that child rearing entails.

Social factors like those studied by Coulton and her colleagues (1995) clearly contribute to child abuse, but they are only part of the puzzle. Although maltreatment *is* more common among families living in poverty, it does not occur in a majority of these families and it does occur in middle-class families, too. Consequently, we need to look for additional factors to explain why abuse occurs in some families but not others.

Today, we know that parents who abuse their children:

■ were, as children, sometimes maltreated themselves (Simons et al., 1991).

■ have high expectations for their children but do little to help them achieve these goals (Trickett et al., 1991).

■ rely upon physical punishment to control their children (Trickett & Kuczynski, 1986).

Overall, then, the typical abusing parent often had an unhappy childhood and has limited understanding of effective parenting techniques.

To place the last few pieces in the puzzle, we must look at the abused children themselves. The discussion in Module 14.1 of reciprocal influence between parents and children should remind you that children may inadvertently, through their behavior, bring on their own abuse. In fact, infants and preschoolers are more often abused than older ones, probably because they are less able to regulate aversive behaviors that elicit abuse (Belsky, 1993). You've probably heard stories about a parent who shakes a baby to death because the baby won't stop crying. Because younger children are more likely to cry or whine excessively—behaviors that irritate all parents sooner or later—they are more likely to be the targets of abuse.

Children are most likely to be maltreated when their culture condones physical punishment, their parents lack effective child-rearing skills, and their own behavior is often aversive.

For much the same reason, children who are frequently ill are more often abused. When children are sick, they're more likely to cry and whine, annoying their parents. Also, when children are sick, they need medical care, which means additional expense, and they can't go to school, which means that parents must arrange alternate child care. By increasing the level of stress in a family, sick children can inadvertently become the targets of abuse (Sherrod et al., 1984).

Obviously the children are not at fault and do not deserve the abuse. Nevertheless, normal infant or child behavior can provoke anger and maltreatment from some parents.

Thus, cultural, parental, and child factors all contribute to child maltreatment. Any single factor will usually not result in abuse. For instance, a sick infant who cries constantly would not be maltreated in countries where physical punishment is not tolerated. Maltreatment is likely only when cultures condone physical punishment, parents lack effective skills for dealing with children, and a child's behavior is frequently aversive.

PREVENTING MALTREATMENT

The complexity of the contributing factors dashes any hopes for a simple solution to the problem of child maltreatment. Because maltreatment is more apt to occur when several of these contributing factors are present, eradicating child maltreatment would entail a massive effort. First, American attitudes toward "acceptable" levels of punishment and poverty would have to change. American children will be abused as long as physical punishment is considered acceptable and effective and as long as poverty-stricken families live in chronic stress from simply trying to provide food and shelter. Another element would involve dealing with parents, providing counseling and training in parenting skills. Abuse will continue as long as parents remain ignorant of effective methods of parenting and discipline.

It would be naive to expect all of these changes to occur overnight. However, by focusing on some of the more manageable factors, the risk of maltreatment can be reduced, if not eliminated entirely. For example, families can be taught more effective ways of coping with situations that might otherwise trigger abuse (Wicks-Nelson & Israel, 1991). Parents can learn the benefits of authoritative parenting and effective ways of using feedback and modeling (described in Module 14.1) to regulate children's behavior. In role-playing sessions that recreate problems from home, child development professionals can demonstrate more effective means of solving problems, and then parents can practice these themselves.

Social supports also help. When parents know that they can turn to other helpful adults for advice and reassurance, they can more readily manage the stresses of child rearing, stresses that might otherwise lead to abuse. Finally, we need to remember that most parents who have mistreated their children deserve compassion, not censure. In most cases, parents and children *are* attached to each other; maltreatment is a consequence of ignorance and burden, not malice.

Check Your Learning

1. Children who are maltreated frequently have poor peer relationships because
   _____.

2. Cultural and social factors that contribute to child maltreatment include a culture's views toward physical punishment, the incidence of poverty, and a family's
   _____.

3. Programs for preventing maltreatment often try to help families learn
   _____.

Answers: (1) they are too aggressive, (2) social isolation, (3) new ways of coping with situations that might trigger maltreatment

FAMILY RELATIONSHIPS IN PERSPECTIVE

The basic goal of all families is to nurture children until they achieve adulthood, but we've seen in this chapter that families pursue this goal in many different ways and with varying degrees of success. In Module 14.1, we saw that parenting styles differ in warmth and control, that feedback and modeling are powerful means through which parents regulate children's behavior, and that children influence the type of parenting they receive. In Module 14.2, we learned that a child's position in the birth order can affect development and that how well siblings get along with each other depends on the parents and the children's temperament, sex, and age. In Module 14.3, we discovered that the effects of divorce on children are broad and last for years, and that children and parents in blended families face special challenges. Finally, in Module 14.4, we found that child maltreatment, which affects virtually all aspects of children's development, is caused by cultural, parental, and child factors.

In this chapter, I want to emphasize the theme that *children help determine their own development.* This may seem to be an unusual chapter to emphasize this theme because, after all, we usually think of how parents influence their children. But several times in this chapter we've seen that parenting is determined, in part, by children themselves. We saw that parents change their behavior as their children grow older, and they adjust their behavior depending upon how their children respond to previous efforts to discipline. And, in discussing causes of child maltreatment, we discovered that younger and sick children often unwittingly place themselves at risk for abuse because of their behavior. Constant whining and crying is trying for all parents and prompts a small few to harm their children.

Of course, parents do influence their children's development in many important ways. But effective parenting recognizes that there is no all-purpose formula that works for all children or, for that matter, for all children in one family. Instead, parents must tailor their child-rearing behavior to each child, recognizing his or her unique needs, strengths, and weaknesses.

THINKING ABOUT DEVELOPMENT

1. Suppose that you heard the host of a local talk radio show say, "What's wrong with American youth today is that parents don't discipline the way they used to. 'Spare the rod and spoil the child' made sense before and still makes sense today." If you called in, what would you say in response to the host's remarks?

2. Piaget had three children. If he reared them according to the basic principles of his theory, what parental style do you think he would have used?

3. Most research on sibling relationships is based on families with two children because these families are easier to find than families with three or more children and because there's only one sibling relationship to consider. Think how the conclusions about sibling relationships that were described in Module 14.2 might need to be modified to apply to larger families.

4. Suppose you were asked to prepare a brochure for mothers who have recently divorced and will have custody of their children. What advice would you give them about the trials and tribulations of being a single parent?

5. A sociologist claims that child maltreatment would vanish if poverty were eliminated. Do you agree? Why or why not?

SEE FOR YOURSELF

Many students find it hard to believe that parents actually use the different styles described in Module 14.1. To observe how parents differ in their warmth and control, visit a place where parents and children interact together. Shopping malls and fast-food restaurants are two good examples. Observe parents and children, then judge their warmth (responsive to the child's needs versus uninterested) and degree of control (relatively controlling versus uncontrolling). As you observe, decide if parents are using feedback and modeling effectively or not. You should observe an astonishing variety of parental behavior—some effective and some not. See for yourself!

RESOURCES

For more information about . . .

 *ways to help children deal with divorce,* try Neil Kalter's *Growing up with Divorce* (Free Press, 1990) which describes practical ways for parents to help their children deal with the stresses of divorce

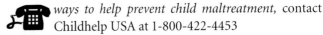 *ways to help prevent child maltreatment,* contact Childhelp USA at 1-800-422-4453

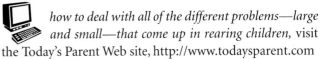 *how to deal with all of the different problems—large and small—that come up in rearing children,* visit the Today's Parent Web site, http://www.todaysparent.com

KEY TERMS

authoritarian parenting *362*
authoritative parenting *362*
blended family *378*
counterimitation *365*
disinhibition *365*
dispensing-family-wisdom
   grandparents *366*

distant grandparents *366*
formal grandparents *366*
fun-seeking grandparents *366*
indifferent-uninvolved parenting
   362
indulgent-permissive parenting *362*
inhibition *365*

joint custody *377*
negative reinforcement trap *364*
punishment *364*
reinforcement *363*
surrogate-parent grandparents *366*
time-out *364*

 **UMMARY**

MODULE 14.1:
PARENTING

DIMENSIONS AND STYLES
One dimension of parenting is the degree of parental warmth: Children clearly benefit from warm, caring parents. Another dimension is control. Neither too much nor too little control is desirable. Effective parental control involves setting appropriate standards and enforcing them consistently.

    Combining warmth and control yields four parental styles: (a) authoritarian parents are controlling but uninvolved, (b) authoritative parents are controlling but responsive to their children, (c) indulgent-permissive parents are loving but exert little control, and (d) indifferent-uninvolved parents are neither warm nor controlling. Authoritative parenting seems best for children, for both cognitive and social development.

PARENTAL BEHAVIOR
Parents influence development by reinforcing and punishing children's behavior. Sometimes parents fall into the negative reinforcement trap in which they inadvertently reinforce behaviors that they want to discourage.

    Punishment suppresses behaviors but does not eliminate them, and it often has side effects. Time-out is one useful form of punishment.

    Children sometimes imitate parents' behavior directly; sometimes they behave in ways that are similar to what they have seen (disinhibition), and sometimes in ways that are the opposite of what they've seen (counterimitation).

CULTURAL INFLUENCES AND FAMILY CONFIGURATION
Child rearing is influenced by culture and family configuration. Compared to American parents, Chinese parents are more controlling and less affectionate. In African American families, grandmothers often live with their daughters, an arrangement that eases the cost burden of housing and child care and benefits children because grandmothers can play an active role in child rearing. Research on gay and lesbian parents suggests that they are more similar to heterosexual parents than different and that their children develop much like children reared by heterosexual couples.

CHILDREN'S CONTRIBUTIONS
Parenting is influenced by characteristics of children themselves. For example, as children grow, parents display affection more discretely and are less controlling.

MODULE 14.2:
BROTHERS AND SISTERS

FIRSTBORN, LATERBORN, AND ONLY CHILDREN
Firstborn children often are more intelligent and more likely to go to college, but laterborn children are more popular and more innovative. Only children are comparable to children with siblings on most dimensions and better off on some, such as achievement and autonomy.

QUALITIES OF SIBLING RELATIONSHIPS

The birth of a sibling can be stressful for older children, particularly when parents ignore their older child's needs. Siblings get along better when they are of the same sex, believe that parents treat them similarly, enter adolescence, and have parents who get along well.

MODULE 14.3:
DIVORCE AND REMARRIAGE

FAMILY LIFE AFTER DIVORCE

In the months after a divorce, a mother's parenting is often less effective and her children behave immaturely. By 2 years after the divorce, family life is much improved. At 6 years after the divorce, mother-daughter relationships are often very positive but mother-son relationships are often conflict-filled.

IMPACT OF DIVORCE ON CHILDREN

A divorce can harm children in many ways, ranging from school achievement to adjustment. The impact of divorce stems from less supervision of children, economic hardship, and conflict between parents. Children often benefit when parents have joint custody following divorce or when they live with the same-sex parent.

BLENDED FAMILIES

When a mother remarries, daughters sometimes have difficulty adjusting because the new stepfather encroaches on an intimate mother-daughter relationship. A father's remarriage can cause problems because children fear that the stepmother will disturb intimate father-child relationships and because of tension between the stepmother and the noncustodial mother.

MODULE 14.4:
PARENT-CHILD RELATIONSHIPS GONE AWRY

CONSEQUENCES OF MALTREATMENT

Children who are maltreated sometimes suffer permanent physical damage. Their peer relationships are often poor, and they tend to lag behind in cognitive development and academic performance.

CAUSES OF MALTREATMENT

A culture's views on violence, poverty, and social isolation can foster child maltreatment. Parents who abuse their children are often unhappy, socially unskilled individuals. Younger, unhealthy children are more likely to be targets of maltreatment.

PREVENTING MALTREATMENT

Prevention should target each of the factors that contribute to child maltreatment. In reality, prevention programs often focus on providing families with new ways of coping with problems and providing parents with resources to help them cope with stress.

Peers, Media, and Schools

IF YOU STAND OUTSIDE A KINDERGARTEN CLASSROOM ON THE FIRST DAY OF SCHOOL, YOU'LL PROBABLY SEE SOME CHILDREN IN TEARS, FEARFUL OF FACING A NOVEL ENVIRONMENT ON THEIR OWN. WHAT MAY SURPRISE YOU IS THAT MANY PARENTS, TOO, are struggling to hold back their tears. Why? Parents realize that when their children begin school, they are taking an important step toward independence. Other forces now become influential in children's lives, sometimes challenging parents' influence. Among these forces are children's agemates (their peers), the media, and school itself. In this chapter, we'll examine these forces and see how they affect children. We'll look at peer influence in Module 15.1. Next, in Module 15.2, we'll see how the media—particularly television—contribute to children's development. Finally, Module 15.3 focuses on schools, where most American children spend 13 or more years of their lives.

PEERS

Learning Objectives

- **When do youngsters first begin to play with each other and how does play change during infancy and the preschool years?**
- **Why do children become friends and what are the benefits of friendship?**
- **What are the important features of groups in childhood and adolescence? How do groups influence individuals?**
- **Why are some children more popular than others? What are the causes and consequences of being rejected?**

> Only 36 hours had passed since campers arrived at Crab Orchard Summer Camp. Nevertheless, groups had already formed spontaneously, based on the campers' main interests: arts and crafts, hiking, and swimming. And, within each group, leaders and followers had already emerged. This happened every year, but the staff was always astonished at how quickly a "social network" emerged.

The groups that form at summer camps—as well as in schools and neighborhoods—represent one of the more complex forms of peer relationships: Many children are involved and there are multiple relationships. We'll examine these kinds of interactions later in the module. Let's begin, though, by looking at the earliest peer interactions, which usually begin in the context of play.

THE JOYS OF PLAY

If you watch two 5-month-olds, hoping to see some social interaction, you'll be disappointed. The infants will look at each other, but you won't observe anything that qualifies as an interaction. However, at about 6 months, the first signs of peer interaction appear: Now an infant may point to or smile at another infant (Hartup, 1983).

The next big step in social interaction usually occurs soon after the first birthday. Look at the boys in the photo. Each has his own toy but is watching the other play, too. **The photograph illustrates *parallel play,* youngsters playing alone but each maintaining a keen interest in what other children are doing.** During parallel play, exchanges between youngsters begin to occur. When one talks or smiles, the other usually responds (Howes, Unger, & Seidner, 1990).

Beginning at roughly 15 to 18 months, toddlers no longer just watch one another at play. *Simple social play* **emerges, in which youngsters engage in similar activities, talk or smile at one another, and offer each other toys.** Play is now truly interactive (Howes & Matheson, 1992). An example of simple social play would be two 20-month-olds pushing toy cars along the floor, making "car sounds" and periodically trading cars.

Towards the second birthday, *cooperative play* begins: Now children organize their play around a distinct theme and take on special roles based on the theme. For example, children may play "hide-and-seek" and alternate roles of hider and finder, or they may have a tea party and alternate being the host and guest (Parten, 1932).

The pie charts show how the nature of young children's play changes dramatically in a few years. These charts are based on observing 1- to 5-year-olds interacting

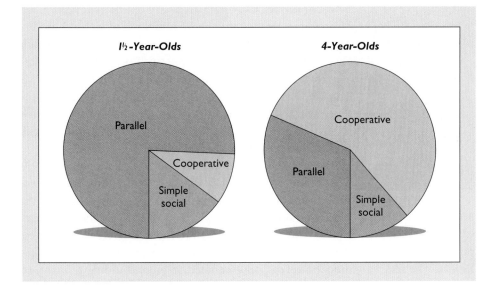

with their peers at a day-care center (Howes & Matheson, 1992). The 1½-year-olds spend the vast majority of their time in parallel play, and other forms of play are relatively rare. By the time children are 3½ to 4 years old, parallel play is much less common and cooperative play is the norm. Cooperative play typically involves peers of the same gender, a preference that increases until, by age 6, youngsters choose same-sex playmates about two-thirds of the time (LaFreniere, Strayer, & Gauthier, 1984).

Parental Influence. Conflicts are surprisingly common in cooperative play: Preschoolers often disagree, argue, and sometimes fight. Children play more cooperatively and longer with parents present to help iron out conflicts that emerge (Mize, Pettit, & Brown, 1995; Parke & Bhavnagri, 1989). When young children can't agree on what to play, a parent can negotiate a mutually acceptable topic. When both youngsters want to play with the same toy, a parent can arrange for them to share. In effect, parents provide the scaffolding for their preschoolers' play (see Module 6.3), smoothing the interaction by providing some of the social skills that preschoolers lack.

Parents also influence the success of their children's peer interactions in a much less direct manner. Perhaps you remember from Module 10.3 that children's relationships with peers are most successful when, as infants, children had a secure attachment relationship with their mother (Ladd & LeSieur, 1995). Why does quality of attachment predict the success of children's peer relationships? One view is that a child's relationship with his or her parents is the internal working model for all future social relationships. When the parent-child relationship is high quality and emotionally satisfying, children are encouraged to form relationships with other people. Another possibility is that a secure attachment relationship with the mother makes an infant feel more confident about exploring the environment, which typically provides more opportunities to interact with peers. These two views are not mutually exclusive; both may contribute to the relative ease with which securely attached children interact with their peers (Hartup, 1992b).

Parents enhance their children's peer interactions directly by scaffolding these interactions and indirectly by forging secure attachments with their children in infancy.

Make-Believe. During the preschool years, cooperative play often takes the form of make-believe. Between 2 and 3 years, children begin to have telephone conversations with imaginary partners or, like the youngsters in the photo, pretend to drive a make-believe car. For example, Harris and Kavanaugh (1993) studied how children use props in make-believe, such as pretending that a Popsicle stick is a spoon or a toothbrush. They asked youngsters to pretend to brush a toy bear's teeth with the Popsicle stick or to use it to stir the bear's tea. Most 28-month-olds did so readily, but few 21-month-olds did.

The change that Harris and Kavanaugh (1993) observed between 21 and 28 months fits Piaget's account of the sensorimotor period (see pages 145–147 in Module 6.2). The ability to use symbols emerges in the last sensorimotor substage, which spans 18 to 24 months. The younger children in the study were in the earliest phases of symbolic development, so they weren't cognitively capable of make-believe. The older children, however, had graduated to preoperational thought, so make-believe was within their grasp.

Make-believe play is not only entertaining for children; it also allows them to explore topics that frighten them. Children who are afraid of the dark may reassure a doll who is also afraid of the dark. By explaining to the doll why she need not be afraid, children come to understand and regulate their own fear of darkness. Or children may pretend that a doll has misbehaved and must be punished, which allows them to experience the parent's anger and the doll's guilt. With make-believe, children explore other emotions as well, including joy and affection (Gottman, 1986).

For many preschool children, make-believe play involves imaginary companions. These children can usually describe their imaginary playmates in some detail,

Make-believe allows children to explore emotional topics that frighten them.

mentioning sex and age as well as the color of their hair and eyes. Imaginary companions were once thought to be fairly rare and a sign of possible developmental problems. But more recent research shows that nearly two-thirds of all preschoolers report imaginary companions (Taylor, Cartwright, & Carlson, 1993). Moreover, the presence of an imaginary companion is actually associated with many *positive* social characteristics: Preschoolers with imaginary companions tend to be more sociable and have more real friends than preschoolers without imaginary companions. Furthermore, vivid fantasy play with imaginary companions does *not* mean that the distinction between fantasy and reality is blurred: Children with imaginary companions can distinguish fantasy from reality just as accurately as youngsters without imaginary companions (Taylor et al., 1993).

In the course of cooperative play, children discover that they prefer to play with some children over others. This is a first step toward friendship, the focus of the next section.

FRIENDSHIP

By 4 or 5 years of age, most children claim to have a "best friend." If you ask them how they can tell a child is their best friend, their response will probably resemble 5-year-old Kara's:

Interviewer:	Why is Kelly your best friend?
Kara:	Because she plays with me. And she's nice to me.
Interviewer:	Are there any other reasons?
Kara:	Yeah, she lets me play with her dolls.

Of course, older children and adolescents also have best friends, but they describe them differently. Here is a typical 13-year-old's response:

Interviewer:	Why is Leah your best friend?
Shauna:	She helps me. And we think alike. My mom says we're like twins!
Interviewer:	What else tells you that she's your best friend?
Shauna:	Because I can tell her stuff—special stuff, like secrets—and I know that she won't tell anybody else.
Interviewer:	Anything else?
Shauna:	Yeah. If we fight, later we always tell each other that we're sorry.

For both Kara and Shauna, best friends have common interests and like each other. However, Shauna's friendship with Leah has other features as well. Older children and adolescents believe that loyalty, trust, and intimacy are important ingredients of friendship. Also, adolescents, much more so than children, believe that friends should defend one another. And they believe, just as strongly, that friends should not deceive or abandon one another (Newcomb & Bagwell, 1995).

The emphasis on loyalty in adolescent friendships apparently goes hand in hand with the emphasis on intimacy: If a friend is disloyal, adolescents are afraid that they may be humiliated because their intimate thoughts and feelings will become known to a much broader circle of people (Berndt & Perry, 1990).

Intimacy is more common in friendships among girls, who are more likely than boys to have one exclusive "best friend." Because intimacy is at the core of their friendships, girls are also more likely to be concerned about the faithfulness of their friends and to worry about being rejected (Buhrmester & Furman, 1987).

The emergence of intimacy in adolescent friendships means that friends also come to be seen as sources of social and emotional support. Levitt, Guacci-Franco, and Levitt (1993) asked African American, European American, and Hispanic American 7-, 10-, and 14-year-olds to whom they would turn if they needed help or were bothered by something. For all ethnic groups, 7- and 10-year-olds relied upon close family members—parents, siblings, and grandparents—as primary sources of support, but not friends. However, 14-year-olds relied upon close family members less often and said they would turn to friends instead. Because adolescent friends share intimate thoughts and feelings, they can provide support during emotional or stressful periods.

Who Becomes Friends? Like the friends shown in the photo, most friends are alike in age, gender, and race (Hartup, 1992a). Because friends are supposed to treat each other as equals, friendships are rare between an older, more experienced child and a younger, less experienced child. Because children typically play with same-sex peers (see Module 13.3), boys and girls rarely become friends.

Friendships are more common between children from the same race or ethnic group than between children from different groups, reflecting racial segregation in American society. Friendships among children of different groups are more common in schools where classes are smaller (Hallinan & Teixeira, 1987). Evidently, when classes are large, children select friends from the large number of available same-race peers. When fewer same-race peers are available in smaller classes, children more often become friends with other-race children. Interracial friendships are usually confined to school, unless children come from integrated neighborhoods. That is, when children live in different, segregated neighborhoods, their friendship does not extend to out-of-school settings (DuBois & Hirsch, 1990).

Of course, friends are not only alike in age, sex, and race. Children and adolescents are usually drawn together because they have similar attitudes towards school, recreation, and the future (Newcomb & Bagwell, 1995). Tom, who enjoys school, likes to read, and plans to go to Harvard, will probably not befriend Barry, who thinks that school is stupid, listens to his disc player constantly, and plans to quit high school to become a rock star. As time passes, friends become more similar in their attitudes and values (Kandel, 1978).

Consequences of Friendship. Friends are good and good for you. Researchers consistently find that children benefit from having good friends. Compared to children who lack friends, children with good friends have higher self-esteem and are less likely to be lonely and depressed. In addition, children with good friends more often act prosocially—sharing and cooperating with others (Hartup, 1992a). Finally, children with good friends tend to cope better with life stresses, such as the transition from elementary school to middle school or junior high (Berndt & Keefe, 1995).

When children have good friends, they are more likely to behave prosocially and are better adjusted.

Thus, friends are *not* simply special playmates and companions. They are important resources. Children learn from their friends and can turn to them for support in times of stress. Friendships are one important way peers influence development. Peers also influence development through groups, the topic of the next section.

GROUPS

As was the case at the summer camp in the opening vignette, whenever strangers are brought together, they form groups. Psychologist Muzafer Sherif and his colleagues (1961) used this phenomenon to conduct what turned out to be a landmark study of children's groups at The Robbers Cave State Park in Oklahoma. The boys in this study did not know one another before coming to camp. They were put in two groups that were equal in terms of several criteria thought to be important to the camp setting, such as height and weight, athletic ability, and previous camping experience. For the first week, the two groups were kept apart and did not know of the other's existence. Both groups spent their time in traditional camp activities that required considerable cooperation, such as transporting boats and other camping equipment, and organizing hikes, campfires, and meals.

After just a few days, leaders emerged within each group. Boys acquired nicknames and the groups themselves acquired names, Rattlers and Eagles. Each group established norms to regulate behavior within the group. For example, boys who complained about minor injuries or being homesick were teased for not being "tough."

At the end of the first week, it was arranged that the groups discover each other. Each insisted that the other had intruded on its "turf," which helped solidify the emerging feelings of group membership. Each group insisted on challenging the other in baseball, so a game was planned, along with other competitions (such as tent pitching and cleaning the cabins). Prizes were announced for the winners.

Preparing for these events further solidified group loyalties, and activities that had once been avoided—cleaning the cabins, for example—were now pursued vigorously because they contributed to the goal of establishing the group's superiority. In this phase, boys became antagonistic to members of the other group. During the competitions, boys heckled and cursed the other group. After losing to the Rattlers in the first baseball game, members of the Eagles found the Rattlers' flag at the ball field. They burned it and hung the remnants for the Rattlers to find. One Eagle said, "You can tell those guys *I* did it if they say anything. I'll fight 'em!" Relations deteriorated so rapidly between the groups that in just a few days the boys abandoned displays of good sportsmanship and refused to eat together in the same mess hall. And stereotypes formed. Rattlers were convinced that Eagles were unfriendly and sneaky. Of course, Eagles felt the same way about Rattlers.

After about two weeks, the final phase of the experiment began. The objective now was to reduce the hostility between the groups. First, the two groups participated in enjoyable, noncompetitive events, such as watching a movie or shooting firecrackers together. This approach failed completely, and the antagonism that marked recent interactions continued unabated.

The second approach involved creating common goals for the two groups that required cooperation. When the boys wanted to see a popular movie, the staff said that the camp could not afford the rental. After some debate, the two groups agreed to contribute equally to the cost of the movie. A few days later, a truck that was to be used for picking up supplies would not start. A Rattler suggested that they use a rope to pull the truck to start it. As the photo shows, all group members joined in and, after a few tries, started the truck (which was in working condition all along). The boys congratulated one another, and the groups intermingled.

Another time, the staff deliberately mispacked gear for a camping trip, so that each group had extra pieces of equipment that were missing from the other group's gear. The Rattlers and Eagles immediately recognized the problem and promptly swapped gear without argument.

These and other situations involving common goals effectively eliminated the hostility between groups just as rapidly as the competition had elicited it. By the end of the week, Rattlers and Eagles were sitting together in the mess hall. When camp was over, the Rattlers and Eagles asked to travel home on the same bus.

The Robbers Cave study tells us much about group formation and group functioning. Three conclusions are particularly worth remembering. First, when groups of children are brought together, a structure emerges rapidly with individuals having specific roles, for example, as a leader. Second, when groups compete for scarce resources (for example, prizes), individuals' identification with and support for their own group increases. At the same time, they develop negative stereotypes of members of other groups and feel antagonistic towards them. Third, when common goals require that groups cooperate, group boundaries become less pronounced and hostility between groups ceases.

Though it's been nearly 50 years since Sherif's study at Robbers Cave, groups remain prominent in the social landscape of late childhood and adolescence. Two types of groups are particularly common as children enter adolescence. **A *clique* consists of 4 to 6 individuals who are good friends and, consequently, tend to be similar in age, sex, race, and interests.** Members of a clique spend time together and often dress, talk, and act alike. Cliques are often part of a larger group, too. **A *crowd* is a larger group of older children or adolescents who have similar values and attitudes and are known by a common label.** Maybe you remember some of the different crowds from your own youth? "Jocks," "preppies," "burnouts," "nerds," and "brains"—adolescents use these or similar terms to refer to crowds of older children or adolescents.

Some crowds have more status than others. For example, students in many junior and senior high schools claim that the "jocks" are the most prestigious crowd whereas the "burnouts" are among the least prestigious. Self-esteem in older children and adolescents often reflects the status of their crowd. During the school years, youth from high-status crowds tend to have greater self-esteem than those from low-status crowds (Brown & Lohr, 1987).

> *Some crowds have greater social status than others; youth from high-status crowds tend to have greater self-esteem than youth from low-status crowds.*

Why do some students become nerds while others join the burnouts? Parenting style (discussed in Module 14.1) is part of the answer. A study by Brown and his colleagues (1993) examined the impact of three parental practices on students' membership in particular crowds. The investigators measured the extent to which parents emphasized academic achievement, monitored their children's out-of-school activities, and involved their children in joint decision making. When parents emphasized achievement, their children were more likely to be in the popular, jock, and normal crowds and less likely to be in the druggie crowd. When parents monitored out-of-school behavior, their children were more likely to be in the brain crowd and less likely to be in the druggie crowd. Finally, when parents included their children in joint decision making, their children were more likely to be in the brain and normal crowds and less likely to be in the druggie crowd. These findings were true for African American, Asian American, European American, and Hispanic American children and their parents.

What seems to happen is that when parents use the practices associated with authoritative parenting—control coupled with warmth—their children become involved with crowds that endorse adult standards of behavior (for example, normals, jocks, brains). But, when parents' style is neglecting or permissive, their children are less likely to identify with adult standards of behavior and, in fact, become involved with crowds like druggies that disavow adult standards.

Group Structure. Groups—whether in school, at a summer camp, or anyplace else—typically have a well-defined structure. **Most groups have a *dominance hierarchy* consisting of a leader to whom all other members of the group defer.** Other members know their position in the hierarchy. They yield to members who are above them in the hierarchy and assert themselves over members who are below them. A dominance hierarchy is useful in reducing conflict within groups because every member knows his or her place.

What determines where members stand in the hierarchy? With children, especially boys, physical power is often the basis for the dominance hierarchy. The leader is usually the member who is the most intimidating physically (Pettit et al., 1990). Among girls and older boys, hierarchies are often based on individual traits that relate to the group's main function. At Crab Orchard Summer Camp, for example, the leaders most often are the children with the greatest camping experience. Among Girl Scouts, girls chosen to be patrol leaders tend to be bright, goal oriented, and have new ideas (Edwards, 1994). These characteristics are appropriate because the primary function of patrols is to help plan activities for the entire troop of Girl Scouts. Thus, leadership based on key skills is effective because it gives the greatest influence to those with the skills most important to group functioning (Hartup, 1983).

Peer Pressure. Groups establish norms—standards of behavior that apply to all group members—and groups may pressure members to conform to these norms. Such "peer pressure" is often characterized as an irresistible, harmful force. The stereotype is that teenagers exert enormous pressure on each other to behave antisocially. In reality, peer pressure is neither all powerful nor always evil. For example, most junior and senior high students *resist* peer pressure to behave in ways that are clearly antisocial, such as stealing (Brown, Lohr, & McClenahan, 1986). Peer pressure can be positive, too; peers often urge one another to participate in school activities, such as trying out for a play or working on the yearbook, or become involved in community-action projects, such as Habitat for Humanity.

Peer pressure is most powerful when the standards for appropriate behavior are not clear-cut. Taste in music and clothing, for example, is completely subjective, so youth conform to peer group guidelines, as you can see in the all too familiar sight shown in the photo—girls all wearing "in" clothing.

Similarly, standards on smoking, drinking, and using drugs are often fuzzy. Drinking is a good case in point. Parents and groups like SADD (Students Against Driving Drunk) may discourage teens from drinking, yet American culture is filled with youthful models who drink, seem to enjoy it, and suffer no apparent ill effects. To the contrary, they seem to enjoy life even more. With such contradictory messages, it is not surprising that youth look to their peers for answers (Chassin et al., 1986). Consequently, some youth *will* drink (or smoke, use drugs, or have sex) to conform to *their* group's norms; others will abstain, again, reflecting their group's norms.

POPULARITY AND REJECTION

Eileen is definitely the most popular child in her class. Other youngsters always want to play with her and sit near her at lunch or on the school bus. In contrast, Jay is the *least* popular child in the class. When he tries to join a game of four-square, the others quit. Students in the class dislike Jay as much as they like Eileen.

Popular and rejected children like Eileen and Jay can be found in every classroom and neighborhood. In fact, studies of popularity (Newcomb, Bukowski, & Pattee, 1993) reveal that most children can be placed in one of five categories:

- *Popular children* are liked by many classmates.

- *Rejected children* are disliked by many classmates.

- *Controversial children* are both liked and disliked by classmates.

- *Average children* are liked and disliked by some classmates but without the intensity found for popular, rejected, or controversial children.

- *Neglected children* are ignored by classmates.

What determines who's hot and who's not? Why is a child popular, rejected, controversial, average, or neglected? Smarter and physically attractive children are more often popular (Johnstone, Frame, & Bouman, 1992). However, the most important ingredient in popularity is social skill. Popular children are better at initiating social interactions with other children. They are more skillful at communicating and better at integrating themselves into an ongoing conversation or play session. Popular children also seem relatively gifted in assessing and monitoring their own social impact in various situations and in tailoring their responses to the requirements of each new social situation (Crick & Dodge, 1994; Wentzel & Asher, 1995). For example, a study by Wentzel and Erdley (1993) showed that popular children had better social skills. Sixth- and seventh-grade boys and girls were asked to evaluate their peers' prosocial behavior, antisocial behavior, and popularity. Popular youngsters were more likely than unpopular children to share, cooperate, and help and less likely to start fights and break rules.

Why do some children fail in their efforts to be popular and end up in one of the other categories—rejected, controversial, average, or neglected? We know the most about rejected children. Rejected children tend to be socially unskilled. Many rejected children are aggressive, attacking their peers without provocation (Dodge, Bates, & Pettit, 1990). Other rejected youngsters have poor self-control and are often disruptive in school (French, 1988, 1990). When conflicts arise, rejected children often become angry and retaliate (Bryant, 1992).

Being well liked seems straightforward: Be pleasant and friendly, not obnoxious. Share, cooperate, and help instead of being disruptive. Are these rules specific to American children or do they apply more generally? The "Cultural Influences" feature has the answer.

Cultural Influences: **KEYS TO POPULARITY**

In America, popular children seem to know how to get along with others. These results don't apply just to American children; they hold for children in many cultures around the world, including Canada, European countries, Israel, and China. Sometimes, however, popular children have other characteristics that are unique to their cultural setting. In Israel, for example, popular children are more likely to be assertive and direct than in other countries (Krispin, Sternberg, & Lamb, 1992). In China, popular children are more likely to be shy than in other countries (Chen, Rubin, & Li, 1995). Evidently, good social skills are at the core of popularity in most countries, but other features may also be important, reflecting culturally specific values. ■

Consequences of Rejection. No one enjoys being rejected. In fact, repeated peer rejection in childhood can have serious long-term consequences (DeRosier, Kupersmidt, & Patterson, 1995; Parker & Asher, 1987). Rejected youngsters are more likely than youngsters in the other categories to drop out of school, commit juvenile offenses, and suffer from psychopathology. The "Focus on Research" feature describes one study that showed some of the long-term effects of popularity and rejection.

Focus on Research: LONG-TERM CONSEQUENCES OF POPULARITY AND REJECTION

Who were the investigators and what was the aim of the study? Is the outcome of development similar for popular and unpopular children? Or do popularity and rejection steer children down different developmental paths? Patricia Morison and Ann Masten (1991) wanted to answer these questions.

How did the investigators measure the topic of interest? Morison and Masten identified popular and rejected children by asking children in grades 3 to 6 to nominate classmates for roles in an imaginary class play. Popular children were defined as those who were frequently nominated for roles like "a good leader," "everyone likes to be with," and "has many friends." Rejected children were those frequently nominated for roles like "picks on other kids," "too bossy," and "teases other children too much." Seven years later, the children and their parents completed questionnaires measuring academic achievement, social skill, and self-worth.

Who were the children in the study? Initially, 207 children in grades 3 to 6 were tested, and 183 of them completed the questionnaires 7 years later.

> *When children are rejected, they usually do less well in school, have lower self-esteem, and are more likely to have behavioral problems.*

What was the design of the study? This study was correlational because Morison and Masten were interested in the relation that existed naturally between two sets of variables: popularity and rejection at the first testing and academic achievement, social skill, and self-worth at the second. The study was longitudinal because children were tested twice, once in grades 3 to 6 and again 7 years later.

Were there ethical concerns with the study? No. The general purpose of the study was explained and then parents and children consented to participate.

What were the results? The table shows the correlations between popularity and rejection in grades 3 to 6 and academic achievement, social skill, and self-worth measured 7 years later. Children who were popular in grades 3 to 6 were doing well in school, were socially skilled and had high self-esteem. In contrast, children who were rejected in grades 3 to 6 were not doing well in school and had low self-esteem.

Correlations between Boys' and Girls' Popularity and Rejection in Grades 3 to 6 and Academic Achievement, Social Skill, and Self-Worth

Outcome	Popularity in grades 3–6	Rejection in grades 3–6
Academic Achievement	.27	−.25
Social Skill	.24	.03
Self-Worth	.24	−.22

What did the investigators conclude? Popular children fit in with groups instead of trying to make groups adjust to them. When conflicts arise with peers, popular children try to understand the problem and provide useful solutions. Over time, popular children's prosocial skill pays long-term dividends; unfortunately, rejected children's lack of prosocial skill has a price as well. ■

Rejected children often have an aggressive interpersonal style that reflects, in part, how their parents interact.

Causes of Rejection. Peer rejection can be traced, at least in part, to parental influence (Ladd & LeSieur, 1995). Children see how their parents respond to different social situations and often imitate these responses later. Parents who are friendly and cooperative with others demonstrate effective social skills for their youngsters. Parents who are belligerent and combative demonstrate much less effective social skills. In particular, when parents typically respond to interpersonal conflict like the couple in the photo—with intimidation or aggression—their children may imitate them, hampering their development of social skills and making them less popular in the long run (Keane, Brown, & Crenshaw, 1990).

Parents' disciplinary practices also affect their children's social skill and popularity. Inconsistent discipline—punishing a child for misbehaving one day and ignoring the same behavior the next—is associated with antisocial and aggressive behavior, paving the way to rejection (Dishion, 1990). Consistent punishment that is tied to parental love and affection is more likely to promote social skill and, in the process, popularity (Dekovic & Janssens, 1992).

In sum, parenting can lead to an aggressive interpersonal style in a child, which in turn leads to peer rejection. But the implication is that by teaching youngsters (and their parents) more effective ways of interacting with others, we can make rejection less likely. With improved social skills, rejected children would not need to resort to antisocial behaviors. Rejected children (and other types of unpopular children) can be taught how to initiate interaction, communicate clearly, and be friendly. They can also be discouraged from behaviors that peers dislike, such as whining and fighting. This training is very similar to the training given aggressive adolescents, who are typically unpopular (see Module 12.4). Training of this sort *does* work. Rejected children can learn skills that lead to peer acceptance and thereby avoid the long-term harm associated with being rejected (LaGreca, 1993; Mize & Ladd, 1990).

Check Your Learning

1. Toddlers who are 12 to 15 months old often engage in _____ play, which consists of playing separately but looking at one another and sometimes communicating verbally.

2. One of the advantages of _____ play is that children can use it to explore topics that frighten them.

3. Beginning in adolescence, friendships include an emphasis on _____.

4. As groups form, a _____ typically emerges, with the leader at the top.

5. Peer pressure is most powerful when _____.

6. Compared to unpopular children, popular children are usually _____.

Answers: (1) parallel, (2) make-believe, (3) loyalty, trust, and intimacy, (4) dominance hierarchy, (5) standards for appropriate behavior are vague, (6) more skilled socially

ELECTRONIC MEDIA

Learning Objectives

- How does watching television affect children's attitudes and behavior?
- How does TV-viewing influence children's creativity and cognitive development?
- How are computers used in school and what are their effects on instruction?
- How do computer and video games affect children?

Whenever Dorothy visited her granddaughters, Sadie and Molly, she was struck by the amount of time the girls spent watching television. Many of the programs they watched were worthwhile (their mother had strict rules about which programs they could and could not see). Nevertheless, Dorothy wondered if such a steady diet of video stimulation might somehow be harmful. And, how different, she thought, from her own TV-less childhood in the 1930s!

Think about some of the technological developments that today's children take for granted that were completely foreign to youngsters growing up in the 1970s, let alone in Dorothy's era, the 1930s. Your list would probably include VCRs, cable TV, CD players, video-game players, personal computers, and the World Wide Web. More forces than ever before can potentially influence children's development. In generations past, children learned their culture's values from parents, teachers, religious leaders, and print media. These sources of cultural knowledge are still with us, but they coexist with new technologies that do not always portray parents' values. Two of these technologies—television and computers—are the focus of this module. As we look at their influence, we'll see if Dorothy's concern for her granddaughters is well founded.

TELEVISION

The cartoon exaggerates TV's impact on American children, but only somewhat. After all, think about how much time you spent in front of a TV while you were growing up. If you were a typical U.S. child and adolescent, you spent much more time watching TV than interacting with your parents or in school. The numbers tell an incredible story. School-age children spend about 25 hours each week watching TV (Nielson, 1990). Extrapolated through adolescence, the typical American high-school graduate has watched 20,000 hours of TV—the equivalent of 2 full years of watching TV 24 hours daily! No wonder social scientists and lay people alike see TV as an important contributor to the socialization of American children.

For most youngsters, viewing time increases gradually during the preschool and elementary-school years, reaching a peak at about 11 to 12 years of age. Boys watch more TV than girls. Also, children with lower IQs watch more than those with higher IQs; children from lower-income families watch more TV than children from higher-income families (Huston, Watkins, & Kunkel, 1989).

It is hard to imagine that all this TV-viewing would have no effect on children's behavior. After all, 30-second TV ads are designed to influence children's preferences in toys, cereals, and hamburgers, so the programs themselves ought to have even more impact. In this section, we'll see how TV influences children's attitudes, behavior, and thinking.

MRS. HORTON, COULD YOU STOP BY SCHOOL TODAY?"

*© 1995 Martha F. Campbell.
Reprinted with permission.*

Influence on Attitudes and Social Behavior. Children are definitely influenced by what they see on TV. Module 12.4, for example, described how some children become more aggressive after viewing violence on television, and Module 13.3 discussed how children adopt gender stereotypes from TV. Television can definitely have negative effects, but can TV be put to prosocial goals? Can TV-viewing help children learn to be more generous and cooperative and have greater self-control? Yes, according to early laboratory studies. In these experiments, children were more likely to act prosocially after they watched brief films in which a peer acted prosocially (Liebert & Sprafkin, 1988). For example, children were more likely to share or more likely to resist the temptation to take from others after they watched a filmed peer sharing or resisting temptation.

In one of the early laboratory studies on the impact of TV-viewing on prosocial behavior, Bryan and Walbek (1970) gave third- and fourth-grade children a prize for playing a game. Then the children watched a film about another child who had received the same prize and was asked to donate some of the prize to charity. In one version of the film, the child agreed, but in another version, the child did not. The children in the study were then given the opportunity to donate a portion of their winnings to the same charity shown in the film. Children were much more

Children can learn prosocial behavior from television—they are more likely to be cooperative and generous after having seen TV characters act this way.

likely to donate when they saw the film about the generous child than when they saw the film about the greedy one. Thus, from watching others who were generous, children learned to be generous themselves.

Research with actual TV programs leads to the same conclusion. Youngsters who watch TV shows that emphasize prosocial behavior, such as *Mister Rogers' Neighborhood,* are more likely to behave prosocially. In fact, a comprehensive analysis revealed that the impact of viewing prosocial TV programs is much greater than the impact of viewing televised violence (Hearold, 1986). Boys, in particular, benefit from viewing prosocial TV, perhaps because they usually are much less skilled prosocially than girls.

Although research indicates that prosocial behavior *can* be influenced by TV-watching, two important factors restrict the actual prosocial impact of TV-viewing. First, prosocial behaviors are portrayed far less frequently than aggressive behaviors, so opportunities to learn prosocial behaviors from television are limited. Second, the relatively small number of prosocial programs compete with other kinds of television programs and other non-TV activities for children's time, so children simply may not watch the few prosocial programs that are televised. Consequently, we are far from harnessing the power of television for prosocial uses.

Influence on Consumer Behavior. Sugary cereals, hamburgers and french fries, snack foods, toys, jeans, and athletic shoes . . . A phenomenal number of TV advertisements for these products are directed towards children and adolescents. A typical youth may see more than 50 commercials a day! Children as young as 3 years can distinguish commercials from programs, though preschoolers believe commercials are simply a different form of entertainment—one designed to inform viewers. Not until age 8 or 9 do most children understand the persuasive intent of commercials. At the same time, children also begin to realize that commercials are not always truthful (Liebert & Sprafkin, 1988). They understand that a toy rocket will not really fly or that a doll will not really talk, contrary to how they're shown in commercials.

Even though children gradually understand the real intent of commercials, this doesn't undermine their effectiveness as sales tools with children (Donkin, Neale, & Tilston, 1993). Children grow to like many of the products advertised on TV and, like the youngster in the photograph, urge parents to buy products they've seen on television. In one study (Greenberg, Fazel, & Weber, 1986), for example, more than 75 percent of the children reported that they had asked their parents to buy a product they had advertised on TV. And more often than not, parents had purchased the product for them!

This selling power of TV has long concerned advocates for children because so many commercials are for foods that have little nutritional value and are associated with problems such as obesity and tooth decay. The U.S. government once regulated the amount and type of advertising on children's TV programs (Huston et al., 1989), but today the responsibility falls largely to parents.

Influence on Creativity. Like Dorothy, the grandmother in the opening vignette, many American children growing up in the 1930s and 1940s listened to radio instead of watching television. During these years, radio included adventure, comedy, musical, sports, and news programs. When TV was introduced, many of these programs were transferred with minor changes to the new medium. Some early critics noted that whereas radio programs required listeners to generate their own mental images, TV provided viewers with ready-made images. Would this difference stifle viewers' creativity? Years later, we know the answer is yes. Although some studies find no link between amount of TV-viewing and creativity, about half find a negative relation: As children watch more TV, they tend to be less creative on tests of divergent thinking like those described in Module 8.3 (Valkenburg & van der Voort, 1994, 1995).

What explains this negative relation? Perhaps, as the early critics observed, the problem lies with TV's ready-made images, which mean children need not make their own. Another possibility is that children who watch a lot of TV have less time for other activities that do stimulate creative thinking, such as reading (Valkenburg & van der Voort, 1994). Whatever the explanation, Dorothy is right to be concerned about her granddaughters: Creativity can be harmed by excessive TV-viewing.

Influence on Cognition. The year 1969 was a watershed in the history of children's television. That year marked the appearance of a program designed to use the power of video and animation to foster such skills as recognizing letters and numbers, counting, and vocabulary building in preschool children. Evaluations conducted in the early years showed that the program achieved its goals. Preschoolers who watched the show regularly were more proficient at the targeted academic skills than preschoolers who watched infrequently. Regular viewers also adjusted to school more readily, according to teachers' ratings (Bogatz & Ball, 1972).

By now, of course, you know that we're talking about Big Bird, Bert, Ernie, and other members of the cast of *Sesame Street,* shown in the photo on page 404. Since appearing in 1969, *Sesame Street,* produced by Children's Television Workshop, has

helped educate generations of preschoolers. Today, mothers and fathers who watched *Sesame Street* as preschoolers are watching with their own youngsters.

More recent studies confirm that *Sesame Street* remains effective. Rice and her colleagues (1990), for example, found that children who had watched *Sesame Street* frequently at age 3 had larger vocabularies as 5-year-olds than those who had watched infrequently.

Building on the success of *Sesame Street,* Children's Television Workshop has developed a number of other successful programs. *Electric Company* teaches reading skills; *3-2-1 Contact* focuses on science and technology, and *Square One TV* teaches mathematics (Fisch & McCann, 1993). Other public television programs include *Reading Rainbow,* which introduces children's books; *Where in Time is Carmen Sandiego?,* which teaches history; and *Bill Nye the Science Guy,* which makes science lessons fun and exciting. Programs like these leave little doubt that children *can* learn academic skills and useful social skills from TV, particularly by following the guidelines in the "Making Children's Lives Better" feature.

Making Children's Lives Better: **GET THE KIDS OFF THE COUCH!**

 If you know a child who sits glued to the TV screen from after school until bedtime, has his or her own remote control, and reads the contents of *TV Guide* from cover to cover, it's time to take action. Here are some suggestions:

1. Children need absolute rules concerning the amount of TV and the types of programs that they can watch. These rules must be enforced consistently!

2. Children shouldn't fall into the trap of "I'm bored, so I'll watch TV." Children should be encouraged to know what they want to watch *before* they turn on the TV set.

3. Adults should watch TV with children and discuss the programs. Parents can, for example, express their disapproval of a character's use of aggression and suggest other means of resolving conflicts. Parents can also point to the stereotypes that are depicted. The aim is for children to learn that TV's account of the world is often inaccurate and that TV should be watched critically.

4. Parents need to be good TV viewers themselves. The first two tips listed here apply to viewers of all ages! When a child is present, parents shouldn't watch violent programs or others that are inappropriate for the young. And parents should throw away the remote control so that they, too, watch TV deliberately and selectively, instead of simply mindlessly flipping between channels. ▨

TV can be beneficial *if* parents monitor their youngsters' viewing, and *if* they insist that the television industry improves the quality and variety of programs available for children and adolescents. In the next section, we'll see that both guidelines apply as well to computers. Like television, computers can influence children positively or negatively, depending upon how they are used.

COMPUTERS

How has the new computer technology influenced children? Are computers just expensive toys? Yes, say some, pointing to the proliferation of video games. Others, however, cite the benefits of computers in schools. In this section, we'll look at both uses.

Video Games. According to one recent survey of U.S. adolescents, about two-thirds of girls and nearly 90 percent of boys play video games at least 1 to 2 hours each week (Funk, 1993). Nevertheless, we know relatively little about the impact of video games on children. Many of the popular games, such *Mortal Kombat, Doom,* and *Quake* are violent, with players killing game characters in extraordinarily gruesome ways (Funk, 1993). Just as exposure to televised violence can make children behave more aggressively, playing violent video games can cause children to be more aggressive (Irwin & Gross, 1995).

Some parents fear that video games consume too much of their children's time and divert their attention from schoolwork, other activities, and peers. Although a relatively small number of children develop an overwhelming need to play video games (termed by researchers "video-game addiction"), the more common pattern is for a period of intense play after a new game or system is purchased, followed soon by a return to other activities (Fisher, 1994; Funk, 1992). In general, how often children play video games does not seem to influence their peer relationships or their grades. One exception is that boys who frequent video arcades often have lower grades. This may reflect a third variable, however—lack of parental supervision. Parents who allow their sons to spend hours "hanging out" at video arcades may also not be overly concerned about their sons' progress in school (Funk, 1992; Sakamato, 1994).

We're far from a full understanding of the impact of video games on children, but it seems fair to say that video games are relatively benign, as long as parents monitor the content of the games and the amount of time that children spend playing them.

Computers in the Classroom. New technologies—whether TV, videotape, or pocket calculator—soon find themselves in the classroom. Personal computers are no exception; virtually all American public schools now use personal computers to aid instruction. As one computer advocate put it, "We are moving rapidly toward a future when computers will comprise the dominant delivery system in education. . . . Not since the invention of the printing press has a technological device borne such implications for the learning process" (Bork, 1985, p. 1).

A primary function of computers in the schools is as a tutor (Lepper & Gurtner, 1989). Children use computers to learn reading, spelling, arithmetic, science, and social studies. Computers allow instruction to be individualized and interactive. Students proceed at their own pace, receiving feedback and help when necessary.

Computers are used in schools as tutors, as a medium for experiential learning, and as tools that allow children to accomplish traditional academic tasks more simply.

Computers are also a valuable medium for experiential learning (Lepper & Gurtner, 1989). Simulation programs allow students to explore the world in ways that would be impossible or dangerous otherwise. Students can change the law of gravity or see what happens to a city when no taxes are imposed.

Finally, the computer is a multipurpose tool that can help students achieve traditional academic goals (Steelman, 1994). A graphics program can allow artistically untalented students to produce beautiful illustrations. A word-processing program can relieve much of the drudgery associated with revising, thereby encouraging better writing. The "Real Children" feature shows how one youngster was helped this way.

Real Children: **A WORD PROCESSOR SAVES ROBERT'S WRITING**

 Throughout elementary school, Robert had hated to write. From a two-paragraph essay to a two-page report, he dreaded them all. The reasons were simple. First, Robert's penmanship was awful: Teachers always complained that they simply could not read his scribbles. Second, Robert was a lousy speller: His completed assignments always contained many misspelled words. Teachers often liked the ideas that Robert expressed in his writing, but his grades on written assignments were always low because of his penmanship and poor spelling.

All this changed in seventh grade. Robert's English class attended a weekly writing lab in which all students had computers with word-processing software. Robert's typing was painfully slow but it was worth the effort because the laser printer made his assignments look spectacular. And the spell checker meant that Robert could eliminate many of his misspelled words. When the spell checker flagged a word and presented alternate spellings, Robert would use the dictionary to determine which one he needed. (Of course, this wasn't foolproof; once he wrote that "Alexander the Great was seriously ignored in battle.") Robert's grades now began to reflect his excellent ideas, and he began to write more and more. When Robert went to high school, he began to write for the school newspaper and, in his senior year, became the editor: A success story possible because the computer helped Robert focus on the creative aspects of writing, not the tedious aspects. ■

Despite success stories like Robert's, some critics fear that computers eliminate an important human element in learning. To some, " . . . a classroom in which children spend the day plugged into their own individual desktop computers seems a chilling spectacle" (Lepper & Gurtner, 1989, p. 172). Many worry that computers isolate students from each other and from the teacher and that learning becomes a solitary activity. In reality, students interact with each other more when computers are introduced into the classroom, not less (Pozzi, Healy, & Hoyles, 1993). As the photo shows, students often cluster around one student as he or she works and they often consult the class "expert" on a particular program. Teachers, freed from many of the drill-type tasks that occupy the school day, can turn their attention to more creative aspects of instruction.

Check Your Learning

1. Preschool children believe that commercials _____.

2. Youngsters who are frequent viewers of *Sesame Street* typically improve their academic skills and, according to their teachers, _____.

3. When children play violent video games, they _____.

4. Computers are used in schools as tutors, _____, and to help students accomplish traditional academic tasks more simply.

Answers: (1) represent a different, informative type of program but do not understand their intent to persuade, (2) adjust to school more readily, (3) become more aggressive, (4) as a medium for experiential learning

CHOOLS

Learning Objectives

- **How do the size of a school and the size of classes affect students?**
- **How do traditional and open classrooms compare?**
- **What are the benefits of attending a junior high or middle school?**
- **What are the effects of grouping students by ability?**
- **What are some of the trademarks of effective teaching?**

Christine's cousins always teased her about going to a "hick" junior high school. Her school, which served a small town in a rural area, did have far fewer students than her cousins', located in a wealthy suburb. Yet Christine was able to play on the softball, basketball, and track teams; she sang in the choir, and she was vice president of student council. Her cousins were always "cut" from sports teams and were never elected to student government. Frankly, she never understood why they bragged so much about their school.

Roosevelt High School, in the center of Philadelphia, has an enrollment of 3,500 students in grades 9 to 12. Opened in 1936, the building shows its age: The rooms are drafty, the desks are decorated with generations of graffiti, and new technology means an overhead projector. East Ottawa High School, in an affluent suburb of Grand Rapids, Michigan, has an enrollment of 1,800 students in grades 9 to 12. The building is brand new and has elaborate computer facilities, an observatory, and a television in every classroom. Plainview School, in Plainview, South Dakota (population 8,752) has 42 students enrolled in grades 1 to 12. The school consists of one large room where all students are taught by the same teacher.

These are hypothetical schools, but they could be real. American schools are as heterogeneous as the students in them. Schools can be old and plain or modern and high-tech; they can be small and intimate like Christine's or large and impersonal. Do these variations affect what children can accomplish in school? Sometimes, as we shall see in this module.

SCHOOL AND CLASS SIZE

Historically, American schools had far fewer pupils than they do today. However, just as local department stores have given way to Wal-Mart, K-Mart, and the like, many smaller community elementary and secondary schools have been replaced by much larger, consolidated schools like the one in the photo. Con-

solidation is often justified on economic grounds and on the educational grounds that a larger school can offer more to students than its smaller counterpart. In fact, students apparently do not learn more in larger schools. The typical result from research is that students in smaller and larger schools do equally well on measures of scholastic achievement (Rutter et al., 1979).

School size does have an impact on social behavior, but the edge goes to smaller schools, not larger ones. Smaller schools have many of the same extracurricular activities—sports, music, student government—that are found in larger schools, but a smaller enrollment means that students like Christine in the opening vignette have more opportunity to participate. Thus, a substantially greater percentage of students are involved in extracurricular activities in smaller schools than in larger schools (Lindsay, 1984).

Students attending small schools often have more opportunities for leadership roles; students in small classes usually progress more in reading and math.

Because students in smaller schools are involved in more school activities, they have more opportunities to have the responsibilities that come with group membership and the special challenges associated with leadership. These opportunities are less common in larger schools. Consequently, students in larger schools are more likely to feel anonymous—like a student with a number, not a name—which helps explain why antisocial behavior is more common in larger schools (Rutter et al., 1979).

The same idea—"smaller is better"—also applies to class size, but with a catch. A fairly small class—fewer than 20 students—has clear benefits. Reading and math achievement improves in classes of this size (Finn & Achilles, 1990). When classes are this small, teachers spend less time on discipline and more on instruction. Plus, in small classes, teachers are better able to individualize instruction, matching their teaching to the specific needs of each student (Cahan et al., 1983).

When classes swell to more than approximately 20 students, the impact of class size largely disappears (Hedges & Stock, 1983). That is, students in classes of 30, for example, do not learn noticeably more than students in classes of 40 or 50. Why? Once teachers can no longer tailor their teaching to individuals, they teach to the group, and this approach is essentially as effective with 50 students as it is with 30.

CLASSROOM ORGANIZATION AND ATMOSPHERE

When schools were designed in the early 1900s, classrooms resembled the one in the photo, with desks organized in rows so that windows could provide adequate light and ventilation (Sommer, 1969). Today, classrooms are lighted and ventilated artificially; nevertheless, straight rows of desks remain common in American schools. When classrooms are organized this way, teachers direct more of their attention to children seated in the front and middle of the room than to children seated in the back (Adams, 1969). When desks are arranged in a circle, teachers direct their attention more evenly, leading to more student participation in class (Rosenfield, Lambert, & Black, 1985).

The arrangement of a classroom may seem like a trivial issue, but it often reflects a teacher's philosophy or approach to education. More often than not, teachers who organize their rooms in traditional rows adhere to a traditional philosophy of education. Teachers who put desks in a circle or in groups of four or five more often support an open-classroom philosophy. These philosophies go far beyond the placement of desks in the room; they differ on a number of key points (Minuchin & Shapiro, 1983):

Features of Traditional and Open-Classroom Philosophies

Features	Traditional Classrooms	Open Classrooms
Aim of instruction	Acquiring knowledge	Acquiring knowledge; learning to work with others; personal growth
Role of the teacher	Leads students through the learning process	Structures an environment in which students learn on their own
Daily schedule	Teacher organizes the day	Students choose from different activities
Individual versus collaborative learning	Students work alone	Students work alone and with others
Evaluation	Based on absolute standards and in relation to other students	Based on each student's improvement

When traditional and open classrooms are compared, students from traditional classrooms typically have somewhat better scores on achievement tests (Giaconia & Hedges, 1982). However, open classrooms have their benefits, too. Students in open classrooms tend to be more independent, more cooperative, more accepted by their peers, and they like school more (Walberg, 1986).

Both traditional and open classrooms have their merits. An open classroom promotes social development and personal growth whereas a traditional classroom typically results in greater scholastic achievement. Many of today's best classrooms, therefore, fall somewhat between either a purely traditional or purely open approach (Aitken, Bennett, & Hesketh, 1981).

THE TRANSITION TO SECONDARY SCHOOL

The 42 students at the hypothetical Plainview School mentioned earlier are unusual; today, few American students complete their primary and secondary education in a single school building. You probably attended an elementary school, a junior high or middle school, and a high school. School systems with junior highs follow a 6-3-3 plan (years spent in each school); systems with middle schools follow a 5-3-4 plan. Junior highs developed in the early 1900s to accommodate growing enrollments and respond to the special needs of young adolescents. Middle schools were created in the 1960s, as children began to reach puberty at a younger age.

Research does not give either the 6-3-3 or the 5-3-4 arrangement a decided advantage. Surprisingly, both fall short of a much older arrangement, 8-4. Simmons and Blyth (1987) conducted a 5-year longitudinal study of nearly 1,000 students in Milwaukee. Some attended elementary school through eighth grade, then went directly to a high school. Others went to elementary school through sixth grade, then went to junior high and high schools. Compared to seventh grade students in the 8-4 system, seventh graders in the 6-3-3 systems viewed school less positively, had lower grades and achievement scores, and participated in fewer extracurricular activities. Among girls, seventh graders in the 6-3-3 system had lower self-esteem and were less likely to be leaders in extracurricular activities than seventh graders in the 8-4 system.

How can we understand these unexpected results? The key is that the transition to a new school is stressful for students. In the 6-3-3 and 5-3-4 arrangements, students make this transition first as they are just entering adolescence. At this age, youth are already trying to adjust to their changing bodies, to changing responsibilities, and to changing expectations. Elementary schools are often intimate and friendly whereas junior high and middle schools seem impersonal and bureaucratic by comparison. The transition from the friendly elementary-school environment to the impersonal junior-high or middle-school environment is yet another adjustment during a time that is already trying. For students in the 8-4 arrangement, the shift to high school is challenging, but comes later in adolescence when most youth are better able to meet the challenge. The shift may be particularly trying for girls, who are more troubled than boys by bodily changes brought about by puberty.

Reverting to 8-4 schools nationwide is not practical, but we can make the transitions in 6-3-3 and 5-3-4 systems less abrupt. The key is for junior high and middle schools to create a warmer, more personal atmosphere so that students don't feel lost among the masses. One approach is to create "teams" within schools. A junior high school with 300 seventh graders, for example, might be divided into 3 teams of 100 students. A group of teachers would work exclusively with each team of students, who have all of their classes together. Teachers and students alike thus come to know each other well. In effect, under a common roof, there are three school units that have the supportive atmosphere of an elementary school, an arrangement that eases the transition to junior high or middle school (Felner & Adan, 1988).

> *The transition from elementary school to junior high or middle school is less stressful when junior high or middle schools create teams to help foster a more personal school climate.*

ABILITY GROUPING

Bluebirds, rabbits, and seashells—innocent sounding but these are typical of the names assigned to groups of students who differ in ability. Based on standardized tests of achievement, students are often divided into above-average, average, and below-average ability groups. **Grouping by ability, often known as** *tracking,* **is common in American schools, particularly when classes are too large for teachers to individualize instruction.** The idea is that if teachers cannot gear their teaching to individual children, then the next best thing is to create groups of youngsters of comparable ability and adjust the instruction accordingly.

The usual outcomes of this practice are not encouraging. As you might expect, bluebirds, rabbits, and seashells are poor disguises for the real identities of these groups, which, as the cartoon shows, children quickly discover. When they do, the self-esteem of children in the low-ability group drops. In addition, despite the spe-

SAFE HAVENS © 1993. Reprinted with special permission of King Features Syndicate.

cialized instruction that low-ability children receive, they do not catch up; instead, they fall farther behind children in the other groups. These results, when combined with the fact that more-talented youngsters progress well in classes with less-talented students, suggests that ability grouping has relatively little merit in elementary schools (Oakes, Gamoran, & Page, 1992).

TEACHERS

Take a moment to recall your teachers in elementary school, junior high, and high school. Some you probably remember fondly. They were enthusiastic, innovative, and made learning fun. You may remember others with bitterness. They seemed to have lost their love of teaching and children, making class sheer drudgery. Your experiences tell you that some teachers are better than others, but what is it that makes an effective teacher? Personality and enthusiasm are *not* the main factors. Although you may enjoy warm and eager teachers, classroom management skills matter most when it comes to students' achievement. Students learn the most when teachers can devote most of their time to instruction. When teachers spend a lot of time disciplining students or when students do not move smoothly from one class activity to the next, instructional time is wasted and students are apt to learn less (Brophy & Good, 1986).

Effective teachers manage classrooms efficiently so that classroom time can be devoted to instruction instead of to discipline.

How can teachers manage classrooms well? Reinforcing appropriate behavior—through praise or token rewards—is an effective technique for elementary-school children (Kazdin, 1982). Tokens can be exchanged for simple trinkets (combs, pencils, rings) or food (candy, cookies). Or an entire class may be rewarded with a party or field trip when a specified number of tokens is earned. The token system has the advantage that peers urge one another to behave properly for the common good.

Teachers' Expectations. We all make impressions when we first meet others, and this happens at the start of a new school year, too. Are teachers able to keep their first impressions of students from interfering with their objectivity? Not always. Teachers often treat high- and low-ability children differently (Minuchin & Shapiro, 1983; Ritts, Patterson, & Tubbs, 1992). High-ability children

- receive more attention and instruction from teachers

- get more opportunities and more time to respond

- get more praise when they answer correctly and less criticism when they err

When teachers give high-ability students more attention, opportunities, and praise, it only serves to confirm their expectancies about their students. The more-able students improve but the less-able students—who receive less instruction, have less time to answer in class, and receive less praise for being correct—fall farther behind. Different expectations for success thus result in different teaching, which leads to the expected outcome—a self-fulfilling prophecy (Raudenbusch, 1984).

Of course, teachers will always have impressions of their students' abilities, but they must avoid letting the impression of "David as he is now" become the expectation that "David will always be this way."

Peers as Tutors. The photo at the top of page 412 shows a common scene in elementary schools; one child helping another. In many schools this happens informally:

A youngster who is stuck on a problem seeks a friend's help. **Some schools, however, have formal programs of *peer tutoring* in which older or more-capable students tutor younger or less-capable students.** Children who are tutored in this fashion *do* learn. What may surprise you is that tutors often improve as much or even more than the tutees, evidently because teaching helps tutors organize their knowledge (Topping & Whiteley, 1993). The benefits of tutoring are not limited to learning. Tutors and tutees are often more motivated for schoolwork and have more positive attitudes toward school.

The effectiveness of peer tutoring also bears on the issue of ability grouping. Proponents of tracking often charge that high-ability students lose out when placed in a classroom that includes students from all ability levels. In fact, in such a classroom, the most-capable students can tutor the less-capable and everyone benefits.

Check Your Learning

1. An advantage of attending a smaller school is that students have more _____.

2. Among the advantages of an open classroom are that students tend to be more independent and more cooperative; the primary disadvantage is that _____.

3. Girls in junior high schools may have lower self-esteem because _____.

4. When students are tracked, low-ability children lose self-esteem and _____.

5. Students are most likely to achieve when their teacher is _____.

Answers: (1) opportunities to participate in school activities, (2) they have lower scores on achievement tests, (3) the stress associated with entering a new school occurs at a trying time in their lives, (4) fall farther behind students in higher-ability groups, (5) skilled in organizing and managing a classroom

PEERS, MEDIA, AND SCHOOLS
IN PERSPECTIVE

Maybe now you better understand parents who shed tears as their children go off to kindergarten? Tearful parents know that peers, media, and schools are indeed influential forces in children's development. In Module 15.1, we saw the emergence of play during the toddler and preschool years and the emergence of friendship. We also learned how groups influence children and why some youngsters are popular and others aren't. In Module 15.2, we discovered that television and computers can benefit children but often don't. In Module 15.3, we learned that many factors influence children's experiences in schools, including class and school size, classroom organization, and teachers.

In this last chapter of the book, I want to remind you that *early development is related to later development but not perfectly.* Children who are rejected by their peers are, over time, more likely to do poorly in school, to have lower self-esteem, and to have behavioral problems. Of course, not all rejected children suffer this fate. Some do well in school, have high self-esteem, and avoid behavioral problems. These positive outcomes are more common when children learn more effective skills for interacting with others. As we've seen many times in previous chapters, early experiences often point children toward a particular developmental path, but later experiences can cause them to change course.

THINKING ABOUT DEVELOPMENT

1. How might children's temperament, which was described in Module 10.2, influence the development of their play with peers?

2. How can developmental change in the nature of friendship be explained by Piaget's stages of cognitive development, discussed in Module 6.2?

3. Use the difference between divergent and convergent thinking, explained in Module 8.3, to describe the impact of TV-viewing on children's creativity and cognitive development.

4. Suppose that a candidate for your local school board contends that (a) open classrooms are harmful, (b) tracking should be implemented in grades K–12, and (c) computers in classrooms are a waste of money. How might you respond?

5. How do factors associated with effective schools (Module 15.3) relate to the factors responsible for cultural differences in mathematics achievement (Module 7.3)?

SEE FOR YOURSELF

The best way to understand differences in classroom organization and atmosphere is to visit some actual elementary-school classrooms. Try to arrange to visit three or four rooms in at least two different schools. (Usually you can do this by speaking with the school's principal.) Take along the table on page 409 that lists the characteristics of traditional and open classrooms. Watch how the teachers and children interact. Then, for each of the five features in the table, decide if the room is primarily traditional, primarily open, or in between. If possible, ask the teacher about traditional and open classroom philosophies and how he or she would describe his or her own classroom. Later, you can determine if the teachers' descriptions of their rooms match your evaluations. See for yourself!

RESOURCES

For more information about . . .

 what makes some schools more effective than others, read Edward Fiske's *Smart Schools, Smart Kids* (Simon and Schuster, 1991) which examines some exceptional U.S. schools to discover the key ingredients to a successful school

ways to improve TV programs for children, contact The Center for Media Education, a nonprofit organization dedicated to improving the quality of the electronic media, 1-202-628-2620

use of computers and other technology in schools, visit the Web site of Twenty-First Century Teachers, a nationwide volunteer initiative to encourage teachers to use technology in their teaching, http://www.21ct.org/

KEY TERMS

clique *396*
cooperative play *390*
crowd *396*

dominance hierarchy *396*
parallel play *390*
peer tutoring *412*

simple social play *390*
tracking *410*

SUMMARY

MODULE 15.1:
PEERS

THE JOYS OF PLAY

Children's first real social interactions, at about 12 to 15 months, take the form of parallel play, in which infants play alone while watching each other. A few months later, simple social play emerges, in which toddlers engage in similar activities and interact with one another. At about 2 years, cooperative play organized around a theme becomes common. Make-believe play is also common and, in addition to being fun, lets children examine frightening topics in a nonthreatening way.

FRIENDSHIP

Friendships among preschoolers are based on common interests and getting along well. As children grow, loyalty, trust, and intimacy become more important features in their friendships. Friends are usually similar in age, sex, race, and attitudes. Children with friends are more skilled socially and better adjusted.

GROUPS

Older children and adolescents often form cliques—small groups of like-minded individuals—that become part of a crowd. Some crowds have higher status than others and members of higher-status crowds often have higher self-esteem than members of lower-status crowds.

Common to most groups is a dominance hierarchy, a well-defined structure with a leader at the top. Physical power often determines the dominance hierarchy, particularly among boys. However, with older children and adolescents, dominance hierarchies are more often based on skills that are important to group functioning.

Peers are particularly influential in areas where standards of behavior are unclear, such as tastes in music or clothing, or concerning drinking, using drugs, and sex.

POPULARITY AND REJECTION

Popular children are socially skilled. They generally share, cooperate, and help others; they are unlikely to behave antisocially (fight or whine). Some children are rejected by their peers because they are too aggressive. These children are often unsuccessful in school and have behavioral problems. Their aggressive style of interacting can often be traced to parents who are belligerent or inconsistent in their discipline.

MODULE 15.2:
ELECTRONIC MEDIA

TELEVISION

Youngsters who frequently watch prosocial TV become more skilled socially, and preschoolers who watch *Sesame Street* improve their academic skills and adjust more readily to school. However, children who watch TV frequently tend to be less creative.

COMPUTERS

Most children play video games, but we still know relatively little about their impact. Children are more aggressive after playing violent video games. Computers are used in school as tutors, to provide experiential learning, and as a multipurpose tool.

MODULE 15.3:
SCHOOLS

SCHOOL AND CLASS SIZE

School size does not affect achievement, but smaller schools often are better for students' social development because they provide more opportunities to participate in school activities and fewer opportunities to feel anonymous. Classes of 20 or fewer students foster achievement; when classes have more than 20 students, size of class is not related to achievement.

CLASSROOM ORGANIZATION AND ATMOSPHERE

Traditional classrooms emphasize the acquisition of knowledge by students working alone under a teacher's direction. Open classrooms also emphasize knowledge acquisition, as well as learning to work with others and personal growth; students often work together, and the teacher's role is to structure an environment in which students can learn on their own. Traditional classrooms seem to promote academic achievement, but open classrooms foster social and personal development.

THE TRANSITION TO SECONDARY SCHOOL

The transition to middle school or junior high is often stressful because it is yet another change to which students must adjust during adolescence, a stressful time in their lives. Creating "teams" in middle or junior high schools can create a more personal environment that reduces some of the stress associated with this transition.

ABILITY GROUPING

Tracking does not help less-capable students, who continue to fall behind. Furthermore, better students progress well in classes that include students with a range of abilities.

TEACHERS

Effective teachers organize and manage classrooms so that class time is devoted to instruction not discipline. Teachers often form impressions of their students, which can sometimes give rise to self-fulfilling prophesies in which students succeed (or fail) in part because the teacher expected them to succeed (or fail). Students can learn from being tutored and from tutoring others.

Glossary

accommodation   According to Piaget, changing existing knowledge based on new knowledge.

achievement status   The identity status in Marcia's theory in which adolescents have explored alternative identities and are now secure in their chosen identities.

active gene-environment relation   The phenomenon in which individuals actively seek environments related to their genetic makeup.

active-passive child issue   The issue of whether children are simply at the mercy of the environment (passive child) or actively influence their own development through their own unique individual characteristics (active child).

activity   The dimension of temperament defined by the tempo and vigor of a child's movement during play.

adolescent egocentrism   The self-absorption that is characteristic of teenagers as they search for identity.

age of viability   The age at which a fetus can survive because most of its bodily systems function adequately; typically at 7 months after conception.

aggression   Behavior meant to harm others.

allele   A variation of a specific gene.

altruism   Prosocial behavior, such as helping and sharing, in which the individual does not benefit directly from his or her behavior.

amniocentesis   A prenatal diagnostic technique that involves withdrawing a sample of amniotic fluid through the abdomen using a syringe.

amnion   An inner sac in which the developing child will rest.

amniotic fluid   Fluid in the amnion that cushions the embryo and maintains a constant temperature.

androgens   Hormones secreted by the testes that influence aggressive behavior.

androgynous   Having a combination of gender-role traits that includes both instrumental and expressive behaviors.

animism   Crediting inanimate objects with life and lifelike properties such as feelings.

anorexia nervosa   A persistent refusal to eat, accompanied by an irrational fear of being overweight.

anoxia   Lack of oxygen during delivery, typically because the umbilical cord becomes pinched or tangled during delivery.

assimilation   According to Piaget, taking in information that is compatible with what one already knows.

attachment   The affectionate, reciprocal relationship that is formed at about 6 or 7 months between an infant and his or her primary caregiver, usually the mother.

attention   Processes that determine which information will be processed further by an individual.

auditory threshold   The quietest sound that a person can hear.

authoritarian parenting   A style of parenting that combines high levels of control and low levels of warmth toward children.

authoritative parenting   A style of parenting that combines a moderate degree of control with being warm and responsive toward children.

automatic processes   Cognitive activities that require virtually no effort.

autosomes   The first 22 pairs of chromosomes.

avoidant attachment   A relationship in which infants turn away from their mothers when they are reunited following a brief separation.

axon   A tubelike structure that emerges from the cell body and transmits information to other neurons.

babbling   Speechlike sounds that consist of vowel-consonant combinations.

basal metabolic rate   The speed with which the body consumes calories.

basic cry   A cry that starts softly and gradually becomes more intense; often heard when babies are hungry or tired.

Black English   A dialect of standard English spoken by some African Americans that has slightly different grammatical rules than standard English.

blended family   A family consisting of a biological parent, a stepparent, and children.

breech presentation   A birth in which the feet or bottom are delivered first, before the head.

cardinality principle   The counting principle that the last number name denotes the number of objects being counted.

cell body   The center of the neuron that keeps the neuron alive.

centration   Narrowly focused thought characteristic of Piaget's preoperational stage.

cephalocaudal principle   The principle that growth occurs from the head first and then down the spine.

cerebral cortex   The wrinkled surface of the brain that regulates many functions that are distinctly human.

cesarean section (C-section)   A surgical procedure in which an incision is made in the abdomen to remove the baby from the uterus.

chorion   An outer sac in which the developing child will rest during prenatal development.

chorionic villus sampling (CVS)   A prenatal diagnostic technique that involves taking a sample of tissue from the chorion.

chromosomes   Threadlike structures in the nucleus of the cell that contain genetic material.

clique   Small groups of friends who are similar in age, sex, race, and interests.

codominance   The situation in which one allele does not completely dominate another.

cohort effects   A potential problem in cross-sectional studies in which differences between age groups (cohorts) may result from environmental events, not developmental processes.

componential subtheory   In Sternberg's triarchic theory, the idea that intelligence depends on basic cognitive processes.

components   Fundamental cognitive processes that, in Sternberg's componential subtheory, are the basis of intelligence.

comprehension   The process of extracting meaning from a sequence of words.

concrete operational stage   The third of Piaget's stages, from 7 to 11 years, in which children first use mental operations to solve problems and to reason.

cones Specialized neurons in the back of the eye that detect wavelength and, therefore, color.

constricting An interaction style, common among boys, in which one child tries to emerge as the victor by threatening or contradicting the others, by exaggerating, and so on.

contextual subtheory In Sternberg's triarchic theory, the idea that intelligent behavior involves adapting to an environment to achieve one's goals.

continuity-discontinuity issue An issue concerned with whether a developmental phenomenon follows a smooth progression throughout the life span or a series of abrupt shifts.

conventional level The second level of reasoning in Kohlberg's theory, where moral reasoning is based on society's norms.

convergent thinking Using information to arrive at one standard, correct answer.

cooing Early vowel-like sounds that babies produce.

cooperative play Play that is organized around a theme, with each child taking on a different role; begins at about 2 years of age.

corpus callosum A thick bundle of neurons that connects the two cerebral hemispheres.

correlation coefficient A statistic that reveals the strength and direction of the relation between two variables.

correlational study A research design in which investigators look at relations between variables as they exist naturally in the world.

counterimitation A type of observational learning in which the child observes and learns what should not be done.

critical period A time in development when a specific type of learning can take place; before or after the critical period, the same learning is difficult or even impossible.

cross-sectional study A research design in which people of different ages are compared at the same point in time.

crowd A large group including many cliques that have similar attitudes and values.

crowning The appearance of the top of the baby's head during labor.

crystallization The first phase in Super's theory of career development, in which adolescents use their emerging identities for ideas about careers.

culture-fair intelligence tests Tests designed to reduce the impact of different experiences by including items based on experiences common to many cultures.

deductive reasoning Drawing conclusions from facts; characteristic of formal operational thought.

dendrite The end of the neuron that receives information; it looks like a tree with many branches.

deoxyribonucleic acid (DNA) A molecule composed of four nucleotide bases that is the biochemical basis of heredity.

dependent variable The behavior that is observed after other variables are manipulated.

depression A disorder characterized by pervasive feelings of sadness, irritability, and low self-esteem.

differentiation Distinguishing and mastering individual motions.

differentiation theory A theory of perceptual development formulated by Gibson in which perception reflects children's growing ability to identify the features that distinguish complex patterns.

diffusion status The identity status in Marcia's theory in which adolescents do not have an identity and are doing nothing to achieve one.

disinhibition A type of observational learning in which all behaviors like those observed are more likely after observation.

disorganized (disoriented) attachment A relationship in which infants don't seem to understand what's happening when they are separated and later reunited with their mothers.

dispensing-family-wisdom grandparents Grandparents who assume an authoritarian position and dispense information and advice to parents and child alike.

dispositional praise Praise that links a child's altruistic behavior to an underlying altruistic disposition.

distant grandparents Grandparents who have little contact except on holidays, birthdays, or other family celebrations.

divergent thinking Thinking in novel and unusual directions.

dizygotic (fraternal) twins Twins that are the result of the fertilization of two separate eggs by two sperm.

dominance hierarchy An ordering of individuals within a group in which group members with lower status defer to those with greater status.

dominant The form of an allele whose chemical instructions are followed.

Down syndrome A disorder, caused by an extra chromosome, in which individuals are mentally retarded and have a distinctive appearance.

ecological theory A view that human development cannot be separated from the environmental contexts in which development occurs.

ectoderm The outer layer of the embryo, which will become the hair, outer layer of skin, and nervous system.

ego According to Freud, the rational component of the personality; develops during the first few years of life.

egocentrism Difficulty in seeing the world from another's point of view; typical of children in Piaget's preoperational stage.

electroencephalogram (EEG) A pattern of brain waves recorded from electrodes that are placed on the scalp.

embryo The name given to the developing baby once the zygote is completely embedded in the uterine wall.

emotionality The aspect of temperament that refers to the strength of the infant's emotional response to a situation, the ease with which that response is triggered, and the ease with which the infant can be returned to a nonemotional state.

empathic orientation According to Eisenberg, a level of prosocial reasoning common in some children and many adolescents in which their thinking considers the injured child's perspective and how their own actions would make the child feel.

empathy Experiencing another person's feelings.

empirical approach An approach to perception in which sensory experience is the building block of all perception and, ultimately, all knowledge.

enabling An interaction style, common among girls, in which children's actions and remarks tend to support others and to sustain the interaction.

endoderm The inner layer of the embryo, which will become the lungs and the digestive system.

epiphyses Ends of bone tissue, which are formed first before the center is formed.

equilibration According to Piaget, the process by which children reorganize their schemes and, in the process, move to the next developmental stage.

ethological theory A theory in which development is seen from an evolutionary perspective and behaviors are examined for their survival value.

evocative gene-environment relation The phenomenon in which different genotypes evoke different responses from the environment.

exosystem According to Bronfenbrenner, social settings that influence one's development even though one does not experience them firsthand.

experiential subtheory In Sternberg's triarchic theory, the idea that intelligence is revealed on both novel and familiar tasks.

experiment A systematic way of manipulating factors that a researcher thinks cause a particular behavior.

expressive style A style of language learning that describes children whose vocabularies include many social phrases that are used like one word.

expressive traits Psychological characteristics that describe a person who is focused on emotions and interpersonal relationships.

familial mental retardation A form of mental retardation that does not involve biological damage but represents the low end of the normal distribution of intelligence.

fast mapping The fact that children make connections between new words and referents so quickly that they can't be considering all possible meanings.

fetal alcohol syndrome (FAS) A disorder affecting babies whose mothers consumed large amounts of alcohol while they were pregnant.

fetal medicine The branch of medicine that deals with treating prenatal problems before birth.

fine-motor skills Motor skills associated with grasping, holding, and manipulating objects.

foreclosure status The identity status in Marcia's theory in which adolescents have an identity that was chosen based on advice from adults, rather than one that was a result of personal exploration of alternatives.

formal grandparents Grandparents who see their role in traditional terms, expressing a strong interest in the grandchild, but maintaining a hands-off attitude toward child rearing.

formal operational stage The fourth of Piaget's stages, from roughly age 11 into adulthood, in which children and adolescents can apply mental operations to abstract entities, allowing them to think hypothetically and reason deductively.

frontal cortex A brain region that regulates personality and goal-directed behavior.

fun-seeking grandparents Grandparents who see themselves as a primary source of fun for their grandchildren and who avoid more serious interactions.

gender constancy Children's understanding, between 4 and 7 years, that maleness and femaleness do not change over situations or according to personal wishes.

gender labeling Children's understanding, by 2 or 3 years, that they are either boys or girls, and their use of these words to label themselves.

gender-schema theory A theory that children learn gender roles by first deciding if an object, activity, or behavior is female or male, then using this information to decide whether they should learn more about the object, activity, or behavior.

gender stability Children's understanding, during the preschool years, that gender does not change: Boys become men and girls become women.

gender stereotypes Beliefs and images about males and females that are not necessarily true.

gene A group of nucleotide bases that provide a specific set of biochemical instructions.

genotype A person's hereditary makeup.

germ disc A small cluster of cells near the center of the zygote that develops into the baby.

gifted Traditionally, individuals with intelligence test scores of at least 130.

grammar A language's rules for combining words to create sentences.

grammatical morphemes Words or endings of words that make a sentence grammatical.

habituation Becoming unresponsive to a stimulus that is presented repeatedly.

hedonistic orientation According to Eisenberg, a level of prosocial reasoning common in preschool and elementary-school children in which they emphasize pursuing their own pleasure.

hemispheres The right and left halves of the cortex.

heterozygous When the genes for any hereditary characteristic differ from each other.

homozygous When the genes for any hereditary characteristic are the same.

hormones Chemicals released by glands throughout the body that travel in the bloodstream to act on other body parts.

Huntington's disease A type of dementia.

id According to Freud, the element of personality that wants immediate gratification of bodily wants and needs; present at birth.

illusion of invulnerability The belief, common among adolescents, that misfortune only happens to others.

imaginary audience Adolescents' feeling that their behavior is constantly being watched by their peers.

imitation (observational learning) Learning that takes place simply by observing others.

immanent justice A characteristic of the stage of moral realism in which children believe that breaking a rule always leads to punishment.

implantation The process in which the zygote burrows into the uterine wall and establishes connections with a woman's blood vessels.

implementation The third phase in Super's theory of career development, in which individuals now enter the work force.

imprinting   Learning that occurs during a critical period soon after birth or hatching, as demonstrated with chicks creating an emotional bond with the first moving object seen.

independent variable   The factor that is manipulated by the researcher in an experiment.

indifferent-uninvolved parenting   A style of parenting that provides neither warmth nor control and minimizes the amount of time parents spend with children.

indulgent-permissive parenting   A style of parenting that offers warmth and caring but little parental control over children.

infant-directed speech   Speech that adults use with babies that is slow and loud and has exaggerated changes in pitch.

infant mortality   The number of infants out of 1,000 births who die before their first birthday.

information-processing theory   A view that human cognition consists of mental hardware and software.

inhibition   A type of observational learning in which all behaviors like those observed are less likely after observation.

instrumental traits   Psychological characteristics that describe a person who acts on and influences the world.

integration   Linking individual motions into a coherent, coordinated whole.

intelligence quotient (IQ)   A ratio of mental age to chronological age, multiplied by 100.

internal working model   An infant's understanding of how responsive and dependable the mother is; thought to influence close relationships throughout the child's life.

interposition   A perceptual cue to depth based on the fact that nearby objects partially obscure more distant objects.

intonation   A pattern of rising and falling pitch in speech or babbling that often indicates whether the utterance is a statement, question, or command.

in vitro fertilization   The technique of fertilizing eggs with sperm in a petri dish and then transferring several of the fertilized eggs to the mother's uterus where they might implant in the lining of the uterine wall.

joint custody   When both parents retain legal custody of their children following a divorce.

learning disability   When a child with normal intelligence has difficulty mastering at least one academic subject.

linear perspective   A perceptual cue to depth based on the fact that parallel lines appear to come together at a single point in the distance.

locomotion   The ability to move around in the world.

longitudinal study   A research design in which a single cohort is studied over multiple times of measurement.

long-term memory   A permanent storehouse for memories that has unlimited capacity.

macrosystem   According to Bronfenbrenner, the cultural and subcultural settings in which the microsystems, mesosystems, and exosystems are embedded.

mad cry   A more intense version of a basic cry.

mainstreaming   A practice in elementary and secondary schools in which children with Down syndrome and other children with disabilities are placed in regular classes.

maturational theory   The view that child development reflects a specific and prearranged scheme or plan within the body.

memory strategies   Activities that improve remembering.

menarche   The onset of menstruation.

mental age (MA)   In intelligence testing, a measure of children's performance corresponding to the chronological age of those whose performance equals the child's.

mental operations   Cognitive actions that can be performed on objects or ideas.

mental retardation   A disorder in which, before 18 years of age, individuals have substantially below average intelligence and problems adapting to an environment.

mental rotation   One aspect of spatial ability involving the ability to imagine how an object will look after it has been moved in space.

mesoderm   The middle layer of the embryo, which will become the muscles, bones, and circulatory system.

mesosystem   According to Bronfenbrenner, the interrelations between different microsystems.

microsystem   According to Bronfenbrenner, the people and objects that are present in one's immediate environment.

monozygotic (identical) twins   Twins that result when a single fertilized egg splits to form two new individuals.

moral realism   A stage described by Piaget that begins at about 5 years and continues through age 7, in which children believe that rules are created by wise adults and, therefore, must be followed and cannot be changed.

moral relativism   A stage described by Piaget that begins at about age 8, in which children understand that rules are created by people to help them get along.

moratorium status   The identity status in Marcia's theory in which adolescents are still examining different alternatives and have yet to find a satisfactory identity.

motor skills   Coordinated movements of the muscles and limbs.

Müller-Lyer illusion   The tendency to see a line with inward-facing arrows as longer than the same line with outward-facing arrows.

myelin   A fatty sheath that surrounds neurons in the central nervous system and allows them to transmit information more rapidly.

myelinization   The process by which neurons in the central nervous system are wrapped in myelin; begins in prenatal development and is completed in adolescence.

naturalistic observation   A method of observation in which children are observed as they behave spontaneously in a real-life situation.

nature-nurture issue   An issue concerning the manner in which genetic and environmental factors influence development.

needs-oriented orientation   According to Eisenberg, a level of prosocial reasoning common in some preschool and many elementary-school children in which they are concerned about others' needs and want to help.

negative reinforcement trap A situation in which parents often unwittingly reinforce the very behaviors they want to discourage; particularly likely between mothers and sons.

neo-Piagetian theories Theories of cognitive development that share Piaget's basic assumptions about cognitive development.

neural plate A flat group of cells present in prenatal development that becomes the brain and spinal cord.

neuron A cell that is the basic unit of the brain and nervous system that specializes in receiving and transmitting information.

niche-picking The process of deliberately seeking environments that are compatible with one's genetic makeup.

non-REM sleep Sleep in which heart rate, breathing, and brain activity are steady.

one-to-one principle The counting principle that states that there must be one and only one number name for each object counted.

operant conditioning A view of learning, proposed by Skinner, that emphasizes reward and punishment.

organic mental retardation Mental retardation that can be traced to a specific biological or physical problem.

orienting response The response to an unfamiliar or unusual stimulus in which a person startles, fixates the eyes on the stimulus, and shows changes in heart rate and brain-wave patterns.

overextension When children define words more broadly than adults do.

overregularization Children's application of rules to words that are exceptions to the rule; used as evidence that children master grammar by learning rules.

pain cry A cry that begins with a sudden, long burst, followed by a long pause and gasping.

parallel play When children play alone but are aware of and interested in what another child is doing; occurs soon after the first birthday.

passive gene-environment relation The phenomenon in which parents pass on genotypes to their children and provide much of the early environment for their young children.

peer tutoring A program in which older or more capable students tutor younger or less capable students.

period of the fetus The longest period of prenatal development, extending from the ninth week after conception until birth.

personal fable The feeling of many adolescents that their feelings and experiences are unique and have never been experienced by anyone else before.

phenotype The physical, behavioral, and psychological features that are the result of the interaction between one's genes and environment.

phenylketonuria (PKU) An inherited disorder in which babies are born lacking a liver enzyme.

phonemes Unique speech sounds that can be used to create words.

phonological awareness The ability to hear the distinctive sounds associated with specific letters.

placenta The structure through which nutrients and wastes are exchanged between the mother and the developing child.

polygenic inheritance When phenotypes are the result of the combined activity of many separate genes.

population A broad group of children that are the usual focus of research in child development.

positron emission tomography (PET-scan) A procedure that shows the amount of activity in various regions of the brain by monitoring levels of radioactive glucose.

postconventional level The third level of reasoning in Kohlberg's theory, in which morality is based on a personal moral code.

preconventional level The first level of reasoning in Kohlberg's theory, where moral reasoning is based on external forces.

prejudice A view of other people, usually negative, based on their membership in a specific group.

premature infant A baby born before the 38th week after conception.

prenatal development The many changes that turn a fertilized egg into a newborn human.

preoperational stage The second of Piaget's stages, from 2 to 7 years, in which children first use symbols to represent objects and events.

primary circular reaction According to Piaget, when infants accidentally produce pleasant events that are centered on the body and then try to recreate the events.

private speech Comments that are not intended for others but serve the purpose of helping children regulate their behavior.

propositions Ideas created during reading by combining words.

prosocial behavior Any behavior that benefits another person.

proximodistal principle The principle that growth occurs first from the center of the body and then out to the extremities.

psychodynamic theory A view first formulated by Sigmund Freud in which development is largely determined by how well people resolve conflicts they face at different ages.

psychometricians Psychologists who specialize in the measurement of psychological characteristics such as intelligence and personality.

psychosocial theory A theory proposed by Erik Erikson in which personality development is the result of the interaction of maturation and societal demands.

puberty A collection of physical changes that marks the onset of adolescence, such as the growth spurt and the growth of breasts or testes.

punishment Applying an aversive stimulus (e.g., a spanking) or removing an attractive stimulus (e.g., TV-viewing); an action that discourages the reoccurrence of the response that it follows.

rapid-eye-movement (REM) sleep Irregular sleep in which an infant's eyes will dart rapidly beneath the eyelids, while the body is quite active.

reaction range The phenomenon that a particular genotype can interact with various environments to produce a range of phenotypes.

recessive An allele whose instructions are ignored when it is combined with a dominant allele.

referential style A style of language learning that describes children whose vocabularies are dominated by names of objects, persons, or actions.

reflexes Unlearned responses that are triggered by specific stimulation.

reinforcement A consequence that increases the likelihood that a behavior will be repeated in the future.

relative size A perceptual cue to depth based on the fact that nearby objects look substantially larger than objects in the distance.

reliable As applied to tests, when test scores are consistent from one testing time to another.

resistant attachment A relationship in which, after a brief separation, infants want to be held but are difficult to console.

retinal disparity A perceptual cue to depth based on the fact that when a person views an object, the retinal images in the left and right eyes differ.

sample A group of children drawn from a population that participates in research.

savants Individuals with mental retardation who are quite talented in one domain.

scaffolding A teaching style in which adults adjust the amount of assistance that they offer, based on the learner's needs.

scheme According to Piaget, a mental structure that organizes information and regulates behavior.

schizophrenia A psychological disorder in which individuals hallucinate, have confused language and thought, and often behave bizarrely.

school phobia An overwhelming fear of going to school and active resistance to attending school.

scientific method A method of study that involves systematic observation, testing alternative hypotheses, and sharing results with the scientific community.

script The means by which people remember common events consisting of sequences of activities.

secondary circular reaction According to Piaget, when infants accidentally produce interesting events with objects and then try to repeat those events.

secular growth trends Changes in physical development from one generation to the next; for example, the fact that people in industrialized societies are larger and are maturing earlier than in previous generations.

secure attachment A relationship in which infants have come to trust and depend on their mothers.

self-concept Attitudes, behaviors, and values that a person believes make him or her a unique individual.

self-control The ability to rise above immediate pressures and not give in to impulse.

self-efficacy The belief that one is capable of performing a certain task.

self-esteem A person's judgment and feelings about his or her own worth.

self reports Children's answers to questions about specific topics.

semantic bootstrapping hypothesis A view that children rely on their knowledge of word meanings to discover grammatical rules.

sensorimotor stage The first of Piaget's four stages of cognitive development, which lasts from birth to approximately 2 years, in which infants progress from responding reflexively to using symbols.

sensory and perceptual processes The means by which the nervous system receives, selects, modifies, and organizes stimulation from the world.

sensory memory A type of memory in which information is held in raw, unanalyzed form very briefly (no longer than a few seconds).

sequential processing A scale on the K-ABC intelligence test that assesses how well a child integrates information over time.

severe malnourishment A state in which children weigh less than 60 percent of the average body weight for their age.

sex chromosomes The 23rd pair of chromosomes; these determine the sex of the child.

short-term storage space In Case's neo-Piagetian theory, a memory used to store schemes whose size increases with age.

sickle cell trait A disorder in which individuals show signs of mild anemia only when they are seriously deprived of oxygen; occurs in individuals who have one dominant allele for normal blood cells and one recessive sickle cell allele.

simple social play Play that begins at about 15 to 18 months; toddlers engage in similar activities as well as talk and smile at each other and offer each other toys.

simultaneous processing A scale on the K-ABC intelligence test that measures how well a child integrates different information at the same time.

size constancy The realization that an object's actual size remains the same despite changes in the size of its retinal image.

small-for-date infants Newborns who are substantially smaller than would be expected based on the length of time since conception.

sociability The dimension of temperament defined by preference for being with other people.

social cognitive theory A theory developed by Albert Bandura in which children use reward, punishment, and imitation to try to understand what goes on in their world.

social conventions Arbitrary standards of behavior agreed to by a cultural group to help coordinate interactions of individuals within the group.

social referencing A phenomenon in which infants in an unfamiliar or ambiguous environment look at their mother or father, as if searching for cues to help them interpret the situation.

social role A set of cultural guidelines about how one should behave, especially with other people.

social smiles Smiles that first appear at about 2 months of age, when infants see another human face.

specification The second phase in Super's theory of career development, in which adolescents learn more about specific lines of work and begin training.

spina bifida A disorder in which the embryo's neural tube does not close properly during the first month of pregnancy.

stable-order principle The counting principle that states that number names must always be counted in the same order.

stereotyped, approval-focused orientation According to Eisenberg, a level of prosocial reasoning common in many elementary-school children and adolescents in which they behave as they think society would expect "good people" to behave.

stranger anxiety An infant's wariness in the presence of an unfamiliar adult, typically observed at about 6 months of age.

structured observation Observation taken in a setting created by the researcher so that it will elicit the behavior of interest.

sudden infant death syndrome (SIDS) A disorder in which a healthy baby dies suddenly, for no apparent reason, typically occurring between 2 and 4 months of age.

superego According to Freud, the moral component of the personality that has incorporated adult standards of right and wrong.

surrogate-parent grandparents Grandparents who assume many of the normal roles of parents.

systematic desensitization A therapeutic technique that associates deep relaxation with progressively more anxiety-provoking situations.

systematic observation A method of observation in which investigators watch children and carefully record what they do or say.

telegraphic speech A style of speaking common in 1-year-olds that includes only words directly relevant to meaning.

temperament A consistent style or pattern of behavior.

teratogen An agent that causes abnormal prenatal development.

tertiary circular reaction According to Piaget, repeating old schemes with new objects.

texture gradient A perceptual cue to depth based on the fact that the texture of objects changes from coarse but distinct for nearby objects to finer and less distinct for distant objects.

theory An organized set of ideas that is designed to explain development.

theory of mind An intuitive understanding of the connections between thoughts, beliefs, intentions, and behavior; develops rapidly in the preschool years.

thyroxine A hormone essential for the development of nerve cells.

time-out Punishment that involves removing a child who is misbehaving to a quiet, unstimulating environment.

toddlers Young children who have just learned to walk.

tracking Placing schoolchildren with similar abilities in classes together.

triarchic theory A theory of intelligence proposed by Sternberg that includes componential, experiential, and contextual subtheories.

ultrasound A prenatal diagnostic technique that involves bouncing sound waves off the fetus to generate an image of the fetus.

umbilical cord A structure containing veins and arteries that connects the developing child to the placenta.

underextension When children define words more narrowly than adults do.

validity As applied to tests, the extent to which the test measures what it is supposed to measure.

visual acuity The smallest pattern that one can distinguish reliably.

visual cliff A glass-covered platform that appears to have a "shallow" side and "deep" side; used to study infants' depth perception.

word recognition The process of identifying a unique pattern of letters.

working memory A type of memory in which a small number of items can be stored briefly.

zone of proximal development The difference between what children can do with assistance and what they can do alone.

zygote The fertilized egg.

References

Ackerman, B. P. (1993). Children's understanding of the speaker's meaning in referential communication. *Journal of Experimental Child Psychology, 55,* 56–86.

Aboud, F. E. (1993). The developmental psychology of racial prejudice. *Transcultural Psychiatric Research Review, 30,* 229–242.

Adams, R. J. (1995). Further exploration of human neonatal chromatic-achromatic discrimination. *Journal of Experimental Child Psychology, 60,* 344–360.

Adams, R. J., & Courage, M. L. (1995). Development of chromatic discrimination in early infancy. *Behavioural Brain Research, 67,* 99–101.

Adams, R. S. (1969). Location as a feature of instructional interaction. *Merrill-Palmer Quarterly, 15,* 309–321.

Adler, N. (1994). *Adolescent sexual behavior looks irrational—but looks are deceiving.* Washington, DC: Federation of Behavioral, Psychological, and Cognitive Sciences.

Ainsworth, M. D. S. (1978). The development of infant-mother attachment. In B. M. Caldwell & H. N. Ricciuti (Eds.), *Review of child development research* (Vol. 3). Chicago: University of Chicago Press.

Ainsworth, M. S. (1993). Attachment as related to mother-infant interaction. *Advances in Infancy Research, 8,* 1–50.

Aitken, M., Bennett, S. N., & Hesketh, J. (1981). Teaching styles and pupil progress: A re-analysis. *British Journal of Educational Psychology, 51,* 187–196.

Ales, K. L., Druzin, M. L., & Santini, D. L. (1990). Impact of maternal age on the outcome of pregnancy. *Surgery, Gynecology & Obstetrics, 171,* 209–216.

Allen, L., Cipielewski, J., & Stanovich, K. E. (1992). Multiple indicators of children's reading habits and attitudes: Construct validity and cognitive correlates. *Journal of Educational Psychology, 84,* 489–503.

Amato, P. R., & Keith, B. (1991). Parental divorce and the well-being of children: A meta-analysis. *Psychological Bulletin, 110,* 26–46.

American Association on Mental Retardation. (1992). *Mental retardation: Definition, classification, and systems of supports* (9th ed.). Washington, DC: American Association on Mental Retardation.

American Psychiatric Association. (1987). *Diagnostic and statistical manual of mental disorders* (3rd ed., Rev.). Washington, DC: Author.

Ames, G. J., & Murray, F. B. (1982). When two wrongs make a right: Promoting cognitive change by social conflict. *Developmental Psychology, 18,* 894–897.

Anand, K. J., & Hickey, P. R. (1987). Pain and its effect in the human neonate and fetus. *New England Journal of Medicine, 31,* 1321–1329.

Anastasi, A. (1988). *Psychological testing* (6th ed.). New York: Macmillan.

Anastopoulos, A. D., Guevremont, D. C., Shelton, T. L., & DuPaul, G. J. (1992). Parenting stress among families of children with attention deficit hyperactivity disorder. *Journal of Abnormal Child Psychology, 20,* 503–520.

Anastopoulos, A. D., Shelton, T. L., DuPaul, G. J., & Guevremont, D. C. (1993). Parent training for attention deficit hyperactivity disorder: Its impact on parent functioning. *Journal of Abnormal Child Psychology, 21,* 581–596.

Anglin, J. M. (1993). Vocabulary development: A morphological analysis. *Monographs of the Society for Research in Child Development, 58* (10, Serial No. 238).

Antonarakis, S. E., & the Down Syndrome Collaborative Group. (1991). Parental origin of the extra chromosome in trisomy 21 as indicated by analysis of DNA polymorphisms. *New England Journal of Medicine, 324,* 872–876.

Apgar, V. (1953). A proposal for a new method of evaluation of the newborn infant. *Current Researches in Anesthesia and Analgesia, 32,* 260–267.

Arterberry, M., Yonas, A., & Bensen, A. S. (1989). Self-produced locomotion and the development of responsiveness to linear perspective and texture gradients. *Developmental Psychology, 25,* 976–982.

Asendorpf, J. B. (1991) Development of inhibited children's coping with unfamiliarity. *Child Development, 62,* 1460–1474.

Ashcraft, M. H. (1982). The development of mental arithmetic: A chronometric approach. *Developmental Review, 2,* 212–236.

Aslin, R. N. (1987). Visual and auditory discrimination in infancy. In J. D. Osofsky (Ed.), *Handbook of infant development* (2nd ed.). New York: Wiley.

Attie, I., Brooks-Gunn, J., & Petersen, A. C. (1990). A developmental perspective on eating disorders and eating problems. In M. Lewis & S. M. Miller (Eds.), *Handbook of developmental psychopathology.* New York: Plenum Press.

Au, T. K., & Glusman, M. (1990). The principle of mutual exclusivity in word learning: To honor or not to honor? *Child Development, 61,* 1474–1490.

Averill, J. A. (1980). A constructivist view of emotion. In R. Plutchik & H. Kellerman (Eds.), *Emotion: Theory, research, and experience: Vol. 1. Theories of emotion.* New York: Academic Press.

Baddeley, A. (1996). Exploring the central executive. *Quarterly Journal of Experimental Psychology: Human Experimental Psychlogy, 49,* 5–28.

Baenninger, M. A., & Newcombe, N. (1989). The role of experience in spatial test performance: A meta-analysis. *Sex Roles, 20,* 327–344.

Baer, D. M., & Wolf, M. M. (1968). The reinforcement contingency in preschool and remedial education. In R. D. Hess & R. M Baer (Eds.), *Early education.* Chicago: Aldine.

Bailey, J. M., Bobrow, D., Wolfe, M., & Mikach, S. (1995). Sexual orientation of adult sons of gay fathers. *Developmental Psychology, 31,* 124–129.

Baillargeon, R. (1987). Object permanence in 3½- and 4½-month-old infants. *Developmental Psychology, 23,* 655–664.

Baillargeon, R. (1994). How do infants learn about the physical world? *Current Directions in Psychological Science, 3,* 133–140.

Baker, C. (1993). *Foundations of bilingual education and bilingualism.* Clevedon, England: Multilingual Matters.

Baker, L., & Brown, A. L. (1984). Metacognitive skills and reading. In P. D. Pearson (Ed.), *Handbook of Reading Research, Part 2.* New York: Longman.

Bancroft, J., Axworthy, D., & Ratcliffe, S. (1982). The personality and psycho-sexual development of boys with 47-XXY chromosome constitution. *Journal of Child Psychology and Psychiatry, 23,* 169–180.

Bandura, A. (1977). *Social learning theory.* Englewood Cliffs, NJ: Prentice Hall.

Bandura, A. (1986). *Social foundations of thought and action: A social-cognitive theory.* Englewood Cliffs, NJ: Prentice Hall.

Bandura, A., & Mischel, W. (1965). Modification of self-imposed delay of reward through exposure to live and symbolic models. *Journal of Personality and Social Psychology, 2,* 698–705.

Bandura, A., Ross, D., & Ross, S. A. (1963). Imitation of film-mediated aggressive models. *Journal of Abnormal and Social Psychology, 66,* 3–11.

Bandura, A., & Walters, R. H. (1963). *Social learning and personality development.* New York: Holt, Rinehart & Winston.

Banks, M. D., & Dannemiller, J. L. (1987). Infant visual psychophysics. In P. Salapatek & L. Cohen (Eds.), *Handbook of infant perception* (Vol. 1). Orlando, FL: Academic Press.

Barenboim, C. (1981). The development of person perception in childhood and adolescence: From behavioral comparisons to psychological constructs to psychological comparisons. *Child Development, 52,* 129–144.

Barkley, R. A. (1990). Attention deficit disorders: History, definition, and diagnosis. In M. Lewis & S. M. Miller (Eds.), *Handbook of developmental psychopathology.* New York: Plenum Press.

Barkley, R. A. (1994). Impaired delayed responding: A unified theory of attention deficit hyperactivity disorder. In R. A. Barkley (Ed.), *Disruptive behavior disorders in childhood.* New York: Plenum Press.

Barkley, R. A., DuPaul, G. J., & Costello, A. (1993). Stimulant medications. In J. Werry & M. Aman (Eds.), *Handbook of pediatric psychopharmacology.* New York: Plenum Press.

Barr, H. M., Streissguth, A. P., Darby, B. L., & Sampson, P. D. (1990). Prenatal exposure to alcohol, caffeine, tobacco, and aspirin: Effects on fine and gross motor performance in 4-year-old children. *Developmental Psychology, 26,* 339–348.

Barton, M. E., & Tomasello, M. (1991). Joint attention and conversation in mother-infant-sibling triads. *Child Development, 62,* 517–529.

Bartsch, K., & Wellman, H. M. (1995). *Children talk about the mind.* New York: Oxford University Press.

Baskett, L. M. (1985). Sibling status effects: Adult expectations. *Developmental Psychology, 21,* 441–445.

Bates, E., Bretherton, I., & Snyder, L. (1988). *From first words to grammar: Individual differences and dissociable mechanisms.* New York: Cambridge University Press.

Bates, E., & MacWhinney, B. (1987). Competition, variation, and language learning. In B. MacWhinney (Ed.), *Mechanisms of language acquisition* (pp. 157–193). Hillsdale, NJ: Erlbaum.

Bates, J. E. (1987). Temperament in infancy. In J. D. Osofsky (Ed.), *Handbook of infant development* (2nd ed.). New York: Wiley.

Baumrind, D. (1975). *Early socialization and the discipline controversy.* Morristown, NJ: General Learning Press.

Baumrind, D. (1991). Parenting styles and adolescent development. In R. M. Lerner, A. C. Petersen, & J. Brooks-Gunn (Eds.), *Encyclopedia of adolescence.* New York: Garland.

Bayley, N. (1970). Development of mental abilities. In P. H. Mussen (Ed.), *Carmichael's manual of child psychology.* New York: Wiley.

Bayley, N. (1993). *Bayley scales of infant development: Birth to two years* (2nd ed.). San Antonio TX: Psychological Corporation.

Beal, C. R., & Belgrad, S. L. (1990). The development of message evaluation skills in young children. *Child Development, 61,* 705–712.

Beck, M. (1994, January 16). How far should we push Mother Nature? *Newsweek,* 54–57.

Becker, B. J. (1986). Influence again: An examination of reviews and studies of gender differences in social influence. In J. S. Hyde & M. C. Linn (Eds.), *The psychology of gender differences: Advances through meta-analysis.* Baltimore: Johns Hopkins University Press.

Behnke, M., & Eyler, F. D. (1993). The consequences of prenatal substance use for the developing fetus, newborn, and young child. *International Journal of the Addictions, 28,* 1341–1391.

Bellinger, D., Leviton, A., Waternaux, C., Needleman, H., & Rabinowitz, M. (1987). Longitudinal analyses of prenatal and postnatal lead exposure and early cognitive development. *New England Journal of Medicine, 316,* 1037–1043.

Belsky, J. (1993). Etiology of child maltreatment: A developmental-ecological analysis. *Psychological Bulletin, 114,* 413–434.

Belsky, J., Fish, M., & Isabella, R. A. (1991). Continuity and discontinuity in infant negative and positive emotionality: Family antecedents and attachment consequences. *Developmental Psychology, 27,* 421–431.

Belsky, J., Steinberg, L., & Draper, P. (1991). Childhood experience, interpersonal development, and reproductive strategy: An evolutionary theory of socialization. *Child Development, 62,* 647–670.

Bem, S. L. (1984). Androgyny and gender schema theory: A conceptual and empirical integration. In T. B. Sonderegger (Ed.), *Nebraska symposium on motivation: Psychology and gender.* Lincoln: University of Nebraska Press.

Bem, S. L. (1989). Genital knowledge and gender constancy in preschool children. *Child Development, 60,* 649–662.

Berenbaum, S. A., & Snyder, E. (1995). Early hormonal influences on childhood sex-typed activity and playmate preferences: Implications for the development of sexual orientation. *Developmental Psychology, 31,* 31–42.

Berg, W. K., & Berg, K. M. (1987). Psychophysiological development in infancy: State, startle, and attention. In J. D. Osofsky (Ed.), *Handbook of infant development* (2nd ed.). New York: Wiley.

Berk, L. E. (1992). Children's private speech: An overview of theory and the status of research. In R. M. Diaz & L. E. Berk (Eds.), *Private speech: From social interaction to self-regulation.* Hillsdale, NJ: Erlbaum.

Berko, J. (1958). The child's learning of English morphology. *Word, 14,* 150–177.

Berko Gleason, J. (Ed.), (1989). *The development of language* (2nd ed.). Columbus, OH: Merrill.

Berkowitz, L. (1989). Frustration-aggression hypothesis: Examination and reformulation. *Psychological Bulletin, 106,* 59–73.

Berkowitz, M. W., & Gibbs, J. C. (1985). The process of moral conflict resolution and moral development. In M. W. Berkowitz (Ed.), *Peer conflict and psychological growth* (pp. 71–84). San Francisco: Jossey-Bass.

Berndt, T. J., & Keefe, K. (1995). Friends' influence on adolescents' adjustment to school. *Child Development, 66,* 1312–1329.

Berndt, T. J., & Perry, T. B. (1990). Distinctive features and effects of adolescent friendships. In R. Montemeyer, G. R. Adams, & T. P. Gullotta, (Eds.), *From childhood to adolescence: A transition period?* London: Sage.

Bernier, J. C., & Siegel, D. H. (1994). Attention deficit hyperactivity disorder: A family ecological systems perspective. *Families in Society, 75,* 142–150.

Berry, J. W. (1993). Ethnic identities in plural societies. In M. E. Bernal & G. P. Knight (Eds.), *Ethnic identity: Formation and transmission among Hispanics and other minorities.* Albany: State University of New York Press.

Bertenthal, B. I., Campos, J. J., & Kermoian, R. (1994). An epigenetic perspective on the development of self-produced locomotion and its consequences. *Current Directions in Psychological Science, 3,* 140–145.

Best, D. L., Williams, J. E., Cloud, J. M., Davis, S. W., Robertson, L. S., Edwards, J. R., Giles, H., & Fowles, J. (1977). Development of sex-trait stereotypes among young children in the United States, England, and Ireland. *Child Development, 48,* 1375–1384.

Bialystok, E. (1988). Levels of bilingualism and levels of linguistic awareness. *Developmental Psychology, 24,* 560–567.

Bigler, R. S., & Liben, L. S. (1990). The role of attitudes and interventions in gender-schematic processing. *Child Development, 61,* 1440–1452.

Bigner, J. J., & Jacobsen, R. B. (1989). Parenting behavior of homosexual and heterosexual fathers. *Journal of Homosexuality, 18,* 173–186.

Birch, L. L. (1991). Obesity and eating disorders: A developmental perspective. *Bulletin of the Psychonomic Society, 29,* 265–272.

Birch, L. L., & Fisher, J. A. (1995). Appetite and eating behavior in children. *Pediatric Clinics of North America, 42,* 931–953.

Birnholz, J. C., & Benacerraf, B. R. (1983). The development of human fetal hearing. *Science, 222,* 516–518.

Bisanz, G. L., Das, J. P., Varnhagen, C. K., & Henderson, H. R. (1992). Structural components of reading time and recall for sentences in narratives: Exploring changes with age and reading ability. *Journal of Educational Psychology, 84,* 103–114.

Black-Gutman, D., & Hickson, F. (1996). The relationship between racial attitudes and social-cognitive development in children: An Australian study. *Developmental Psychology, 32,* 448–456.

Blash, R. R., & Unger, D. G. (1995). Self-concept of African-American male youth: Self-esteem and ethnic identity. *Journal of Child and Family Studies, 4,* 359–373.

Block, J. (1976). Debatable conclusions about sex differences. *Contemporary Psychology, 21,* 517–522.

Block, J. H. (1978). Another look at sex differentiation in the socialization behaviors of mothers and fathers. In J. Sherman & F. L. Denmark (Eds.), *Psychology of women: Future directions for research* (pp. 29–87). New York: Psychological Dimensions.

Block, J. H. (1983). Differential premises arising from differential socialization of the sexes: Some conjectures. *Child Development, 54,* 1335–1354.

Block, J. H., Gjerde, P. F., & Block, J. H. (1991). Personality antecedents of depressive tendencies in 18-year-olds: A prospective study. *Journal of Personality and Social Psychology, 60,* 726–738.

Bogatz, G. A., & Ball, S. (1972). *The second year of "Sesame Street": A continuing evaluation.* Princeton, NJ: Educational Testing Service.

Bohannon, J. N., MacWhinney, B., & Snow, C. (1990). No negative evidence revisited: Beyond learnability or who has to prove what to whom. *Developmental Psychology, 26,* 221–226.

Boivin, M., Vitaro, F., & Gagnon, C. (1992). A reassessment of the self-perception profile for children: Factor structure, reliability, and convergent validity of a French version among second- through sixth-grade children. *International Journal of Behavioral Development, 15,* 275–290.

Bork, A. (1985). *Personal computers for education.* New York: Harper & Row.

Bornstein, M. H. (1981). Psychological studies of color perception in human infants: Habituation, discrimination and categorization, recognition, and conceptualization. *Advances in Infancy Research, 1,* 1–40.

Bornstein, M. H. (1989). Information processing (habituation) in infancy and stability in cognitive development. *Human Development, 32,* 129–136.

Bornstein, M. H. (1997). Stability in mental development from early life: Methods, measures, models, meanings, and myths. In G. E. Butterworth & F. Simion (Eds.), *The development of sensory, motor, and cognitive capacities in early infancy: From sensation to cognition.* Hove, England: Psychology Press.

Bouchard, T. J., & McGue, M. (1981). Familial studies of intelligence: A review. *Science, 212,* 1056.

Bowlby, J. (1969). *Attachment and loss* (Vol. 1). New York: Basic Books.

Boyer, C. B., & Hein, K. (1991). AIDS and HIV infection in adolescents: The role of education and antibody testing. In R. M. Lerner, A. C. Petersen, & J. Brooks-Gunn (Eds.), *Encyclopedia of adolescence* (Vol. 1). New York: Garland.

Bradley, L., & Bryant, P. E. (1983). Categorizing sounds and learning to read—a causal connection. *Nature, 301,* 419–421.

Bradley, R. H., Caldwell, B. M., & Rock, S. L. (1988). Home environment and school performance: A ten-year follow-up and examination of three models of environmental action. *Child Development, 59,* 852–867.

Bradley, R. H., Caldwell, B. M., Rock, S. L., Casey, P. M., & Nelson, J. (1987). The early development of low-birthweight infants: Relationship to health, family status, family context, family processes, and parenting. *International Journal of Behavioral Development, 10,* 301–318.

Bradley, R. H., Caldwell, B. M., Rock, S. L., Ramey, C. T., Barnard, K. E., Gray, C., Hammond, M. A., Mitchell, S., Gottfried, A. W., Siegel, L., & Johnson, D. L. (1989). Home environment and cognitive development in the first 3 years of life: A collaborative study involving six sites and three ethnic groups in North America. *Developmental Psychology, 25,* 217–235.

Brainerd, C. J. (1996). Piaget: A centennial celebration. *Psychological Science, 7,* 191–203.

Brand, E., Clingempeel, W. G., & Bowen-Woodward, D. (1988). Family relationships and children's psychological adjustment in stepmother and stepfather families. In E. M. Hetherington & J. D. Arasten (Eds.), *Impact of divorce, single parenting and stepparenting on children* (pp. 299–324). Hillsdale, NJ: Erlbaum.

Braungart, J. M., Plomin, R., DeFries, J. C., & Fulker, D. W. (1992). Genetic influence on tester-rated infant temperament as assessed by Bayley's Infant Behavior Record: Nonadoptive and adoptive siblings and twins. *Developmental Psychology, 28,* 40–47.

Brazelton, T. B. (1984). *Brazelton Behavior Assessment Scale* (Rev. ed.). Philadelphia: Lippincott.

Brazelton, T. B., Nugent, J. K., & Lester, B. M. (1987). Neonatal behavioral assessment scale. In J. D. Osofsky (Ed.), *Handbook of infant development* (2nd ed). New York: Wiley.

Bretherton, I. (1992). The origins of attachment theory: John Bowlby and Mary Ainsworth. *Developmental Psychology, 28,* 759–775.

Brigham, J. C., & Spier, S. A. (1992). Opinions held by professionals who work with child witnesses. In H. Dent & R. Flin (Eds.), *Children as witnesses.* New York: Wiley.

Brody, G. H., Stoneman, A., & McCoy, J. K. (1994). Forecasting sibling relationships in early adolescence from child temperaments and family processes in middle childhood. *Child Development, 65,* 771–784.

Brody, N. (1992). *Intelligence* (2nd ed.). San Diego, CA: Academic Press.

Bronfenbrenner, U. (1979). *The ecology of human development.* Cambridge, MA: Harvard University Press.

Bronfenbrenner, U. (1989). Ecological systems theory. In R. Vasta (Ed.), *Annals of child development* (Vol. 6). Greenwich, CT: JAI Press.

Bronfenbrenner, U. (1995). Developmental ecology through space and time: A future perspective. In P. Moen, G. H. Elder, Jr., & K. Luscher (Eds.), *Examining lives in context: Perspectives on the ecology of human development.* Washington, DC: American Psychological Association.

Bronson, G. W. (1991). Infant differences in rate of visual encoding. *Child Development, 62,* 44–54.

Brooks-Gunn, J. (1988). Antecedents and consequences of variations in girls' maturational timing. *Journal of Adolescent Health Care, 9,* 1–9.

Brooks-Gunn, J., Klebanov, P. K., & Duncan, G. J. (1996). Ethnic differences in children's intelligence test scores: Role of economic deprivation, home environment, and maternal characteristics. *Child Development, 67,* 396–408.

Brooks-Gunn, J., Klebanov, P. K., Liaw, F., & Spiker, D. (1993). Enhancing the development of low-birthweight premature infants: Changes in cognition and behavior over the first three years. *Child Development, 64,* 736–753.

Brophy, J. E., & Good, T. L. (1986). Teacher behavior and student achievement. In M. C. Wittrock (Ed.), *Handbook of research on teaching* (3rd ed.). New York: Macmillan.

Brown, B. B., & Lohr, M. J. (1987). Peer-group affiliation and adolescent self-esteem: An integration of ego-identity and symbolic-interaction theories. *Journal of Personality and Social Psychology, 52,* 47–55.

Brown, B. B., Lohr, M. J., & McClenahan, E. L. (1986). Early adolescents' perceptions of peer pressure. *Journal of Early Adolescence, 6,* 139–154.

Brown, B. B., Mounts, N., Lamborn, S. D., & Steinberg, L. (1993). Parenting practices and peer group affiliation in adolescence. *Developmental Psychology, 64,* 467–482.

Brown, J. R., & Dunn, J. (1992). Talk with your mother or your sibling? Developmental changes in early family conversations about feelings. *Child Development, 63,* 336–349.

Brown, R. (1973). *A first language: The early stages.* Cambridge, MA: Harvard University Press.

Bryan, J. H., & Walbek, N. B. (1970). Preaching and practicing generosity: Children's actions and reactions. *Child Development, 41,* 329–353.

Bryant, B. K. (1992). Conflict resolution strategies in relation to children's peer relations. *Journal of Applied Developmental Psychology, 13,* 35–50.

Bryant, B. K., & Crockenberg, S. B. (1980). Correlates and dimensions of prosocial behavior: A study of female siblings with their mothers. *Child Development, 51,* 529–554.

Buhrmester, D., & Furman, W. (1987). The development of companionship and intimacy, *Child Development, 58,* 1101–1113.

Buhrmester, D., & Furman, W. (1990). Perceptions of sibling relationships during middle childhood and adolescence. *Child Development, 61,* 1387–1398.

Bullock, M., & Lütkenhaus, P. (1990). Who am I? The development of self-understanding in toddlers. *Merrill-Palmer Quarterly, 36,* 217–238.

Burns, A., & Scott, C. (1994). *Mother-headed families and why they have increased.* Hillsdale, NJ: Erlbaum.

Buss, A. H., & Plomin, R. (1975). *A temperamental theory of personality development.* New York: Wiley-Interscience.

Buss, A. H., & Plomin, R. (1984). *Temperament: Early developing personality traits.* Hillsdale, NJ: Erlbaum.

Butler, R. (1992). What young people want to know when: The effects of mastery and ability on social information seeking. *Journal of Personality and Social Psychology, 62,* 934–943.

Button, E. J., Sonuga-Burke, E. J. S., Davis, J., & Thompson, M. (1996). A prospective study of self-esteem in the prediction of eating problems in schoolgirls: Questionnaire findings. *British Journal of Clinical Psychology, 35,* 193–203.

Cahan, L. S., Filby, N. N., McCutcheon, G., & Kyle, D. W. (1983). *Class size and instruction.* New York: Longman.

Cairns, R. B., Cairns, B. D., Neckerman, H. J., Ferguson, L. L., & Gariépy, J.-L. (1989). Growth and aggression: 1. Childhood to early adolescence. *Developmental Psychology, 25,* 320–330.

Caldwell, B. M., & Bradley, R. H. (1994). Environmental issues in developmental follow-up research. In S. L. Friedman & H. C. Haywood (Eds.), *Developmental follow-up.* San Diego, CA: Academic Press.

Calkins, S. D., Fox, N. A., & Marshall, T. R. (1996). Behavioral and physiological antecedents of inhibited and uninhibited behavior. *Child Development, 67,* 523–540.

Camara, K. A., & Resnick, G. (1988). Interparental conflict and cooperation: Factors moderating children's post-divorce adjustment. In E. M. Hetherington & J. D. Arasten (Eds.), *Impact of divorce, single parenting and stepparenting on children.* Hillsdale, NJ: Erlbaum.

Campbell, F. A., & Ramey, C. T. (1994). Effects of early intervention on intellectual and academic achievement: A follow-up study of children from low-income families. *Child Development, 65,* 684–698.

Campbell, R., & Sais, E. (1995). Accelerated metalinguistic (phonological) awareness in bilingual children. *British Journal of Developmental Psychology, 13,* 61–68.

Campos, J. J., Hiatt, S., Ramsay, D., Henderson, C., & Svejda, M. (1978). The emergence of fear on the visual cliff. In M. Lewis & L. Rosenblum (Eds.), *The origins of affect.* New York: Plenum Press.

Canfield, R. L., & Smith, E. G. (1996). Number-based expectations and sequential enumeration by 5-month-old infants. *Developmental Psychology, 32,* 269–279.

Capaldi, D. M., & Patterson, G. R. (1991). Relation of parental transitions to boys' adjustment problems: 1. A linear hypothesis. 2. Mothers at risk for transitions and unskilled parenting. *Developmental Psychology, 27,* 489–504.

Capelli, C. A., Nakagawa, N., & Madden, C. M. (1990). How children understand sarcasm: The role of context and intonation. *Child Development, 61,* 1824–1841.

Carey, S. (1978). The child as a word learner. In M. Halle, J. Bresnan, & G. Miller (Eds.), *Linguistic theory and psychological reality.* Cambridge, MA: MIT Press.

Carey, S. (1992). Becoming a face expert. In V. Bruce, A. Cowey, A. W. Ellis, & D. I. Perrett (Eds.), *Processing the facial image.* Oxford, England: Clarendon Press.

Carlson, C. L., Pelham, W. E., Milich, R., & Dixon, J. (1992). Single and combined effects of methylphenidate and behavior therapy on the classroom performance of children with attention deficit hyperactivity disorder. *Journal of Abnormal Child Psychology, 20,* 213–232.

Carpenter, P. A., & Daneman, M. (1981). Lexical retrieval and error recovery in reading: A model based on eye fixations. *Journal of Verbal Learning and Verbal Behavior, 20,* 137–160.

Carroll, J. B. (1993). *Human cognitive abilities: A survey of factor-analytic studies.* New York: Cambridge University Press.

Carroll, J. L., & Loughlin, G. M. (1994). Sudden infant death syndrome. In F. A. Oski, C. D. DeAngelis, R. D. Feigin, J. A. McMillan, & J. B. Warshaw (Eds.), *Principles and practice of pediatrics.* Philadelphia: Lippincott.

Casaer, P. (1993). Old and new facts about perinatal brain development. *Journal of Child Psychology and Psychiatry, 34,* 101–109.

Case, R. (1985). *Intellectual development: Birth to adulthood.* Orlando, FL: Academic Press.

Case, R. (1992). *The mind's staircase: Exploring the conceptual underpinnings of children's thought and knowledge.* Hillsdale, NJ: Erlbaum.

Case, R. (1995). Capacity-based explanations of working memory growth: A brief history and reevaluation. In F. E. Weinert & W. Schneider (Eds.), *Memory performance and competencies.* Mahwah, NJ: Erlbaum.

Caspi, A., Henry, B., McGee, R. O., Moffitt, T. E., & Silva, P. A. (1995). Temperamental origins of child and adolescent behavior problems: From age three to age fifteen. *Child Development, 66,* 55–68.

Cattell, R. B. (1965). *The scientific analysis of personality.* Baltimore: Penguin.

Ceci, S. J., & Bruck, M. (1993). Suggestibility of the child witness: A historical review and synthesis. *Psychological Bulletin, 113,* 403–439.

Cerella, J., & Hale, S. (1994). The rise and fall in information-processing rates over the life span. *Acta Psychologica, 86,* 109–197.

Chandler, M., & Moran, T. (1990). Psychopathy and moral development: A comparative study of delinquent and nondelinquent youth. *Development and Psychopathology, 2,* 227–246.

Chao, R. K. (1994). Beyond parental control and authoritarian parenting style: Understanding Chinese parenting through the cultural notion of training. *Child Development, 65,* 1111–1119.

Chapman, P. D. (1988). *Schools as sorters: Lewis M. Terman, applied psychology, and the intelligence testing movement, 1890–1930.* New York: New York University Press.

Chase-Lansdale, P. L., Brooks-Gunn, J., & Zamsky, E. S. (1994). Young African-American multigenerational families in poverty: Quality of mothering and grandmothering. *Child Development, 65,* 373–393.

Chase-Lansdale, P. L., Cherlin, A. J., & Kiernan, K. E. (1995). The long-term effects of parental divorce on the mental health of young adults: A developmental perspective. *Child Development, 66,* 1614–1634.

Chase-Lansdale, P. L., & Hetherington, E. M. (1990). The impact of divorce on life-span development: Short- and long-term effects. In P. B. Baltes, B. L. Featherman, & R. M. Lerner, (Eds.), *Life-span development and behavior* (Vol. 10). Hillsdale, NJ: Erlbaum.

Chassin, L., Presson, C. C., Montello, D., Sherman, S. J., & McGrew, J. (1986). Changes in peer and parent influence during adolescence: Longitudinal versus cross-sectional perspectives on smoking initiation. *Developmental Psychology, 22,* 327–334.

Chen, X., Rubin, K. H., & Li, Z. (1995). Social functioning and adjustment in Chinese children. *Developmental Psychology, 31,* 531–539.

Cherlin, A. J., Furstenberg, F. F., Chase-Lansdale, P. L., Kiernan, D. E., Robins, P. K., Morrison, D. R., & Teitler, J. O. (1991). Longitudinal studies of effects of divorce on children in Great Britain and the United States. *Science, 252,* 1386–1389.

Chess, S., & Thomas, A. (1986). *Temperament in clinical practice.* New York: Guilford Press.

Chi, M. T. H. (1978). Knowledge structures and memory development. In R. Siegler (Ed.), *Children's thinking: What develops?* Hillsdale, NJ: Erlbaum.

Children's Defense Fund. (1996). *The state of America's children yearbook, 1996.* Washington, DC: Author.

Chilman, C. S. (1983). *Adolescent sexuality in a changing American society* (2nd ed.). New York: Wiley.

Chisholm, J. S. (1983). *Navajo infancy: An ethological study of child development.* New York: Aldine.

Chomitz, V. R., Cheung, L. W. Y., & Lieberman, E. (1995). The role of lifestyle in preventing low birth weight. *The Future of Children, 5,* 121–138.

Chomsky, N. (1957). *Syntactic structures.* The Hague, The Netherlands: Mouton.

Chugani, H. T., & Phelps, M. E. (1986). Maturational changes in cerebral function in infants determined by 18FDG positron emission tomography. *Science, 231,* 840–843.

Cipani, E. (1991). Educational classification and placement. In J. L. Matson & J. A. Mulick (Eds.), *Handbook of mental retardation* (2nd ed.). New York: Pergamon Press.

Clarke, A. M., & Clarke, A. D. (1989). The later cognitive effects of early intervention. *Intelligence, 13*, 289–297.

Clarke-Stewart, K. A. (1989). Infant day care: Maligned or malignant? *American Psychologist, 44*, 266–273.

Clarke-Stewart, K. A., & Fein, G. G. (1983). Early childhood programs. In P. H. Mussen (Ed.), *Handbook of child psychology* (Vol. 2). New York: Wiley.

Clifton, R., Perris, E., & Bullinger, A. (1991). Infants' perception of auditory space. *Developmental Psychology, 27*, 187–197.

Cohen, S., & Williamson, G. M. (1991). Stress and infectious disease in humans. *Psychological Bulletin, 109*, 5–24.

Colby, A., Kohlberg, L., Gibbs, J. C., & Lieberman, M. (1983). A longitudinal study of moral development. *Monographs of the Society for Research in Child Development, 48* (Whole No. 200).

Cole, D. A. (1991). Preliminary support for a competency-based model of depression in children. *Journal of Abnormal Psychology, 100*, 181–190.

Collaer, M. L., & Hines, M. (1995). Human behavioral sex differences: A role for gonadal hormones during early development? *Psychological Bulletin, 118*, 55–107.

Condry, J. C., & Ross, D. F. (1985). Sex and aggression: The influence of gender label on the perception of aggression in children. *Child Development, 56*, 225–233.

Conger, R. D., Patterson, G. R., & Ge, X. (1995). It takes two to replicate: A mediational model for the impact of parents' stress on adolescent adjustment. *Child Development, 66*, 80–97.

Coopersmith, S. (1967). *The antecedents of self-esteem.* San Francisco: Freeman.

Cornwell, K. S., Harris, L. J., & Fitzgerald, H. E. (1991). Task effects in the development of hand preference in 9-, 13-, and 20-month-old infant girls. *Developmental Neuropsychology, 7*, 19–34.

Costin, S. E., & Jones, D. C. (1992). Friendship as a facilitator of emotional responsiveness and prosocial interventions among young children. *Developmental Psychology, 28*, 941–947.

Coulton, C. J., Korbin, J. E., Su, M., & Chow, J. (1995). Community level factors and child maltreatment rates. *Child Development, 66*, 1262–1276.

Cox, M. J., Owen, M. T., Henderson, V. K., & Margand, N. A. (1992). Prediction of infant-father and infant-mother attachment. *Developmental Psychology, 28*, 474–483.

Craig, K. D., Whitfield, M. F., Grunau, R. V. E., Linton, J., & Hadjistavropoulos, H. D. (1993). Pain in the preterm neonate: Behavioural and physiological indices. *Pain, 52*, 287–299.

Crick, N. R., & Dodge, K. A. (1994). A review and reformulation of social information-processing mechanisms in children's social adjustment. *Psychological Bulletin, 115*, 74–101.

Crick, N. R., & Grotpeter, J. K. (1995). Relational aggression, gender, and social-psychological adjustment. *Child Development, 66*, 710–722.

Crook, C. (1987). Taste and olfaction. In P. Salapatek & L. Cohen (Eds.), *Handbook of infant perception* (Vol. 1). Orlando, FL: Academic Press.

Crowder, R. G. (1982). *The psychology of reading.* New York: Oxford University Press.

Crowley, K., & Siegler, R. (1993). Flexible strategy use in young children's tic-tac-toe. *Cognitive Science, 17*, 531–561.

Cummings, E. M., Iannotti, R. J., & Zahn-Waxler, C. (1989). Aggression between peers in early childhood: Individual continuity and developmental change. *Child Development, 60*, 887–895.

Cunningham, F. G., MacDonald, P. C., & Gant, N. F. (1989). *Williams obstetrics* (18th ed.). London: Appleton & Lange.

Curtiss, S. (1989). The independence and task-specificity of language. In M. H. Bornstein & J. S. Bruner (Eds.), *Interaction in human development* (pp. 105–137). Hillsdale, NJ: Erlbaum.

Damon, W., & Hart, D. (1988). *Self-understanding in childhood and adolescence.* New York: Cambridge University Press.

Dannemiller, J. L., & Hanko, S. A. (1987). A test of color constancy in 4-month-old infants. *Journal of Experimental Child Psychology, 44*, 255–267.

Dannemiller, J. L., & Stephens, B. R. (1988). A critical test of infant pattern preference models. *Child Development, 59*, 210–216.

Davidson, K. M., Richards, D. S., Schatz, D. A., & Fisher, D. A. (1991). Successful in utero treatment of fetal goiter and hypothyroidism. *New England Journal of Medicine, 324*, 543–546.

DeCasper, A. J., & Spence, M. J. (1986). Prenatal maternal speech influences newborns' perception of speech sounds. *Infant Behavior and Development, 9*, 133–150.

Dekovic, M., & Janssens, J. M. (1992). Parents' child-rearing style and child's sociometric status. *Developmental Psychology, 28*, 925–932.

Dellas, M., & Jernigan, L. P. (1990). Affective personality characteristics associated with undergraduate ego identity formation. *Journal of Adolescent Research, 5*, 306–324.

DeLoache, J. S. (1984). Oh where, oh where: Memory-based searching by very young children. In C. Sophian (Ed.), *Origins of cognitive skills.* Hillsdale, NJ: Erlbaum.

Dennis, W., & Dennis, M. G. (1940). The effects of cradling practices upon the onset of walking in Hopi children. *Journal of Genetic Psychology, 56*, 77–86.

DeRosier, M. E., Kupersmidt, J. B., & Patterson, C. J. (1995). Children's academic and behavioral adjustment as a function of the chronicity and proximity of peer rejection. *Child Development, 65*, 1799–1813.

deVilliers, J. G., & deVilliers, P. A. (1985). The acquisition of English. In D. I. Slobin (Ed.), *The cross-linguistic study of language acquisition.* Hillsdale, NJ: Erlbaum.

Diamond, M., Johnson, R., Young, D., & Singh, S. (1983). Age-related morphologic differences in the rat cerebral cortex and hippocampus: Male-female; right-left. *Experimental Neurology, 81*, 1–13.

DiBlasio, F. A., & Benda, B. B. (1990). Adolescent sexual behavior: Multivariate analysis of a social learning model. *Journal of Adolescent Research, 5*, 449–466.

Dishion, T. J. (1990). The family ecology of boys' peer relations in middle childhood. *Child Development, 61*, 874–892.

Dockrell, J., & McShane, J. (1993). *Children's learning difficulties: A cognitive approach.* Cambridge, MA: Blackwell.

Dodge, K. A., Bates, J. E., & Pettit, G. S. (1990). Mechanisms in the cycle of violence. *Science, 250*, 1678–1683.

Dodge, K. A., & Crick, N. R. (1990). Social information-processing bases of aggressive behavior in children. *Personality and Social Psychology Bulletin, 16*, 8–22.

Donkin, A. J. M., Neale, R. J., & Tilston, C. (1993). Children's food purchase requests. *Appetite, 21*, 291–294.

Downey, J., Elkin, E. J., Ehrhardt, A. A., Meyer-Bahlburg, H. F. L., Bell, J. J., & Morishima, A. (1991). Cognitive ability and everyday functioning in women with Turner's syndrome. *Journal of Learning Disabilities, 24*, 32–39.

Drabman, R. S., & Thomas, M. H. (1976). Does watching violence on television cause apathy? *Pediatrics, 52*, 329–331.

Dryfoos, J. G. (1990). *Adolescents at risk: Prevalence and prevention.* New York: Oxford University Press.

DuBois, D. L., & Hirsch, B. J. (1990). School and neighborhood friendship patterns of blacks and whites in early adolescence. *Child Development, 61*, 524–536.

Dumas, J. E., LaFreniere, P. J., & Serketich, W. J. (1995). "Balance of power": A transactional analysis of control in mother-child dyads involving socially competent, aggressive, and anxious children. *Journal of Abnormal Psychology, 104*, 104–113.

Dunham, P. J., Dunham, F., & Curwin, A. (1993). Joint-attentional states and lexical acquisition at 18 months. *Developmental Psychology, 29*, 827–831.

Dunn, J., Brown, J. R., & Maguire, M. (1995). The development of children's moral sensibility: Individual differences and emotion understanding. *Developmental Psychology, 31,* 649–659.

Dunn, J., & Kendrick, C. (1981). Social behavior of young siblings in the family context: Differences between same-sex and different-sex dyads. *Child Development, 52,* 1265–1273.

Dunn, J., Slomkowski, C., & Beardsall, L. (1994). Sibling relationships from the preschool period through middle childhood and early adolescence. *Developmental Psychology, 30,* 315–324.

Eagly, A. H. (1995). The science and politics of comparing women and men. *American Psychologist, 50,* 145–158.

Eaton, W. O., Chipperfield, J. G., & Singbeil, C. E. (1989). Birth order and activity level in children. *Developmental Psychology, 25,* 668–672.

Eaton W. O., & Enns, L. R. (1986). Sex differences in human motor activity level. *Psychological Bulletin, 100,* 19–28.

Edwards, C. A. (1994). Leadership in groups of school-age girls. *Developmental Psychology, 30,* 920–927.

Eisenberg, N. (1982). The development of reasoning regarding prosocial behavior. In N. Eisenberg (Ed.), *The development of prosocial behavior.* New York: Academic Press.

Eisenberg, N. (1986). *Altruistic emotion, cognition, and behavior.* Hillsdale, NJ: Erlbaum.

Eisenberg, N. (1988). The development of prosocial and aggressive behavior. In M. H. Bornstein & M. E. Lamb (Eds.), *Developmental psychology: An advanced textbook* (2nd ed.). Hillsdale, NJ: Erlbaum.

Eisenberg, N., Carlo, G., Murphy, B., & Van Court, P. (1995). Prosocial development in late adolescence: A longitudinal study. *Child Development, 66,* 1179–1197.

Eisenberg, N., Fabes, R. A., Schaller, M., Carlo, G., & Miller, P. A. (1991). The relations of parental characteristics and practices to children's vicarious emotional responding. *Child Development, 62,* 1393–1408.

Eisenberg, N., & Miller, P. A. (1987). The relation of empathy to prosocial and related behaviors. *Psychological Bulletin, 101,* 91–119.

Eisenberg, N., & Shell, R. (1986). Prosocial moral judgment and behavior in children: The mediating role of cost. *Personality and Social Psychology Bulletin, 12,* 426–433.

Elicker, J., Englund, M., & Sroufe, L. A. (1992). Predicting peer competence and peer relationships in childhood from early parent-child relationships. In R. D. Parke & G. W. Ladd (Eds.), *Family-peer relationships: Modes of linkage.* Hillsdale, NJ: Erlbaum.

Elkind, D. (1978). *The child's reality: Three developmental themes.* Hillsdale, NJ: Erlbaum.

Elkind, D., & Bowen, R. (1979). Imaginary audience behavior in children and adolescents. *Developmental Psychology, 15,* 38–44.

Ellis, W. K., & Rusch, F. R. (1991). Supported employment: Current practices and future directions. In J. L. Matson & J. A. Mulick (Eds.), *Handbook of mental retardation* (2nd ed.). New York: Pergamon Press.

Elmer-DeWitt, P. (1994, January 17). The genetic revolution. *Time,* 46–53.

Engle, R. W., Carullo, J. J., & Collins, K. W. (1991). Individual differences in working memory for comprehension and following directions. *Journal of Educational Research, 84,* 253–262.

Enns, J. T. (1990). Relations between components of visual attention. In J. T. Enns (Ed.), *The development of attention.* Amsterdam: North Holland.

Epstein, L. H., & Cluss, P. A. (1986). Behavioral genetics of childhood obesity. *Behavior Therapy, 17,* 324–334.

Epstein, L. H., McCurley, J., Wing, R. R., & Valoski, A. (1990). Five-year follow-up of family-based behavioral treatments for childhood obesity. *Journal of Consulting and Clinical Psychology, 58,* 661–664.

Epstein, L. H., & Wing, R. R. (1987). Behavioral treatment of childhood obesity. *Psychological Bulletin, 101,* 331–342.

Erel, O., & Burman, B. (1995). Interrelatedness of marital relations and parent-child relations: A meta-analytic review. *Psychological Bulletin, 118,* 108–132.

Erikson, E. H. (1968). *Identity: Youth and crisis.* New York: Norton.

Ervin-Tripp, S. (1970). Discourse agreement: How children answer questions. In J. R. Hayes (Ed.), *Cognition and the development of language.* New York: Wiley.

Etaugh, C., & Liss, M. B. (1992). Home, school, and playroom: Training grounds for adult gender roles. *Sex Roles, 26,* 129–147.

Fagot, B. I. (1985). Changes in thinking about early sex role development. *Developmental Review, 5,* 83–98.

Falbo, T., & Polit, E. F. (1986). Quantitative review of the only child literature: Research evidence and theory development. *Psychological Bulletin, 100,* 176–186.

Falbo, T., & Poston, D. L., Jr. (1993). The academic, personality, and physical outcomes of only children in China. *Child Development, 64,* 18–35.

Farver, J. M., & Branstetter, W. H. (1994). Preschoolers' prosocial responses to their peers' distress. *Developmental Psychology, 30,* 334–341.

Feingold, A. (1993). Cognitive gender differences: A developmental perspective. *Sex Roles, 29,* 91–112.

Feldman, D. H., & Goldsmith, L. T. (1991). *Nature's gambit.* New York: Teachers College Press.

Feldman, S. S., & Wentzel, K. R. (1990). The relationship between parental styles, sons' self-restraint, and peer relations in early adolescence. *Journal of Early Adolescence, 10,* 439–454.

Felner, R. D., & Adan, A. M. (1988). The School Transitional Environment Project: An ecological intervention and evaluation. In R. H. Price, E. L. Cowan, R. P. Lorion, & J. Ramos-McKay (Eds.), *14 ounces of prevention: A casebook for practitioners.* Washington, DC: American Psychological Association.

Fergusson, D. M., Horwood, L. J., & Shannon, F. T. (1987). Breastfeeding and subsequent social adjustment in six- and eight-year-old children. *Journal of Child Psychology and Psychiatry, 28,* 376–386.

Field, T. M. (1990). *Infancy.* Cambridge, MA: Harvard University Press.

Field, T. M., & Widmayer, S. M. (1982). Motherhood. In B. J. Wolman (Ed.), *Handbook of developmental psychology.* Englewood Cliffs, NJ: Prentice Hall.

Finn, J. D., & Achilles, C. M. (1990). Answers and questions about class size: A statewide experiment. *American Educational Research Journal, 27,* 557–577.

Fisch, S., & McCann, S. K. (1993). Making broadcast television participative: Eliciting mathematical behavior through *Square One TV. Educational Technology Research and Development, 41,* 103–109.

Fischer, K. W., & Farrar, M. J. (1987). Generalizations about generalization: How a theory of skill development explains both generality and specificity. *International Journal of Psychology, 22,* 643–677.

Fisher, C. B., & Brone, R. J. (1991). Eating disorders in adolescence. In R. M. Lerner, A. C. Petersen, & J. Brooks-Gunn (Eds.), *Encyclopedia of adolescence* (Vol. 1). New York: Garland.

Fisher, S. (1994). Identifying video game addiction in children and adolescents. *Addictive Behaviors, 19,* 545–553.

Fivush, R. (1991). Gender and emotion in mother-child conversations about the past. *Journal of Narrative and Life History, 1,* 325–341.

Flaks, D. K., Filcher, I., Masterpasqua, F., & Joseph, G. (1995). Lesbians choosing motherhood: A comparative study of lesbian and heterosexual parents and their children. *Developmental Psychology, 31,* 105–114.

Flavell, J. H. (1985). *Cognitive development* (2nd ed.). Englewood Cliffs, NJ: Prentice Hall.

Flavell, J. H. (1996). Piaget's legacy. *Psychological Science, 7,* 200–203.

Flavell, J. H., Green, F. L., & Flavell, E. R. (1989). Development of knowledge about the appearance-reality distinction. *Monographs of the Society for Research in Child Development, 51* (1, Serial No. 212).

Fox, N. A. (1991). If it's not left, it's right. *American Psychologist, 46,* 863–872.

Fox, N. A., Kimmerly, N. L., & Schaffer, W. D. (1991). Attachment to mother/attachment to father: A meta-analysis. *Child Development, 62*, 210–225.

Frankenburg, W. K., & Dobbs, J. B. (1969). The Denver Developmental Screening Test. *Journal of Pediatrics, 71*, 181–191.

French, D. C. (1988). Heterogeneity of peer-rejected boys: Aggressive and nonaggressive subtypes. *Child Development, 53*, 976–985.

French, D. C. (1990). Heterogeneity of peer-rejected girls. *Child Development, 61*, 2028–2031.

Friend, M., & Davis, T. L. (1993). Appearance-reality distinction: Children's understanding of the physical and affective domains. *Developmental Psychology, 29*, 907–914.

Frye, D. (1993). Causes and precursors of children's theories of mind. In D. F. Hay & A. Angold (Eds.), *Precursors and causes in development and psychopathology*. Chichester, England: Wiley.

Fulker, D. W., DeFries, J. C., & Plomin, R. (1988). Genetic influence on general mental ability increases between infancy and middle childhood. *Nature, 336*, 767–769.

Funk, J. B. (1992). Video games: Benign or malignant? *Journal of Developmental and Behavioral Pediatrics, 13*, 53–54.

Funk, J. B. (1993). Reevaluating the impact of video games. *Clinical Pediatrics, 32*, 86–90.

Furstenburg, F. F., Brooks-Gunn, J., & Morgan, S. P. (1987). *Adolescent mothers and their children in later life*. Cambridge, England: Cambridge University Press.

Furstenburg, F. F., & Teitler, J. O. (1994). Reconsidering the effects of marital disruption: What happens to children of divorce in early adulthood? *Journal of Family Issues, 15*, 173–190.

Gable, S., & Isabella, R. A. (1992). Maternal contributions to infant regulation of arousal. *Infant Behavior and Development, 15*, 95–107.

Galler, J. R., & Ramsey, F. (1989). A follow-up study of the influence of early malnutrition on development: Behavior at home and at school. *Journal of the American Academy of Child and Adolescent Psychiatry, 28*, 254–261.

Galler, J. R., Ramsey, F., & Forde, V. (1986). A follow-up study of the influence of early malnutrition on subsequent development: IV. Intellectual performance during adolescence. *Nutrition and Behavior, 3*, 211–222.

Garbarino, J., & Kostelny, K. (1992). Child maltreatment as a community problem. *Child Abuse and Neglect, 16*, 455–464.

Gardner, H. (1983). *Frames of mind: The theory of multiple intelligences*. New York: Basic Books.

Gardner, H. (1993). *Multiple intelligences: The theory in practice*. New York: Basic Books.

Garner, P. W., Jones, D. C., & Palmer, D. J. (1994). Social cognitive correlates of preschool children's sibling caregiving behavior. *Developmental Psychology, 30*, 905–911.

Garvey, C., & Berninger, G. (1981). Timing and turn taking in children's conversations. *Discourse Processes, 4*, 27–59.

Gash, H., & Morgan, M. (1993). School-based modifications of children's gender-related beliefs. *Journal of Applied Developmental Psychology, 14*, 277–287.

Geisel, T. (1960). *Green eggs and ham, by Dr. Seuss*. New York: Beginner Books.

Gelman, R. (1969). Conservation acquisition: A problem of learning to attend to relevant attributes. *Journal of Experimental Child Psychology, 7*, 167–187.

Gelman, R., & Meck, E. (1986). The notion of principle: The case of counting. In J. Hiebert (Ed.), *Conceptual and procedural knowledge: The case of mathematics*. Hillsdale, NJ: Erlbaum.

Ghim, H. (1990). Evidence for perceptual organization in infants: Perception of subjective contours by young infants. *Infant Behavior and Development, 13*, 221–248.

Giaconia, R. M., & Hedges, L. V. (1982). *Identifying features of open education*. Stanford, CA: Stanford University Press.

Gibbs, J. C., Clark, P. M., Joseph, J. A., Green, J. L., Goodrick, T. S., & Makowski, D. (1986). Relations between moral judgment, moral courage, and field independence. *Child Development, 57*, 185–193.

Giberson, P. K., & Weinberg, J. (1992). Fetal alcohol syndrome and functioning of the immune system. *Alcohol Health and Research World, 16*, 29–38.

Gibson, E. J. (1969). *Principles of perceptual learning and development*. New York: Appleton-Century-Crofts.

Gibson, E. J., & Walk, R. D. (1960). The "visual cliff." *Scientific American, 202*, 64–71.

Gilligan, C. (1982). *In a different voice: Psychological theory and women's development*. Cambridge, MA: Harvard University Press.

Gilligan, C., & Attanucci, J. (1988). Two moral orientations: Gender differences and similarities. *Merrill-Palmer Quarterly, 34*, 223–237.

Gillis, J. J., Gilger, J. W., Pennington, B. F., & DeFries, J. C. (1992). Attention deficit disorder in reading-disabled twins: Evidence for a genetic etiology. *Journal of Abnormal Child Psychology, 20*, 303–315.

Glick, P. C. (1989). The family life cycle and social change. *Family Relations, 38*, 123–129.

Glick, P. C., & Lin, S. (1986). Recent changes in divorce and remarriage. *Journal of Marriage and the Family, 48*, 737–747.

Goldenberg, R. L., & Klerman, L. V. (1995). Adolescent pregnancy—another look. *New England Journal of Medicine, 332*, 1161–1162.

Goldman, S. R. (1989). Strategy instruction in mathematics. *Learning Disability Quarterly, 12*, 43–55.

Goldsmith, H. H., & Harman, C. (1994). Temperament and attachment: Individuals and relationships. *Current Directions in Psychological Science, 3*, 53–57.

Goodnow, J. J. (1992). *Parental belief systems: The psychological consequences for children*. Hillsdale, NJ: Erlbaum.

Goodwyn, S. W., & Acredolo, L. P. (1993). Symbolic gesture versus word: Is there a modality advantage for onset of symbol use? *Child Development, 64*, 688–701.

Goswami, U., & Bryant, P. (1990). *Phonological skills and learning to read*. London: Erlbaum.

Gottesman, I. I. (1963). Genetic aspects of intelligent behavior. In N. R. Ellis (Ed.), *Handbook of mental deficiency*. New York: McGraw-Hill.

Gottesman, I. I. (1993). Origins of schizophrenia: Past as prologue. In R. Plomin & G. E. McClearn (Eds.), *Nature, nurture, and psychology*. Washington, DC: American Psychological Association.

Gottlieb, L. N., & Mendelson, M. J. (1990). Parental support and firstborn girls' adaptation to the birth of a sibling. *Journal of Applied Developmental Psychology, 11*, 29–48.

Gottman, J. M. (1986). The world of coordinated play: Same- and cross-sex friendships in children. In J. M. Gottman & J. G. Parker (Eds.), *Conversations of friends*. New York: Cambridge University Press.

Graber, J. A., Brooks-Gunn, J., Paikoff, R. L., & Warren, M. P. (1994). Prediction of eating problems: An 8-year study of adolescent girls. *Developmental Psychology, 30*, 823–834.

Granrud, C. E. (1986). Binocular vision and spatial perception in 4- and 5-month-old infants. *Journal of Experimental Psychology: Human Perception and Performance, 12*, 36–49.

Greenberg, B. S., Fazel, S., & Weber, M. (1986). *Children's view on advertising*. New York: Independent Broadcasting Authority Research Report.

Greenberg, M. T., & Crnic, K. A. (1988). Longitudinal predictors of developmental status and social interaction in premature and full-term infants at age two. *Child Development, 59*, 554–570.

Greenough, W. T., & Black, J. E. (1992). Induction of brain structure by experience: Substrates for cognitive development. In M. R. Gunnar & C. A. Nelson (Eds.), *Minnesota symposia on child psychology*. Hillsdale NJ: Erlbaum.

Groen, G. J., & Resnick, L. B. (1977). Can preschool children invent addition algorithms? *Journal of Educational Psychology, 69*, 645–652.

Guerra, N. G., & Slaby, R. G. (1990). Cognitive mediators of aggression in adolescent offenders: 2. Intervention. *Developmental Psychology, 26*, 269–277.

Guilford, J. P. (1967). *The nature of human intelligence*. New York: McGraw-Hill.

Guillemin, J. (1993). Cesarean birth: Social and political aspects. In B. K. Rothman (Ed.), *Encyclopedia of childbearing.* Phoenix, AZ: Oryx Press.

Gurucharri, C., & Selman, R. L. (1982). The development of interpersonal understanding during childhood, preadolescence, and adolescence: A longitudinal follow-up study. *Child Development, 53,* 924–927.

Guttmacher, A. F., & Kaiser, I. H. (1986). *Pregnancy, birth, and family planning.* New York: New American Library.

Hagen, J. W. (1967). The effect of distraction on selective attention. *Child Development, 38,* 685–694.

Hagen, J. W., & Hale, G. A. (1973). The development of attention in children. In A. D. Pick (Ed.), *Minnesota symposia on child psychology* (Vol 7). Minneapolis: University of Minnesota Press.

Hahn, W. (1987). Cerebral lateralization of function: From infancy through childhood. *Psychological Bulletin, 101,* 376–392.

Halford, G. S. (1988). A structure mapping approach to cognitive development. In A. Demetriou (Ed.), *The neo-Piagetian theories of cognitive development: Toward an integration.* Amsterdam: North Holland.

Hall, G. S. (1904). *Adolescence, I.* New York: Appleton.

Hall, J. A., & Halberstadt, A. G. (1981). Sex roles and nonverbal communication skills. *Sex Roles, 7,* 273–287.

Hallinan, M. T., & Teixeira, R. A. (1987). Opportunities and constraints: Black-white differences in the formation of interracial friendships. *Child Development, 58,* 1358–1371.

Halpern, D. F. (1986). *Sex differences in cognitive abilities.* Hillsdale, NJ: Erlbaum.

Halpern, J. J., & Luria, Z. (1989). Labels of giftedness and gender-typicality: Effects on adults' judgments of children's traits. *Psychology in the Schools, 26,* 301–310.

Hammill, D. D. (1990). On defining learning disabilities: An emerging consensus. *Journal of Learning Disabilities, 23,* 74–84.

Harris, L. J. (1983). Laterality of function in the infant: Historical and contemporary trends in theory and research. In G. Young, S. J. Segalowitz, C. M. Corter, & S. E. Trehub (Eds.), *Manual specialization and the developing brain.* New York: Academic Press.

Harris, P. L., & Kavanaugh, R. D. (1993). Young children's understanding of pretense. *Monographs of the Society for Research in Child Development, 58* (1, Serial No. 231).

Harris, P. L., Brown, E., Marriot, C., Whithall, S., & Harmer, S. (1991). Monsters, ghosts, and witches: testing the limits of the fantasy-reality distinction in young children. *British Journal of Developmental Psychology, 9,* 105–123.

Harter, S. (1985). *Manual for the self-perception profile for children.* Denver, CO: University of Denver.

Harter, S. (1988). Developmental processes in the construction of the self. In T. D. Yawkey & J. E. Johnson (Eds.), *Integrative processes and socialization: Early to middle childhood.* Hillsdale, NJ: Erlbaum.

Harter, S. (1990). Self and identity development. In S. S. Feldman & G. R. Elliott (Eds.), *At the threshold: The developing adolescent.* Cambridge, MA: Harvard University Press.

Harter, S. (1994). Developmental changes in self-understanding across the 5 to 7 shift. In A. Sameroff & M. M. Haith (Eds.), *Reason and responsibility: The passage through childhood.* Chicago: University of Chicago Press.

Harter, S., & Monsour, A. (1992). Developmental analysis of conflict caused by opposing attributes in the adolescent self-portrait. *Developmental Psychology, 28,* 251–260.

Harter, S., & Pike, R. (1984). The pictorial scale of perceived competence and social acceptance for young children. *Child Development, 55,* 1969–1982.

Harter, S., Whitesell, N. R., & Kowalski, P. S. (1992). Individual differences in the effects of educational transitions on young adolescents' perceptions of competence and motivational orientation. *American Educational Research Journal, 29,* 777–807.

Hartup, W. W. (1983). Peer relations. In P. H. Mussen (Ed.), *Handbook of child psychology* (Vol. 4). New York: Wiley.

Hartup, W. W. (1992a). Friendships and their developmental significance. In H. McGurk (Ed.), *Contemporary issues in childhood social development.* London: Routledge.

Hartup, W. W. (1992b). Peer relations in early and middle childhood. In V. B. Van Hasselt & M. Hersen (Eds.), *Handbook of social development: A lifespan perspective.* New York: Plenum Press.

Haviland, J. M., & Lelwica, M. (1987). The induced affect response: 10-week-old infants' responses to three emotion expressions. *Developmental Psychology, 23,* 97–104.

Hayes, D. P. (1988). Speaking and writing: Distinct patterns of word choice. *Journal of Memory and Language, 27,* 572–585.

Hearold, S. (1986). A synthesis of 1,043 effects of television on social behavior. In G. Comstock (Ed.), *Public communications and behavior* (Vol. 1, pp. 65–133). New York: Academic Press.

Hedges, L. V., & Nowell, A. (1995). Sex differences in mental test scores, variability, and numbers of high-scoring individuals. *Science, 269,* 41–45.

Hedges, L. V., & Stock, W. (1983). The effects of class size: An examination of rival hypotheses. *American Education Research Journal, 20,* 63–85.

Henshaw, S. K. (1993). Teenage abortion, birth, and pregnancy statistics by state, 1988. *Family Planning Perspectives, 25,* 122–126.

Hernandez, D. J. (1997). Child development and the social demography of childhood. *Child Development, 68,* 149–169.

Herrnstein, R. J., & Murray, C. (1994). *The bell curve: Intelligence and class structure in American life.* New York: Free Press.

Hetherington, E. M. (1972). Effects of father absence on personality development in adolescent daughters. *Developmental Psychology, 7,* 313–326.

Hetherington, E. M. (1988). Family relations six years after divorce. In K. Pasley & M. Ihinger-Tallman (Eds.), *Remarriage and stepparenting: Current research and theory* (pp. 185–205). New York: Guilford Press.

Hetherington, E. M. (1989). Coping with family transitions: Winners, losers and survivors. *Child Development, 60,* 1–14.

Hetherington, E. M. (1993). An overview of the Virginia Longitudinal Study of Divorce and Remarriage with a focus on early adolescence. *Journal of Family Psychology, 7,* 39–56.

Hetherington, E. M., Cox, M., & Cox, R. (1982). Effects of divorce on parents and children. In M. E. Lamb (Ed.), *Nontraditional families* (pp. 233–288). Hillsdale, NJ: Erlbaum.

Hetherington, S. E. (1990). A controlled study of the effect of prepared childbirth classes on obstetric outcomes. *Birth, 17,* 86–90.

Hirshberg, L. M., & Svejda, M. (1990). When infants look to their parents: I. Infants' social referencing of mothers compared to fathers. *Child Development, 61,* 1175–1186.

Hoff-Ginsberg, E. (1990). Maternal speech and the child's development of syntax: A further look. *Journal of Child Language, 17,* 85–99.

Hoffman, M. L. (1988). Moral development. In M. H. Bornstein and M. E. Lamb (Eds.), *Developmental psychology: An advanced textbook* (2nd ed.). Hillsdale, NJ: Erlbaum.

Hoge, D. D., Smit, E. K., & Hanson, S. L. (1990). School experiences predicting changes in self-esteem of sixth- and seventh-grade students. *Journal of Educational Psychology, 82,* 117–127.

Hogge, W. A. (1990). Teratology. In I. R. Merkatz & J. E. Thompson (Eds.), *New perspectives on prenatal care.* New York: Elsevier.

Holden, G. W. (1988). Adults' thinking about a child-rearing problem: Effects of experience, parental status and gender. *Child Development, 59,* 1623–1632.

Horowitz, F. D., & O'Brien, M. (1986). Gifted and talented children: State of knowledge and directions for research. *American Psychologist, 41,* 1147–1152.

Howard, M., & McCabe, J. B. (1990). Helping teenagers postpone sexual involvement. *Family Planning Perspectives, 22,* 21–26.

Howe, N., & Ross, H. S. (1990). Socialization perspective taking and the sibling relationship. *Developmental Psychology, 26,* 160–165.

Howes, C., & Matheson, C. C. (1992). Sequences in the development of competent play with peers: Social and social pretend play. *Developmental Psychology, 28,* 961–974.

Howes, C., Unger, O., & Seidner, L. B. (1990). Social pretend play in toddlers: Parallels with social play and with solitary pretend. *Child Development, 60,* 77–84.

Hudson, J. (1988). Children's memory for atypical actions in script-based stories: Evidence for a disruption effect. *Journal of Experimental Child Psychology, 46,* 159–173.

Huesmann, L. R. (1986). Psychological processes promoting the relation between exposure to media violence and aggressive behavior by the viewer. *Journal of Social Issues, 42,* 125–139.

Huston, A. C. (1983). Sex typing. In P. H. Mussen (Ed.), *Handbook of child psychology* (Vol. 4). New York: Wiley.

Huston, A. C., Donnerstein, E., Fairchild, H., Feshbach, N. D., Katz, P. A., Murray, J. P., Rubinstein, E. A., Wilcox, B. L., & Zuckerman, D. (1992). *Big world, small screen: The role of television in American society.* Lincoln: University of Nebraska Press.

Huston, A. C., Watkins, B. A., & Kunkel, D. (1989). Public policy and children's television. *American Psychologist, 44,* 424–433.

Hutchins, E. (1983). Understanding Micronesian navigation. In D. A. Gentner & A. Stevens (Eds.), *Mental models.* Hillsdale, NJ: Erlbaum.

Huttenlocher, J., Haight, W., Bryk, A., Seltzer, M., & Lyons, T. (1991). Early vocabulary growth: Relation to language input and gender. *Developmental Psychology, 27,* 236–248.

Huttenlocher, P. R. (1990). Morphometric study of human cerebral cortex development. *Neuropsychologia, 28,* 517–527.

Hyde, J. S. (1984). How large are gender differences in aggression? A developmental meta-analysis. *Developmental Psychology, 20,* 722–736.

Hyde, J. S., Fennema, E., & Lamon, S. J. (1990). Gender differences in mathematics performance: A meta-analysis. *Psychological Bulletin, 107,* 139–155.

Hyde, J. S., & Linn, M. C. (1988). Gender differences in verbal ability. *Psychological Bulletin, 104,* 53–69.

Hymel, S., Rubin, K. H., Rowden, L., & LeMare, L. (1990). Children's peer relationships: Longitudinal prediction of internalizing and externalizing problems from middle to late childhood. *Child Development, 61,* 2004–2021.

Inhelder, B., & Piaget, J. (1958). *The growth of logical thinking from childhood to adolescence.* New York: Basic Books.

Institute of Medicine. (1990). *Nutrition during pregnancy.* Washington, DC: National Academy Press.

Irwin, R. A., & Gross, A. M. (1995). Cognitive tempo, violent video games, and aggressive behavior in young boys. *Journal of Family Violence, 10,* 337–350.

Izard, C. E. (1991). *The psychology of emotions.* New York: Plenum Press.

Jacklin, C. N. (1989). Female and male: Issues of gender. *American Psychologist, 44,* 127–133.

Jacklin, C. N., & Maccoby, E. E. (1978). Social behavior at thirty-three months in same-sex and mixed-sex dyads. *Child Development, 49,* 557–569.

Jackson, N. E., & Butterfield, E. C. (1986). A conception of giftedness designed to promote research. In R. J. Sternberg & J. E. Davidson (Eds.), *Conceptions of giftedness.* Cambridge, England: Cambridge University Press.

Jacobs, J. E. (1991). Influence of gender stereotypes on parent and child mathematics attitudes. *Journal of Educational Psychology, 83,* 518–527.

Jacobson, J. L., Jacobson, S. W., & Humphrey, H. E. B. (1990). Effects of in utero exposure to polychlorinated biphenyls and related contaminants on cognitive functioning in young children. *Journal of Pediatrics, 116,* 38–45.

Jaeger, E., & Weinraub, M. (1990). Early nonmaternal care and infant attachment: In search of process. In K. McCartney (Ed.), *Child care and maternal employment: A social ecology approach.* San Francisco: Jossey-Bass.

Jensen, M. D., Benson, R. C., & Bobak, I. M. (1981). *Maternity care.* St. Louis, MO: C. V. Mosby.

Johanson, R. B., Rice, C., Coyle, M., Arthur, J., Anyanwu, L., Ibrahim, J., Warwick, A., Redman, C. W. E., & O'Brien, P. M. S. (1993). A randomized prospective study comparing the new vacuum extractor policy with forceps delivery. *British Journal of Obstetrics and Gynecology, 100,* 524–530.

Johnston, F. E. (1986). Somatic growth of the infant and preschool child. In F. Falkner & J. M. Tanner (Eds.), *Human growth: A comprehensive treatise* (pp. 3–24). New York: Plenum Press.

Johnstone, B., Frame, C. L., & Bouman, D. (1992). Physical attractiveness and athletic and academic ability in controversial-aggressive and rejected-aggressive children. *Journal of Social and Clinical Psychology, 11,* 71–79.

Jusczyk, P. W. (1995). Language acquisition: Speech sounds and phonological development. In J. L. Miller & P. D. Eimas (Eds.), *Handbook of perception and cognition: Vol. 11. Speech, language, and communication.* Orlando, FL: Academic Press.

Jusczyk, P. W., & Aslin, R. N. (1995). Infants' detection of the sound patterns of words in fluent speech. *Cognitive Psychology, 29,* 1–23.

Kagan, J., Arcus, D., Snidman, N., Feng, W. Y., Hendler, J., & Greene, S. (1994). Reactivity in infants: A cross-national comparison. *Developmental Psychology, 30,* 342–345.

Kaijura, H., Cowart, B. J., & Beauchamp, G. K. (1992). Early developmental change in bitter taste responses in human infants. *Developmental Psychobiology, 25,* 375–386.

Kail, R. (1990). *The development of memory in children* (3rd ed.). New York: Freeman.

Kail, R. (1991). Developmental change in speed of processing during childhood and adolescence. *Psychological Bulletin, 109,* 490–501.

Kail, R. (1992). Development of memory in children. In L. R. Squire (Ed.), *Encyclopedia of learning and memory.* New York: Macmillan.

Kail, R. (1995). Processing speed, memory, and cognition. In F. E. Weinert & W. Schneider (Eds.), *Memory performance and competencies.* Mahwah, NJ: Erlbaum.

Kail, R., & Bisanz, J. (1992). The information-processing perspective on cognitive development in childhood and adolescence. In R. J. Sternberg, & C. A. Berg (Eds.), *Intellectual development.* New York: Cambridge University Press.

Kail, R., & Park, Y. (1990). Impact of practice on speed of mental rotation. *Journal of Experimental Child Psychology, 49,* 227–244.

Kamerman, S. B. (1993). International perspectives on child care policies and programs. *Pediatrics, 91,* 248–252.

Kandel, D. B. (1978). Homophily, selection, and socialization in adolescent friendships. *American Journal of Sociology, 84,* 427–436.

Kaplan, P. S., Goldstein, M. H., Huckeby, E. R., & Cooper, R. P. (1995). Habituation, sensitization, and infants' responses to motherese speech. *Developmental Psychobiology, 28,* 45–57.

Karniol, R. (1989). The role of manual manipulative states in the infant's acquisition of perceived control over objects. *Developmental Review, 9,* 205–233.

Kaufman, A. S. (1979). *Intelligent testing with the WISC-R.* New York: Wiley.

Kaufman, A. S., & Kaufman, N. L. (1983a). *K-ABC administration and scoring manual.* Circle Pines, MN: American Guidance Service.

Kaufman, A. S., & Kaufman, N. L. (1983b). *K-ABC interpretive manual.* Circle Pines, MN: American Guidance Service.

Kazdin, A. E. (1982). Applying behavioral principles in the schools. In C. R. Reynolds & T. B. Gutkin (Eds.), *The handbook of school psychology.* New York: Wiley.

Keane, S. P., Brown, K. P., & Crenshaw, T. M. (1990). Children's intention-cue detection as a function of maternal social behavior: Pathways to social rejection. *Developmental Psychology, 26,* 1004–1009.

Kearney, C. A., & Silverman, W. K. (1995). Family environment of youngsters with school refusal behavior: A synopsis with implications for assessment and treatment. *American Journal of Family Therapy, 23,* 59–72.

Kenrick, D. T. (1987). Gender, genes, and the social environment. In P. C. Shaver & C. Hendrick (Eds.), *Review of Personality and Social Psychology, 8*, 14–43.

Kiernan, K. E. (1992). The impact of family disruption in childhood on transitions made in young adult life. *Population Studies, 46*, 213–234.

Kim, Y. H., & Goetz, E. T. (1994). Context effects on word recognition and reading comprehension of good and poor readers: A test of the interactive compensatory hypothesis. *Reading Research Quarterly, 29*, 178–188.

Kimball, M. M. (1986). Television and sex-role attitudes. In T. M. Williams (Ed.), *The impact of television* (pp. 265–301). New York: Academic Press.

Kimball, M. M. (1989). A new perspective on women's math achievement. *Psychological Bulletin, 105*, 198–214.

Kinsbourne, M. (1989). Mechanisms and development of hemisphere specialization in children. In C. R. Reynolds & E. Fletcher-Janzen (Eds), *Handbook of clinical child neuropsychology*. New York: Plenum Press.

Klapper, J. T. (1968). The impact of viewing "aggression": Studies and problems of extrapolation. In O. N. Larsen (Ed.), *Violence and the mass media*. New York: Harper & Row.

Klatzky, R. L. (1980). *Human memory* (2nd ed.). San Francisco: Freeman.

Knight, B. C., Baker, E. H., & Minder, C. C. (1990). Concurrent validity of the Stanford-Binet: Fourth Edition and Kaufman Assessment Battery for Children with learning disabled students. *Psychology in the Schools, 27*, 116–125.

Kochanska, G. (1995). Children's temperament, mothers' discipline, and security of attachment: Multiple pathways to emerging internalization. *Child Development, 66*, 597–615.

Kochanska, G., & Radke-Yarrow, M. (1992). Inhibition in toddlerhood and the dynamics of the child's interaction with an unfamiliar peer at age five. *Child Development, 63*, 325–335.

Kogan, N. (1983). Stylistic variation in childhood and adolescence: Creativity, metaphor, and cognitive style. In P. H. Mussen (Ed.), *Handbook of child psychology* (Vol. 3). New York: Wiley.

Kohlberg, L. (1966). A cognitive-developmental analysis of children's sex-role concepts and attitudes. In. E. E. Maccoby (Ed.), *The development of sex differences*. Stanford, CA: Stanford University Press.

Kohlberg, L. (1969). Stage and sequence: The cognitive-developmental approach to socialization. In D. Goslin (Ed.), *Handbook of socialization theory and research* (pp. 347–480). Chicago: Rand McNally.

Kohlberg, L., & Ullian, D. Z. (1974). Stages in the development of psychosexual concepts and attitudes. In R. C. Friedman, R. M. Richart, & R. L. Van Wiele (Eds.), *Sex differences in behavior*. New York: Wiley.

Kolata, G. (1990, February 6). Rush is on to capitalize on test for gene causing cystic fibrosis. *The New York Times*, p. C3.

Kolb, B. (1989). Brain development, plasticity, and behavior. *American Psychologist, 44*, 1203–1212.

Kopp, C. B. (1982). The antecedents of self-regulation. *Developmental Psychology, 18*, 199–214.

Kopp, C. B., & McCall, R. B. (1982). Predicting later mental performance for normal, at-risk, and handicapped infants. In P. B. Baltes & O. G. Brim (Eds.), *Life-span development and behavior* (Vol. 4). New York: Academic Press.

Kopp, C. B. (1987). The growth of self-regulation: Caregivers and children. In N. Eisenberg (Ed.), *Contemporary topics in developmental psychology*. New York: Wiley.

Korbin, J. E. (1987). Child abuse and neglect: The cultural context. In R. E. Helfer & R. S. Kempe (Eds.), *The battered child* (4th ed., pp. 23–41). Chicago: University of Chicago Press.

Kowal, A., & Kramer, L. (1997). Children's understanding of parental differential treatment. *Child Development, 68*, 113–126.

Krebs, D., & Gillmore, J. (1982). The relationship among the first stages of cognitive development, role-taking abilities, and moral development. *Child Development, 53*, 877–886.

Krispin, O., Sternberg, K. J., & Lamb, M. E. (1992). The dimensions of peer evaluation in Israel: A cross-cultural perspective. *International Journal of Behavioral Development, 15*, 299–314.

Kuhl, P. K. (1993). Early linguistic experience and phonetic perception: Implications for theories of developmental speech perception. *Journal of Phonetics, 21*, 125–139.

Kupersmidt, J. B., & Coie, J. D. (1990). Preadolescent peer status, aggression, and school adjustment as predictors of externalizing problems in adolescence. *Child Development, 61*, 1350–1362.

Ladd, G. W., & LeSieur, K. D. (1995). Parents and children's peer relationships. In M. H. Bornstein (Ed.), *Handbook of parenting: Vol. 4. Applied and practical parenting* (pp. 377–410). Mahwah, NJ: Erlbaum.

LaFreniere, P., Strayer, F. F., & Gauthier, R. (1984). The emergence of same-sex affiliative preferences among preschool peers: A developmental/ethnological perspective. *Child Development, 55*, 1958–1965.

LaGreca, A. M. (1993). Social skills training with children: Where do we go from here? *Journal of Clinical Child Psychology, 22*, 288–298.

Lamb, M. E., Sternberg, K. J., & Prodromidis, M. (1992). Nonmaternal care and the security of infant-mother attachment: A reanalysis of the data. *Infant Behavior and Development, 15*, 71–83.

Lamborn, S. D., Mounts, N. S., Steinberg, L., & Dornbusch, S. M. (1991). Patterns of competence and adjustment among adolescents from authoritative, authoritarian, indulgent, and neglectful families. *Child Development, 62*, 1049–1065.

Lampinen, J. M., & Smith, V. L. (1995). The incredible (and sometimes incredulous) child witness: Child eyewitnesses' sensitivity to source credibility cues. *Journal of Applied Psychology, 80*, 621–627.

Langlois, J. H., & Downs, A. C. (1980). Mothers, fathers, and peers as socialization agents of sex-typed play behaviors in young children. *Child Development, 51*, 1237–1247.

Lanza, E. (1992). Can bilingual two-year-olds code-switch? *Journal of Child Language, 19*, 633–658.

Lau, S. (1989). Sex role orientation and domains of self-esteem. *Sex Roles, 21*, 415–422.

Laursen, B., & Collins, W. A. (1994). Interpersonal conflict during adolescence. *Psychological Bulletin, 115*, 197–209.

Leichtman, M. D., & Ceci, S. L. (1995). The effects of stereotypes and suggestions on preschoolers' reports. *Developmental Psychology, 31*, 568–578.

LeMare, L. J., & Rubin, K. H. (1987). Perspective taking and peer interaction: Structural and developmental analyses. *Child Development, 58*, 306–315.

Lepper, M. R., & Gurtner, J. (1989). Children and computers. *American Psychologist, 44*, 170–178.

Levine, L. E. (1983). Mine: Self-definition in 2-year-old boys. *Developmental Psychology, 19*, 544–549.

Levitt, A. G., & Utman, J. A. (1992). From babbling towards the sound systems of English and French: A longitudinal two-case study. *Journal of Child Language, 19*, 19–49.

Levitt, M. J., Guacci-Franco, N., & Levitt, J. L. (1993). Convoys of social support in childhood and early adolescence: Structure and function. *Developmental Psychology, 29*, 811–818.

Levy, G. D., & Boston, M. B. (1994). Preschoolers' recall of own-sex and other-sex gender scripts. *Journal of Genetic Psychology, 155*, 367–371.

Levy, G. D., Taylor, M. G., & Gelman, S. A. (1995). Traditional and evaluative aspects of flexibility in gender roles, social conventions, moral rules, and physical laws. *Child Development, 66*, 515–531.

Levy, J. (1976). A review of evidence for a genetic component in the determination of handedness. *Behavior Genetics, 6*, 429–453.

Lewis, M. (1987). Social development in infancy and early childhood. In J. D. Osofsky (Ed.), *Handbook of infant development*. New York: Wiley.

Lewis, M. (1992). *Shame: The exposed self.* New York: Free Press.

Lewis, M., Alessandri, S. M., & Sullivan, M. W. (1992). Differences in shame and pride as a function of children's gender and task difficulty. *Child Development, 63,* 630–638.

Lewis, M., & Brooks-Gunn, J. (1979). *Social cognition and the acquisition of self.* New York: Plenum Press.

Lewis, M., Ramsay, D. S., & Kawakami, K. (1993). Differences between Japanese infants and Caucasian American infants in behavioral and cortisol response to inoculation. *Child Development, 64,* 1722–1731.

Liben, L. S., & Signorella, M. L. (1993). Gender-schematic processing in children: The role of initial interpretations of stimuli. *Developmental Psychology, 29,* 141–149.

Liebert, R. M., & Sprafkin, J. (1988). *The early window: Effects of television on children and youth.* New York: Pergamon Press.

Lin, C. C., & Fu, V. R. (1990). A comparison of child-rearing practices among Chinese, immigrant Chinese, and Caucasian-American parents. *Child Development, 61,* 429–433.

Linden, M. G., Bender, B. G., Harmon, R. J., Mrazek, D. A., & Robinson, A. (1988). 47, XXX: What is the prognosis? *Pediatrics, 82,* 619–630.

Lindsay, P. (1984). High school size, participation in activities, and young adult social participation: Some enduring effects of schooling. *Educational Evaluation and Policy Analysis, 6,* 73–83.

Linn, M. C., & Peterson, A. C. (1985). Emergence and characterization of sex differences in spatial ability: A meta-analysis. *Child Development, 56,* 1479–1498.

Livesley, W. J., & Bromley, D. B. (1973). *Person perception in childhood and adolescence.* New York: Wiley.

Lobel, M., Dunkel-Schetter, C., & Scrimshaw, S. C. (1992). Prenatal maternal stress and prematurity: A prospective study of socioeconomically disadvantaged women. *Health Psychology, 11,* 32–40.

Lord, S. E., Eccles, J. S., & McCarthy, K. A. (1994). Surviving the junior high transition: Family processes and self-perception as protective and risk factors. *Journal of Early Adolescence, 14,* 162–199.

Lovett, M. W., Borden, S. L., Deluca, T., Lacerenza, L., Benson, N. J., & Brackstone, D. (1994). Treating the core deficits of developmental dyslexia: Evidence of transfer of learning after phonologically- and strategy-based reading programs. *Developmental Psychology, 30,* 805–822.

Lovett, S. B., & Pillow, B. H. (1996). Development of the ability to distinguish between comprehension and memory: Evidence from goal-state evaluation tasks. *Journal of Educational Psychology, 88,* 546–562.

Ludemann, P. M. (1991). Generalized discrimination of positive facial expressions by seven- and ten-month-old infants. *Child Development, 62,* 55–67.

Ludemann, P. M., & Nelson, C. A. (1988). Categorical representation of facial expressions by 7-month-old infants. *Developmental Psychology, 24,* 492–501.

Luthar, S. S., Zigler, E., & Goldstein, D. (1992). Psychosocial adjustment among intellectually gifted adolescents: The role of cognitive-developmental and experiential factors. *Journal of Child Psychology and Psychiatry and Allied Disciplines, 33,* 361–373.

Lyons-Ruth, K., Alpern, L., & Repacholi, B. (1993). Disorganized infant attachment classification and maternal psychosocial problems as predictors of hostile-aggressive behavior in the preschool classroom. *Child Development, 64,* 572–585.

Lytton, H., & Romney, D. M. (1991). Parents' differential socialization of boys and girls: A meta-analysis. *Psychological Bulletin, 109,* 267–296.

Maccoby, E. E. (1984). Socialization and developmental change. *Child Development, 55,* 317–328.

Maccoby, E. E. (1988). Gender as a social category. *Developmental Psychology, 24,* 755–765.

Maccoby, E. E. (1990). Gender and relationships: A developmental account. *American Psychologist, 45,* 513–520.

Maccoby, E. E., Buchanon, C. M., Mnookin, R. H., & Dornbusch, S. M. (1993). Postdivorce roles of mothers and fathers in the lives of their children. *Journal of Family Psychology, 7,* 24–38.

Maccoby, E. E., & Jacklin, C. N. (1974). *The psychology of sex differences.* Stanford, CA: Stanford University Press.

Maccoby, E. E., & Jacklin, C. N. (1980). Sex differences in aggression: A rejoinder and reprise. *Child Development, 51,* 964–980.

Maccoby, E. E., & Martin, J. A. (1983). Socialization in the context of the family: Parent-child interaction. In P. H. Mussen (Ed.), *Handbook of child psychology* (Vol. 4). New York: Wiley.

Main, M., & Cassidy, J. (1988). Categories of response to reunion with the parent at age 6: Predictable from infant attachment classifications and stable over a 1-month-period. *Developmental Psychology, 24,* 415–426.

Malina, R. M. (1990). Physical growth and development during the transitional years (9–16). In R. Montemayor, G. R. Adams, & T. P. Gullotta (Eds.), *From childhood to adolescence: A transitional period* (pp. 41–62). Newbury Park, CA: Sage.

Malinosky-Rummell, R., & Hansen, D. J. (1993). Long-term consequences of childhood physical abuse. *Psychological Bulletin, 114,* 68–79.

Mandel, D. R., Jusczyk, P. W., & Pisoni, D. B. (1995). Infants' recognition of the sound patterns of their own names. *Psychological Science, 6,* 314–317.

Mange, A. P., & Mange, E. J. (1990). *Genetics: Human aspects* (2nd ed.). Sunderland, MA: Sinhauer Associates.

Mangelsdorf, S. C. (1992). Developmental changes in infant-stranger interaction. *Infant Behavior and Development, 15,* 191–208.

Mangelsdorf, S. C., Gunnar, M., Kestenbaum, R., Lang, S., & Andreas, D. (1990). Infant proneness-to-distress temperament, maternal personality, and mother-infant attachment: Associations and goodness of fit. *Child Development, 61,* 820–831.

Mangelsdorf, S. C., Shapiro, J. R., & Marzolf, D. (1995). Developmental and temperamental differences in emotional regulation in infancy. *Child Development, 66,* 1817–1828.

Marcia, J. E. (1980). Identity in adolescence. In J. Adelson (Ed.), *Handbook of adolescent psychology.* New York: Wiley.

Marcia, J. E. (1991). Identity and self-development. In R. M. Lerner, A. C. Petersen, & J. Brooks-Gunn (Eds.), *Encyclopedia of adolescence* (Vol. 1). New York: Garland.

Marcus, G. F., Pinker, S., Ullman, M., Hollander, M., Rosen, T. J., & Xu, F. (1992). Overregularization in language acquisition. *Monographs of the Society for Research in Child Development, 58*(4, Serial No. 228).

Marcus, J., Maccoby, E. E., Jacklin, C. N., & Doering, C. H. (1985). Individual differences in mood in early childhood: Their relation to gender and neonatal sex steroids. *Developmental Psychobiology, 18,* 327–340.

Markovits, H., & Vachon, R. (1989). Reasoning with contrary-to-fact propositions. *Journal of Experimental Child Psychology, 47,* 398–412.

Markstrom-Adams, A. (1989). Androgyny and its relation to adolescent well-being: A review of the literature. *Sex Roles, 21,* 325–340.

Marsh, H. W., Chessor, D., Craven, R., & Roche, L. (1995). The effects of gifted and talented programs on academic self-concept: The big fish strikes again. *American Educational Research Journal, 32,* 285–319.

Marshall, E. (1995). Gene therapy's growing pains. *Science, 269,* 1050–1052.

Martin, C. L. (1989). Children's use of gender-related information in making social judgments. *Developmental Psychology, 25,* 80–88.

Martin, C. L., & Halverson, C. F. (1987). The roles of cognition in sex roles and sex typing. In D. B. Carter (Ed.), *Current conceptions of sex roles and sex typing: Theory and research.* New York: Praeger.

Martin, C. L., & Little, J. K. (1990). The relation of gender understandings to children's sex-typed preferences and gender stereotypes. *Child Development, 61,* 1427–1439.

Martin, R. P., Olejnik, S., & Gaddis, L. (1994). Is temperament an important contributor to schooling outcomes in elementary school? Modeling effects of temperament and scholastic ability on academic achievement. In W. B. Casey & S. C. McDevitt (Eds.), *Prevention and early intervention.* New York: Brunner/Mazel.

Maurer, D., & Maurer, C. (1988). *The world of the newborn.* New York: Basic.

McCall, R. B. (1989). Commentary. *Human Development, 32,* 177–186.

McCall, R. B., Applebaum, M. I., & Hogarty, P. S. (1973). Developmental changes in mental performance. *Monographs of the Society for Research in Child Development, 38*(Whole No. 150).

McCormick, C. M., & Maurer, D. M. (1988). Unimanual hand preferences in 6-month-olds: Consistency and relation to familial-handedness. *Infant Behavior and Development, 11,* 21–29.

McGee, R., Stanton, W. R., & Sears, M. R. (1993). Allergic disorders and attention deficit disorder in children. *Journal of Abnormal Child Psychology, 21,* 79–88.

McGee, R., Williams, S., & Feehan, M. (1992). Attention deficit disorder and age of onset of problem behaviors. *Journal of Abnormal Child Psychology, 20,* 487–502.

McHale, S. M., Bartko, W. T., Crouter, A. C., & Perry-Jenkins, M. (1990). Children's housework and psychosocial functioning: The mediating effects of parents' sex-role behaviors and attitudes. *Child Development, 61,* 1413–1426.

McKusick, V. A. (1995). *Mendelian inheritance in man: Catalogs of autosomal dominant, autosomal recessive, and X-linked phenotypes* (10th ed.). Baltimore: Johns Hopkins University Press.

McManus, I. C., Sik, G., Cole, D. R., Kloss, J., Mellon, A. F., & Wong, J. (1988). The development of handedness in children. *British Journal of Developmental Psychology, 6,* 257–273.

McNally, S., Eisenberg, N., & Harris, J. D. (1991). Consistency and change in maternal child-rearing practices and values: A longitudinal study. *Child Development, 62,* 190–198.

McNaughton, S., & Leyland, J. (1990). The shifting focus of maternal tutoring across different difficulty levels on a problem solving task. *British Journal of Developmental Psychology, 8,* 147–155.

Meilman, P. W. (1979). Cross-sectional age changes in ego identity status during adolescence. *Developmental Psychology, 15,* 230–231.

Mennella, J. A., & Beauchamp, G. K. (1996). The human infant's response to vanilla flavors in mother's milk and formula. *Infant Behavior and Development, 19,* 13–19.

Meyer, D. R., & Garasky, S. (1993). Custodial fathers: Myths, realities, and child support policy. *Journal of Marriage and the Family, 55,* 73–79.

Meyers, R. (1983). *D.E.S., the bitter pill.* New York: Putnam.

Miller, J. G., & Bersoff, D. M. (1992). Culture and moral judgment: How are conflicts between justice and interpersonal responsibilities resolved? *Journal of Personality and Social Psychology, 62,* 541–554.

Miller, K. F., Smith, C. M., Zhu, J., & Zhang, H. (1995). Preschool origins of cross-national differences in mathematical competence: The role of number-naming systems. *Psychological Science, 6,* 56–60.

Miller, P. A., Eisenberg, N., Fabes, R. A., & Shell, R. (1996). Relations of moral reasoning and vicarious emotion to young children's prosocial behavior toward peers and adults. *Developmental Psychology, 32,* 210–219.

Miller, P. M., Danaher, D. L., & Forbes, D. (1986). Sex-related strategies of coping with interpersonal conflict in children aged five to seven. *Developmental Psychology, 22,* 543–548.

Miller, S. A., & Brownell, C. A. (1975). Peers, persuasion, and Piaget: Dyadic interaction between conservers and nonconservers. *Child Development, 46,* 992–997.

Mills, R. S. L., & Grusec, J. E. (1989). Cognitive, affective, and behavioral consequences of praising altruism. *Merrill-Palmer Quarterly, 35,* 299–326.

Minuchin, P. P., & Shapiro, E. K. (1983). The school as a context for social development. In P. H. Mussen (Ed.), *Handbook of child psychology: Vol. 4.* New York: Wiley.

Mischel, W. (1970) Sex-typing and socialization. In P. H. Mussen, (Ed.) *Carmichaels' manual of child psychology* (Vol. 2). New York: Wiley.

Mischel, W., & Ebbesen, E. (1970). Attention in delay of gratification. *Journal of Personality and Social Psychology, 16,* 329–337.

Mischel, W., Shoda, Y., & Rodriguez, M. L. (1989). Delay of gratification in children. *Science, 244,* 933–938.

Mitchell, J. E., Baker, L. A., & Jacklin, C. N. (1989). Masculinity and femininity in twin children: Genetic and environmental factors. *Child Development, 60,* 1475–1485.

Miura, I. T., Kim, C. C., Chang, C. M., & Okamoto, Y. (1988). Effects of language characteristics on children's cognitive representation of number: Cross-national comparisons. *Child Development, 59,* 1445–1450.

Mize, J., & Ladd, G. W. (1990). A cognitive social-learning approach to social skill training with low-status preschool children. *Developmental Psychology, 26,* 388–397.

Mize, J., Pettit, G. S., & Brown, E. G. (1995). Mothers' supervision of their children's peer play: Relations with beliefs, perceptions, and knowledge. *Developmental Psychology, 31,* 311–321.

Moats, L. C., & Lyon, G. R. (1993). Learning disabilities in the United States: Advocacy, science, and the future of the field. *Journal of Learning Disabilities, 26,* 282–294.

Molfese, D. L., & Burger-Judisch, L. M. (1991). Dynamic temporal-spatial allocation of resources in the human brain: An alternative to the static view of hemisphere differences. In F. L. Ketterle (Ed.), *Cerebral laterality: Theory and research. The Toledo symposium.* Hillsdale, NJ: Erlbaum.

Montgomery, G. T. (1992). Comfort with acculturation status among students from south Texas. *Hispanic Journal of Behavioral Sciences, 14,* 201–223.

Moore, B. S., Underwood, B., & Rosenhan, D. L. (1973). Affect and altruism. *Developmental Psychology, 8,* 99–104.

Moore, K. L., & Persaud, T. V. N. (1993). *Before we are born* (4th ed.). Philadelphia: W. B. Saunders.

Morgan, B., & Gibson, K. R. (1991). Nutritional and environmental interactions in brain development. In K. R. Gibson & A. C. Peterson (Eds.), *Brain maturation and cognitive development: Comparative and cross-cultural perspectives.* New York: Aldine de Gruyter.

Morgane, P. J., Austin-LaFrance, R., Bronzino, J. D., Tonkiss, J., Diaz-Cintra, S., Cintra, L., Kemper, T., & Galler, J. R. (1993). Prenatal malnutrition and development of the brain. *Neuroscience and Biobehavioral Reviews, 17,* 91–128.

Morison, P., & Masten, A. S. (1991). Peer reputation in middle childhood as a predictor of adaptation in adolescence: A seven-year follow-up. *Child Development, 62,* 991–1007.

Morris, R. K. (1994). Lexical and message-level sentence context effects on fixation times in reading. *Journal of Experimental Psychology: Learning, Memory, and Cognition, 20,* 92–103.

Morton, J., & Johnson, M. H. (1991). CONSPEC and CONLERN: A two-process theory of infant face recognition. *Psychological Review, 98,* 164–181.

Naigles, L. G., & Gelman, S. A. (1995). Overextensions in comprehension and production revisited: Preferential-looking in a study of dog, cat, and cow. *Journal of Child Language, 22,* 19–46.

National Research Council. (1987). *Risking the future: Adolescent sexuality, pregnancy, and childbearing* (Vol. 1). Washington, DC: National Academy Press.

National Research Council (1989). *Recommended dietary allowances* (10th edition). Washington, DC: National Academy Press.

Nelson, K. (1973). Structure and strategy in learning to talk. *Monographs of the Society for Research in Child Development, 38* (No. 149).

Neugarten, B. L., & Weinstein, K. K. (1964). The changing American grandparent. *Journal of Marriage and the Family, 26,* 299–304.

Newcomb, A. F., Bukowski, W. M., & Pattee, L. (1993). Children's peer relations: A meta-analytic review of popular, rejected, neglected, controversial, and average sociometric status. *Psychological Bulletin, 113,* 99–123.

Newcomb, A. F., & Bagwell, C. L. (1995). Children's friendship relations: A meta-analytic review. *Psychological Bulletin, 117,* 306–347.

Newman, L. S., Cooper, J., & Ruble, D. N. (1995). Gender and computers: 2. Interactive effects of knowledge and constancy on gender-stereotyped attitudes. *Sex Roles, 33,* 325–351.

Newport, E. L. (1991). Contrasting conceptions of the critical period for language. In S. Carey & R. Gelman (Eds.), *The epigenesis of mind: Essays on biology and cognition* (pp. 111–130). Hillsdale, NJ: Erlbaum.

Niebyl, J. R. (1991). Drugs in pregnancy and lactation. In S. G. Gabbe, J. R. Niebyl, & J. L. Simpson (Eds.), *Obstetrics: Normal and problem pregnancies* (2nd ed.). New York: Churchill Livingstone.

Nielson, A. C. (1990). *Annual Nielsen report on television: 1990.* New York: Nielson Media Research.

Oakes, J., Gamoran, A., & Page, R. N. (1992). Curriculum differentiation: Opportunities, outcomes, and meanings. In P. W. Jackson (Ed.), *Handbook of research on curriculum.* New York: Macmillan.

Offer, D., Ostrov, E., Howard, K. I., & Atkinson, R. (1988). *The teenage world: Adolescents' self-image in ten countries.* New York: Plenum Press.

Ohlendorf-Moffat, P. (1991, February). Surgery before birth. *Discover,* 59–65.

Okagaki, L., & Sternberg, R. J. (1993). Parental beliefs and children's school performance. *Child Development, 64,* 36–56.

Oller, D. K. (1986). Metaphonology and infant vocalizations. In B. Lindblom & R. Zetterstrom (Eds.), *Precursors of early speech.* Basingstoke, England: Macmillan.

Oller, D. K., & Eilers, R. E. (1988). The role of audition in infant babbling. *Child Development, 59,* 441–449.

Pacifici, C., & Bearison, D. J. (1991). Development of children's self-regulations in idealized and mother-child interactions. *Cognitive Development, 6,* 261–277.

Padilla, A. M., Lindholm, K. J., Chen, A., Duran, R., Hakuta, K., Lambert, W., & Tucker, G. R. (1991). The English-only movement. Myths, reality, and implications for psychology. *American Psychologist, 46,* 120–130.

Palca, J. (1991). Fetal brain signals time for birth. *Science, 253,* 1360.

Parazzini, F., Luchini, L., La Vecchia, C., & Crosignani, P. G. (1993). Video display terminal use during pregnancy and reproductive outcome—a meta-analysis. *Journal of Epidemiology and Community Health, 47,* 265–268.

Park, K. A., & Waters, E. (1989). Security of attachment and preschool friendships. *Child Development, 60,* 1076–1081.

Parke, R. D. (1990). In search of fathers: A narrative of an empirical journey. In I. Sigel & G. Brody (Eds.), *Methods of family research.* Hillsdale, NJ: Erlbaum.

Parke, R. D., & Bhavnagri, N. P. (1989). Parents as managers of children's peer relationships. In D. Belle (Ed.), *Children's social networks and social supports.* New York: Wiley.

Parker, J. G., & Asher, S. R. (1987). Peer relations and later personal adjustment: Are low-accepted children at risk? *Psychological Bulletin, 102,* 357–389.

Parten, M. (1932). Social participation among preschool children. *Journal of Abnormal and Social Psychology, 27,* 243–269.

Patterson, C. J. (1992). Children of lesbian and gay parents. *Child Development, 63,* 1025–1042.

Patterson, G. R. (1980). Mothers: The unacknowledged victims. *Monographs of the Society for Research in Child Development, 45*(5, Serial No. 186).

Patterson, G. R. (1984). Microsocial process: A view from the boundary. In J. C. Masters & K. Yarkin-Levin (Eds.), *Boundary areas in social and developmental psychology.* New York: Academic Press.

Pearson, J. L., Hunter, A. G., Ensminger, M. E., & Kellam, S. G. (1990). Black grandmothers in multigenerational households: Diversity in family structure and parenting involvement in the Woodlawn community. *Child Development, 61,* 434–442.

Pederson, D. M., & Wheeler, J. (1983). The Müller-Lyer illusion among Navajos. *Journal of Social Psychology, 121,* 3–6.

Pennington, B. F., Groisser, D., & Welsh, M. C. (1993). Contrasting cognitive deficits in attention deficit hyperactivity disorder versus reading disability. *Developmental Psychology, 29,* 511–523.

Perfetti, C. A., & Curtis, M. E. (1986). Reading. In R. F. Dillon & R. J. Sternberg (Eds.), *Cognition and instruction.* Orlando, FL: Academic Press.

Peterson, L. (1983). Role of donor competence, donor age, and peer presence on helping in an emergency. *Developmental Psychology, 19,* 873–880.

Petrie, R. H. (1991). Intrapartum fetal evaluation. In S. G. Gabbe, J. R. Niebyl, & J. L. Simpson (Eds.), *Obstetrics: Normal and problem pregnancies* (2nd ed.). New York: Churchill Livingstone.

Pettit, G. S., Bakshi, A., Dodge, K. A., & Coie, J. D. (1990). The emergence of social dominance in young boys' play groups: Developmental differences and behavioral correlates. *Developmental Psychology, 26,* 1017–1025.

Pettito, L. A., & Marentette, P. F. (1991). Babbling in the manual mode: Evidence for the ontogeny of language. *Science, 251,* 1493–1496.

Phinney, J. S. (1989). Stage of ethnic identity in minority group adolescents. *Journal of Early Adolescence, 9,* 34–49.

Phinney, J. S. (1990). Ethnic identity in adolescents and adults. *Psychological Bulletin, 108,* 499–514.

Phinney, J. S. (1996). When we talk about American ethnic groups, what do we mean? *American Psychologist, 51,* 918–927.

Phinney, J. S., & Chavira, V. (1992). Ethnic identity and self-esteem: An exploratory longitudinal study. *Journal of Adolescence, 15,* 271–281.

Piaget, J. (1929). *The child's conception of the world.* New York: Harcourt, Brace.

Piaget, J. (1952). *The origins of intelligence in children.* New York: International Universities Press.

Piaget, J., & Albertini, B. von. (1950–1952). Recherches sur le développement des perceptions. XI. L'illusion de Müller-Lyer. [Researches on the development of the perceptions. 11. The Müller-Lyer illusion]. *Arch. Psycholog., Genève, 33,* 1–48.

Piaget, J., & Inhelder, B. (1956). *The child's conception of space.* Boston: Routledge & Kegan Paul.

Pickens, J. (1994). Perception of auditory-visual distance relations by 5-month-old infants. *Developmental Psychology, 30,* 537–544.

Plomin, R., DeFries, J. C., & McClearn, G. E. (1990). *Behavioral genetics: A primer* (2nd ed.). New York: W. H. Freeman.

Plomin, R., Owen, M. J., & McGuffin, P. (1994). The genetic basis of complex human behaviors. *Science, 264,* 1733–1739.

Plomin, R., & Rowe, D. C. (1979). Genetic and environmental etiology of social behavior in infancy. *Developmental Psychology, 15,* 62–72.

Pollitt, E. (1994). Poverty and child development: Relevance of research in developing countries to the United States. *Child Development, 65,* 283–295.

Porter, R. H., Makin, J. W., Davis, L. B., & Christensen, K. M. (1991). An assessment of the salient olfactory environment of formula-fed infants. *Physiology and Behavior, 50,* 907–911.

Potter, M. C. (1966). On perceptual recognition. In J. S. Bruner et al. (Eds.), *Studies in cognitive growth.* New York: Wiley.

Potter, M. C., Moryada, A., Abrams, I., & Noel, A. (1993). Word perception and misperception in context. *Journal of Experimental Psychology: Learning, Memory, and Cognition, 19,* 3–22.

Poulin-Dubois, D., Serbin, L. A., Kenyon, B., & Derbyshire, A. (1994). Infants' intermodal knowledge about gender. *Developmental Psychology, 30,* 436–442.

Poulson, C. L., Kymissis, E., Reeve, K. F., Andreatos, M., & Reeve, L. (1991). Generalized vocal imitation in infants. *Journal of Experimental Child Psychology, 51,* 267–279.

Powers, S. W., & Roberts, M. W. (1995). Simulation training with parents of oppositional children: Preliminary findings. *Journal of Clinical Child Psychology, 24,* 89–97.

Powlishta, K., Serbin, L. A., Doyle, A., & White, D. R. (1994). Gender, ethnic, and body type biases: The generality of prejudice in childhood. *Developmental Psychology, 30*, 526–536.

Pozzi, S., Healy, L., & Hoyles, C. (1993). Learning and interaction in groups with computers: When do ability and gender matter? *Social Development, 2*, 222–241.

Priel, B., & deSchonen, S. (1986). Self-recognition: A study of a population without mirrors. *Journal of Experimental Child Psychology, 41*, 237–250.

Ramey, C. T., & Campbell, F. A. (1991). Poverty, early childhood education, and academic competence: The Abecedarian experiment. In A. Huston (Ed.), *Children reared in poverty*. New York: Cambridge University Press.

Ramey, C. T., & Ramey, S. L. (1990). Intensive educational intervention for children of poverty. *Intelligence, 14*, 1–9.

Ramos-Ford, V., & Gardner, H. (1991). Giftedness from a multiple intelligence perspective. In N. Colangelo & G. A. Davis (Eds.), *Handbook of gifted education*. Boston: Allyn and Bacon.

Ramsey, P. G. (1995). Growing up with the contradictions of race and class. *Young Children, 50*, 18–22.

Rathunde, K. R., & Csikszentmihalyi, M. (1993). Undivided interest and the growth of talent: A longitudinal study of adolescents. *Journal of Youth and Adolescence, 22*, 385–405.

Raudenbusch, S. W. (1984). Magnitude of teacher expectancy effects on pupil IQ as a function of credibility of expectancy induction: A synthesis from 18 experiments. *Journal of Educational Psychology, 76*, 85–97.

Reich, P. A. (1986). *Language development*. Englewood Cliffs, NJ: Prentice Hall.

Reid, D. H., Wilson, P. G., & Faw, G. D. (1991). Teaching self-help skills. In J. L. Matson & J. A. Mulick (Eds.), *Handbook of mental retardation* (2nd ed.). New York: Pergamon Press.

Ricciuti, H. N. (1993). Nutrition and mental development. *Current Directions in Psychological Science, 2*, 43–46.

Rice, M. L., Huston, A. C., Truglio, R., & Wright, J. (1990). Words from "Sesame Street": Learning vocabulary while viewing. *Developmental Psychology, 26*, 421–428.

Ritts, V., Patterson, M. L., & Tubbs, M. E. (1992). Expectations, impressions, and judgments of physically attractive students. *Review of Educational Research, 62*, 413–426.

Rodgers, J. L., & Rowe, D. C. (1993). Social contagion and adolescent sexual behavior: A developmental EMOSA model. *Psychological Review, 100*, 479–510.

Roffwarg, H. P., Muzio, J. N., & Dement, W. C. (1966). Ontogenetic development of the human sleep-dream cycle. *Science, 152*, 604–619.

Rogoff, B., Mistry, J., Goncu, A., & Mosier, C. (1993). Guided participation in cultural activity by toddlers and caregivers. *Monographs of the Society for Research in Child Development, 58* (8, Serial No. 236).

Rooks, J. P., Weatherby, N. L., Ernst, E. K. M., Stapleton, S., Rosen, D., & Rosenfield, A. (1989). Outcomes of care in birth centers: The national birth center study. *New England Journal of Medicine, 321*, 1804–1811.

Roopnarine, J. (1992). Father-child play in India. In K. MacDonald (Ed.), *Parent-child play*. Albany: State University of New York Press.

Rose, S. A. (1994). From hand to eye: Findings and issues in infant cross-modal transfer. In D. J. Lewkowicz & R. Lickliter (Eds.), *The development of intersensory perception*. Hillsdale, NJ: Erlbaum.

Rose, S. A., & Feldman, J. F. (1995). Prediction of IQ and specific cognitive abilities at 11 years from infancy measures. *Developmental Psychology, 31*, 685–696.

Rosenfield, P., Lambert, N. M., & Black, A. (1985). Desk arrangement effects on pupil classroom behavior. *Journal of Educational Psychology, 77*, 101–108.

Rosenthal, D. A., & Feldman, S. S. (1992). The relationship between parenting behaviour and ethnic identity in Chinese-American and Chinese-Australian adolescents. *International Journal of Psychology, 27*, 19–31.

Rotenberg, K. J., & Mayer, E. V. (1990). Delay of gratification in Native and White children: A cross-cultural comparison. *International Journal of Behavioral Development, 13*, 23–30.

Rothbaum, F., & Weisz, J. R. (1994). Parental caregiving and child externalizing behavior in nonclinical samples: A meta-analysis. *Psychological Bulletin, 116*, 55–74.

Rotto, P. C., & Kratochwill, T. R. (1994). Behavioral consultation with parents: Using competency-based training to modify child noncompliance. *School Psychology Review, 23*, 669–693.

Rovee-Collier, C. (1987). Learning and memory in infancy. In J. D. Osofsky (Ed.), *Handbook of infant development* (2nd ed.). New York: Wiley.

Rovee-Collier, C., Evancio, S., & Earley, L. A. (1995). The time window hypothesis: Spacing effects. *Infant Behavior and Development, 18*, 69–78.

Rowe, D. C. (1994). No more than skin deep. *American Psychologist, 49*, 215–216.

Ruble, D. N. (1988). Sex-role development. In M. H. Bornstein & M. E. Lamb (Eds.), *Developmental psychology: An advanced textbook* (2nd ed., pp. 411–460). Hillsdale, NJ: Erlbaum.

Ruble, D. N., Boggiano, A. K., Feldman, N. S., & Loebl, N. H. (1980). Developmental analysis of the role of social comparison in self-evaluation. *Developmental Psychology, 16*, 105–115.

Ruble, T. L. (1983). Sex stereotypes: Issues of changes in the 1970s. *Sex Roles, 9*, 397–402.

Rumelhart, D. E., & McClelland, J. L. (1981). Interactive processing through spreading activation. In A. M. Lesgold & C. A. Perfetti (Eds.), *Interactive processes in reading*. Hillsdale, NJ: Erlbaum.

Russell, J. A., & Paris, F. A. (1994). Do children acquire concepts for complex emotions abruptly? *International Journal of Behavioral Development, 17*, 349–365.

Rutter, M., & Garmezy, N. (1983). Developmental psychopathology. In P. H. Mussen (Ed.), *Handbook of child psychology* (Vol. 4). New York: Wiley.

Rutter, M., Maughan, B., Mortimore, P., & Ouston, J. (1979). *Fifteen thousand hours: Secondary schools and their effects on children*. Cambridge, MA: Harvard University Press.

Rymer, R. (1993). *Genie*. New York: HarperCollins.

Saffran, J. R., Aslin, R. N., & Newport, E. L. (1996). Statistical learning by 8-month-old infants. *Science, 274*, 1926–1928.

Sagi, A., van IJzendoorn, M. H., Aviezer, O., Donnell, F., & Mayseless, O. (1994). Sleeping out of home in a kibbutz communal arrangement: It makes a difference for infant-mother attachment. *Child Development, 65*, 992–1004.

Sakamato, A. (1994). Video game use and the development of sociocognitive abilities in children: Three surveys of elementary school students. *Journal of Applied Social Psychology, 24*, 21–42.

Salganik, L. H., Phelps, R. P., Bianchi, L., Nohara, D., & Smith, T. M. (1993). *Education in states and nations: Indicators comparing U.S. states with the OECD countries in 1988*. Washington, DC: U.S. Government Printing Office.

Savage-Rumbaugh, E. S., Murphy, J., Sevcik, R. A., Brakke, K. E., Williams, S. L., & Rumbaugh, D. M. (1993). Language comprehension in ape and child. *Monographs of the Society for Research in Child Development, 58*(3–4, Serial No. 233).

Savin-Williams, R. C., & Demo, D. H. (1984). Developmental change and stability in adolescent self-concept. *Developmental Psychology, 20*, 1100–1110.

Saxe, G. B. (1988). Candy selling and math learning. *Educational Researcher, 17*, 14–21.

Scarr, S. (1992). Developmental theories for the 1990s: Development and individual differences. *Child Development, 63*, 1–19.

Scarr, S. (1993). Biological and cultural diversity: The legacy of Darwin for development. *Child Development, 64*, 1333–1353.

Scarr, S., & McCartney, K. (1983). How people make their own environments: A theory of genotype environment effects. *Child Development, 54*, 424–435.

Schleidt, M., & Genzel, C. (1990). The significance of mother's perfume for infants in the first weeks of their life. *Ethology and Sociobiology, 11*, 145–154.

Schneider, M. L. (1992). The effect of mild stress during pregnancy on birthweight and neuro-motor maturation in rhesus monkey infants

(*Macaca mulatta*). *Infant Behavior and Development, 15*, 389–403.

Schneider, W., & Bjorklund, D. F. (1997). Memory. In W. Damon (Ed.), *Handbook of child psychology* (Vol. 2). New York: Wiley.

Schnorr, T. M., Grajewski, B. A., Hornung, R. W., Thun, M. J., Egeland, G. M., Murray, W. E., Conover, D. L., & Halperin, W. E. (1991). Video display terminals and the risk of spontaneous abortion. *New England Journal of Medicine, 324*, 727–733.

Schramm, W., Lyle, J., & Parker, E. B. (1961). *Television in the lives of our children.* Stanford, CA: Stanford University Press.

Scott, W. A., Scott, R., & McCabe, M. (1991). Family relationships and children's personality: A cross-cultural, cross-source comparison. *British Journal of Social Psychology, 30*, 1–20.

Sears, R. R. (1975). Your ancients revisited: A history of child development. In E. M. Hetherington (Ed.), *Review of child development research* (Vol. 5). Chicago: University of Chicago Press.

Segall, M. H., Dasen, P. R., Berry, J. W., & Poortinga, Y. (1990). *Human behavior in global perspective.* New York: Pergamon Press.

Seidman, E., Allen, L., Aber, J. L., Mitchell, C., & Feinman, J. (1994). The impact of school transitions in early adolescence on the self-system and perceived social context of poor urban youth. *Child Development, 65*, 507–522.

Seifer, R., Schiller, M., Sameroff, A. J., Resnick, S., & Riordan, K. (1996). Attachment, maternal sensitivity, and infant temperament during the first year of life. *Developmental Psychology, 32*, 12–25.

Selman, R. L. (1980). *The growth of interpersonal understanding: Developmental and clinical analyses.* New York: Academic Press.

Selman, R. L. (1981). The child as a friendship philosopher: A case study in the growth of interpersonal understanding. In S. R. Asher & J. M. Gottman (Eds.), *The development of children's friendships.* Cambridge, England: Cambridge University Press.

Selman, R. L., & Byrne, D F. (1974). A structural-developmental analysis of levels of role-taking in middle childhood. *Child Development, 45*, 803–806.

Sénéchal, M., Thomas, E., & Monker, J. (1995). Individual differences in 4-year-old children's acquisition of vocabulary during storybook reading. *Journal of Educational Psychology, 87*, 218–229.

Serbin, L. A., Powlishta, K. K., & Gulko, J. (1993). The development of sex typing in middle childhood. *Monographs of the Society for Research in Child Development, 58* (Serial No. 232).

Shatz, M., & Gelman, R. (1973). The development of communication skills: Modifications in the speech of young children as a function of listener. *Monographs of the Society for Research in Child Development, 38*(5, Serial No. 152).

Shaw, G. M., Schaffer, D., Velie, E. M., Morland, K., & Harris, J. A. (1995). Periconceptional vitamin use, dietary folate, and the occurrence of neural tube defects. *Epidemiology, 6*, 219–226.

Shelov, S. P. (1993). *Caring for your baby and young child: Birth to age 5.* New York: Bantam.

Sherif, M., Harvey, O. J., White, B. J., Hood, W. R., & Sherif, C. W. (1961). *Intergroup conflict and cooperation.* Norman, OK: University Book Exchange.

Sherrod, K. B., O'Connor, S., Vietze, P. M., & Altemeier, W. A., III. (1984). Child health and maltreatment. *Child Development, 55*, 1174–1183.

Shiwach, R. (1994). Psychopathology in Huntington's disease patients. *Acta Psychiatrica Scandinavica, 90*, 241–246.

Shoda, Y., Mischel, W., & Peake, P. K. (1990). Predicting adolescent cognitive and self-regulatory competencies from preschool delay of gratification: Identifying diagnostic conditions. *Developmental Psychology, 26*, 978–986.

Shuter-Dyson, R. (1982). Musical ability. In D. Deutsch (Ed.), *The psychology of music.* New York: Academic Press.

Siegel, L. S. (1994). Working memory and reading: A life-span perspective. *International Journal of Behavioral Development, 17*, 109–124.

Siegler, R. S. (1981). Developmental sequences within and between concepts. *Monographs of the Society for Research in Child Development, 46* (2, Serial No. 189).

Siegler, R. S. (1986). Unities in strategy choices across domains. In M. Perlmutter (Ed.), *Minnesota symposia on child development* (Vol. 19). Hillsdale, NJ: Erlbaum.

Siegler, R. S. (1988). Strategy choice procedures and the development of multiplication skill. *Journal of Experimental Psychology: General, 117*, 258–278.

Siegler, R. S. (1989). Mechanisms of cognitive development. *Annual Review of Psychology, 40*, 353–379.

Siegler, R. S. (1991). *Children's thinking* (2nd ed). Englewood Cliffs, NJ: Prentice Hall.

Siegler, R. S., & Jenkins, E. (1989). *How children discover new strategies.* Hillsdale, NJ: Erlbaum.

Siegler, R. S., & Robinson, M. (1982). The development of numerical understandings. In H. W. Reese & L. P. Lipsitt (Eds.), *Advances in child development and behavior* (Vol. 16). New York: Academic Press.

Siegler, R. S., & Shrager, J. (1984). Strategy choices in addition and subtraction: How do children know what to do? In C. Sophian (Ed.), *Origins of cognitive skills.* Hillsdale, NJ: Erlbaum.

Signorella, M. L., Bigler, R. S., & Liben, L. S. (1993). Developmental differences in children's gender schemata about others: A meta-analytic review. *Early gender-role development. Developmental Review, 13*, 147–183.

Signorielli, N., & Lears, M. (1992). Children, television, and conceptions about chores: Attitudes and behaviors. *Sex Roles, 27*, 157–170.

Silverman, I. W., & Ragusa, D. M. (1990). Child and maternal correlates of impulse control in 24-month-old children. *Genetic, Social, and General Psychology Monographs, 116*, 435–473.

Simmons, R., & Blyth, D. (1987). *Moving into adolescence.* New York: Aldine de Gruyter.

Simons, R. L., Whitbeck, L. B., Conger, R. D., & Chyi-In, W. (1991). Intergenerational transmission of harsh parenting. *Developmental Psychology, 27*, 159–171.

Simpson, E. L. (1974). Moral development research: A case study of scientific cultural bias. *Human Development, 17*, 81–106.

Skinner, B. F. (1957). *Verbal behavior.* New York: Appleton-Century-Crofts.

Slate, J. R., Jones, C. H., & Dawson, P. (1993). Academic skills of high school students as a function of grade, gender, and academic track. *High School Journal, 76*, 245–251.

Slobin, D. I. (1985). Cross-linguistic evidence for the language-making capacity. In D. I. Slobin (Ed.), *The cross-linguistic study of language acquisition: Vol. 2. Theoretical issues.* Hillsdale, NJ: Erlbaum.

Smetana, J. G., & Braeges, J. L. (1990). The development of toddlers' moral and conventional judgments. *Merrill-Palmer Quarterly, 36*, 329–346.

Smetana, J. G., Killen, M., & Turiel, E. (1991). Children's reasoning about interpersonal and moral conflicts. *Child Development, 62*, 629–644.

Snarey, J. R. (1985). Cross-cultural universality of social-moral development: A critical review of Kohlbergian research. *Psychological Bulletin, 97*, 202–232.

Snow, M. E., Jacklin, C. N., & Maccoby, E. E. (1983). Sex-of-child differences in father-child interaction at one year of age. *Child Development, 54*, 227–232.

Sokolov, J. L. (1993). A local contingency analysis of the fine-tuning hypothesis. *Developmental Psychology, 29*, 1008–1023.

Solley, C. M. (1966). Affective processes in perceptual development. In A. H. Kidd & J. L. Rivoire (Eds.), *Perceptual development in children.* New York: International Universities Press.

Sommer, R. (1969). *Personal space.* Englewood Cliffs, NJ: Prentice Hall.

Sonnenschein, S. (1988). The development of referential communication: Speaking to different listeners. *Child Development, 59*, 694–702.

Sophian, C., & Wellman, H. M. (1987). The development of indirect search strategies. *British Journal of Developmental Psychology, 5*, 9–18.

Spearman, C. (1904). "General intelligence" objectively determined and measured. *American Journal of Psychology, 15*, 201–293.

ence, J. T. (1985). Achievement American style: The rewards and costs of individualism. *American Psychologist, 40,* 1285–1295.

oufe, L. A., & Fleeson, J. (1986). Attachment and the construction of relationships. In W. W. Hartup & Z. Rubin (Eds.), *Relationships and development.* Hillsdale, NJ: Erlbaum.

oufe, L. A., & Waters, E. (1976). The ontogenesis of smiling and laughter: A perspective on the organization of development in infancy. *Psychological Review, 83,* 173–189.

oufe, L. A., & Wunsch, J. P. (1972). The development of laughter in the first year of life. *Child Development, 43,* 1324–1344.

ilkas, A., & Gavaki, E. (1995). The importance of ethnic identity: Self-esteem and academic achievement of second-generation Greeks in secondary school. *Canadian Journal of School Psychology, 11,* 1–9.

Stanovich, K. E. (1993). Dysrationalia: A new specific learning disability. *Journal of Learning Disabilities, 26,* 501–515.

Stattin, H., & Magnusson, D. (1989). The role of early aggressive behavior in the frequency, seriousness, and types of later crime. *Journal of Consulting and Clinical Psychology, 57,* 710–718.

Stedman, J. D. (1994). Revision strategies employed by middle level students using computers. *Journal of Educational Computing Research, 11,* 141–152.

Steinberg, L. (1990). Autonomy, conflict, and harmony in the family relationship. In S. S. Feldman & G. R. Elliott (Eds.), *At the threshold: The developing adolescent.* Cambridge, MA: Harvard University Press.

Steinberg, L., Lamborn, S. D., Dornbusch, S. M., & Darling, N. (1992). Impact of parenting practices on adolescent achievement: Authoritative parenting, school involvement, and encouragement to succeed. *Child Development, 63,* 1266–1281.

Stenberg, C., & Campos, J. (1990). The development of anger expressions in infancy. In N. Stein, B. Leventhal, & T. Trabasso (Eds.), *Psychological and biological approaches to emotion.* Hillsdale, NJ: Erlbaum.

Stern, M., & Karraker, K. H. (1989). Sex stereotyping of infants: A review of gender labeling studies. *Sex Roles, 20,* 501–522.

Sternberg, R. J. (1977). *Intelligence, information processing, and analogical reasoning.* Hillsdale, NJ: Erlbaum.

Sternberg, R. J. (1985). *Beyond IQ: A triarchic theory of human intelligence.* Cambridge, England: Cambridge University Press.

Sternberg, R. J. (1987). Implicit theories: An alternative to modeling cognition and its development. In J. Bisanz, C. J. Brainerd, & R. Kail (Eds.), *Formal methods in developmental psychology.* New York: Springer-Verlag.

Sternberg, R. J., Wagner, R. K., Williams, W. M., & Horvath, J. A. (1995). Testing common sense. *American Psychologist, 50,* 912–927.

Stevenson, H. W., & Lee, S. (1990). Contexts of achievement. *Monographs of the Society for Research in Child Development, 55* (1–2, Serial No. 221).

Stevenson, H. W., Parker, T., Wilkinson, A., Hegion, A., & Fish, E. (1976). Longitudinal study of individual differences in cognitive development and scholastic achievement. *Journal of Educational Psychology, 68,* 377–400.

Stevenson, H. W., & Stigler, J. W. (1992). *The learning gap.* New York: Summit Books.

Stevenson, M. R., & Black, K. N. (1995). *How divorce affects offspring: A research approach.* Madison, WI: Brown & Benchmark.

Stewart, L., & Pascual-Leone, J. (1992). Mental capacity constraints and the development of moral reasoning. *Journal of Experimental Child Psychology, 54,* 251–287.

Stewart R. B., Mobley, L. A., Van Tuyl, S. S., & Salvador, W. A. (1987). The firstborn's adjustment to the birth of a sibling: A longitudinal assessment. *Child Development, 58,* 341–355.

Stice, E., & Barrera, M., Jr. (1995). A longitudinal examination of the reciprocal relations between perceived parenting and adolescents' substance use and externalizing behaviors. *Developmental Psychology, 31,* 322–334.

Stifter, C. A., & Fox, N. A. (1990). Infant reactivity: Physiological correlates of newborn and 5-month temperament. *Developmental Psychology, 26,* 582–588.

Straus, M. A., & Kantor, G. K. (1987). Stress and child abuse. In R. E. Helfer & R. S. Kempe (Eds.), *The battered child* (4th ed.). Chicago: University of Chicago Press.

Strauss, M. S., & Curtis, L. E. (1984). Development of numerical concepts in infancy. In C. Sophian (Ed.), *Origins of cognitive skills.* Hillsdale, NJ: Erlbaum.

Strayer, J., & Schroeder, M. (1989). Children's helping strategies: Influences of emotion, empathy, and age. In N. Eisenberg (Ed.), *New directions for child development: Empathy and related emotional responses* (Vol. 44). San Francisco: Jossey-Bass.

Streissguth, A. P., Barr, H. M., Sampson, P. D., & Bookstein, F. L. (1994). Prenatal alcohol and offspring development: The first fourteen years. *Drugs & Alcohol Dependence, 36,* 89–99.

Stunkard, A. J., Sorensen, T. I. A., Hanis, C., Teasdale, T. W., Chakraborty, R., Schull, W. J., & Schulsinger, F. (1986). An adoption study of human obesity. *New England Journal of Medicine, 314,* 193–198.

Sullivan, L. W. (1987). The risks of the sickle-cell trait: Caution and common sense. *New England Journal of Medicine, 317,* 830–831.

Sullivan, S. A., & Birch, L. L. (1990). Pass the sugar, pass the salt: Experience dictates preference. *Developmental Psychology, 26,* 546–551.

Super, C. M. (1981). Cross-cultural research on infancy. In H. C. Triandis & A. Heron (Eds.), *Handbook of cross-cultural psychology: Vol. 4. Developmental psychology.* Boston: Allyn and Bacon.

Super, C. M., Herrera, M. G., & Mora, J. O. (1990). Long-term effects of food supplementation and psychosocial intervention on the physical growth of Colombian infants at risk of malnutrition. *Child Development, 61,* 29–49.

Super, D. E. (1976). *Career education and the meanings of work.* Washington, DC: U.S. Offices of Education.

Super, D. E. (1980). A life span, life space approach to career development. *Journal of Vocational Behavior, 16,* 282–298.

Tager-Flusberg, H. (1989). Putting words together: Morphology and syntax in the preschool years. In J. Berko Gleason (Ed.), *The development of language* (2nd ed.). Columbus, OH: Merrill.

Tanner, J. M. (1970). Physical growth. In P. H. Mussen (Ed.), *Carmichael's manual of child psychology* (3rd ed.). New York: Wiley.

Tanner, J. M. (1990). *Fetus into man: Physical growth from conception to maturity* (2nd ed.). Cambridge, MA: Harvard University Press.

Taylor, M., Cartwright, B. S., & Carlson, S. M. (1993). A developmental investigation of children's imaginary companions. *Developmental Psychology, 29,* 276–285.

Taylor, M., & Gelman, S. A. (1989). Incorporating new words into the lexicon: Preliminary evidence for language hierarchies in two-year-old children. *Child Development, 60,* 625–636.

Taylor, R., Casten, R., Flickinger, S. M., Roberts, D., & Fulmore, C. D. (1994). Explaining the school performance of African-American adolescents. *Journal of Research on Adolescence, 4,* 21–44.

Taylor, R. D. & Roberts, D. (1995). Kinship support and maternal and adolescent well-being in economically disadvantaged African-American families. *Child Development, 66,* 1585–1597.

Teller, D. Y., & Bornstein, M. H. (1987). Infant color vision and color perception. In P. Salapatek & L. Cohen (Eds.), *Handbook of infant perception* (Vol. 1). Orlando, FL: Academic Press.

Thelen, E., & Ulrich, B. D. (1991). Hidden skills. *Monographs of the Society for Research in Child Development, 56* (1, Serial No. 223).

Thelen, E., Ulrich, B. D., & Jensen, J. L. (1989). The developmental origins of locomotion. In M. H. Woollacott & A. Shumway-Cook (Eds.), *Development of posture and gait across the life span.* Columbia: University of South Carolina Press.

Thomas, A., Chess, S., & Birch, H. G. (1968). *Temperament and behavior disorders in children.* New York: New York University Press.

Thomas, H., & Kail, R. (1991). Sex differences in the speed of mental rotation and the X-linked genetic hypothesis. *Intelligence, 15,* 17–32.

Thomas, J. R., & French, K. E. (1985). Gender differences across age in motor performance: A meta-analysis. *Psychological Bulletin, 98,* 260–282.

Thompson, G. G. (1952). *Child psychology.* Boston: Houghton Mifflin.

Thompson, R. A., & Limber, S. (1991). "Social anxiety" in infancy: Stranger wariness and separation distress. In H. Leitenberg (Ed.), *Handbook of social and evaluation anxiety.* New York: Plenum Press.

Thurstone, L. L., & Thurstone, T. G. (1941). Factorial studies of intelligence. *Psychometric Monograph* (No. 2).

Tisak, M. (1993). Preschool children's judgments of moral and personal events involving physical harm and property damage. *Merrill-Palmer Quarterly, 39,* 375–390.

Toda, S., & Fogel, A. (1993). Infant response to the still-face situation at 3 and 6 months. *Developmental Psychology, 29,* 532–538.

Topping, K., & Whiteley, M. (1993). Sex differences in the effectiveness of peer tutoring. *School Psychology International, 14,* 57–67.

Treboux, D., & Busch-Rossnagel, N. A. (1990). Social network influence on adolescent sexual attitudes and behaviors. *Journal of Adolescent Research, 5,* 175–189.

Trickett, P. K., Aber, J. L., Carlson, V., & Cicchetti, D. (1991). Relationship of socioeconomic status to the etiology and developmental sequelae of physical child abuse. *Developmental Psychology, 27,* 148–158.

Trickett, P. K., & Kuczynski, L. (1986). Children's misbehaviors and parental discipline strategies in abusive and nonabusive families. *Developmental Psychology, 22,* 115–123.

Trickett, P. K., & McBride-Chang, C. (1995). The developmental impact of different forms of child abuse and neglect. *Developmental Review, 15,* 311–337.

U.S. Bureau of the Census. (1994). *Marital status and living arrangements: March 1993.* Washington, DC: U.S. Government Printing Office.

U.S. Bureau of the Census (1995a). *Population Profile of the United States: 1995.* Washington, DC: U.S. Government Printing Office.

U.S. Bureau of the Census. (1995b). *Statistical abstract of the United States* (115th ed.). Washington, DC: U.S. Government Printing Office.

U.S. Department of Health and Human Services. (1995). *Vital statistics of the United States, 1992.* Washington, DC: U.S. Government Printing Office.

Valkenburg, P. M., & van der Voort, T. H. A. (1994). Influence of TV on daydreaming and creative imagination: A review of research. *Psychological Bulletin, 116,* 316–339.

Valkenburg, P. M., & van der Voort, T. H. A. (1995). The influence of television on children's daydreaming styles: A 1-year-panel study. *Communication Research, 22,* 267–287.

van den Boom, D. C. (1994). The influence of temperament and mothering on attachment and exploration: An experimental manipulation of sensitive responsiveness among lower-class mothers with irritable infants. *Child Development, 65,* 1457–1477.

van IJzendoorn, M. H., Goldberg, S., Kroonenberg, P. M., & Frenkel, O. J. (1992). The relative effects of maternal and child problems on the quality of attachment: A meta-analysis of attachment in clinical samples. *Child Development, 63,* 840–858.

van IJzendoorn, M. H., & Kroonenberg, P. M. (1988). Cross-cultural patterns of attachment: A meta-analysis of the Strange Situation. *Child Development, 59,* 147–156.

Vaughn, B. E., Kopp, C. B., & Krakow, J. B. (1984). The emergence and consolidation of self-control from eighteen to thirty months of age: Normative trends and individual differences. *Child Development, 55,* 990–1004.

Ventura, S. J., Martin, J. A., Hartin, A., Taffell, S. M., Mathews, T. J., & Clarke, S. C. (1994). Advance report of final natality statistics, 1992. *National Center for Health Statistics, Monthly Vital Statistics Report, 43.*

Verma, I. M. (1990). Gene therapy. *Scientific American, 263,* 68–84.

Volling, B. L., & Belsky, J. (1992). The contribution of mother-child and father-child relationships to the quality of sibling interaction: A longitudinal study. *Child Development, 63,* 1209–1222.

Vorhees, C. V., & Mollnow, E. (1987). Behavior teratogenesis: Long-term influences on behavior. In J. D. Osofsky (Ed.). *Handbook of infant development* (2nd ed.). New York: Wiley.

Voyer, D., Voyer, S., & Bryden, M. P. (1995). Magnitude of sex differences in spatial abilities: A meta-analysis and consideration of critical variables. *Psychological Bulletin, 117,* 250–270.

Vurpillot, E. (1968). The development of scanning strategies and their relation to visual differentiation. *Journal of Experimental Child Psychology, 6,* 632–650.

Vygotsky, L. S. (1978). *Mind in society: The development of higher psychological processes* (M. Cole, V. John-Steiner, S. Scribner, & E. Soubermen, Eds.). Cambridge, MA: Harvard University Press.

Vygotsky, L. S. (1986). *Thought and language* (A. Kozulin, Trans.). Cambridge, MA: MIT Press. (Original work published in 1934)

Waber, D. P. (1977). Sex differences in mental abilities, hemispheric lateralization, and rate of physical growth at adolescence. *Developmental Psychology, 13,* 29–38.

Wachs, T. D. (1983). The use and abuse of environment in behavior-genetic research. *Child Development, 54,* 396–407.

Wagner, N. E., Schubert, H. J. P., & Schubert, D. S. P. (1985). Family size effects: A revision. *Journal of Genetic Psychology, 146,* 65–78.

Wagner, R. K., Torgesen, J. K., & Rashotte, C. A. (1994). Development of reading-related phonological processing abilities: New evidence of bidirectional causality from a latent variable longitudinal study. *Developmental Psychology, 30,* 73–87.

Walberg, H. J. (1986). Synthesis of research on teaching. In M. C. Wittrock (Ed.), *Handbook of research on teaching* (3rd ed.). New York: Macmillan.

Walker, L. J. (1980). Cognitive and perspective-taking prerequisites for moral development. *Child Development, 51,* 131–139.

Walker, L. J., & Taylor, J. H. (1991). Family interactions and the development of moral reasoning. *Child Development, 62,* 264–283.

Walker, L. J. (1995). Sexism in Kohlberg's moral psychology? In W. M. Kurtines & J. L. Gewirtz (Eds.), *Moral development: An introduction.* Boston: Allyn and Bacon.

Ward, S. L., & Overton, W. F. (1990). Semantic familiarity, relevance, and the development of deductive reasoning. *Developmental Psychology, 26,* 488–493.

Warren, A. R., & McCloskey, L. A. (1993). Pragmatics: Language in social contexts. In J. Berko Gleason (Ed.) *The development of language* (3rd. ed., pp. 195–238). New York: Macmillan.

Warren-Leubecker, A., & Bohannon, J. N. (1989). Pragmatics: Language in social contexts. In J. Berko Gleason (Ed.), *The development of language* (2nd ed., pp. 327–368). Columbus, OH: Merrill.

Waters, H. F. (1993, July 12). Networks under the gun. *Newsweek,* 64–66.

Wechsler, D. (1991). *Manual for the Wechsler Intelligence Test for Children-III.* New York: Psychological Corporation.

Wegman, M. E. (1994). Annual summary of vital statistics—1993. *Pediatrics, 95,* 792–803.

Weinberg, M. K., & Tronick, E. Z. (1994). Beyond the face: An empirical study of infant affective configurations of facial, vocal, gestural, and regulatory behaviors. *Child Development, 65,* 1503–1515.

Weisner, T. S., & Wilson-Mitchell, J. E. (1990). Nonconventional family lifestyles and sex typing in six-year-olds. *Child Development, 61,* 1915–1933.

Wellman, H. M. (1992). *The child's theory of mind.* Cambridge, MA: MIT Press.

Wellman, H. M. (1993). Early understanding of mind: The normal case. In S. Baron-Cohen, H. Tager-Flusberg, & D. J. Cohen (Eds.), *Understanding other minds: Perspectives from autism.* Oxford, England: Oxford University Press.

Wellman, H. M., Cross, D., & Bartsch, K. (1986). Infant search and object permanence: A meta-analysis of the A not B error. *Monographs of the Society for Research in Child Development, 51* (3, Serial No. 214).

Welsh, M. C., Pennington, B. F., & Groisser, D. B. (1991). A normative-developmental study of executive function: A window on prefrontal function in children. *Developmental Neuropsychology, 7,* 131–149.

Wentzel, K. R., & Asher, S. R. (1995). The academic lives of neglected, rejected, popular, and controversial children. *Child Development, 66,* 754–763.

Wentzel, K. R., & Erdley, C. A. (1993). Strategies for making friends: Relations to social behavior and peer acceptance. *Developmental Psychology, 29,* 819–826.

Werker, J. F., & Lalonde, C. E. (1988). Cross-language speech perception: Initial capabilities and developmental change. *Developmental Psychology, 24,* 672–683.

Werner, E. (1994). Overcoming the odds. *Journal of Developmental and Behavioral Pediatrics, 15,* 131–136.

Werner, H. (1948). *Comparative psychology of mental development.* Chicago: Follet.

Werner, L. A., & Bargones, J. Y. (1992). Psychoacoustic development of human infants. *Advances in Infancy Research, 7,* 103–145.

Wertsch, J. V., & Tulviste, P. (1992). L. S. Vygotsky and contemporary developmental psychology. *Developmental Psychology, 28,* 548–557.

Whitehurst, G. J., & Vasta, R. (1975). Is language acquired through imitation? *Journal of Psycholinguistic Research, 4,* 37–59.

Whitehurst, G. J., & Vasta, R. (1977). *Child behavior.* Boston: Houghton Mifflin.

Whiting, J. W. M., & Child, I. L. (1953). *Child training and personality: A cross-cultural study.* New Haven, CT: Yale University Press.

Whitney, E. N., Cataldo, C. B., & Rolfes, S. R. (1987). *Understanding normal and clinical nutrition* (2nd ed.). St. Paul, MN: West.

Whitney, E. N., & Hamilton, E. M. N. (1987). *Understanding nutrition* (4th ed). St. Paul, MN: West.

Wicks-Nelson, R., & Israel, A. C. (1991). *Behavior disorders of childhood* (2nd ed.). Englewood Cliffs, NJ: Prentice Hall.

Widom, C. S. (1989). Does violence beget violence? A critical examination of the literature. *Psychological Bulletin, 106,* 3–28.

Wigfield, A., Eccles, J. S., Mac Iver, D., Reuman, D. A., & Midgley, C. (1991). Transitions during early adolescence: Changes in children's domain-specific self-perceptions and general self-esteem across the transition to junior high school. *Developmental Psychology, 27,* 552–564.

Williams, J. E., & Best, D. L. (1990). *Measuring sex stereotypes: A thirty-nation study* (Rev. ed.). Newbury Park, CA: Sage Publications.

Willinger, M. (1995). Sleep position and sudden infant death syndrome. *Journal of the American Medical Association, 273,* 818–819.

Wilson, C. C., Piazza, C. C., & Nagle, R. (1990). Investigation of the effect of consistent and inconsistent behavioral example upon children's donation behavior. *Journal of Genetic Psychology, 151,* 361–376.

Wilson, M. (1989). Child development in the context of the black extended family. *American Psychologist, 44,* 380–383.

Wilson, R. S. (1986). Growth and development of human twins. In F. Falkner & J. M. Tanner (Eds.), *Human growth: A comprehensive treatise* (Vol. 3). New York: Plenum Press.

Winer, G. A., Craig, R. K., & Weinbaum, E. (1992). Adults' failure on misleading weight-conservation tests: A developmental analysis. *Developmental Psychology, 28,* 109–120.

Winner, E. (1988). *The point of words.* Cambridge, MA: Harvard University Press.

Wintre, M. G., & Vallance, D. D. (1994). A developmental sequence in the comprehension of emotions: Intensity, multiple emotions, and valence. *Developmental Psychology, 30,* 509–514.

Wolfe, D. A. (1985). Child-abusive parents: An empirical review and analysis. *Psychological Bulletin, 97,* 462–482.

Wolff, P. H. (1987). *The development of behavioral states and the expression of emotions in early infancy.* Chicago: University of Chicago Press.

Wolraich, M. L., Lindgren, S. D., Stumbo, P. J., Stegink, L. D., Appelbaum, M. I., & Kiritsy, M. C. (1994). Effects of diets high in sucrose or aspartame on the behavior and cognitive performance of children. *New England Journal of Medicine, 330,* 301–307.

Wong-Fillmore, L., Ammon, P., McLaughlin, B., & Ammon, M. S. (1985). *Learning English through bilingual instruction.* Rosslyn, VA: National Clearinghouse for Bilingual Education.

Woollacott, M. H., Shumway-Cook, A., & Williams, H. (1989). The development of balance and locomotion in children. In M. H. Woollacott & A. Shumway-Cook (Eds.), *Development of posture and gait across the life span.* Columbia: University of South Carolina Press.

Worobey, J., & Blajda, V. M. (1989). Temperament ratings at 2 weeks, 2 months, and 1 year: Differential stability of activity and emotionality. *Developmental Psychology, 25,* 257–263.

Wynn, K. (1996). Infants' individuation and enumeration of actions. *Psychological Science, 7,* 164–169.

Yonas, A., & Owsley, C. (1987). Development of visual space perception. In P. Salapatek & L. Cohen (Eds.), *Handbook of infant perception* (Vol. 2). Orlando, FL: Academic Press.

Zahn-Waxler, C., Cole, P. M., & Barrett, K. C. (1991). Guilt and empathy: Sex differences and implications for the development of depression. In J. Garber & K. Dodge (Eds.), *The development of emotion regulation and dysregulation* (pp. 243–272). Cambridge, England: Cambridge University Press.

Zahn-Waxler, C., Radke-Yarrow, M., Wagner, E., & Chapman, M. (1992). Development of concern for others. *Developmental Psychology, 28,* 126–136.

Zelazo, N. A., Zelazo, P. R., Cohen, K. M., & Zelazo, P. D. (1993). Specificity of practice effects on elementary neuromotor patterns. *Developmental Psychology, 29,* 686–691.

Zelazo, P. R. (1983). The development of walking: New findings and old assumptions. *Journal of Motor Behavior, 15,* 99–137.

Zelazo, P. R., Weiss, M. J., Papageorgiou, A. N., & Laplante, D. P. (1989). Recovery and dishabituation of sound localization among normal-, moderate-, and high-risk newborns: Discriminant validity. *Infant Behavior and Development, 12,* 321–340.

Zigler, E., & Finn-Stevenson, M. (1992). Applied developmental psychology. In M. H. Bornstein & M. E. Lamb (Eds.), *Developmental psychology: An advanced textbook.* Hillsdale, NJ: Erlbaum.

Zigler, E., & Hall, N. W. (1989). Physical child abuse in America: Past, present, and future. In D. Cicchetti & V. Carlson (Eds.), *Child maltreatment: Theory and research on the causes and consequences of child abuse and neglect.* New York: Cambridge University Press.

Zimiles, H., & Lee, V. E. (1991). Adolescent family structure and educational progress. *Developmental Psychology, 27,* 314–320.

Zuraivin, S. J. (1991). Research definitions of child physical abuse and neglect: Current problems. In R. H. Starr, Jr., & D. A. Wolfe (Eds.), *The effects of child abuse and neglect.* New York: Guilford Press.

Acknowledgments

PHOTOGRAPHS

Cover (bottom center and bottom right-middle photo) Brian Vikander; (lower right - left photo) Peter Brandt; (upper right) Teena Albert; (right center) Nita Winter; (top left and top center) Erika Stone; (center-middle photo) Phoebe Ferguson, Ltd.; (lower left) Carl Fischer; (lower right - right photo) Hunter Freeman Studio; (left center) Dennis Degnan/Westlight

About the Author Page xviii, Courtesy of Robert V. Kail

Chapter 1 Page xx Barbara Campbell, Gamma Liaison, Inc.; p. 3 Margaret Miller, Photo Researchers, Inc.; p. 6 AP/Wide World Photos; p. 7 (top) Nina Leen, Life Magazine. Copyright Time Inc. Time-Life Picture Agency; (bottom) Corbis-Bettman; p. 8 Jon Erikson; p. 9 (top) Susan Hogue; (bottom) Bob Daemmrich, The Image Works; p. 10 (top) Albert Bandura; (bottom) Corbis-Bettman; p. 12 AP/Wide World Photos; p. 25 Will and Deni McIntyre/Science Source, Photo Researchers, Inc.; p. 27 Barbara Campbell, Gamma Liaison, Inc.

Chapter 2 Page 30 Nancy Richmond, The Image Works; p. 32 (top) Dr. Gopal Murti/Science Photo Library, Custom Medical Stock Photo; (bottom) Francis Leroy, Biocosmos/Science Photo Library, Photo Researchers, Inc.; p. 33 (top) David Phillips, Photo Researchers, Inc.; (middle) Alexander Tsiaras/Science Source, Photo Researchers, Inc.; (bottom) Biophoto Associates, Photo Researchers, Inc.; p. 37 Porterfield-Chickering, Photo Researchers, Inc.; p. 42 Laura Dwight, Peter Arnold, Inc.; p. 46 Bob Daemmrich, Stock Boston; p. 49 Nancy Richmond, The Image Works

Chapter 3 Page 50 T. Henstra, Photo Researchers, Inc.; pp. 53, 54 (left) Lennart Nilsson; p. 54 (right) Petit Format/Nestle/Science Source, Photo Researchers, Inc.; p. 59 Laura Dwight; p. 61 Washington University School of Medicine; p. 66 Medichrome/The Stock Shop, Inc.; p. 70 Lawrence Migdale, Photo Researchers, Inc.; p. 71 Margaret Miller, Photo Researchers, Inc.; p. 74 Robert Kail; p. 75 Innervisions; p.80 T. Henstra, Photo Researchers, Inc.

Chapter 4 Page 82 Bob Daemmrich, Stock Boston; p. 85 Tony Freeman, PhotoEdit; p. 89 Stock Boston; p. 90 Byron/Monkmeyer, Monkmeyer Press; p. 91 M. Granitsas, The Image Works; p. 93 (top) David Woo, Stock Boston; (bottom) Tony Freeman, PhotoEdit; p. 94 M. Douglas, The Image Works; p. 98 (top) Alexander Tsiaras, Stock Boston; (bottom) Dr. Michael E. Phelps, U.C.L.A. School of Medicine; p. 99 Peter Menzel, Stock Boston; p. 103 Dexter Gormley; p.104 FeliciaMartinez, PhotoEdit; p. 105 Erika Stone, Photo Rearchers, Inc.; p. 106 (top) Rick Browne, Stock Boston; (bottom) Mitch Reardon, Photo Researchers, Inc.; p. 109 Bob Daemmrich, Stock Boston

Chapter 5 Page 112 Laura Dwight; p. 117 Russell C. Hamilton, Cornell University; p. 120 (top) Dion Ogust, The Image Works; (bottom) Michael Iamborrino, Medichrome; (bottom) Michael Tamborrino, Medichrome/The Stock Shop, Inc.; p. 123 Courtesy of Arthur Ginsburg, Vision Sciences Research, San Ramon, CA; p. 124 Innervisions; p. 125 (top) Joe Sohm, The Image Works; (middle) Tadao Kimura, The Image Bank; (bottom) Bob Daemmrich, Stock Boston; p. 126 John William Banagan, The Image Bank; p. 135 Coco McCoy, Rainbow; p.138 Laura Dwight

Chapter 6 Pages 140, 143, 146 (top) Laura Dwight; p. 146 (bottom) Gary Goodman, Picture Cube, Inc.; pp. 148, 150 Tony Freeman, Pho-
toEdit; p. 152 Richard Hutchings, Photo Researchers, Inc.; p. 161 (top) Dr. Michael Cole, courtesy of A.R. Luria; (bottom) D. Young-Wolff, Photo Edit; p. 162 Eric. A. Weissman, Stock Boston; p. 165 Laura Dwight

Chapter 7 Page 166 Mary Kate Denny, Tony Stone Images; p. 171 Bob Daemmrich, Stock Boston; p. 173 Courtesy of Carolyn Rovee-Collier; p. 174 Shackman, Monkmeyer Press; p. 175 Amy Etra, PhotoEdit; p. 177 Gale Zucker, Stock Boston; pp. 178, 182 Tony Freeman, PhotoEdit; p. 183 Laura Dwight; p. 186 Elizabeth Zuckerman, PhotoEdit; p. 189 Gottlieb, Monkmeyer Press; p. 192 Mary Kate Denny, Tony Stone Images

Chapter 8 Page 194 Lawrence Migdale, Tony Stone Images; p. 198 Paul L. Merideth; p. 199 (top) Macduff Everton; (bottom) Anna E. Zuckerman, PhotoEdit; p. 203 Laura Dwight; p. 209 Myrleen Ferguson, PhotoEdit; p. 213 Okoniewski, Gamma-Liaison, Inc.; p. 216 MacPherson, Monkmeyer Press; 219 Lawrence Migdale, Tony Stone Images

Chapter 9 Page 222 Robert Brenner, PhotoEdit; p. 225 (top) Dreyfuss, Monkmeyer Press; (bottom) Barbara Filet, Tony Stone Images; pp. 228, 229 Laura Dwight; p. 230 Lawrence Migdale, Stock Boston; p. 232 (top) Tom Prettyman/PhotoEdit; (bottom) Elena Rooraid/PhotoEdit; p. 237 Susan Kuklin, Photo Researchers, Inc.; p. 240 Tony Freeman, Photo Edit; p. 246 Robert Brenner, PhotoEdit

Chapter 10 Page 248 Robert E. Daemmrich, Tony Stone Images; p. 251 (top left) Laura Dwight; (top center) Michael Newman, PhotoEdit; (top right) Comstock; (bottom) Peter Southwick, Stock Boston; p. 252 Robert Kail; p. 253 Bob Daemmrich, Stock Boston; p. 257 Robert Kail; p. 258 Myrleen Ferguson, PhotoEdit; p. 259 Innervisions; p. 260 Steve Starr, Stock Boston; p. 263 Mark Richards, PhotoEdit; p. 264 (top) William Hamilton, Johns Hopkins University; (bottom), Laura Dwight; p. 265 Laura Dwight; p. 268 Boulton-Wilson, Jerobaum, Inc.; p. 271 Robert E. Daemmrich, Tony Stone Images

Chapter 11 Page 272 Bruno Maso, Photo Researchers, Inc.; p. 274 Santana, Tony Stone Images; p. 277 Comstock; p. 278 Richard Hutchings, PhotoEdit; p. 280 Mark Richards, PhotoEdit; p. 281 Myrleen Ferguson, PhotoEdit; p. 286 Laura Dwight; p. 287 Bob Daemmrich: p. 290 D. & I. MacDonald, Picture Cube, Inc.; p. 295 David Young-Wolff, PhotoEdit; p. 296 Bob Daemmrich, Stock Boston; p. 298 Bruno Maso, Photo Researchers, Inc.

Chapter 12 Page 300 Bob Daemmrich, Tony Stone Images; p. 303 Elizabeth Hathon, The Stock Market; p. 307 Laura Dwight; p. 309 Tony Freeman, PhotoEdit; p. 312 John Boykin, Picture Cube, Inc.; p. 313 David R. Frazier Photolibrary, Inc.; p. 315 Michael Sulik, Picture Cube, Inc.; p. 316 Andrew M. Levine, Photo Researchers, Inc.; p. 317 Lawrence Migdale, Lawrence Migdale/PIX; p. 318 Martin Adler, Panos Pictures; p. 320 Amy Etra, PhotoEdit; p. 322 Laura Dwight; p. 323 Mark Walker, Picture Cube, Inc.; p. 324 John Coletti, Picture Cube, Inc.; p. 329 Bob Daemmrich, Tony Stone Images

Chapter 13 Page 330 Kim Robbie, The Stock Market; p. 334 D. Young-Wolff, PhotoEdit; p. 337 (top) Mark Downey, Mark Downey/Lucid Images; (bottom) Bernard Wolf, Monkmeyer Press; p. 338 Stephen Collins, Photo Researchers, Inc.; p. 341 Tony Freeman, PhotoEdit; p. 342 (top, left) Catherine Ursillo, Photo Researchers, Inc.; (top, right) Alan & Sandy Carey, Photo Researchers,

Inc.; (bottom) Elizabeth Crews, Elizabeth Crews Photography; p. 345 Gabe Palmer, The Stock Market; p. 346 Goodwin, Monkmeyer Press; p. 349 Elizabeth Crews, Elizabeth Crews Photography; p. 351 Denise Marcotte, Stock Boston; p. 352 Nancy Sheehan, PhotoEdit; p. 356 Kim Robbie, The Stock Market

Chapter 14 Page 358 Frank Wing, Gamma-Liaison, Inc.; p. 361 Jean Hangarter, Picture Cube, Inc.; p. 362 Stewart Cohen, Tony Stone Images; p. 364 Laura Dwight; p. 367 Pam Francis, Gamma-Liaison, Inc.; p. 368 Charles Thatcher, Tony Stone Images; p. 370 (bottom) Bachmann, PhotoEdit; p. 371 Susanne Szasz, Photo Researchers, Inc.; p. 372 Cathlyn Melloan, Tony Stone Images; p. 379 Michael Newman, PhotoEdit; p. 380 Courtesy of San Francisco Child Abuse Council; p. 381 (top) S. Agricola, The Image Works; (bottom) Alan S. Weiner, Gamma-Liaison, Inc.; p. 385 Frank Wing, Gamma-Liaison, Inc.

Chapter 15 Page 388 Pascal Crapet, Tony Stone Images; p. 390 David M. Grossman; p. 392 Laura Dwight; p. 393 D. Young-Wolff, PhotoEdit; p. 395 Robert Kail; p. 397 Richard Hutchings, Photo Researchers, Inc.; p. 400 Bob Daemmrich, Stock Boston; p. 403 Tony Freeman, PhotoEdit; p. 404 R. Termine/CTW, Everett Collection; p. 406 David. M. Grossman; p. 407 Tony Freeman, PhotoEdit; p. 408 Corbis-Bettman; p. 412 Robert Finken, Picture Cube, Inc.; p. 414 Pascal Crapet, Tony Stone Images

CARTOONS, FIGURES AND TABLES

Chapter 1 Page 15 *Hi and Lois* © 1993. Reprinted with special permission of King Features Syndicate

Chapter 2 Page 45 From I. Gottesman (1963). Genetic aspects of intellectual behavior. In N.R. Ellis (Ed.), *Handbook of mental deficiency.* New York: McGraw-Hill. Reprinted courtesy of Norman R. Ellis

Chapter 3 Pages 55, 64 From Moore and Persaud (1993). *Before we are born,* Philadelphia: W.B. Saunders. Reprinted with permission; p. 77 *Hi and Lois* © 1994. Reprinted with special permission of King Features Syndicate

Chapter 4 Page 88 From Whitney et al., *Understanding normal and clinical nutrition* (2nd ed.). Belmont, CA: Wadsworth Publishing Co. Copyright by Wadsworth Publishing Co. Reprinted with permission; p. 89 From *Fetus into man: Physical growth from conception to maturity* by J.M. Tanner. Cambridge, MA: Harvard University Press, Copyright © 1978 by J.M. Tanner by the Presidents and Fellows of Harvard College. Reprinted by permission of the publisher; p. 97 From R.J. Lemire et al., (1975). *Normal and abnormal development of the human nervous system.* New York: HarperCollins Publishers. Reprinted with permission of Lippincott-Raven Publishers; p. 107 From P. Zelazo et al., (1993) Specificity of practice effects on elementary neuromotor patterns. *Developmental Psychology, 29,* 686-691. Copyright © 1993 by the American Psychological Association. Reprinted with permission

Chapter 5 Page 128 From H. Ghim, Evidence for perceptual organization in infants. *Infant Behavior and Development, 13,* 221-248. Copyright by Ablex Publishing Corporation. Reprinted by permission; p. 130 From J. Morton & M.H. Johnson (1991). CONSPEC and CONLERN: A two-process theory of infant face recognition. *Psychological Review, 98,* 164-181. Copyright © 1991 by the American Psy-

chological Association. Reprinted with permission; p. 133 Adapted from J.W. Hagen (1972). Strategies for remembering. In S. Farnam-Diggory (Ed.), *Information processing in children.* New York: Academic Press. Copyright by Academic Press, Inc. Reprinted with permission

Chapter 6 Page 157 Adapted from R.S. Siegler (1981). Developmental sequences within and between concepts. *Monographs of the Society for Research in Child Development, 46,* Serial No. 189, 7. Copyright © Society for Research in Child Development, Inc. Reprinted with permission

Chapter 7 Page 177 From *The Development of memory in children,* 3E, by R. Kail. © 1990 by W.H. Freeman and Co. Used with permission

Chapter 8 Page 197 Adapted from J. B. Carroll (1993). *Human cognitive abilities: A survey of factor-analytic studies.* New York: Cambridge University Press. Copyright Cambridge University Press. Reprinted with permission of Cambridge University Press; p. 206 (top) From B. Bloom (1964) *Stability and change in human characteristics.* New York: John Wiley and Sons. Copyright by Benjamin S. Bloom. Reprinted with permission; p. 206 (bottom) Adapted from R.S. Wilson (1983). The Louisville twin study: Developmental synchronies in behavior. *Child Development, 54,* 298-316. Copyright © Society for Research in Child Development, Inc. Reprinted with permission; p. 212 *The New Yorker Magazine;* p. 214 creativity measurement test - Copyright by Scholastic Testing Service, Inc. Bensonville, IL. Reprinted with permission. (Test completed by Laura Kail)

Chapter 9 Page 227 Reprinted by permission of Johnny Hart and Creators Syndicate

Chapter 11 Page 276 Copyright by Axel Scheffler. Reprinted with permission of Axel Scheffler and Blackwell Publishers; p. 280 Reprinted by permission of Bunny Hoest, Wm. Hoest Enterprises, Inc.; p. 286 Adapted from S. Harter & R. Pike (1984). The pictorial scale of perceived competence and social acceptance for young children. *Child Development, 55,* 1973. Copyright © Society for Research in Child Development, Inc. Reprinted with permission

Chapter 12 Page 302 *Calvin and Hobbes* © 1993 Watterson. Distributed by Universal Press Syndicate. Reprinted with permission. All rights reserved; p. 304 From Y. Shoda, W. Mischel, & P.K. Peake (1994). Predicting adolescent cognitive and self-regulatory competencies from preschool delay of gratification: Identifying diagnostic conditions. *Developmental Psychology, 26,* 978-986. Copyright © by the American Psychological Association. Reprinted with permission; p. 311 Adapted from A. Colby et al. (1983). A longitudinal study of moral development. *Monographs of the Society for Research in Child Development, 48* (Whole #200), 46. Copyright © Society for Research in Child Development, Inc. Reprinted with permission; p. 326 From N.R. Crick & K.A. Dodge (1994). A review and reformulation of social information processing mechanisms in children's social adjustment. *Psychological Bulletin, 115,* 74-101. Copyright © 1994 by the American Psychological Association. Reprinted with permission

Chapter 13 Page 340 From J.W. Pellegrino & R. Kail (1982), Process analyses of spatial aptitude. In R. Sternberg, (ed.) *Advances in the psychology of human intelligence, Vol. 1.* Hillsdale, NJ: Lawrence Erlbaum Associates. Copyright by Lawrence Erlbaum Associates. Reprinted with permission; p. 349 Adapted from C.L. Martin & C.F. Halvorsen, Jr. (1981). A schematic processing model of sex typing and stereotyping in children. *Child Development, 52,* 1121. Copyright © Society for Research in Child Development, Inc. Reprinted with permission

Chapter 14 Page 370 *Peanuts* © 1993. Reprinted with permission of United Feature Syndicate

Chapter 15 Page 399 Adapted from R. Morison & A.S. Masten (1991). Peer reputation in middle childhood as a predictor of adaptation in adolescence: A seven-year follow-up. *Child Development, 62,* 1001. Copyright © Society for Research in Child Development, Inc. Reprinted with permission; p. 401 © Martha F. Campbell. Reprinted with permission; p. 410 *Safe Havens* © 1993. Reprinted with special permission of King Features Syndicate

Name Index

Subject Index